MENEKET RIVKAH

EDWARD E. ELSON CLASSIC

MENEKET RIVKAH

A Manual of Wisdom and Piety for Jewish Women
by Rivkah bat Meir

Edited with an Introduction and Commentary
by Frauke von Rohden

Translation of *Meneket Rivkah* by Samuel Spinner

Translation of Introduction and Commentary by Maurice Tszorf

2009 • 5769
Philadelphia

The Jewish Publication Society
2100 Arch Street, 2nd floor
Philadelphia, PA 19103
www.jewishpub.org

Design and Composition by El Ot Pre Press & Computing Ltd. Tel Aviv.

Manufactured in the United States of America

09 10 11 12 13   10 9 8 7 6 5 4 3 2 1

Library of Congress Cataloging-in-Publication Data:

Tiktiner, Rivkah bat Me'ir.
  [Menekes Rivkeh. English & Yiddish]
  Meneket Rivkah : a manual of wisdom and piety for Jewish women / by Rivkah bat Meir ; edited with an introduction and commentary by Frauke von Rohden. – 1st ed.
     p. cm.
  Includes bibliographical references and index.
  ISBN 978-0-8276-0835-1
  1. Jewish women–Conduct of life–Early works to 1800. 2. Jewish women–Religious life–Early works to 1800. 3. Jews–Czech Republic–Prague–History–16th century. 4. Jews–Czech Republic–Prague–History–17th century. 5. Tiktiner, Rivkah bat Me'ir. Menekes Rivkeh. I. Rohden, Frauke von. II. Tiktiner, Rivkah bat Me'ir. Simhes Toyreh lid. III. Title.
  BM726.T5513 2008
  296.7082–dc22
                        2008018112

JPS books are available at discounts for bulk purchases for reading groups, special sales, and fundraising purchases. Custom editions, including personalized covers, can be created in larger quantities for special needs. For more information, please contact us at marketing@jewishpub.org or at this address: 2100 Arch Street, Philadelphia, PA 19103.

Dedicated to my parents

"...we must reconstitute another discourse, rediscover the silent murmuring, the inexhaustible speech that animates from within the voice that one hears, re-establish the tiny, invisible text that runs between and sometimes collides with them."

Michel Foucault, *The Archeology of Knowledge*

ACKNOWLEDGMENTS

I would like to thank the Berliner Förderprogramm Frauenforschung (Berlin Support Program for Women Studies). Without its generous grant and financing for my extended research in Jerusalem and two trips to Prague, this work would not have come into existence.

I would also like to express my gratitude to all employees of the Central Archives for the History of the Jewish People and the Jewish National University Library, both in Jerusalem, especially to Hadassah Assouline and Avraham David; the archive of the Prague Jewish community, especially to Alexander Putík; the archive of the Prague municipality; the Alte Bibliothek (Old Library) of the University of Erlangen, where I had free access to the copy of *Meneket Rivkah* and the friendly assistance of its staff; and finally to Heidi Stern, who offered her hospitality and engaged in fruitful talks while I stayed in Erlangen.

I am, of course, solely responsible for all shortcomings of my work, but I would like to give special credit to the many people in Germany and in Israel who helped me with their valuable suggestions and participated in many intense discussions. I am unable to list all their names, but I would like to express my great appreciation to them all. I would like to especially thank my doctoral advisor, Michael Brocke, who followed the progress of my work with ongoing interest and constructive criticism; Edward Fram, who provided me with important ideas for the structure of my work; Cheryl Tallan, with whom I shared ideas over a great distance; Chava Turniansky, with whom I had fertile discussions on Old Yiddish literature; Gerold Necker, who provided important help correcting the Yiddish text; and Gottfried Reeg, who invested great efforts in typesetting the Yiddish text and preparing the Yiddish subject index. I am grateful for the help and constant encouragement from Ralph Winkle, who assisted me in the process of recasting my thesis into a book.

I would like to express my sincere gratitude to my translators, Samuel Spinner and Maurice Tszorf, for their accurate and advertent translations. The numerous comments provided by Maurice Tszorf were of great help and it was a pleasure to work with him. My sincere thanks to Rena Potok and Janet Liss of The Jewish Publication Society, who demonstrated care and patience during the development and production phases of this book.

I owe special thanks to Andrea Behrends, with whom I had many intelligent discussions on my dissertation project, from its outset. Her friendship and support were invaluable.

During the last several years, this work and my daughter, Yola, have grown and flourished. My greatest appreciation goes to Yola for her readiness to adapt so beautifully during our months in Jerusalem, thus enabling me to conduct my archive research, as well as for her patience with me as I spent so much time at my desk instead of going inline skating with her.

CONTENTS

PREFACE

When working on Old Yiddish moral literature of the 16th and 17th centuries, one repeatedly runs into the name of Rebecca Tiktiner and the remark that this educated woman authored a book of moral conduct. In fact, the moral-homiletic book *Meneket Rivkah* (Rebekah's nurse), written by this author who referred to herself as Rivkah bat Meir, was the first extensive book ever written by a Jewish woman. At a time when quite a few Jewish women could neither read nor write, and the first educated ones among them hesitantly began to print their self-composed prayers, Rivkah bat Meir's authorship of a normative book was no matter to be taken for granted. The same would most probably apply to her work as well. Although she was part of a long tradition of experienced women who stood out for their thorough knowledge and introduced other women into matters of liturgy and religion, she was the only one to have been referred to as a "preacher and female rabbi" (*darshanit ve-rabbanit*).

From the end of the 19th century until the late 1970s, *Meneket Rivkah* was considered lost. Although scholarly interest in Yiddish literature and the general and intellectual history of women has increased during the past thirty years, upon its rediscovery *Meneket Rivkah* has received very little attention. This was a fate that Rivkah bat Meir's book shared with the Yiddish *musar* literature in general. The reason may be found in the lack of modern editions, which would have made the texts accessible to a broad scholarly audience. The more profound reasons for such a marginal approach to the research of Old Yiddish literature, however, must be searched for in history.

The majority of the representatives of the *Wissenschaft des Judentums* (the Science of Judaism), which marked the beginning of modern research of Judaism in the middle of the 19th century, already despised the Yiddish language as "jargon," or, to quote Abraham Geiger, "most pathetic gibberish." This verdict placed these researchers in the tradition of the *maskilim* of the 18th century, who, in defense of the purity of languages, fought decisively against the "Jewish-German" language as a hybrid between Hebrew and German. The majority of the German-Jewish scholars of the 19th and early 20th centuries turned their attention to the history of traditional rabbinic Judaism and its Hebrew literature, or turned to esoteric and exotic phenomena such as Jewish mysticism. At the same time, they deliberately erased from their canon the very existence of the Yiddish language and literature, which had been the province of their own parents or grandparents.

In an attempt to correct the obvious lack of research of Eastern European history and Yiddish literature, the *Yidisher Visnshaftlekher Insitut* (YIVO) was founded in

Berlin in 1925, later establishing its residence in Vilna. In the wake of World War II, the New York YIVO branch, which had been established the same year, became the main seat of the organization.

Even here, however, research of Old Yiddish literature developed only slowly; and the fact that moral literature was only marginally noted may be regarded in the tradition of the Science of Judaism: From the outset, its representatives perceived the moral literature as secondary in comparison to the halakhic, exegetic, theosophical, and mystical currents of rabbinic literature.

Another circumstance must be taken into consideration in regard to modern research in this context in Germany. Research of Judaism, newly established during the 1960s in the wake of the Holocaust, succeeded, more or less consciously, the Science of Judaism and accepted its canon of research. After the destruction of European Jewry, the new Yiddish research was carried on mostly by non-Jewish scholars and was developed in close adherence to German studies. Thus the emphasis was originally on the examination of the language and the history of its literature: both the more secular Yiddish works and those more religiously oriented were examined in regard to their relationship to the German language and its connections to the European narrative traditions. But even in modern editions and in examinations of this religious Yiddish literature to this day, the relationship to Yiddish moral literature, or rabbinic literature, was barely examined. Thus there has been a lack of research acknowledging Yiddish literature as Jewish traditional literature.

The work presented here constitutes the first modern edition of *Meneket Rivkah*, based upon its first Prague print of 1609. One purpose of the new edition is to make the original text and its English translation not only accessible to a wide cross-disciplinary audience, but also to a broader audience of readers interested in the history of Jewish women. In addition, this work examines the relationship between *Meneket Rivkah* and rabbinic literature, the exegetic, homiletic, and narrative traditions the author quotes so extensively. It further places *Meneket Rivkah* within its contemporary Yiddish and Hebrew moral literature. My research, however, does not provide a linguistic examination that could attribute *Meneket Rivkah* to Western or Eastern Yiddish.

Two discoveries that I made proved to be of particular significance, providing information about the hitherto unknown reception of *Meneket Rivkah* and the status of the author within her society. First, I was able to show that the book was still quoted a hundred years after its publication in works that assumed a certain familiarity with and distribution of the work. Second, a hitherto unknown entry in a Prague memory book (*Sefer Hazkarot*) confirms that Rivkah bat Meir was able to perform as an author and preacher for women, not from a marginalized yet advantageous position as a widow or unmarried woman who would have been relieved from obligations toward a husband or children, but as a married woman, from within society, coping with the same challenges as other women of her time. This information provides a more precise reflection of the variety of the life choices available to Ashkenazic women in the early modern era, which otherwise has been only dimly illuminated.

The introduction is divided into five sections. The first two sections describe the historical and cultural context of Rivkah bat Meir, her activity as preacher and teacher in the tradition of a female conveyer of knowledge, and her literary work and its reception.

The third section shows that *Meneket Rivkah* does not merely constitute a morality book: its distinct homiletic and exegetic character also establishes it within the scholarly rabbinical literature. Within the exegetic-homiletic passages, Rivkah bat Meir both modified classic male-dominated interpretations and introduced completely independent readings. This is interesting not only because of the relatively limited education among Ashkenazic women in the early modern era, but more significantly because Rivkah bat Meir was one of the few female voices expressing the views of women of her time.

The fourth section illuminates certain ideals of conduct for women and reflects specifically female attitudes of the period, though it does not provide a complete summary of all virtues and social practices described in the book. Unlike most authors of moral works of the 16th and 17th centuries, Rivkah bat Meir derived practical demands of conduct from actual experience and by an analysis of contemporary conduct, thus presenting a chiefly pragmatic discourse rather than the orthodox discourse of rabbinic literature.

The fifth section discusses the research history of *Meneket Rivkah,* showing how, during the 19th and to some extent the 20th century after its rediscovery, the book was practically excluded from history as a result of the low esteem traditionally conferred on moral literature, particularly as it related to the history of women. This description is followed by a presentation of the research of Yiddish moral literature to this day.

The present edition includes both the Yiddish text and its translation into English. The introduction and commentary overlap at times, but I believe such repetitions to be helpful so that the reader does not need to return continuously to the introduction for relevant information. In addition, the commentary offers comprehensive quotes from the contemporary moral literature, thus establishing both the common and the distinctive features of *Meneket Rivkah*.

Finally, this edition provides explanations of the principles used in editing and translating the work, a list of the abbreviations in *Meneket Rivkah*, a scriptural index, English and Yiddish subject indexes, and a reproduction of the Yiddish original of the *Simḥes Toyre Lid*, the only known additional text written by Rivkah bat Meir.

INTRODUCTION

Rivkah bat Meir

The Lives of Jewish Women in the Early Modern Era

Ashkenazic women in the early modern era[1] lived their lives along paths determined by religion and social conventions, as was the case for their Christian contemporaries. Their path through life was predetermined to a great extent. In their youth, daughters, like sons, helped their fathers in earning a living if it consisted of manual work such as fixing and mending pawned goods like old clothes. For Jewish girls from poor backgrounds, childhood at home ended in their early youth when they became maids, which they usually remained until they married.[2] Girls from wealthy families left their home only when they married, usually at the age of about 15, which followed two or more years of engagement, which was earlier than for girls from poor families.[3] It was typical that girls, regardless of social background, were not allowed to choose their husbands. Marriages were arranged by the parents of the couple according to economic and social criteria. Although girls had a halakhically vested right to object to a match, this right was useless in most cases because the engaged couple would usually not meet before the wedding often enough to get to know each other.[4]

The purpose of marriage arrangements was to connect wealthy and scholarly families, in order to allow them to mutually profit from joining economic forces and from garnering respect and influence within the community.[5] Daughters from these homes, who were educated to become adequate brides for sons of similar backgrounds, had significantly easier access to Jewish education.[6] Together with their brothers they enjoyed lessons in the Bible at home. Sometimes they could even study Hebrew, which provided them with the capability of reading Jewish religious literature. Educated girls would sometimes work as typesetters and printers in their fathers' and husbands' print shops,[7] less often as nurses or medical doctors, the latter of which had previously been a relatively common occupation for Jewish women during the Middle Ages.[8] However, many Jewish women in the early modern era could neither write nor read at all in any language.[9]

Knowledge was in fact widely transmitted orally. Mothers of all social levels would teach their daughters the blessings and prayers as they knew them, the laws of kashrut, and the laws relating to menstruation (*niddah*), which they would be subjected to as married women. In addition, the girls would acquire knowledge in the finances of a

1

household, food storage, cooking, needlework, and child care. Every Jewish woman was expected to have such skills and knowledge, regardless of whether she was likely to run a large household with maids and servants or to be a "poor householder" (*Meneket Rivkah*, 33a) in a small, overcrowded home.

Caring for children and their education constituted an important part of a Jewish woman's household work. Infant mortality rates were very high and many women died at a young age, often during childbirth or soon after. This necessitated that widowed husbands find new wives quickly, especially if there were young children in their families to raise. Divorce, though not common, was another reason for remarriages.

With Jewish law (*halakhah*) setting narrow limits on the rights of Jewish women, they would often call upon civil courts, particularly in matters of inheritance and personal property rights.[10] Jewish men would do the same, although for different reasons. Many women worked in their husbands' businesses,[11] but according to Jewish law their income was the exclusive property of their husbands; as such, women were rarely listed in the tax registers. However, if a man was away on business trips or ill, his wife would often replace him, and in case of his death she might even take over his trade or business completely.[12] In times without any social security, the activity of widows in trade or pawn broking was a necessity born out of economic insecurity. Successful and rich women such as the businesswoman Glikl bas Judah Leib (Glueckel of Hameln, d. 1724)[13] or the court Jewess Esther Liebmann[14] were exceptions, not the rule.

Pious women would take part in prayer services just as pious men did. In many places there were particularly learned women who would pray with the female communities and explain the commandments to them. Women had no access to official or liturgical positions, but they did participate in running the synagogues by assuming certain tasks, such as keeping the keys to the synagogue, supervising the *mikveh* (ritual bath), or serving as *gabba'it* (administrator of the community's charity fund). Sometimes they would function as generous contributors of ritual objects for the synagogue. Often women were forced to miss prayer services in order to attend to their small children or because of other household tasks. Pious women, however, would still say the Yiddish *thinnot* (*tkhines*, special prayers for women) at home. At first, these individual Yiddish prayers were written by men for female and unlearned male readers, but from the end of the 16th century, *thinnot* were increasingly written by learned women, who would introduce into them their own experiences and expressions of female spirituality.[15]

Younger women respected older and more experienced women as consultants. In cases of uncertainties and questions regarding the practical application of *halakhah*, they often functioned as mediators between the young women and the rabbis. Pious and educated women collected information from Yiddish morality books, and they read Yiddish Bible translations as well as devotional literature. But even adventurous romances taken from Christian narrative writing were popular, and were read aloud to women, men, and children who were not capable of reading during social gatherings.[16]

Prague at the Time of Rivkah bat Meir

In the second half of the 16th century, the Jewish community of Prague went through a period of extraordinary economic and cultural expansion,[17] following Emperor Rudolf II's protective edict for Bohemia's Jews that included a comprehensive right to settle in Prague. Many Jews from Germany, Poland, and Moravia subsequently moved there, and by the end of the 16th century, the Jewish community of Prague developed into the second-largest Jewish community in Christian Europe after Rome, with an estimated population of 3,000.

Both the Bohemian chamber and the emperor regarded the Jews of Prague as a welcome financial resource for exploitation. They depended particularly upon the merchant Mordecai Markus Meisel (d. 1601), whose legendary wealth not only made him the greatest benefactor of the Jewish community but also one of the main financiers of the court. His loans were indispensable for Emperor Rudolf's war plans. Thus the protection and privileges of the Jewish community depended, to a great degree, on Meisel's money.[18]

However, few people enjoyed economic success; most Jews of Prague probably lived in relative poverty. The community did have the privilege of extensive self-administration, but it was subject to various forms of dependency on the magistrate of Prague and the court. The resulting internal tensions within the community erupted in sometimes bitter disputes, particularly in the 1570s.[19]

There are many and varied reports regarding the extremely confined living conditions inside the Jewish Quarter. Real estate prices were astronomically high and a family of several members would often live in a single room and a small chamber. The outbreak of epidemics, such as the plague of 1589, was one of the consequences. But the Jewish Quarter was not a ghetto in the usual meaning of the word; there were no curfews or gates that could be bolted. Sometimes they were allowed to purchase plots outside the district.

In addition, Jews were granted the privilege to engage in crafts, which made contact with the non-Jewish population of Prague more possible than it would have been as the result of a trader–client relationship. In that sense, it has been documented that Jewish women in 16th-century Prague were active in various professions. An index of letters of safe conduct in Prague for the year 1546 mentions a female butcher, case maker, hat seller, market vendor, and innkeeper. The section of services lists a children's nurse, a female cantor, cooks, and kitchen maids.[20] The municipal archive of Prague for the 1520s through the 1540s lists female goose merchants, one seamstress, and one cube maker.[21] However, an assessment roll from 1540 lists only one woman among 54 Jews.[22] This suggests that women performed their work on a small scale and were therefore not liable for tax payments, or that many of them performed their work on behalf of their husbands or a male relative.

The economic prosperity of the growing community led to an influx of important rabbis and scholars to Prague, who opened yeshivot that attracted students from all over Europe. In addition, Prague became an important center for Hebrew and Yiddish letterpresses.

Another significant institution and point of reference in the life of the Jewish community of Prague was the *ḥevra kaddisha* (holy society), founded in 1564, which cared for the ill and dying, buried the dead, and supported bereaved family members. It organized social activities such as acts of penance, celebrations, lectures, and religious study groups. In addition, it provided loans, assumed godparenthood (*sandeka'ut*) for newborn boys, and engaged in marriage brokering. Sylvie-Anne Goldberg advocates the thesis that the *ḥevra kaddisha* of Prague was in control of the entire social and religious life of Prague's Jewish community, and "embodied the standards of the urban life-world," providing it "power even over the conscience of the families and individuals."[23] Goldberg's thinking, however, focuses on traditional political channels. Thus, she ignores the possibilities for informal, non-institutionalized sources of influence and claims of leadership based on experience, seniority, erudition, and social status.

One should also not forget the moral-normative discourse, which was conducted on the written level, namely as moral literature. Had the *ḥevra kaddisha* in fact been an overpowering moral authority, one would expect that Prague morality books, such as those by Moses Henokhs Altshul[24] or Rivkah bat Meir, would at least mention the *ḥevra kaddisha*, and that the authors would attempt to reconcile their own behavior with the moral authority of the *ḥevra kaddisha*. This did not happen, however.

After the city became the permanent seat of the emperor in 1584, Prague was the most important Central European center of commerce. It was a multiethnic and multicultural milieu, which resulted in multiple opportunities for Jews to observe foreign ways of life and to come in contact with different social groups, and allowed for the development of new perceptions and social activities. At the same time, it became necessary for Jews to differentiate themselves from others and to emphasize their own principles in everyday life, including on the literary level.

Origin and Family

Regrettably, little is known about the origin, life, and work of Rivkah bat Meir. There exist, however, two epigraphic sources that provide information about her biography. One is her memorial entry initiated by her family in the memorial book of the Prague Altneushul; the other is the epitaph on her gravestone at the old Jewish cemetery in Prague. That epitaph reads as follows:[25]

(1) רבקה בת מהר״ר (2) מאיר טיקאטין (3) נפטרה כ׳ה׳ ניסן (4) לפרט ר׳ב׳ק׳ה׳ ה׳א׳ב׳ן׳.
(5) הזאת ת׳נ׳צ׳ב׳ה׳: (6) רבות בנות עשו (7) חיל ואת עלית על (8) כלנה: בטח בה לבנו
(9) כאביגיל בחייה (10) בזכותה להגינה: (11) קרבן כליל כאיל: (12) במות לכפר׳ ניתנה:
(13) היתה דורשת יום (14) וליל׳ לנשים בכל (15) קריה נאמנ׳: זלגה (16) עין כל נפיק ועייל
(17) כאשר נגנזה ונט (18) מנה:

(1) Rivkah, daughter of our teacher (2) and master, Rabbi Meir Tikotin (3) She passed away on the 25th day of Nissan [April 13] (4) according to the count of

"Rivkah this stone"[26] [1605]. (5) May her soul "be bound up in the bundle of life."[27] (6) Many women have (7) done well, but you surpass them (8) all.[28] We put our confidence in her.[29] (9) Just like Abigail[30] she provided (10) protection through her merit. (11) A whole sacrifice,[31] like a ram. (12) She atoned with her death.[32] (13) She preached day and (14) night to the women in every (15) faithful city.[33] (16) The eye of every passerby and oncoming person wept,[34] (17) as concealed and buried (18) she was.

In addition to the date of death, the inscription provides an indication that she belonged to a scholarly family. Her father's title was *mhr"r*, the acronym for *morenu ha-rav rabbi*—"our teacher and master, Rabbi—."[35] In the 16th century, the granting of titles was by no means standardized, so it is not completely clear what function or status this title implies. Meir Tikotin was undoubtedly a scholar, but he did not necessarily hold the position of a rabbi.[36] The appearance on the title page of *Meneket Rivkah* of the title *Ga'on*, which was commonly conferred only upon incumbent rabbis or heads of yeshivot, was possibly a mistake that referred to the author's late father. If Meir Tikotin had actually borne this title, Rivkah bat Meir would have used it elsewhere as well. But in her *Simḥes Toyre Lid* she mentions the name of her deceased father only as *mhr"r Meir zz"l* ("our teacher and master, Rabbi Meir, may the memory of the righteous be a blessing").[37]

As the daughter of a learned father, Rivkah bat Meir most probably studied the Hebrew language and the Torah as a child, and she may also have studied the basics of rabbinic literature. Her study would not likely have included Gemara, however, which traditionally was taught only to boys. In any case, she quotes almost no traditional Aramaic material, and so it may be concluded that she did not understand Aramaic.[38]

Tikotin, as part of her father's name, indicates his origin in the Polish town of Tykocin, near Bialystok, where a Jewish community had existed since the early 16th century. The Germanized spelling "Tiktiner," as it appears on the posthumous title page of *Meneket Rivkah*, reflects the name of the town Tiktin as it was called by its originally White Russian population.[39] However, the patronymic does not prove that Rivkah bat Meir was herself born in Tykocin, or that she grew up there, particularly since her father could already have inherited this name.[40] Khone Shmeruk, on the other hand, regarded this toponym and the usage of Eastern Yiddish words such as *nebbekh*, *zayde*, and *davenen*, which appear in *Meneket Rivkah*, as evidence of her Polish origin. It should be noted that the word *nebbekh* ("regrettably," "alas") is found very early in Western Yiddish, and its origin may even be Czech.[41] The originally Slavic word *zayde* ("grandfather") is used exclusively in a long account, which, by her own words, was communicated to her orally, and she may have wished to retain the linguistic style of the original storyteller.[42] In any case, the parallel term *dayde* was widely used in Bohemian-Moravian Yiddish already in the 16th century. She therefore might not have perceived *zayde* as a foreign word, and therefore did not replace it.[43] The word *davenen*[44]—to pray—is, in fact, a marker of Eastern Yiddish.[45] Another Yiddish morality book, however, contains both *davenen* and its Western Yiddish parallels *beten* and *oren*,[46] such that a certain mixing of Western and Eastern Yiddish may be assumed for the linguistic border regions. In any case, the existence of these words cannot be read as evidence for Rivkah bat Meir's origin from Poland, although this cannot be excluded.

Her report about various experiences in *Rayser Land*[47] allows for the assumption that Rivkah bat Meir spent some time in other regions. This geographical designation is unusual, therefore the region cannot be located beyond doubt. It most probably corresponds to the designations *Rayssen*, *Raysin*, or *Rusya*, which refer to the Ukrainian Rus (Ruthenia), and which were common in contemporary Yiddish and Hebrew sources. Since the middle of the 16th century, this region saw a significant growth of Jewish communities.[48] Assuming that her accounts are not fictitious—a technique she might have employed to distance her writings from direct criticism of her readers—it still remains unclear whether she is referencing her country of origin or merely a region where she once lived.

The formulations on the gravestone suggest that she spent at least some time in Prague. She referred to her readers as women "in every faithful city," which probably indicates Prague and its surrounding communities.[49] She performed her activities with great commitment ("day and night"), and thus acquired high esteem within the Prague community. This is impressively expressed in the epitaph's modification of the biblical verse, "Her husband puts his confidence in her" (Prov. 31:1) into "We put our confidence in her" (line 8). Her piety and perfection received particular praise in line 11, where she is called a "whole sacrifice, like a ram," comparing her death to a sin offering of her contemporaries; indeed, her death was deeply mourned by her family as well as by the entire community (lines 15–17).[50]

Further information about the author can be found in *Sefer Hazkarot*, the memory book of the Altneushul. The memory book contains an entry for every deceased individual whose families made a charitable donation to the synagogue. The memorial entry for Rivkah bat Meir which was hitherto unknown to be included and which I was able to discover, reads as follows:[51]

(1) יזכור אלקים נשמת הזקינה רבנית מרת רבקה בת מהר"ר מא[י]ר

(2) בעבור שנתן בעלה הר"ר [בצ]ל[ל]{א}ל [בר]וך ∼ ∼ ∼ ∼ ∼

(3) לצדקה וגם היתה דורשת בכל {קרייה נאמנה} בע[ב]{ור זה תהא}

(4) נשמתה צרורה בצרור החיים עם [נש[מו]תם] איו"י [שרה ר]ב[קה רח]ל

(5) ולאה ועם שאר צדיקים וצ[ד]קני[ו]ת הטהורי[ם] {בג}ן עדן ונאמר אמן.

(1) May the Lord remember the soul of the elder, the Rabbanit Madam Rivkah, daughter of our teacher and master, Rabbi Meir (2) for that her husband, the master, Rabbi [Beza]l{e}l [Bar]ukh contributed ∼ ∼ ∼ ∼ (3) for charity. She preached in every {faithful city}. For {this merit} (4) her soul {shall be} bound up in the bundle of life with [the souls] of Abraham, Isaac, and Jacob, [Sarah, Ri]v[ka, Rache]l (5) and Leah, and all the other righteous and pure men and [women] {in Gan} Eden, and let us say "Amen."

The inscription indicates that Rivkah bat Meir died in old age, and thus it may be assumed that she was born in the first half of the 16th century. The fact that the name of her husband is mentioned is evidence of the fact that she did not become widowed at an early age, which would have enabled her to teach and preach. Her husband's name should probably be read as Bezalel Barukh or Bezalel Henokh. However, no further details about a man with this name can be found in prosopographic literature.[52] Her husband's title *ha-rav rabbi* indicates that although he had received traditional rabbinic training, he did not hold any outstanding position and did not officiate as a rabbi. Such a person would have usually been designated as *Ga'on*, whereas other scholars of higher education would have been called *ḥaver*—member—or *morenu*—our teacher.

We do not know whether Rivkah bat Meir had children or not. On the one hand, the memorial entry implies that she did not have any (surviving) children, because in the Altneushul as elsewhere, the *Sefer Hazkarot* would usually mention all members of the core family as donors. Here, however, only the name of her husband is mentioned, with the appropriate singular verb "[he] contributed," followed by a short illegible passage. In context it is far more likely that this passage represents the donation rather than the names of children. On the other hand, the only place in *Meneket Rivkah* where the author speaks about herself seems to indicate the existence of children or grandchildren: "If I only should merit seeing my children's children perform such good deeds."[53] Although this formulation is mainly a linguistic convention to emphasize the example set by experienced and righteous women, it is unlikely that she would have used this phrase if she had never had children or if her own children had died childless.[54] At most, the available evidence suggests the possibility that any son or daughter passed away during her lifetime after bearing their own children.

Rivkah bat Meir in the Tradition of Female Transfer of Knowledge

In the memorial entry, Rivkah bat Meir is denoted as *ha-rabbanit* (the female rabbi or female teacher). On the title page of *Meneket Rivkah* she is referred to as *ha-darshanit* (the female interpreter or female preacher).[55] Both titles are surprising, particularly since they cannot be regarded as merely honorary. Nor do they constitute official titles set forth in the community ordinance, or designate an official position. This is true particularly for the title of Rabbanit, which is not the same as the common honorary title of a rabbi's wife, since her husband most probably did not hold the office of a rabbi. As it was not unusual for the Rebbetzin to instruct women on behalf of their husbands in questions on the laws concerning menstruation, this honorary title undoubtedly served as the model for Rivkah bat Meir's designation as Rabbanit. This is further confused by the fact that the gravestones in the Prague cemetery designate wives of rabbis almost without exception with the honorary title of Rabbanit, without indication of their erudition or whether they taught women.[56] Only in Italy at that time were erudite women who were not married to rabbis given the designation of Rabbanit.[57] Therefore, in the case of Rivkah bat Meir, Rabbanit must be understood as a functional title, not meaning a "rabbi's wife" but "rabbi" in the sense of scholar and teacher.

The degree to which the titles designate her teaching and preaching activity is likewise indicated in her formulations, where she announces her own interpretation: "I could also expound (*oys legen*) the verse and teach (*darshen*) it as follows."[58]

Although these titles constitute a unique innovation for women, Rivkah bat Meir's work falls within a long tradition of female teaching of religious knowledge. Several decades later, Hannah bat Judah Leib (Loeb) Katz wrote a Yiddish sermon that resulted from her experience as teacher of and preacher to women.[59] The sermon's title page notes that Hannah bat Judah "had composed (*gekloyben*) her sermon from the *Sefer ha-Musar* and other midrashim, as well as the Gemara." Thus, this sermon, too, stands in the tradition of women as teachers. In a certain sense it can be regarded as a continued development of *Meneket Rivkah*. While Rivkah bat Meir, perhaps out of modesty, gave her sermons the form of a morality book, Hannah bat Judah described her moral and homiletic statements with self-confidence as a "lovely sermon," their combination with various prayers emphasizing her homiletic competence.

It may be assumed, however, that at all times there were learned Jewish women who transferred their knowledge of liturgy and religion to less learned women.[60] Beginning in the early modern period, such women were called *firzogerin* ("woman who prompts") in Eastern Europe. In Ashkenaz and northern Italy in particular, there is evidence for such activity since the Middle Ages. Eleazar of Worms, in his elegy for his wife Dolce, killed by Crusaders in 1197, reports as follows:

> She sings hymns and prayers, she recites petitions, daily [she says] confession, "*nishmat kol ḥai*" and "*ve-khol ma'aminim*." She says the "*pittum ha-ketoret*" and the Ten Commandments; in all the towns she taught women [so they can] chant songs; she knows the order of the morning and evening prayers, and she comes early to the synagogue and stays late.[61]

We do not know when, and under what conditions, the practice of women instructing other women became institutionalized and highly respected.[62] Their work most probably consisted of explaining the liturgy to other women, translating prayers and at least parts of the sermon, praying with them and singing hymns (which is why in early sources they were sometimes referred to as "cantors"). The index of letters of safe-conduct of the city council of Prague for the year 1546 lists, for example, a "female cantor Rypka," most probably referring to a *firzogerin*.[63]

The reading of the Torah was an established element of the liturgy, and so it is possible that able *firzogerins* instructed women in this task. The inscriptions on the gravestones in Prague mention not only women who performed their "prayer with devotion," but also such who "pondered over the Torah" or spent time "studying the Torah."[64] Even in Prague in the 16th century, women undoubtedly taught Torah to other women, just as they composed prayers for one another and prayed together. The epitaph on the gravestone of Rivkah bat Shabbtai, who died in 1579, says: "The pious woman, whose charm was the jewel of her lips, for she taught and explained the prayer book of the holidays to the daughters of Israel."[65] Clearly some *firzogerins* also composed prayers for specific women's needs in a language they understood. A Yiddish *thinne*, printed in Prague in 1600, may have been such a prayer. Beneath its title *Eyn gor sheyne thinne* (A very beautiful *thinne*) we find the note, "[This *thinne*] was for a long time kept secret among a group of pious women; they let it remain among themselves, and let no one copy it. Now they have rethought the matter, and have brought it for publication."[66] Although this *thinne*, as well as the Yiddish collection of prayers entitled *Thinnah Zu* published in Prague in 1590,[67] was published anonymously, it would seem to have been written by a woman. Without further research regarding female authorship, knowledge about the tradition of Jewish female cantors, teachers, and preachers remains veiled. Though a small number of published works survive, most of these women's activities were strictly oral in nature.[68]

We also lack information regarding the connection between communal prayer and moral instruction. Was this a task of the *firzogerins* from the start? I think it is more likely that women's moral instruction to other women began in the 16th century as Hebrew sermons became increasingly important in Jewish society. It was only then that the obvious communicative connection between prayer and religious-moral instruction was reflected in Yiddish literature. Evidence for such development can be found not only in the moral sermon of Hannah bat Judah, but also in the 16th-century Hebrew-Yiddish morality book *Mishlei Ḥakhamim*, which was composed for unlearned male readers and which contained at the end a Yiddish *thinne*.[69]

We do not know where and under what circumstances Rivkah bat Meir functioned as preacher and teacher. As a member of the Altneushul she may have used the women's section there for that purpose in her later years, after a wing was added for women along two sides of the main prayer hall some time around 1598.[70] This room was equipped with high, narrow, horizontal openings through which it was possible for the women to follow the services without being able to view the main prayer hall. If Rivkah bat Meir did not teach in the women's section, it is conceivable that she provided her lessons in another room in the synagogue, or in a different synagogue, or in private homes.[71]

We also do not know whether she was paid for her instruction or how often she taught. Similarly, it is not clear what the phrase "every faithful city" on her epitaph refers to in regard to how far she traveled for her teaching. It probably refers to communities close to Prague, such as Lieben, Kolin, and Leitmeritz, since these cities were among the few in the region where Jewish families were allowed to settle from the middle of the 16th century. And also unknown is whether Rivkah bat Meir was assigned students by a rabbi, her synagogue, or the *ḥevra kaddisha* (which organized study groups for men), or whether she acted independently.

That Rivkah bat Meir's name appears in the *Sefer Hazkarot* of the Altneushul, however, suggests a connection to preachers there whose homilies may have influenced her own sermons.[72] During the last 30 years of her life, the Altneushul included Yehudah Liwa (Loew) ben Bezalel, the famous Maharal (d. 1609), who was the head of a yeshivah in Prague and who held the position of Chief Rabbi as of 1599,[73] as well as Isaac ben Isaiah Meling (d. 1583), who was also the head of a yeshivah and, in addition, a judge on the Jewish court. Rivkah bat Meir may also have been acquainted with the preachers Isaac ben Abraham Chayes (d. approx. 1615),[74] who was Chief Rabbi of Prague during the 1580s, and Mordecai ben Abraham Jaffe (d. 1612),[75] who taught and preached in Prague during the 1590s, as well as the Polish preacher Ephraim Luntshitz (d. 1619), who only came to Prague in 1604 but whose printed sermons had been disseminated earlier.[76] All of these men were famous in their time. To examine if, and to what extent, the works or sermons of these rabbis and preachers influenced Rivkah bat Meir's interpretations and homilies would require a separate study.[77]

The Maharal, for example, initiated study groups for less learned men with emphasis on the Mishnah, which he considered to have been neglected. Following the death of the Maharal, the community ordinance of 1611 made the participation of all men in such study groups obligatory. Regardless of the assessment of the influence of these rabbis and preachers, it is in any case certain that Rivkah bat Meir worked during a time and in an environment where sermons enjoyed high esteem.

From Teacher to Writer

Even assuming a longstanding Jewish tradition of learned women teachers, one might ask what caused Rivkah bat Meir to exceed the tradition of oral instruction by setting her words down in writing. One of the basic reasons was certainly the letterpress, which made the inexpensive distribution of written material possible for the first time. Perhaps prints of Yiddish *thinnot* produced during the period were an additional incentive for Rivkah bat Meir to write down her own moral-homiletical instruction. In fact, her literary activity may have begun with the writing of prayers, since she also wrote a liturgical hymn in addition to the posthumously published *Meneket Rivkah*: *Simhes Toyre Lid*, a hymn for Simhat Torah, was handed down in three slightly different versions, one of which may have been printed during her lifetime.[78] Yiddish *Toyre lider* were very popular in the 16th century and were printed in many editions.[79] Women, and probably men as well, sang the *Toyre Lid* on Simhat Torah, the last day of Sukkoth, during preparations for the ceremony of *hakafot*, the presentation of the Torah scrolls in the synagogue, and possibly during the ensuing exuberant procession around the synagogue.[80]

In writing her *Simhes Toyre Lid*, Rivkah bat Meir adhered strictly to the predetermined structure of the *Toyre lider*, written in rhyming couplets and in two parts. The beginning of the verses in the first part are in alphabetical order, one line for each letter, and in the second part the first letters of each line form an acrostic of her name.[81] The first part praises God's oneness, His creative power, and His Torah, the universal source for consolation and redemption. The second part describes an eschatological feast prepared by God[82] where all generations, including pregnant women and women in childbirth, come together peacefully and eat delicious food, and where girls and boys dance together until finally, after sundown, they all walk in God's light. The alphabetically arranged verses and the rhythmic repetition of the Hallelujah at the end of each verse give the poem a harmonic unity, reflecting both God's oneness and the unity of humanity. The joyful harmony radiating from the image of the feast and the simultaneous strict compliance with the predetermined formal structure show that Rivkah bat Meir was skilled in handling this genre as well.

It is likely that Rivkah bat Meir wrote additional literary texts beyond her *Simḥes Toyre Lid* and *Meneket Rivkah*, but according to current research no other works have survived. On the other hand, there is no evidence for the claim that Rivkah bat Meir translated *Ḥovot ha-Levavot* by Bahya ibn Paquda into Yiddish.[83]

The great popularity of Yiddish morality books, which increased enormously during the 16th century, contributed to a great degree to Rivkah bat Meir's decision to compose her own such work. In her Hebrew *piyyut*, written as an introduction to *Meneket Rivkah*, she contemplates her personal reasons for writing a Yiddish book.[84] It is conspicuous that she does not, as in other morality books, mention the general gaps in women's knowledge or their lack of knowledge in Hebrew, but she does explain her own desire to transmit her knowledge to others. She describes in poetic language the decision-making process that led to the creation of her book and the goals she wishes to pursue, employing multiple biblical allusions along the way. She has the requisite authority to do so, she writes self-confidently, because she is able to comply with God's precepts ("enabling the fulfillment of Your words. I will follow after You and confirm Your words"), wherefore God's grace will fall upon her, and upon all persons, who live according to His commandments ("merit gazing upon the beauty of Your face").

The author implies that she considers it her moral obligation to pass along her knowledge about the correct implementation of the commandments by noting that "important figures and pious saints had to leave in their youth," which constituted a penance for failing to prevent infringements of the Torah. Such prevention, she suggests, could have kept misfortune from befalling not only individuals but the entire Jewish community.[85] Immediately afterward, she criticizes housewives, who, according to her own alleged observation,[86] did not prevent various infringements of halakhic rules for the home: "I would not have written this, but as we say, 'One does not punish unless he has also warned.' This means, 'One does not harm anyone by warning him that such a thing must never occur.'"[87]

One could read this remark as Rivkah bat Meir's justification for a woman to write a morality book, because until that time only learned men had undertaken that task. However, here she aligns herself not with experienced and respected housewives, but with pious men and scholars who bore the responsibility of preventing infringements of the Torah, be it in their roles as rabbis, lay leaders, or teachers. She places this self-reflection at the end of the first chapter, apparently to bolster her claim that she should formulate normative social practices and ideals of conduct in the course of the ensuing six chapters.

The great importance that moral instruction held for her is reflected in her hope that it will provide her with merit, which is essential to obtaining a place in the world to come: "This is why all pious women and men should be scrupulous about all of their actions—about every word and every step. And whoever should pay attention to my words, perhaps I will gain some merit from them."[88]

The little word "perhaps" gives this statement a mixture of self-confidence and modesty, which is typical for Rivkah bat Meir. In a different place, she quotes the rabbinic list of opportunities for obtaining merit. However, instead of the item "writing books" listed there, she writes that one should "purchase religious books"—perhaps out of modesty, in order not to praise her own authorship.[89]

Self-confidence presented with modesty certainly made it easier for her to be accepted by women. Her experience as teacher, together with her sensibility, finds expression particularly in a passage that reads like her educational program: she writes that admonitions are to be formulated with great sensitivity and should not criticize a person as a whole, in order to avoid a defensive reaction. Moreover, one should assume a basic benevolence and integrity of the person being admonished. Thus she compares the frequent praise of her mainly "righteous," "God-fearing," and "pious" female readers with the ignorance of other "young" and "inexperienced" women, in order to be able to inconspicuously include the first group in directing the admonitions and instructions against the latter.[90]

At the same time, Rivkah bat Meir claims a high degree of authority and obedience when she demands as a matter of fact: "Therefore every pious woman should take care to follow what I wrote in the first chapter."[91] This claim of authority is also expressed in her homiletic rhetoric and her exegetic style.

Meneket Rivkah

Authorship and Provenance

Yiddish morality books that were translated in the 16th century from the Hebrew were often published anonymously because their legitimacy was considered in doubt.[92] Further, the date of such works is usually a matter of speculation. In contrast, it is stated specifically on the title page of *Meneket Rivkah* that Rivkah bat Meir wrote the book on her own and that it is not a copy or a compilation, referring to "the respected woman who conceived and wrote this book. . . . Who has ever heard of or seen such a novelty; has it ever happened in countless years, that a woman has written something of her own accord? And she has read numerous verses and midrashim."

Other Yiddish moral-halakhic works of the era contained disclaimers regarding authorship. In *Eyn shoyn Froyenbuykhleyn* (A beautiful women's booklet),[93] for example, the anonymous author justifies the publication of his book by writing, "And it is not as if somebody composed the book by himself and made it up in his own mind. He merely searched and extracted it from all books" (*Eyn shoyn Froyenbuykhleyn*, 2a). Similarly, the anonymous editor of the morality book *Sefer Middot* (Book of traits) defends his activity as a mere edition or translation: "Thus I have taken it on, with God's help, and have published it, although I should not have accepted such a task" (*Sefer Middot*, 99b).

Rivkah bat Meir's authorship is thus undisputed, but the period during which she wrote *Meneket Rivkah* can only be roughly determined. The only certain *terminus ante quem* is the year of her death, 1605. The determination of the *terminus post quem* is significantly more difficult. In two places (*Meneket Rivkah*, 12a, 24a) she mentions the book *Orḥot Ẓaddikim* (Ways of the righteous), which was initially printed in Prague in 1581. Even if only one of the quotes can be related to that book, and she perhaps borrowed the other quote from the *Sefer Middot*, which was initially printed in 1542, we can exclude the idea that *Meneket Rivkah* was written immediately after 1542, since the very title *Orḥot Ẓaddikim* was simply unknown to the author until 1581.[94]

On folios 4a and 10a, the author mentions *Froyen Bukh* (Women's book) and *Vroyen Bikhel* (Women's booklet). An anonymous book entitled *Eyn shoyn Froyenbuykhleyn* was printed in Basel only in 1602. This book is an almost unchanged reprint of the Yiddish *Seder Miẓvot ha-Nashim* (Order of women's commandments) by Benjamin Slonik, a compendium of halakhic instructions for women that was printed in Krakow in 1577, 1585, and 1595 and that belonged to a corpus of various books dealing with the duties of women that was widely disseminated and highly popular in the 16th century.[95] Therefore, the author's formulations such as "we also find in the *Froyen Bukh*" and "it is in the *Vroyen Bikhel*" do not necessarily refer to any specific title, particularly not to *Eyn shoyn Froyenbuykhleyn* of 1602. It may rather be assumed that all works of the *Miẓvot Nashim* corpus were popular even before 1602 under the generic name of *Froyen Bukh* or *Froyenbuykhleyn*.[96] Thus, the short version *Miẓvot Nashim* (Venice, 1552) was published with the subtitle *Vroyen Buykhleyn*. Consequently, when the author of *Brantshpigl* (Burning mirror), printed in 1596, states, "even if you found it in a *vroyen bikhel*," this could not refer to the work printed in 1602.[97] Thus, since Rivkah bat Meir's reference does not necessarily relate to the edition of 1602, 1581 must be assumed as the *terminus post quem*.

Prints

Today, one copy each of the different prints of *Meneket Rivkah* is known to exist.[98] The colophon on the title page of the first print indicates that it was prepared in 1609 by the printer Gershom ben Bezalel Katz,[99] who was the head of the famous Prague Gersonide print shop. *Meneket Rivkah* was undoubtedly a minor book produced by this shop, and it is likely that an employee rather than Katz himself prepared the print. Among those employees were Yekutiel ben David (Zalman Zetzer [type-setter]), who began there in 1597, Mordecai ben Jacob Zetzer, who began in 1609, and Judah ben Alexander ha-Kohen (Loeb Zetzer, or Loeb Presentziher [press puller]),[100] one of whom may have been the actual printer and thus the author of the title page of *Meneket Rivkah*.

The print shop owners often acted as the publishers or patrons of the print, but sometimes they cooperated with other patrons who would finance a specific job.[101] In the case of *Meneket Rivkah*, Azariah Ziskind ben Samuel Zanvil Taymer is noted in the colophon below the preface as a patron of the printing. Nothing is known about his identity and his connection to Rivkah bat Meir, nor is it clear how literally to take the words written about him there, in which it states that he took "his life in his hands" when he "poured money from his purse to publish this book" (*Meneket Rivkah*, 2a). Perhaps this refers only to a higher than usual monetary outlay for the printing, since the author was not able to share the expenses. Indeed, the complete failure of a book could lead to financial disaster for those involved. But it is also possible that such a description merely served to honor the patron for his assistance. That nine years later, in 1618, the book was published in a second edition indicates that *Meneket Rivkah* was in fact a commercial success.

The book was printed in quarto and the title page was decorated with a simple, rectangular decorative frame, not unusual for Yiddish prints or for small format Hebrew Gersonide prints.[102] The first title page also contains a number of small rosettes and scrolls. The latter can likewise be found next to the headers and the chapter names. Instead of the typical format that used Hebrew square print for Bible quotes, all Hebrew quotes were also set in italics and emphasized by round brackets. While the decorations suggest an adherence to certain aesthetic principles, there are also inconsistent, missing,[103] and incorrect[104] headings, numerous misprints, missing round brackets, and incorrect pagination,[105] all of which indicate that the print was not carefully executed.

The Krakow print of 1618 was executed in an even simpler manner, and with fewer decorations. Although it contains small orthographic deviations from the Prague print,[106] the contents and page breaks are identical. The folios are unpaginated and without decoration, and the only editorial additions are chapter headings. The name of the printer, Joseph Samuel ben Mordecai Grozmark, is inserted in the colophon at the end of folio 36a. The surviving Krakow copy has a faulty binding, such that the second chapter, with the exception of the first page, and approximately half of the third chapter (fols. 9a–17a) are not included. In their place are nine folios of the Yiddish translation of *Pirkei Avot*, initially published in Krakow in 1617.

Dissemination and Reception

As is the case for all works published in the 16th and 17th centuries, no reliable statements are possible regarding the print run and radius of dissemination of *Meneket Rivkah*. It is also difficult to reconstruct the history of its reception. *Meneket Rivkah* was by far less widely disseminated than the morality books *Brantshpigl* or *Lev Tov* (Good heart), which emerged around the turn of the 17th century and which were reprinted many times, even 100 years after first publication.[107] In her memoirs from the early 18th century, the merchant woman from Hamburg, Glikl bas Judah Leib (Glueckel of Hameln), suggested that her children read both these morality books,[108] and women, and probably sometimes men, continued to do so for generations.

However, the more modest impact of *Meneket Rivkah* cannot be seen as evidence of poor reception. In fact, *Meneket Rivkah* was not forgotten even 100 years after its publication. In 1715, the Hebrew-Yiddish morality book *Meshiv Ḥema—Minhagim Eshet Ḥayil* (Allayer of wrath—Customs of the capable wife) by Isaac ben Berl Zoref from Nikolsburg (Mikulov in Moravia) was published in Frankfurt-am-Main.[109] The Yiddish title page recommends the book with the words: "You should not be regretful about your sparse money, because it contains a beautiful story, which itself is worth that money." This is a reference to the almost literal rendition of the story about the honoring of parents, which appears in *Meneket Rivkah* on folios 16a–18a. In *Minhagim Eshet Ḥayil*, together with the source, ends on folio 13b: "This story is printed in the book *Meneket Rivkah*." Isaac ben Berl also uses almost literally, but without indication of its source, the parable of the gardener and his garden (*Minhagim Eshet Ḥayil*, 4a), which appears in *Meneket Rivkah* on 4b.[110] The later book also bears the stylistic influence of *Meneket Rivkah*. Although the description of events—real or fictitious—or personal experiences is rather unusual in moral literature, Isaac ben Berl reports concrete events, as does Rivkah bat Meir in several places. In one case, Isaac ben Berl may not have had firsthand knowledge of an event that reportedly took place in Nikolsburg; he may have merely read of it, and it is by no means certain that it actually took place as described.[111] But just like Rivkah bat Meir, he used the implication of real, authentic experiences in order to lend his moral instructions greater vividness and legitimacy.

Despite its evident influence on Isaac ben Berl, *Meneket Rivkah* most probably had its greatest effect among women in the 17th century, and perhaps even beyond, to women who bought the book, borrowed it from a friend or relative, or inherited it from their mothers and grandmothers years later. They read it—or had it read to them—for moral instruction, for pious self-assurance, and as pleasurable literature. They commented on it, analyzed it, and accepted or rejected its moral admonitions among their girlfriends and relatives. They read from it to their children and grandchildren until the book slowly vanished from the shelves. In light of the fact that *Meneket Rivkah* was published in two editions and was still known 100 years later, it must be concluded that the book had a certain readership, though its overall effect remains largely unknown and may never be fully clarified.

Structure

The book consists of 36 folio pages, which, compared to other morality books of the 16th century, makes it of average length.[112] The title follows the Jewish scholarly tradition of referring to the author's name, often in combination with a Bible quote. The title *Meneket Rivkah* refers to Genesis 35:8, which describes how Deborah, Rebekah's nurse, died near Beth El. The meaning of this location, where God appeared to Jacob and gave him the name Israel (Gen. 35:9f.), and which is considered in rabbinic literature to be identical with Rebekah's place of death (Bereshit Rabbah 81.5), thus grants Rebekah's nurse special significance and dignity, as well.[113] It is possible that Rivkah bat Meir was aware of Rabbi Moses ben Nahman's interpretation of Genesis 35:8, where he assumes that the nurse was responsible for the upbringing of Jacob's children, and that Jacob wished to support her in her old days. An adequate description of the author's tasks, namely the instruction and support of inexperienced children and young women, certainly fit the honored position of the nurse.

The preface is preceded not only by this quote from Genesis, but by a quote from Deuteronomy 32:13 ("He fed him honey from the crag"), where the verb assumes the Hebrew root of *meneket*. This attributes an additional interpretation to the title of the book: just as God nursed the people in the desert by letting them suck honey from a rock, so does the book supply essential nourishment to female readers. Nevertheless, it is not clear whether this motto was placed in the text by the author or the printer, nor even if either person was aware of the verse's rabbinic interpretation of "crag" as a reference to the six orders of the Mishnah.[114] If this had been the intent of quoting Deuteronomy here, the implication would have been that *Meneket Rivkah* consisted of the most dignified of intellectual food.

The book's seven chapters detail the ideals of conduct and social practices for married women within their domestic world. The first chapter (12 pages) is the only one that does not deal with any specific social relationship but instead with a general female moral precept regarding the "wisdom of the soul" and the "wisdom of the body." This roughly follows the pattern of many morality books of that time, in which the fear of God constitutes the subject of the introduction or first chapter, as in *Brantshpigl* and *Sefer Middot*, or of the concluding chapter, as in *Orhot Zaddikim*. Just as the fear of God constitutes an ethical-religious principle and not an ideal of conduct, so is Rivkah bat Meir's concept of wisdom an ethical principle. The second chapter (12 pages) describes a woman's conduct toward her husband; the third chapter (eight pages) discusses her conduct toward her parents; and the fourth chapter (five pages) discusses her conduct toward her in-laws. The fifth chapter, by far the longest (18 pages), deals with a woman's conduct toward her children; the sixth chapter (four pages) deals with her conduct toward her daughters-in-law; and the concluding seventh chapter (nine pages) deals with her conduct toward the non-familial residents of the home, such as guests, boarders, and house staff.

In the first chapter, the author presents the composition of her book by comparing it to the temple candelabrum:

> The meaning must be as follows: the body of the *menorah* indicates a woman; the six arms are the six chapters that I will write, God willing, after this chapter, and all of which relate to a woman. That is to say that she should follow the six chapters along with the first, which is (like) a body to the other six chapters. (*Meneket Rivkah*, 5b)

The author uses the menorah here as a double metaphor. On one hand, the body of the candelabrum stands for the woman with her social relationships, as described in the following six chapters, while on the other it is a metaphor for the first chapter itself, which assumes a central position as the key to understanding the rest of the book. The comparison of the book with a menorah indicates the high status she attributed to the first chapter, but it is also evidence of Rivkah bat Meir's literary education. The division into seven chapters was a popular form of organization, particularly in Hebrew ethical works. In *Menorat ha-Ma'or* (Candelabrum of light), for example, Isaac Abohav (14th century) used the same seven-armed candelabrum as his model, even referring to his chapters as *nerot* (lamps); another example is the *Sefer ha-Musar* (Book of ethics) by Judah Khalaz (Constantinople, 1537). The multiple editions of *Menorat ha-Ma'or* in the 16th century are evidence of its lasting popularity, serving as a manual for preachers and a welcome text for learned readers who lived in locations without a preacher.[115]

Both the sequence and structure of the chapters reflect an intentionally stringent composition. The first chapter begins with a homily of a very young woman who, upon marrying, leaves her parents' home behind, and with it her childhood. The following chapters are ordered according to the importance of the woman's social obligations and her phases in life. The end of the last chapter of *Meneket Rivkah* reflects its beginning: the subject of the last homily is the old woman, who may go in peace to the world to come (*olam ha-ba*).

Part of the book's composition is its almost complete lack of redundancies, and there are numerous references throughout to issues that have already been mentioned[116] or are yet to be discussed.[117] For that reason, the author frequently assumes the rabbinic convention of abbreviating statements.[118] Occasionally she does so upon adding the remark that there is sufficient evidence in the rabbinic literature, not because the author has exceeded her authority or because of a lack of understanding among her female readers. In one case she breaks off her exposition with the explanation that the number seven is "very deep and far-reaching" (*Meneket Rivkah*, 5b). This corresponds to the conventional rhetorical formulation, used in the exegetic literature as endings for mystical or philosophical subjects. In Yiddish moral literature as well, simple interpretations but especially such kabbalistic subjects are broken off.[119] It is much more surprising that following this section Rivkah bat Meir explains additional examples for the number seven. Agnes Romer Segal has pointed out that it was this form of reduction that made the mention of complex contexts or halakhic problems possible in the first place.[120] It is therefore likely that the author was torn between the rabbinic convention that did not approve of transferring esoteric knowledge to unlearned persons, particularly women, and her wish to pass on her extensive knowledge to other women.

The stringently organized composition of *Meneket Rivkah*, as well as the book's linguistic and stylistic uniformity, indicate beyond doubt that the author left behind a complete copy of her work.

The Literary Style: Between Morality Book and Homiletic Work

The Homiletic Style

The choice of words on the title page, according to which *Meneket Rivkah* contains both "words of moral instruction" (*divrei musar*)[121] and "good biblical interpretations" (*gute pshatim*) (1b), is certainly good advertising, but it does not mislead potential buyers. Already in its time, the book was received as a moral *and* exegetic-homiletical work, and rightly so.[122] In fact, one of the special characteristics of *Meneket Rivkah* is that its description of ideals of conduct and social practices are embedded in at times lengthy narrative and preaching, which sometimes contain specifically exegetic elements. The thoroughness of these homiletic passages displays a striking difference with other Yiddish morality books, for example *Brantshpigl* (Krakow, 1596), although the latter offers a much larger scope of opinions and *aggadot* from rabbinic literature. Its author, Moses Henokhs Altshul, lines them up in mostly abbreviated form, because his emphasis is on encyclopedic completeness of rabbinic textual evidence for any respective subject. Rivkah bat Meir, on the other hand, paraphrases rabbinic literature comparatively rarely, and instead performs a detailed processing of various exegetical originals that she uses to bolster her moral statements. This gives her book a slower, homiletical rhythm.

Biblical exegesis is a firm part of all Jewish preaching, in which there is no clear-cut division whatsoever between exegetical[123] and homiletical[124] passages that resemble the midrash and sometimes pass immediately into each other. The author is sometimes led by the classic rabbinic homily, such as when she introduces a sermon with a Bible quote (*petiḥah*) and its interpretation in order to build a bridge to the verse from the weekly Torah reading that she wishes to interpret. Similar to the eschatological concluding formulation (*ḥatimah*) common in rabbinic homily, Rivkah bat Meir closes these passages with a verse from the Prophets and relates her admonitions to human behavior in "this world."[125]

One particularly long homily (8b–10a) opens with Proverbs 12:4, presenting the *eshet ḥayil*, the "capable wife," following with a sequence of talmudic interpretations (8b). She connects these with another long exegetical chain (9b) by picking up again on Psalms 32:6 from the previous interpretation. This focus is on the word *zot*—female "this." The author presents a total of 12 verses containing this word. On one hand she relates *zot* to the pious, modest woman whose children are rewarded for her merits, and on the other hand she relates it to Torah, in the sense of scholarship. She considers both equally desirable. She also inserts two exegetical digressions into the homily. In the first, she describes in detail why Leah had just as much merit as Rachel, even though she was loved less than the latter. This is an original interpretation by the author for which there is no precedent in rabbinic literature.[126] In the second excursus (9b), which concludes the homily, she states that an impecunious daughter from a scholarly family should not be rejected as a potential marriage partner. Thus the second excursus, which is structured similarly to the eschatological end of the rabbinic homily, relates explicitly to the present by criticizing a marriage policy guided by economic considerations. However, the first excursus can be placed in the practical world as well, considering that arranged marriages did not always result in successful and happy relationships. The author emphasizes, however, that a woman is by no means less meritorious for not being loved. Perhaps this was a consolation for women readers living in unhappy marriages to know that they could earn as much merit and social respect through piety as women living in happy marriages.

The author begins another homily (19b–20b) connected to women's experience with a verse from the Prophets (Jer. 17:7), which presents the subject of the homily according to which trust in God is better than trust in a person. Through an exegetical chain of verses from Psalms she moves to the next subject, which is that one should trust a rebuking but well-meaning person rather than a conspicuously friendly but hypocritical person. She substantiates the sometimes positive effect of painful criticism and the often negative effect of alleged praise with a midrash (20a) about Balaam. For that purpose, the author turns to the problem of the bad blessing, and vice versa, the good curse, which is suggested in the story of Balaam. For clarification, she states a second midrash (20b) that deals with the existence of Israel in exile. Rivkah bat Meir's version of the second midrash is unusual in its combination of various rabbinic versions. By processing these versions stylistically (such as dramatization by direct speech), and in conclusion turning to the present, her version takes on a significantly stronger homiletical character. This is most discernible in the version in the midrash *Panim Aḥerim*, where the situation of the exile takes on a central position, whereas in the versions transmitted by the Yalkut and Talmud, the truth of biblical praises takes precedence.[127] The homily begins with a mention of the exile, where man should rely on God's mercy. The verse that opens the subject matter—"He who trusts in the LORD" (19b)—introduces the following interpretations, similar to a *petiḥah*, which the author finally uses in order to span a bridge to the weekly Torah reading of Balak. Relying on the truthfulness of biblical curses is like the trustful acceptance of well-meant rebuking admonitions. The concluding prophetic *ḥatimah* formula is missing, but the author refers admonishingly to the present at the end of the homily:[128]

> And so we see well that the curse of Ahijah of Shiloh was a blessing and good advice to Israel in exile. . . . We see the same thing every day in front of our own eyes—wicked people who have no fear of God, as are common due to our many transgressions, and who provoke disputes between people, including between daughter-in-law and mother-in-law . . . from which nothing good comes—only disputing and quarreling. (*Meneket Rivkah*, 20b)

The homiletical character of Rivkah bat Meir's instructions and sermons is likewise emphasized by the liturgical references at the end of each chapter. While chapters three, five, and six end with a prayer for redemption, or for return to Zion, or, as in chapter three, for individual redemption by one's own merits, the author quotes biblical verses bearing specific significance in the prayer services at the end of chapters one, two, four, and seven. These liturgical references become particularly distinct at the end of the last chapter, which the author concludes with a quote from Proverbs 3:17. In the Ashkenazi rituals during the early modern period, this verse was recited during both the removal of the Torah from, as well as its return to the ark.[129] It can hardly be assumed, then, that this conclusion would be pure coincidence. Instead, at the end of the reading of *Meneket Rivkah*, the author is most probably referencing the end of the Torah reading.

Female Rhetoric

The narrative style of *Meneket Rivkah* contributes to its homiletical character. But the narrative element is not supported by a lavish number of paraphrases of rabbinic *aggadot*, as is the case, for example, in *Brantshpigl*.[130] Compared to *Brantshpigl* and *Meneket Rivkah*, *Sefer Middot* takes a middle position. Particularly in its first two-thirds, only a limited number of fairly long tales, from rabbinic and non-rabbinic sources, illustrate and interpret the respective topic, while in the last third a large number of shorter rabbinic tales follow one another.[131] The relatively limited number of *aggadot* in *Meneket Rivkah* is not necessarily a result of material from the *aggadot* having been transmitted mainly in Aramaic, and the author thus not having understood them, since there were sufficient Hebrew transmissions of *aggadot* in Hebrew ethical literature or Yiddish translations in morality books—not to mention the existence of oral transmissions. However, the *aggadot* paraphrased by Rivkah bat Meir are actually based on the Hebrew transmissions. The only exception is the tale of the wives of Korah and On ben Pelet (10a–10b), which was transmitted in Aramaic both in the midrash and in the parallel talmudic transmission.

The main reason behind the author's sparse use of rabbinic narrative material is the fact that it was not common in women's rhetoric. Since access to rabbinic literature was barred to most Jewish women, they were acquainted with only a very limited section of its narrative treasure, and were accustomed to seasoning their speech with other oral traditions such as biblical metaphors, vernacular proverbs,[132] popular tales, and narrative reports of everyday experiences. In any case, these oral stylistic devices offered the same, or at least comparable, rhetorical function as the rabbinic *aggadot*. Just like the latter, they served a linguistic-aesthetic purpose, as well as providing a metaphoric interpretation and illustration of theological and moral topics.

Thus, the composition of the narrative material reflects the rhetoric women were familiar with. Of the 15 tales, six originate in rabbinic literature,[133] four are tales from moral literature,[134] one is biblical (where the author may have used a midrash), and three others constitute eyewitness reports.[135] It is remarkable that no other Yiddish morality book makes use of such detailed personal reports, and that the author grants them similar didactical weight as parables from other literary sources. In addition, the text contains a long tale (16a–18a) that has its origins in Christian narrative tradition. Besides the aforesaid inclusion in *Meshiv Hema—Minhagim Eshet Ḥayil*, evidence of this tale is found only in an extremely abbreviated version in *Brantshpigl*, and it stands out because of its unusual length. The tale in question is a European wandering tale that was known in many parts of Western and Central Europe during the early modern period.[136] Its essential moral aspect is that the hope for support from their adult children should not cause parents to trust them blindly (see the proverb on 16a and 17b). This version contains specific Jewish details (such as the *Kaddish* and a rabbi),[137] and places a new moral emphasis whereby parents will be treated by their children in the same manner in which they themselves treated their own parents. The moral can be found in this version in *Brantshpigl*, too, but evidence for a connection between a Yiddish adaptation and a new moral, which is also supported by a rabbinic opinion (*Meneket Rivkah*, 18a), can be found only here.

The narrative, homiletical style of *Meneket Rivkah* allows us to assume that the homilies correspond at least in part to sermons actually given by Rivkah bat Meir. Yet one must still assume a more or less high degree of stylistic editing occurred when the words were put down in written form. Though there are 39 times in which she describes her activity as writing,[138] there are also 16 references to oral transmission in terms such as "talk," "say," or "speak."[139] Her designation of the chapters, too, indicates editing of oral material. Usually, the author uses the common Hebrew word *sha'ar*[140] for "chapter," but in one place she refers to a chapter with the word *shi'ur* (lesson).[141] The originally oral version can be recognized in the relatively frequent way she addresses her readers as "my dear women,"[142] and the even more frequent indirect address in rhetoric that is appellative, admonishing, enticing, sometimes almost imploring: "This is as our beloved Torah wishes, and, praise God, as we have clearly, explicitly, and straightforward in front of us: if we would only want to do it and to keep it in mind properly, then we could have this world as well as the world to come" (*Meneket Rivkah*, 11b).

It cannot be determined with certainty whether it was Rivkah bat Meir herself who created her homilies. Since she repeatedly references them to the female world and intersperses specifically female experiences, however, it is probable that the homilies were the author's original creations. But even in cases where she falls back on written or oral sources she adjusts them to a woman's everyday life, which gives us insight into her preaching skills.

The Exegetic Style

Several passages put less emphasis on the didactic-homiletical use of Bible quotes and more on their actual explanation and interpretation. In these exegetical sections, the author frequently uses terminology and methods borrowed from rabbinic discussions. One of these rabbinic terms is the word *peshat*—meaning the literal understanding of the Bible, or simply "explanation"—which she applies both to interpretations from other sources and to her own.[143] She often introduces the presentation of an exegetic problem with the Aramaic word *kashya*[144]—objection, difficulty, problem—and resolves it by the use of rabbinic terms such as *hakesh*—draw a parallel (4b), *mima nafshekha*—no matter the situation (11b; 28a), *afilu hakhi*—even in this case (16a), *kefel lashon*—pleonasm (4a, 34b), or *metarez*—explains (4b). One method of interpretation popular in rabbinic exegesis, and one which she uses particularly frequently, is the principle of *a fortiori*, which she designates with the term *mikol she-ken*—literally, all the more[145]—and she also applies the numerical operations of *gematria*[146] and *notarikon* as exegetical methods.[147] The skillful use of these terms shows that Rivkah bat Meir must have received a solid training in rabbinic exegesis.

Occasionally the author legitimizes her own interpretation not with the help of other verses or another traditional interpretation, but through a Yiddish proverb or expression.[148] This was by no means a common practice in Yiddish moral literature. Similar to *Meneket Rivkah,* only the distinctly didactical narrative *Brantshpigl* made frequent use of proverbs.[149] Apart from their aesthetic-rhetorical function, proverbs have been defined as pieces of everyday wisdom with a normative influence, clad in poetic forms.[150] This means in the exegetical context that proverbs, because of their normative effect, can support a statement or claim and thus fulfill a similar function as verses from the Bible or quotes from rabbinic literature.

Ultimately, the few albeit sometimes very detailed exegetical passages served a moral-didactical purpose. In these passages, particularly by the application of rabbinic terminology, Rivkah bat Meir provides evidence of her erudition and familiarity with rabbinic discourse, which is meant to emphasize not her moral authority but her authority as exegete. This is expressed most directly in her repeated formulation, "but I would like to explain the verse in such a way."[151]

Sources and Their Editing

By presenting below the literary sources evidently used in *Meneket Rivkah*, I do not mean to postulate that Rivkah bat Meir used them as direct and immediate patterns for paraphrasing. On one hand, it is difficult to identify any concrete original sources, because the author translated all Hebrew material into Yiddish except for Bible quotes, and thus edited outside texts. On the other hand, the majority of the rabbinic material was transmitted in several more or less deviating versions, which hardly allows determination of the original source. Thus, when I mention sources below, I merely refer to the earliest or most popular written form of an interpretation or narrative passage contained in *Meneket Rivkah*.

In addition, we cannot be entirely sure of the author's work method in this regard. It was probably not her standard procedure to copy directly from a specific book or to directly paraphrase it. In light of the large number of works to which she had access, it is likely that she extemporized from her earlier reading. Perhaps she only knew many of the rabbinic texts from oral discussion, and thus the actual source was unknown to her. If so, then the author's designation of a source makes clear its relevance to her, particularly in the case of a work from outside traditional rabbinic literature that must have been highly regarded by her and her readers. The large number and range of sources thus gives us insight into Rivkah bat Meir's high standard of education. Her method of processing the sources tells us about her specific understanding of them, and thus of her understanding of women and their world. Last but not least, her method provides a more precise understanding of her work as teacher and preacher.

The overwhelming majority of the quotes are taken from the Bible. The verses are immediately translated ("*doz iz taytsh*") into common, clear Yiddish. Often the translation is replaced by an explanation, which corresponds to the usual practice of Yiddish moral literature,[152] and because the Yiddish verb *taytshen* means both "translate" and "explain."[153] Only rarely is a translation or explanation omitted completely. Occasionally, the quotes deviate from the masoretic text, which, aside from misprints, is probably due to the author's faulty recollection of a verse, given her impression of a specific interpretation.[154]

The quoting of rabbinic literature corresponds to the common practice in morality books of that time. Instead of providing a concrete source, the author merely presents indications such as "our sages said," "the midrash explains,"[155] or, more often, "the Gemara explains." The latter is by no means always followed by quotes from the Talmud; instead, it is often a midrash or a combination of various transmissions. This implies that Rivkah bat Meir considered the Gemara a generic term for the totality of rabbinic literature,[156] perhaps because of the common perception of rabbinic literature as united, since all of its works were studied together in the yeshivot by the scholarly male elite. The only rabbinic work the author mentions by name is the midrash *Yalkut*

Shimoni, which, unlike older, anonymously transmitted midrashim, is the work of a known author.[157]

Of the authors of the exegetical literature, the author names only Rashi.[158] Otherwise she simply refers to the "commentators" (*mefarshim*) as a source.[159] One of them can be identified undoubtedly as Abraham Ibn Ezra. The general impression is that Rivkah bat Meir, particularly in the first chapter, referred to several terms and interpretations from Ibn Ezra without naming him.[160] The phrase "wisdom of the soul" (*hokhmat ha-neshamah*), which is found in Ibn Ezra on Ecclesiastes 7:21 and on Daniel 4:28, as well as in a passage of *Orhot Zaddikim* (57a) (which she likewise names), deserves particular attention. In both sources it means "peace of the soul" or "internal enlightenment." For its counterpart, "wisdom of the body" (*hokhmat ha-guf*), no evidence is found that it exists in the rabbinic or ethical literature, suggesting that it is a neologism by the author.[161] Although *Orhot Zaddikim* does mention physical needs in the aforesaid context, they are designated as *ta'avot ha-guf* (desires of the body), which other authors consider to be antagonists of the "wisdom of the soul." Thus these terms, as used by Ibn Ezra and in *Orhot Zaddikim*, adhere to the Neoplatonic and kabbalistic world of ideas, whereas the author, in her application of these concepts, seeks to harmonize them with the tradition of Aristotle. She understands them as positive, mutually complementing physical and religious-social necessities, which correspond more to the ethics of Sa'adya Ga'on's or Maimonides's "Golden Mean."[162]

Maimonides (Moshe ben Maimon, or Rambam) is the only other rabbinic authority mentioned by the author as a source besides Rashi. She cites almost literally a medical-ethical piece of advice from his halakhic Mishnah commentary without naming it. Rivkah bat Meir certainly knew Maimonides as one of the greatest philosophers and halakhic authorities in Judaism, and she was probably also aware of the fact that he had been a renowned physician. It must remain unclear, however, if she did not mention his name for the same reason she refrained from any halakhic discussion (that is, the rabbinic prohibition for women to deal with *halakhah*), or because she simply did not know that this very passage originated from Maimonides.[163]

The third most frequently used type of source in *Meneket Rivkah*, after biblical and rabbinic literature, is ethical literature. From this genre she most often mentions the Hebrew ethical-kabbalistic book *Reshit Hokhmah*[164] (The Beginning of wisdom) by Eliyahu de Vidas (16th century), which gained popularity in the 16th and 17th centuries.[165] Although quotes from this work are translated paraphrases, their contents are rendered precisely.[166] One passage constitutes a literal translation, which gives the impression that the author had the source at hand.[167] Another morality book she quotes is the aforementioned *Orhot Zaddikim*,[168] which she may have confused with the Yiddish *Sefer Middot* that she mentions in a different place.[169]

The author provides numerous quotes from the medieval ethical work *Sefer Hasidim* (Book of the pious).[170] Two of her paraphrases have not been located, or have not been located with certainty,[171] but two additional passages can be related unequivocally.[172] However, the presentation of the following passages by the author raises a number of questions:

Sefer Ḥasidim writes, one may not speak of or believe things such as: One should not take fire from (a place where) a woman is lying in childbed; or one may not perform a (circumcision) on any particular day. Or (one must not say), "The magpie is crowing— we'll have guests"; or, "The fire lit up and can not be extinguished—the guest who is coming will drown."[173]

This passage is quoted in the context of a warning against superstitions, and with its heavy formulations and faulty syntax, deviates distinctively from the author's otherwise skillful Yiddish. In fact, the translation of the respective Hebrew passage of the *Sefer Ḥasidim* deviates significantly from the passage presented here:

One should not take fire twice [from the hearth], if a sick person is in the house, or during the nine days, which a woman in childbed spends there.... If one sees a coal fire lighting up, one (should not) say, "We will have a guest," or if it is extinguished with water, "The guest will fall into the water."[174]

Unless she was working from a completely corrupt manuscript, it is hardly conceivable that Rivkah bat Meir could have misunderstood the Hebrew *Sefer Ḥasidim* to such a degree. Even if she was not familiar with the custom of a woman remaining in childbed for nine days, and she therefore brought the warning in connection with circumcision, the question of the missing unequivocal reference to the sick person remains. Somewhat mysterious is the missing translation of the divinatory explanation of the fire, and the confusion of *agelster* (magpie) with the original *esh gaḥelet* (coal fire). It must be assumed that the author did not use an accurate Hebrew version of *Sefer Ḥasidim* as her source, but that she knew this passage from oral transmission or a supposedly Yiddish translation. That translation, however, was not only faulty or clumsy, but also offered an interesting contemporary adaptation, which included Central European superstitions. An indication to that effect is the mention of the magpie, to which early modern popular belief in Poland and Germany ascribed special divinatory abilities.[175]

Aside from these Hebrew works, the author quotes two Yiddish books: the already-mentioned Yiddish morality book *Sefer Middot*, and a *Vroyen Bikhel*.[176] The quoting of Yiddish books, as in the suggestion to "accustom herself to read Yiddish books" (*Meneket Rivkah*, 6a), is completely unusual in moral literature of the 16th century. I am aware of no other work of moral literature of that time that displays such a positive attitude toward this genre. This positive attitude is expressed by the author, for example, when she legitimizes one of her central ethical ideas, that is, the woman's responsibility for her deeds. At one such place, Rivkah bat Meir points to the many pieces of evidence that justify this idea. However, she does not provide any biblical or rabbinic source of evidence, but only the *Vroyen Bikhel*, which is part of the moral-halakhic *Miẓvot Nashim* (Women's commandments) corpus.[177] This attitude demonstrates the high regard she had for the Yiddish moral-halakhic literature, which was probably shared by the majority of women at the time. This is also clear from the plethora of editions published of this literature during the 16th century, that these were a response to the unlearned masses' immense need for easily understood summaries of important daily rules.[178] The fact that the rabbinic elite had vehemently rejected the

Yiddish moral-halakhic literature since its beginnings in the late 14th century was clearly of no concern to those who produced or read these works. What the rabbis feared more than the profanation of holy texts by their reproduction in the spoken language was the loss of their own monopoly on authority. Thus, their main objection was against the possibility that the unlearned, including women, could be tempted to decide relevant halakhic questions by themselves. The Maharil, Jacob ben Moses Molin (Moelln; d. 1427), for example, sharply refused in one of his responsa to accede to the request of an author for permission to write a Yiddish compendium of the laws on menstruating women:

> I must reply to my esteemed and beloved R. Hayim.... I was greatly amazed that it should have occurred to you to compose a work in the language of Ashkenaz, as you plan. And we already regret those who have preceded you since any layman who knows how to read Rashi's commentary or a *maḥzor* ... and people alike will glance at the works of great Rabbis such as *Sha'arei Dura* [halakhic compilation of prohibitions and permissions (*issur ve-heter*) from the 14th century].... *They will make practical legal rulings from such works.* And now you have come, adding to all this ... [a book] for the ignorant, and for women ... in order to instruct them on the basis of your Yiddish work in matters of menstrual laws and stains ... even though we see many works dealing with laws of ritual prohibitions, menstrual laws, *ḥallah*, and laws of Pesaḥ and festivals.[179]

Halakhic authority could only be obtained by male scholars capable of studying the Hebrew body of laws. Therefore the Maharil noted in his responsum that oral transmission of knowledge would be sufficient for women. Consequently, up to the middle of the 16th century, most Yiddish moral-halakhic works were published anonymously, and their authors attempted to downplay their roles as mere compilers. For their legitimacy, they referred to other authoritative halakhic works, to acknowledged—or anonymous—authorities, or even to their learned wives.[180] In addition, they repeatedly called upon the female readers, should they have any doubts, to turn to the rabbi, or his wife, but at least to their own husbands.[181] The publisher of *Eyn shoyn Froyenbuykhleyn*, which is similar to this type of literature, justified himself with the words: "He first obtained the permission of the rabbis, so that he should not perform an abomination, and, God forbid, instruct someone in the wrong way."[182]

The general suspicion against this literature, which most likely was the justified or unjustified suspicion against women's halakhic observance, was not resolved even 200 years after the Maharil.[183] Thus, Moses Henokhs Altshul, the author of *Brantshpigl*, was eager to warn the women:

> And even if you find in a *froyen bikhleyn* something that is pure, or impure, do not abide by it. King Solomon says in Proverbs, "Do not rely on your own understanding" (Prov. 3:5).... Perhaps you believe that you would understand, but you don't. No woman should make decisions. Choose an old understanding Jewess, and send her to the rabbi.[184]

This rejection may have been another reason why Rivkah bat Meir completely abstained from any halakhic discussion, although in connection with the "wisdom of the body," a compilation of halakhic rules of *niddah* (the regulations and rituals concerning a menstruating woman) would certainly have been appropriate. But in avoiding such a discussion she does not cite her lack of authority in halakhic matters as the reason, which would have been the norm in Yiddish moral literature; remarkably, she merely notes regarding menstruation, "I do not need to write much about this subject, because every woman knows well enough herself how she should conduct herself."[185] In so doing, the author skirted the displeasure of the rabbinic authorities, but her casual quoting of a Yiddish moral-halakhic work still provides some insight into her positive attitude, and perhaps that of most women and unlearned men, toward this literature.

One can only guess the sources of some of the author's thoughts and interpretations. This is true, for example, of the source of her idea of a "seventh millennium" as a Shabbat Millennium (*Meneket Rivkah*, 5b), which was not at all common in rabbinic literature. The *shemitah* millennium in the kabbalistic teaching of the *shemitot*, according to which a cosmic cycle of the millennia constantly creates new worlds, gained a certain popularity. This was the basic idea of the 13th century *Sefer ha-Temunah* (Book of the image), which was known only to a small circle of kabbalists in the 16th century.[186] One outspoken adherent of this teaching was Mordecai ben Abraham Jaffe (d. 1612) from Prague, who preached there from 1592 until 1596 as the successor of the Maharal. Thus, there is a possibility that Rivkah bat Meir, to the extent that the book was unknown to her, may have heard this idea from a preacher or rabbi.[187]

Her source for the interpretation of the word *sullam* (ladder) in Genesis 28:12 as *mamon* (money), according to the method of *gematria*, is likewise uncertain. The author cites a "midrash" as the source, but no work of the rabbinic literature contains this *gematria*. Its earliest evidence can be found in the *Sefer Gematriyot* by Yehudah he-Ḥasid from the 13th century, which only existed in manuscript until the modern era, the interpretations of which were included in later, though marginal, Ashkenazi Torah commentaries.[188] In this case, too, it remains uncertain how the author learned of this interpretation.

Another idea that Rivkah bat Meir relied upon, and that was also unusual in the moral literature of the 16th century, is that of the first female creation, Lilith (9a). The author quotes a midrash as her source, possibly referring to the *Alfa Beta de-Ben Sira*. However, this rabbinic work was controversial because of its polemic and cutting satirical character (Maimonides was one of its strongest opponents), and it remained unmentioned in the contemporary moral literature except for *Brantshpigl*, which Rivkah bat Meir could have cited as a reference. However, she did not do so and did not even derive her information tacitly from it because she supplies information which does not appear in *Brantshpigl*. Thus, she must have drawn her information about Lilith from some other source.[189] Perhaps her reference to the midrash actually refers to the *Zohar*, which incorporated the tradition of *Alfa Beta de-Ben Sira*. The tale of Lilith only became known to a broader audience through the popularization of the *Zohar* during the 17th century. Until then it was known only to a narrow kabbalist circle. Although Rivkah bat Meir was obviously familiar with some ideas of the *Zohar*,[190] it is doubtful that she knew the Aramaic *Zohar* from her own reading. Thus in this case, too, it cannot be determined whether knowledge of the tale of Lilith was based on the *Zohar*, which may have been transmitted to her orally, or in fact on *Alfa Beta de-Ben Sira*. Be that as it may, the esoteric interpretations and ideas presented in *Meneket Rivkah* provide a clear indication of Rivkah bat Meir's high level of education, which included the knowledge of ideas and works that were unknown to the great majority of women and unlearned men of her time.

Compared with elaborate, comprehensive morality books from the 16th century, *Meneket Rivkah* contains a similar range of genres as sources, whereas the shorter, less elaborate works quote from a significantly smaller corpus, made up exclusively of the Bible, midrashim, Talmud, and the exegetical literature. Each of the elaborate works, however, presents the individual author's choice of specific works of such genres. And thus we find in the Hebrew ethical works *Sefer Mizvot* (Book of duties) by Maimonides,[191] and, relatively frequently, books from the medieval circle of the *Hasidei Ashkenaz*, such as *Sefer Hasidim* (Book of the pious; printed first in 1538) and *Sefer ha-Rokeah* (Book of the apothecary; printed first in 1505).[192] Other genres are not quoted by either Rivkah bat Meir or by other authors. Two unusual exceptions underline this rule: only a single morality book names *Sefer ha-Refu'ot* (Book of remedies),[193] a book about natural history and medicine, and one other morality book mentions a medical book allegedly entitled *Sefer Ba'alei Hayyim* (Book of animals).[194]

The extensive *Brantshpigl*, on the other hand, uses highly varied, wide-ranging source material. Its author not only quotes frequently from the Bible and talmudic literature,[195] but also from medieval, Sephardic literature, from Maimonides among others,[196] and particularly from the ethic-philosophical works of *Hovot ha-Levavot*[197] (Duties of the heart; printed first in 1489) by Bahya ibn Paquda, *Shevilei Emunah*[198] (Paths of faith; printed first in 1518) by Meir ben Isaac Aldabi, the aforementioned *Menorat ha-Ma'or*[199] (1514), and *Sefer ha-Musar*[200] (1537) by Judah Khalaz. Although unnamed, *Sefer Musarei ha-pilozofim* (Book of the philosophers' ethics, 1562) or *Tikkun Middot ha-Nefesh* (Improvement of the moral qualities, 1550) by Solomon ibn Gabirol,[201] and Abraham bar Hiyya's *Hegyon ha-Nefesh* (Meditation of the soul)[202] may be assumed to have been used as sources. Moses Henokhs Altshul mentions the *hakhmei ha-kabbalah* (sages of the Kabbalah) at least 70 times, referring usually to the *Sefer ha-Zohar*[203] (Book of splendor; printed first from 1558–60). In addition to Sephardic works, he quotes only a few Ashkenazi books, such as *Sefer Hasidim* (1538)[204] and possibly *Reshit Hokhmah* (1579), which he does not mention by name, but where some of his exegetical and narrative explanations can be found.

This great abundance of quoted literature alone shows that Moses Henokhs's purpose was by no means merely the description of contemporary ideals of conduct, but also, and often predominantly, an encyclopedic compilation of rabbinic and philosophical moral standards and ethic-kabbalistic ideas—ultimately, the order of the body of Jewish knowledge of unlearned Jewish men and women of the 16th century.

This unmentioned program influenced the demands of conduct formulated in his book. Other morality books, too, succeed repeatedly in astonishing readers with descriptions of ideals that are incompatible with historic reality. I, therefore, consider it appropriate to examine more closely the context of the ideas presented in the morality books, and their methods of discourse.

The Discourse of the Morality Books

Academics in the humanities have held for some time now that society and socially conscious behavior are not bound by a rigid set of standards. As such, a central research
question has focused on how individuals' different experiences have shaped their social
conditions. Rather than moving as pawns according to fixed rules, women, men, and
children are considered active participants in determining social rules and outcomes
through their own interpretations and decisions. This has often been described as a
negotiation process, in the course of which a society's existing mores are interpreted
and evaluated on the basis of individual and collective experiences, thereby redeter-
mining correct and incorrect social conduct.[205]

In the framework of this praxeological view of society, in which authors of moral
literature are also considered acting subjects, the female and male readers of this literature are not mere passive consumers but also actors, determining their actions more
or less in accordance with the described ideals of conduct and social practices. The
influence of morality books was greater the more closely they corresponded to the
practical interests of the reading audience, and the more quickly they could convince
that audience of the truth and correctness of the described ways of conduct. The
question as to which social practices are essential for a pious Jewish way of life took
on a new form of discourse in the 16th century: that of popular moral literature.[206]
With the appearance and increasing popularization of this literature, the majority of
Jewish society, women and unlearned men gained access to various areas of Jewish
knowledge for the first time.

While moral-halakhic literature considered itself an extract of what was then considered valid *halakhah*, the moral-didactical literature formulated ideals of conduct and
social practices that were not determined by religious law. Similar to the *halakhah* itself,
these ideals of conduct also needed to be adapted to the changing requirements of
everyday life, and could only be transformed into socially conscious actions if they
could be integrated into existing thought, connotation, and acting schemes.

A closer look at the popular moral literature of the 16th century, however, shows
that even its authors who wrote at the same time and in the same cultural environment
had different, sometimes incompatible, understandings of socially conscious actions,
and by no means coincided in the formulation of ideals of conduct. The question arises
as to what the reasons were for these moral divergences, and what they meant for the
practical application of the texts.

I consider the discourse analysis developed by Michel Foucault, which is best
understood as a theory-guided analysis grid or tool for the understanding of social
processes, as particularly well-suited for the examination of these divergences.[207]
Foucault himself understood discourse as an act of calling into question, in a specific
historical phase, what was until then regarded as the truth, and thus as a social practice
that produces generally binding truths and thus constitutes social reality.[208] Since truth
cannot be produced at random, every society has a "politics of truth," containing a set
of already existing and accepted interpretation patterns and social conventions, on

the basis of which a discourse is proven true. In this context, Foucault regarded the categories "power" and "discourse" as interdependent: social power relationships produce a specific discourse. At the same time, the discourse produces power relationships by producing concepts of social action. However, in order to generate a discourse, or in order to take power over a discourse, specific regulations must be observed. In that sense, certain taboos must be respected in order to prevent random wild growth of the discourse, and certain socially determined and determining limits of knowledge may not be overstepped. When transferred to Jewish moral literature, this means that the intangibility of rabbinic normative authority is never questioned, and the field of exclusive rabbinic knowledge, namely the *halakhah*, may never be invaded by unauthorized persons—women and unlearned men.

As a backdrop to Foucault's notion of discourse, Rüdiger Schnell developed in his study on gender discourses during the early modern period a practicable model for the analysis of the discourse of individual morality books.[209] He worked out that the gender discourses conducted in the moral literature are not determined solely by the author's gender perspective, but mainly by the respective usage and communication form of the text. For that purpose, text features such as the intention of the statement, manner of speech, usage of sources, and reader must be analyzed. These will show whether the respective text pursues a pragmatic discourse with practically oriented interest in every-day situations and practical instructions for action, or whether it conducts a speculative-dogmatic discourse that deals in a scientific-dialectical manner with standards and ideals led by canonized literary traditions. However, some texts do not pursue an integrated discourse, but instead fluctuate between studied observation and an attempt at practical application.

The examination of texts based on discourse analysis and usage orientation opens up a new perspective on the reasons for the differing ideals of conduct and social practices in Jewish moral literature. In fact, part of Yiddish moral literature tended to use the pragmatic discourse by referring comparatively less to transmitted literary standards than to the Hebrew morality books of the same period, and was therefore more open toward existing ideals of conduct. The Hebrew as well as part of the Yiddish moral literature was guided by the orthodox[210] rabbinic moral discourse, and the patterns of action and ideals handed down with it were often anachronistic and therefore not practicable in the 16th century. However, I would not limit this phenomenon to Yiddish works translated from Hebrew, because large parts of original Yiddish works, for example, *Brantshpigl*, conducted an orthodox moral discourse. On the other hand, the orthodox discourse should not be regarded as something absolutely static, because, as the example of the *halakhah* shows, even an orthodox discourse had to undergo careful adjustments to new social, economic, and technical conditions, and to changing values and mentalities, if it wished to retain its normative authority.

Chava Turniansky gave the first important indication of the discourse dependency of moral literature, although she used different terms to describe this aspect. She emphasized that Yiddish moral literature underwent a basic change toward the end of the 16th and the beginning of the 17th centuries. This was the time of the first original

Yiddish moral writings that were not translations from the Hebrew, and which, although they quoted extensively from rabbinic literature, did not depend directly on any older Hebrew morality book.

> The liberation from the dependency on a specific text that usually originated in another time, and in faraway places, allowed the Yiddish moral literature to establish closer connections to daily life at the time, and the place, where they had been written. Consequently, it put a greater emphasis on the description of reality, and on its criticism, whereas the share taken by descriptions of religious standards, and of abstract ideals, decreased.[211]

This important observation, however, only reflects the tendency of a small number of works, since, although Turniansky characterizes the Yiddish morality books as "works of reference" and "guides," she is forced to realize that in most of them, the description of the ideal outweighs the portrayal of reality.[212]

In fact, many morality books, including original Yiddish ones, continued the orthodox discourse of the Hebrew ethical books. That may have been because, to their authors, the concrete, practicable daily behavior was less important than the transfer of traditional knowledge, as is the case with *Brantshpigl*, or because they felt an obligation toward the normativity and the legitimacy of the rabbinic ethical works, feeling that the description of new patterns of conduct that had become a fact long before would be illegitimate. I would negate the question as to whether the Ashkenazi authors in the early modern period were aware of the fact that many of the rabbinic or medieval ideals of conduct were hardly topical and appropriate in their time, when social conditions did not correspond to those of medieval Levant or Spain, because nowhere do the authors reflect on the discrepancies between traditional ideals and contemporary ways of conduct.

Contemporary and outdated instructions and ideals of conduct, such as pragmatic and orthodox discourse, often coexist peacefully. One particularly impressive example is Moses Henokhs Altshul's narration that women, upon leaving the house, cover their faces and leave only openings for the eyes.[213] This instruction cannot be found in any contemporary morality book. In fact, Ashkenazi women in the early modern period would never have considered wearing a veil.[214] Rather, Altshul took this behavioral prescription from the Sephardic *Menorat ha-Ma'or* (13th century), which, at the time belonged to the canon of ethical literature and became part of the normative foundation for most orthodox moral discourses.[215]

By comparing *Meneket Rivkah* with the moral-didactical *Brantshpigl* we find particularly clear evidence that the behavioral practices described in works conducting an orthodox discourse reflected the place and time of their creation only in a limited way. They collect, in a very comprehensive manner, the ideals of conduct and practical behavioral demands in regard to many, if not all, areas of Jewish life. Noteworthy about these works is the fact that their authors, Moses Henokhs Altshul[216] and Rivkah bat Meir, lived in Prague at the same time and probably knew each other personally. Both were known and respected in the Jewish community to the extent that they held public positions. Moses Henokhs, too, was a scholar, even though he did not function as rabbi, preacher, or teacher; instead, according to contemporary sources, he held the position of a community scribe and *shul klopfer*—the beadle, who would knock on people's doors in order to summon them to the morning prayer.[217] *Brantshpigl* was written and printed twice (Krakow, 1596; Basel, 1602) during the lifetime of Rivkah bat Meir.[218] However, no direct dependency between *Meneket Rivkah* and *Brantshpigl* can be discerned. Neither quotes the other work and there is no proof for any immediate reception. Despite the many thematic issues in common between the two works, they only rarely overlap in the manners of conduct demanded by the authors, because *Brantshpigl* emphasizes the rabbinic orthodox discourse and only occasionally prescribes modes of everyday behavior.

However, orthodox discourse is not marked only by the quantity of the rabbinic sources quoted. While *Brantshpigl* and *Orḥot Zaddikim* refer relatively frequently and in detail to rabbinic literature, *Sefer Middot* or *Sefer Oraḥ Ḥayyim* (Book of the way of life), which often conduct an orthodox discourse, paraphrase rabbinic source material far more tersely. At the same time, all of these works were first and foremost compendia of knowledge; their function was less as practical guides than as reference works where readers could find information on traditional normative statements regarding contemporary daily topics.

Rivkah bat Meir, on the other hand, conducts a generally pragmatic discourse with concrete instructions of behavior, oriented toward women's daily routines. The rabbinic discourse in her exegetic-homiletic passages, where she makes references to the traditional knowledge base, did not postulate on any specific, outdated ideals of conduct for the present, but provided a foundation for contemporary ideals and practices and perhaps illustrated them. Her main concerns were actual, contemporary ideals of conduct and the demand for corresponding action, which she did not adjust to traditional standards but supported with the help of traditional methods, namely exegesis and sermon.

Feminizing Exegesis

Since its beginnings, Jewish exegesis has reinterpreted both the written Torah (*Torah she-bikhtav*, the Bible) and the orally transmitted Torah (*Torah she-be'al peh*, the rabbinic literature). The interpretations of canonical exegetes from the Middle Ages essentially determined the later understanding of the Bible and rabbinic literature, even though the social values that formed the foundation of these older rulings had long ceased to correspond to social realities. Furthermore, whatever contradictions existed within these interpretations, which had arisen over centuries and within different cultural frameworks, they shared the fact that they had all been created by male scholars. Without exception, women were mere objects of interpretations with no direct influence on the formulation and evaluation of their prescribed behavior, ideals, or symbolic attributions.

Based on the traditional openness toward new interpretations, it is therefore not surprising that Rivkah bat Meir, experienced as preacher and teacher, occasionally arrives at completely new interpretations.[219] It is refreshing to find that her interpretations sometimes broaden rabbinic interpretations, though only very subtly, introducing a certain female element.[220] There are, however, other rabbinic interpretations that she modifies more distinctly, or sometimes she conducts a fundamental reinterpretation, manifesting an explicitly female aspect, so that we can even speak of a feminization of exegesis. My notion of "feminization" refers not to the introduction of classical gender ideology concerning femininity, as it can be found in the male-encoded texts written exclusively by men, but to the opportunity to write and the actual practice of writing women's own constructions of femininity, female ideals, and role models into these texts.

In rabbinic literature (for example, Bereshit Rabbah 17.8), the woman's role in the creation of a child is considered to be less than that of the man. Rabbinic exegesis culls evidence for this theory from the secondary creation of the woman out of Adam's rib (Gen. 2:22), suggesting that the woman is merely the "house" or "vessel" for the male seed. Male superiority as primary progenitor, at the same time, is attributed to his primary creation from earth (Gen. 2:7).[221] However, in an unusual, almost ironic manner, Rivkah bat Meir uses precisely these verses to derive the supposition that the role of the woman, at least when it comes to creating pious and god-fearing children, is, in fact, greater than that of the man:

> I have a difficulty here: Why did he use the word *binyan*, which means build, in reference to the woman, and in reference to the man he uses the word "*va-yazar*" (Gen. 2:7), which means in Yiddish, and he created—? It seems to me that the essence of "building" lies with the woman, as I wrote above. (*Meneket Rivkah*, 5a)

The author refers here to her earlier detailed description (3b–4a) of the female "house" as the location of her body-related ideals of conduct, deriving unequivocally that the woman has the greater part in the successful upbringing of the children that are instructed by her in the home. Because, according to the author, the virtuous handling of the female body (menstruation and pregnancy) takes on a high priority, there must be a female part in Creation, which is negated in rabbinic literature.[222] Through this broadening of the traditional interpretation of Genesis 2:7 and Genesis 2:22, which gave man absolute priority, Rivkah bat Meir added an active, socially cultivating function to the woman's purely biological function.

Besides the aforesaid broadening, *Meneket Rivkah* likewise contains interpretations by the author that differ even more fundamentally from traditional exegesis. In rabbinic literature, Genesis 3:16: "And to the woman He said, 'I will make most severe your pangs in childbearing; in pain shall you bear children. Yet your urge shall be for your husband, and he shall rule over you,'" is interpreted as an accumulation of curses that were laid upon Eve as atonement for her guilt for having eaten the forbidden fruit and having induced Adam to do the same.[223] As with rabbinic interpretations, scarcely any contemporary Yiddish morality book can avoid mentioning that Eve, by her actions, brought death into the world and was therefore punished with many sorts of pain. This interpretation pattern can be found particularly frequently in *Brantshpigl*.[224] *Eyn shoyn Froyenbuykhleyn* drastically places Eve and consequently all women on one level with "murderers," and as such, the book says that a woman must repent for 40 years, until menopause, with monthly fasting and menstrual pain.[225]

Therefore, it is all the more conspicuous that Rivkah bat Meir mentions only marginally the component of physical pain as punishment. She does quote the traditional interpretation of "in pain" as the pain of birth and menstruation; however, she does not consider that interpretation as penance for guilt, but instead refers to women's natural character since animals, too, are capable of pregnancy and birth. Her obvious discomfort with the rabbinic interpretation causes her instead to provide her own interpretation. While citing the rabbinic interpretation of "your pangs" as the efforts and the work of child rearing, she also gives her own interpretation of "your pangs" as menstruation, and thus as distress resulting from the unwanted absence of pregnancy. In her interpretation of "in pain" as work, she could be drawing a parallel to Adam's curse, which also appears in the highly popular homiletical Bible commentary *Ze'enah u-Re'enah* (*Zenne Renne*; Go forth and gaze) from the early 17th century. The latter says in regards to Genesis 3:16 that a hard-working woman takes over part of Adam's curse, which weakens her curse and consequently her pain during childbirth.[226]

In her examination of rabbinic female images, Judith Baskin dedicates herself extensively to the rabbinic cursing of women.[227] Regarding the laws of *niddah*, which is also perceived by the rabbis as a curse and penance for Eve's sin, she asks: "Did women view these duties as special opportunities for sanctity, or as deserved reminders of Eve's sin?"[228] She concludes that these questions cannot be answered because of the lack of female voices in the period of rabbinic literature, but Rivkah bat Meir's interpretation now provides a female voice, maintaining an unequivocal point of view in this matter. As opposed to authors of rabbinic literature and contemporary moral literature, Rivkah bat Meir never describes the female pains and efforts of pregnancy and birth as "curse" or "punishment," let alone believes that the respective commandments should serve as a kind of cyclical reminder for women of some kind of original "sin," for which they had to "repent." Instead, she uses the term "retaliation" (*Meneket Rivkah*, 22a), which is used in rabbinic literature as well. However, she immediately removes the punishing element through a detailed interpretation and proves its ultimately positive meaning: "The more distress you have raising your children, the more reward I will give you" (ibid.), as divine repayment leads to special merits.

In the context of the negative rabbinic explanation of female duties, Baskin further remarks: "We do not see a similar construction of male duties as burdens or punishments rather than as avenues to righteousness." As opposed to the rabbinic point of view, Rivkah bat Meir interprets the female pains that ultimately lead to merit as a true avenue to righteousness: the greater the difficulty of child rearing, the more successful it will be, producing more pious children. Therefore the mother will receive more merit (*Meneket Rivkah*, 22a).

The author also distances herself from the misogynist rabbinic interpretation of female conduct in another context. She considers the problem of the choice of words in Judges 4:6 by asking why Deborah was not at the side of her husband, Barak (10b).[229] With that question she implicitly refers to the criticism stated in the Talmud (B. Megillah 14b) regarding Deborah's "sending" for her husband. For this presumptuous behavior she was punished by receiving the humiliating name *Devorah*, which means "bee." The author refutes the rabbinic criticism by noting that specific circumstances, namely the divine gift of prophecy (10b), required spatial separation such that Deborah had to call for her husband to come to her. Her complementary interpretation of the behavior of Barak, who had gone with Deborah in order to remain at his wife's side, corresponds to this positive interpretation of Deborah. According to the biblical text, however, Barak went with Deborah by the order of God.

Feminization is again displayed in the meaning of positive presentations of female actions in her version of a rabbinic tale.[230] In the rabbinic version of this *aggadah*, a woman gives her husband, who is in a problematic situation, good advice with the help of a biblical verse. In a later rabbinic version in *Reshit Hokhmah*, which is the one quoted by Rivkah bat Meir, this good advice was completely omitted. Rivkah bat Meir's version, on the other hand, not only contains the good advice, but also the detail that her husband, as well as a rabbi who had been asked for counsel and had provided worse guidance, thanked her afterward for her scholarly argument. This may be read as an indication of the author's opinion that female erudition deserves respect and acknowledgment from male scholars.

Perhaps Rivkah bat Meir's interpretations already corresponded to common female perception; perhaps she only brought them to women through her sermons. As a pious woman, she would certainly never have propagated the neglect of the commandments or other female duties. However, her interpretations provide a positive concept of femininity as a natural process, the more difficult part of which leads to garnering even more merit. No other contemporary morality book presents such a positive aspect of women and female piety.

Ideals of Conduct and Social Practices

Female Addressees

Like the moral-halakhic books of the *Mizvot Nashim* corpus, Rivkah bat Meir had a solely female audience in mind and therefore, like the authors of those books, she selected what she considered ideals of conduct for women, which she tailored to the world of her intended readers. That the intended readership existed only of women becomes more clear from the fact that she often addressed her readers directly by expressions like "dear women" (18b) and similar terms. The policy of addressing the readers directly was not common for Yiddish morality books at all. Detailed description of the target audience was usually left for the title pages. Most of these address women *and* men as, for example, on the title page of *Brantshpigl*, "Come here, you pious people . . . men, women, or young maidens," or on that of *Sefer Oraḥ Ḥayyim*, "When you own this little book, every man and woman will know what you need to do. . . . In addition, I have also written it in Yiddish for servants and maids." The same applies to *Ze'enah u-Re'enah*, the Hebrew title page (Hanau, 1622) of which reads: "This work comes to serve, with all its might and with all its power, men and women, so that they may find peace of mind, and that they may understand the words of the living God in easier and more comfortable language." The title page of one of books intended for an exclusively male audience, *Den Muser un' Hanhoge*, speaks fairly neutrally about "how a person should conduct himself."

Although Rivkah bat Meir addresses "every man and woman near to me" (2a) in her introduction, this formulation most likely constitutes more of a concession to poetic *piyyut* style than to an actual expectation of male readers. Accordingly, it is very rare that her descriptions include male ideals of conduct.[231]

The ideals of conduct that she formulates generally apply to all Jewish women. But her criticisms and instructions address the young and inexperienced,[232] explicitly excluding older, experienced, and pious women from her admonitions. This differentiation is expressed in the more ordinary, everyday Yiddish expressions she uses for inexperienced young women—*yunge vayberlekh*, or for pious women—*frume froyen*, reserving the dignified Hebrew for exemplary, truly righteous women—*nashim zadkaniyot*.[233]

The differentiation of the target audience according to age is quite common in moral literature. Many title pages address their audience as "women and young maidens" or "big and small."[234] Moses Henokhs Altshul in *Brantshpigl* is unique in dividing his readers into the rabbinic categories "learned" and "unlearned" as he describes his reading audience as "women and men, who are like women, in that they cannot learn much."[235]

The age and social affiliation of those the author addresses in *Meneket Rivkah* are reflected in the descriptions of their domestic world. The reader is an urban citizen of the propertied class, whose husband is a merchant dealing with money or merchandise. This constellation includes all age groups of married women. At the beginning of her marriage the young wife lives in the house of her in-laws, or at least in close proximity to them. In later years she herself will bear the responsibility for a large household, including servants and a cook, though the woman will likely still participate in the domestic production process, often consisting of needlework (33b) or linen manufacture, which is, however, not described in further detail. She raises the children and in later years will instruct her daughter-in-law. The size and economic prosperity of the household allow her to lead a bourgeois lifestyle. She buys books, is charitable toward the poor, and houses impoverished boarders and Torah students. Only rarely does the author address poor women or women without their own money, advising them as to how they can give charity despite their meager resources.[236] The woman's domestic and work environments are closely tied to various social relationships that form the frame of reference for the female ideals of conduct described by the author.

General Moral Ideals of Conduct

Rather than provide a comprehensive overview of the author's ideals of conduct and social practice, the following sections cover those I consider of particular interest and importance, along with historical and literary background information.

In the first chapter, Rivkah bat Meir describes a few general ideals of conduct, discussing, first of all, the "good deeds" (*ma'asim tovim*) that, according to Jewish tradition, are held in particularly high moral esteem. These include charity, such as financial support of impoverished members of the Jewish community (widows, orphans, poor brides) and visiting scholars, but also the performance of nonmaterial works of charity, such as visiting sick people and membership in a burial society (*ḥevra kaddisha*). Because these acts of charity are considered fundamental and thus applicable to both men and women, the author does not list them individually, but she does mention them in various contexts as a demand to perform "Torah and good deeds."[237]

Occasionally, when speaking of "good deeds," the author implies generally correct behavior that is expected from both men and women, but she frequently makes her demands specifically for women. These include maintaining one's physical health,[238] using piety as a model for children (4b–5a, 6a), avoiding inadvertent sins (7a), maintaining domestic cleanliness (7b), and avoiding cursing and swearing (7b, 11b).[239] While the first four virtues are discussed in other morality books, the last virtue is different. Most contemporary morality books often criticize particularly women because of their frequent swearing and mentioning of God's name. They sometimes substantiate their warning by claiming that menstruating women were not allowed to pronounce God's name at all.[240] Rivkah bat Meir, on the other hand, makes no mention of a special women's inclination to swear or curse, or of an implicit prohibition for menstruating women to mention God's name at all, thus following the actual *halakhah* and ruling less restrictively than other contemporary morality books.

In cases of the disregard of general ideals of conduct, Rivkah bat Meir expresses concrete criticism toward the behavior of both men and women. She denounces, for example, the fact that daughters from wealthy homes are preferred as marriage partners, whereas pious but non-wealthy daughters from scholarly families are rejected (9b). She criticizes the lack of responsibility for compliance with commandments, be it by housewives or by representatives of the community and the land (7a). Typical of her style, however, she uses not criticism but admonitions and requests, as well as praise for pious women.

Corresponding to the general ideals of conduct specified in the first chapter, the author emphasizes at the end: "This is why all pious women and men should be scrupulous about all of their actions—about every word and every step" (8a).

The Woman's Ideals of Conduct

In her discussion of female ideals of conduct, Rivkah bat Meir orients herself along practical, daily, and social modes of conduct. She avoids both halakhic discussions of female duties and descriptions of religious customs. One basic difference from other morality books is the author's demands for compliance with her prescribed ideals without simultaneously issuing dire warnings in the event of inappropriate conduct. Other moral literature, in contrast, like earlier rabbinic literature, frequently warns that a woman's inappropriate conduct will lead to her children turning out badly, becoming sick or even dying. Perhaps Rivkah bat Meir, as a preacher for women who must have frequently confronted children's illnesses and deaths and their parents' grief in the Prague community, considered such threats unnecessary and inconsiderate.[241]

The author begins her description of female ideals of conduct with a model of the "God-fearing woman," who represents the exemplarily virtuous woman in all morality books of the 16th and 17th centuries.[242] What is unusual about Rivkah bat Meir's use of this model image is its integration into a female moral philosophy through application of her own unprecedented concepts. The pious woman stands out through her "wisdom of the body" and "wisdom of the soul."[243] While "wisdom of the body" stands for the individual fulfillment of body-related commandments, such as compliance with the *niddah* commandments, and consumption of healthy—not merely kosher—food, "wisdom of the soul" is differentiated as a religious-ethical concept.[244] This implies, next to appropriate social conduct such as honesty in trade and charity, fulfillment of the religious-ethical duties (*mitzvot*) and good deeds (*ma'asim tovim*). The fundamental virtues appear in rabbinic literature mostly in connection with the exclusively male behavioral ideal of *talmud Torah* or, in short, *Torah* (studying the Holy Scriptures). Although the author regards comprehensive knowledge for girls with a positive eye, it comes as no surprise that she does not include *talmud Torah* in the concept of the "wisdom of the soul," since this would have been tantamount to open rebellion against the *halakhah*.[245] Only if the "wisdom of the soul" and the "wisdom of the body" are in balance will the ideal of the "intelligent woman" be obtained, upon which the woman may expect as reward a share in the world to come, as well as children who turn out well and are socially respected (4a).

Rivkah bat Meir does not write of a comprehensive ethical system insofar as she does not raise questions regarding the freedom of decision. Nevertheless, her work is the first within the Yiddish moral literature to assay a comprehensive systematic description of female ethics according to her own consistent terminology.

The individual ideals of the pious woman's conduct relate exclusively to the woman herself and to her domestic world. It is therefore conspicuous that "domesticity," as a female virtue, is not discussed on its own anywhere in the book.[246] In contrast, the importance attributed to female domesticity in many contemporary moral works can be seen in the negative female stereotype of the "tramp" (*yaz'anit*), an expression already used in the rabbinic literature to stigmatize non-domestic women.[247] At the same time, women are warned against roaming around outside, because they might meet the same fate as Jacob's daughter, Dinah, who was raped by Shechem. Moses Henokhs Altshul, in particular, describes the *yaz'anit* with her generally immoral conduct as a reverse image of the domestic, modest, and thus wise woman who subordinates herself to her husband. Rivkah bat Meir, too, falls back on the popular stereotype and uses its counterpart to characterize a young, inexperienced woman who "does not accept admonition, and will not be obedient."[248]

The lack of the ideal of domesticity in *Meneket Rivkah* is particularly conspicuous, because the author of *Brantshpigl*, a contemporary of Rivkah bat Meir and also a resident of Prague, strictly demands it. He even regards it as a prerequisite for female modesty, which he believes is best preserved if the woman never leaves the house.[249] This strict gender stereotyping, however, was not so much a result of Moses Henokhs's care for the woman's modesty but rather for that of the man, based on Henokhs's downright obsessive fear of the "evil inclination" (*yezer ha-ra*) and a man's impure thoughts, which would inevitably be aroused upon looking at a woman. This fear appears already in rabbinic literature,[250] but I have found no parallel in contemporary moral literature to Moses Henokhs's warnings. For example, he recommends that a mother bringing her children to the rabbi's house for lessons "just let them run inside" instead of going inside herself, so as to avoid triggering "impure thoughts" in the rabbi.[251] Rivkah bat Meir, on the other hand, suggests that it is well and appropriate for the woman to ask the rabbi about her child's conduct in order to monitor his development.[252]

Considering Rivkah bat Meir's pragmatic approach, the complete lack of a discussion of an ideal of domesticity is actually not surprising, since, after all, the women of Prague constantly had to leave their houses in order to shop in the markets, go to the laundry, visit friends or relatives, and sometimes earn a living. What is perhaps more astonishing is that she does not provide any instructions for conduct in public. She only discusses the pros and cons of a young mother's visit to the synagogue, and from what age she should take her children along, yet she does not mention the woman's modest conduct on the way to the synagogue.[253] Her descriptions of the external appearance of the woman are correspondingly terse. The author mentions that the woman should be "modest" (7b) with her hair, but she does not describe this in any detail. Instead, she quickly ends the subject with, "I do not even need to write or emphasize their necessity" (7b), implying that she considers women knowledgeable enough about modest appearances. In contrast, *Brantshpigl,* in describing in detail which parts of a woman's body may under no circumstances be visible, is actually presenting a halakhic discourse on the subject rather than a description of the female dress code of the time.[254] Rivkah bat Meir may have omitted any discussion of public conduct because of her book's self-imposed thematic limitations. But even works that allegedly discuss women's conduct in public often provide only a small number of vague statements. Another reason may be that the subject is less one of religious Jewish standards than of general standards within the respective cultural environment; these were generally well known and handled in the framework of daily practice rather than in the moral literature of the time.

The author is consistent in her avoidance of discussing conduct in public places, but just as consistent in not generally rejecting the notion of a woman being in public. Only in one specific case does she explicitly oppose it, mainly in the case of an idle, talkative woman "sit[ting] in front of the door," which is also repeatedly criticized by Moses Henokhs.[255] The street in front of the door in the Jewish Quarter in Prague was not only a result of the cramped living conditions, but also a prime place of social life, providing ample opportunity for encounters and communication. But it also could have been a starting point for immoral conduct: women and men could establish contact, which could spiral out of the control of the public in which they were first meeting.

Rivkah bat Meir's exclusive focus on domestic life resulted in her complete neglect of female wage-earning outside the house. Although there is ample evidence that the Jewish women of Prague in the 16th century were active in the areas of commerce, craft, and services, almost none of the authors of that era's morality books mention this, even where they discuss the conduct of women in public.[256]

An exception is the author of *Brantshpigl*, who discusses the earning activities of women in detail. He regards it as positive only in combination with domestic reproduction, allowing women to contribute "a little" to the economic security of the home and to give money to charity. In addition, he believes this work from within the home can have a morally disciplining effect on women by preventing them from harmful idleness. Women's work outside the house, on the other hand, he regards in an unequivocally negative light, because it is a danger to their modesty and, to the extent to which it turns women into families' providers, because it constitutes a threat to the patriarchal hierarchy of marriage.[257] Rivkah bat Meir does not discuss wage earning conducted outside the house, but it may be assumed that she would have arrived at a pragmatic point of view in which female modesty and work outside the house would be considered compatible, since she does not regard women as constantly exposed to moral jeopardy.

At any rate, some of Rivkah bat Meir's descriptions allow the indirect conclusion that women did contribute to their husbands' earning activities. In such a case, she recommends that the woman could support poor people as a pawnbroker, perhaps providing interest-free loans. This example can otherwise be found in only two works that were written for men, and it could be understood as an indication that women participated in their husbands' domestic pawnbroker business, or perhaps even ran their own such business and were therefore able to perform similar charity as the men.[258]

Another detail from the economic realm is the author's criticism of Jewish employers who prefer to hire Christian workers rather than impoverished Jews.[259] It is possible that Rivkah bat Meir voiced this criticism because she believed that women, as a result of their participation in craft (perhaps not only domestic), were able to exert practical or at least moral influence on their husbands regarding the question of economic efficiency. In another place, the author most obviously assumes that women have an influence on their husbands' economic activities, namely where she reproaches some women for tolerating their husbands' lack of honesty out of material greed.[260]

The question as to why the contemporary morality books deal so little with the phenomenon of female economic activity can be answered, in my opinion, by pointing out their mainly orthodox discourse (see above). When discussing ostensibly daily practical behavioral modes, they in fact often oriented themselves toward the statements of the canonized, rabbinic-ethical literature, perceiving women in an image that was determined by medieval, Ibero-Islamic culture, where domestic seclusion of women constituted the norm. Morality books rarely conducted a pragmatic discourse, taking into consideration the often indispensable activity of women outside the house, in commerce or services, in medieval and early modern Ashkenaz. Most authors probably never discerned this discrepancy between reality and ideal, and the female and male readers were either not conscious of it or generously ignored it. In that sense, even a person such as the successful merchant woman Glikl bas Judah Leib, who traveled over long distances in order to visit fairs, necessitating her being in contact with male merchants or inn-keepers and being away from home for several weeks, could recommend *Brantshpigl* to her children with a clear conscience.[261]

Regarding domestic earning activities, Rivkah bat Meir, like Moses Henokhs, considers it morally justified.[262] In contrast, however, she does not emphasize the advantage of additional economic security to the home provided by the women with the help of self-earned money, and she points out instead that money could enable them to perform charity independently. This aspect was probably based on the fact that women often did not have their own money. As a consequence, the author recommends elsewhere that women can perform charity in a non-material form (34a), or that they can support their needy parents (18a). She does not specify the character of domestic earning activity, while Moses Henokhs mentions the manufacture of clothes and linen.[263] The domestic production of fabrics and other handicraft products corresponds with the mercantilist modes of production in the early modern period, in which all family members participated, and which Rivkah bat Meir probably also had in mind as domestic earning activity.

Domestic activity naturally included housework in the narrow meaning of the word, as well as raising and caring for children. The latter included nursing by the mother. This ideal is not formulated in any other morality book, and even *Brantshpigl*, which at least discusses possible disadvantages of employing a wet-nurse, does so mainly from the halakhic point of view, insofar as the kashrut of the milk coming from a Christian wet-nurse is not guaranteed.[264] Rivkah bat Meir ignores the halakhic aspect, as well as any added health-related or emotional value that the mother's nursing could have for the child and the mother. Instead, she emphasizes that successful nursing will reward the mother with social appreciation, given that society will stigmatize her as "incapable" and she may lose her "reputation" (22b) if she fails to comply with this ideal. This is why she points out that practicing the correct nursing technique is so important, and why using a wet-nurse is so extremely harmful to the mother's successful nursing.[265]

A woman's good reputation, obtained by virtuousness, was obviously an important indicator for her social esteem and her prestige. This can be seen in a different example. After their bar mitzvahs, talented boys who were slated for intense talmudic studies would be sent to a yeshivah that would often be located far away from home, and a family would take them in as boarders. The author points out that only a respected woman with a "good reputation" would be entrusted with Torah students.[266] The reference to a woman's reputation seems to be the author's way of making the idea of providing lodging for a student appealing. The accommodation of Torah pupils may not have been popular everywhere, and some perhaps tried to avoid this moral obligation.[267] Thus, the author does not attribute this conduct to economic hardship but to selfishness and a lack of esteem for erudition. On the other hand, a woman's good reputation did increase her social prestige, which she (as opposed to men) could not normally obtain by erudition. Therefore, Rivkah bat Meir compares the esteem of such women with that of the economically successful merchant (*Meneket Rivkah*, 33a). Another parallel, perhaps not intended by the author but even clearer, can be drawn to a scholar's social esteem: just as a recognized, scholarly rabbi assembles students at his yeshivah, thus increasing his prestige, so the home of a righteous, virtuous woman will be a popular address for Torah students, and she will thus be in possession of a widely visible source of social prestige.

Ideals of Conduct toward the Husband

The woman's main conjugal task is to help and support her husband. This applies first and foremost to the support of the male ideal of erudition, *talmud Torah*, as requested by other morality books as well.[268]

The greatest space in the book is given, however, to the ideals of conduct with which the woman supports her husband in his commercial life, since she "should be helpful to him in all things" (*Meneket Rivkah*, 12b) and "bring her husband to good deeds, and discourage him from bad things" (11a). In this context, the body-soul motive returns, although it is not conceptually differentiated in the same way as in the case of female ethics: the husband and father must care for the entire family's physical need, and for that purpose he must be economically successful. However, in doing this he may not neglect his "soul" and allow himself to be economically dishonest, which would implicitly be interpreted as impious.

The economic ideals of conduct that apply to men and women are occasionally interwoven with ideas of an economic moral concept, which can be found in rabbinic literature and in contemporary morality books: Property obligates one to perform charity, and its purpose is to obtain a place in the world to come (11b). Social envy is considered a bad trait, because it leads to dishonest obtainment of wealth (11b). Wealth, however, like economic success or failure in general, depends solely on divine providence. Dishonesty in commerce may, in addition, result in social sanctions such as excommunication by *ḥerem*, or in divine punishment such as *Geihinnom* (12b–13a).[269]

On the other hand, Rivkah bat Meir's demand that the woman encourage, indeed implore, her husband to be honest in commerce (11a), to not commit perjury (11a), to not get involved in a dispute (11a) or waste money carelessly (13b), is highly unusual among contemporary morality books. The fact that she allows the woman legitimate knowledge of her husband's business affairs and even a certain control over them speaks to her perception of marriage as an equal partnership.[270] She may not regard the woman as having equal rights, though a marriage is considered of equal value to both parties. Both husband and wife bear a mutual responsibility toward each other. This includes the woman's right to forbid her husband to behave badly:

If her child sees something improper done, he says, "My mother did not permit me to do something like that." Her husband, too, when he sees another man doing something improper, says, "I won't do that—my wife also wouldn't permit me to do it." (*Meneket Rivkah*, 21a)

The notion that a woman's rights with regard to her children parallels her rights toward her husband is unsupported by Moses Henokhs, based on his reading of rabbinic sources in which the wife is subordinate to the husband; thus, he speaks of her position as one of the household, closer to that of the children and servants.[271] In an almost ironic reversal, however, Rivkah bat Meir compares the authority of the woman over her husband with that over a child, since she can permit or forbid her husband any indecorous behavior.[272] She should, however, criticize her husband's improper conduct "amicably" (14a). The author of *Brantshpigl* also grants the woman the right of admonition, though uttered as a friendly request even in a flagrantly immoral case such as unfaithfulness within the marriage.[273]

Most contemporary popular morality books of its time place the conjugal power structure and the mutual responsibility of the marriage partners is placed at the center of the discussion about marriage. Thus, they regard the support of the husband in his compliance with mitzvot and other religious ideals of conduct as first and foremost among the woman's most important conjugal duties.[274] Even so, Moses Henokhs Altshul is the only author who describes this support as "*dinen*" (serving). It is not merely a special term for "helping," but designates the woman's unequivocally subordinate position in marriage,[275] a point of view held in the moral literature as well.[276] He demands particularly in pragmatic contexts that the wife "serves," and he substantiates his claim with numerous examples so that it may not be regarded as mere orthodox discourse. On the other hand, Rivkah bat Meir reserves "*dinen*" for the religious context or, in the secular realm, exclusively for the work performed by servants.[277] The fact that she does not assume the semantics of "serving" in connection with concrete behavioral instructions is certainly no coincidence, although she does, on the level of the orthodox discourse, follow its rigid ideas:

> That is to say if he has found a woman who is subservient to her husband, and has a lower opinion of herself than her husband, and follows him, and does not think, "He is beneath me," that man has found something good through God, blessed be His name. (*Meneket Rivkah*, 13b)

This passage is found in connection with the popular rabbinic interpretation of Ecclesiastes 7:26, 28, and Proverbs 18:22 (*Meneket Rivkah*, 13b–14a). Only in this exegetical context does Rivkah bat Meir postulate that the woman must be "subservient" and should have a "lower opinion of herself," that is, must subject herself to the requirements of her husband. Her interpretation that a woman who "will not yield" to her husband and wants to be the same as him is "more bitter than death" generally repeats the rabbinic interpretation. She follows this further by stating that a woman who wants to be "more" than her husband is "totally out of order." At this point the author introduces a different rabbinic interpretation of Ecclesiastes 7:28, the verse regarding the woman who is "totally unheard of," now acknowledging that these women have a particular piety, which somewhat mitigates the preceding negative interpretation.[278] However, the author leaves this exegetical passage uncommented on and does not derive from it any practical behavioral demand for female subservience.

In a different place, Rivkah bat Meir reflects the restrictive orthodox discourse in a similar manner. Although by quoting Genesis 3:16, "and he shall rule over you," she indicates the legitimacy of male dominance in marriage (*Meneket Rivkah*, 14a), she does not derive from it any practices aiming at female obedience. Instead, she adds interpretations that speak of special female merits or gifts, such as that of prophecy, that obligate the man to respect his wife.[279] At this point, her opinion differs distinctly from that of Moses Henokhs, who regards Genesis 3:16 as evidence for the man's traditional right to beat his wife—an opinion that, in the 16th century, was still held in some scholarly circles, though it by no means constituted generally accepted *halakhah*. Yet it did reflect the orthodox discourse of the moral literature.[280]

Like *Meneket Rivkah*, most other morality books of its time dealt only marginally with conjugal love and sexuality. Usually only the ethic-halakhic works discussed sexuality, and even then only in regard to its halakhic implications, albeit in great detail. Romantic love, however, was neglected by the moral literature because marriages were arranged according to strictly economic and educational concerns. Although conjugal love was definitely desired, it was regarded as secondary for the successful marriage, and was associated more with a friendly, trustful, and respectful relationship than with romantic and passionate emotions.[281] Apart from that, moral literature was in any case not the place for discussions about intimate, uncontrolled passions.

All the same, the author recommended tersely that conjugal intercourse should be conducted with "love and affection" (*Meneket Rivkah*, 14b). This may not have been a sinful image. However, within and around the moral literature in which authors worried about appropriate morals, such formulations appeared only rarely. More frequently found, however, was the warning, shaped by the orthodox discourse, of intercourse incited by lust, in connection with the urgent reminder that intercourse should only be conducted in fulfillment of the commandment, "Be fertile and increase."[282]

Ideals of Conduct toward Parents and In-Laws

The coexistence of several generations under one roof is rarely mentioned in contemporary moral literature, although elderly parents or in-laws would most likely spend their last years in the household of one of their adult children. Since the close domestic contact to parents and in-laws was especially significant in the female experience, it comes as no surprise that only a female author raises the topic. However, of all one's social relationships, the ideals of conduct toward parents and in-laws are the least differentiated by gender, since the same conduct would be expected from both the woman and the man. It is conspicuous that the author should rely heavily on talmudic and popular tales in discussing conduct toward parents, thus attributing a universal and timeless meaning to the parent-child relationship.

Since the new bride usually lived at her husband's residence after marriage, only a small number of the ideals of conduct and social practices relate to her own parents. This relationship is founded upon respect (*Meneket Rivkah*, 14b–15a) and honor (15b), which also means that the woman should support her parents financially or at least offer them assistance, even after the wedding. Although according to *halakhah* a married woman is not allowed to support her parents financially against her husband's will, Rivkah bat Meir calls upon the woman to convince her husband to allow her to provide such help.[283]

The author provides more concrete behavioral instructions regarding a woman's relationship with her mother-in-law, which has halakhic implications as well as practical ones, for not only is the young married couple living at the husband's residence, but the man assumes the authority over the woman in place of her parents. Since, according to the customs of those days, the bride and groom married at a very young age, the practical authority would initially be held by the mother-in-law, whose instructions and teachings, the author emphasizes, the young bride should follow.[284] It is consistent, however, that Rivkah bat Meir, in the sixth chapter, also extends moral instruction to the mother-in-law herself. Although the mother-in-law is not among the target audience of the book, given her age and status as an experienced and pious woman, she is admonished to receive her daughter-in-law with forbearance and benevolence.

The author criticizes not only the overly strict mother-in-law, but also young couples who rely on the support of the husband's parents or those who feel disadvantaged by their parents' alleged preference for siblings, causing the couple to be jealous (*Meneket Rivkah*, 19b). Such common details are not mentioned in other morality books, but they are typical for the author's pragmatic style of sticking close to reality.

Generally, old people are hardly mentioned specifically in contemporary moral literature. Only in connection with "honoring one's father and mother" and showing respect toward the elderly are they designated by their age. Sometimes "pious old women" are considered specifically in the context of the commandments regarding *niddah*, where they take on the function of acting as role models for young women, and sometimes as guardians of young women's modesty in public. With respect to this connection, the author of *Brantshpigl* criticizes what he considers the excessive forbearance of the elderly toward the indecent conduct of young women.[285] In contrast, Rivkah bat Meir describes old people exclusively in a respectful manner. Quoting the Talmud, she writes that the actions of an old woman within the family can only be positive to the residents for domestic peace and harmony.[286] Although the author's description indicates frequent conflicts between the generations, she nevertheless idealizes relationships with the elderly. This certainly follows orthodox rabbinic discourse, but it may also appear in her writing due to the author's own advanced age and her natural empathy with those of her generation.

Ideals of Conduct in Child Education

The most discussed social relationship in *Meneket Rivkah* is that between mother and child, focusing on education and moral development. Although Rivkah bat Meir addresses her practical instructions to the mother, she expresses the opinion that the father, too, is responsible for his children's successful upbringing and piety, an opinion generally shared by contemporary morality books.[287] Thus, *Meneket Rivkah* and works contemporary to it agree that both mother and father are rewarded for good parenting in the upbringing of children, and conversely, in the event of failing to properly educate their children, they are punished.

One problem when examining child education in the early modern period is understanding which ideals were targeted for boys and which for girls, because the morality books do not clearly differentiate this even though education of the sexes was not identical. *Brantshpigl* is one of the few that differentiates explicitly between *kinder mans namen* ("male children") and *maydlekh* ("girls") in prayers for the education of children.[288] *Meneket Rivkah*, in contrast, is one of the morality books that simply applies the Yiddish *kinder* or the Hebrew *banim*, words that may mean "sons" or "male children" but also "children" in general, making it unclear whether any specific ideals of education apply only to boys or to girls, as well. Only *tokhter*, *maydel* (both Yiddish), or *bat* (Hebrew), meaning "daughter" and "girl," make the distinction clear.[289]

Rivkah bat Meir differentiates between ideals of the "body" and the "soul" in discussing the morally correct education of children (22a). But unlike the "wisdom of the body" and the "wisdom of the soul," paradigms of female ethics, these terms in the context of children's education are not part of a system that provides practical instructions.

The author notes that the correct handling of a child's body includes careful hygiene (22b) and nursing of the child by its own mother (22a), thus extending the behavioral demands to the maternal body. Mothers must bear the pain of nursing and must sufficiently practice the nursing technique (22a–b). At the same time, she urgently warns the mother not to allow the child to become too attached to her, which is already the case when she "takes the child to her, even once" (22b), most likely referring to taking the child into her bed at night. It is not clear whether the author warns of such conduct because the child could contract "the illness that one shall not name," a warning that appears in the Talmud related to having sexual intercourse in the presence of the child, or whether this merely reflects the fear that the child might inadvertently be suffocated in its sleep.[290] In addition, she criticizes other practices regarding illnesses, such as the use of incantations by Christian women, and the lack of supervision over small children, which is particularly rebuked because of the danger of injury.

Regarding the child's "soul," which the author designates as education toward "good behavior" (25a), *Meneket Rivkah* presents a hodgepodge of social-religious virtues without always differentiating between the mother's ideals of conduct and those of the child. This is because virtuous parents would certainly be rewarded with virtuous children. The author's advocacy of corporal punishment (25a–26a) in order to assert one's educational ideals is consistent with the moral literature of that time.[291]

At the beginning of her description of religious ideals of education, the author summarizes by stating that children should participate in prayer services, perform good deeds, and commit themselves to study (*talmud Torah*) (19a). Although the author, in the ensuing description, speaks repeatedly of *kind* (child), describing social behavioral ideals that apply to both genders, the mention of *talmud Torah* indicates the traditional educational discourse for boys. She notes, in fact, in her conclusion that the aforesaid applies to "sons" (29a), whereas daughters should be educated in diligence (29a) and hospitality (29b), the only two female educational ideals that she emphasizes. Thus maternal ideals, such as speaking with children about the Torah (24a) and God's kindness (27b), and demanding Hebrew lessons for "children" (24b) may not include girls.

Rivkah bat Meir's ignorance of a specific educational regimen for girls is probably best understood in the context of the rabbinic rejection of female erudition in her time. This was not mitigated by the fact that knowledge of the commandments for Shabbat, kashrut, and *niddah*, as well as prayers and blessings, were obligatory for all girls as well as boys, even though girls were taught this practical knowledge through direct instruction. In addition, the knowledge of other commandments, as well as the ability to read the Torah, was definitely desired for girls from scholarly families, as this was very useful for them as potential wives of rabbis. Thus, a fair number of girls participated in the lessons for boys provided by a hired teacher (*melammed*), although those lessons did not always lead to the complete ability to read or write Hebrew, not even for boys.[292]

According to *halakhah*, the father, based on Deuteronomy 11:19, was permitted to teach his daughter Torah, although he was not obligated to do so.[293] In addition, the rabbinic statement that the instruction of a daughter in Gemara would be tantamount to triviality or immorality (*tiflut*) was commonly accepted, and independent study of rabbinic texts by girls and women was considered the same way.

Since girls and women were excluded from institutionalized instruction and the study of rabbinic scriptures, Rivkah bat Meir suggested that they should "listen to learning" (4b). Such a suggestion cannot be found in any of the morality books that I have seen from that era. It shows how much the author appreciated the opportunity to obtain knowledge, even if only by participating passively in men's domestic studies in order to learn both the religious literature and the Hebrew language.

Another opportunity to learn was through "listening" to sermons (4b). In principle, women were considered exempt from participation in the prayer services, which constitute a time-bound obligation.[294] At the same time, there are rabbinic sources of that time that argue that women are also subject to the commandment of daily prayer, and that the service performed in the synagogue is more important than private prayer. Although many contemporary morality books agreed, their authors must have been well aware that women and unlearned men would hardly understand the Hebrew spoken in sermons.[295] It may, however, be assumed that the author, in her suggestion to the women to participate in the prayer services, took into consideration the Yiddish translation, and the explanations by the *firzogerin*—a privilege that was not accessible to unlearned men.

An interesting demand by the author, for which there is no correspondence either in rabbinic or contemporary moral literature, is the demand that when it comes to learning the prayers, the mother should not rely solely on the rabbi, but should herself control that at home (23b). The mother's active support of the lessons presupposes Rivkah bat Meir's trust in women's sufficient knowledge and educational level. Other morality books, on the other hand, were hardly prepared to concede intellectual capabilities to women. The author of *Ze'enah u-Re'enah*, for example, explains that women are responsible for raising the children, and since it is assumed that women are not intellectually capable of studying, they can only help their sons obtain an education by taking them to the lessons.[296]

In sum, it can be stated that the author, herself a learned woman and teacher of girls and women, does not express any explicit demand that girls should know the Hebrew language or provide any specific program for girls' education. This may be because she did not wish to oppose rabbinic opinion, and indeed, the majority of Jewish society probably regarded female erudition as unnecessary or even harmful. It is likewise possible that she regarded the existing possibilities of education for girls, depending on the knowledge of their parents, as sufficient through daily, casual appropriation of Hebrew idioms, through copying daily mitzvot and *halakhot*, repeating blessings and prayers, as well as listening to domestic learning, sermons, and the Yiddish explanations of the *firzogerin*. In a society that was ambivalent toward or completely rejected the idea of female erudition, and where even learned women were only able and willing to move within the limits set by the powerful rabbinic leaders, there was simply no room for the development of a program of female education.

Ideals of Conduct toward House Staff and Boarders

According to Rivkah bat Meir and the authors of other morality books contemporary to hers, one of the most important tasks of the housewife was the supervision of the household. This included her moral responsibility for the household staff (31b), which the author derives from the commandment of altruistic love (32a) and the ideal of the capable wife (*eshet ḥayil*) (33b–34a). Since the early modern period, the designation of *gezind* does not relate only to the maids and servants working in the house, but also to all other non-related residents of the house, such as boarders and orphans.[297] All these disparate individuals are lumped together because there was hardly any difference between the working and living areas of maids and servants and those of other non-related residents of the house. Maids and servants began working at a young age.[298] Thus, household staff, orphans, and young Torah students had to be brought up and instructed by the master of the house, and particularly by the mistress of the house.[299] While orphans were frequently (and with hardly any opposition) given the tasks of maids and servants, Rivkah bat Meir criticizes the fact that Torah students, too, were sometimes called to perform housework, given that they were supposed to commit themselves completely to their studies, and taking them in as boarders was considered a good deed.[300] The authors of other books discuss this subject only marginally, if at all. Moses Henokhs explicitly rejects the idea of having Torah students perform housework, but his statements on this issue are conspicuously short, perhaps because he had little insight or interest in daily household arrangements.[301]

While Rivkah bat Meir emphasizes the proper behavior toward Torah students (32a–33b) and the poor and beggars (33b–35b), she also discusses, albeit only briefly, the orphans who were often taken into the house, in the context of the education of one's own children (26a). She only touches marginally on the household staff in regard to the question as to what degree a cook would be capable of fulfilling the mitzvah of supporting Torah students (23b). On the other hand, the mention of behavioral ideals regarding the household staff within moral literature of the time is completely unusual, and probably results from the fact that Rivkah bat Meir was more sensitive in perceiving the requirements and duties of the household staff than male authors.[302]

In any event, the moral literature of that time only rarely mentions the household staff, and then mostly under halakhic aspects, because the danger of a violation of *halakhah* was particularly great for cooks. In that sense, the author emphasizes violations by Christian cooks (7a–b). She does not, however, enter into halakhic details, but instead rebukes negligent housewives who do not sufficiently fulfill their responsibility for the preservation of kashrut. Moral literature, however, mentions Christian cooks only rarely, possibly because they were rarely employed or because people preferred to conceal their employment, either of which could be due to the halakhic prohibition of *bishul goyim* (unsupervised cooking by non-Jews). It may be assumed that for this reason many a Christian cook worked under the cover of a maidservant. *Brantshpigl*, for example, designates a housemaid that worked as a cook with the Hebrew word *shifha* (maid).[303]

The author adds a number of virtues to the ideals of conduct toward non-related residents of the house who spend only limited time there. She mentions, in addition, hospitality (34a–b, 36a) and charity toward beggars and the poor. Both ideals of conduct have a high status in many Hebrew and Yiddish moral works, and they are considered, in fact, mitzvot rather than virtues.[304] On the other hand, Rivkah bat Meir's emphatic advice that a woman can be charitable in non-material form, by helping out with her own hands, with good advice or a friendly word, or by simply praying for somebody, has no parallel in the moral literature of that time (33b–34a, 34b, 35b), and she clearly took into consideration those women who did not have their own money.

Summary

The subtle differences between *Meneket Rivkah* and morality books contemporary to it in their description of ideals of conduct and social practices are part of a continuous, dynamic process in which certain attributes and values regarding, for example, femininity, masculinity, marriage, or education of children are negotiated. These negotiation processes unfold in day-to-day communication, but they manifest themselves in written moral literature, too.

The description of virtues that can be implemented in daily life required a style that corresponded to daily experience and was connected to reality. As such, morality books typically discussed, in a more or less comprehensive manner, the ideals of conduct and social practices realistic in their time.

The moral-halakhic *Mizvot Nashim* texts also provided day-to-day practical behavior patterns, but they were limited to a small halakhic area, and in addition, their style often had casuistic characteristics. These works, like most moral-didactical books, conducted an orthodox, rabbinic discourse, with regard to social behavior patterns exceeding that discourse, reflected mostly traditional ideals of conduct that had been transmitted from canonical Hebrew moral literature.

Besides the contextual circumstances, the discourse in all morality books, including *Meneket Rivkah*, was dependent on their intended function. While the moral-halakhic works were conceived as practical guides and their female and male readers were expected to strictly follow their instructions, the moral-didactical works were meant rather as manuals for moral action. The latter had been drawn up as works of reference for various daily topics, in which female and male readers could find information regarding normative statements from traditional literature, or regarding ideals of conduct—depending on whether the emphasis was on orthodox-rabbinic or pragmatic, day-to-day discourse.

The frequent parallel existence of both discourses could have led to conflict. Traditional ideas, for example, of female submission and domesticity and the phenomena of that era, such as the woman's responsibilities in the house, in commercial life, or in religious-cultural life, had to be integrated. But female and male readers of the moral literature may not even have perceived this potential conflict, or may have simply ignored it, since even the authoritative binding power of moral literature did have its limits.

The realization that most Yiddish morality books of the 16th and 17th centuries conducted a mainly rabbinic-orthodox discourse contains important implications regarding the use of moral literature as a cultural-historical source. It must be differentiated whether a text refers back to transmitted norms, which sometimes reflect ideals that were formulated centuries earlier in the context of a completely different culture, or whether it refers to actual contemporary ideals and social practices.

This examination of *Meneket Rivkah* has shown to what extent the pragmatic and the orthodox discourses coexist here. In the moral-didactical passages, Rivkah bat Meir provided pragmatic behavioral demands that belonged to the world of women in their own time, instead of deriving anachronistic and ultimately unusable practices from the rabbinic or medieval ethical literature.

In the exegetical and homiletical passages, on the other hand, Rivkah bat Meir conducted an orthodox rabbinic discourse, insofar as she used traditional interpretations and biblical and rabbinic role models and their modes of action in order to substantiate and legitimize moral ideas of her time. Where she thought it necessary, the author supported the traditional interpretations with her own emphasis from a female perspective, or provided fundamentally new interpretations. In this way she reproduced, for example, the rabbinic view of the woman's subservient conjugal position. At the same time, she softened the respective rabbinic interpretations of the conceited woman who strives for equality by pointing to positive female figures and their modes of action.

Ringing from these adaptations and reformulations we hear a distinctly female voice formulating female self-perceptions and interpretations. These deviate sometimes significantly from the perceptions contained in the morality books written by men. This applies likewise to the reformulation of specific female ideals of conduct. The occasional reformulation of female virtues, however, cannot be generalized in the sense that Rivkah bat Meir designed a completely new female morality. The behavioral demands for women described in *Meneket Rivkah* correspond in most areas to those of morality books of that era, to the extent to which they are considered there at all.

In *Meneket Rivkah*, pragmatic and rabbinic discourses are often intertwined in a mutually complementary manner without ever really mixing. The author's success in generally holding on to the pragmatic discourse, despite the exegetic-homiletical orientation, results most probably from her familiarity with her audience, and even more so from her experience and skill as teacher and preacher.

On Research

Meneket Rivkah in Research: A Case Study of Women Written Out of History

Thanks to the famous Hebraist Johann Christoph Wagenseil, roughly a century after the publication of *Meneket Rivkah*, the existence of a Yiddish author of the early modern period and her learned work has never been completely forgotten. It is all the more conspicuous then, that modern scholarship has allowed knowledge of this learned author to atrophy in comparison to the attention given her by scholars of the 18th century. Three main factors that characterize research of Old Yiddish literature are responsible for this development. First, the work was written in Yiddish with Hebrew quotations, which presented a certain barrier. Second, an important factor may have been the traditional lack of interest in Yiddish moral literature, most probably a consequence of the low status attributed to Hebrew ethical literature, which was never unreservedly accepted in the canon of rabbinic literature and was therefore neglected by scholarly research. Third, there was the notorious marginalization of women as a result of the focus on literary works written by and for men, such that books produced for a female readership received little attention. This marginalization applied also to male-dominated historiography, which showed almost no interest in the experiences and lives of women until the beginning of the last third of the 20th century. These factors, taken together, were responsible for the process of writing women out of history, which the research history of *Meneket Rivkah* is a perfect example of.

Christian Hebraists were the first to devote themselves to *Meneket Rivkah*, in part because the occupation with popular works written in the vernacular seemed particularly helpful for their missionary intentions. Wagenseil (1633–1705), however, as a scholar of biblical and rabbinic literature in his capacity as professor of Oriental languages and Hebrew, had a true interest in the Jewish way of life as well. His main work, the translation and commentary on the Mishnah tractate *Sotah*, was published in 1674.[305] In this work, he quotes a number of Yiddish books such as the *Maysse Bukh* (Basel, 1602) and *Lev Tov* (Prague, 1620).[306] In connection with the mention of a learned woman in that tractate, Wagenseil notes that in the last century there lived a famous female scholar, "Rebecca Tiktiner." Besides quoting her on the bathing of infants, nursing by the natural mother, and Abraham's hospitality, he likewise quotes her exegetical passage on Genesis 3:16. As proof for Rivkah bat Meir's work as scholar and teacher, he quotes the title page of *Meneket Rivkah* in its Latin translation.[307] Although by no means attracted to the Yiddish language,[308] Wagenseil's interest in all facets of Jewish culture caused him to emphasize in an unbiased manner the phenomenon of a learned female author and preacher. He even had the Prague Rabbi Issachar Beer Perlhefter live as a teacher in his house in 1674 in order to learn more about the Jewish religion.[309] For a short while, Perlhefter's learned wife, Bella, taught Wagenseil's daughter dancing lessons and, like her husband, corresponded with Wagenseil in Hebrew. She, too, came from Prague, and it is conceivable that she gave Wagenseil a copy of *Meneket Rivkah*.[310]

Fourteen years after Wagenseil's death, *Meneket Rivkah* enjoyed even more profound attention from another Hebraist, Johann Konrad Lufft, in his dissertation "On the Polish Rebecca. The Rare Example of a Learned Woman within the Jewish People."[311] Lufft reports that he used Wagenseil's copy of *Meneket Rivkah*, which, after Wagenseil's death, had been sold to the University of Altdorf together with part of his library.

Lufft notes that, in addition to Wagenseil, Rivkah bat Meir had already been mentioned favorably by the Hebraists Bartolocci, Wolff, and Schudt.[312] He also names a second Krakow publication from the year 1618, known to him through the work *Siftei Yeshenim* (languages of the elders) by the "Polish rabbi Shabbtai Strimer."[313] Lufft provides many details on the contents of *Meneket Rivkah* and particularly emphasizes its scholarly style. But the reception of his Latin-language dissertation remained limited over a long period of time to the small circle of Christian Hebraists.

This changed only 150 years later with Meyer Kayserling and his 1879 book on Jewish women. It was he, however, who blurred Rivkah bat Meir's footprints for a long time to come. He reported that the "Polish woman Rebekkah Tiktiner" had written a "book of morals" on women's duties and that she was a learned preacher who had acquired a "certain fame." But he also wrote that her book has "long been lost" and that the dissertation of the "Rostock Professor G. G. Zellner [*sic*]" does not provide "much information beyond her mere name."[314] Kayserling could have concluded, based on his knowledge of Lufft's dissertation, that this was not simply just another "book of morals," but a scholarly, moral-homiletical book, and that the work was not "lost" but probably in the possession of the University of Nuremberg, which, after the dissolution of the University of Altdorf in 1809, had obtained its complete library stock. The consequence of Kayserling's statements was that *Meneket Rivkah* was considered a mere compilation of women's duties that was lost to any further research.

Gustav Karpeles, in his popular description, surprisingly mentions the "learned Madam Rebekkah Tiktiner" in connection with translations from Hebrew into "Jewish-German."[315] He did not provide evidence for his claim that Rivkah bat Meir translated Bahya ibn Paquda's *Ḥovot ha-Levavot* (Duties of the heart), but it was accepted by most subsequent authors. Karpeles declared the year 1609 as the date of publication of *Ḥovot ha-Levavot*, allegedly translated by Rivkah bat Meir, but because this was the very year of the first print of *Meneket Rivkah*, it may be assumed that he had merely been confused. He refers back to Kayserling and adds, in passing, that Rivkah bat Meir "also wrote a popular morality book about women's duties, bearing the strange title Meneketh Ribka."[316]

The next time we find mention of Rivkah bat Meir is in Israel Zinberg's 1926 *Altyiddishe literatur*, which contained another mistake that was taken over by subsequent research. Zinberg wrote that the book had been "extremely rare" already at the time of Wagenseil.[317] This mistake goes back to his wrong translation of the title of Lufft's dissertation. Zinberg related "rariori exemplo" to *Meneket Rivkah* instead of to the author herself, whereas Lufft's title speaks of a "rare example" of a learned Jewess, not of a rare copy of her book. Zinberg's mistake gave the impression that any search for an extant copy was not promising, implying that only a few decades after its publication the book had become difficult to find and therefore had little notable reception, a statement that basically marginalized it retroactively. He did not, however, ignore Rivkah bat Meir's significance. He pointed out that she was a *firzogerin* who obtained great respect through her erudition, that her morality book contained numerous quotations from the midrashim and the Gemara, and that she had been the "first Yiddish female author."

Shortly after Zinberg, Max Weinreich mentioned *Meneket Rivkah* in the context of his research on Wagenseil. His reaction to Wagenseil's remarks is a typical example of "writing women out of history." Rather than mentioning Rivkah bat Meir's scholarship and her work as the first Yiddish book written by a woman, he merely castigates Wagenseil's inability to "formulate his thoughts concisely" and his "arbitrarily accumulated knowledge," in short, his lack of scientific methodology.[318] Weinreich thus missed the opportunity to impart what is actually important and extraordinary about *Meneket Rivkah*.

Since 1954, when Simḥa Assaf quoted from it in his edition of primary source texts, modern scholarship could have been at least aware of the existence of the (incomplete) Krakow print of *Meneket Rivkah*. Assaf translated individual behavioral instructions of the "female rabbi and preacher" regarding child education into Hebrew, but he too did not point out the exegetical and homiletical character of the book. Additionally, he did not indicate where the copy was located, although attentive reading of his descriptions could easily have led to the library of the Jewish Theological Seminary in New York.[319] But it took almost another quarter-century before it was discovered there, simultaneously by Sondra Henry and Emily Taitz, and by Khone Shmeruk. While Henry and Taitz mainly emphasized the outstanding significance of a female Yiddish author in the 16th century, they only touched on the fact that the book contained moral instructions, passages from the Mishnah and Talmud, and poems.[320]

Shmeruk, on the other hand, was the first and, to this day, only scholar to scrutinize *Meneket Rivkah* itself, even if he had only the incomplete New York copy of the Krakow print. He described Rivkah bat Meir's scholarly, rabbinic style and assumed that she was born in Tykocin and that she was the wife of a rabbi. Judging by the sources she quoted, he justly assumed 1581 as the earliest date for the composition of the book. His assumption that it had been written in Poland, prior to her move to Prague, was however, purely speculative. Although Shmeruk was aware of the particular significance of Rivkah bat Meir as the first female Jewish author, he handled the subject in his first article rather negligently. He therefore missed the fact that the book was actually a faulty binding, and he subsequently assumed that the author "in the second and third chapters translated and narrated extensively from *Pirkei Avot*."[321] Three years later, however, he corrected and deepened his description and indicated the existence of an additional copy of *Meneket Rivkah* in the University of Erlangen library.[322] In 1980, Hermann Süß became the first modern researcher to describe Wagenseil's copy of the first Prague print, which he had discovered in the framework of his reconstruction of the Wagenseil library.[323] In 1992, Meir Wunder published the text of *Meneket Rivkah* for the first time in the form of a book, but as photocopied material of the incomplete New York copy.[324]

Most subsequent examinations that mentioned Rivkah bat Meir and her book did not acknowledge this publication or Shmeruk's research. This applies likewise to the edition of Rivkah bat Meir's epitaph by Otto Muneles in 1988, which was of great significance for research: it provided details about the author herself for the first time, since until then the focus had been exclusively on her book. The epitaph documented that the author had been highly esteemed during her lifetime for her work as teacher and preacher. In addition, it clarified unequivocally the question regarding the author's date of death.[325]

Thus in the 19th and early 20th centuries, it was mainly the lack of sensibility for the extraordinary fact of a learned Jewish female author in the 16th century that resulted in a decreasing level of knowledge about, and an increasingly skewed portrait of, the work and its author. In the German and English secondary literature in the last half of the 20th century, insufficient perception of Hebrew research literature is the main reason for this declining level of knowledge. In most cases only Kayserling, Karpeles, and Zinberg were acknowledged, but not Shmeruk or Muneles. That is how it was possible that *Meneket Rivkah* could be transformed into a "morality book on the instruction of children"[326] or even into a "book about childcare and child education."[327]

Jean Baumgarten, a French scholar of Old Yiddish literature, reviewed Shmeruk, but he also wrote only a few lines about Rivkah bat Meir in the context of female authors. He quoted a passage from *Meneket Rivkah* about "the teaching mother," but without acknowledging the fact that this was a well-polished homiletic passage.[328]

Shoshana Zolty takes neither Shmeruk nor Muneles nor Wunder into consideration, but she translates the Yiddish quotation used by Assaf and acknowledges Rivkah bat Meir extensively as an educator of women, a scholar, a preacher, and a lyricist who she claims was known throughout Jewish-German society. Her presentation distorted *Meneket Rivkah* somewhat by attributing to it "poems in Hebrew and Yiddish, and her own responsa related to women's halakhic problems." The latter is precisely what *Meneket Rivkah* does not contain.[329]

In recent years, only Emily Taitz, Sondra Henry, and Cheryl Tallan have rendered correctly the current state of research.[330]

Following the traces left by Rivkah bat Meir and her work in the research literature, the causes for the decrease and distortions of knowledge over the course of time become clear. Lack of interest in Yiddish literature, particularly in Yiddish moral literature, in the social and intellectual history of women, and also in Hebrew research literature have contributed, sometimes unconsciously, sometimes systematically, to the process of writing women out of history. In this regard, the reception and understanding of Rivkah bat Meir and her book are in no way unusual. Another example is the story of the aforementioned Hannah bat Judah Leib Katz. Her printed sermon has been preserved and she was frequently mentioned in older research literature, but she seems to have been forgotten by modern research literature.[331]

One of the main factors contributing to this situation was the categorization, since the 19th century, of Old Yiddish literature as "women's literature." Although factually not even correct, this designation created a stigma in a male-dominated scholarly world that perceived, in large part, only literature from learned male elites as adequate subjects for research. Already in 1882, Max Grünbaum[332] flatly designated Old Yiddish literature as "women's literature." Shmuel Niger adopted this assessment, and established the "feminine character" of the Old Yiddish literature and particularly of old moral literature. He wrote that only the Yiddish language possesses the "necessary softness and sweetness" required for this genre, and the style of the works is "soft and lyrical, intimate, folksy, and feminine," and addresses the "spirit and imagination" of women, or of simple men, but not their intellect.[333] This description may tell us much about Niger's ideas on femininity, but it gives us only very little concrete information about the style of the morality books themselves. Although the term "women's literature" is meant to imply both stylistic and content-related features, the actual difference between that and "men's literature" was never examined.[334]

Although Niger, Erik,[335] Weinreich,[336] and Zinberg[337] (the latter particularly emphatic) pointed out that Yiddish moral literature was by no means written only for women, but for men as well (some texts were even written exclusively for men), the flat assessment of Yiddish literature as "literature for women" remains widely disseminated to this day. Chava Turniansky, on the other hand, believes that Old Yiddish literature formed from the start a literary genre for all men and women of Jewish society, with the exception of the small elite of learned men—for obvious reasons: "Education—in whichever form—could not provide the entire population with a level of language skills that would have allowed direct access to the Hebrew language treasures of the cultural canon. Only part of the society obtained the ability to read this language, and understand it unrestrictedly. Even if the number of those, who obtained neither of the two abilities, is unknown, it was certainly not insignificant."[338]

However, the attribution of popular, female, and non-scholarly characteristics to the Yiddish literature cannot be blamed on modern research alone. Many works of the genre, even if described on their title pages as having been written for women, had men as readers, because men who were not sufficiently educated in Hebrew had only Yiddish books from which to learn. Thus non-Hebrew works, though they were often regarded with rabbinic disdain, whether because of the uncontrolled dissemination of halakhic knowledge or the rejection of "inconsequential" or "immoral" stories, were widely read. Rabbinic disdain had entered to some extent into general opinion because *talmud Torah* was such a powerful male ideal in the early modern era that it influenced the perception of Yiddish literature that it could possibly be written for and read by women, even if it actually had a wider readership than officially assumed.[339] Similar confusion has arisen with regard to the typographic designation *vaybertaytsh* (women's Yiddish), in which most of these books had been printed. This cursive script was very popular as *mashket* (decorative style) in sixteenth-century Italy and was also used for printing popular Hebrew morality books for male readers (for example, *Iggeret Derekh ha-Shem* [Correspondence about God's way] by Moses of Trani [Venice, 1553] and *Sefer Ḥayyei Olam* [Book of the eternal life, Sabbioneta, 1552]). Only with the beginning of the following century was it referred to as *vaybertaytsh*—an act of semantic gendering, establishing Yiddish literature as non-scholarly, non-rabbinic, and non-male literature. Modern research partially carried on this marginalization of Yiddish literature, and therefore it is often perceived to this day as a historically peripheral phenomenon rather than what it really was: the literature of the majority of Ashkenazi society.[340]

Old Yiddish Moral Literature in Research

Yiddish moral literature leads a rather sad, shadowy existence in scholarly circles. The lack of modern editions, which could make these texts known and thus facilitate further research in the fields of Yiddish studies, Jewish studies, literary criticism, and social and cultural studies, is a particular impediment on top of the general lack of interest in popular Yiddish literature.[341] To this day, modern editions of only two Old Yiddish morality books exist, *Sefer Brantshpigl* and *Seder Mizvot ha-Nashim*.[342] It is therefore hardly surprising that the moral literature is sometimes not even perceived as an element of Yiddish literature. Erika Timm, for example, who earned great merits for her intensive research of Old Yiddish, does not even mention Yiddish moral literature in a study in which she undertook to "illuminate the scope and variety of Italo-Ashkenazi literature,"[343] even though Yiddish moral-halakhic literature had its beginnings in Italy. The earliest handwritten evidence from the early 16th century contains Italian words, and their earliest prints, such as *Mizvot Nashim* (Venice, 1552 and 1588), were produced there.[344]

Hebrew ethical literature, on the other hand, has enjoyed significant attention during the past decades. However, that too applied only to texts that were created in the center of rabbinic scholarship and adopted by it.[345] Popular Hebrew morality books created outside of rabbinic discourse and presenting an orthopraxic orientation were likewise rarely acknowledged by research. These books are similar to the moral-halakhic works for women. They, too, were printed mainly in the 16th century, and compiled halakhic laws and social ideals for their male readers. Often these works comprised rather terse lists of norms and regulations, almost like accounting sheets,[346] although sometimes they were decorated with narrative or homiletical details.[347]

Joseph Dan, in his examination of rabbinic ethical literature, shows that it does not represent a unified and conforming genre. Rather, it is a heterogeneous, even contradictory literary genre, reflecting like almost no other the intellectual and religious movements and personal experiences of individuals and society. The "riddle of the Hebrew ethical literature" of the Middle Ages and the early modern period consists of its ability to integrate "many extreme radical and even seemingly heretical schools of thought" into constructive, traditional Jewish ethics.[348] Despite its diversity, Dan outlines four major trends: the philosophical-ethical literature, the Ashkenazi hasidic-ethical literature, the kabbalistic-ethical literature, and the mystical-ethical literature. He describes the ideological, orthodox orientation as its most important common characteristic. As opposed to orthopraxic texts, the rabbinic ethical texts do not explain *which* conduct is requested, but *why* a specific conduct is requested.[349]

The impoverished state of research into old Yiddish moral literature has not even yet discovered its own "riddle," if I may be allowed to fall back on Dan's formulation. Until now there have been hardly any attempts to systematize the main categories of this equally heterogeneous literature, although the authors of the older research literature were certainly conscious of the great formal and content-related differences in old Yiddish moral literature.

Israel Zinberg, for example, differentiated merely between "moral books" of the 16th and 17th centuries and "moral books in the form of storybooks," for the didactical *exempla* literature of the 17th century.[350] In his detailed description of the different contents and goals of Yiddish moral literature, he did not create any classification that would have taken into consideration its content-related and stylistic differences.

Max Eric also knew only one designation, *musser-seforim*, for the Yiddish morality books, which followed on principle a "religious purpose" and displayed a "clerical tendency,"[351] with which he may have referred to its normative orientation. He ignored, however, the difference between a rather religious-legal, halakhic orientation on the one hand, and a rather social-normative one on the other.

Hartmut Dinse attempted a chronological systematization of Yiddish moral literature according to functional aspects. He differentiated between the "early *musar* literature" of the 16th century, which together with other liturgy and narrative genres, he designated as "women's literature," and the "critical *musar* literature" of the 17th century, which dealt with social and pedagogical problems and was therefore, he says, written for a male audience.[352] The early *musar* literature was composed, according to Dinse, mainly of "abstract ethical writings" that were limited to the three classical women's duties, *ḥallah* (taking of a portion of dough to be baked), *niddah* (menstruation laws), and *hadlakat nerot* (kindling of the Shabbat candles). The objection that has to be made here is that this limitation applies only to the moral-halakhic texts, while the contents of didactical morality books of the 16th century, such as *Sefer Middot* (1542) and *Brantshpigl* (1596), are not concerned with *halakhah* at all but rather criticize common behavioral patterns, whereas Dinse saw such criticism limited to the "critical *musar* literature" of the 17th century.[353]

Chava Turniansky was the first to raise attention to another moral genre, namely the Songs of Dispute (*shirei vikuaḥ*). Her expanded view brought her to differentiate between morality books (*sifrei musar*), which offered a comprehensive occupation with everyday topics, and moral songs (*shirei musar*), which, according to Turniansky, form the only genre to deal with only one area. However, she considered the *Mizvot Nashim* works as morality books, although most of them deal with only women's duties, so that ultimately she too avoided a differentiation of the actual moral literature.[354]

In his comprehensive description of Old Yiddish literature, Jean Baumgarten indicated formal and content-related idiosyncrasies, as well as the different purposes of the various morality books. But he did not offer any systematization, instead using only the generic term "morality books" for all Yiddish moral works.[355]

The only prior examination that comes close to the "riddle" of Yiddish moral literature and to its solution, with the help of an albeit implied systematization, was presented by Agnes Romer Segal in her content-related stylistic analysis of the texts of the *Mizvot Nashim* corpus. She described these texts as "work[s] of minimal scope containing minimal descriptions of the most basic laws with very little halakhic elaboration. The non-legal material is also minimal, consisting mainly of a few exemplary stories from the midrash . . . and some words of direct ethical teaching."[356] Consequently, she characterized these books as "works of women's commandments" and "legal works."[357]

On the other hand, she described another, extended version from this corpus, the *Seder Mizvot ha-Nashim* by Benjamin Slonik (Krakow, 1577), as a "work [that] defies definition as a *book of 'laws and customs'* for it has all the attributes of *didactic-ethical musar* literature."[358] According to Romer Segal, Slonik's text distinguishes itself by the greater thematic range, the more detailed explanations of the mitzvot on the basis of concrete everyday situations, the long moral passages, and its decidedly social orientation. At the same time, Romer Segal considers his style to be livelier as a result of narrative passages, and more "rabbinic" because of the use of Hebrew literature and Hebrew-Aramaic terms from talmudic discussion. She also sees his work as significantly more didactical because of redundancies and vivid examples, as compared to texts that deal with commandments relating to women. Not least, she says, it stands out with its coherent ethical concept that integrates negative and positive aspects of the woman.[359] Romer Segal concludes that these "particular literary and stylistic features qualify Slonik's work as a forerunner of the original comprehensive works of *musar* literature that arose in Yiddish at the very close of the 16th century."[360]

Among those "comprehensive" and "didactic-ethical works," she includes *Brantshpigl* (Krakow, 1596) and *Lev Tov* (Prague, 1620). Although Romer Segal does not explicitly point out that these works, with their extended contents, were written for an extensive reading audience, including men, she does describe accurately the functional change they underwent. While the classical texts on women's commandments limited themselves more or less to the transfer of practical *halakhah* and women's religious duties, the didactical morality books provided for women and unlearned men "access to a wealth of Jewish knowledge and literary tradition."[361]

I agree with Romer Segal's implicit systematization and the differentiation between moral-halakhic works and moral-didactical works. These terms do not imply that halakhic works neglect a didactic function; the latter works, however, more prominently employ didactical strategies such as narrative material and rhetorical devices, the use of rabbinic discourse, exegetic and homiletic passages, and vivid descriptions of daily life.

Moral-halakhic books such as *Seder Mizvot ha-Nashim* (1552) and *Den Muser un' Hanhoge* (1538) have been printed since the middle of the 16th century. At the same time, they are embedded in a history that reaches even further back, as indicated by the responsa from the 14th or early 15th century, when the codification of practical *halakhah* in the Yiddish language was already officially rejected.[362] Despite that, moral-halakhic books were published in great number, a fact that explains the desire of the unlearned majority both for halakhic instruction, as well as for participation in the moral discourse. The discrepancy between the rejection of the Yiddish moral-halakhic works by the rabbinic authorities and the dissemination of such texts in the vernacular, which was considered necessary, had a decisive influence on the form and contents of these works.[363] This meant that their authors compiled the halakhic laws in a concise, clear form and refrained from mixing them with descriptive or narrative passages, in order not to create even the smallest suspicion of being too entertaining or careless.

The moral-didactical works did not provide any practical *halakhot*, and therefore they did not need to limit themselves stylistically. They were published since the middle of the 16th century beginning with *Sefer Middot* (1542). Although it constituted an adaptation of a Hebrew moral book, it stood apart through its significantly stronger narrative, didactic style. This included the frequent use of rabbinic *aggadot* and popular interpretations, vivid examples, and a narrower orientation along ideals of daily behavior and social practices. This is also true of books such as *Sefer ha-Gan* (Book of the Garden, ca. 1579) and *Sefer Orah Hayyim* (Book of the way of life, 1602), which constituted adaptations from the Hebrew, but also of original Yiddish works such as *Eyn shoyn Froyenbuykhleyn—Seder Mizvot ha-Nashim* (1577). The narrative-didactical style is even more characteristic of *Brantshpigl* and *Lev Tov*, which were published at the end of the 16th and the beginning of the 17th centuries. The authors of the Yiddish morality books were often presumably not rabbis. However, in their capacity as scholars, itinerant preachers, or learned community employees, they were in direct contact with the members of the community, and reacted to their desire for knowledge, explanations, and instruction with an appropriate classical, but to an increasing degree homiletical and moral-didactical style. During the 17th century, the moral-didactical books adopted an increasingly narrative and devotional character by leaning stylistically on the *exempla* literature. Books like *Ẓukhtshpigl* (Mirror of discipline, 1609) by Seligman Ulma Guenzburger and *Simḥat ha-Nefesh* (Enjoyment of life, 1709–1727) by Elchanan Hendel Kirchan may thus be designated as moral-devotional works.

Like every systematization, this too is based on an ideal that rarely exists in pure form. Transitory and mixed forms are more frequently found, of which some must be regarded as special. In that sense, *Meneket Rivkah* is not a classical representative of the moral-didactical literature, such as *Brantshpigl* or *Lev Ṭov*, since its content range is not nearly as comprehensive. Because of its moral orientation and its distinctive didactical rhetoric, *Meneket Rivkah* must without doubt be attributed to the moral-didactical literature. Considering, however, its unusually strong homiletical style, *Meneket Rivkah* can most definitely be positioned on the border between moral-didactical and moral-homiletical works.[364] Its stylistic affinity to the homiletic Yiddish Bible commentary *Ẓe'enah u-Re'enah* cannot be overlooked.[365] Rivkah bat Meir could not have known this work, because its first print appeared after her death.[366] The decisive reason for their similar characteristics seems to me to lie with the fact that both Jacob ben Isaac and Rivkah bat Meir were preachers, being in close contact to a pious non-elite audience who asked for religious instruction and practical moral guidance.

Notes to the Introduction*

* "Fol." refers to *Meneket Rivkah*, if no other book is quoted.

1. In Jewish historiography, the beginning of the modern era is often placed in the 18th century, as by Katz, or in the 17th century, as by Ben Sasson; see J. Katz, *Tradition and Crisis: Jewish Society at the End of the Middle Ages* (New York, 1993); H. H. Ben Sasson, *Hagut ve-hanhagah: Hashkafoteihem ha-ḥevratiyot shel yehudei Polin be-shilhei yemei ha-benayim* (Jerusalem, 1959). I follow here the convention of general historiography, which usually sets the beginning of the modern era around the year 1500, as in A. Funkenstein, *Perceptions of Jewish History* (Berkeley, 1993), and Y. H. Yerushalmi, *Zakhor. Jewish History and Jewish Memory* (Seattle, 1982).

2. E. Horowitz, "Jüdische Jugend in Europa: 1300–1800" (Jewish Youth in Europe: 1300–1800), in G. Levi and J.-C. Schmitt (eds.), *Geschichte der Jugend*, vol. 1 (Frankfurt-am-Main, 1996), pp. 113–165; G. D. Hundert, "Jewish Children and Childhood in Early Modern East Central Europe," in D. Kraemer (ed.), *The Jewish Family* (New York, 1989).

3. Glikl bas Judah Leib was engaged in the year 1658 at the age of about 12 and was married at the age of 14. She then lived one year with her husband in the house of her in-laws before they had their own home; see Ch. Turniansky, *Glikl. Ẓikhronot 1691–1719* (Jerusalem, 2006); N. Z. Davis, "Glikl bas Judah Leib: Arguing with God," in *Women on the Margins: Three Seventeenth-Century Lives* (Cambridge, Mass., 1995), chap. 1, pp. 5–62.

4 R. Berger, *Sexualität, Ehe und Familienleben in der jüdischen Moralliteratur, 900–1900* (Sexuality, Marriage, and Family Life in Jewish Moral Literature, 900–1900) (Wiesbaden, 2003).

5. Cf. F. Rohden, "Jüdische Ehe zwischen religiöser Norm und Alltagswahrnehmung im 16. Jahrhundert" (Jewish Marriage between Religious Norms and Daily Life Perceptions in the Sixteenth Century), in A. Holzem and I. Weber (eds.), *Ehe, Familie, Verwandtschaft* (Münster, 2008).

6. "Education" here means the specific form of erudition, defined by male, rabbinic standards, which Jewish women and girls could only obtain in a limited scope anyway. The knowledge and intellectual capabilities that women obtained through their work, the house, and the business did not count as education in the traditional sense. This, however, should not lead to the assumption that women, who by these standards were "uneducated," did not have any knowledge or intellect; see B. Whitehead, *Women's Education in Early Modern Europe: A History 1500–1800* (New York, 1999), x–xii.

7. Ch. Turniansky, "Maydlekh in der altyidisher literatur" (Girls in Old Yiddish Literature), in W. Röll and S. Neuberg (eds.), *Jiddische Philologie. Festschrift für Erika Timm* (Tübingen, 1999), p. 18; S. Henry, E. Taitz, C. Tallan (eds.), *The JPS Guide to Jewish Women, 600 B.C.E.–1900 C.E.* (Philadelphia, 2003), pp. 135–137, 142, 145.

8. Henry et al., *Guide*, p. 152.

9. I. Fishman, *The History of Jewish Education in Central Europe: From the End of the Sixteenth to the End of the Eighteenth Century* (London, 1944); cf. the frequent call in *Brantshpigl* to women, who cannot read, to have the book read to them; see S. Riedel (ed.), Moses Henochs Altschul-Jeruschalmi, "Brantspigel" (Frankfurt-am-Main, 1993), pp. 10, 21, 22, 72 (cited below as *Brantshpigl*).

10. *Brantshpigl, passim.*

11. M. Toch, "Die jüdische Frau im Erwerbsleben des Spätmittelalters" (The Jewish Woman in the Economic Life of the Late Middle Ages), in J. Carlebach (ed.), *Zur Geschichte der jüdischen Frau in Deutschland* (Berlin, 1993), pp. 37–48.

12. Henry et al., *Guide*, p. 149f.

13. Turniansky, *Glikl*; Davis, "Glickl."

14. Henry et al., *Guide*, p. 143f.

15. D. Kay, *Seyder Tkhines: The Forgotten Book of Common Prayer for Jewish Women* (Philadelphia, 2004); Ch. Weissler, *Voices of the Matriarchs: Listening to Prayers of Early Modern Jewish Women* (Boston, 1998), pp. 3–35.

16. Regarding the reading practices of women, and reading material for women, see J. Baumgarten, *Old Yiddish Literature,* ed. and trans. J. C. Frakes (New York, 2005), chap. 3; Turniansky, "Maydlekh," *passim.*

17. Regarding the history of the Jewish community of Prague in the early modern period, see G. Bondy and F. Dvorsky, *Zur Geschichte der Juden in Böhmen, Mähren, Schlesien von 906–1620* (On the History of the Jews of Bohemia, Moravia, Silesia 906–1620) (Prague, 1906); B. Brilling, "Die Prager jüdische Gemeinde als Fürsprecherin und Vertreterin des deutschen Judentums im 16. und 17. Jahrhundert" (The Jewish Community of Prague as Advocate and Representative of German Jewry in the Sixteenth and Seventeenth Century), in *Theokratia* 3 (1973–75) (Leiden, 1979), pp. 185–198; S.-A. Goldberg, *Crossing the Jabbok: Illness and Death in Ashkenazi Judaism in Sixteenth through Nineteenth Century Prague* (Berkeley, 1996); J. Herman, "Die wirtschaftliche Betätigung und Berufe der Prager Juden vor ihrer Ausweisung im Jahre 1541" (Economic Activity and Professions of the Jews of Prague prior to Their Expulsion in the Year 1541), in *Judaica Bohemiae* 4, 1 (1968), pp. 20–63; J. Herman, "The Conflict between Jewish and Non-Jewish Population in Bohemia before the 1541 Banishment," in *Judaica Bohemiae*, 6, 1 (1970), pp. 39–53; J. Israel, *European Jewry in the Age of Mercantilism, 1550–1750* (Oxford, 1985); T. Jakobovits, "Die jüdischen Zünfte in Prag" (The Jewish Guilds in Prague), in *Jahrbuch der Gesellschaft für Geschichte der Juden in der czechoslovakischen Republik* 8 (1936), pp. 57–68; S. H. Lieben, "Frumet Meisel, ebenbürtige Gattin ihres Mannes Mordechai Meisel" (Frumet Meisel, a Wife Equal to Her Husband Mordecai Meisel), in *Monatsschrift für Geschichte und Wissenschaft des Judentums* 75 (1931), pp. 374–377; O. Muneles (ed.), *Prague Ghetto in the Renaissance Period* (Prague, 1965); A. Stein, *Die Geschichte der Juden in Böhmen und Mähren* (The History of the Jews of Bohemia and Moravia) (Brünn, 1904); G. Wolf, "Zur Geschichte der Juden in Österreich. Gemeindestreitigkeiten in Prag von 1567–1678" (On the History of Jews in Austria. Community Conflicts in Prague, 1567–1678), in *Zeitschrift für die Geschichte der Juden in Deutschland* 1 (1887), pp. 309–320; G. Wolf, "Zur Geschichte der Juden in Österreich. Verzeichnis der Prager Juden, ihrer Frauen, Kinder und Dienstboten im Jahre 1546" (On the History of Jews in Prague, Their Wives, Children, and Servants, in the Year 1546), in *Zeitschrift für die Geschichte der Juden in Deutschland* 1 (1887), pp. 177–190.

18. G. Veltri, "'Ohne Recht und Gerechtigkeit': Rudolf II. und sein Bankier Markus Meyzl" (Without Law and Justice: Rudolf II and His Financier, Markus Meisel), in G. Veltri and A. Winkelmann (eds.), *An der Schwelle zur Moderne. Juden in der Renaissance* (Leiden, 2003), pp. 233–255.

19. Herman, "Conflict," p. 46ff.; Wolf, "Gemeindestreitigkeiten" (Community Conflicts), p. 310ff.

20. Wolf, "Verzeichnis" (Register), p. 178ff.

21. Herman, "Wirtschaftliche Betätigung" (Economic Activities), p. 57ff.

22. Wolf, "Verzeichnis" (Register), p. 189.

23. S.-A. Goldberg, "Von der (Prager) Judenstadt zum jüdischen Prag" (From the Jewish Quarter in Prague to Jewish Prague), in M. Graetz, *Schöpferische Momente des Judentums* (Heidelberg, 2000), pp. 222 and 225; Goldberg, *Crossing,* p. 111ff.

24. Regarding the author of *Brantshpigl*, see n. 218.

25. This slightly faulty rendition of the inscription is found in O. Muneles, *Epitaphs from the Ancient Jewish Cemetery of Prague* [Heb.] (Jerusalem, 1988), p. 161, no. 61. The tall stone is decorated by surrounding strapwork, a pointed gable, and attached rosettes and rocailles. The last two lines are separated from the epitaph by a horizontal strapwork. The inscription is written in alternate rhyme; various letters (in ll. 8, 11, 13, 15–17) are marked by notches (except in l. 6 where the *resh* could not be marked for lack of space) and result in the phrase *Rivkah z"l v"n* , probably the abbreviation for *zikhronah li-vrakhah ve-nezah* (of blessed memory and for eternity).

26. See Josh. 24:27. The letters *Rivkah ha-even* are marked as a chronostichon by abbreviation marks: 365 (1605). The final *nun* was chiseled into the strapwork on the side.

27. I Sam. 25:29.

28. Prov. 31:29.

29. Prov. 31:11.

30. Abigail is the role model of a pious, wise woman; see I Sam. 25:3ff.

31. See Yalkut, §992: "The prayer of the pious is more beautiful than a whole sacrifice." The word *kalil* is hardly legible, of the two *lamedim* only the top notches are legible. The distance between the two *lamedim* is greater than required for a *yud*.

32. See Bamidbar Rabbah 8.2: "And the sacrificial ram of atonement." Spiritualization of death as atonement for the sins of the present or of an earlier generation can be found already in rabbinic literature; see Y. Sanhedrin 6, 2: "May my death be an atonement for everybody."

33. See Isa. 1:21, 26.

34. See M. Sotah 7:8.

35. This abbreviation differs from *mhvr"r*, which stands for *morenu ha-rav ve-rav rabbeinu* (our teacher, the master and our great Rabbi), applied to the head of a yeshivah; Turniansky, however, interprets this rather as a common misreading of *mvhr"r*; cf. Turniansky, *Glikl*, p. 20, n. 66. Concerning the different titles, cf. Katz, *Tradition*, p. 167.

36. Muneles, *Epitaphs*, p. 28, pointed out that in Prague in the 16th century, a title did not, in most cases, designate any specific function but rather, as an expression of a formalized address, denoted the social position of its bearer; see the title *mh"r* (*morenu ha-rav*—our teacher, the master) of the printer Gershom ben Bezalel Katz on the title page.

37. See Appendix, ll. 59–79; a translation of the *Simhes Toyre Lid* is included in Kay, *Seyder Tkhines*, pp. 220–223.

38. Aramaic statements from B. Shabbat 23b are quoted exclusively on fol. 33b. In the light of their downright proverbial quality, she may have known them as part of the vernacular.

39. M. Weinreich, *History of the Yiddish Language* (Chicago/London, 1980), p. 586.

40. Kh. Shmeruk, "The First Jewish Authoress in Poland: Rivkah Tiktiner and Her Works" [Heb.], *Gal-Ed*, 27–28 (1978), p. 14, derives from the father's designation of origin that Rivkah bat Meir was born and raised in Poland, and came to Prague only in later years. This must, however, be regarded as speculation.

41. Weinreich, *History*, p. 542f.; fols. 12a/11 and 16a/23 (Yiddish text).

42. Fol. 17a/7 and 20, fol. 18a/3 (Yiddish text). The expressions *tet* resp. *tate*—father, or *tet leben*—dear father, more commonly used in Eastern Yiddish, appear only in the tale; see fols. 17b/1, 18a/2 (Yiddish text). In addition, the word is also common in German; see, for example, "lieber tetel" in a Christian medieval manuscript of the same tale.

43. Weinreich, *History*, p. 547f. Weinreich transcribes *zeyde* and *deyde*.

44. Fols. 23b/24 and 27b/23 (Yiddish text).

45. Weinreich, *History*, p. 726.

46. For example, in the anonymous Yiddish translation of the original Hebrew *Sefer ha-Gan* by Isaac ben Eliezer (Krakow, ca. 1579; Hanau, ca. 1620; Prague, 1657), fols. 6b, 11b (*davenen*), fols. 5a, 7a (*oren*); see W. Röll, "Zum 'Sefer ha-Gan' Jizhaks ben Elieser" (On *Sefer ha-Gan* by Isaac ben Eliezer), *Trierer Beiträge* 2 (1977), pp. 35–41. around 1620, Prague

47. Fol. 7a/25 (Yiddish text).

48. See commentary on p. 105/2.

49. The expression *kiryah ne'emanah* is taken from Isa. 1:21, 26, referring to Jerusalem. Although it is grammatically incorrect, and therefore rather improbable, that *be-khol kiryah ne'emanah* should also mean "in the entire faithful city"—i.e., only in Prague.

50. The gravestone is located in direct proximity of the gravestone of the famous financier, community elder, and patron Mordecai Markus Meisel (d. 1601), which may be an indication of her high esteem.

51. *Sefer Hazkarot* (MS 113), fol. 33a, entry no. 174; the table of contents lists on fol. 45a the name *Rivkah bat mhr"r Meir*. The writing of the entry is very faded, and at some points completely illegible. Infrared photography did not provide any considerable improvement of legibility: in my transcription, letters set in square brackets indicate questionable readings; letters in curly brackets are emendations that are not legible in the original; a tilde denotes an illegible word.

52. S. Muneles, *Epitaphs;* O. Muneles, "Zur Prosopographie der Prager Juden im 15. und 16. Jahrhundert" (On the Prosopography of Fifteenth and Sixteenth Century Jews of Prague), *Judaica Bohemiae* 2, 1 (1966), pp. 3–13; S. Hock and D. Kaufmann, *Die Familien Prags* (The Families of Prague) (Pressburg, 1892).

53. Fol. 8a.

54. In Yiddish, grandchildren are mostly called *enikel*, see 17a/7 (Yiddish text).

55. Contemporary sources use the male form *ha-darshan* rather rarely, although a figure from the 17th century is known as Judah Isaac ben Jacob Darshan, whose medical book of prescriptions *Mezil Nefashot* was printed in 1651. *Ha-darshan* appears as a functional title already in the rabbinic literature (e.g., B. Bava Batra 119b). Community preachers or itinerant preacher, were, in Central Europe, designated as *maggid*, as in the case of the itinerant preacher Jacob ben Isaac Ashkenazi from Janow, the author of *Ze'enah u-Re'enah* (Hanau, 1622); cf. the anonymous, Hebrew-Yiddish homiletic commentary to the prophets, *Sefer ha-Maggid* (Lublin, 1623); regarding *maggid*, see I. Zinberg, *A History of Jewish Literature*, vol. 7: *Old Yiddish Literature from Its Origins to the Haskalah Period* (New York, 1975), p. 129; Ch. Turniansky, "Ha-derashah veha-derashah bikhtav ke-metavkhot beyn ha-tarbut ha-kanonit le-veyn ha-kahal ha-rahav" (Sermons and Written Sermons as Mediators between the Canonical Culture and the Broad Public), in B. Z. Kedar (ed.), *Ha-tarbut ha-amamit. Kovez mehkarim* (Jerusalem, 1996), pp. 183–185, 191f.; Baumgarten, *Old Yiddish*, pp. 113–121, 240.

56. See Muneles, *Epitaphs;* the only exception is the daughter of the Maharal, Feigele, who died in 1629 and who was married to a rabbi: "scholarly through reason and insight in all laws of the Gemara"; ibid., p. 303, no. 199.

57. See H. Adelman, "The Literacy of Women in Early Modern Italy," in B. J. Whitehead, *Women's Education in Early Modern Italy* (New York/London, 1999), p. 142; J. R. Baskin, *Women of the Word: Jewish Women and Jewish Writing* (Detroit, 1994), p. 64.

58. Fol. 2b/12 (Yiddish text); "interpret," see also fols. 20a, 21b, 33b, 34a, 35b. Regarding the contemporary understanding of *darshen*, see *Sefer Middot*, fol. 96a: "*ayn talmid hokhem der do darsht doz maynt der ander loyt lernt*" (a scholar who *darsht*, this means, who teaches other people). Teaching, however, was also understood as preaching; see commentary on p. 93/10.

59. Hardly anything is known about the author: the colophon on the title page of her sermon, *Eyn hipshe droshe* ("A lovely sermon," printed in Amsterdam, no date, probably beginning of the 17th century), reads, "From the widow Hannah bat *mvh"r* Judah Leib (Loeb) Katz, to the widow of *mvh"r* Isaac Ashkenaz [*sic*] *z"l*. One copy is in the Bodleian Library in Oxford (Steinschneider, *Catalogus*, no. 49; Opp. 8° 124), and contains 15 pages (fols. 2a–9a). The short sermon is followed by a *Tefillah le-Shabbat* from fol. 6b, a Yiddish translation of the *Mah Tovu* prayer from fol. 7b, and a *thinne* for the blowing of the shofar at the beginning of the month of Elul from fol. 8a; see M. Kayserling, *Die jüdischen Frauen in der Geschichte, Literatur und Kunst* (Jewish Women in History, Literature, and Arts) (Leipzig, 1879; reprint, Hildesheim, 1991), p. 152; E. Korman, *Yidishe Dikhterins* (Jewish Women Poets) (Chicago, 1928), p. 22.

60. Regarding the role of women in the synagogue, see S. Grossman and R. Haut (eds.), *Daughters of the King. Women and the Synagogue: A Survey of History, Halakhah, and Contemporary Realities* (Philadelphia, 1992).

61. Quoted according to Henry et al., *Guide*, p. 77; see A. Grossman, *Pious and Rebellious: Jewish Women in Medieval Europe* (Waltham, Mass., 2004), p. 285. Since the days of Dolce this activity does not seem to have changed much until the late 19th century, when the Yiddish-Hebrew writer Mendele Mokher Seforim described the literary image of such a woman with the words: "It was she who showed the women how to pray: what hymns to say, when to rise, when to stand on tip-toe in the *Kedushah* prayer.... And in fact it was hardly possible to keep from fainting when Sarah read. She would read with great emotion, her melody melting the soul and pulling at the heart strings;" quoted according to E. Taitz, "Women's Voices, Women's Prayers: The European Synagogue of the Middle Ages," in Grossman/Haut, *Daughters*, p. 67.

62. Regarding medieval and early modern period female leaders, see Sh. P. Zolty, *And All Your Children Shall be Learned: Women and the Study of Torah in Jewish Law and History* (Northvale, N.J., 1993), pp. 174f., 179–186, 195f.; Grossman, *Pious*, p. 285; Henry et al., *Guide*, pp. 73–197; Taitz, *Women's Voices*, pp. 62–65; Zinberg, *History*, p. 23f. Regarding women teachers in the Levant in the 16th century, see R. Lamdan, *A Separate People: Jewish Women in Palestine, Syria and Egypt in the Sixteenth Century* (Leiden, 2000), p. 110.

63. The list has the German word "Kantorin;" Wolf, "Verzeichnis" (Register), p. 187. It seems doubtful to me whether this could refer to Rivkah bat Meir. Assuming a minimum age of 25 for this task, this "Rypka" would have to have reached the age of 84 years in 1605, which may not be out of the question, but would nevertheless be exceptional.

64. Muneles, *Epitaphs*, p. 114, no. 11 (from 1492); p. 130, no. 30 (from 1531); p. 132, no. 33 (from 1533); p. 150, no. 52 (from 1546); p. 151, no. 52b (from 1547); p. 302f., no. 199 (from 1629). It must be pointed out that the gravestones specified by Muneles constitute only a fraction of those that existed at that time.

65. Muneles, *Epitaphs*, p. 214, no. 114. It is unclear whether Rachel, who passed away in 1654 and who was the wife of the famous Prague rabbi and scholar Lipman Heller, helped her husband by teaching on her own: "The rabbi's wife supports her husband: To learn, as well as to teach old and young"; see Muneles, *Epitaphs*, p. 329, no. 217.

66. JNUL R8° 894501, quoted according to Weissler, *Voices*, p. 24.

67. Kh. Shmeruk, *Sifrut yidish be-polin: Mehkarim ve-iyyunim historiyim* (Yiddish Literature in Poland: Research and Historical Analysis) (Jerusalem, 1981), p. 51. Regarding religious and secular poems by women since the Middle Ages, see G. Hasan-Rokem, T. S. Hess and Sh. Kaufman, *The Defiant Muse: Hebrew Feminist Poems from Antiquity to the Present. A Bilingual Anthology* (New York, 1999), pp. 63–81.

68. Regarding the *thinnot*, see Weissler, *Voices*; regarding Jewish female authors, see Baskin, *Women*; Hasan-Rokem et al., *Defiant Muse*; S. Henry and E. Taitz, *Written Out of History: Our Jewish Foremothers* (New York, 1978 [1988³]); Korman, *Dikhterins*; Weissler, *Voices*; Zolty, *Children*.

69. *Doz iz ayn hipshe thinne di men al tog zogen zol*, in *Mishlei Hakhamim* (Prague, ca. 1616; first edition Venice, 1566), fols. 15a–16a.

70. M. Vilimkova, "Seven Hundred Years of the Old-New-Synagogue," in *Judaica Bohemiae* 5, 2 (1969), pp. 72–83.

71. At the time of Rivkah bat Meir there were five synagogues in Prague: Altshul, Altneushul, Neue Shul (since 1599), the Meisel Synagogue (since 1591), and the Pinkas Synagogue (since 1535); see Vilimkova, "Seven Hundred Years."

72. Regarding the rabbis of the Altneushul, see O. Muneles, "Die Rabbiner der Altneuschul" (The Rabbis of the Altneushul), *Judaica Bohemiae* 5, 2 (1969), p. 110.

73. Many of his sermons range among his printed work, such as *Drush Na'eh* (1589).

74. Among others, he wrote a book compiling *aggadot* derived from B. Gittin (1573), and rhyming commentaries on Pesah (1587), and on the *Yore De'ah* of Shulhan Arukh (1591).

75. He wrote, among others, *Levushim* (1590–1604), a work in ten volumes, one half of which was halakhically oriented, the other half consisting of partially kabbalistic inspired commentaries of the Torah, and other commentators; see commentary on p. 98/4 and the section "Sources and Their Editing."

76. *Ir Gibborim* (Basel, 1580); *Olelot Efrayim* (Lublin, 1590); *Orah le-Hayyim* (Lublin, 1595); *Keli Yakar* (Lublin, 1602).

77. The examination could also show whether there existed a connection between the activities of Rivkah bat Meir and the Maharal's didactical program, which was very similar to the pedagogical ideas of the Bohemian

scholar Amos Comenius; see A. F. Kleinberger, "The Didactics of Rabbi Loew of Prague," *Scripta Hierosolymitana* 13 (1963), pp. 32–55; M. Fox, "The Moral Philosophy of the Maharal," in D. B. Cooperman (ed.), *Jewish Thought in the Sixteenth Century* (Cambridge, Mass., 1983), pp. 167–185.

78. See appendix, n. 1; according to Shmeruk, "Jewish Authoress", p. 19, he knew only of two prints, but because of several corrupted words in both prints, he also assumed the existence of an earlier third print.

79. See Baumgarten, *Old Yiddish*, p. 268, n. 21, p. 273f.; Zinberg, *History*, p. 285ff.; Shmeruk, *Sifrut yidish*, chapter 2.

80. Regarding the *hakafot* see I. Elbogen, *Der jüdische Gottesdienst in seiner geschichtlichen Entwicklung* (Hildesheim, 1995) (*Jewish Liturgy: A Comprehensive History,* trans. R. P. Scheindlin) (Philadelphia, 1993), p. 200 (page number refers to German edition); A. Ya'ari, *Toldot ḥag simḥat torah* (History of the Feast Simhat Torah) (Jerusalem, 1989), pp. 276–293.

81. On this matter, see K. Hellerstein, "The Name in the Poem: Yiddish Women Poets," in *Shofar* 20, 3 (spring 2002), pp. 32–52, p. 34f.

82. See the eschatological feast in Isa. 25:6.

83. Thus mentioned first in G. Karpeles, *Geschichte der jüdischen Literatur* (History of Jewish Literature), 2 vols. (Berlin, 1909), p. 333; see below, section "Meneket Rivkah in Research." The first Yiddish translation of *Ḥovot ha-Levavot* was published only in 1698 in Sulzbach; see Baumgarten, *Old Yiddish*, p. 218, n. 35.

84. See pp. 80/5–81/4.

85. Fol. 7a/21ff. (Yiddish text). It remains unclear which events or persons the author refers to, particularly since it is not certain whether she refers to events that took place in Prague.

86. The use of other witness reports is unusual in the Yiddish moral literature of the 16th century, but in the Hebrew ethical literature of the early modern period it became increasingly common to back up moral demands with empirical findings; see J. Dan, *Sifrut ha-derush veha-musar* (Jerusalem, 1975), p. 14. Additional eyewitness reports in fols. 7b and 23a–b.

87. Fol. 7b/10ff (Yiddish text).

88. Fol. 8a; also 18b.

89. See commentary on p. 169/12.

90. Fols. 3b, 7b, 8a, 18a, 18b, 22b, 23a, and 30a.

91. Fol. 21b.

92. Regarding the rejection of the Yiddish moral literature, see below, section "Sources and Their Editing."

93. Due to the transcription rules applied here, the title should read *Ayn shoyn Froyenbuykhlayn*; however, this is rather uncommon in secondary literature; for this reason, the transcription follows the more common spelling.

94. See commentary on p. 124/7.

95. E. Fram, *My Dear Daughter: Rabbi Benjamin Slonik and the Education of Jewish Women in Sixteenth-Century Poland* (Cincinnati, 2007); A. Romer Segal, "Yiddish Works on Women's Commandments in the Sixteenth Century," *Studies in Yiddish Literature and Folklore,* Monograph Series 1986 (7), p. 54f.

96. An additional print of *Seder Mizvot ha-Nashim* under the title of *Eyn shoyn Froyenbuykhleyn* was produced in 1627 in Hanau; a similar book from the *Mizvot Nashim* corpus, *Seder Nashim,* by Samuel Shmelke from Prague, was printed in 1629, subtitled *Vayber Bukh.*

97. *Brantshpigl,* p. 247. The translation of Riedel's transcript is mine.

98. The copy from the 1609 Prague print is found in the old library of the University of Erlangen (Wagenseil Collection, VK 90/1); the copy from the 1618 Krakow print is in the library of the Jewish Theological Seminary, New York (SHF 1878:12 RB 5715).

99. He was the great-grandchild of Gershom ben Solomon ha-Kohen, the man who established the Gersonides printer family in 1512 with the beginning of Hebrew letterpress; B. Nosek, "Katalog mit einer Auswahl hebräischer Drucke Prager Provenienz" (Catalogue with a Selection of Hebrew Prints of Prague Provenance), *Judaica Bohemiae* 10, 1 (1977), pp. 17–25; S. H. Lieben, "Der hebräische Buchdruck in Prag im 16. Jahrhundert" (Hebrew Book Printing in Sixteenth Century Prague), in S. Steinhertz, *Die Juden in Prag* (Prague, 1927), pp. 88–126; see commentary on p. 80/10.

100. Nosek, "Katalog," p. 19f.

101. Ibid., p. 24. Besides Gershom ben Bezalel himself, Abraham ben Simon Heida, Moses Utitz ben Eliezer, and Gershom ben Solomon Poper participated in financing a print in 1609.

102. Ibid., p. 25.

103. Fols. 9a, 10b, 11a, 12b.

104. Fols. 14b, 15a–19a, 22b, 23a, 24b, 29b, 30b–31b.

105. Fol. 25a.

106. Frequently a *vav* instead of an *aleph* as a middle vowel, a *heh* instead of a *yud* as a final vowel, a *sin* instead of a *zayin*, a missing or additional *ayin* as a vowel symbol, or an *aleph* as a final letter of a word; more rarely a conjunction or preposition was added or omitted: all these deviations exist.

107. Between 1596 and 1706, six prints of *Brantshpigl* were published; and at least 11 additional prints of *Lev Tov* (Prague, 1620; Krakow, 1641; Amsterdam, 1651 and others) by Isaac ben Eliakim of Poznan, which, as opposed to *Brantshpigl,* also took into consideration the life of Polish rural communities, were published until 1709; see Y. Vinograd, *Thesaurus of the Hebrew Book: Listing of Books Printed in Hebrew Letters since the Beginning of Hebrew Printing circa 1469 through 1863* (Jerusalem, 1993), vol. 1, p. 65; Baumgarten, *Old Yiddish*, pp. 208, 212–215; Zinberg, *History*, p. 159ff.

108. Turniansky, *Glikl*, p. 27; Glikl bas Judah recommends likewise that those "who can study" should read Hebrew morality books (*sifrei muser*).

109. In this matter see Baumgarten, *Old Yiddish*, p. 224, n. 42; regarding bilingual moral literature, see Ch. Turniansky, *Sefer massah u-merivah shel Aleksander ben Yizhak Pfafenhofen* (Jerusalem, 1985), pp. 126–144.

110. There is also agreement between Rivkah bat Meir in her criticism of overly permissive parents and Isaac ben Berl in his disapproval of too lenient mothers; see commentary on p. 83/4.

111. See fols. 2b–3b: "A nice story took place in our times in the holy, splendid community of Nikolsburg.... As it has been printed earlier."

112. Cf. the morality books (each also in quarto) *Sefer Middot*: 99 fols.; *Brantshpigl*: 198 fols.; *Lev Tov*: 134 fols.; *Sefer Orah Hayyim*: 22 fols.; *Meshiv Hema—Minhagim Eshet Hayil*: 19 fols.; *Mishlei Hakhamim* and *Sefer Hayyei Olam*: 11 fols. The moral-halakhic texts, however, mostly turn out shorter, and, except for the first, were printed in octavo: *Den Muser un' Hanhoge*: 36 fols.; *Iggeret Derekh ha-Shem*: 13 fols.; *Sefer Hayyei Olam*: 11 fols.; *Mizvot Nashim* (Venice, 1552): 52 fols.; *Mizvot Nashim* (Venice, 1588): 38 fols.; *Eyn shoyn Froyenbuykhleyn*: 54 fols.

113. This nurse is mentioned first in Gen. 24:59. After Rebekah decided to go with Abraham's slave and become Isaac's wife, the nurse was sent along with her.

114. See commentary on p. 80/14.

115. First print, Constantinople, 1514; additional prints, Venice, 1544, 1594, 1595, and 1602; see below, n. 199.

116. Fols. 4a, 5a, 8a, 10a, 14a, 21b, 30a, 33b, 34b. In fol. 15b the author paraphrases the preceding section, structuring the passage as a whole.

117. Fols. 3b, 5b, 32b.

118. Fols. 3b, 5a, 5b, 7b, 8b, 10a, 10b, 12a, 22b, 32b. See commentary on p. 97/6–7.

119. For example, *Brantshpigl*, pp. 13, 27, 48, 59, 66, 81, 152, 245, 250, 268, 309, 311, 314, 344, 360, 398, 410, 435.

120. Romer Segal, "Yiddish Works," p. 57, n. 7.

121. See *sifrut ha-musar* for "moral literature," "ethical literature"; the noun *musar* stands in the Bible for "castigation," "admonition," or "behavioral teaching"; see Prov. 1:8 and Prov. 12:1. From this the meanings "ethics," "aretology," and "moral" were derived; see Even Shoshan, *Ha-milon*, p. 647.

122. Similar in *Brantshpigl* was the double characterization "*unter vayzung un' ler*" on the title page and in the text: see ibid., pp. 1, 24, 38.

123. For example, fols. 5a, 8b–9a, 13b, 15a, 21b–22a, 28b, 35b–36a.

124. For example, fols. 9a–10a, 19b–20b, 33b–34b.

125. Fols. 2b–3a, 3b–5a, 8b–10a, 13b–14a, 19b–21a, 21b–22a, 30b–31b, 35b–36a. Regarding rabbinic homily, see D. Lenhard, *Die rabbinische Homilie. Ein formanalytischer Index* (The Rabbinic Homily. A Form Analytic Index) (Frankfurt-am-Main, 1998); D. Stern, *Parables in Midrash. Narrative and Exegesis in Rabbinic Literature* (Cambridge, Mass., 1994), pp. 154–166.

126. See commentary on p. 113/8–9. Regarding the rabbinic interpretation of Leah, see J. R. Baskin, *Midrashic Women: Formations of the Feminine in Rabbinic Literature* (Hanover, N.H., 2002), pp. 145–149.

127. See commentary on pp. 147/16; 149/3.

128. Similar structure is found in the comparison between newlyweds and their new family, and Abraham and Sarah in foreign lands, in a short homily in fol. 2b.

129. M. Nulman, *The Encyclopedia of Jewish Prayer* (Northvale, N.J., 1993), pp. 336 and 358.

130. About one half of *Brantshpigl* consists of quotes or paraphrases from the Talmud and midrashim; a large part thereof are tales, of which some were condensed into one or two lines, in order to describe an exemplary situation; see F. v. Rohden, *Zur Jiddischen Mussar-Literatur im 16. Jahrhundert: Die Konstruktion von Weiblichkeit und Männlichkeit im Brantshpigl von Moshe Henochs Altschul* (On Sixteenth-Century Yiddish Moral Literature: The Construction of Female and Male in the *Brantshpigl* by Moses Henokhs Altschul), master's thesis, Free University of Berlin, 1997, pp. 76–79; M. Gaster, "The Maasehbuch and the Brantspiegel," in S. W. Baron and A. Marx (eds.), *Jewish Studies in the Memory of G. A. Kohut* (New York, 1935), pp. 270–278.

131. Most probably of rabbinic origin are the tales of the *Sefer Middot* in fols. 10a, 19b, 42a, 44a, 45b, 46a, 57a, 57b, 58a, 64a, 72b, 73b, 74b, 94a, 94b, 95a, 95b, 96a, 96b; some originate in the environment of the *Hasidei Ashkenaz*: 15a, 67a; from the German or European tradition of storytelling: 38a, 46a, 57a. In accordance with its origin, *Sefer ha-Gan* falls back on many tales from the environment of *Hasidei Ashkenaz*; *Eyn shoyn Froyenbuykhleyn*, strongly related to the moral-halakhic literature, on the other hand, uses only a few tales, which are exclusively of rabbinic origin. In some morality books, the *aggadot* have a mainly devotional character, rather than a midrashic character, for example in *Sefer Orah Hayyim* and *Sefer Mishlei*.

132. Because of the normative quality of proverbs, the author uses them frequently, like Bible verses. Therefore I relate to the following proverbs in connection with the exegetical style.

133. Fols. 10a–10b, 13a, 15b, 15b–16a, 20b, 34b–35a.

134. Fols. 12a, 25a, 28a, 33a.

135. Fols. 7a–7b, 7b, 23a–24a.

136. M. Koch, *Der Schlegel. Zur Novelle von Rüdiger von Hünchoven: Kritische Ausgabe, Untersuchungen und Übersetzung* (The Club: On the Novella by Rüdiger von Hünchoven: Critical Edition, Studies and Translation) (Münster/Hamburg, 1993); Röhrich, *Lexikon*, p. 1100.

137. In *Brantshpigl* the specifically Jewish details are missing; see the commentary on p. 138/12.

138. Fols. 3b, 4a, 5a, 7b, 8a, 10a–b, 11a, 12b, 13b, 14a, 15b, 18b, 19a, 21a–b, 22a–b, 30a, 31a, 32a–b, 34b, 36a; various folios contain multiple references.

139. Fols. 3b, 5b, 18a–b, 21b, 22b, 23a, 28b, 29a, 30a, 32a, 33b; various folios contain multiple references.
140. Fols. 5b, 8b, 21b.
141. Fol. 30a.
142. Fols. 8a, 13a, 18b.
143. Fol. 28b; see, among others, fols. 3a, 13b, 20a.
144. Fols. 3b, 5a, 12b, 28b, 30a, 33b.
145. See the thirteen *middot* of R. Yishmael; fols. 3b, 4a, 5a, 7b, 11a, 13b, 14a, 16a, 19a, 24b, 26b, 27b.
146. Fols. 11b, 13b, 32b.
147. Fols. 9a, 28a, 28b, 34b.
148. Fols. 12b, 13b, 14a, 16a (twice), 23b, 26a, 30a.
149. *Brantshpigl*, pp. 18, 37, 80, 83, 99, 118, 120, 137, 151, 157f., 164, 168, 173, 191f., 273, 282, 337, 342, 358, 371f., 380, 402, 449; see also *Mishlei Hakhamim*, no. 52; *Sefer Middot*, fol. 45a.
150. B. Kirshenblatt-Gimblett, "Toward a Theory of Proverb Meaning," *Proverbium* 22 (1973), pp. 821–827; R. G. Warnock, "Proverbs and Sayings in Early Yiddish Literature," in W. Röll and S. Neuberg (eds.), *Jiddische Philologie. Festschrift für Erika Timm* (Tübingen 1999), p. 195.
151. Fol. 35a; same or similar in fols. 2b, 3b, 6b, 21b, 33b, 34a, 35b.
152. The author of *Brantshpigl*, for example, offered almost no translation of Bible verses into common spoken Yiddish; instead, he preferred a word-by-word transfer into Yiddish, preserving the Hebrew syntax, a method corresponding to the teaching practice in Torah schools.
153. Weinreich, *History*, p. 223.
154. For example, fols. 4a/21, 5a/12, 6a/3, 12b/5, 13b/9, 20a/29, 28b/1, 32b/20, 35b/21, 36a/12, 16 (Yiddish text).
155. Fols. 2b/7, 4a/27, 6a/14, 9a/19, 11b/16, 12b/19, 20a/1, 7, 20b/9.15, 26b/3, 32a/18, 34b/25, 35b/9 (Yiddish text).
156. Fols. 8a/8, 8b/8, 11, 9a/2ff., 13a/1, 15a/7, 16a/25, 19a/4, 25b/13, 26a/23, 25, 28a/1, 28b/4, 29a/10; unequivocally wrong attribution of the rabbinic source: 8b/8, 9a/2 (Yiddish text).
157. Fols. 3a, 35a. The compiler of this anthology was Shimon ha-Darshan (13th century) from Frankfurt; printed in Saloniki, 1521–26; Venice, 1566.
158. Fols. 3a, 4b, 9b, 31a.
159. Fols. 4b, 5a, 8b, 10a (*parshanim*).
160. See commentary on pp. 98/4; 99/1–2; 99/10; 109/18; 112/17; 114/10; 119/4; 132/9; 146/7.
161. See commentary on pp. 87/7 and 90/11.
162. Neoplatonic ethics exerted significant influence on Jewish moral doctrine mainly through Bahya's *Hovot ha-Levavot* ("Duties of the heart"); an overview of the Aristotelian and Neoplatonic influences on Jewish moral literature is provided by Berger, *Sexualität* (Sexuality), pp. 34–40; see also the commentary on pp. 87/7; 90/11.
163. Fol. 4a/1f.
164. Fols. 4a, 6a, 21b, 25a, 25b, 26a, 26b, 27a, 33b, 34a.
165. First print in Venice, 1579; an abridged version was published 1600 in Venice under the title *Reshit Hokhmah Kazar*. According to J. Dan, *Jewish Mysticism and Jewish Ethics* (Seattle, 1986), p. 24, it was the most popular and most influential ethical book of the 16th century in general.
166. Only the attribution on pp. 100/2 and 193/5 is erroneous; see respective commentary.
167. Fol. 34a/25 (Yiddish text).
168. Fols. 12a, 24a; the first print of *Orhot Zaddikim* was prepared in Prague, 1581; regarding the confusion, see above in section "Authorship and Provenance."
169. Fols. 14b, 19a; first print of *Sefer Middot* (Isny, 1542; Krakow, 1582).
170. First print of Bologna, 1538; various manuscripts of the significantly longer version (MS Parma) were disseminated in the 16th century.
171. Fols. 28a, 7a.
172. Fols. 23a, 33a.
173. Fol. 23a/10; see commentary on p. 157/9.
174. *Sefer Hasidim*, § 59.
175. See commentary on p. 159/9 and 10.
176. Fols. 4a, 10a; regarding *Vroyen Bikhel* see above, section "Authorship and Provenance."
177. See commentary on p. 115/17.
178. See Romer Segal, *Yiddish Works*.
179. Quoted according to Romer Segal, *Yiddish Works*, p. 39; emphasis is mine. See also Grossmann, *Pious*, p. 288, and the commentary on pp. 101/12 and 175/11.
180. The "respected female rabbi" as authoritative figure is mentioned in *Mizvot Nashim* (Venice, 1552). A compilation of the "safety measures" meant to protect from rabbinic attacks is in Romer Segal, *Yiddish Works*, p. 41ff.
181. The call, in works written for women, to ask the rabbi in cases of doubt, naturally addresses women. Accordingly, works that were written for non-scholarly male readers, such as *Sefer ha-Gan*, require the same behavior from men; see commentary on p. 88/9.
182. *Eyn shoyn Froyenbuykhleyn*, fol. 2a.
183. The rejection of the moral-halakhic literature was ultimately assumed by the complete Yiddish literature. The reasons are manifold and, regrettably, cannot be elaborated here. It is noted, however, that even Yiddish morality books expressed disapproval of Yiddish literature; see in *Eyn shoyn Froyenbuykhleyn*, fol. 37a: "Therefore, dear daughter, note what I have written, and do not think that this is only mockery [*geshpay*], like other Yiddish

books that were written in order to pass the time. . . . To read this is better for you, your body, and your soul, [better than] all [other] Yiddish books that exist, and [better] than all morality [*shtrof*] books."

184. *Brantshpigl*, p. 247.

185. Fol. 3b; see commentary on p. 88/9.

186. A print from Krakow, 1549, is uncertain; see G. Scholem, *Zur Kabbala und ihrer Symbolik* (Frankfurt-am-Main, 1973) (On the Kabbalah and Its Symbolism [New York, 1965]), pp. 105–116; *Encyclopedia Judaica*, s. v. Sefer ha-Temunah.

187. Regarding Jaffe see L. Kaplan, "R. Mordekhai Jaffe and the Evolution of Jewish Culture," in D. B. Cooperman (ed.), *Jewish Thought in the Sixteenth Century* (Cambridge, Mass./London, 1983), pp. 266–282.

188. See commentary on p. 122/8.

189. See the commentary to 9b/20. *Brantshpigl* does not quote the traditionally attributed verses, which can, however, be found in *Meneket Rivkah*. Therefore *Brantshpigl* as source for Rivkah bat Meir is out of the question.

190. See commentary on pp. 97/2; 99/5; 113/2. *Reshit Hokhmah*, too, quotes the kabbalistic material from the *Zohar* in Aramaic.

191. *Sefer Middot*, fols. 78b, 84b, 97b; an additional mention of Maimonides is in fol. 32b.

192. *Sefer Middot*, fols. 61b, 89b; *Sefer Orah Hayyim*, fol. 20a; *Sefer ha-Gan*, fol. 3a.

193. *Sefer Orah Hayyim*, fol. 17b, here also the medical knowledge of Maimonides is mentioned; it is unclear which book is referred to with *Sefer Refu'ot*; regarding Yiddish medical works, see Baumgarten, *Old Yiddish*, pp. 431–359.

194. *Eyn shoyn Froyenbuykhleyn*, fol. 38b. This refers probably to a Hebrew translation of the Greek commentary by Galen on the Hippocratic Treatise "Air, Water and Places," which had been prepared by Solomon ha-Me'ati in the late Middle Ages; see Veltri, *Magie und Halakha: Ansätze zu einem empirischen Wissenschaftsbegriff im spätantiken und frühmittelalterlichen Judentum* (Tübingen, 1997); for the title, cf. *Sefer Iggeret Ba'alei Hayyim* (Mantua, 1557), which is however a Hebrew anthology of fables.

195. About two-thirds of *Brantshpigl* consists of quotes and paraphrases of this literature.

196. From *Moreh Nevukhim* and *Mishneh Torah*: pp. 24, 25, 73, 83, 179, 384, 426.

197. *Brantshpigl*, pp. 404, 419.

198. *Brantshpigl*, pp. 340, 341.

199. *Brantshpigl*, p. 313. He probably used *Menorat ha-Ma-or* by Isaac Abohav, which constituted the basis for the book by the same title by Israel Al-Nakawa, which was also published in the 14th century, and was disseminated in manuscript form until the 17th century. The Yiddish morality book *Lev Tov* by Isaac ben Eliakim (Prague, 1620) includes the last chapter of Al-Nakawa's work in Yiddish translation, confirming some distribution of his work.

200. *Brantshpigl*, pp. 223, 291.

201. *Brantshpigl*, pp. 105, 150, 228, 305, 355, 403, 443, and elsewhere; quoted as *musarei ha-pilozofyah* ("the admonitions of philosophy") or *hakhmei ha-musar* ("the sages of admonition"). All source references are according to the editor; see Riedel, "Brantspigel."

202. *Brantshpigl*, p. 291; quoted as *hakhmei ha-mehkar* ("the sages of research").

203. Ibid., passim.

204. Ibid., pp. 4, 16, 55, 84, 112, 127, 155, 184, 216, 233, 314, 357, 394, 397, 440.

205. See P. Bourdieu, *Practical Reason: On the Theory of Action* (Cambridge, 1998).

206. These works were "popular" because they had been written in the Yiddish vernacular. Simple Hebrew works, too, that were read by a non-rabbinic male reader audience with basic education can be considered as popular, because, like the Yiddish books, they did not contain any complex casuistical, philosophical, or theological discussions, as did the non-popular works, produced and adapted only by the scholarly elites.

207. H. Bublitz, A. Bührmann, Chr. Hanke, A. Seier (eds.), *Das Wuchern der Diskurse: Perspektiven der Diskursanlayse Foucaults* (The Proliferation of Discourses: Perspectives on Foucault's Discourse Analysis) (Frankfurt-am-Main, 1999), pp. 10–22.

208. See M. Foucault, *The Order of Things: An Archaeology of Human Sciences* (New York, 1973).

209. R. Schnell, *Frauendiskurs, Männerdiskurs, Ehediskurs: Textsorten und Geschlechterkonzepte in Mittelalter und Früher Neuzeit* (Female Discourse, Male Discourse, Marriage Discourse: Literary Genres and Gender Concepts in the Middle Ages and in the Early Modern Age) (Frankfurt-am-Main/New York, 1998), p. 22ff.

210. I prefer the term "orthodox" over the term "dogmatic" as used by Schnell, because the latter transmits, as he intended, the connotation of Christian dogmatism. "Orthodox" should not imply that the issue is the *one* correct idea, but rather standards that had been negotiated in the rabbinic tradition and were transmitted as such. The orthodox discourse may also be understood as a rabbinic or scholarly discourse. In the center of the pragmatic discourse, on the other hand, are realistic modes of behavior, and behavioral ideals that are oriented toward reality. The term "orthopraxic," too, does not relate to the *one* mode of behavior as the only possible correct one, but to the totality of the respectively implemented and practicable activities. Therefore, both the halakhic commandments and the moral behavioral instructions are to be understood as "orthopraxic."

211. Turniansky, *Sefer Massah*, p. 60; translation mine.

212. Ibid., p. 61.

213. *Brantshpigl*, p. 98.

214. See the extensive image material in D. Wolfthal, *Picturing Yiddish: Gender, Identity, and Memory in the Illustrated Yiddish Books of Renaissance Italy* (Leiden, 2004).

215. Berger, *Sexualität*, p. 116, located the origin of this behavioral demand in *Menorat ha-Ma'or*. She, too, notes the astounding match, but does not explain this obvious discrepancy between the behavioral ideal and the actual practices within a morality book.

216. Moses Henokhs Altshul lived from ca. 1540 to ca. 1630; in research literature, the name of the author is often noted incorrectly as Altshuler (-Yerushalmi). All contemporary sources, however, name the author exclusively as "Altshul" or, abridged, as "a'sh" insofar as the family name is mentioned at all; see Muneles, *Epitaphs*, pp. 309f. and 431; A. Kisch, *Testament*, p. 131; A. Kisch, "Megillat purei ha-kela'im. The Chronicle of Henokh Altshul" [Heb.], in *Jubelschrift zum Siebzigsten Geburtstage des Professors Dr. Heinrich Graetz* (Breslau, 1887), p. 52. The name "Altshuler," on the other hand, is not documented at all in the 16th and 17th centuries in Prague; see Hock/Kaufmann, *Familien*. The additional appellation *ish yerushalmi* is mentioned only on three title pages of *Brantshpigl* (Prague, 1610; Hanau, 1626; Frankfurt-am-Main, 1676), but it is unclear whether it is a matronym or an honorary title for pilgrims to Jerusalem. None of these title pages contain at the same time the name Altshul; therefore the double name must be regarded as the invention of Carmoly, who may have misread the Hebrew *ish* on the title page as "a'sh [yerushalmi]"; see E. Carmoly, "Gallerie der Rabbiner" (Gallery of Rabbis), in *Der Israelit. Ein Central-Organ für das orthodoxe Judenthum* 5 (1867), p. 81; 10 (1867), pp. 164f. There is no evidence for Carmoly's and Riedel's assumption regarding the origin of Moses Henokhs from a Sephardi family, and it must therefore be regarded as speculation; Riedel, "Brantspigel," p. xv.

217. A. Kisch, "Das Testament des Mardochai Meysels" (The Testament of Mordecai Meisel), *Monatsschrift für Geschichte und Wissenschaft des Judenthums* 37 (1892), p. 87; Kisch, "Megillat," p. 52. As such, he was assigned various tasks within the community, such as official witness for the conclusion of contracts. In that sense he was also witness for Mordecai Meisel's testament; see Kisch, ibid.

218. Regarding *Brantshpigl* see Riedel, "Brantspigel"; M. Erik, "Bletlekh tzu der geshikhte fun der elterer yidisher literatur un kultur" (Papers on the History of the Older Yiddish Literature and Culture), *Journal on Jewish History, Demography and Economy, Literary Research, Language Research, and Ethnography* 1 (1926), pp. 173–177; Gaster, *Maasehbuch*; M. Rosenfeld, "'Der Brandspiegel': An Unknown Edition, and the Identification of Its Author" [Heb.], in *Kiryat Sefer* 55 (1980), pp. 617–621; F. v. Rohden, "'Für Frauen und Männer, die wie Frauen sind.' Weibliche und männliche Verhaltensideale im *Brantshpigl* des Moses Henochs Altschul" ('For Women and Men Who Are Like Women.' Female and Male Ideals of Conduct in *Brantshpigl* by Moses Henokhs Altshul), in *Neuer Anbruch. Minima Judaica* 1 (Berlin, 2001), pp. 175–190; Baumgarten, *Old Yiddish*, pp. 208–215. Five additional prints appeared until 1706, no evidence for any later reprint exists.

219. Interpretations that are partially or, most probably, completely the author's own interpretations can be found on fols. 2b, 3a–b, 5a, 6b, 10b, 12b, 13b, 20a, 21a–b, 22a, 28b, 30a, 33b, 34a, 35a–b.

220. In that sense, the prominent interpretation of Prov. 18:22 ("He who finds a wife has found happiness, and has won the favor of the LORD") is interpreted literally in the rabbinic literature, whereby here the "good wife," too, enjoys the benefit of divine benevolence; see the commentary on p. 111/5. Another interpretation, introducing women into a traditionally "womanless" perspective, is that of Songs 8:8, 9, which rabbinic literature interprets as Torah or allegorically as Israel, but Rivkah bat Meir sees as a young, orphaned woman; see the commentary on p. 84/9.

221. For example B. Niddah 31b; see commentary on p. 95/7–10.

222. See Baskin, *Midrashic Women*, pp. 18 and 66–67.

223. See commentary on pp. 151/19 and 153/12.

224. See commentary on p. 153/12.

225. See commentary on p. 153/12.

226. Fol. 21b; see commentary on p. 152/13.

227. Baskin, *Midrashic Women*, pp. 73–79.

228. Ibid., p. 73.

229. See commentary on p. 119/6.

230. See commentary on p. 128/1.

231. Fols. 3b, 11a, 21a, 32b. The first chapter is an exception; see above, section "Sources and Their Editing."

232. Fol. 8a; see also fols. 3b, 13a, 18a, 22b.

233. Fol. 8a; see also fols. 3b, 7b, 18b, 23a.

234. *Eyn shoyn Froyenbuykhleyn* mentions "dear wives" (2a) or "dear daughter" (3a) as female reader; *Sefer Middot* addresses its readers as "dear children" (6b, 72a) or "dear son" (72a).

235. See commentary on p. 79/1.

236. Fols. 18a, 33b–34a; regarding the awareness that prosperity is permanently in jeopardy, see fol. 27a.

237. Fols. 6b, 8a, 19b, 21a, 24a, 26a, 27b, 29a, 30a, 31a, 32a, 35b. Regarding the understanding of "Torah," see further below in this section.

238. See commentary on pp. 89/2; 89/7; 98/11.

239. See commentary on pp. 106/14; 121/17.

240. *Brantshpigl*, p. 391, *Eyn shoyn Froyenbuykhleyn*, fol. 49b.

241. See the commentary on p. 103/3–4

242. See the commentary on p. 91/6.

243. Regarding the terms, see above, section "Sources and Their Editing."

244. See commentary on pp. 87/7; 90/11.

245. See commentary on pp. 164/4; 93/9–10.

246. The house is considered only occasionally in the discussion, and even then only indirectly; see the commentary on pp. 83/10 and 85/20 (domesticity), 149/2 (work) and 161/6 (child upbringing).

247. See commentary on p. 85/20.

248. Fol. 3a.

249. Cf. *Brantshpigl*, p. 123, as well as the complete 17th chapter. *Brantshpigl* requests a certain measure of domesticity also from men, for reasons of modesty; see the commentary on p. 129/18. Regarding the discussion of public conduct in moral literature, see also Berger, *Sexualität*, pp. 110–118. Regarding the female behavior ideals in *Brantshpigl*, see Rohden, *Frauen*, p. 178ff.

250. For example M. Sotah 1, 5; Y. Sotah 3, 4; B. Shabbat 62a; B. Sanhedrin 75a.

251. See commentary on p. 167/17.

252. Fol. 25b; cf. 32a (the woman should ask the boy, but perhaps also the rabbi).

253. Fols. 23b and 27b–28a.

254. This is in contrast to contemporary texts that express criticism of overly glamorous, extravagant women's clothing, the discussion of which obscures concern about social peace within the community, one in which many suffered from great socio-economical inequality. See the commentary on p. 107/10.

255. See commentary on p. 160/2–3.

256. Regarding women in commerce and craft, see Herman, *Wirtschaftliche Betätigung* (Economic Activity), p. 57ff.; see Toch, *Frau* (Woman), p. 38ff.; Lieben, *Frumet Meisel*, p. 374; Wolf, *Verzeichnis* (Register), p. 178ff.

257. See commentary on p. 194/2.

258. See commentary on p. 195/13.

259. Fol. 34a.

260. Fol. 13a.

261. See n. 108.

262. See commentary on p. 194/2.

263. *Brantshpigl*, p. 305.

264. See commentary on p. 155/1.

265. Fols. 22a–b; to the extent to which nursing is discussed in Jewish moral literature, it mostly warns of the harmful influence exerted by nonkosher food given the child through the milk, or of the transfer of negative motherly emotions (such as anger) onto the child; see Berger, *Sexualität*, pp. 161f., 278ff.

266. Fols. 31b and 31b.

267. Fols. 32a and 32b.

268. See commentary on pp. 110/10; 112/13.

269. See commentary on pp. 104/11; 126/4, 11–12.

270. See commentary on pp. 120/15; 151/2 ("not permit").

271. See commentary on p. 132/1.

272. Similar choice of words is documented in 14a/25ff. (Yiddish text).

273. See commentary on p. 129/18.

274. See commentary to footnote 276; see Berger, *Sexualität*, pp. 197–207, particularly p. 204.

275. See commentary on p. 131/10.

276. See commentary on pp. 110/9; 120/15; 127/10; 131/10.

277. Rivkah Bat Meir uses "to serve" to refer to a maid's work (p. 105/7) and in reference to approaching God (p. 174/2).

278. See commentary on p. 131/1.

279. The author frequently illustrates the virtues she has formulated with examples from the Bible and Talmud of pious and righteous women who supported their husbands in an exemplary manner: Rachel and Leah (9a–9b), Ruth (9b), On ben Pelet's wife (10a), Deborah and Bityah, Pharaoh's daughter (10b), Sarah (14a), and Yosse bar Halafta's wife (13a); see the commentary on p. 128/1.

280. While Joseph Caro, Bet Yosef, *Even ha-Ezer*, 154,15 rejected the beating of a woman on principle, Moses Isserles granted the man the right to beat his wife "moderately" if she curses him or humiliates his parents; see the commentary on p. 132/1.

281. See in this matter the detailed description in Berger, *Sexualität*, pp. 129–145, 189–197.

282. See commentary on p. 133/9.

283. See commentary on p. 142/23.

284. See commentary on p. 143/15.

285. See commentary on p. 201/10.

286. See commentary on pp. 201/10; 202/12.

287. See fol. 6b and the commentary on p. 103/3–4.

288. See commentary on p. 145/18.

289. See commentary on p. 164/4.

290. See commentary on p. 156/18.

291. See commentary on p. 165/12; concerning beating of children, cf. Berger, *Sexualität*, pp. 287–295.

292. We can only presume how educated girls obtained their knowledge. Turniansky assumes that Old Yiddish literature constituted the most important medium for the transmission of knowledge for girls and women, who did not master either the Hebrew language nor the German or Latin scripts; lessons given by male teachers, which included the transmission of the script and language of the local country, as in the case of Italo-Ashkenazi girls, was most probably not common in Poland and Germany; see Turniansky, *Maydlekh*, pp. 9 and 17.

293. See B. Kiddushin 30a: "'And teach them to your children' (Deut. 11:19): [this means] your sons, not your daughters"; see M. Sotah 3, 4; Shulhan Arukh, *Talmud Torah*, 246, 6. The men's obligation to study Torah was derived from Josh. 1:8 and was successively transformed into the male ideal of lifelong study of the Jewish traditional literature, *talmud Torah*.

294. Accordingly, M. Kiddushin 33b; see in this matter R. Biale, *Women and Jewish Law: An Exploration on Women's Issues in Halakhic Sources* (New York, 1984), pp. 12, 17–24.

295. See commentary on p. 93/9–10; 164/4.

296. See commentary on pp. 161/6; 179/5.

297. Grimm, *Dictionary*, vol. V, p. 4109; E. Timm, "Verwandtschaftsbezeichnungen im Jiddischen, kontrastiv zum Deutschen betrachtet" (Examination of Kinship Terms in Yiddish as Opposed to German), in J. Jährling, U. Mewes, E. Timm (eds.), *Röllwagenbüchlein. Festschrift für Walter Röll zum 65. Geburtstag* (Tübingen, 2002), p. 454.

298. Horowitz, *Jugend* (Youth), p. 139f.; see the overview of the age of Jewish household staff, in Berger, *Sexualität*, pp. 317–329.

299. In *Brantshpigl*, household staff is used only in the narrow sense; see the commentary on p. 198/12. Particular emphasis is given the educational task, as with the master of the house toward the young maids and servants, but also toward orphans and students; see *Brantshpigl*, pp. 5, 45, 93, and other places. They have in common their claim for accommodation and welfare; see ibid., pp. 41, 134, 238, 301, and elsewhere.

300. See commentary on p. 187/15.

301. *Brantshpigl*, p. 132; regarding Torah students in the context with household staff, see also *Sefer Middot*, fols. 41b–42a.

302. According to an index of letters of safe conduct to Prague, in the year 1546 more than a quarter of the Jewish households (35 out of 127; 10 others had a maid) employed a Jewish female cook or a Jewish kitchen maid. Jews were prohibited from employing Christian household staff, thus they are not listed in official documents; see Wolf, *Verzeichnis* (Register), p. 182ff.

303. See commentary on p. 105/12.

304. See commentary on pp. 196/26; 202/4.

305. J. C. Wagenseil, *Sota, hoc est, liber Mischnicus de uxore adulterii suspecta, una cum Libri En Iacob excerptis Gemarae, versione latina…Accedunt correctiones Lipmannianae* (Altdorf, 1674).

306. Ibid., p. 491.

307. Ibid., p. 490.

308. He, too, rejected Yiddish as being mutilated German; see Zinberg, *History*, p. 44, n. 32.

309. B. Weinryb, "Historisches und Kulturhistorisches aus Wagenseils hebräischem Briefwechsel" (Historical and Cultural-Historical Material from Wagenseil's Hebrew Correspondence), *Monatsschrift für Geschichte und Wissenschaft des Judentums* 83 (1939), pp. 329–334.

310. Another possibility is that he purchased the copy in the year 1666 in Amsterdam, where, he noted, he would purchase "rare books" from sellers who were preparing to journey to the Holy Land after Shabbtai Zevi had declared himself the Messiah; see H. Süß, *Raritäten der jiddischen Literatur des sechzehnten und siebzehnten Jahrhunderts in der Universitätsbibliothek; Ausstellungsbegleittext* (Rarities in Sixteenth- and Seventeenth-Century Yiddish Literature in the University Library [accompanying text for the exhibition]) (Erlangen, 1980), p. 2.

311. *De Rebecca Polona. Eruditarum in Gente Judaica Foeminarum Rariori Exemplo* (Altdorf, 1719). The dissertation is occasionally and mistakenly attributed to the chairman of the dissertation committee, Gustav Georg Zeltner, instead of to the doctoral candidate Lufft; the title page reads: "praeside Gustavo Georgio Zeltner […] disputabit Ioh. Conradus Lufft"; it is given correctly, however, in Shmeruk, *Jewish Authoress*, p. 14, and Y. Levine Katz, "Nashim lamdaniyot birushalayim" (Learned Women in Jerusalem), *Mabua* 26 (1994), p. 115.

312. Giulio Bartolocci, *Bibliotheca Magna Rabbinica…de scriptoribus et scriptis hebraicis, ordine alphabetico hebraice et latine digestis*, 4 vols. (Rome, 1675–93), here vol. 4, fol. 362b; Johann Christoph Wolff, *Bibliotheca Hebraea*, 4 vols., (Hamburg, 1715–33), here vol. 4; no. 1908; Johann Jakob Schudt, *Jüdische Merkwürdigkeiten*, (Frankfurt-am-Main, 1714–18), here vol. 4, p. 226; see Lufft, *Rebecca*, p. 5.

313. Lufft, *Rebecca*, p. 18. He probably referred to the bibliographic work *Siftei Yeshenim* (Amsterdam, 1680) by Shabbtai Bass.

314. Kayserling, *Jüdische Frauen* (Jewish Women), p. 152. A reprint of Kayserling's book was published in 1980.

315. Karpeles, *Geschichte* (History), p. 332f. He mentions this immediately before that he complains about the deteriorating taste that characterizes the imitators of the "books of morals" *Brantshpigl*, *Sefer Middot*, and *Eyn shoyn Froyenbuykhleyn*.

316. Karpeles, *Geschichte*, p. 333.

317. Zinberg, *History*, p. 241.

318. Weinreich, *Geschichte*, p. 122f.

319. S. Assaf, *Mekorot le-toledot ha-ḥinnukh be-yisra'el* (Sources on the History of Jewish Education), 4 vols. (Tel Aviv, 1954), IV, p. 45f. His statement that he received photographs of the title page and a few pages "from I. Rivkind" pointed to the library of JTS, were Rivkind worked as librarian; see *Encyclopedia Judaica*, s.v. Rivkind. This copy had previously been in possession of S. Y. Agnon, who gave it to the JTS library after it had survived a fire in his house in Homburg in 1924; see Henry/Taitz, *History*, p. 93f. Prior to Assaf, Rivkah bat Meir was mentioned by Shelomo Ashkenazi, who had taken his statements from Kayserling and Karpeles; see Sh. Ashkenazi, *Ha-Ishah be-aspeklariyat ha-yahadut* (The Woman as Reflected in Judaism), 2 vols. (Tel Aviv, 1979), p. 121.

320. Henry/Taitz, *Written*, p. 93.

321. Shmeruk, *Jewish Authoress*, p. 16. He extracted the missing beginning of the third chapter from Lufft's transcript; he assumed a "missing page" was the reason for the missing beginning of the third and fourth chapters.

322. Shmeruk, *Sifrut yidish*, pp. 56–62, 64–70, 101f.

323. Süß, *Raritäten*, p. 13. A consequence of this reconstruction was that *Meneket Rivkah* was documented on microform; see H. Bobzin, H. Süß (eds.), *Sammlung Wagenseil. Gesamtedition nach dem Verkaufskatalog von 1708* (Wagenseil Collection. Complete Edition according to the Sales Catalogue from 1708) (Erlangen, 1996).

324. M. Wunder, *Ateret Rivkah. Arba'ah thinnot nashim 'im tirgum li-leshon ha-kodesh ve-sefer ha-musar Meneket Rivkah*. (Jerusalem, 1992), pp. 77–147.

325. Muneles, *Epitaphs*, p. 161. Shmeruk's research was not acknowledged in the edition of the epitaphs that appeared posthumously in the year 1988 in Muneles's name, which only used Wagenseil's quotes. Based on a misreading of the year by Hock/Kaufmann, *Familien*, p. 153, the secondary literature assumed until then that 1550 was the year of her death.

326. N. Shepherd, *A Price below Rubies: Jewish Women as Rebels and Radicals* (Cambridge, Mass., 1993), p. 47.

327. M. Vilimkova, *Die Prager Judenstadt* (The Jewish Quarter of Prague) (Hanau, 1981), p. 158.

328. Baumgarten, *Old Yiddish*, p. 61 and p. 227, n. 47. Similarly short in Hellerstein, *Name*, p. 34f.

329. Zolty, *Children*, p. 198. The only "poem" in *Meneket Rivkah* is the Hebrew *piyyut* that is used as an introduction.

330. Henry et al., *Guide*, pp. 147–149; Kay, *Seyder Tkhines*, pp. 21–22. Cf. Levine Katz, "Nashim," pp. 98 und 115; she, however, mistakenly assumes Rivkah bat Meir was the author of the title page. Ruth Berger used the incomplete Krakow print, albeit quoting frequently from the latter; see Berger, *Sexualität*, pp. 4, 165, and *passim*.

331. Regarding Hannah bat Judah, see n. 59.

332. M. Grünbaum, *Jüdischdeutsche Chrestomathie. Zugleich ein Beitrag zur Kunde der hebräischen Literatur* (Jewish-German Anthology and Contribution to the Lore of Hebrew Literature) (Leipzig, 1882, reprint Hildesheim, 1969), p. 194: "Other works, too, that were written in this 'Weiberdeutsch' (women's Yiddish) constitute literature for women insofar as it is intended for women, since it may be assumed for every man that he is at least capable . . . of reading Rashi." His text collection was strongly influenced by German language research of old Yiddish literature.

333. Sh. Niger, Sh. Zucker, "Yiddish Literature and the Female Reader," in J. Baskin, *Women of the Word: Jewish Women and Jewish Writing* (Detroit, 1994), p. 79f.; this abridged translation of an article by Niger (from 1913) completely ignored the newest research, with the exception of mentioning Henry/Taitz, *Written*; cf. the Yiddish original in Sh. Niger, "Di yidishe literatur un di lezerin" (Yiddish Literature and the Female Reader), *Der Pinkes* 1 (1913), pp. 85–138, p. 85. Regarding gender classification of "women and uneducated men," which was already a rabbinic feature (*nashim ve-amei ha-arez*), see Weissler, *Voices*, pp. 52–55.

334. In the late 1970s, the demand of feminists for a specific literature, written only by women, resulted in the use of the term "women's literature." However, since its distinctive feature remained rather vague, the term used today is "literature written by women"; S. Weigel, *Die Stimme der Medusa. Schreibweisen in der Gegenwartsliteratur von Frauen* (The Voice of the Medusa. Modes of Writing in Contemporary Literature by Women) (Reinbek, 1983), p. 23.

335. Erik, *Bletlekh* (Papers), p. 173. His ambivalent approach on this question is reflected in his opinion that the "genuine encyclopedias" of the Yiddish moral literature, such as *Lev Tov* and *Brantshpigl*, are "works for the woman," a view that cannot be upheld, at least not based on their contents.

336. Weinreich, *History*, p. 276f.

337. Zinberg, *History*, p. 124f.

338. Turniansky, *Ha-derashah*, p. 183.

339. See Weinreich, *History*, p. 275.

340. See the lucid description of this process for the Old Yiddish literature in J. C. Frakes, *The Politics of Interpretation: Alterity and Ideology in Old Yiddish Studies* (Albany, 1989), pp. 7, 15f., and *passim*.

341. Regarding the causes for the ignorance toward moral literature, particularly Yiddish moral literature, see also chapter 5.

342. Riedel's edition still presents the Yiddish text only in transliteration and does not offer any commentary, with the exception of a short introduction. It does, however, provide a great number of references to the biblical and rabbinic literature. The Hebrew edition and English translation of *Seder Mizvot ha-Nashim* appeared just prior to the completion of this book and unfortunately could not be taken into consideration; see E. Fram, *My Dear Daughter*.

343. E. Timm, "Das jiddischsprachige literarische Erbe der Italo-Aschkenasen" (The Yiddish Literary Heritage of Italian Ashkenazim), in M. Graetz, *Schöpferische Momente des europäischen Judentums* (Heidelberg, 2000), p. 167.

344. Romer Segal, *Yiddish Works*, p. 44. Another popular moral genre that is also documented in Italy in the 16th century is the Yiddish *vantshpigl* ("wall mirrors"), such as the *Mareh lekashet ha-neshamah* (Mantua, 1591). They may have existed earlier, because Soncino had printed a similar didactical Hebrew calendar page already in 1496; see J. R. Markus, "Etishe Vantshpigln," *Yivo Bleter* 21 (1943), p. 202.

345. Regarding the Hebrew ethical literature, see Dan, *Sifrut ha-Derush*; J. Elbaum, "Aspects of Hebrew Ethical Literature in Sixteenth Century Poland," in D. B. Cooperman (ed.), *Jewish Thought in the Sixteenth Century* (Cambridge, Mass., 1983), pp. 146–166.

346. For example, the anonymous *Sefer Hayyei Olam* (Venice and Sabbioneta, 1552).

347. For example, *Iggeret Derekh ha-Shem* by Mose of Trani (Venice, 1553), or the Yiddish-Hebrew *Mishlei Hakhamim* by Judah bar Israel Regensburg, called Leib Sheberl of Lumpenburg (Prague, around 1616).

348. J. Dan, *Jewish Mysticism and Jewish Ethics* (Seattle, 1986), p. 1.

349. Ibid., p. 13. Jacob Elbaum pointed out, in addition, that its theosophical-ethical orientation corresponded well to the sermon, which is why many Hebrew ethical books of the 16th century contained a strong homiletical element; see Elbaum, *Aspects*, p. 153.

350. Zinberg, *History*, p. 141.

351. Erik, *Bletlekh* (Papers), p. 173.

352. H. Dinse, *Die Entwicklung des jiddischen Schrifttums im deutschen Sprachgebiet* (The Development of Yiddish Literature in the German Speaking Area) (Stuttgart, 1974), p. 91; regarding Dinse's use of the term "women's literature," see earlier in this chapter. Despite his problematic stand, German language research continues to make occasional reference to Dinse, who transferred the popular connotation of "women's literature" onto its authors and then drew the conclusion that they "did not have any great knowledge" and were not "mis-educated by Talmud and Torah studies." He thus followed the notorious separation between male-scholarly literature on the one hand and female-popular literature on the other; see ibid., p. 69f. There is no need to enter into the details of his questionable negative connotation of Jewish scholarship.

353. Ibid., p. 117f.

354. Turniansky, *Sefer Massah*, pp. 58–61, particularly p. 61.

355. Baumgarten, *Old Yiddish*, pp. 207, 222.

356. Romer Segal, *Yiddish Works*, p. 44.

357. Ibid., p. 39f.

358. Ibid., p. 47. My emphasis.

359. Ibid., p. 48f.

360. Ibid., p. 50.

361. Ibid., p. 51. Shortly before, however, the author mentions that both versions "come[s] to serve the same end"; see ibid., p. 46.

362. See above, section "Sources and Their Editing." Regarding the moral-halakhic literature, see Baumgarten, *Old Yiddish*, p. 224f.

363. The rabbinic elite does not seem to have generally rejected the popularization of the *halakhah*, but rather specifically the female elements of *halakhah*, since it was crucial for control over the female body and female sexuality. After all, in the middle of the 16th century, the Yiddish book *Brit Melah* (Prague, n.d.; Krakow, 1665) by the Prague rabbi Yom Tov Lipman Heller (d. 1654) was published, in which he compiled the halakhic rules regarding the salting and watering of meat, which are relevant for kashrut.

364. See chapter 3.

365. *Ze'enah u-Re'enah* is the best known and most frequently printed work of the Old Yiddish literature in general. The oldest preserved print (Hanau/Basel, 1622) was preceded, according to its title page, by three prints, which are assumed to be Lublin (1615) as well as Krakow (1618 and 1620); in the 17th century alone, 16 additional editions were published; see Baumgarten, *Old Yiddish*, pp. 113–121; J. Baumgarten, *Le Commentaire sur la Torah* (The Torah Commentary): *Tseenah ureenah de Jacob ben Isaac Achkenazi de Janow* (Lagrasse, 1987); cf. S. Neuberg, *Aspekte der jiddischen Sprachgeschichte am Beispiel der "Zenerene"* (Aspects of the History of the Yiddish Language Using the Example of "Zenerene") (Hamburg, 1999).

366. The author of *Ze'enah u-Re'enah*, the itinerant preacher Jacob ben Isaac Ashkenazi from Janow, died around 1628 in Prague, where he may have spent his last decades; see Baumgarten, *Commentaire*, p. 15. Ashkenazi's mention of a contemporary rabbinic authority, of "Rabbi Loew of Prague," in *Ze'enah u-Re'enah*, was unusual in literature and may be interpreted as an expression of his special connection to Prague; see Baumgarten, *Commentaire*, p. 292. That Rivkah bat Meir and Ashkenazi knew each other personally must be regarded as highly speculative; however, the possibility cannot be ruled out completely.

שער הראשון

דאש ווערט רירן וויא זיך מין משה זאל פירן · וויא זיא מין גון זאל
צירן · די מיר בטאה כטב וויל פר ליך :

דוד המלך ע"ה (האט גשריבן מין (תהילים (דען פסוק (
שאתי בת ורמי והט מנֶךֶ וַשְׂכְחִי שַׁאַך וּבֵית וְיִתְאַו הַמֶּלֶךְ יָפְיֵךְ כִּי הוּא אֲדֹנַיִךְ
והשתחוי לו (דאש מיז טייטש היר איר לו אין טאכטר מזל זיך נייג מזרן מזל
פר געט דיין פאלק מזל האיז דיין פאטר דא ווערט דער קיניג הקנה דיין
מונהייט גילוסטן דען ער מיו דיין הער מזל נייג דיך לו מיק דאש אדרט גיט
מו מין פרשה לך לך עש גיט מון מברהם מזל שרה דא מיא (הקנה האט
היישן מויט מירן לנד גין דא האט אר לו זיא גיזאגט זיא זאלן פר געשן מיר פאטר
מזל אנטר מזל מיר אשפחה (רְבָּה לוער (זיא זאלן זיך ארחיק זיין לון
מין עלטרין אנשיפ דא ווערט הקנה גילוסטן מירי שונהייט דאש אייכט מירי
אנשיפ טובע (מויך אנן מיך רפן פסוק מזו מויש ליגן מזל מוו דרטן די
דוד האלך עה (דען פסוק גיזאנט האט מויך מין בת ישראל דיא מין אמן
האט גינואן דיא מזל זיך מוו מין (דרך פיר כשאן מזל מויך טיין תכלית (
גידענקין דאש אייכט מֶה דאש זיא מזל פר געשן דיא (אנשיפ (מזל וומל טמגן
דיא זיא ביא מיר עלטרין האבין גיהט דען איר זיהן מלי טמג מו מין פאטר מזל
מוטר מיר קינד פר ענטפרין וון עש שון גלייך ניט רעכט טוט (אכח מהבה (
מו דער פסוק גיט (עַל כָל פְטָעִים תכסה מהבה (דרוק גה דער (איזוער זיא
זאלין דיא זעלביגן טיבוטין פר געשן מזל זאל זיך גוטה (אנשיפ טובע (
מן כשנין דרחן גיט דר פסוק (וְיִתְאַו הַמֶּלֶךְ יָפְיֵךְ (דאש אייכט הקבה ווערט
לושט האבין לו רייכי אנשיפ טובע מו דר פסוק מוך גיט (הַדֵּךְ יָפַה רַמֶּיָתִי (
דאש מיז טייטש דוא ביסט שן אין גיזעלין איט (אנשיפ טובע (מו דער פסוק
מויך וויטר גיט כל כבודה בת מלך פני אה אמבצות זהב לבושה (דש מיז טייטש
ושן מין משה אין גכונה מיז מזל בליבט מין מירן היגד דא רעכנט זיא
הקנה פר מין טאכטר איר מז דיא זיך נירט איט מייטל גיק גמלד דרוין גיטדר
איזוער וויטר (תַחַת מַבוֹתֶיךָ יַהֵיו בָנֵיךָ (דאש מיז טייטש דוא ווערטט לראה
קיבדר האבן די דא ווערין (אֲוַלֶא מַקַם מַשָׁתַהָא (זיין איט מירי אנשיפ טובע (
נון

MENEKET RIVKAH

NOTES ON THE TRANSLITERATION, TRANSLATION, EDITION OF THE YIDDISH TEXT, AND YIDDISH INDEX

1. Transliteration

The transliteration of Hebrew and Yiddish words and names follows the *Encyclopaedia Judaica* (Jerusalem, 1972); in some cases the Yiddish transliteration follows the standard YIVO rules. Hebrew words that have entered the English language are rendered according to *Merriam Webster's Collegiate Dictionary*, 11th edition (Springfield, Mass., 2003). Biblical names are rendered according to the NJPS; the books of the Bible are abbreviated according to *The Chicago Manual of Style*, 15th edition (Chicago, 2003). Hebrew titles of morality books have been transliterated according to the above rules.

2. Translation

Additions in the translation are indicated by parentheses; words emended within the edition have been set within square brackets, if translated.

The expression *"dos iz taitsh"* is used in two different instances: following Bible quotations, where it indicates a translation ("this means in Yiddish"), or as an explanation ("this means"). The transition from translation to explanation is often smooth; depending on the author's intent I have decided to take one or the other direction.

The translation of the Bible quotations follows the New Jewish Publication Society edition. In a few cases I have followed the author's own understanding of the verse.

The addition of "see" preceding quotations from the Bible and Rabbinic literature indicates a quotation that differs slightly from the masoretic text or the Rabbinic text. The addition "cf." indicates a Bible quotation that differs significantly from the masoretic text.

3. Edition of the Yiddish Text

P 1609 indicates the Prague edition of 1609 (Erlangen copy). K 1618 indicates the Krakow edition of 1618 (New York copy). M. indicates the Mishnah; B. and Y. refer to the Babylonian and Jerusalem Talmuds, respectively.

The book title of the Prague edition appeared as a column title and is rendered here as a title.

The last page (fol. 36a) was taken from K 1618.

Wrong or missing header lines in the text (fols. 5b; 9a; 10b; 11a; 12b; 14b–17a; 18a–19a; 20b; 21a; 22b; 23a; 24b; 30b; 31a; 32b) and wrong or missing folio indications (fols. 21a; 22a; 23a–end) are emended.

The missing chapter numbers for the first and second chapters have been added. In some cases, empty lines have been inserted before or after chapter headings (fols. 2b; 8b; 29b; 31b).

All emendations and conjectures have been set inside square brackets. The concomitant apparatus indicates the respective readings in P 1609 and K 1618.

The *rafe* setting is assumed from both editions, and is not corrected. Quotes from the edition in the commentary do not render the *rafe*.

Bible quotations are printed in letters that appear with extra spaces between them. The parentheses surrounding the Bible quotes from P 1609 are retained, and missing parentheses have not been replaced.

In Bible quotations, only obvious printing errors, not deviations from the masoretic text, have been corrected, which also conforms with the Yiddish translation or spelling based on Yiddish pronunciation: such deviations are indicated in the commentary.

Missing abbreviation symbols have been added without comment. Common present-day abbreviations are used (Avraham Even-Shoshan, *Ha-Milon he-Ḥadash*, vol. 4 [Jerusalem: Kiryat Sefer, 1988]).

Line and page breaks have been preserved throughout in the text edition, in accordance with P 1609 and K 1618.

Missing letters are indicated in the reference material with braces { }.

Empty brackets (line fillers) from the original text appear as parentheses; gaps are not rendered.

Unclear readings are indicated by a small circle "o" above the letter.

The Erlangen copy (P 1609) contains various handwritten glosses, none of which are rendered: some Bible quotations are mentioned as marginal notes (fols. 2b–3b), and there are intra-linear insertions of letters or words in Bible quotations (fols. 3b; 5b; 7a; 8b). Up to fol. 28b, the vowels in most Bible quotations were inserted manually; later only occasionally. Beginning on fol. 14b, and also on 18b, 20b–22a, 23a, and 26a–27a, some Bible quotations, individual words, or entire sentences were underlined in the original text. On fols. 22b–24b, almost all lines were manually inserted with supralinear dots. Sometimes sections were marked at the beginning or end of the line by small double bars (fols. 11b; 12a; 13a; 14a; 21a–23a); none of these markings have been reproduced.

4. Yiddish Index

The Yiddish index is ordered by subject; wherever possible, the spelling of words listed therein follows the original Yiddish. This spelling, however, was not standardized; therefore, in cases where more than one spelling for a given word has been used, the index lists the most common form. In those cases, when a certain form is not documented at all (such as an infinitive), the most likely spelling is used.

LIST OF ABBREVIATIONS

God willing	אם ירצה השם	אי"ה
Amen. So may be His will.	אמן כן יהי רצונו	אכי"ר
Two		ב'
Temple	בית המקדש	ב"ה
Blessed be he	ברוך הוא	ב"ה
Due to our many transgressions	בעוונותינו הרבים	בעו"ה
Gan Eden	גן עדן	ג"ע
The Tetragrammaton, the LORD	יהוה	ה'
God, blessed be His name	השם יתברך	ה"י
The Holy One, Blessed be He	הקדוש ברוך הוא	הקב"ה
The master, Rabbi	הרב, רב	הר"ר
God protect us	השם ישמרינו	הש"י
God, blessed be He	השם יתברך	הש"י
God, blessed be He	השם יתברך	השי"ת
Six		ו'
Etc.	וגומר	וג'
And so forth	וכוליה	וכו'
And deeds	ומעשים	ומ'
Seven		ז'
His/her/their memory be a blessing	זכרונו\ה\ם לברכה	ז"ל
The memory of the righteous be a blessing	זכרון צדיק לברכה	זצ"ל
God forbid	חס ושלום	ח"ו
The Tetragrammaton, the LORD	יהוה	וי'
Blessed be His name	יתברך שמו	י"ש
Blessed be His name	יתברך שמו	ית"ש
Twenty-four		כ"ד
All the more so	כל שכן	כ"ש
To the lesser reckoning	לפרט קטן	לפ"ק
Conduct, deeds	מעשים	מ'
Our teacher and master, Rabbi	מורינו הרב רבי	מהר"ר
All the more so	מכל שכן	מכ"ש
Peace be upon him/her	עליו\ה השלום	ע"ה

Idol worship	עבודה זרה	ע״ז
By, through	על ידי	ע״י
Peace be upon him/her	עליו\ה שלום	ע״ש
The Holy One, Blessed be He	קדוש ברוך הוא	קב״ה
One hundred and nine		ק״ט
Reb	רב	ר׳
Meaning	רצה לומר	ר״ל
Rabbi Solomon ben Isaac, Rashi	רבי שלמה בן יצחק	רש״י
Acrostic	ראשי תיבות	ר״ת
Torah scholar	תלמיד חכם	ת״ח
Praise to God	תהילה לאל	ת״ל
A teaching says	תלמוד לומר	ת״ל

TRANSLATION AND COMMENTARY

Meneket Rivkah

Listen, dear, esteemed, pious women. Take a look at this Yiddish book, and read it so that one shall place one's trust in God the Almighty, and in all one's deeds rely on Him.

5 Because you have known the respected woman who conceived and wrote this book, the Rabbanit and preacher Madam Rivkah, may her memory be a blessing, daughter of the sage, our teacher and master, Rabbi Meir Tiktiner, may his memory be a blessing. Her intentions were focused exclusively on the fear of God day and night, and her thoughts were by no

1b

1   *Meneket Rivkah.* (מנקת רבקה :1). Regarding the title see the Introduction, the section entitled "Structure." Next to the masoretic plene style of writing, the defective rabbinic writing is also common in literature. The title page is adorned with a simple decorative frame surrounding the text. The text itself follows the rhyme pattern aa aa (*–oyen*) bb bb (*–akht*) cc cc (*–ehen, –ezen*) de (*–uken, –aynen*) de (*–uken, –ayzen*) ff ff f (*–im*). Excluded from the rhyme are the name of the author, the eulogy, and the colophon, containing the printing location and the name of the printer, inserted between a and b.

2   *Women.* (פרוייאן :2). On women as readers, see the section "Female Addressees" in the Introduction. Like most authors of morality books, Rivkah bat meir specified the sex of the intended readership but was reticent on its intellectual background. Only the author of *Brantshpigl* elaborates: "The book was made in Yiddish for women, and for men who are like women, in that they are not capable of much learning. Then, when they read the book on a Sabbath, or on a Holy Day, they may understand what they are reading. After all, our books are written in the Holy Tongue, and may sometimes contain casuistic arguments (*pilpul*) taken from the Gemara. They could not understand this" (*Brantshpigl*, p. 25).

4   *Conceived and wrote.* (גיטרכט אוני' גימכט :7). See the section "Authorship and Provenance" in the Introduction. Cf. the formulation in *Eyn shoyn Froyenbuykhleyn*, fol. 2a, that the anonymous author uses as justification for drafting an ethic-halakhic book: "אוני' ניט דז איינר האט דאז ביכליין דער טראכט. אודר העט עז אויז דען קאפא גימאכט. נוי ערט גיקלויבט אוני' אויז אלין ספרים ביקומן. אוני' פער רשות פון רבנים גינומן. דז מיר ניט טונן גריוזן. אוני—זאלטן איינן חס ושלום און רעכט אונטר וויזן."—"And it is not as if anybody had made up this book himself, and in his own head. He merely collected it and took it out from all the books. Beforehand, he obtained permission from the rabbis, so that we may not perform an atrocity, and instruct someone wrongly, God forbid."

    Regarding copying and translating books cf. *Sefer Middot*, fol. 99b, where the anonymous translator substantiates his work: "זא האב איך מיך אונטר שטאנדן מיט דער הוילף גוטש יתברך דעש אלמעכטיגן אוני' האב עז אם טאג גיברוכט אוני' וויא איך מיך זוילך דינג ניט אן נעמן זולט."—"Thus I have taken it on, with God's help, and I have brought it out to daylight, although I should not have taken on such a thing."

5   *Rabbanit and preacher.* (הרבנית הדרשנית :5-6). Regarding this designation, see the section "Origin and Family" in the Introduction.

6   *Meir Tiktiner.* (מאיר טיקטינר :6). Regarding her father, see the section "Origin and Family" in the Introduction.

means of grandeur. Who has ever heard of or seen such a novelty; has it ever happened in countless years, that a woman has written something of her own accord? And she has read numerous verses and midrashim. I let it, therefore, be printed, so that every woman who wishes to read it can buy and possess a copy. (She) named the book *Meneket Rivkah* to be a

5 commemoration for herself, and in honor of all women. It shows that a woman can also compose words of ethical instruction and good biblical interpretations as well as many men. She divided her book into seven chapters. She was brief and did not lengthen her words. In the merit of this, may you merit the redemption of the Messiah, in which the *Shekhinah* will once again delight in Israel. Amen, so may it be His will.

10 Here in Prague, according to the lesser reckoning (1609), by the printer Gershom, the son of our teacher and master, Rabbi Bezalel Katz, may the memory of the righteous be a blessing.

2a
Book

Introduction of the Rabbanit
Rebekah's Nurse[1]—He fed him honey from the crag.[2]

15 I have marked well,[3] and I have pondered in my heart, I have raised my voice and spoke.[4] Now I have come,[5] today I have gone out. I have found a well of water,[6] and have rolled the

---

10   ***Here in Prague.*** (פ׳ה פ׳ראג :23). The abbreviation marks designate the letters as a chronostichon.

10   ***Gershom.*** (גרשם :24). Member of the Prague printer family that established, in 1512, the first Hebrew printshop in Central Europe. In 1589 Gershom ben Bezalel, together with his father, printed the sermons of the Maharal under the title *Derush Na'eh*, and in 1596, two years after having assumed the management of the printshop, published the Maharal's *Netivot Olam*. In 1610 he ended his printing activity; cf. Lieben, "Buchdruck" (Book Printing), pp. 88–126; Nosek, "Katalog" (Catalogue), pp. 17–25.

2a

14   ***He fed him.*** (ויניקהו :3). Yalkut, § 944: "'To feast on the yield of the earth' (Deut. 32:13)—that is the Bible. 'He fed him honey from the crag' (ibid.)—that is the Mishnah. 'And oil from the flinty rock' (ibid.)—that is the Talmud." Cf. Sifrei Devarim, § 317.

     The verses Deut. 32:13 and Gen. 35:8 are title and motto of the following preface. This is a *piyyut* in rhyme: 11 verses rhyme with *-iti*, *-eti*, *-ati*, or *-oti*; interrupted by two verses with *-avi*; three verses with *-orakh* (see below), and 20 verses with *-ekha*.

15   ***I have marked well.*** (ראה ראיתי :4). The first letters of each Bible quote in this line make up the name Rivkah. This acronym and other poetic stylistic devices (such as rhyme, alphabetic rows, and meter) are common for *piyyutim*; cf. Elbogen, *Gottesdienst* (Liturgy), pp. 290–295; cf. Hellerstein, "The Name in the Poem," pp. 32–52.

large stone from the well.[7] I drank from it, but I continued to thirst. I said in my heart: I shall go and bring [water] to every man and woman near to me. My bones rejoice[8] that they shall drink for many long years, in order to fulfill what is said: "Drink water from your own cistern."[9] Blessed be they who bless You,[10] and all who seek refuge in Your shade.[11]

5 That which You have promised me through Your Prophets, shall not be absent from the mouth of Your children's children.[12] I am Your handmaid,[13] daughter of Your servant.[14] You have spread Your wings over me[15] so that I shall not be ashamed of Your precepts. Your steadfast love is great toward me,[16] enabling the fulfillment of Your words. I will follow after You and confirm Your words[17] that are [written] in Your Torah.[18] I have no good but

10 You,[19] so draw me after You.[20] I regard Your ways,[21] for Your word is a lamp to my feet,[22] for You are just in Your judgment,[23] for You are near to all who call You.[24] All who desire to hold You in awe shall merit gazing upon the beauty of Your face.[25]

Put up a palanquin to raise Reb Azariah, called Ziskind, son of the master, Rabbi Samuel, called Reb Zanvil Taymer, from the holy congregation of Poznan, who took his life in his hands

15 and poured money from his purse to publish this book in order to bring merit to all people.

1   *I continued to thirst.* (צמיתי 6:). Here, a spelling with *aleph* instead of the middle *yud* would have been correct; cf. however the spelling in Judg. 4:19. The letter *yud* has been inserted in order to adjust the word visually to the rhyme with –*iti*, yet both forms are pronounced *zameti*.

3   *For many long years.* (לימים אורך 7:). *Le-yamim orekh*. The common form would be *le-orekh yamim*, as in Ps. 23:6; 93:5; Lam. 5:20; here, the words were rearranged to enable the rhyme. In order for *orekh* to rhyme with *mi-borkha* (Yiddish text, line 8), it would have to be pronounced *orkha*, which is grammatically wrong. The intention was probably a visual rhyme; see below.

4   *Blessed be they who bless You.* (ומברכך מבורך 8:). The second verbal form, *mevorakh*, plays with the visually identical form of the preceding rhyme word; that, however, must be pronounced *mi-borkha*.

5   *Your Prophets.* (נביאך 8-9:). Possible intentions may be both the singular and the defective plural, both with the personal suffix; in both cases the word would be pronounced *nevi'ekha*.

6   *Your handmaid.* (אמתיך 9:). Unusual plene spelling, rendering the vocalization with an *atnakh*, thus changing the actual pronunciation *amatkha* that adjusts to the rhyme with –*ekha*; cf. Deut. 5:14; Lev. 25:6.

9   *[Written].* (ככתו[ן] 11:). The reading due to Prague 1609, *ba-katu'* (in the Scripture), is also possible, because of the following "in Your Torah"; this would be redundant, however, and therefore less sensible.

13   *Put up a palanquin.* (ואפריון נמטי להנעלה 17:). Literally "Bring a canopy for footwear"; a rabbinic expression of particular esteem; cf. B. Bava Metzi'a 119a.

13   *Azariah.* (עזריא 18:). Regarding the patron, see "Prints" in the Introduction.

14   *Took his life in his hands.* (שם נפשו בכפו 18:). Cf. I Sam. 28:21. The expression means "exposed himself to risks."

2b

Chapter One

This will speak of how a woman should behave, and how she should adorn her body, so that her soul should not be lost.

King David, peace be upon him, wrote in Psalms the verse, "Take heed, lass, and note, [incline] your ear: forget your people and your father's house,[26] and let the king be aroused by your beauty; since [he] is your lord, bow to him."[27] This means in Yiddish, listen to me, my daughter and see, incline your ears. Forget your people and your father's house, then the King, the Holy One, blessed be He, will desire your beauty; since he is your master, bow to him. The midrash[28] in the weekly Torah reading Lekh Lekha relates this to Sarah and Abraham, and how they were commanded by the Holy One, blessed be He, to leave their land. Namely, He told them to forget their father and mother and family, meaning they should distance themselves from the behavior of their parents. Then the Holy One, blessed be He, will find your beauty desirable, for example, your good deeds. I could also

2b

2   **Adorn.** (‏צירן‏ :2).   Regarding the individual care of a woman for her body and her soul, see the commentary on pp. 87/7 and 90/11.

S. in *Eyn shoyn Froyenbuykhleyn*, fol. 2a, the words chosen by the author to describe the intentions of the publication: ‏דרום האבן מיר איין שין פרויין ביכליין טון דר ווילן. צו‏ ‏בעשרונג דען לייב אונ' צו צירונג דר זילן.‏"—"Therefore we have chosen a fine women's booklet for the enhancement of the body, and as an adornment of the soul." Further on (fol. 3a–b), its author discusses the significance of the correct treatment of body and soul, in order to obtain a share in the coming world.

S. *Brantshpigl*, p. 3: "Thus should one conduct himself: If his body is soiled, he shall wash it. . . . The same way, the soul must be washed by repentance and good deeds, if it has been soiled with sins or wrong conduct, making it too heavy to rise to the place, from whence it was taken."

9   **Midrash.** (‏מדרש‏ :7).   S. Tanḥuma, Lekh Lekha 3, following the interpretation of Ps. 45:11f.: "Thus Abraham lived among the idolaters. The Holy One, blessed be He, told him: Why do you dwell among the evil, leave them, and let the world know of your good deeds, as is written, 'Go forth' (Gen. 12:1)." The exegetic details (father, mother, family, parents) are not mentioned in the Midrash, and they constitute decorative speech used by the author, possibly influenced by Bereshit Rabbah 63.4 that speaks of the ungodliness and deceptiveness of Rebekah's father and brother, whom she left in order to follow Eliezer.

S. Rashi on Ps. 45:12: "'The King, the Holy One, blessed be He, will desire your beauty.' Then the Holy One, blessed be He, will find your beauty, i.e., your good deeds, desirable."

9   **Lekh Lekha.** (‏לך לך‏ :8).   Weekly Torah reading, Gen. 12:1–17:27.

13   **Beauty.** (‏שונהייט‏ :11).   S. *Den Muser un' Hanhoge*, fol. 32a–b, no. 98: ‏אל תשבח‏" ‏אשה ביפיה ובטוב מעשה יאשרוה השומעי' — ניט דו זולט לובן אין ורויא מיט איר שונהייט‏

expound the verse and teach it as follows: King David, peace be upon him, spoke the verse about a daughter of Israel, who took a man. She should thus take up a (new) path and think of (its) aim, meaning, she should forget the deeds and good days she had with her parents.

For we perceive every day, that due to the strength of love, a father and mother defend their child, even when it behaves poorly, as the verse says, "Love covers up all faults."[29] About this the Psalm says that she should forget her errors and should take up good deeds. The verse is referring to the verse "Let the king be aroused by your beauty."[30] This means that the Holy One, blessed be He, will desire your good deeds, as this verse also says, "Ah, you are fair, my darling."[31] This means, my beloved, you are beautiful with good deeds. The verse goes on and says, "The king's daughter is all glorious within: her clothing is of

---

אבר גוטי מעשים די זי אן איר הוט זא זולן זי לובן די עש הארן.״—"Do not praise a woman through her beauty; instead, those who hear of her good deeds should praise her. You shall not praise a woman through her beauty, instead, the good deeds that she does, shall be praised by those, who hear of it."

4   *Father and mother.* (מוטר אונ׳ פאטר :16-17). S. *Meshiv Ḥema—Minhagim Eshet Ḥayil*, fol. 2a–b: דרום ״אונ׳ ניט אלז ווי איין טייל ווייבר די האבן רחמנות אויף אירה קינדר. שטראפין זיא ניט. וועז זיא גלייך ניט רעכט טונה. דז אנדרה לייט צו זעהין. אונ׳ זאגין עז די א מוטר קריגט זיא מיט דיא זעלבגה. אונ׳ איבר העלפט אירה קינדר אין פנים אריין אזו ווערין דיא קינדר נאך ערגר.״—"Not like some women, who pity their children, and fail to admonish their children even when they conduct themselves incorrectly. When other people see this and tell the mother, she quarrels with them. She helps her children to save face, but this makes them even worse." Regarding the warning of forbearing conduct toward children, see the commentary on p. 165/12.

6   *Psalm.* (מזמור :18). The reference is to Ps. 45:11, to which Prov. 10:12 is here referred.

6   *Good deeds.* (גוטה מעשים טובים :19). The bilingual pleonasm "good (Yiddish) good (Hebrew) deeds" indicates that the author understood *ma'asim tovim* to be the technical term for adequate, normative conduct, which is why she added the qualifying adjective "good."

8   *Good deeds.* (מעשים טובים :22). S. Tanḥuma, Tetsaveh 1: "Rav said: See how the Holy One, blessed be He, praises the congregation of Israel in His midst, 'Ah, you are fair, my darling' (Songs 1:15). Behold, you are beautiful by deeds, behold, you are beautiful by the deeds of your fathers, behold, you are beautiful in the home, behold, you are beautiful in the field."

10   *King's daughter.* (בת מלך :23). Ps. 45:14 became the *locus classicus* for the interpretation of female virtue as domesticity; see *Brantshpigl*, p. 102: "'The king's daughter is all glorious within' (Ps. 45:14).... This is to be understood in such a manner, that she would always remain in the home, even if she were a royal princess with sufficient servants and maids, it would be a great honor to her, to remain in the home and not to sit outside the door." Similar remark in *Brantshpigl*, p. 123; see the commentary on p. 85/20 (domesticity), on p. 194/2 (work) and on p. 161/6 (child upbringing).

Rabbinic literature offers a less unique interpretation; see, e.g., Tanhuma (Warsaw), Va-yishlaḥ 6: "'The king's daughter is all glorious within' (Ps. 45:14). Rabbi Yose said: If the woman conducts herself virtuously in the home, she is worthy of marrying a high

wrought gold."[32] This means, when a woman is modest and remains in her house, then the Holy One, blessed be He, will appreciate her as a daughter, more than one who adorns herself with pure gold. The Psalm goes further, "Your sons will succeed your ancestors."[33] This means that you will have pious children who will fill the place of their forebears with

3a

5 their good deeds. And so we see that King David, peace be upon him, spoke of a daughter of Israel who should accustom herself to the proper path. King Solomon, peace be upon him, said on that subject in Song of Songs, "We have a little sister, whose breasts are not yet formed. What shall we do for our sister when she is spoken for?[34] If she be a wall, we will build upon it a silver battlement; if she be a door, we will panel it in cedar."[35] Rashi[36]

10 explains as follows: it deals with the nation of Israel in exile. When the nations of the world harbor evil plans against Israel, Israel should be like a wall, and they will be unable to do anything to them. However, the Yalkut[37] writes that it deals with the Torah, which is

priest, and to bring up high priests, as is written, 'The king's daughter is all glorious within' (ibid.) etc. If she keeps herself glorious even inside the house: 'her clothing is of wrought gold' (ibid.)." Other places, e.g., Y. Yoma 38d; Va-yikra Rabbah 20.11; Yalkut, § 525.

2   *Adorns.* (צירט :25). Ps. 45:14 is used as additional evidence that external beauty emerges only as a result of appropriate conduct. The interpretation construes a contradiction between the virtuous, domestic royal princess, and the woman adorning herself with golden jewelry, although the verse only speaks of one person.

3a

6   *Proper Path.* (גוטן דרך :2). Corresponds with the Hebrew technical term *derekh erez*—"tradition (literally: path) of the land," used in the rabbinic discourse to indicate the traditions of the land that were adopted as normative conduct.

    S. *Brantshpigl*, p. 13: "I do think, however, that the women nowadays are smart and will choose the proper path, and will do everything that is good, and not bad: (namely) the conduct and virtues that you find here, in accordance with our Torah, and with the decisions of our sages."

9   *Rashi.* (רש"י :4). S. Rashi on Songs 8:8: "'Whose breasts are not yet formed'— this corresponds with what is said on the exile in Egypt, 'Your breasts became firm' (Ezek. 16:7), when the time of redemption has come. But this, 'Whose breasts are not yet formed' (Songs 8:8) (means): the time for lovers has not yet arrived. 'What shall we do for our sister when she is spoken for' (ibid.): When the nations that surround her whisper in order to deprave her, this relates to, as it is written, 'Let us wipe them out as a nation' (Ps. 83:5)."

10   *Explains.* (פשט :5). Interpretation method referring to the literal meaning of a word, although here a symbolic *derash* rather than *peshat* interpretation is applied. In common usage, the term was generally used as a synonym for "explanation." Accordingly, this is how the author uses it for her interpretations; see the commentary on p. 85/4.

12   *Yalkut.* (ילקוט :7). S. Yalkut, § 994: "'We have a little sister' (Songs 8:8), that is the Torah, as it is written, 'Say to Wisdom, "You are my sister"' (Prov. 7:4). Small in

likened to a woman, as another verse says, "Say to Wisdom, 'You are my sister.'"[38] This means in Yiddish, tell wisdom, you are my sister. She is called "little," which means that the Torah appears small, but is large with commandments.

I could also explain the verse as follows: King Solomon, peace be upon him, spoke of a daughter of Israel who is still young. What should we do with our sister, on the day when we must speak with her? Will she hold herself like a wall? That means, will she maintain proper standards in all of her actions, as is appropriate for a daughter of Israel? If so, she will be privileged with children who are Torah scholars, and will be as prestigious as a silver building. And when it says, "Whose breasts are not yet formed,"[39] the verse means one who is orphaned at a young age, and has become an orphan without mother or father—"breasts" means "father." This orphan must be disciplined more than others.

Or the verse refers to one who comes into a foreign country, far away from her parents—an inexperienced and ill-mannered woman is like an orphan. And so when the verse says, "If she be a wall,"[40] it means that she should be like a wall that stands even when it is shot. In other words, it means that she will accept admonition, and will allow herself to be disciplined and turned toward her good.

The verse goes further, "We will build upon it a silver battlement"[41]—upon her will be built a palace of pure silver. This means that she will be highly valued. The verse goes on, "If she be a door."[42] This means that if she does not accept admonition, and will not be obedient, she will be a tramp, one who runs around outside, who we could compare to a

appearance, and great in deeds. 'Whose breasts are not yet formed' (Songs 8:8), like a woman, but she nurses the entire world, as it is written, 'Let her breasts satisfy you at all times' (Prov. 5:19)."

4   ***Explain.*** (פשט :10). Partial interpretations of Songs 8:8f. can be found, among others, in Bereshit Rabbah 39.3; Shir ha-Shirim Rabbah (Vilna), 8.3; they interpret the verses allegorically in regards to the dangers that Israel and its existence in the exile are subjected to; at times they are adorned with female metaphors; see Shir ha-Shirim Zuta 8, 8: "'We have a little sister' (Songs 8:8) etc. This is Hiskia's generation, which resembles a beautiful woman. 'Whose breasts are not yet formed' (Songs 8:8). It (the generation) was also pretty, but its deeds were not good."

Songs 8:8f. is not interpreted allegorically, rather in the meaning of a young, somewhat orphaned woman, or a woman living far away from her parents, and who is particularly dependent on admonitions for proper conduct, in order to obtain respect.

10   ***Father.*** (פאטר :17). Now follows the homiletic connection between Songs 8:8 and Gen. 49:25, without, however, any mention of the verse that plays with the similarity between *shadayim* (breasts) and *Shaddai* (the name of God); cf. Gen. 49:25.

S. Rashi: "'Blessings of the breast and womb' (Gen. 49:25); that is the blessing of the father and the mother." Same in Bereshit Rabbah 87.7.

20   ***Tramp.*** (יוצאנית :27). Literally "one who stayes off the house." The word designates an incorrigible woman, who will not accept any admonitions (see above). In rabbinic literature, she is particularly associated with lack of virtuousness, see *Reshit Ḥokhmah*, I, p. 198, §4: "'Gave her no share of understanding' (Job 39:17). A tramp

3b

board of fir that is full of worm holes. That is to say, she will not be able to endure. About that King Solomon, peace be upon him, spoke the verse, "The wisdom of women builds

(*yaz'anit*) that does not conduct herself modestly, and that is not shy, is not even worthy to marry an ignoramus."

S. Tanḥuma (Warsaw), Va-yishlaḥ 7: "Now Dinah, the daughter whom Leah had borne . . . went out' (Gen. 34:1). (It says) not 'the daughter of Jacob,' because the scripture struggles with her mother: since Leah is a tramp (*yaz'anit*), she, too, is a tramp (*yaz'anit*). Similar in Bereshit Rabbah 80.1 and B. Eruvin 100b.

S. Rashi on Gen. 1:28: "'And master it' (Gen. 1:28). A *vav* is missing in order to teach you that the man shall master the woman, so that she may not be a tramp, but also to teach you that it is the way of man, not that of woman, to subject himself to the duty of fertility and procreation." The word is also mentioned in highly negative connotation in the moral literature; e.g., *Brantshpigl* uses *unshtetigerin*—tramp—and *zonah*—whore— synonymously; for *yaz'anit* see *Brantshpigl*, p. 99f.: "Much evil comes from it, as with Dinah, who went out and became a tramp. . . . And with a woman who confronts every- body and wants to do everything herself, who interferes with everything, and who wants everything to be her way, who does not care about anybody, regardless of the time, and who says, 'This is what I am, and this is my opinion.' King Solomon says in Proverbs (*sic*), 'You had the brazenness of a street woman (*ishah zonah*)' (Jer. 3:3). This means in Yiddish, and the brazenness of a tramp. It always ends badly, when one insists on having one's own way." Cf. ibid., pp. 15; 45f.; 93f.; 114; 123; 243; 304f.; 336.

S. the misogynous maxim in *Mishlei Ḥakhamim*, 13b; no. 70, which emphasizes, in its last and most narrative paragraph, both the woman's depravity, and the importance of domesticity: ״חכם אחד כתב על פתח ביתו בכתיבה גסה יהי רצון שלא יכנס פה דבר שלא יהא עלי למשא. עבר חכם אחר וכתב תחתיו אם יש לך אשה לפתוח פתח אחר אל תעמוד מהרה חושה: [. . .] איין חכם וואר איבר זיינר הויז טיר שרייבן. גאט געב דז אלז ביז פון זיינר טיר זאלט איושן בלייבן. דא וואר איין אנדרר חכם דער פיר גיפארן. דאש טעט אים בנג און צארן. און שריב דרונטר וען דו דיך דאז האשט פיר גינומן. וען דיין וייב אויש גיט צו וועלכר טיר זאל זיא ווידר קומן.הײמן״—"A wise man wrote on his door in rough (Hebrew) letters: 'May it be His will, that nothing shall enter here which may become a burden to me.' Another wise man passed by, and wrote underneath: 'If you have a wife, open another door that she may not dare to hurry around restlessly.' . . . (This means in Yiddish:) A wise man had written over his door, God help that all evil remain outside his door. Then another wise man came traveling. He became worried and angry, and wrote underneath, If you have such an intention: If your wife leaves the house, through which door shall she reenter?"

3b

1   ***Board.*** (טאביל 1:).   Cf. the metaphor at Rashi on Songs 8:8: "'We will panel it in cedar' (Songs 8:9)—Women behind a door, or rotten wooden planks, and a worm gnaws and eats it."

2   ***Wisdom.*** (חכמת 3:).   The masoretic text in Prov. 14:1 reads *ḥakhmot*.

S. *Brantshpigl*, p. 45, where the woman's wisdom is interpreted in respect to her conduct as wife and mother: "King Solomon (says) in Proverbs, 'The wisdom of women builds her house' (Prov. 14:1). . . . This is to mean: If the woman serves her husband diligently, admonishes him, and urges him to do good, and she gets the servants and her children used to do everything for the honor of God—then she will have built a nice

her house, but [folly] tears it down with its own hands."[43] In Yiddish this means, the wisdom of women builds her house, but a foolish woman runs her house wantonly.

I have a difficulty with this verse. It speaks of "wisdom" in the plural, and just after it says, "she builds her house" in the singular. Therefore I can also interpret the verse as follows: it spoke of two aspects related to a woman. First, about the wisdom of the body—a woman must use wisdom regarding her body, as I will, God willing, write about later. Second, about the wisdom of the soul, as I will also, God willing, write about later, each in its proper place.

---

house. The house shall stand forever, and she shall enjoy the present world and the world to come."

1   ***Own hands.*** (בידה 3:).   The masoretic text of Prov. 14:1 differs slighty.

3   ***I have a difficulty.*** (איז מיר קשה 4:).   *Iz mir kashe* is similar to the Aramaic expression *hai kashya*—this poses a difficulty—from the rabbinic discussion. The author's problem lies with the assumed use of numbers in Prov. 14:1: she regards the subject wisdom (*hakhmot*) as a plural because it seems to have a plural ending, while the predicate is singular. However, *hakhmot* constitutes a lexical variant of *hokhmah* and is in fact singular; cf. Gesenius, *Handwörterbuch*, p. 230; Even Shoshan, I, p. 391. She solves the problem by deriving from "wisdoms" a "wisdom of the body" (the female body regulations; see below), and a "wisdom of the soul" (ideals of social conduct; see below); see also the commentary on pp. 90/11 and 122/6. Regarding the equation of body and house see fol. 5a, and the respective commentary on p. 95/5–9.

3   ***Wisdom.*** (חכמת 5:).   As above, defective spelling of *hakhmot* due to the Yiddish pronunciation. In the Erlangen copy (Krakow, 1618), a *vav* was added by hand.

7   ***Wisdom of the soul.*** (חכמת הנשמה 8:).   Regarding the term, see Ibn Ezra on Eccles. 7:21: "He said to the wise man: If you wish to find peace, 'Don't pay attention to everything' (Eccles. 7:21) that the people say. If someone reviles you, even if it is your slave, do not pay attention to their words. If you are scornful, the light of the wisdom of the soul (*hokhmat ha-neshamah*) will become dark." Similar in ibid. on Dan. 4:28. Cf. the commentary on pp. 90/11 and 122/6.

S. *Orhot Zaddikim*, fol. 57a (chapter on the fear of God): כך ענין הנשמה היא בת מלך״
נפוחה באדם מכסא הכבוד והובאה בגוף המלוכלל אשר חשקו רב מאד לעולם הזה ויש לו כמה
מיני תאות עד שנקבע הנשמ׳ שהיא בת המלך ביניהם ונמשכת אחר תאוות הגוף ושוכחת אביה
העליון ובעת שמראים לה שמים, וכוכבים, וחמה, ולבנה, היאך מתנהגי׳ הם במנהג שוה ואומר
לה שהיא נבראת מאותו שברא אותה אז היא מתעלה יותר ויותר ובעת שמלמדין אותה סוד
יחוד הק״בה וסוד **חכמת הנשמה** אז היא לובשת בגדי מלכות ונכנס׳ בסוד היראה״. —"Such is
also the matter of the soul. It is the king's daughter, breathed into man, from the throne of glory into the dirty body that has a great desire for this world. The body has many lusts, until the soul is drowned therein, because it is the daughter of the king among them, and is drawn away by the *body's lusts*, and it forgets its superior father. If it is shown the sky, the stars, the sun, and the moon, and how they all behave by the same tradition, and it is told that it was created by the same One that created all those, it rises higher and higher. It is taught the secrets of the oneness of the Holy One, blessed be He, and the secret of the *wisdom of the soul*, it dons the royal attire and enters the secret of the fear of God" (my emphasis). Cf. the section "Sources and Their Editing" in the Introduction.

Now I would like to return to the verses, and to speak of a daughter of Israel—specifically a young person who is not yet very experienced—and how she should conduct herself in relation to her body. Great wisdom resides there, as the verse says, "The wisdom of women builds her house"[44]—meaning the body, which is called "her house." There is also a *piyyut* from Yom Kippur that mentions a householder who has left his house orphaned—here too (the house) refers to a body. And so it says that a woman requires great wisdom in relation to her body. This is not the case for a man, who does not need to, the way a woman must, observe one time after the other. I do not need to write much about this subject, because every woman knows well enough herself how she should conduct herself.

5 *Piyyut.* (פויט :13). The spelling *payet* is based on the Yiddish pronunciation. It is unclear which *piyyut* is referred to in which house is interpreted as body.

8 *Time.* (צייט :17). This refers to the menstruation period and the subsequent period of the seven white days. During both of these *niddah* periods, the woman is subject to various restrictions in her conduct with her husband and in the religious realm; cf. Biale, *Women and Jewish Law*, p. 153ff.

9 *Knows.* (וויש :18). Contrary to Rivkah bat Meir, other morality books doubt the women's knowledge, see *Brantshpigl*, p. 245: "Because they do not have the understanding to compare one thing with another, or to fully understand a matter, they could make a mistake and (decide) that an impure woman is pure, or that a pure woman is impure. That, too, is a great sin."

S. ibid., p. 34: "I ask all pious, God-fearing women, not to judge or decide by yourselves if you are impure or pure, if there is any doubt. The welfare of us all depends on it.... Even if you find something, in a women's booklet, about pure or impure, do not abide by it.... A woman should not decide. Pick an old understanding Jewess, and send her to the Rabbi, who has studied the laws and knows them, and he will say whether you are pure or impure. Important laws are dependent on the *halakhah* regarding the *niddah*."

S. *Eyn shoyn Froyenbuykhleyn*, fol. 10a, in connection with the beginning of the white days: "רען דיא שמועה גיט ניט אזו לייכט צו. אז עטליכי ורויאן ווינן וועלין."—"Because the story is not as easy as some women would like to believe."

S. ibid., fol. 30b: "אונ' וון מן גלייך דיא מיא ניט שפארט אונ' זאלט אלש אן שרייבן דאך ווער עז דען ווייברן גאר צו הערב דיא זאך. דיא קענטן דיא זאך ניט הלבר ור שטין דרום גיב איך אייך איין עצה אלן ווייבר דש זיא רעבט מינטליך לערנ' אונ' דש איטליכי ורויא פרעגט נאך איר סדר ווא זיא זיך זאל האלטן."—"Even if one would make the effort to write it all down, it would still be too difficult for women, since they would not be able to understand even half of it. Therefore I advise you and all women to seek oral advice from the rabbis. Every woman should ask about her time determination, and how to follow it."

S. ibid., fol. 49b: "דיא פרויאן זאלן גיוואָרנט זיין דש זי דאז ספר פער אוינן הלטן אונ' דש זי אופט דרינן לייאן דש זי וואול דרינן בקי ווערן זיין דש זי זאלן וויסן ווי זיא זיך האלטין זאלין מיט אל אירי זאכין דען איר עולם הבא העננגט אן דעם. דאך זאלן די ווייבר גיהיט זיין בייא אירן חיות דאש וועג אין אין איין זאך צו קומט די זא שווער איז דש זי זאלן נישט פסקנן אונ' זאלן איין רב דרום פראגן."—"The women should be warned to keep the book in mind, and read in it often, in order to know it well. They should know how to conduct themselves in all matters, because their world to come depends on it. However, the women must by their lives be careful not to decide any difficult matters by themselves. Instead, they must then ask a Rabbi." Similar on fols. 21a, 30b, 47a.

Cf. the rare warning, directed at unlearned men, of their own decisions in the *Sefer ha-Gan*, fol. 10b, in connection with the prohibition of lending money against interest:

She should be prudent and sparing, but during her period she should be careful not to damage her body, otherwise she will not be able to make herself pure. In this regard, King Solomon, peace be upon him, said, "Folly tears it down with its own hands."[45] This means, foolishness destroys her house willfully. On this a verse says, "Every clever man acts know-
5 ledgeably."[46] This means in Yiddish, every prudent person does everything with sense and reason. The Gemara[47] explains this verse: "A righteous person knows the needs of his beast."[48] It means every pious Jew knows what his cattle needs, all the more so his wife. [Our] sages, may their memories be a blessing, also write much about the things that a person should be alerted to: that he should take care of his body and eat nothing unhealthful. If he should,
10 God forbid, become sick, he cannot fulfill many of the commandments he otherwise

4a

can when he is healthy. Maimonides[49] writes on this matter that the verse "He who guards

"אונ' אידר מאן זאל דראן גיוואָרנט זיין אוב אין איין זעלכש צו קעם אז ער זול איין רב דרום ורעגן אז ער אין דרויז בישייד דיא סברות אונ' אלי אונטער שייד אונ' וויא מן זיך זול הלטן אז ער ניט אום רעכט דינן קאן טאן." —"And every man shall be warned that if something like that occurs to him, that he shall ask a Rabbi, so that he may tell him his opinion and explain to him all the differences, and tell him how to conduct himself, and prevent him from wrongdoing."

2   *Damage.* (פר דערבט: 20). The moral books mention, on various occasions, that particularly women should not restrict themselves too much physically; see *Brantshpigl*, p. 253: "There are women who fast on the same day (that they go to the ritual bath), so that nothing is stuck between their teeth. I, however, think it is better to eat and not to fast." This description by Moses Henokhs Altshul contradicts his own immediately preceding image of women, who do not know the rules well or who do not observe them strictly.

    S. ibid., p. 317: "However, to eat little, or to fast repeatedly, is not right at all, particularly for women with a weak constitution. King Solomon says in Proverbs, 'A cruel man makes trouble for himself' (Prov. 11:17). . . . This means, one should not torment one's body too much, and not plague one's flesh."

    Not specifically for women, on the other hand, in the *Sefer Middot*, fol. 24b: "אויך זול איינר ניט צו ויל ואַשטן ביש דאש ער שוואך ווערט. זו קאן ער אבר אבר הקדוש ברוך הוא ניט דינן." —"One should also not fast too much, until one feels weakness, because then one cannot serve the Holy One, blessed be He."

6   *Gemara.* (גמרא: 23). S. B. Ketubbot 63a: "She heard of his (i.e., her husband, Rabbi Akiva's) return home (after twelve years) and went out to greet him. Her neighbors said to her, borrow pretty clothes, and dress yourself. But she said: 'A righteous man knows the needs of his beast' (Prov. 12:10). As she approached him, she threw herself to the ground, and kissed his feet." Similar in B. Nedarim 50a; Kallah Rabbati, 9, 20.

7   *Sages.* (חכמים: 25). Regarding the discussion of food and health, cf. B. Ḥullin; *Yore Deʻah* in Arbaʻa Turim and Shulḥan Arukh; Maimonides, *Moreh Nevukhim*, 3, 48; Nahmanides on Lev. 11:9. *Reshit Ḥokhmah*, I, p. 198f., explains the detrimental effect of bad foods on a mother's milk and of the effect of specific foods and beverages on children's characteristics.

    4a

11   *Maimonides.* (מיימני: 1). S. Mishneh Torah, *Hilkhot Deʻot*, 4:15: "Most of man's illnesses result only from bad eating, or from overfilling the stomach and eating

his mouth and tongue guards himself from trouble,"[50] means that one should guard his tongue from slander and his mouth from unhealthful foods, since many illnesses, God forbid, come from them. Therefore the verse uses a pleonasm, "his mouth and his tongue," in order to show that it applies all the more so for a woman. On this [King] Solomon,

5 peace be upon him, said, "Folly tears it down with its own hands."[51] This means, foolishness destroys her house willfully. King Solomon, peace be upon him, also said on this matter, "A house is built by wisdom, and is established by understanding;[52] by knowledge are its rooms filled with all precious and beautiful things."[53] This means in Yiddish, with wisdom the house will be built. That is to say, this also refers to the wisdom of the body,

10 which is compared to a house, as I wrote above. With reason is it maintained—this is the wisdom of the spirit, which is the soul—(this means) how a woman should take care of her soul. And with good sense her rooms will be filled with precious and valuable ornaments.

insufficiently minced food, even if the food is good. This is what Solomon meant when he said, in his wisdom, 'He who guards his mouth and tongue, guards himself from trouble' (Prov. 21:23). This means he should guard his mouth from eating bad food, or from eating to oversaturation, and (guard) his tongue from speaking, except when necessary." In this context, Maimonides does not mention slander.

3   *Pleonasm.* (כפל לשון :4).   The expression *kefel lashon* originates from the rabbinic discourse.

4   *All the more so.* (מכל שכן :4).   Expression from rabbinic discourse. While the warning of unhealthy eating and slander is earlier (fol. 3b) related specifically to men and women, the author here refers back to the preceding (fol. 3b) demand, whereby women must take more care of their bodies than men. The implied connection between food and specifically female biology is made in *Brantshpigl*, p. 273: "A pregnant woman must be careful not to be too wild or to pretend that she knows everything better. Also, when she nurses, she should not eat food that is unhealthy, and instead only food that strengthens the heart and fills the brain. Because during the entire pregnancy and nursing period, the child feeds of the mother's food. If she observes the things that I describe, the child will be easy to bring up, because it will have a good nature, and something good will become of it."

11   *Wisdom of the spirit.* (חכמת הנפש :11-10).   This is the only occasion where this expression is used, probably as a result of a mistake by the author or the printer, as a synonym for *hokhmat ha-neshamah.*

On *hokhmat ha-nefesh* see Ibn Ezra on Ps. 17:16 (regarding the difference between simple dreams and divine visions): "Not when the stomach is full, because that is only a dream in the waking phase. However, such vision is not a vision of the eye, rather a vision with awakened consciousness: these are the true visions of God. But such things will only be understood by one who has studied the wisdom of the spirit (*hokhmat ha-nefesh*)."

The term became known also through the book *Hokhmat ha-Nefesh* by Eleazar of Worms (12th century), which gained popularity, however, only after its first printing in the 19th century. In this book, the author designs a human psychology for which he discusses the significance of dreams, the relationship between the soul and the divine world, and the fate of the soul after death; cf. Scholem, *Jüdische Mystik* (Jewish Mysticism), p. 97. As to the terms, see the commentary on pp. 87/7 and 122/6.

This means to say that when she directs her body and soul in the proper paths, she will merit children who will be held to be more precious and valuable than pure gold.

On this one does not need to bring many proofs; we can also learn it from the verse, "He established households for them."[54] This means in Yiddish, and he makes them houses. This verse is located in relation to Jochebed and Miriam, where this verse also appears, "And because the midwives feared God."[55] This means that since they had fear of God in them, God, may He be blessed, [built] such houses for them, from which they merited to have children who became priests, Levites, and kings. And so it also says regarding Bezalel, who descended from Miriam, "He has endowed him with a divine spirit of knowledge, ability, and skill."[56] This means in Yiddish, and the spirit of God filled him with reason, insight, and wisdom. About this it is written in *Reshit Ḥokhmah*:[57] be it a man or a woman— the one who is God-fearing will merit to have the divine spirit rest upon her. Therefore

---

5   *Jochebed and Miriam.* (יוכבד אונ׳ מרים :17). Exod. 1:21 refers to the midwives Shiphrah and Puah, who are mentioned by name in Exod. 1:15; as to their interpretation as Jochebed and Miriam, the mother and sister of Moses, see B. Sotah 11b: "Shiphrah, that is Jochebed. Why was she named Shiphrah? Because she beautifies the child (derivation of Heb. *shifrah*—beauty). Another interpretation: Shiphrah, because in her days, Israel was fertile (derivation of Heb. *she-parah*—who was fertile), and multiplied. Puah, that is Miriam. Why was she named Puah? Because she parturiates (with the mother) (derivation of Heb. *pa'ah*—open the mouth; scream) and brings out the child."
These interpretations can also be found in *Brantshpigl*, pp. 75 and 341f.

6   *Fear of God.* (יראת שמים :18). See also the introductory chapter of *Brantshpigl*, p. 2, "'Come my sons, listen to me, I will teach you what it is to fear the LORD' (Ps. 34:12). 'The beginning of wisdom is the fear of the LORD; all who practice it gain sound understanding' (Ps. 111:10). King David, peace be upon him, said, the beginning of wisdom is the fear of God. Those who practice it, will gain sound understanding, praise of Him is everlasting. This means that whoever wishes to obtain God's wisdom and understanding must fear God and follow His commandments, as the holy Torah commands, (then) praise of him is everlasting."

8   *Priests.* (כהנים :19). S. B. Sotah 11b: "'And because the midwives feared God, He established households for them' (Exod. 1:21). Rav and Shemuel (discussed, and) one of them said: (this means) houses of the priests and Levites, and the other said: (it means) houses of kings."

8   *Bezalel.* (בצלאל :20). The *aggadah* construes Bezalel's descent from Miriam by equating her with Azubah, Bezalel's grandmother; cf. Shemot Rabbah 1.17, whereby Bezalel particularly inherited her wisdom, and Shemot Rabbah 1.16: "And Bezalel, who was filled with wisdom, descended from Miriam, 'I have endowed him with a divine spirit' (Exod. 31:3) etc."

9   *Knowledge.* (בדעת :21). The masoretic text of Exod. 35:31 differs slightly.

11   *Reshit Ḥokhmah.* (ראשית חכמה :23). S. *Reshit Ḥokhmah*, I, p. 646, §72: "If man abides by all mentioned virtues of grace, and by the other virtues discussed in this section, then the spirit of holiness will rest upon him."

every woman should hold herself in holiness and purity. As our sages write, everything depends upon a woman. As we also find in the *Froyen Bukh*,[58] much depends on the woman's thoughts. There is a midrash[59] about this verse in Ki Tavo, "Blessed shall be the issue of

4b

your womb, and the produce of your soil."[60] This means in Yiddish, the fruit of your stomach and the fruit of your earth will be blessed. Draw a parallel between "fruit of the [womb]" and "fruit of the earth"—the verse compares the fruit of the stomach to the fruit of the earth. This means as follows: when a gardener wants his garden to bear good fruit or good and tasty vegetables, he has to work hard and with great diligence. He must plough

1 ***Sages.*** (חכמים: 25). The formulation stating that "all depends on the woman" is not substantiated in rabbinic literature; see below.

2 ***Froyen Bukh.*** (פרואין בוך: 26). Cf. 10a: *Vroyen Bikhel*; cf. the section "Authorship and Provenance" in the Introduction.

2-3 ***Woman's thoughts.*** (אשה מחשבה: 27). Expression commonly used in *Eyn shoyn Froyenbuykhleyn*, e.g., fol. 5a: (!) ״אונ׳ דרום איז דיא ורויא בישאפן גיווארן אין דער ציהיטן זאג (!) אם וורייא טאג שפוט. נוהנט צו דען היילוגן שבת. צו ווייזן דז אן דען ורויען איז די —בישעפנש פאלינט גאר. דרום זיכשטו וואל דז אן דער ורויאן מחשבה ליגט דיא גנץ גנץ וועלט.״ "Woman was created on (the sixth day), late in the day on Friday, shortly before the holy Sabbath, in order to demonstrate that creation was completed with women. This may make you realize that the entire world depends on the woman's thoughts." *Eyn shoyn Froyenbuykhleyn* also mentions the importance of "thought," i.e., the correct attitude, in respect to the upbringing of children (fols. 6b; 34b; 38b), and the woman's conduct toward her husband (positive influence and modest sexuality; fols. 32b; 33a), which will be rewarded with pious and well-behaved children.

3 ***Midrash.*** (מדרש: 27). S. Devarim Rabbah 3.5: "Why does he compare the fruit of the body with the fruit of the soil? The Holy One, blessed be He, said: As the fruit of your soil grow generously, so shall the fruit of your body grow generously." Same in Yalkut, §848. Cf. Deut. 7:13.

3 ***Ki Tavo*** (כי תבא: 27). Weekly Torah reading, Deut. 26:1–29:8.

4b

5 ***Draw a parallel.*** (הקיש: 2). Term taken from the rabbinic discourse; interpretation on the grounds of equal or parallel setting.

7 ***Gardener.*** (גערטנר: 3). Cf. also the interpretations of Adam's work in *Gan Eden*, in Sifrei Devarim, §41; Pirkei de-Rabbi Eliezer, chap. 11; Yalkut, §22 on Gen. 2:15. The Midrash interprets the verse saying that what is meant is not the cultivation of *Gan Eden* itself, but that Adam studied the Torah and kept all the mitzvot. The source of the narrative details, and the transfer of the image (work in *Gan Eden*) onto the mother's work of raising her children (as an equivalent to Adam's *talmud Torah*), may possibly be the author herself.

  In *Meshiv Ḥema—Minhagim Eshet Ḥayil*, fol. 4a, the allegory of the gardener is repeated almost literally, but without mention of *Meneket Rivkah* as its source.

the field well, and must dig out all the harmful roots so that none remain. When the field is completely clear, he must first pick out the seeds so that no other grains are present. Then he can sow nicely in his garden. A woman is the same way: if she wants to have pious, upright children who will be raised to serve God and be God-fearing, she must improve
5   herself with her good deeds, and distance herself from evil deeds.

    Although she is always obligated in these things, she must be especially careful as soon as she becomes pregnant—even more than at other times—not to lie or gossip. She must also not steal, even when it is only a small thing, because the child could, God forbid, be raised to do the same. Such a woman should take on good deeds; she should listen gladly to
10   learning; and she should go to sermons. Thus will her children be raised to act the same

7   ***Pregnant.*** (טראגין 12:). The idea that the conduct of the pregnant and nursing woman exercises an influence on her child's character was widely shared during the early modern era; *Brantshpigl*, p. 302: "When the women are pregnant, they should only do good and pray to the Holy One, blessed be He. At the time of King David, the women prayed for strong children that would be undaunted in times of war, and would be dignified among the people, in order to obtain power," cf. Berger, Sexualität, pp. 250–269.

7-8   ***Lie*** [...] ***gossip*** [...] ***steal.*** בגניבה נעמן [...] רכילות טרייבן [...] ליגן 13:). Lying, gossiping (partially not unequivocally distinguished from *lashon ra*—slander), and stealing are harshly criticized in most Hebrew and Yiddish moral books. The first two, particularly, are even considered the gravest forms of social misconduct. In *Sefer Middot,* fol. 68b (similar on fols. 48a; 54a, 74a, 84a, 88a, particularly 69a–71a), gossip is described as the greatest sin: he who gossips is worse than a thief, and is on a level with a murderer, idolater, or adulterer, which is why he, like perpetrators of these three main sins, deserves the penalty of death (fol. 69a). Same in B. Sanhedrin 90a and *Reshit Ḥokhmah,* I, p. 262, §70. *Sefer Middot* explains as the reason for such rigor that murder or adultery are committed in the heat of passion and are regretted after the fact, whereas gossip is perpetrated consciously and continuously.
    S. *Brantshpigl*, p. 377: "But (the Rabbis) all agree that the Holy One, blessed be He, will hate no man more than the one who gossips or quarrels with other people." Similar in *Sefer Middot*, fol. 72a.
    Regarding lying, see for example *Brantshpigl*, p. 387: "And there is no difference between big and small lies. Even the smallest lie can lead to much evil. Even in case of life or death, one cannot trust (a liar) and not rely on his words. The people hate a liar."
    Regarding stealing, see *Brantshpigl*, p. 406: "If father and mother have this evil trait, and simply take whatever they want, the children will in most cases turn out like them. From a very young age they feel they must touch everything and squeeze it. One should make great efforts to teach them to stop it."

9-10   ***Listen gladly to learning.*** (הערין צו לערנן 15:). It is unclear whether this refers only to the immediate instruction of girls and women, as practiced by Rivkah bat Meir and other *firzogerins*, or whether it also refers to the men's in-house studies. No contemporary work besides *Meneket Rivkah* explicitly demands the participation of girls and women in any studies, even if only by passive listening.
    Regarding the education of girls, see the commentary on p. 164/4.

10   ***Sermons.*** (דרשות 15:). Even contemporary rabbinic sources call upon women to participate in the sermons given in synagogues; see *Reshit Ḥokhmah,* I, p. 197, §1. At the

way. As we find in our holy Torah, it is written relating to our mother Rebekah, "But the children struggled in her womb."[61] Rashi[62] gives the meaning as follows: When she passed by (houses) of idol worship, Esau wanted to come out, and when she passed by synagogues and study halls, Jacob wanted to come out. This explains where Esau's (behavior) came from. Jacob was pious since her thoughts were focused on Torah and good deeds. Esau, however, grew up crooked because the righteous woman sinned by passing by houses of idol worship. Although she had no intention of doing so, she still should not have passed them by, because by this she committed a sin.

As the Gemara[63] says, one should rather go to a whorehouse than to a house of idol worship. We learn this from the verse, "Do not come near the doorway of her house,"[64] which the Gemara[65] explains as idol worship. (The verse) means in Yiddish, you should not

time, the sermons, most probably given in Hebrew, could not be understood by either women or unlearned men; see *Brantshpigl*, p. 3: "There are also some who cannot always come to hear the sermon, in order to listen to the admonitions and instructions, so that they may learn how pious people are supposed to conduct themselves. And even if they go, it is often of no use to them, because they do not understand all that is said in the sermons. They include interpretations of the weekly Torah reading, Midrashim and stories, most of them in Hebrew. This applies particularly, if a *Targum* or kabbalistic material is presented. They also speak of obligations that women are not obligated to fulfill."

It is unclear, whether *Brantshpigl*'s request that unlearned men participate in the sermon nonetheless also applies to women; see ibid., p. 289: "Even if a person cannot read, he should still go to the synagogue, if the community is there. One should listen in silence and concentration, speak every benediction with dedication, and say 'Amen,' recite the *Kedushah* and the benediction."

The moral literature concedes, however, that women, despite the endorsement of communal prayer, often cannot go to the synagogue because of their domestic chores, particularly their care for small children, which constitutes their highest precepts; see the commentary on p. 159/22.

2   *Rashi.* (רש״י :18). S. Rashi on Gen. 25:22: "As she passed the gates of the teachings of the (divine) name, Jacob struggled to get out. As she passed the gates of idolatry, Esau struggled to get out."

The details of the description are more similar to Bereshit Rabbah 63.6: "'But the children struggled in her womb' (Gen. 25:22): When she stood before the synagogues and the houses of teaching, Jacob struggled to get out, as it is written, 'Before I created you in the womb, I selected you' (Jer. 1:5). When she passed the houses of idolatry, Esau pushed and struggled to get out, as it is written, 'The wicked are defiant from birth' (Ps. 58:4)."

3   *Synagogues.* (כנסיות :19). The Yiddish spelling is based on the Yiddish pronunciation.

4   *Explains.* (מתורץ :20). The term originates from the rabbinic discussion. Yiddish spelling is based on the Yiddish pronunciation.

5a

go near the door of a house of idol worship. Our commentators have many explanations on that verse that I do not need to write here.

All the more so, all other women must distance themselves from all that is not good. The following verse spoke on this matter, "The wisdom of women builds her house, but [folly] tears it down with its own hands."[66] We also learn it from the verse, "The LORD fashioned the rib."[67] This means, and he builds the rib that he took from the man. I have a difficulty here: Why did he use the language of *binyan* which means build, in reference to the woman, and in reference to the man he uses the word "*va-yaẓar*,"[68] which means in Yiddish, and he created—? It seems to me that the essence of building lies with the woman, as I wrote above. We learn this also from [our] mother Sarah, who said to Abraham, when she gave him Hagar, "Perhaps I shall be built up through her."[69] This means in Yiddish, maybe I will be built through her—she uses the language of *binyan* because she also wanted to build the world. For that reason Rachel also used the same language, "Perhaps I shall also be built up,"[70] just as Sarah merited. That is why we also say in the Seven Benedictions

1   *Commentators.* (מפרשים :27). Cf. Rashi on Prov. 5:6; *Avot de-Rabbi Natan*, A, chap. 2; Ba-midbar Rabbah 9.6; Yalkut, § 551.

    In the Yiddish midrash *Sefer Mishlei*, fol. 11a, the first part of Prov. 5:8 is interpreted as idolatry, the second part, which is quoted here, is interpreted as "evil woman."

5a

7   *Binyan* [...] *build.* (בוייאן [...] בניין :6). The author translates the noun *binyan*—building—with the verb "build." The exegetic connection between building a house, in Prov. 14:1 (*bantah*), and in creating a woman, in Gen. 2:22 (*va-yiven*), is made through the common root *b-n-h* (build; create). As to the rabbinic equalization of the female body with a house or vessel, cf. B. Niddah 31b.

8   *Va-yaẓar.* (ויצר :7). Cf. Gen. 2:19.

9   *Essence.* (עיקר :7). The idea of the woman as bearer of the main share in the creation of human life is presented by the author as her own interpretation ("it seems to me"). Her linguistic interpretation, which plays with the similarity between the roots of *b-n-h* (build) and *b-y-n* (realize; understand) is possibly influenced by B. Niddah 45b: "'And the LORD God fashioned the rib.' This teaches us that the Holy One, blessed be He, gave the woman more insight than He gave man."

10   *Above.* (אובן :8). See 3b–4a. Against the background of the interpretation of a "built house" and "building" as metaphors for the female body, the author ranks the woman's share in the emergence of human life higher than that of the man, because of her bodily processes (menstruation, pregnancy).

11   *I shall be built.* (איבנה :9). The interpretation plays with the polysemic root *b-n-h*, which means, in the Paʿal, "build," in the Nifʿal "become pregnant," "have children."

13   *Perhaps.* (אולי :12). The word is not included in Gen. 30:3; influenced by Gen. 16:2.

14   *Sarah.* (שרה :12). Both Sarah and Rachel only became pregnant late in life, by divine grace.

prayer, "And He prepared for him, from himself, an eternal building." This means that God, blessed be He, wants a person to direct his thoughts toward an eternal building. This refers to children, one after the other; or (it) refers to the soul, whose building is in the world to come, for eternity.

5 The verse that King Solomon, peace be upon him, said, "Wisdom has built her house, She has hewn her seven pillars,"[71] could also follow the interpretation that I wrote above, namely, that a woman should focus her thoughts on both the body and the soul. This is now the meaning of the verse: the prudent woman builds her house with seven columns. What does the verse mean by referring specifically to seven columns? It seems to me that

10 the intention of the verse was to speak specifically of seven columns, since our commentators,[72] as is known, have written that our dear God, blessed be His name, loves sevens.

At the creation of the universe, the Creator, blessed be His name, created the world in six days, and sanctified the seventh day. Additionally, he commanded us with the holidays— seven days of Passover and Sukkot; every seventh year, a *shemitah* year; a jubilee year follows

15 seven *shemitah* years; seven books of the Torah; in the seventh month, Rosh Hashanah;

---

1 *Prepared.* (והתקין : 13). The formulation is similar to the fourteenth benediction *Boneh Yerushalayim*; see *Mahzor Vitry*, 83: "Blessed be You, Lord, our God, King of the World, who created man by His image, by the image of His appearance, and has erected for him an eternal building. Blessed be You, Lord, creator of man."

8 *Prudent.* (קלוגי : 19). This is the beginning of a new interpretation of Prov. 9:1, where *hakhmot* is no more understood as plural, rather, by the exegetic connection between Prov. 14:1 and Prov. 9:1, as singular.

10 *Commentators.* (מפרשים : 22). S. Va-yikra Rabbah 23.11: "All forms of the number seven are dear to the world above." There, as well as in other rabbinic sources, various series of the number seven are described, of which, however, none corresponds with the series presented here. A large collection of sevens is found in *Ozar Midrashim*, p. 238, chap. 4: "Seven double consonants: *b-g-d-k-p-r-t*, which hold seven worlds, seven heavens, seven countries, seven seas, seven rivers, seven deserts, seven days, seven weeks, seven years, seven years of *Shemitah*, seven years of the *yovel*, and the (seventh) palace of the Holy One. Accordingly, the number seven is the dearest in heaven."
In the moral literature one mostly finds other forms of sevens; cf. *Brantshpigl*, p. 55; *Ze'enah u-Re'enah* on Lev. 9:1, p. 561; both in the context of the interpretation of Prov. 9:1.

14 *Shemitah.* (שמיטית : 26). Yiddish spelling *shmites* is based on Yiddish pronunciation. Regarding the year of *Shemitah*, see also Midrash Tehillim 72:2; *Ozar Midrashim*, p. 238, chap. 4; see also Deut. 15:1–2.

15 *Seven books.* (זיבן ספרים : 26). Regarding the counting of the Torah as seven books (with the segmentation of Numbers into three separate books: Num. 1:1–10:34; Num. 10:35–36; Num. 11:1–end), cf. B. Shabbat 116a; Va-yikra Rabbah 11.3; Yalkut, §729. Similar in *Sefer Mishlei*, fol. 20a.

15 *Seventh month.* (חדש השביעי : 27-26). According to the Bible (Exod. 12:1ff.), the counting of the calendar months begins in spring with the month of Nissan. The beginning of the year, on the other hand, is in the fall, in the seventh month, Tishri (Lev. 23:24).

out of seven deserts, the Holy One, blessed be He, chose the Sinai desert; from seven

5b

lands he took the Land of Israel. Moses, our teacher, the seventh of the Patriarchs, was privileged with the giving of the Torah; King David, the seventh brother, was privileged with kingship. The Holy One, blessed be He, also created seven heavens, and chose the seventh for his dwelling. God, blessed be He, let Joseph the Righteous understand the dream of seven cows and seven ears of corn. There are many more examples of sevens, not all of which I want to write here, since they all have one meaning. Their meaning is very deep and far-reaching, so that we cannot say much about it. This is also why we convert a dream to good seven times, and why we say, "The Lord is our God" seven times on Yom

1   *Seven deserts.* (זיבן מדברות :27). Cf. Midrash Tehillim 9:2; *Oẓar Midrashim*, p. 238.

5b

1-2   *Seven lands.* (זיבן לענדר :1). See *Midrash Mishlei*, 9:1; Yalkut, §944; *Oẓar Midrashim*, p. 238.

2   *Moses, our teacher.* (משה רבינו :1). Moses as "seventh father" does not correspond with chronology, and he is therefore not substantiated as such by the rabbinic sources; see Kallah Rabbati, 1:16: "I have concluded my bond with seven fathers, these are Abraham, Isaac, Jacob, Moses, Aaron, Phinehas and King David." The tradition of the seven fathers became known as the seven *Ushpizin*—guests—on Sukkot, particularly by their adaptation into the *Zohar*, III, 104a–b (which has Phinehas instead of Joseph). In the *Seder Ushpizin,* which has been included in the prayer books, the patriarchs are listed in chronological order.

3   *King David.* (דוד המלך :2). According to I Sam. 16:10f., Jesse showed Samuel his seven sons, but Samuel chose only the eighth, David.

4   *Seven heavens.* (זיבן הימל :4). The idea of God having created seven heavens, and having chosen the seventh for his own abode, is highly popular in rabbinic literature; cf. B. Menaḥot 39a; *Midrash* Tehillim 72:2; *Oẓar Midrashim*, p. 237.

6   *Seven cows and seven ears of corn.* (שבע פרות אונ' שבע שבלם :5). Cf. Gen. 41:1ff. The defective spelling for *shibbolim* is unusual.

6-7   *Not all.* (ניט אל :6). See the conventional rhetorical figure that ends mystical or philosophical subjects, e.g., Ibn Ezra on Exod. 2:1: "I shall not expand on it, but the understanding will understand." It is all the more surprising that the following lines contain additional examples for usage of the number seven.

8-9   *Convert a dream to good.* (חלום מטיב :8). Various prayer books (cf. Baer, Siddur Avodat Yisrael, p. 578f.) contain the so-called *seder hatavat ḥalom*—the order of turning a bad dream to good. Cf. B. Berakhot 55b, whereby three dream readers are to confirm the positive meaning of the dream by the sevenfold recitation of Bible verses containing words composed of the root *ṭet-vav-bet* (good).

9   *The Lord is our God.* (ה' הוא האלהים :9-8). Cf. the *Neʿilah* prayer at the end of Yom Kippur: the sevenfold praying of ה' הוא האלהים emphasizes God's oneness.

Kippur. And also for this reason, Balaam the Wicked had the intention of building seven altars, in order to destroy the nation of Israel, whose focus is directed entirely toward sevens, and has its dwelling in the seventh world, which is a single Shabbat, toward the world to come, which is the seventh millennium.

5　About this, Job says, "He will deliver you from six troubles; In seven no harm will reach you."[73] This means in Yiddish, God, blessed be He, will save you from six troubles. This means that in the 6,000 years that the earth has stood, as well as in the seventh millennium, you will not know to report of any evil. Referring to this King Solomon, peace be upon him, also alluded to "The wisdom of women has built her house, She has hewn

10　her seven pillars."[74] That is why he also uses the feminine, because the unflawed woman, who keeps her seven clean (days) correctly, will merit to have children who will achieve

1-2　　　*Seven altars.* (זיבן מזבחות :10). See Num. 23:1ff.

3　　　*Seventh world.* (עולם השביעי :12-11). Regarding the idea that a world was created on every day of creation, and that therefore the Sabbath constitutes the seventh world, see *Pirkei de-Rabbi Eliezer*, 19: "The Holy One, blessed be He, created six worlds, in which war and peace alternate, and the seventh world is a Sabbath and the peace of eternal life."

4　　　*Seventh millennium.* (אלף השביעי :12). S. B. Sanhedrin 97a: "The teaching is according to Rav Katina: As the seventh year is left out once every seven years, so the world leaves out one millennium every seven thousand years." Cf. also Ibn Ezra on Lev. 31:13. A supporter of the teaching of the *Shemitah* millennium was the Prague scholar Mordecai b. Abraham Jaffe; see the section "Sources and Their Editing" in the Introduction.

5　　　*Troubles.* (צרה :13). The masoretic text of Job 5:19 differs slightly.

9　　　*Wisdom of women.* (חכמת נשי׳ :16). The misquote of Prov. 9:1 is founded on a conflation of Prov. 14:1 and Prov. 9:1. It is conspicuous that the Prague author Samuel Shmelke ben Ḥayyim opens the introduction of his *Seder Nashim-Vayberbukh* (Prague, 1620) with the same misquote of Prov. 9:1. The seven pillars are interpreted as the days on which the woman dresses in white, which corresponds with the seven clean days (see below). *Eyn shoyn Froyenbuykhleyn* does not quote Prov. 9:1.

11　　　*Seven clean (days).* (שבעה נקיים :18). The seven days following the termination of menstruation, during which the woman is subject to various restrictions (see Lev. 15:28), and at the end of which she concludes the *niddah* phase in the ritual bath; see also B. Niddah 66a. The Hebrew expression, taken from the halakhic context, is occasionally used in the Yiddish ethic-halakhic literature, such as in *Eyn shoyn Froyenbuykhleyn*, fol. 7b; more common in Yiddish, however, is *ziben rayne teg*—seven clean days—, e.g., ibid., fols. 10a, or *vays an legen*—to dress in white—, e.g., ibid., fol. 9b.

　　　See also *Brantshpigl*, p. 252: "Beginning with the moment, in which she has her period, she should examine herself for seven days. On the seventh day she is pure. She should then don white, clean clothing and put white sheets (on the bed). After having cleaned or washed herself, she dons better clothes than during the first seven days, and she does not need to stay all that far away from her husband." Similar in ibid., pp. 255, 260. On *niddah* see also the commentary on p. 162/8.

this, and will have faith in the Unique One, blessed be He, who is the one Lord of the [six Ends]. This too is an allusion to the significance of sevens. And it is also the meaning of the *menorah* that God, blessed be His name, ordered Moses to make, commanding him, "And mount its seven lamps."[75] But since he said, "So for all six branches issuing from the
5 menorah,"[76] the meaning must be as follows: the body of the *menorah* indicates a woman; the six branches are the six chapters that I will write, God willing, after this chapter, and all of which relate to a woman. That is to say that she should follow the six chapters along with the first, which is (like) a body to the other six chapters. Thus every woman should focus

6a

her intentions, so that she should merit having children who will be able to acquire the
10 seven steps. That is what the verse means with "She has hewn her seven pillars."[77] About such a woman, another verse says, "She is not worried for her household because of snow;

1   ***This.*** (ראש : 19). The reference of the predicative demonstrative pronoun is not unequivocal; it either relates to the idea of the seventh millennium (see above), or to the belief in God's oneness and rule (see below).

1-2   **[*Six Ends*]**. (ושש קצוות] :20). S. Ibn Ezra on Songs 5:15: "'His legs are': The (one divine) body, of which the world was created. 'Like marble pillars': Because he has six ends." Similar in *Ozar Midrashim*, p. 237.
         The term is borrowed from the mythical idea of the divine image of man; so, e.g., in the *Hekhalot* literature, cf. Schäfer, *Synopse* [Parma], fol. 6a/28 (*Massekhet Hekhalot*).

3   ***Make.*** (העלה : 20). The masoretic text of Exod. 25:37 differs distinctly.

4   ***So.*** (כן : 23). Cf. Exod. 37:19.

5   ***Body.*** (גוף : 24). The equalization of the body of the *menorah* with the woman's body is described in further detail on fol. 6b. Here, describing the *menorah* as a body, from which six further arms extend, the author, in the interpretation of the number seven, moves on to the one-plus-six concept.
         See accordingly *Zohar*, I, p. 264: "'In the image of God He created him; male and female He created them' (Gen. 1:27). And these are (the six ends of the male body): the right and the left leg, the right and the left hand, the body, and the circumcised foreskin. These, however, are only six, although you said seven. They become seven with his woman."

7   ***Chapters*** (שערים : 25). Here the author puts the seven chapters of her book into the exegetic context to her one-plus-six concept, cf. the section "Structure" in the Introduction.

         6a

10   ***Seven steps.*** (מעלות ז' :1). S. Ezek. 40:22 (Seven steps to the temple). The identification of the seven steps with seven heavens is common; see also the commentary on p. 97/4. Regarding the seven steps as seven levels (classes) of righteous in *Gan Eden*, cf. *Ozar Midrashim*, p. 94.
         Cf. the theosophical explanation of the seven steps in Ibn Ezra on Exod. 23:20.

For her whole household is dressed in crimson,"[78] which means that she does not need to fear *Geihinnom*, as the verse says, "Like a snowstorm in Zalmon."[79] *Reshit Ḥokhmah*[80] explains it that way, and King David, peace be upon him, also says, "Your wife shall be like a fruitful vine within your house."[81] In Yiddish this means, your wife will be like a grapevine that stands by the side of your house. The Gemara[82] explains the verse as follows: Just as a fruitful vine is to be blessed, so a fruitful woman is to be blessed.

When one sees a well-behaved child, one says: "To the well-being of the mother who carried that child!" King David, peace be upon him, said about this, "I became your charge at birth; from my mother's womb You have been my God."[83] This means, while I was still in my mother's womb, I knew that you are my God, because of my mother's good thoughts. God, may He be blessed, spoke on this matter to Jeremiah the Prophet, peace be upon him, "Before I created you in the womb, I selected you."[84] This means, before I created you in your mother's belly, I loved you. In this regard, the midrash[85] explains the

1   *Dressed in crimson.* (לבוש שני 3:). The masoretic text of Prov. 31:21 differs slightly. Instead of the translation, what follows is the interpretation of *sheleg*—snow—as *Geihinnom* with Ps. 68:15: "When Shaddai scattered the kings, it seemed like a snowstorm in Zalmon." The connection between the verses is created by the Hebrew root sh-l-g. The biblical spelling *shani*—crimson in Prov. 31:21 may also be read as the Yiddish *shne*—snow; cf. the interpretation of Prov. 31:21 on fol. 33b and the respective commentary.

2   *Reshit Ḥokhmah.* (ראשית חכמה 4:). Most probably attributed by mistake to *Reshit Ḥokhmah*; see ibid., I, p. 267, §75: "Fierce fire, snow, and stormy winds set out from this palace, to judge the evil ones, as it is written, 'It seemed like a snowstorm in Zalmon' (Ps. 68:15)." Same on fol. 33b.

3   *Your wife.* (אשתך 5:). The second half of verse Ps. 128:3, "Your sons, like olive saplings around your table," is not quoted, but it implicitly forms the transfer to the following homily, which deals with the children's piety as a result of their mother's good thoughts.
S. Midrash Tehillim 128:3: "'Your wife shall be like a fruitful vine' (Ps. 128:3). When is your wife like a fruitful vine? When she is modest 'within your house' (ibid.), then 'your sons shall be like olive saplings' (ibid.)."

5   *Gemara.* (גמרא 7:). This interpretation constitutes a compilation of various rabbinic sources; see Va-yikra Rabbah 36.2: "What is the meaning of this vine? It brings forth grapes, it brings forth raisins. Such is Israel: among them there are Torah scholars, Mishnah scholars, Talmud scholars, *aggadah* scholars. What is the meaning of this vine? It brings forth wine, and it brings forth vinegar. The one requires a benediction, as does the other. Such is Israel: they must speak a blessing over the good as well as over the evil."
S. Ruth Zuta 4, 11: "Every one who marries an unflawed woman (*ishah kesherah*), is, as if he fulfilled the entire Torah, from the beginning to the end, and of him it is said, 'Your wife shall be like a fruitful vine' (Ps. 128:3) etc. Therefore, the (praise) of the *eshet ḥayil* (Prov. 31:10) was written from *aleph* to *tav*. The generations shall be delivered only by the merit of the righteous women that live in that (generation)."
Same in Yalkut, §606. Similar interpretations of Prov. 128:3 among others, in Bereshit Rabbah 63.3; Shemot Rabbah 16.2.

13   *Midrash.* (מדרש 14:). S. Midrash Tehillim 68:14: "'In assemblies bless God' (Ps. 68:27). These are the children. 'From the fountain of Israel' (ibid.). These are the

verse, "Bless God, the LORD, O you who are from the fountain of Israel."[86] In Yiddish this means, praised be God, blessed be His name, from the source of Israel. This means that children in the womb praise God, blessed be His name, which means that when [Israel] went through the sea, the children sang, "This is my God and I will glorify Him."[87] This

5   means in Yiddish, this is my God and I will glorify Him. The child let the breast out of his mouth and sang *Shirah*. We learn all of this from the verse, "God, from the fountain of Israel"[88]—even the baby in the womb sang *Shirah*. King Solomon, peace be upon him, said on this, "Let your fountain be blessed; Find joy in the wife of your youth."[89] This means, your origin will be blessed if you rejoice with your wife.

10   This refers to a respectable woman, whose thoughts are occupied only with good. Such a woman should associate only with pious people and should accustom herself to read Yiddish books. If she cannot read, then she should listen to others read or listen to sermons, as we find with Deborah the Prophetess, who said, "My heart is with Israel's leaders."[90] This means, my heart is attached to the scholars of Israel. She was privileged that the

15   salvation of Israel occurred through her, because she favored the scholars.

6b

The meaning of the *menorah* could also be that a good woman can be compared to it, just as a good woman can be compared to our Torah, since we learn from the verses,

---

unborn inside their mothers. This comes to teach us that every individual pointed to the *Shekhinah* with his finger and said, 'This is my God, and I will exalt him' (Exod. 15:2)."

4   *I will glorify him.* (ואנוויהו :17). The masoretic text of Exod. 15:2 reads slightly different.

4   *Children.* (קינדר :17). Allusion to Exod. 15:1.

12   *Yiddish books.* (טייטשי ספרי' :24). Cf. in *Eyn shoyn Froyenbuykhleyn*, fol. 24a, the call to read Yiddish books, so as not to commit a transgression. Otherwise, Yiddish ethic literature does not call to read Yiddish books. There is, however, the call to read contemporary books, as in the *Sefer Middot*, fols. 6a; 56b; 84b; *Eyn shoyn Froyenbuykhleyn*, fol. 37a; *Brantshpigl*, pp. 25; 72 and in other places; *Iggeret Derekh ha-Shem*, fol. 12b.

12   *Sermons.* (דרשות :25). See the commentary on p. 93/10.

14   *Scholars.* (לערנר :27). The translation of *ḥokekei*—leaders, legislators—in Judg. 5:9 with "scholars" emphasizes the author's argumentation that esteem of scholarship are part of the woman's good thoughts.

6b

16   *Meaning.* (כוונה :1). Recourse to the exegetic equalization of the *menorah* with the woman in 5b. To that end, the homiletic detour through the equalization of the good woman with the Torah is chosen hereafter.

17   *Verses.* (פסוקים :3). This most probably refers to Prov. 14:1 and Prov. 9:1.

"Wisdom has built her house."[91] This refers to the Torah as well as to a good woman. King Solomon, peace be upon him, ended Proverbs with (the praise of) "The Woman of Valor" and therefore ordered it alphabetically. He did that nowhere else in [Proverbs], in order that one should know that a good woman is equal to the entire Torah. Just as the Torah
5 without one letter cannot exist, so too a good woman should be complete with only good deeds toward God, blessed be His name, and toward people.

And just as our beloved Torah wishes us to follow its commandments so that it can give us our recompense, so too a good woman would wish to see her children become upright. That is why she is also similar to the pure *menorah* which is, in Yiddish, the pure cande-
10 labrum. God, may He be blessed, showed to Moses, our teacher, in heaven how it should be made, and commanded him to make it from one piece of clear, pure gold. Now, since it was made in one piece, and from clear, pure gold, that gold had to be all the same, and the very best. One can find many different kinds of gold: Hungarian gold, gold crowns, and Rhenish gold. I also wanted to say that for the buds, goblets, and flowers that were designed on (the
15 *menorah*), I could not use any other gold, since it had to be made of one piece.

This is also the significance of a woman: if her thoughts are good and her husband's thoughts are also good, they will have children who will be unblemished and pure in their piety. For that reason the verse says, "So for all six branches issuing from the menorah."[92] This is an allusion to the fact that the children of such a woman will be unflawed.
20 I could also mention a different meaning—the *menorah* has been compared to olive oil. It is well known, an established fact perennially, at all times, that the capsules of the *menorah* into which the oil was poured needed to be pure, along with the olive oil as well as the wicks. When it was all prepared such that everything was pure, the light burned

---

4   *Is equal.* (גיוואגן 6:). Regarding the traditional equalization of Prov. 31:10–31, the only section of Proverbs set alphabetically, with the entire Torah; cf. also Yalkut, §§ 964; 606.

5   *Letter.* (אות 7:). Regarding the rabbinic idea, the Torah could not continue to exist if it were to be missing merely one letter or word; cf. Y. Sanhedrin 20c; Va-yikra Rabbah 19.3.

10   *Moses, our teacher.* (משה רבינו 12:). Allusion to Exod. 25:31ff.

13   *Many different kinds of gold.* (פילר ליי גאלד 16:). Being the emperor's residence (since 1584) and important central European center of commerce, many foreign emissaries and merchants resided in Prague, which is why many different currencies were in use. Dealing with and exchange of foreign currency constituted an important source of income for the Jews; cf. Herman, "Wirtschaftliche Betätigung" (Economic Activities), p. 34ff.

16-17   *Husband's thoughts.* (מאנש מחשבה 20:). The share of the man's good thoughts in the successful education of the children is rarely found in moral literature; see the commentary on p. 103/3–4.

7a

more clearly and purely, even when only a drop (of pure oil) was in them. But when something wasn't clean, whether the capsules into which one poured the oil, or the olive oil, or the wicks, then the light would burn darkly and would burn out early. So too a woman and her husband, if they are pious and upright and have many good deeds, will have upright
5   children, who also will have many good deeds and will be luminaries in the Torah. (The Torah) is here compared to a light, and the flame of the light is compared to a soul, as the verse says, "The soul of man is the lamp of the LORD."[93]

Sometimes it happens that the flame extinguishes, although the lamp, the oil, and the wicks are all clean. This happens, for example, when a wind blows through a window,
10 although one could easily have prevented it. So too when the father and the mother are pious, and the child is a jewel, a wind can come through a window, God protect us, and

7a

3-4   ***And her husband. (אויך דער מאן‎‎ :5).*** Regarding the mainly caring education by the mother, and punishing education by the father, cf. *Brantshpigl*, pp. 15; 26; 50; 72; 123; 154; and *Reshit Ḥokhmah*, III, p. 55, §§1ff.; regarding the educational responsibility of both parents, cf. *Brantshpigl*, pp. 301f.; 305; 331; 338ff.; regarding the idea that the father's help is rather subordinate, cf. ibid., p. 343.

Regarding fatherly help in the education toward piety and erudition, cf. ibid., p. 257. Regarding the father's main share as provider of economic security to the children, cf. ibid., p. 41; regarding the man's educational tasks, *Sefer Middot* lists the beating of the children (fol. 27b), and prohibiting gossip and lies (fol. 76b). *Eyn shoyn Froyenbuykhleyn*, fol. 6a, describes that the woman educates the children, since the man is not at home during the day (cf. fol. 23b: here the author implies that the woman is always at home). *Sefer Middot*, fol. 22b, formulates that the woman educates the children on behalf of the man.

The mother's and father's responsibility is reflected in the reward for good education, and in the punishment that they will suffer in the event of non-fulfillment of their educational tasks, or in the event of the bad example they provide by their own social misconduct. Regarding the bad character of children of a mother who divorces herself, cf. *Brantshpigl*, p. 399; regarding illness or death of children as a result of bad education by the mother, ibid., p. 106; the indecent man, too, is in danger of ending up with impious children (ibid., p. 107) or leprous children (ibid., pp. 246, 259). See *Sefer Middot*, fol. 97b, whereby women obtain their share in the world to come solely by good education of children; same in *Reshit Ḥokhmah*, III, p. 197, §1.

5   ***Luminaries. (לייכטן‎ :6).*** See the blessing following the lighting of the Sabbath candles in *Eyn shoyn Froyenbuykhleyn*, fol. 4a: ‏"אונ׳ דער נאך זאל זי זאגן די [ברכה] יהי רצון שיהיו בני מאירים בתורה ובמלאכת שמים: דז איז אין טויטשין עז זאל זיין ווילן זיין דאז זי זאלן לייכטן מיין קינדר אין דער תורה אונ׳ אין וערק דש הימל."‏—"After that, she should say the (blessing): May it be the will that my sons shall shine in matters of Torah and in the performance of mitzvot. This means in Yiddish, may it be His will that my children shall shine in matters of Torah and in the work of heaven."

9   ***Window. (פענשטר‎ :12).*** The image of the lethal draft through the window, for the death of the child as a result of inadvertent sins, is possibly influenced by Jer. 9:20.

extinguish the flame. This means that one sinned unintentionally. But whoever plans ahead can certainly prevent wind from coming to the light.

So must a woman be warned to pay attention to her house servants, so that, God forbid, no sins take place in her house. Even if she had no part in it, she should not have to atone for it, God forbid. As it says in the *Sefer Ḥasidim*: If, God forbid, a sin occurs in his house, and there was someone who could have prevented it but did not, he must, God protect us, pay the consequences.

If sins take place in a city, the individual who can prevent them but does not must, God forbid, pay for them. If a sin takes place in a country, the greatest figure of the generation who can prevent it must, due to our many transgressions, pay for it. We have seen how recently, due to our many transgressions, such important figures and pious saints had to leave in their youth, due to our many transgressions—may God, blessed be He, remove his rod from us. He should remove his wrath from us.

5   *Sefer Ḥasidim.* (ספר חסיד׳ 16:). Similar in *Sefer Ḥasidim*, § 538: "Somebody had a slave or a maid in the house, whether non-Jewess or Jewess, and the master of the house ordered his son: 'May you be warned that you shall send her away!' After the master of the house died, the son said that mishap has happened by her hands, which thus had helped to commit a sin. He therefore asked a sage what he should do. The sage replied: 'It is an obligation to abide by the words of a deceased. (This applies) to matters that do not lead to sin. However, if a sin is committed by any matter, it need not be abided by.'" Here is the aspect of the master's responsibility of the house missing, as well as his warning preceding the sin, which is the topic of *Sefer Ḥasidim*, § 592: "Who is a wise advisor? He who knows how to provide good advice that does not lead to an impediment. And if an impediment occurs, despite having given good advice, then, because the impediment occurred, it was not good advice, and he is not a wise advisor, which is only he who knows how to warn, that his advice shall not lead to sin, and to no evil."

7   *Pay the consequences.* (באד אויז גיסין 19:). Literally: Pour out the bath (tub). References for this expression, meaning "pay the consequences of an unpleasant matter," exist ever since the 16th century; cf. Röhrich, *Lexikon*, vol. 1, p. 131.

10   *Due to our many transgressions.* (בעו״ה 20:). The expression reflects the widespread idea that individuals, or a group, must pay for Israel's sins, and be punished; here it receives the additional meaning that because of the sins of individuals even more sins are committed; cf. below and fols. 7b; 9b; 13a; 16a; 18a; 20b; 26a; 26b; 32b.

11   *Important figures.* (גדולי הדור 22:). The characteristic linguistic style ("we have seen") indicates an allusion to real events; it is unclear whether reference to any personalities of Prague is made and to which. Joseph Ashkenazi (d. 1577) left Prague in 1560, after he intended to ban Maimonides on the grounds of heresy, whereupon he himself was threatened with the ban. The sensational departure of the *Maharal* to Poznan in 1592 was a result of conflicts within the community. These are commonly referenced for the 16th century, particularly from the 1530s (between the Horowitz family and part of the community), and the 1570s, in connection with the election of the community Elders; cf. Goldberg, *Crossing*, p. 93f.; Herman, "Conflict," p. 46f., Wolf, "Geschichte," (History), p. 311ff.

12   *Remove.* (יסיר 23:). See Job 9:34.

I must write yet about something I have seen—a great desecration of God's name, which takes place, due to our many transgressions, with Christian maids in *Rayser* Land. I have seen this great impurity: On Friday night, after everyone had gone to sleep, she washed the dishes in a basin used for dairy. Her mistress also kept cows, and would rinse off the

7b

dishes in the milk basin. Then I also saw that they slaughtered geese, and the Christian maid took the heads and put them in the basin for dairy products and poured hot water over them. I told this to her mistress, who answered, "I don't believe it—she's served here for many years."

2   ***Christian maids.*** (שקצות 25:). *Shikses*, pejorative Yiddish term for "gentile women," derived from *shekez*—disgusting, abomination; cf. Deut. 7:26 regarding the designation of idols, or Lev. 7:21 and other places regarding the designation of all impure prohibited animals. The usage of this word is unusual in the Yiddish moral literature. Instead, common designation is *goyah*—gentile woman, as on fol. 23a. Cf. *Brantshpigl*, e.g., pp. 221, 243, 416; *Eyn shoyn Froyenbuykhleyn*, fols. 12b; 17b; *Sefer Middot*, fols. 78a; 88b; here, as on fol. 7b, it serves as rhetorical enforcement of the "great desecration of God's name" by the Christian maids.

     Cf. the critical statements regarding Christian servants, particularly Christian cooks, in *Brantshpigl*, p. 135: "If you have a gentile man or woman in the house, you must have your eyes everywhere, even if they had been with Jews for a long time. One must constantly be on the watch to keep them from doing things that are *trefe*, because they cannot be trusted.... It would be preferable to manage without them.... One cannot allow a gentile maid to cook by herself, because one would not prevent (a transgression)."

     Cf. ibid., p. 135ff.; regarding the rejection of Christian wet-nurses, because of their *trefe* milk, see ibid., p. 136; regarding the warning of Christian nannies, who take children along to churches and get them used to "idolatry," see ibid., p. 138f.; regarding the warning of Christian maids as sexual threat to servants, boarders, and juvenile sons, see ibid., p. 139.

2   ***Rayser Land.*** (רייסר לנד 25:). The expression is not common, therefore it is uncertain which area the author refers to; Krakow 1618 reads the same. Contemporary literature used the words *Raysen*, such as, Pinkas Va'ad Arba Arazot, wherein Halperin assumes Russia; cf. Halperin, Pinkas, p. 508. An additional 17th century source differentiates between *Ashkenaz, Polin, Pehem, Raysen*—Germany, Poland, Bohemia, *Raysen*; cf. Assaf, *Mekorot*, II, p. 137. The latter probably corresponds with the designation *Rus* or *Rusya* in various historiographic texts from the middle of the 17th century, meaning Ruthenia (Rus), possibly also parts of Belarus, cf. Weinreich, *Bilder* (Pictures), pp. 201, 216 (*Raysen*). Many Jews of the Polish-Lithuanian republic had settled in Ruthenia, particularly since the 1570s, which explains the existence of a relatively tight net of Jewish communities; cf. Stone, *Polish-Lithuanian State*, p. 203f.; Goldberg, *Privileges*, pp. 31–54.

4   ***Dishes.*** (דאז גפעס 26:). Literally "the crockery," "the vessels" here probably refers to the dairy dishes, which the maid and the housewife inserted, together, into a "milk basin". However, since the maid had not correctly separated meat from dairy (see below), rinsing the dairy dishes in a nonkosher basin constituted a transgression of the rules of *kashrut*.

Later something else happened with a different Jewish woman: On Yom Kippur afternoon she had the oven heated up and let the Christian maid stuff chickens, so that when everyone came home from synagogue, everything would be ready. She herself stood there the whole time and directed (the maid), "Do it like this, and like this!" I asked her,

5 "Why did you do this? Isn't it a sin?" She answered, "This is how I've seen it done, and this is how I've always done it."

I would not have written this, but as we say, "One does not punish unless he has also warned." This means, "One does not harm anyone by warning him that such a thing must never occur."

10 This is also what the verse refers to, "The wisdom of women builds her house, but folly tears it down with its own hands."[94] This means that she destroys her house willfully. Therefore every woman should be cautious, and should pay attention to her servants. A woman is responsible for everything: for her husband, for her children, and for her servants. She should specifically not tolerate oaths or, God protect us, curses

15 in her house—the [views] (on this) are not all the same, God protect us. We learn from our Patriarch Jacob that Rachel died for this reason—the righteous man knew nothing

7b

4   ***Do it like this.*** (מכש אזו 8:). The transgression of the *halakhah* is that the housewife gives her maid direct orders, which is fundamentally prohibited on Sabbath and on the religious holidays; cf. Shulḥan Arukh, *Oraḥ Ḥayyim*, 252:1ff. *Sefer Middot*, fol. 91b, describes the "grave sin" of giving non-Jews direct orders on a Sabbath, to light a fire, or to perform other work. The described situation included, in addition, the transgression of the *halakhah* under the aspect of *bishul goyim* (cooking by non-Jews), which prohibits the eating of food that had been prepared exclusively by non-Jews: only if the housewife herself prepares the food, puts it on the fire, and brings it to boil is a gentile woman permitted to conclude the cooking procedure. Cf. Shulḥan Arukh, *Yore Deʿah*, 113.

7   ***One does not.*** (אין 11:). S. B. Sanhedrin 56b: "One may only punish, if the punishment is preceded by a warning." This principle ultimately criticizes the Jewish housewives that do not fulfill their responsibility for the observance of all commandments in the house.

14   ***Oaths*** [...] ***curses.*** (קללות [...] שבועות 16:). Regarding swearing, see the commentary on p. 121/17. *Eyn shoyn Froyenbuykhleyn*, fol. 48b, lists making vows, cursing, and, as the most severe sin, swearing as typically female bad habits.

15   ***[Views].*** (דעות] 17:). The emendation makes sense as the claim of careless "views" regarding cursing is followed by the apotropaic formula "God protect us"; cf. the same expression on fols. 12b; 13b; 32a.

16   ***Our Patriarch Jacob.*** (יעקב אבינו 18:). This refers to the event concerning the *terafim*, the house deities of Rachel's father, Laban, which she steals (Gen. 31:19). Laban accuses Jacob of theft. Jacob denies the accusation and calls for death to befall the real thief, not knowing that it is Rachel who is responsible (Gen. 31:32). Only in the rabbinic literature is a connection made between Rachel's death (Gen. 35:18) and the curse; cf. Bereshit Rabbah 74.4.

about it, but she was punished anyway. All the more so, anyone else should be on guard against this.

Once I saw a woman who lost material from Cologne for a shirt. She began to make a curse that one should make shrouds out of the cloth for the person who stole it. Afterward she found the Cologne cloth, and made a shirt out of it. It wasn't thirty days, due to our many transgressions, before she was laid in the ground along with her shirt. This is why one should be warned about cursing.

A woman should also be cautious with and pay attention to the cleanliness of her house, particularly where one prays, or religious books are, or near the *mezuzah.* Also with her bearing, with her hair, as well as all other issues of modesty, about which I do not even

8a

need to write or emphasize their necessity. It is written in our Torah, "Let Him not find anything unseemly among you."[95] This means in Yiddish, no disgraceful things should be

1   *Punished.* (נענוש :19). Defective conflation of the two passive forms: *ne'enash* in the Nif'al case, and *anush* as passive participle in the Pa'al case—probably based on the Yiddish pronunciation.

3   *I saw.* (איך גזעהן :20). The report extends the preceding warning of the consequences of a curse by the danger that the curse may hit the curser himself; cf. Va-yikra Rabbah 15.7: "Rabbi Levi said: 'Blessings bless their master, and curses curse their master.'"

3   *From Cologne.* (קעלניש :20). "Koelsh" is the designation of a bluish, or blue striped, fabric; cf. Grimm, *Lexikon,* II, p. 1622.

10   *Hair.* (האירן :26). S. in that matter *Brantshpigl*, p. 110f.: "A woman must also handle her hair modestly. None of it shall show and be visible, as that would be a great sin and disgrace. The sages of the Kabbalah write that every woman must guard her modesty very much, particularly in respect to her hair. Much terrible suffering will otherwise descend from heaven on her, on her husband, and on her children, and it brings poverty into their home. It is said, on behalf of Rabbi Shimon ben Yohai, 'If one hair shows on a woman, the evil spirits come, descend (on the house) and spoil everything in the house.'... And if the women would understand what is written in the book *Zohar* on behalf of Rabbi Yehiskiyah, namely how much evil results from a woman showing her hair: her house is cursed, and her children despised—then she would take great care to make sure that not a single hair shows."

S. *Eyn shoyn Froyenbuykhleyn*, fol. 47a–47b: אונ' בפרט דז איין איקלכי פרומי פרויא זול"
אירה טאכטר לערנן אונטר ווייזן ווען זי איין מאן נעמט וויא זיא זיך זול בצניעות אונ' יודיש
האלטן דש זיא ניט זול לאשן זעהן קיין פרעמדן מאן אירי האר נאך אירן לייב נוך אירי בריסט
ניט הרויש לאשן גין נאך אירה פיס ניט בלייס צו זעהן"—"And every woman must particularly teach (and) instruct her daughter, how to conduct herself modestly and in a Jewish way, when she takes a man: that she may not let any strange man see her hair or her body, nor should she allow her breasts or her feet to show."

8a

12   *Disgraceful things.* (ערות דבר :1). Cf. Deut. 24:1.

seen among you. As the verse says, "Since the LORD your God moves about in your camp, let your camp be holy."[96] In Yiddish this means, when [God] moves among your groups, your groups shall be holy. The verse goes on, "Let Him not find anything unseemly among you and turn away from you."[97] If you, God forbid, do not keep your camp pure, or your appearance modest, the *Shekhinah* will, God forbid, be removed from you. If you do, however, keep yourselves holy and pure, the *Shekhinah* will rest upon Israel.

About this issue, it is also said, as the Gemara[98] has it: "The seal of the Holy One, blessed be He, is truth (*EMeT*)." It is composed of the first letter of the alphabet, *aleph*, and the middle letter, *mem*, and the final letter, *tav*. This means that God, blessed be He, was, is, and will be. A verse also says, "Truth is the essence of your word."[99] Here it is meant the *aleph* from *anokhi* (I). If a person, God forbid, does not follow the proper path, and breaks the (law of) *anokhi*, the Holy One, blessed be He, [will take] away the *aleph* from *EMeT*, leaving *MeT* (dead). The Gemara says, "There are three partners in a person: his father, his mother, and the Holy One, blessed be He."[100] In Yiddish this means: three have partnership in a person—the Holy One, blessed be He, the father and the mother. When God, blessed be He, takes away his share—which is the soul, then he is dead. On this matter the verse said, "And turn away from you."[101]

---

5   **Modest.** (צניעות 5:).   Modesty as an ideal of female conduct is mentioned only marginally here, whereas it is otherwise strongly emphasized in moral literature; see also the commentary on pp. 83/10 and 160/23.

7   **Gemara.** (גמרא 8:).   S. B. Shabbat 55a: "Resh Lakish said, 'The letter *tav* is the end of the seal of the Holy One, blessed be He, as Rabbi Ḥanina said: The seal of the Holy One, blessed be He, is truth.' Rabbi Shemuel bar Naḥmani (said), 'These are the men who kept the entire Torah, from *aleph* to *tav.*'" Similar in B. Yoma 69b; B. Sanhedrin 64a.
           Most similar in Bereshit Rabbah 81.2: "What is the seal of the Holy One, blessed be He? Our teacher said in the name of Rabbi Reuven, 'Truth.' What is truth? Resh Lakish said, '*Aleph* is at the beginning, *mem* is in the middle, and *tav* is at the end.' This is taken from, 'I am the first and I am the last' (Isa. 44:6) etc."

11   **Anokhi.** (אנכי 11:).   Cf. Gen. 26:24; Exod. 4:11; Exod. 20:2.5; Deut. 5:6.9; Isa. 43:11.
           Regarding the exegetic connection between *emet* and *anokhi* see Rashi on Ps. 119:160: "'The beginning of your words is truth.' The end of your words testifies the beginning, which is the truth. This is how it was, when the nations heard, 'I am' (Exod. 20:2), and 'You shall have' (Exod. 20:3), and 'You shall not swear' (Exod. 20:7)."

13   **Dead.** (מת 12:).   The interpretation of *emet*, which becomes *met* by dropping the *aleph*, is widespread in the tradition of the creation of the Golem, as in the *Sefer Gematriot* (13th century), from the circle of students of Yehudah he-Ḥasid, and the pseudo Sa'adya commentary to the *Sefer Yezirah*; cf. Scholem, *Kabbala*, p. 233f.; Idel, *Golem*, p. 63f.

13   **Three.** (שלשה 13:).   S. B. Niddah 31a: "Three participate in the human: the Holy One, blessed be He, his father, and his mother. [...] When his time has come to die, the Holy One, blessed be He, withdraws his share, but he leaves them their father's and mother's share." Similar in B. Kiddushin 30b.

This is why all pious women and men should be scrupulous about all of their actions—about every word and every step. And whoever should pay attention to my words, perhaps I will gain some merit from them, as I wrote above, "But it shall go well with them who decide justly; Blessings of good things will light upon them."[102] This means in Yiddish, those who allow themselves to be admonished will be given pleasantness, and good blessings will come to them.

I say all of this only to young women, and God forbid that I should even question the honor of truly righteous women. If I only should merit seeing my children's children perform such good deeds—how they go to synagogue, and pray, and how they treat Torah scholars. God, blessed be His name, should grant that this should last so pleasurably until the coming of our Redeemer, Amen.

8b

Chapter Two

This is the next chapter, which will speak of how a woman should relate to her husband, if they want to grow old with each other with respect.

King Solomon, peace be upon him, says in Proverbs, "A capable wife is a crown for her husband, but an incompetent one is like rot in his bones."[1] This means in Yiddish, a dutiful woman is a crown upon her husband. But an immodest woman, meaning one for whom her husband must be ashamed, she is like decay in his bones. The commentators[2] write that

---

3   *Above.* (פארט 18:). Reference to fol. 6a: The reward of a pious woman are children who turned out well.

5   *Those who allow themselves to be admonished.* (ולמוכיחם 18:). Instead of translating in the active form, the author translates the subject—those who admonish (others)—in the tolerant form "those who allow themselves to be admonished"; (see below), thus turning the verse into an admonition of the readers instead of justifying the author's admonition, as it would in its literal meaning.

9   *Pray.* (תפילית 23:). Yiddish spelling is based on the Yiddish pronunciation.

11   *The coming of our Redeemer.* (ביאות גואלינו 24:). Yiddish spelling; see also the prayer that begins with the words *u-va le-ziyyon goel*—May a redeemer come to Zion; cf. Nulman, *Encyclopedia*, p. 333.

     8b

15   *Capable wife.* (אשת חיל 3:). Prov. 12:4 is the beginning of a long homiletic interpretation of the capable wife up to fol. 9a, the last verse of which is Ps. 32:6.

18   *Commentators.* (מפרשים 6:). S. Ibn Ezra on Prov. 12:4: "'In his bones.' (For which) no remedy has any effect: such is a shameful woman, she is a disgrace to her husband, and she does harm to the property."

just as, God protect us, there is no cure for decayed bones, so too there is no remedy for a husband with an [undutiful] wife. The Gemara[3] explains this verse, "A capable wife is a crown for her husband,"[4] as follows: This is Sarah, from whom God, may He be blessed, took the *yud,* and shared it with Abraham. God gave Abraham a *heh* and gave Sarah a *heh* at
5 the end.

The Gemara[5] goes on to say, "Her husband is adorned by his wife." ([...]) This means that her husband will be recognized at the gate. This means that when he sits among Torah scholars, who are called "[the elders] of the city gates," he will be recognized. (The crown) refers to an unflawed woman who maintains her husband in his studying, as we find in the
10 Gemara:[6] a Torah scholar gave his son a wife. In the morning (after the wedding) he asked

2 *Gemara.* (גמרא :8). S. Bereshit Rabbah 47.1: "Rabbi Yehoshua ben Korḥa said, 'The *yud,* which the Holy One, blessed be He, took from Sarai, was divided into one half for Sarah, and one for Abraham.' Rabbi Shimon ben Yoḥai said, 'The *yud,* which the Holy One took from Sarai, flourished and blossomed before the throne of the Holy One, blessed be He. It said to the Lord of the world: Because I am the smallest among the letters, you have taken me away from Sarah the righteous.'" There is no evidence for such an interpretation in the Talmud.

6 *Gemara.* (גמרא :11). S. Bereshit Rabbah 47.1: "'And God said to Abraham, as for your wife Sarai' (Gen. 17:15) etc. It is written, 'A capable wife is a crown for her husband' (Prov. 12:4). Rabbi Aha said, 'A man is crowned by his wife, but she is not crowned by her husband.'" There is no evidence for such an interpretation in the Talmud.

6 *This means.* (טייטש :11). The translated text is Prov. 31:23: "Her husband is prominent in the gates, As he sits among the elders of the land." During the print, the translation of Bereshit Rabbah 47.1, the exegetic transfer to Prov. 31:23, and its Hebrew quoting were most probably dropped.
The translation of "Elders of the land" as "Torah scholars" is substantiated in Shemot Rabbah 5.12; see also the respective interpretation on fol. 14a.

8 *[The elders] of the city gates.* (זקני] שער ערו :13). Deut. 21:19 reads, "His father and mother shall take hold of him and bring him out to the elders of his town (*el ziknei iro*) at the public place of his community (*el shaar mekomo*)."

9 *Unflawed woman.* (אשה כשרה :14). The woman urging her husband to study is often formulated as a female ideal in moral literature, such as in *Brantshpigl,* pp. 64; 208; *Reshit Ḥokhmah,* I, p. 197, §1; *Eyn shoyn Froyenbuykhleyn,* fol. 16b. Regarding the formulation of the "unflawed woman" in Ruth Zuta 4, 11; see the commentary on p. 100/5.

10 *Gemara.* (גמרא :14). S. B. Berakhot 8a: "'Therefore let every faithful man pray to You upon discovering' (Ps. 32:6). Rabbi Ḥanina said, 'Upon discovering,' that is the woman, as it is written, 'He who finds a wife has found happiness' (Prov. 18:22). Upon sundown after a man married, somebody says to him, 'Has found' or 'Finds?' 'Has found,' as it is written, 'He who finds a wife has found happiness' (Prov. 18:22) etc. 'He who finds,' as it is written, 'Now, I find woman more bitter than death' (Eccles. 7:26) etc." Similar in Tanḥuma, Naso 4; Yalkut, §976.
The narrative formulation, however, corresponds more with the version in Midrash Tehillim 59:3. Similar in *Brantshpigl,* p. 72. It is conspicuous that contrary to rabbinic tradition, Eccles. 7:26 is not quoted here. Cf. fols. 12b and 13b, where Eccles. 7:26 is brought in other exegetic contexts.

him, "What kind of [wife] did you receive, 'he found' or 'he finds'? He answered, "'he found.'" He meant it as follows: The verse says, "He who finds a wife has found happiness, and has won the favor of the LORD."[7] In Yiddish this means, he who finds a pious wife, finds everything good. He gains the goodwill of the Holy One, blessed be He. This means that God, blessed be He, fulfills all their desires. (The father) asked him again, "How do you know that she is pious?" He answered, "I studied the entire night, and she illuminated for me." About this King David, peace be upon him, said, "Therefore let every faithful man pray to You at a time when You can be found."[8] The Gemara[9] gives many explanations of this verse; I do not want to write them here, but I will say, "at a time when you can be found," refers to a woman, because there is no better find than getting an upright wife. This is as King Solomon, peace be upon him, wrote at the end of Proverbs, "What a rare find is a capable wife! Her worth is far beyond that of rubies."[10] This means in Yiddish, a woman who is a heroine—who can find her? She is worth more than if pure gold were her price.

9a

One can win or lose with merchandise, but with a good wife, who can estimate how much good can come from her? The Gemara[11] also says, "He who is without a wife is without

5   ***Their desires. (אירין רצון** :19)***. Contrary to the traditional interpretation, the author applies Prov. 18:22 to a woman, and thus feminizes the exegesis: if she behaves appropriately, God will fulfill her wishes, i.e., she experiences God's benevolence. See the deviating interpretation in *Sefer Mishlei*, fol. 48a: מצא. דר דא גיפינט אייין וורייב אונ' גיפינט "זי גוט אונ' אויז ציכט ווילן כלומ' ער לושט זיך בינוגן דז איז פון גוט אייין מתנה." —"'Has found.' He who has found a wife, and finds that she is good and creates benevolence, it means that he contents himself (with her): it is a gift from God."

8   ***Gemara. (גמרא** :22)***. S. B. Berakhot 8a: "Rabbi Ḥanina said, 'Upon discovering' (Ps. 32:6), that is the woman, as it is said, 'He who finds a wife has found happiness' (Prov. 18:22)."

13   ***Heroine. (העלדין** :26)***. *Eshet ḥayil* (capable woman) is commonly translated in contemporary Yiddish literature as *bider vayb*—diligent woman; dutiful woman—as above; cf. *Brantshpigl*, p. 39 (Prov. 12:4) and p. 45 (Prov. 31:10); *Sefer Mishlei*, fol. 28a (on Prov. 12:4), on the other hand, translates *heldin*—heroine—and on fol. 84b (on Prov. 31:10) as *helde vroy*—a heroic woman. See Rashi on II Chron. 13:2: "She, who was a woman of valor, an industrious woman (*gevartanit*)."

9a

15   ***Gemara. (גמרא** :2)***. S. Midrash Tehillim 59:2: "He who has no wife, will remain without blessing, without life, without joy, without help, without good, without peace. 'Without blessing,' as it is said, 'God blessed them' (Gen. 1:28) at a time, when they were two. 'Without good life,' as it is said, 'Enjoy happiness with a woman' (Eccles. 9:9). 'Without joy,' as it is said, 'Find joy in the wife of your youth' (Prov. 5:18). 'Without help,' as it is said, 'I will make a fitting helper for him' (Gen. 2:18). 'Without good,' as it is said, 'He who finds a wife has found happiness' (Prov. 18:22). 'Without peace,' as it is said, 'You will know that all is well in your tent' (Job 5:24)." Similar in B. Yevamot 62b, where "atonement" and "life" are missing. On the other hand, "atonement" is

good, without blessing, without atonement, without peace, without life, without help, without happiness." This means in Yiddish, he who is without a wife is without good. "Without good," as the verse says, "It is not good for man to be alone"[12]—it is not good that a human should be alone. "Without blessing," as it says, "That a blessing may rest upon your home"[13]—you should allow blessings into your house. "Without atonement," as it says, "To make expiation for himself and for his household"[14]—the priest should ask forgiveness for himself, his wife, and his children. "Without peace," as it says, "You will know that peace is in your tent"[15]—you should know that peace is in your tent. This means that when a woman is in a tent, then there is peace. "Without life," as it says, "Enjoy life with a woman"[16]—see life with your wife. "Without happiness," as it says, "And rejoice with your household,"[17] and so on. (House) means wife: you and your wife should rejoice on the holidays. "Without help," as it says, "I will make a fitting helper for him"[18]—I will make a wife for him, who should help him. The Gemara[19] explains this: "If he merits it—a help; if he does not merit it—against him." This means, if one merits it, she will be a help for him. If he does not merit it, she will always be against him. This is why the verse says, "Therefore let every faithful man pray."[20]

This is why Adam said when God created Eve for him, "This one at last is bone of my

included in Bereshit Rabbah 17.2 and Kohelet Rabbah 9.9. *Brantshpigl*, p. 39f., contains the talmudic version.

13   ***Gemara.*** (גמרא :13).   S. B. Yevamot 63a: "Rabbi Eliezer said: What does it mean, that is written, 'I will make a fitting helper for him' (Gen. 2:18)? If he is worthy, she will help him, if he is not worthy, she will oppose him."

The second part (an unworthy man receives a woman who opposes him) is not found in most moral texts, since they assign the responsibility for the partner mostly to the woman alone. See *Eyn shoyn Froyenbuykhleyn*, fol. 33a (on Eccles. 9:9): "דער פשט איז איין פרום וייב מכט איין פרומן מאן דען דיא פרויא קאן אירן מאן גיווינן צו תורה אוני' מצות אוני' מעשים טובים [. . .] איין ביזי פרויא מכט איין אויך ביז אוני' מכט אים דיא זיל אין אבגרונד העלין קומן."—דער—"The interpretation is that a pious wife can lead her husband to become pious, because the wife can bring her husband to get accustomed to Torah and obligations and good deeds . . . a bad wife will bring him to be evil, as well. She causes his soul to descend into the abyss of hell."

16   ***Therefore.*** (על :15).   The interpretation of Ps. 32:6 opens a particularly long homily (112/16–115/15), which is connected with the preceding interpretation of the capable woman by usage of the interpretation chain in B. Berakhot 8a; see the commentary on p. 110/10. The Hebrew word *zot*—this (feminine)—is in the center of the homily. All in all, twelve verses containing this word are quoted. A homiletic interpretation on *zot* can also be found in *Ze'enah u-Re'enah* on Lev. 16:3, p. 592, which, together with Lev. 16:33, Deut. 4:44, Gen. 17:10, Isa. 56:2, and two interpretations from Va-yikra Rabbah 21.6 and 9, contain a smaller, not identical part of the interpretations specified here.

17   ***This one at last.*** (זאת הפעם :16).   Literally: "this time," traditionally read as the creation of Eve, which was preceded by the creation of Lilith; see Ibn Ezra on Gen. 2:23: "'Then the man said,' so it is said, with 'This one at last' I found a helper for me: (she is) like me, as she had been (taken) from him. The (other) matter is interpreted as Lilith."

bones, and flesh of my flesh. This one shall be called Woman,"[21] and not Lilith, as it is written, "Male and female He created them."[22] As the midrash[23] has it: as soon as he saw that Lilith was not good, he did not want her.

For that reason the verse also writes regarding our Patriarch Jacob, "Wait until the week of this one is over."[24] That is to say, do you mean that only Rachel was a righteous woman? Leah was an equally righteous woman! This is why the verse says, "That one also,"[25] the acrostic of which (*GaM*—also—) spell "body" and "money," with which she was just as pious as Rachel. And so the verse goes on, "And he loved Rachel,"[26]—and he also loved Rachel. With this the verse lets us know that he also loved Leah, but he loved Rachel more, since she was the first in his thoughts. This is why the verse says, "By Your arm You redeemed Your people, the children of Jacob and Joseph. Selah."[27] This means in Yiddish, you have delivered with your arm your people, the children of Jacob and Joseph. The verse

1   *Lilith.* (לילות 17:).   Spelling based on Yiddish pronunciation.

2   *Midrash.* (מדרש 19:).   Regarding Lilith in the rabbinic tradition, cf. also B. Niddah 24b; *Alpha-Beta de-Ben Sira* (Constantinople, 1519; Venice, 1544), 23a–b; 33a–b; *Zohar*, I, 19b, 34b; III, 19a; cf. also Ginzberg, *Legends*, I, p. 65 and V, p. 87.

     S. *Brantshpigl*, p. 51: "'It is not good for man to be alone' (Gen. 2:18)....One may ask, where has the first woman gone, who had been created together with him? They say the first woman was called Lilith. She did not obey her man, and she was arrogant, because she, too, had been created from the soil. Therefore she refused to follow his orders, and replied, 'I am as good as you, God's creation from the soil.' Therefore God, blessed be His name, took her from him, and created another from his body, so that she may obey him, and help him in all matters, as much as she could."

7   *Acrostic.* (ר"ת 22:).   The author uses the rabbinic exegetical method: the first letters of two or more words form a word. The source for this *notarikon "gam"* (also) as *guf* (body) and *mamon* (money) is unclear; cf. fol. 28b. The usage of *notarikon* was very popular in the early modern kabbalistic and homiletic literature; cf. Heilperin, *Ha-Notarikon*. More *notarikonim* on fols. 28a and 34b.

8   *Pious.* (פרום 22:).   The interpretation of Leah as pious woman is also substantiated in *Brantshpigl*, pp. 66 and 81, where Leah is exemplified as a wise, understanding woman. An allusion to Leah's sense of justice as reason for her fertility can be found in Bereshit Rabbah 71.6.

9   *Leah.* (ליאה 24:).   The interpretation, whereby Jacob also loved Leah, has no model in rabbinic literature. Only Bereshit Rabbah 71.2 describes that Leah was eventually accepted by Jacob and his esteem for her increased because of her fertility, but she was otherwise mainly despised for being hypocritical. Here, the plene spelling of the name is unusual.

     S. Tanḥuma, Va-yetse 13: "Leah and Rachel: 'One loved' (Deut. 21:15): that is Rachel, as it is written, 'He loved Rachel' (Gen. 29:30). 'And the other unloved' (Deut. 21:15): that is Leah, as it is written, 'The Lᴏʀᴅ saw that Leah was unloved' (Gen. 29:31)."

11   *Redeemed.* (גאלת 25:).   The special significance of Rachel for Joseph is derived from Ps. 77:16, where the children of Leah, Zilpah, and Bilhah are listed collectively only (*benei Yaakov*) while Rachel's son Joseph is named individually.

12   *Arm.* (ארם 26:).   Metonymic for power or strength; both meanings for *zaroa* can already be found in the Bible.

9b

names only Joseph, because he was Rachel's son, and she was the most important.

　　We also find regarding Ruth that Boaz asked, "To whom does this girl belong?"[28] Rashi[29] asks if it is typical for a righteous man like him to look at women. Rather, as Rashi answers, he asked about her because he noticed her great modesty. And this is why he said,
5　"This girl,"[30] that is to say, "For this every man shall pray."[31] This is why the verse later says, "All the people at the gate and the elders answered, 'May the LORD make the woman who is coming into your house like Rachel and Leah, both of whom built up the house of Israel!'[32] And may your house be like the house of Perez whom Tamar bore to Judah—through the offspring which the LORD will give you by this young woman."[33] This means that when
10　Boaz took Ruth, the people and the entire Sanhedrin gave him a blessing, and said as follows: "God should grant that this woman, who is coming into your house, should be like Rachel and Leah who built the house of Israel"—(the verse) places Rachel before Leah because she was the first in his thoughts. It also says Rachel and Leah and not Sarah or Rebekah because Esau came from them, but no one unworthy came from Rachel and Leah.
15　　It is also written "this (young woman)" here, as the verse[34] goes on to say, your house should be like the house of Perez, who was born by Tamar to Judah, through the seed that God will give you from this young woman.

　　And so it says regarding our Patriarch Jacob, when he gave his children his last will, "And this is what their father said to them."[35] He was indicating that they should pay
20　attention to pious women. As the Gemara[36] explains, "A man should always sell everything he has in order to marry the daughter of a Torah scholar." This means in Yiddish, a man

9b

3　　***Rashi.*** (רש״י 2:). S. Rashi on Ruth 2:5: "Because it was Boaz's way to only ask the women, if they (did) modest and wise things. He saw that she picked up two ears every time, and did not pick up the third ear, so as to enable her to pick the erect ones standing. She left the lying (ears), so as not to have to bend down."

6　　***May.*** (ויהי 7:). Instead of the second part of Ruth 4:11, verse 12 is quoted, containing the central word "this." The connection between the verses emphasized the equalization of Rachel and Leah with Ruth.

10　　***Sanhedrin.*** (סנהדרין 9:). Regarding the translation of "Elders" in Ruth 4:11 with "Sanhedrin," see Ibn Ezra on Deut. 31:9: "'To all the elders of Israel': that is the Sanhedrin."

14　　***Unworthy.*** (פסול 14:). The idea that Sarah and Rebekah are stigmatized because of their descendent Esau is not common in rabbinic literature; see, on the other hand, B. Pesaḥim 56a: "(Jacob) said: That I may not see in my tribe, God forbid, any stigma, as with Abraham, who brought forth Ishmael, and with my father Isaac, who brought forth Esau." The blessings, on the other hand, with which their mother and her deceitful brother bid them farewell, were interpreted as "curses of the godless," and as the reason for Rebekah's long years of infertility; cf. Bereshit Rabbah 60.13.

20　　***Always.*** (לעולם 19:). S. B. Pesaḥim 49a: "Our teachers taught: A man shall always sell all of his assets, in order to marry the daughter of a scholar. Should he die or

should always sell everything he has in order to take a maiden who is the daughter of a Torah scholar. In our times, due to our many transgressions, people see only money—even the daughter of a Torah scholar, if she has no money, will be pushed away with both hands. King David said about this, "A brutish man cannot know, a fool cannot understand this."[37]
5 This means as follows: a fool does not want to know the daughter of a Torah scholar,

10a

and so he will also not merit to have children who will understand the Torah, which is indicated by "this."

So too, Moses, our teacher, peace be upon him, blessed Israel with "This is the blessing."[38] Regarding Aaron the priest [it says], "With this only Aaron shall enter,"[39] in
10 the merit of the Torah, which is called "this," and in the merit of their respectable mother, Aaron and Moses also merited reaching greatness. This is also why Moses, our teacher, merited receiving the Torah, as the verse says, "This is the Teaching that Moses set."[40] And this is why, before his death, Moses, our teacher, peace be upon him, blessed Judah, "And this he said of Judah,"[41] that the kingship of the House of David should come from
15 Tamar, as the commentators[42] assert.

I do not need to write everything here about how all depends on the woman, since it is in the *Vroyen Bikhel*[43] along with many proofs. The [verse] says, "Property and riches are

go into exile, it will be warranted that his sons, too, become scholars. He shall not marry the daughter of an unlearned person. Should he die or go into exile, his sons will become unlearned." On other interpretations, cf. ibid.

10a

6   *Torah.* (תורה :1). Regarding the interpretation of *zot* as Torah, cf. Deut. 4:44 and Bereshit Rabbah 100.12.

10   *Mother.* (מוטר :5). Regarding the idea that Jochebed's sons Moses and Aaron were worthy because of her merits, see Shemot Rabbah 11.6: "What is the merit of the fear (of the Lord)? Torah! Because Jochebed feared, the Holy One, blessed be He, let Moses come forth from her. About him it is written, 'How beautiful he was' (Exod. 2:2). And the Torah, which is called the 'good Teaching,' was given into his hands."

15   *Commentators.* (פרשנים :9). S. Rashi on I Chron. 4:21; Nachmanides on Gen. 38:2; Midrash Tehillim 76:2; Tanḥuma, Va-yeḥi 12.

17   *Vroyen Bikhel.* (ורויאן ביכל :10). S. *Eyn shoyn Froyenbuykhleyn*, 33a: אונ׳ די פרום" פרויא איז אויך די דא קאן מכין קינדר די דא ווערן פרום אונ׳ פערכטר גוט זיין ווילשטו זעהן דז עז וו.אר איז דז אלו אן דר ורויאן ליגט זיך דאש מעשה פון תמר [...] אונ׳ פון איר גוטי כוונה "וועגין ווער זי זוכה זו מלכות פון בית דוד פון איר קאם.—"The pious woman can also cause children to become pious and God-fearing. If you want to see, that it all depends on the woman, then behold the tale of Tamar. . . . Because of her good intentions, she became worthy of bringing forth the royal house of David."

17   *Proofs.* (ראיית :10). Spelling based on Yiddish pronunciation.
    Regarding the examples for the woman's "good thoughts," see *Eyn shoyn Froyenbuykhleyn*, ibid., fol. 38a–b, where Samson's mother (Judg. 13:2ff.), the Shunammite

bequeathed by fathers, but an efficient wife comes from the LORD."[44] In Yiddish this means one can certainly inherit a house and [property] from one's parents, but a prudent woman must be earned from God, blessed be His name.

5   As I wrote above, a woman can prevent much with her wisdom. For one, she must [always] do right regarding her body. She must (also) consider her soul, and remember that this world is not important, but the world to come is. King Solomon, peace be upon him, said about this, "The wisdom of women builds her house, but folly tears it down with its own hands."[45] The Gemara[46] explains this verse as follows: "the wisdom of women" refers to the wife of On ben Pelet, and "foolishness" is Korah's wife. This is why every pious

10   woman should convince her husband not to associate with any bad men. As our sages[47] said,

        (II Kings 4:14ff.), and Hannah (I Sam. 1:2ff.) are mentioned as examples for pious women, whose "good thoughts" relieved them of many years of infertility. See also ibid., fol. 15a–b, where a pious woman needs to go repeatedly to the *tevilah*, because she encounters, on her way home, visions that trigger bad thoughts (sick people, beasts, unlearned), who, by popular belief, have a negative influence on a child to be conceived shortly after. Only after God lets her see the angel Metatron, after the *tevilah*, she conceives who was later to become the Rabbi and "High Priest" Yishmael (cf. *Oẓar Midrashim*, p. 388; 439). For further examples see the commentary on p. 92/2–3.

4   *Above.* (פארט :13). The indication refers to the remarks on the "wisdom of the soul" and the "wisdom of the body"; see the commentary on pp. 87/7 and 90/11.

6   *Important.* (עיקר :16). The concept of "this world" (*olam ha-zeh*), the earthly, transient world of the living, and of the "world to come" (*olam ha-ba*), that of eternity, is widespread in rabbinic literature. In later sources, the latter was also understood as the Messianic times of redemption and resurrection of the dead, cf. M. Avot 4:16. Regarding the idea of man having a share in the world to come because of his merits, cf., e.g., B. Berakhot 51a.

     The greater significance of the world to come as opposed to this world is a widespread topic also in the moral literature; see *Brantshpigl*, p. 35: "There are many verses that prove that this world is nothing, and the world to come is the main thing. And all the good that the Holy One, blessed be He, promised the righteous and the pious, refers to that other world."

     Sefer Middot, fol. 55b: יענר (!) זוישקייש אונ׳ קלארהייט דיא אן גידענקן טאג אל זול איינר״ ואלט אונ׳ זול אויש דעם הערצן שלאגן דיא ליבשאפט דיזר וועלט. אונ׳ ווער דיזם עולם גאנץ ליבא האבן.״—ליבא הוט קאן יענן עולם ניט גאנץ ליבן עולם קאן הוט ליבא—. "One should think of the purity and sweetness of the other world every day, and one should not attach oneself to the love of this world. Whoever loves this world wholeheartedly, cannot love the other world wholeheartedly."

     Similar also in ibid., fols. 33b; 35b; 39b; 53b.

8   *Gemara.* (גמרא :17). S. B. Sanhedrin 110a: "'The wisdom of women builds her house' (Prov. 14:1): that is On ben Pelet's wife. 'Folly tears it down with its own hands' (ibid.): that is Korah's wife." The same also in Rashi on Prov. 14:1.

10   *Sages.* (חכמים :20). S. *Avot de-Rabbi Natan*, A, chap. 1:9: "Nitai ha-Arbeli says: Keep away from an evil neighbor, do not fraternize with an evildoer, and do not doubt (divine) retribution." See ibid., presenting various examples for disastrous connections between men; Korah and On ben Pelet, however, are not mentioned; cf. M. Avot 1:7.

"Distance yourself from a bad neighbor, and do not befriend a wicked man." That is what happened with Korah's wife—she provoked and badgered him to fight with Moses, [our teacher,] peace be upon him, for which she received her due payment. But the wife of On ben Pelet did the opposite—she did not want to allow her husband to fight. When Korah

10b

5   came to call her husband, she stood with her hair out as if she wanted to comb it, to make sure that he would have to run away. That is how she saved her husband.

Or, the verse could mean by "foolishness"[48] etc., Jezebel, the wife of Ahab, who also caused her husband to all sorts of evil. That is why she also found a bad end, along with her husband and her children.

2   ***Korah's wife.*** (קורח וזייב 21:). The wives of Korah and On ben Pelet are not mentioned in Num. 16:1–35, only later, in the Midrash, as negative and positive examples; see Tanḥuma, Korah 24: "Rav said: On ben Pelet's wife saved him. She said to him: What dealings do you have with that group? If Aaron is the High Priest, then you are (his) pupil. He said to her: But I know that the entire community is holy, as it is written, 'For all the community are holy' (Num. 16:3). What did she do? She gave him wine to drink, and had him lie on the bed. Then she sat down in front of her house, and let her hair down. Whoever came to see her husband On, saw her, and turned around (with shame). In the meantime, those (men of Korah) were swallowed by the earth. Where it is written, 'The wisdom of women builds her house' (Prov. 14:1), it refers to the wife of On ben Pelet, and when it says, 'Folly tears it down with its own hands' (ibid.), that is the wife of Korah." Same in B. Sanhedrin 109b–110a; Yalkut, §750.

10b

5   ***Hair.*** (האריין 1:). Various Yiddish texts describe the "hair scene" in further details; cf. *Brantshpigl*, p. 68f., where On ben Pelet's wife removes the hair cover and her veil, in order to clarify to her husband by use of a parable (just like every hair grows out of its own pore, so has God allocated a place to every person; cf. B. Sanhedrin 109b) that he must accept Moses' authority: "While she spoke with him, Korah arrived to call (On ben Pelet), but as he saw her standing with her hair (uncovered), he did not enter, out of shame. Thus On ben Pelet remained in his house, and was saved."

In comparison with the version *Brantshpigl*, On ben Pelet's wife appears less learned here, as she does not use the talmudic parable. At the same time, however, she is more cunning in that she uses her hair strategically as a female lure as in the Midrash, and thus forces the man who sees it to turn away in shame.

Same in *Sefer Mishlei*, fol. 33b on Prov. 14:1: "דא קרח קאם צו אירם גיצעלט אונ' וואלט אירן מאן אן רייצן צו קריגן זא שטעלט זיא זיך אן טיר דז גיצעלט אונ' קעמט אירי האר אין דר וורטן דז קורח ניט זולט הניין גין."—"When Korah came to her tent, planning to goad her husband into quarreling, she stood in the entrance of her tent, combing her hair, so as to prevent Korah from entering."

7   ***Jezebel.*** (איזבל 2:). S. Yalkut, §42: "It said about Jezebel, the daughter of Etbaal, 'Folly tears it down with its own hands' (Prov. 14:1)." Jezebel's actions and her death (I Kings 21:1–29; II Kings 9:30–37) are also mentioned in *Brantshpigl* in connection with the wives of On ben Pelet and Korah; see ibid., p. 69.

But *Reshit Ḥokhmah*[49] writes that "The wisdom of women"[50] refers to Deborah the Prophetess, which is a great surprise for our sages. They are surprised because Phinehas the priest lived in those times, and God, blessed be He, loved him greatly, but let His prophecy rest upon a woman and not on Phinehas. But he[51] writes further, "Heaven and
5   earth witness me," heaven and earth should be my witnesses, that there is no difference between a man and a woman, between a servant and a maid. Whether a man or woman, servant or maid—whoever is upright will merit divine inspiration, as we often see. And also what Pharaoh's daughter Bityah merited for raising Moses, our teacher, peace be upon him,—[God,] blessed be His name, Himself gave her the name Bityah, which means
10   "daughter of God." She also merited entering *Gan Eden* while alive. There is more similar material that I do not want to write down here, because it all belongs in its own place.

Now I would like to write more about how our sages[52] explain why Deborah was called

1   ***Reshit Ḥokhmah.*** (ראשית חכמה :4).   *Reshit Ḥokhmah*, I, p. 9, §18: "His wife Deborah. About her it is written, 'The wisdom of women builds her house' (Prov. 14:1). And about Jezebel, Etbaal's daughter, it is written, 'Folly tears it down with its own hands' (ibid.)."

2   ***Surprise.*** (תמיה :5).   The word is a variant of *temihah*—astonishment, surprise—used particularly in exegetic literature; cf. Even Shoshan, IV, p. 1459.
    Regarding the question about the reason for Deborah's prophetic gift, see Yalkut, §42: "'Deborah...was a prophetess' (Judg. 4:4). But what was the quality of Deborah, who prophesied and judged Israel? Did not Phinehas ben Eleazar hold chair?...The spirit of holiness rests on each and every one, in accordance with his actions. A teaching on behalf of Elijah: They said that Deborah's husband was an unlearned man."

2   ***Phinehas.*** (פנחס :6).   The priest Phinehas ben Eleazar; cf. Judg. 20:28.

4   ***He writes.*** (ער שרייבט :8).   *Reshit Ḥokhmah*, I, p. 9, §18, regarding Deborah's gift of prophecy, which should have been received by her husband in his capacity as acting priest: "Heaven and earth witness me, that the spirit of holiness rests on everybody, according to his actions, whether a stranger or an Israelite, whether man or woman, whether slave or maid." Same in *Seder Eliyahu Rabbah*, 10; Yalkut, §42.

8   ***Bityah.*** (בתיה :13).   Bityah, the daughter of Pharaoh, is not mentioned at the respective place in *Reshit Ḥokhmah*; here she appears as an exemplary woman who, because of her actions (Exod. 2:5–10), entered *Gan Eden* during her lifetime; same in Kallah Rabbati, 3:23.
    Sefer Mishlei does not mention Bityah, but the homiletic *Midrash Eshet Ḥayil* allocates an exemplary female figure to each of the 20 verses in Prov. 31:10–31, and mentions Bityah (on Prov. 31:15) with the remark that she had entered *Gan Eden* during her lifetime; cf. Levine Katz, *Midreshei Eshet Ḥayil*, pp. 111–114 and 347ff. Same in *Brantshpigl*, pp. 57, 72.

10   ***More similar.*** (פיל דער גלייכין :15-14).   Possibly an allusion to Serah bat Asher, who was the only additional woman to enter *Gan Eden* during her lifetime, and whom the traditional literature always mentions in the same breath with Bityah, the daughter of Pharaoh; cf. Levine Katz, ibid.

12   ***Sages.*** (חכמים :16).   *Reshit Ḥokhmah*, I, p. 9, §18, explains the three names of Deborah's husband: Barak (lightning), because his face resembles a lightning bolt;

"The wife of Lappidoth."[53] Who was Lappidoth? Our sages, may their memory be a blessing, say that Lappidoth was Barak. Why was he called Lappidoth? Because Deborah made wicks—*lapidot*—in the Temple and gave them to her husband who lit them. And she made sure that he studied Torah day and night. It was given in thunder and lightning—
5   *lapidot u-verakim*—. Now the question must be posed: If he was her husband, why did she send for him to campaign against Sisera? It sounds as if he were not her husband. But since the prophecy was granted to her, she separated herself from him, which is why she had to send for him. This is also why he said, "If you want to go with me, then I too want to go; but if you do not want to, then I also do not want to go." How could he have said that he
10   wanted to go with another woman? Rather, she was his wife, and only separated herself

11a

from him because he knew that she was a righteous woman. (He said to himself): "Perhaps I will enjoy her merit."

Every pious woman can learn from all the issues that I have written here, that she should bring her husband to good deeds, and discourage him from bad things. She should
15   not tell him about everything that goes wrong in the house—she should excuse him from

Michael, because he made himself small (derivative of the Hebrew root *mem-vav-kaf*); and Lappidoth (torch), because Deborah made for him large wicks that shone like torches (same also in B. Megillah 14a and in other places), so that God may recognize his bond with the perfect; alternately, see below: so as to allow Lappidoth to study the Torah at night as well.

1   *Lappidoth.* (לפידית :21). Spelling based on Yiddish pronunciation.

4   *Thunder and lightning.* (לפידית וברקים :21). S. Tanḥuma (Warsaw), Lekh Lekha 6: "Rabbi Shimon ben Lakish said to him: The Holy One, blessed be He, prefers the proselyte to the troops who stood at Mount Sinai. Why? Because those troops did not accept the kingdom of heaven, despite having seen and heard the lightning and the light, the trembling mountains, and the sound of the trumpets."

See also Exod. 19:16 and Ibn Ezra on Deut. 33:2: "'Lightning flashing at them from His right.' The Torah, which was handed down through fire and lightning."

6   *Send.* (גשיקט :22). The author expounds the problem of the choice of words in Judg. 4:6: She refutes the implied criticism against Deborah for not having been on Barak's side in any case by presenting the special circumstances (prophecy, see below) that necessitated the separation. B. Megillah 14b already criticizes her arrogant conduct of calling her husband to come to her, and claims that her demeaning name, meaning "bee," was a punishment.

11a

11   *Righteous.* (צדקות :1). Spelling based on Yiddish pronunciation.

14   *Him from.* (אימש :4). It is not clear whether the *es* (it) contained in the dative pronoun *ims* means that the woman is supposed to talk her husband out of the quarrel-some interference in the sometimes unbalanced, disharmonic daily routine. The abbreviated Bible quotes in the homiletic version (up to p. 120/74) in fact sound like proverbs, which the wife uses in order to talk her husband out of interfering.

(involvement), since nothing good comes from a fight. As the verse says, "Who cries, 'Woe!' who, 'Alas!,' who has quarrels?"[54] This means in Yiddish, who has pain, who should complain—he who fights. King Solomon, peace be upon him, also said, "To start a quarrel is to open a [sluice]."[55] This means that when one digs a well, the water begins to flow slowly, and afterwards it begins to shoot out with force. So too, God protect us, a fight: it begins with a quarrel over one little word, and later a big fight grows out of it. This is why the verse says, "Before a dispute flares up, drop it."[56] In Yiddish this means, before the fight begins, give it up. This means that one should quickly cut it off. The verse also goes on to say, "For lack of wood a fire goes out, and without a querulous man contention is stilled."[57] This means in Yiddish, if one does not put wood on a fire, the fire goes out and is extinguished. So too if no gossipmonger goes here [and] there (spreading gossip), the fight will be quieted. On this matter the verse goes on, "It is honorable for a man to desist from strife."[58] This means, whoever wants honor should refrain from conflict, and should take interest only in peace. There is much to write about the good that can come from peace.

Now I would like to speak more about how a pious, upright woman should urge her husband toward good, so that he [should] do business with faith. As the verse says, "The righteous man is rewarded with life for his fidelity."[59] This means in Yiddish, a righteous man who does business with faith will live in the world to come. And so the opposite: Whoever does not, God forbid, do business with faith, the Gemara[60] says about him, "He who wrought vengeance against the generation of the Deluge and against the generation of

4   **Well.** (ברונין :7). The parable of the watercourse can be found even more elaborated in *Sefer Mishlei*, fol. 44b, where it ends with the words: "אונ׳ אי מן וערט גיוואר —דיין שנט דא פער לאז דיין קריג דען עז איז ניט מיגליך עז קומט פון קריג זינד אונ׳ שנד." "Before your shame becomes known, you should stop your quarrel, because it is not proper, quarrel is the source of sin and shame."

9   **For lack of.** (באפס :12). Cf. Prov. 15:18.

11   **Gossip.** (רכילת :14). Spelling based on Yiddish pronunciation. See the commentary on p. 93/7–8.

15   **Urge.** (אן הלטין :18). The call upon the woman to urge her husband to be honest in his trading is not common in Yiddish moral books that turn to mainly female readers; see also the commentary on p. 151/2 ("not permit"). The author of *Brantshpigl* demands that the woman urge her husband to study the Torah, to perform good deeds, and to practice modesty and conjugal fidelity. She should also care for his orderly, proper appearance; cf. ibid., pp. 42f., 45, 64, 66, 68, 397. The woman's part in the moral support of his work is merely to disperse his worries by her joyful, satisfied mood and her pretty appearance, so that he may properly attend to his business; ibid., p. 133. The demand for honest trading is expressed in general terms, cf. ibid., pp. 44, 364; the same in *Ze'enah u-Re'enah* on Exod. 38:21, p. 535. In the Hebrew and Yiddish moral literature written mainly for men, the demand for honesty in one's trade is a matter of course; see *Sefer Middot*, fols. 23b; 51a; 61b; 64a; *Den Muser un' Hanhoge*, fol. 3b; *Iggeret Derekh ha-Shem*, fol. 9b; *Sefer Ḥayyei Olam*, fol. 2b; *Sefer ha-Gan*, fol. 7a.

19   **Gemara.** (גמרא :21). S. B. Bava Metzi'a 44a: "He who punished the generation of the Deluge, and the generation of the builder of the Tower of Babylon, he will also

the Tower of Babel will wreak vengeance against he who is not true to his word." That
means in Yiddish, he who punished the generation of the Deluge and the generation of the
Tower of Babel, will punish whoever does not keep his word. All the more so, if one makes,
God forbid, a false oath, and engages in dishonest business. He brings sin to his wife and
5   his children, as the verse says, "Don't let your mouth bring you [into disfavor]."[61] This
means in Yiddish as follows: you should not sin with your mouth so that you do not bring
sin to your flesh and blood. The Gemara[62] also explains the verse, "Lest your bed be taken

11b

from under you."[63] This means in Yiddish, why should your bed be taken from you? Every
pious woman should remember this, and should make sure that her husband is only
10   involved with good deeds.

    The Gemara says about this, that this world and the world to come are like a man
who has two wives. When he does what one wants, the other becomes angry. This world
is the same way: if a man wants to please all people and fulfill all his needs, whether
for food, or drink, or clothing, or housing, or great wealth, or satisfying all of his chil-
15   dren's desires, he must have a lot. And if he does not have the means, then he must,
God forbid, do business dishonestly, and deceive his partner by diverting his share, or
swearing falsely, or forcing his partner to make an oath that would bring him, God forbid,

punish those, who do not live by their word." Also in B. Bava Metzi'a 49a; similar in
B. Bava Metzi'a 47b and elsewhere.

7   *Gemara.* (גמרא :27). S. B. Shabbat 32b: "Rabbi Natan says: Because of the violation of vows, the wife of a man may die, as it is written, 'Lest your bed be taken from under
you when you have no money to pay' (Prov. 22:27). Rabbi says: Because of the violation
of vows, the children die when they are still small, as it is written, 'Don't let your mouth
bring you into disfavor, and don't plead before the messenger that it was an error, but fear
God; else God may be angered by your talk and destroy your possessions' (Eccles. 5:5)."

11b

11   *Gemara.* (גמרא :3). Same in *Mishlei Ḥalchamin*, 5b.

14   *Housing.* (בניינים :6). Literally "buildings."

17   *Oath.* (שבועה :9). The following explanation describes the rabbinic concept of
the false oath (*shevuat shav*), which differentiates between perjury (*shevuat sheker*)—
delivering a false oath, although the truth is known (see below)—and a superfluous oath
(*shevuat shav*)—delivering an oath regarding a known fact (see below); cf. B. Shevuot 21a.
Regarding the oath of women in matters of commerce, cf. Shulḥan Arukh, *Ḥoshen
Mishpat*, 61:3; 87:15.
    Sefer ha-Gan, fol. 9a–b, includes a detailed warning of delivering perjury and oath in
the context of honest trading.
    Ze'enah u-Re'enah on Exod. 20:7, p. 436, explains that perjury is like idolatry: both
delay the arrival of the Messiah.
    Some moral books relate superfluous oaths and the utterance of God's name in vain
explicitly to women, such as *Brantshpigl*, p. 391: "One shall not utter the holy name in

no matter the situation, a punishment. If he is in the right, then he has done wrong by causing his partner to swear a false oath. If he is in the wrong, then the punishment comes from the fact that he has caused his partner to take an oath needlessly. But he who thinks of the world to come can prevent all of this. This is like the following analogy: when

5   one puts more onto one side of a balance than the other, it will outweigh the other. So too when one wants to do more for his body than for his soul—he will have to let go of *Gan Eden* and hold on to *Geihinnom*, God protect us.

The midrash says about "A stairway was set on the ground and its top reached to the sky":[64] *sullam*—stairway—is, in *gematria*, *mamon*—money—. The word *sullam* has the same

10 numeric value as the word *mamon*. That is to say that the Holy One, blessed be He, put money into the world so that through it one can reach heaven. Whomever the Holy One,

---

vain, moreover, one shall not deliver a false oath. . . . Particularly the women shall not utter the name, as at times they are not pure, that means when they are not (at all) permitted to utter the name of God."

Similar in *Eyn shoyn Froyenbuykhleyn*, fol. 49b.

Only the moral book *Iggeret Derekh ha-Shem*, 9b, which was written for men, mentions the limited sovereignty of women for their vows: וישמור מוצא שפתיו במה שנשבע או נדר או בכל נדרי הקדש ונחשבו לו קיום מצוה זו ויפר נדרי אשתו וביתו אם ראוי שיפר אותם.—"He must take care of his utterances, what is being sworn or vowed, or any holy vows. It shall be considered as observance of a mitzvah, if he violates vows made by his wife or other members of his house, believing it is necessary to violate them."

1   ***No matter the situation.*** (ממה נפשך :9). A term from rabbinic discourse, referring to an unreserved, prescriptive case: here it refers to the punishment that will follow in any case. Same on fol. 28a.

6   ***Body*** [...] ***soul.*** (נשמה [...] גוף :14). This is a more detailed description of the concept of the "wisdom of the soul": It includes elements of social conduct such as honesty in trading (see above) and charity (see below); in addition, it must keep the balance with the "wisdom of the body" (see above); cf. the commentary on pp. 87/7 and 90/11; cf. fol. 22b.

8   ***Midrash.*** (מדרש :16). Same on fol. 32b. The earliest source for the interpretation of *sullam* as *mamon* can be found in the book *Sefer Gematriot* by Yehudah he-Ḥasid (12th/13th centuries), fol. 4a: סולם מוצב ארצה בגימ' גלגל הוזר בעולם סולם בגימ' ממון או עוני זה ירים וזה ישפיל שנגזר משמיא די שליטין שמיא במלכות אינשא.—"'A stairway was set on the ground (Gen. 28:12) is in Gematria equivalent to "'The world is a wheel which revolves.' Stairway is in Gematria equivalent to possession or poverty: One goes up, the other comes down, as it has been decided in the heavens, that is how they rule the heavens in the kingdom of man"; cf. Abrams/Ta-Shma, *Sefer Gematri'ot*, fol. 4a. Yehudah he-Ḥasid's interpretation was passed on by various Ashkenazic traditions, and there is evidence to manuscripts going back to the 17th century; see ibid., p. 2ff. It can also be found at R. Jacob from Vienna (14th/15th centuries), who also resided in Moravia; cf. Gellis, *Sefer Tosafot*, vol. III, p. 100f.

9   ***In gematria.*** (בגמטרא :16). A rabbinical interpretation method based on identical numerical values: *sullam* (ladder) and *mamon* (money) both have the numerical value of 136.

blessed be He, blesses with good views, will invest well in charity and benevolence. This is as our beloved Torah wishes, and, praise God, as we have clearly, explicitly, and straight-forward in front of us, if we would only want to do it and to keep it in mind properly, then we could have this world as well as the world to come. As Moses, our teacher, peace be
5   upon him, said: "While you, who held fast to the LORD your God, are all alive today."[65] The Gemara[66] explains this as follows: "How is it possible to adhere to the *Shekhinah*? In that, just as the Holy One, blessed be He, is righteous, so you too are righteous; just as

12a

the Holy One, blessed be He, is merciful, so you shall be merciful; as he is the redeemer of pious ones, so you shall be. From this (one can deduce) the resurrection of the dead from
10   the Torah, as it says, "You are all alive today."[67]

Another explanation: just as one goes up and down a ladder, so too with money. One can quickly become rich or poor, as one merits it, and as is determined for him by God, blessed be His name. One also finds from time to time people who wish to ascend by force higher up the ladder than they belong. Then the person receives a blow, and falls all the way
15   down. This also applies to the person who wishes to become rich by force and does business dishonestly, and puts himself in danger, and buys stolen goods, and many other similar things. And then he quickly loses what he has, even what he had before. As the verse says, "One in a hurry to get rich makes only loss."[68] This means in Yiddish, he who hurries to become rich, has even less.

1   *Good views.* (גוטי דעה 19:). Regarding the connection between *mamon* and benevolence and charity, see B. Peah 15c: "Man gives benefaction with his possessions, and he gives charity both with his possessions, and with his body."

     S. Derekh Ereẓ, 3:3: "If you obtain possessions, be charitable with it, as long as it is in your hand. Acquire with your possessions both this world and the world to come."

6   *Gemara.* (גמרא 24:). Compiled from various sources; see B. Ketubbot 111b: "My teacher, I found improvement for her through the Torah (as it is written), 'You, who held fast to the LORD your God, are all alive today' (Deut. 4:4). But how is it possible, to hold on to the *Shekhinah*? It is written, 'The LORD your God is a consuming fire' (Deut. 4:24). In other words, the scripture says about every person, who marries off his daughter to a scholar, or provides a scholar with income, or supports a scholar from his own income, that he is holding fast to the *Shekhinah*."

     S. Maimonides, Sefer Miẓvot, *Miẓvot Aseh* 8: "'And walk in His ways' (Deut. 28:9). Here we have already a double order, which is, on the one hand, to walk in his path. This is interpreted as follows: Just as the Holy One, blessed be He, is called merciful, so you shall be merciful. Just as the Holy One, blessed be He, is called comforting, so you shall be comforting. Just as the Holy One, blessed be He, is called righteous, so you shall be righteous. Just like the Holy One, blessed be He, is called pious, so you shall be pious."

12a

12   *Determined.* (נגזור 4:). Spelling based on Yiddish pronunciation.
17   *Verse.* (פסוק 9:). The quoted verse is a conflation: see Prov. 28:20 and Prov. 21:5.

One can also find someone who has a good livelihood, and sees that his friend has a different livelihood that he would also like to have, so he envies his friend and competes with him for his sustenance, and allows his own previous sustenance to decline, believing the other is better. And he deprives, alas, his friend of his sustenance, for which he is punished by the Holy One, blessed be He, causing him to lose everything, even that which he had attained with his first livelihood.

In *Orḥot Ẓaddikim*[69] is the following fable written: One can find many different birds in the desert: some are yellow, some are green, and some are red—all kinds of colors. The

5

---

7   ***Orḥot Ẓaddikim.*** **(אורחת צדיקים :17).** The Yiddish spelling is based on the Yiddish pronunciation; same on fol. 24a. A print of the Hebrew book *Orḥot Ẓaddikim* was issued in the year 1743 in Frankfurt-am-Main with the same spelling, being probably a printer's mistake due to the Yiddish pronunciation.

The fable is not included in *Orḥot Ẓaddikim*; it does, however, appear in *Sefer Middot*, fol. 46a. It is possible that the author confused the Hebrew *Orḥot Ẓaddikim* (Prague, 1581) with the Yiddish *Sefer Middot* (Isny, 1542; Krakow, 1582). The chapters of these books are identically structured and bear the same names (merely the last chapter of *Orḥot Ẓaddikim* became the introduction in the *Sefer Middot*), but their contents differ significantly in various places. In any case, the quotes allow the assumption that the author was at least familiar with the *Sefer Middot*; cf. also the quotes on fols. 14b and 19a–b. In fact, *Sefer Middot* was later published under the title *Orḥot Ẓaddikim* (e.g., in Hanau, 1710), and their titles may have switched back and forth since the printing of the books in close chronological proximity, in 1581 and 1582. The relationship between the histories of the origins of the two texts, which probably both originate in a common Hebrew draft titled *Sefer Middot*, is hitherto unclarified; cf. Zinberg, *History*, pp. 148–153; Baumgarten, *Introduction*, p. 264f.

The fable is already contained in *Mishlei Shu'alim* (Mantua, 1557/58) by Berekhyah ha-Nakdan (12th/13th centuries), of which a Yiddish edition by Jacob ben Samuel Kopelman was published in 1583 in Freiburg/Breisgau; cf. Schwarzbaum, *Mishlei Shu'alim*, pp. 178–184. It is also found in the *Ku Bukh* in the edition of Moses ben Eliezer Wallich (Frankfurt, 1697; no. 21 [first print, Sabbioneta, 1555 (unverified); Verona, 1595]); cf. Baumgarten, *Introduction*, p. 394f.

The version in the *Sefer Middot* is significantly longer (323 words as opposed to 98 words here), and it reads in the translation (for comparison of the degree of Hebraization, the Hebrew words are transcribed): "An envious person (*kana'i*) is like a black bird flying in the desert (*midbar*), having only black feathers. In the desert (*midbar*) fly also many other birds with pretty feathers, red, green, and yellow, and other pretty colors. Every time the black bird sees one of those pretty feathers, lost by another bird, lying on the ground, it pulls out one of its own black feathers, and sticks the pretty feathers in its place, until it, too, is covered in pretty feathers. It feels envy (*kin'ah*), because it is so black, and the others are so pretty. So it flew to the other birds, for them to see how pretty it was. But each bird recognized its own feather, which the black bird had stuck on to itself. Then all the birds flew to the black bird, and each pulled out its own feathers, until the black bird had lost all its feathers and remained completely naked. Now it was forced to stand naked in front of all the other birds and it could not fly away, because it did not have any feathers on its body. Not only did it not have the pretty feathers anymore, it had also lost its own black feathers. This happened because it had felt envy (*kin'ah*) toward the other, pretty birds, and did not content itself with the feathers that the Creator, blessed be He

---

raven envies the birds their beautiful colors, and so tears out all his black feathers, and gathers the beautiful feathers that the other birds have dropped, and sticks them into himself. Later the other birds come along, recognize their feathers, and pluck them all out, each bird taking his own feathers, leaving him totally bare and naked.

5   This is why every pious woman should be forewarned, and should hold her husband to good with convincing arguments, because a good woman is responsible for much,

12b

as the proverb says: "A pious wife makes her husband pious."

    The midrash[70] says our Patriarch Jacob brought sin to his daughter Dinah, who was made impure because he did not want to give her to Esau, even though she might have
10 made him pious. And so too, the opposite: A bad woman does not remember that King Solomon, peace be upon him, said, "Wicked woman is more bitter than death."[71] There is an

(*bore yitbarakh*) had created and given to it. This example comes to show that one should not feel envy (*kin'ah*) toward anybody, and that everybody should content himself with what the Holy One, blessed be He (*ha-kadosh barukh hu*) has given him. Such happens to the envious person (*kana'i*): He who feels envy (*kin'ah*) will lose all his possessions (*mamon*), too. He will not succeed in anything, if he feels envy (*kin'ah*), just as it happened to the black bird."

    The stylistic differences between the version in *Meneket Rivkah* and in *Sefer Middot* lie in the use of different words: here it is "raven" instead of "black bird"; "gathers" instead of "finds"; "pluck" instead of "tear"; on one occasion a different Hebrew word is used: *mekane*—he envies—instead of *kin'ah hoben*—feel envy. Deviations in the content are the missing indication to the vanity of the raven, and his inability to fly because of the lost feathers, and in the missing indication here that personal characteristics or possessions are granted by God. However, we have here the introduction of punishment for unsocial conduct (disputing somebody else's basis for livelihood), which in itself is of divine origin.

12b

7   *Proverb.* (שפריך ווארט 1:). Popular Yiddish expression (also on fol. 14a); see *Brantshpigl*, p. 51, where it is said about Eve, in the context of the tale of Lilith, that she was better than Lilith insofar as she was obedient and helpful toward her husband: "Of her one would say in Yiddish, 'A pious woman educates a pious man.'"
    The same proverb appears in *Sefer Mishlei*, fol. 12a (on Prov. 5:18).

8   *Midrash.* (מדרש 2:). S. Tanḥuma, Va-yishlaḥ 19: "When our Patriarch Jacob came with the tribes, Dinah was with him. When the messengers came saying, 'We came to your brother Esau' (Gen. 32:7), Jacob put Dinah into a trunk so that Esau would not see her and take her for his wife. The Holy One, blessed be He, said to him: You withheld her from him, by your life! She would have made an uncircumcised man better, as it is written, 'A friend owes loyalty to one who fails' (Job 6:14). Had she married Esau, she might have turned him into a proselyte."

11   *Wicked woman.* (אשה רעה 5:). The quote is an interpretation; the respective masoretic text of Eccles. 7:26 doesn't contain the word "wicked." Cf. Midrash Tehillim, 59:5: "A different interpretation: 'He who finds a wife has found happiness' (Prov. 18:22). But a wicked wife is more bitter than her." See the commentary on p. 110/10.

objection to be raised—what can be bitterer than death? What it refers to is a bad woman who causes her husband to engage in robbery and assault, depriving others of what is theirs through false oaths and deceit and much more of the same that I do not want to write. Such a woman brings her husband to *Geihinnom*, on which the verse says, "She snares a person of honor."[72] This means that even if he is respected, she will chase him into hell. If, however, she is a good woman, she remembers everything for one purpose: "If I could have everything as I want, and have my every wish and desire, my husband will not deal honestly in business, and then, God forbid, my children will have to pay for it." As the verse says, "Remembering [the guilt] of the parents upon the children."[73] This means in Yiddish, God, blessed be He, remembers the sins of the parents on the children.

At times one finds a woman to whom it does not matter if her husband is excommunicated, as long as she has enough—God protect us from such views. She should, however,

1   ***Objection.*** (קשיא :5). "Difficulty," "objection," "argument." The Aramaic term, used in the rabbinic discourse, describes an exegetic problem; see also 3b; 5a; 28b; 30a; 33b.

2   ***Robbery and assault.*** (גוזל וחומס :7). A word pair commonly found in rabbinic literature; such as in Va-yikra Rabbah 3.1: "He is better, who goes out to work and is charitable with his possession, than he who robs and extorts, and is charitable with the possession of others."

     S. Tanḥuma (Warsaw), Ki Tetse 4: "Esau went out and robbed and extorted. The people cursed him, and within five years, during which he departed from Abraham's way of life, Esau committed two grave sins."

4   ***Geihinnom.*** (גיהנם :10). S. similar choice of words in *Sefer Mishlei*, fol. 15a: "אונ׳ דער דא אום קיישט מיט איינר די דו אין מאן האט וען שון דער זעלביג מענש פאר גאר קעשטליך איז דענוך טוט זיא אים יאגן אין דאז גיהנם."—"And he who fornicates with a woman, who has a husband, and even if he was previously upright, she will send him to *Geihinnom*."

     The author does not argue that the woman, because of her bad influence, could lose her share in the world to come. The mutual dependency of the married couple is discussed in *Brantshpigl*, p. 56f.: "If a righteous man has an evil woman, and if she does not repent, he must wait for her (until she repents, and can then enter into the world to come). If an evil man has a pious wife, and she does not cause him to repent, she must wait for him. If both are pious or bad, and one dies before the other, then one of them must still wait for the other (until they can enter into the world to come, together)."

9   ***Remembering.*** (פוקד :14). Cf. the expression "Visiting the guilt of the parents upon the children" from Exod. 20:5, 34:7; Num. 14:18; Deut. 5:8. The word *avon*—iniquity, transgression—was dropped in the print but is translated here.

11-12   ***Excommunicated.*** (חרמות :16). The banishment, here as punishment for dishonest economic conduct (thus falling into the halakhic category of *niddui*; cf. B. Moed Katan 16a), constitutes a disciplinary sanction used by the religious authority against individual members of the community. It means the partial or total prohibition of mutual interaction between the banned person and the community, up to complete excommunication. The partial excommunication included the limited prohibition of holding a worldly position, of religious tasks (reading from the Torah, participation in communal prayer), and individual issues (circumcision of sons, marriage of children, Jewish burial). However, there are many reports of banned persons disregarding the ban; cf. Katz,

know how far the punishment for someone who has been excommunicated extends. He must tear his clothing, God protect us, and must sit like a mourner on the ground. The midrash says that a person, God protect us, who is excommunicated for one day is excommunicated in heaven for three days. And if he is excommunicated for three days, he must be excommunicated in heaven for a week. And whoever is excommunicated for a week must be excommunicated in heaven for thirty days. And whoever is excommunicated for thirty days must be excommunicated in heaven for a whole year. And whoever is excommunicated for a whole year must be excommunicated for eternity in the world to come. That is why every pious woman should protect her husband from this.

She should be helpful to him in all things, as the verse says, "I will make a fitting helper for him."[74] "If he merits it, we will make him a help; if he [does not] merit it, (she will be) against him."[75] This means as follows: If she wants to, she can help him to *Gan Eden*; if she

---

Tradition, p. 84ff. This is possibly a recount of an event in the history of Prague: in order to escape providing suretyship for Meisel's risky financial transactions, the Prague community banished him in 1592. However, the ban was lifted when Emperor Rudolf assumed suretyship for him; cf. Veltri, "Rudolf II," p. 245.

2   **Tear his clothing.** (קריעה :18). The tearing of a piece of clothing by a mourner, as a symbol of his mourning; cf. B. Moed Katan 22b. Symbolically, this is an expression of mourning over the banished who has, in a way, died a social death, as far as he was excluded from the social and the religious community; regarding the tearing of clothing as a ritual of mourning, cf. Goldberg, *Crossing*, p. 141f.

3   *Midrash.* (מדרש :19). It is unclear whether this is a rabbinic source.

    (()() :23). The two empty brackets serve as line fillers.

10   *Helpful.* (בהילפיג :25). See the commentary on p. 112/13. The ideal conduct, according to which the wife assists her husband in the observation of his obligations, is occasionally described in the moral literature; see *Sefer Middot*, fol. 22b: ‏"ער זול גידענקן דש‏ אין זיין וייבא ביהויט בור זוינדן. דאש ער ניט דארף זנות טרייבן מיט אנדרן וויבן. אונ' דש ער מיט זיינם וייבא קינדר גיווינט. דיא זיא אים דר ציכט אונ' זיא צו אלם גוטן גווינט אונ' זיא קובט אים אונ' טוט אים אל זיין בידורפניש אים היוז צום בעשטן. דרום איז ער מוישיג דאש ער קאן תורה לערנן אונ' מצוות אונ' מעשים טובים קאן טון צום בעשטן דא העלפט זיא אים צו."—"He should take into consideration that his wife saves him from the sin of fornication with other women, which is prohibited to him. He should have children with his wife, who will bring them up on his behalf, and who will raise them to do good. She cooks for him, and tends to all of his needs in the house in the best of manners. Thus he has peace of mind and can learn Torah and fulfill mitzvot, and perform good deeds in the best of manners: she enables him to do all that." Similar on fol. 98a.

    See *Brantshpigl* regarding the woman's marital obligations: Urging her husband to study Torah, ibid., pp. 42, 64; to observe religious obligations, ibid., p. 42f.; to participate in communal prayers, ibid., p. 42f.; to manage the household and the education of children, ibid., pp. 45, 133, and 135; to modesty, ibid., pp. 42 and 66; to moral conduct, ibid., p. 44; to be charitable, ibid., pp. 132, 191, 207, 347.

11   *Merits.* (זכה :26). See the commentary to 9a/13.

13a

does not want to, she helps him to *Geihinnom*. There is a story in the Gemara[76] about Rabbi
Yosse bar Ḥalafta who had a pious wife. He was extremely poor and did not even have
enough for his livelihood. They were so poor that one Friday they did not have enough to
prepare for Shabbat. The pious man was distressed, and went to the fields and prayed that
5 God, blessed be He, should provide for him that he be able to feed his wife and children
from the charity of the people. God, blessed be He, immediately heard his prayer, and
threw down a precious stone. He went directly to his rabbi, Rabbi Shimon ben Yoḥai, and
told him what had happened. He said, "It is very valuable, and you cannot sell it so
quickly—borrow as much as you need for Shabbat against it." That is what he did, and he
10 bought what he needed for Shabbat. When they were about to eat, his wife asked him
where he got the food. She did not want to eat until he told her where he got it from, since
it may not have been acquired honestly. After he told her, she said that she did not want to
eat from the food and that he should promise her that he would redeem the valuable stone.
He should return it, because it was taken from his share in the world to come, and his
15 reward in the world to come would therefore not be complete. And so he went to his rabbi
and told him what his wife had said. He said, "Tell your wife that whatever will be

13a

1   *Gemara.* (גמרא :1).   The story is not substantiated in the Gemara; it is, however, frequently substantiated in the Midrash, with the most detail in Shemot Rabbah 52.3;
see further Tanḥuma, Pekudei 7; Yalkut, §964; similar in Midrash Tehillim 82:8; Yalkut,
§843; *Oẓar Midrashim*, p. 138. The tale is also popular in the moral literature; cf. *Reshit
Ḥokhmah*, III, p. 29f., §6; *Sefer Mishlei*, fol. 86a; *Brantshpigl*, p. 32f.
          The interpretation that turns the course of the tale (p. 129/1) is an example of the
author's abbreviated rabbinic method of interpretation: the reference to the "special world
for himself" of each and every righteous person does not explicitly clarify that this is the
reason for the impossibility for R. Yosse bar Ḥalafta to complete the incomplete merit in
the world to come.
          All sources name Shimon ben Ḥalafta as the protagonist (Yosse bar Ḥalafta's appear-
ances as a halakhic figure is limited mainly to halakhic texts). Like in Shemot Rabbah 52.3,
the woman is assigned an active role here: she is pious and upright when she expresses her
fear that the purchase was unjust; she recognizes the stone as a share in the world to
come; and she is learned, in that she argues using a quote from the scriptures that
convinces the Rabbi; in no other version do her husband and the rabbi thank her for her
wise caution. In the shorter version that appears in *Reshit Ḥokhmah*, III, p. 29f., §6, the
woman's learned argumentation is missing. The version in *Sefer Mishlei*, fol. 86a, is similar
to that in *Reshit Ḥokhmah*: the woman is stingy and envious, because the use of the stone
reduces her husband's share in the world to come as opposed to that of her neighbor. The
version in *Brantshpigl*, p. 32f., is similarly abbreviated: "Rabbi Shimon ben Ḥalafta did not
have anything to eat on the Sabbath. He prayed, and was given a precious pearl. His wife
asked him. 'Where did you get this from?' He said, 'It was handed to me from heaven.'
She answered, 'Return it, because in the end, a pearl will be missing in the crown that will
be put on your head in *Gan Eden*.' So he returned it."

removed from you, I will replenish." She responded that the verse says, "But man sets out for his eternal abode."[77] This means that when a person goes to his world, each righteous one has a special world for himself. They conceded that she was correct and (Rabbi Yosse) returned to the same place and [prayed]. Then a hand came and took the precious stone away. Our sages,[78] may their memory be a blessing, said that the second miracle was greater than the first, since one has often heard that the Holy One, blessed be He, is accustomed to giving. But one has never heard that He has taken back.

Every pious woman should also do this. But, due to our many transgressions, there are few who have such a view, and few who ask from where their husband has acquired something, as long as they have it. And so, my dear, pious women, I ask that you judge me

13b

favorably, because my intention is that others should accept admonition and should engage with it, and that every woman should be satisfied with her husband, and should request of him no more than [God], blessed be His name, bestows on him. As a (Hebrew) proverb says, "He who gives away more than the divine Name has decreed for him—no wonder he goes in tatters." In Yiddish this is also, "He who consumes more than God, blessed be His name, bestows—it is no wonder that he goes in rags." This is why every woman should make sure that her husband does not squander money and does not use more than he has, but not maliciously or with anger, rather only if she sees that he is of good will. As King

5   *Sages.* (חכמים :22). The final interpretation is also found, besides the aforesaid sources (see the commentary on p. 128/1), in B. Ta'anit 25a, but there for a different story of similar structure: "The second miracle was greater than the first. Because there is a decision: Whoever gives something, gives it, and whoever gives something up, does not take back."

    13b

13   *Proverb.* (שפריך ווארט :3). The unusual parallel quote of a Hebrew and respective Yiddish proverb is similar to the usage of a Bible verse with subsequent translation. Similar in *Mishlei Ḥakhamim*, fol. 11a–b: (!) מי שרוצה לפזר יותר מאשר לו נגזר אין להפלי" עליו כי יבוש בחוסר כל ושאין לו בגד ללבוש — ווער דא איז וויל פור צערין מין אז אים גוט ית' איז בישערן דא איז ניט זיך ניט בור וואונדרן אייף זיין ארמוט דער ווייל דש ער מין אז ער בור מאג בור טוט".—"He who wishes to spend more than was decreed to him, should not be surprised when he finds himself in shame, because he has no clothing to wear.—He who consumes more than God, blessed be He, has bestowed upon him, should not wonder about his poverty, because he spends more than is good for him." A German proverb with the keywords "wonder" and "rags" has only been substantiated since the 19th century; cf. Grimm, *Wörterbuch*, vol. 30, p. 1822.

18   *Maliciously or with anger.* (בושיקיט אונ' צאורין :8-7). The request that the woman shall utter justified criticism only in the most gentle words, even in extreme cases such as infidelity, can also be found in *Brantshpigl*, p. 66: "She must not be angry with the husband. If she feels that he leaves the house because of his feelings of lust, because his evil inclination drives him to seek out women or young girls, she should tell

Solomon, peace be upon him, said, "A gentle response allays wrath; a harsh word provokes anger."[79] This means in Yiddish, mild words avert anger, but upsetting words arouse anger. All the more so should a woman faithfully help her husband to keep his possessions together as far as she can or is able to, because when one hand washes the other, both will be clean.

On these issues about which I have written, and about which one finds different views, King Solomon, peace be upon him, also said, "I find the woman more bitter than death."[80] Another time it says, "The one I found among so many was never a woman,"[81] and another time he said, "He who finds a woman has found happiness."[82] This is the explanation of the three verses: In the verse, "He who finds a woman has found happiness,"[83] the word *ishah*—woman—is worth numerically less than the word *ish*—man. That is to say, if he has found a woman who is subservient to her husband, and has a lower opinion of herself than her husband, and follows him, and does not think, "He is beneath me," that man has found something good through God, blessed be His name. The verse goes on to say, "I find the woman more bitter than death."[84] This means, he who finds a wife who wants to be the same as her husband, and will not yield to him, since *ha-ishah*—the woman—has the same numerical value as *ish*, and this wife is more bitter than death. But (in the verse), "The one I found among so many was never a woman,"[85] the wife wants to be more than her husband because *ve-ishah*—and a woman—is worth one more in numerical value than *ish*—such

him gently, 'What do you miss with me? You can live out your lust with me. Even if it is not possible for a few days, it is not for eternity. You transgress the Torah, where it says, "*Lo tin'af.* Thou shalt not fornicate," it says so in many places.' If she speaks to him like this, without anger, it is very honorable, and no shame to her."

1   *Allays.* (משיב :9).   Same on fol. 30b; Prov. 15:1 reads (instead of *meshiv*) *yashiv*. The mistaken use of the present participle instead of the imperfect may be influenced by its use in Proverbs; cf. Prov. 17:13; Prov. 18:13; Prov. 24:26. However, this expression has already been found in rabbinic use; see B. Berakhot 17a: "'A gentle response allays (*meshiv*) wrath' (Prov. 15:1). He who increases peace with his brother, with his neighbor, and with any person, even with a stranger in the market, he will be loved above, and will be popular below." Cf. the book title *Meshiv Ḥema—Minhagim Eshet Ḥayil.*

2   *Mild.* (דעמהפטיגי :10).   The author translates the biblical *rakh*—soft, mild, gentle—in an unusual manner literally as "a lady's style." *Sefer Mishlei*, fol. 36a, translates *rakh* as *vaykhe*—soft.

9   *Explanation.* (פשט :16).   The source for the numerical interpretation of Prov. 18:22; Eccles. 7:26, and Eccles. 7:28 is unclear; regarding the popular interpretation of the verse regarding conjugal hierarchy; cf. Tanḥuma, Naso 4.

11   *Ishah—woman.* (אשה :17).   The numerical value is 306.

11   *Ish—man.* (איש :18).   The numerical value is 311.

16   *Ha-ishah—the woman.* (האשה :23).   The numerical value is 311.

19   *Ve-ishah—and a woman.* (ואשה :25).   The numerical value is 312.

a woman is totally unheard of. Still, our sages[86] explained this verse for the benefit of us women. When the verse says, "The one I found among so many was never a woman,"[87] this

14a

means that Israel made the Golden Calf, and said, "This is your God, Israel."[88] This means in Yiddish, this is your God, Israel. But no woman had any part in it, and none would give their consent to it, as the verse says, "And they took off the rings that were in their ears."[89] This means, all (men) gave their earrings, but the women did not want to give their earrings. That is why we do not find any women among the tribes of the desert.

On the issues about which I wrote above, the verse also says, "Her husband is prominent in the gates."[90] This means that the husband will be recognized in his wife. An upright wife crowns her husband with her good deeds. She should treat him with respect as the proverb says, "If you treat your husband with respect, you [will] also grow old beside him like a queen."

1   *Sages.* (חכמים :27). As opposed to the aforesaid interpretation of *ve-ishah* as "a women unheard of," the author points to a different interpretation of this word from Eccles. 7:28, there, however, not in context with the Golden Calf; see Va-yikra Rabbah 2.1: "'I found only one human being in a thousand' (Eccles. 7:28). That is Moses. 'And the one I found among so many was never a woman' (ibid.). These are the women of the generation of the desert. Rabbi says, the women of the generation of the desert were perfect, because when they heard that they were prohibited to their men, they immediately closed their doors. The Holy One, blessed be He, said, through preciousness they stand by me."

14a

5   *Took off.* (ויתפרקו :3). Cf. the different reading of Exod. 32:3.

6   *But the women.* (אביר דיא ווייבר :4). S. Ba-midbar Rabbah 21.10: "'Take off the gold rings that are on the ears of your wives' (Exod. 32:2). But the women did not want to, and opposed their husbands, as it is written, 'And all the people took off the gold rings' (Exod. 32:3) etc. The women did not participate in the manufacturing of the calf." The interpretation is based on the lack of an explicit mention of the women in Exod. 32:3, thus implying the exclusive participation of the men, although in Exod. 32:2 the women's earrings are mentioned.

8   *Above.* (אובין :6). S. fol. 8b. The context there is that she is a perfect, capable woman, who urges her husband to study; see the commentary on p. 110/9.

10   *Crowns.* (קרינט :8). The interpretation of Prov. 31:23 recurs with Prov. 12:4/1: "A capable wife is a crown for her husband." In the later ethic and epigraphic literature, the verse became the *locus classicus* for the ideal of female submission, but it is only rarely used in moral literature. *Brantshpigl*, p. 61, presents the image of the crown for the ideal woman: "Stand before your man and serve him, as one would stand before a king and serve him. If you will conduct yourself with him like a maid, he will be your servant, and he will adore you, and he will provide for everything that you might need. But if you attempt to rule over him, he will be your master, against your will. Adorn yourself for him, make yourself beautiful, and go to him cleanly, so that he will like what he sees. Be diligent in your actions, so that he may like it, then you will be the crown on his head." See the commentary on p. 111/13.

A woman should think about how it is written in our holy Torah, "And he shall rule over you."[91] We also learn from our mother Sarah that she called her husband "my lord" even though she was more imbued with prophecy than he was, as the [verse] says, "Whatever Sarah tells you, do as she says."[92] This means in Yiddish, everything that she, Sarah, says to you, listen to her voice. Our sages[93] also wrote, "A man should always be cautious with his wife's honor." This means in Yiddish, a man should always be cautious with his wife's honor. The Gemara[94] goes on, "Blessing is only found in a man's house due to his wife, as it says, 'And because of her it went well with Abraham.'"[95] This means that blessing is in a man's house due to his wife's merits. As it is written about Abraham, he was privileged with wealth because of Sarah's merits.

But this is a case of *a fortiori*—she should be cautious with his honor. And every pious woman should be warned not to, God forbid, curse her husband, as one finds among quite a few (women). She could, God forbid, commit a sin, as we find with Michal the daughter of Saul, who sinned against her husband King David, peace be upon him, and so could have

---

1   **And he. (והוא** :11**).** S. the interpretation of Gen. 3:16 in *Brantshpigl*, p. 302: "The Prophet Isaiah said, 'And not to ignore your own kin' (Isa. 58:7)....The sages interpret this as wife, child, and servants. All of these are counted as his kin. It is written in Aḥarei Mot, 'None of you shall come near anyone of his own flesh' (Lev. 18:6). And all that is near to him is his flesh. And if he is angry, he must strike them, because the Torah has given him superiority over them. Of them it is written in Genesis, 'And he shall rule over you' (Gen. 3:16). If she wishes to resist, she will only make it worse."

2   **My lord. (מיין הער** :12**).** Cf. Gen. 18:12.

3   **Prophecy. (נבואה** :12**).** Regarding the idea that Sarah had greater prophetic power than Abraham, see Shemot Rabbah 1.1: "'Do not be distressed (over the boy or your maid; whatever Sarah tells you, do as she says, for it is through Isaac that offspring shall be continued for you)' (Gen. 21:12) etc. From this you can learn, that Abraham was less in prophecy than Sarah." Same in Tanḥuma, (Warsaw), Shemot 1; Rashi on Gen. 21:12.

5   **Sages. (חכמים** :14**).** S. B. Bava Metziʼa 59a: "'It is written, Israel was reduced to utter misery by the Midianites' (Judg. 6:6). Ḥelbo (said): Man shall always honor his wife's dignity, as the blessing is in the house of a man because of his wife only, as it is written, 'And because of her, it went well with Abram' (Gen. 12:16). Therefore Raba told the inhabitants of Maḥoza, 'Honor your wives, that you may become rich.'" Similar in Yalkut, § 68.

7   **Gemara. (גמרא** :16**).** See the commentary above.

9   **Written. (גשריבן** :19**).** See the commentary above. S. also *Midrash Mishlei*, 31:11: "This is what our mother Sarah meant, because of whom Abraham became rich."
       S. Ibn Ezra on Gen. 24:1: "And the Lord blessed Abraham with a long life, and with wealth, and honor, and children, and that is all a man longs for."

12   **Curse. (מקלל** :21**).** Regarding cursing, see the commentary on p. 106/14.

13-14   **Michal the daughter of Saul. (מיכל בת שאול** :23-22**).** Cf. II Sam. 6:16–23. Regarding the explanation of Michal's lack of children as a result of her disrespectful conduct toward David, cf. B. Sanhedrin 24a; Ba-midbar Rabbah 4.20.

no children until her end. This is why every woman should beware not to sin against her husband, and all the more so against other people.

But when she sees him do something improper, she should disallow it, because a pious wife makes her husband pious. She should discuss everything with him amicably, and he
5 will certainly obey her. And if it should be that he will obey her, and she him, and they have

14b

peace and harmony, then they will be privileged together to have good fortune, blessings, and success in all their undertakings for many years. They will merit having children who will be Torah scholars, which is the greatest wealth and happiness. And the Holy One, blessed be He, loves when marriage is consummated in love and affection and in His service
10 in order to observe His holy Torah. This is the purpose of creation, and this should all occur quickly, in our days, Amen. And then this verse will be fulfilled: "In that day there shall be one LORD with one name."[96]

3   *Disallow.* (ניט גשטטין 26:).   Regarding the woman's right to forbid the man a certain conduct, see the commentary on p. 151/1.

3-4   *A pious wife.* (איין ורום וווייב 26:).   See the commentary to 12b/1.

14b

9   *Love and affection.* (באהבה ובחבה 4:).   The couple's feelings during marital intercourse are rarely mentioned; however, in rabbinic literature, mutual consent and the necessary intimacy and attention are mentioned, cf. B. Nedarim 20a–b; B. Eruvin 100b and respectively Rashi; cf. also Boyarin, *Carnal Israel*, p. 120ff.

S. *Brantshpigl*, p. 269: "If she senses that he does not like her, she should make herself pretty for him. If she does not love him, she should remove the rejection from her heart. Our sages write that the intercourse of man and woman shall only take place with great love and friendship, and that the thoughts of both should be pure to the honor of God."

In contrast, the warning of performing marital intercourse for reasons of lust is frequently found; see *Sefer Middot*, fol. 24b: אויך וועו איינר איין וווייבא נימט זו זול ער זיא"
ניט אליין נעמן זיין לושט מיט איר צו האבן וד"ל נוייערט דרום דאש ער קינדר וויל מיט איר האבן
".די׳א הקדוש ברוך הוא איין דינן זולן—"Even if one takes a wife, he should not do it merely to live out his lust with her—and the meaning is understood—rather only because he wants to have children with her, which will also serve the Holy One, blessed be He."

Eyn shoyn Froyenbuykhleyn, fol. 21a: אונ׳ איין איטליכש מענש זאל גיוואורנט זיין. מאן אדר"
וווייב דש זיא איין דער צייט אין דער בייא דער לייגן נישט זאלן רידן נאך קין ביזן גידאנקין זאלין האבן
[...]אונ׳ ער אונ׳ זיא זאלן זיך ניט מכוין זיין צו דער הנאה [...] דש אנדר זאלן זיא מחשבה
".האבן דש זי זי וועלן מקיים זיין מצות פרייה ורביה—"All people, man or woman, shall take care not to talk or have bad thoughts, when they lie with each other.... Neither of them shall be guided by pleasure.... Moreover, they shall keep in mind the commandment of fertility." Similar in *Reshit Hokhmah*, I, p. 494, §80.

11   *In that day.* (ביום 6:).   Zech. 14:9 is used frequently in the liturgy, most prominently at the end of the *Aleinu* prayer recited at the conclusion of each day's three prayer services.

Chapter Three

How a woman and her husband should spend their time with their father and mother, so that God, blessed be His name, should lengthen their years in this world and the world to come.

5   The verse in Proverbs says, "It is for her fear of the LORD that a woman is to be praised."[1] In Yiddish this [means], one should praise a God-fearing woman. It is known to us that *yir'at adonai,* which is fear of God, is essential to people. As *Sefer Middot*[2] writes, just as all the pearls on a string of pearls stay together because of a knot, so too if a person has all the desirable (qualities). If he does not have fear of God, then all is lost. If, however, he has fear

10   of God, then he will certainly have all other good qualities.

2   ***And her husband. (מיט אירין מאן** :9). The chapter deals with the conduct toward parents. Therefore, the Yiddish preposition *mit* (with) must here be read as a conjunction (and) rather than as a relative pronoun. Subsequently the modal verb *zol*—should—is understood as plural.

7   ***Fear of God. (ה'** :13). Regarding fear of God, see the commentary on p. 91/6 and below.

7   ***Sefer Middot. (ספר מדות** :14-13). S. *Sefer Middot*, fol. 4b: אז ווען איינר פערליך״ רייהט אן אין שנור. וען מאן ניט אין קנופפא מאכט אונטן אן דיא שנור. זא בלייבן דיא פערליך ניט דאראן. אונ׳ ואלן אלי אלי העראב. אזו איז אויך גוטש ית׳ בורכט דער האלט אל גוטי מידות. אונ׳ ווער דען קנופפא אויף טוט אונ׳ ניט גוט ית׳ בורכט אויף אים הוט. זא ואלן בון אים אלי גוטי ״מידות אלי אונ׳ ווערק—״It is as if someone threads pearls on a string: If you don't make a knot at the end of the string, the pearls don't remain, they all fall off. It is the same with the fear of God, blessed be He. It holds all (other) virtues. When someone opens the knot, and has no fear of God, blessed be He, he loses them all, all good deeds, and all virtues." Similar in *Brantshpigl,* p. 185. There, the fear of God and humility are equally described as pillars of all other virtues.

S. also the Hebrew parallel records *Orḥot Ẓaddikim,* fol. 3a: לכן יש להודיע לכל כי כל״ יראת כי ומדה מידה כל עם שמים יראת לערב צריך הטובות מידות לידי נפשו להביא הרוצה קשר וקשרו המרגלית חורי תוך שהכניסהו לחוט ודומה המדו׳ כל המחזקת קשר היא השם היא הירראה כך המרגליות. כל יפלו הקשר בהנתק ספק אין המרגליו׳ כל להחזיק בתחתיתו מידות הטובות. כל ממך יבדלו הירראה קשר תתיר ואם המידות כל מחזקת—"Therefore every person, who wishes to lead a virtuous life, must be told that he must combine the fear of God with every individual virtue, because fear of God is the knot that keeps all virtues together. It is like a string on which perforated pearls are strung, and its end closed with a knot, in order to keep the pearls together. Undoubtedly, all pearls would fall off, if the knot were to be cut. Such is the fear (of God), it keeps all virtues together. If the knot of the fear (of God) were to be released, all virtues would fall away from you."

9   ***Desirable. (חפצות** :15). Literally "wishes," "desires"; here used for the desirable ways of conduct; the Hebrew word is not contained either in the appropriate context in the *Sefer Middot,* which has *gute middes*—good qualities, or in *Brantshpigl,* there *tugent*—virtue.

And in our dear Torah it is written, "Revere only the Lord your God."[3] This means in Yiddish, you should fear God, your God. And another verse says, "You shall each revere mother and father."[4] This means in Yiddish, a man should fear his father and mother. The Torah cautioned about the fear of mother and father as well as about its own fear.

The Torah also mentioned it often in the context of the punishment, and wrote, "If he pronounces the name of the Lord he shall be put to death."[5] This means in Yiddish, he who articulates the name with its letters has earned the death penalty. It also says in a verse, "He who insults his father or his mother shall be put to death."[6] This means in Yiddish, he

15a

who curses father or mother—killed, he should be killed.

Regarding honor, it is written in the Torah, "Honor the Lord with your wealth."[7] This means in Yiddish, honor God with your possessions. And regarding father and mother it is written, "Honor your father and your mother."[8] This means in Yiddish, you should honor your father and your mother.

The Holy One, blessed be He, cautioned three times about father and mother as well as about himself: with fear, with punishment, and with honor, as I cited it here. The Gemara[9] teaches here, "Honor of father and mother is greater than that of the Holy One, blessed be He." Honor of father and mother is greater, because the Holy One, blessed be He, warned about it more than His own honor, may He be blessed. It is written, "Honor the Lord

---

1   *The.* (את :18). Similar in Deut. 10:20.

5   *Punishment.* (עונש :21). Regarding the biblical punishments, cf. Lev. 24:15–23.

6   *Pronounces.* (שם :23). S. B. Sanhedrin 66a: "Rabbi Menaḥem said on behalf of Rabbi Yosse: 'If he has thus pronounced the Name, he shall be put to death' (Lev. 24:16). What does the teaching say in this matter? (It says it) in order to teach that he, who curses his father and his mother, is not guilty, unless he curses them with the name (of God)." Same in Yalkut, §§ 609, 658, 825; Mekhilta de-Rabbi Yishmael, *Mishpatim*, 5.

15a

14   *Three times.* (דרייא מאל :4). This means here the three distinct features of the parent-child relationship: "fear" (Prov. 31:30: fol. 14b; Deut. 6:13: ibid.; Lev. 19:13: ibid.), "punishment" (Lev. 24:16: ibid.; Exod. 21:17: ibid.), and "honor" (Prov. 3:9: fol. 15a; Exod. 20:11: ibid.), as well as their three objects, father, mother, and God. The indication paraphrases and structures the preceding statements.

15   *Gemara.* (גמרא :7). Not substantiated in the Talmud; see Yalkut, § 297: "Rabbi Shimon ben Yoḥai says: Most important is honoring father and mother, to which God gives higher priority than his own honoring, as it is written, 'Honor the Lord with your possessions.'" Similar in *Pesikta Rabbati*, 23; *Oẓar Midrashim*, p. 78.

     S. Yalkut, § 932: "Rabbi Shimon ben Yoḥai said: Most important is honoring father and mother, as the scripture compared their honoring with His honoring, the fear of them with the fear of Him, and their curse with His cursing. Such is the law, as these three are part of it."

with your wealth."[10] This means, when you have a lot you are obligated to give a lot, as we find with the sacrifices, offerings, and tithes. But regarding honoring one's father and mother it says, "Honor your father and your mother."[11] Whether you have something or have nothing, you are obligated to do it, even if one must go door to door and beg to support his father and mother.

5

The Gemara[12] also teaches: "Revere only the LORD your God"[13]—(the accusative particle) *et* includes Torah scholars. One must fear a Torah scholar, and honor him and support him, as we find regarding Jehoshaphat, the King of Judah. When he saw a Torah scholar coming, he would stand up from his chair, run up to him, embrace him, and kiss

10

him. The Gemara[14] also says, "All the Prophets only prophesied for him who supports a Torah scholar from his possessions." This means, all the good things that our Prophets foretold for the Jews, and all the consolation that they gave, they spoke them to a person who supports people who study Torah from his possessions, which were given to him by [God], blessed be His name.

15

The *et* located at "honoring one's father and mother"[15] is explained by the Gemara:[16] "The *et* is to include your father's wife." This means that one should honor a stepmother or stepfather because of (the commandment) to honor father and mother. And the other *ve-et* means, "It includes your older brother."[17] One should also honor one's [oldest] brother.

Fear of God is a fundamental part of all of these things. For someone who is God-fearing,

---

4   ***Go door to door.*** (חוזר על הפתחים :12).   S. Tosafot, Kiddushin 31a: "'Honor your father and your mother' (Exod. 20:12). This means whether one has possession or not. If it is so, one must go from door to door and beg, in order to support one's father and mother."

S. *Brantshpigl*, p. 227: "And in the Yerushalmi they write, if one has nothing, he must go and beg. But Rabbenu Tam decides as follows: Every person is obligated to support his father and mother, even if he fears that he must beg." See the commentary on p. 142/23.

6   ***Gemara.*** (גמרא :14).   S. B. Pesaḥim 22b: "He said to them: Just as I received reward for the interpretation (of all accusative particles *et*), I also receive reward for discontinuing (their interpretation). Until Rabbi Akiva came and interpreted (the *et*): 'Revere only the LORD your God' (Deut. 6:13): this includes the scholars." Same in B. Kiddushin 57a; B. Bava Kamma 41b; B. Bekhorot 6b.

8   ***Find.*** (גפינדן :15).   S. B. Ketubbot 103b: "'But who honors those who fear the LORD' (Ps. 15:4). Mar said: That is Jehoshaphat, the king of Judea. When he saw a scholar, he would rise from his throne, embrace and kiss him, and would call him, 'My teacher, my teacher, my master, my master.'" Same in B. Makkot 24a. Cf. II Chron. 20:5.

10   ***Gemara.*** (גמרא :18).   S. B. Berakhot 34a: "All prophets prophesied only for him, who married his daughter off to a scholar, traded with a scholar, or supported a scholar of his possessions." Same in B. Sanhedrin 99a; similar in Rashi on B. Ketubbot 85b.

15   ***Gemara.*** (גמרא :23).   S. B. Ketubbot 103a: "'Honor your father and your mother' (Exod. 20:12). [The *et* of] 'Your father' is to include your father's wife."

17   ***Ve-et.*** (ואת :25).   S. B. Ketubbot 103a: "'And your mother' (Exod. 20:12). The *et* of 'Your' is your mother's husband. The additional 'and' includes your older brother."

15b

one does not need to write much about this. Every pious person knows very well the reward for honoring one's father and mother, what it consists of, and how one should honor them, as well as the great punishment that comes from the opposite, God protect us. That is why one should not write too much about it, so that one does not take it lightly.

5   We find in the Gemara[18] (a story): A man gave his father delicacies to eat, but sinned against him, so that he went to *Geihinnom*. Another let his father grind flour in the mill— heavy labor that involves pulling a millstone, but went to *Gan Eden*. This is how it happened: When the one who gave him delicacies to eat went to buy meat or fish, his father asked him, "How much did this cost?" He then yelled at him, "Why are you asking about

10   that? You don't worry about it, and you also don't give me anything for it!" And when (the father) was eating, he said to him at the table, "Other people do a lot for their children and help them a lot, but in all my days I have gotten nothing from you." This shocked and silenced his father. Who can count all the rude things that people say to their parents? And the other let his father work in the mill, which is very hard labor, but he went to *Gan Eden*,

15   because he consoled his father and told him: "My dear father, I bemoan to God that I am not able to fulfill my obligations toward you. If I were worthy enough for God, blessed be He, to provide me with a small livelihood, I would not let you work so hard." This is why he merited the world to come.

    We also find[19] that Rabbi Tarfon's mother complained about him to the sages that

20   he did not want to do her will. The sages were surprised that such a fine scholar as

---

15b

5   *Gemara.* (גמרא: 4). Most detailed in Tosafot, Kiddushin 31a–b: "One supports his father, but he must leave the world. An interpretation hereof: He (i.e., the son) was punished for having given him the food resentfully. An(other) had him (his father) turn the millstone, which is hard work, but he earned eternal life, because he honored him (his father) with good things, and he had mercy with him. Regarding this, the (Talmud) Yerushalmi tells a tale of two (sons). The tale of one of them says that he fed his father with pheasants. One day his father said, 'From where do you have all this?' To which the son replied, 'Old man, do you care, before it is ground and prepared? So go on and chew and eat like the dogs that eat until they're fat.' Then he let him see how difficult all this was for him. The other one, on the other hand, who turned the mill, had an old father, and ordered him to turn the mill. An interpretation hereto: The king ordered the father to perform forced labor for him. Then his son said to him, 'You turn the mill, and I will perform the forced labor for the king in your place. If he intends to shame you, it is good for you (that I go). If he wants to punish you, it is also good for you (that I go).'" Shorter in Y. Peah 1a, Rashi on B. Kiddushin 31a, and *Brantshpigl*, p. 232. Similar in B. Kiddushin 31a–b and Yalkut, § 297.

19   *Find.* (גפינדן: 20). The story is a conflation of two stories about the mothers of Rabbi Tarfon and Rabbi Yishmael that are frequently transmitted together; most detailed in Tosafot, Kiddushin 31b: "Rabbi Tarfon had a mother. In the Yerushalmi it is written that Rabbi Tarfon's mother once lost her leather sandals in the courtyard. She left her bed, walked outside, and asked him to help her. R. Tarfon put his hands under her feet on the

Rabbi Tarfon should defy his mother. They went and asked him, "Is it true that you do not respect your mother?" He answered, "Ask her how I do not do her will." And so the sages asked her, "What is your complaint about your son?" She began: "This is how he defies me: when he leaves the study hall and washes his feet, I desire to drink the water."

16a

5 The sages said, "Even in this case you should not deny her this desire."

All the more so one should not deny one's father or mother a favor. But, due to our many transgressions, it is all too common not to value one's parents, as the proverb says, "A mother can raise ten children, but ten children cannot support one mother." Everything is too much: whatever they do, or eat, or say is disagreeable. They laugh and mock them,
10 and don't consider that when they grow old, they will be measured by the same standard that they used to measure their parents.

I heard a nice story about the origin of the proverb: "Whoever, during his life, gives away everything he has, will be beaten to death with clubs." The story is as follows:

floor, so that she wouldn't soil her feet, and she walked on his hands. The Yerushalmi also writes about Rabbi Yishmael's mother that every time, when Rabbi Yishmael came from the house of study, she washed his feet and drank the water. When Rabbi Yishmael heard that she did this, he refused it. So she went to the sages and told them that her son, Rabbi Yishmael, did not observe the commandment of honoring his parents. The sages were astonished, and asked Rabbi Yishmael. He told them what had happened, but they ordered him to let her have her will, because that is part of honoring (the parents)." Similar in Y. Peah 15c and *Pesikta Rabbati*, 23; B. Kiddushin 31b includes the tale about Rabbi Tarfon's mother, not, however, the tale of Rabbi Yishmael's mother. One version is included in the *Maysse Bukh* (Gaster), no. 142, which conforms to a great degree with the version in Tosafot, Kiddushin 31b.

16a

5   *Even in this case.* (אפילו הכי :1). Term used in rabbinic discourse.

7   *Proverb.* (שפריכט ווארט :4). Regarding the proverb "A mother can raise ten children, but ten children cannot support one mother," cf. Bernstein, *Jüdische Sprichwörter* (Jewish Proverbs), p. 149.

12   *Story.* (מעשה :8). The tale has been known as a wandering tale in Central Europe since the Middle Ages, and is substantiated for the first time in Rüdiger von Hünchoven's (13th century) tale "Der Schlegel" (the club). However, its structure is different: The grandfather is treated badly by his five children, one after another, until a pious friend comes up with the trick with the chest. Moreover, it does not include the section with the blanket (*koz*). Because of the parallel structure, and the common motive, the latter has been occasionally handed down as *kotzenmaere* (blanket tale) simultaneously with "Der Schlegel." Textual evidence in Old French has also been handed down, besides the Middle High German version of the *kotzenmaere*; cf. Koch, *Der Schlegel*, pp. 273–278.

The proverb used here (see below and 17b) is not included in "Der Schlegel" and was probably added in later versions. It was, however, popular independently of the tale, since

There was a very rich man who had one son. The old father's wife died, and his daughter-in-law took good care of her father-in-law, as is appropriate. The old man saw that he didn't lack anything, and said to his son: "Dear son, I see that I have it as good as I could want with you, praise God. So why should I worry now about my money, and property, and business, and my houses—I'd like to give it all to you, along with all my jewels and obligations." And he gave him the key to everything, and gave him everything he had as a gift. Not long afterward, when the daughter-in-law saw that he no longer had anything, and she had wasted everything through her vanity and deceitfulness, the wicked woman began to nag her husband, and said that she couldn't stand how the old man coughed over the table, it made her sick, and it disgusted her to eat with him. "Tell him that he should sit at the other table; I'll still give him the best and the [nicest] food." The old man, poor thing, had to do it, like it or not. For a while he was given enough, but later they ate once without giving the old man anything. So the son said to his wife, "Why don't you also give anything to my father to eat?" The wicked woman said, "He can wait until

16b

we're finished eating—he won't starve to death." So, alas, he had to wait until the food was already cold, and he was given the bones to gnaw on.

Later on the son became head of the community, and people came in and out of his place. When a matter would be discussed, the old man would sometimes take part in the conversation, just like he used to. The son would not tolerate this, and said to him, "Dear father, don't interfere in everything. People don't like it when someone interferes in their business." Later he said, "Father dear, you are so lazy and idle—I'm ashamed of you in front of other people. Let me ask you, for my sake, to stay in the room where the servants

during the Middle Ages it was posted on a number of city gates in northern Germany, as a warning of risky trading style: "He who gives his children bread while he himself suffers poverty shall be beaten to death with a club"; cf. Röhrich, *Lexikon*, p. 1100.

The tale was adapted for the Jewish culture both lexically and content wise: Instead of a burial "*als ez kristenlíchen zeme*"—as befits Christians (s. Koch, *Schlegel*, Verse 1091f.)—the Kaddish shall be spoken; instead of "*vier burgaere und den pfaffen*"—four citizens and the priest (s. Koch, *Schlegel*, Verse 1081)—the community rabbi, the beadle, the cantor, and the community leaders appear. The frequent appearance of the Eastern Yiddish words *zayde* and its genitive case *zaydes* (Yiddish text: 17a/7, 20, 18a/3) is conspicuous; this might be an indication of the possibility that the author had heard the tale in Eastern Yiddish dialect. A massively abbreviated version of the *kotzenmaere* can be found in *Brantshpigl*, p. 228f. In that version, all Jewish details, the proverb as well as the rabbinic teaching in line 142/6, are missing.

8   *Deceitfulness.* (זייפֿנית 19:). Spelling based on Yiddish pronunciation.

16b

21   *Lazy and idle.* (עבר ובטל 7:). Common is *over batel*—idler, good-for-nothing; e.g., M. Avot 5:21.

are. I'll send in enough for you to eat and drink." The poor man had to do it, like it or not, and went to the other room where the servants and maids were. For a while he was brought food and drink, but then they got tired of it, and forgot him sometimes. The poor man had to take it, wasn't [allowed] to say anything about it, and ate what he was given.

5 The old man also had a little room where he slept. The son said to him, "Father dear, I need the little room—people come to see me, so I need my own room. I'll give you your own chamber." It wasn't long before the cruel wife started to nag her husband: She can't do without the chamber; she needs the chamber because she keeps all kinds of things there. Since he doesn't have anything but a bed anyway, it could just as well go in the small room 10 under the staircase. And so they put his bed in the small room under the staircase. When he wanted to lie down, his bed was so full of dust that it needed to be shaken out, and when he lay down in the room and people would go up and down (the stairs), lots of [dust] would get in his eyes.

After all this, the old man's clothes, poor thing, hung torn from his neck and the father 15 said to his son, "Son dear, winter is coming, and I don't have anything to wear. Make me some clothes." The son responded, "Father dear, why should I make you clothes? You don't go anywhere, anyway. You can just as well sit behind the oven when you get cold,

17a

and I'll give you a good blanket to wrap yourself in." The old man had no choice but to take the blanket.

20 Now, the son had a boy who was now grown up and saw the pitiful state the grandfather was in, and how everyone wished him ill, even the servants and maids. All the servants made fun of him—they saw how his son and daughter-in-law regarded him as beneath them, so they did the same. So the pious grandson went to the grandfather, and said to him: "Dear grandfather, I want to help you out of all your troubles. It will go well if 25 you only follow me, and don't betray me." The old man started to cry, "My dear grandson, God forbid I should do that to you. You don't have to worry."

Then the pious boy went to several God-fearing people, and told them the story that his father and mother treated him with disrespect and not as they are obligated to. "I ask you, please be so good as to lend me money and [jewels] so that they'll see that he still has some- 30 thing. Maybe they'll keep him better, and try to ingratiate themselves with him." The people were amazed by the pious boy's cleverness, and lent him a lot of money, and silver and gold coins, and beautiful jewels. (The boy) made the old man sit in his room and lock himself in from the inside, where he took the money and jewels, and clattered them around. And so the boy went and called his father and mother, and said, "Look what grandpa has.

17a

20 ***Pitiful state.*** (רחמנית :3). Spelling based on Yiddish pronunciation.

He locked himself in the chamber." The son went with his wife and looked in through a hole, and saw the money and jewels. Then the son said to his wife, "You shameless woman! You did this! I would have gotten all this a long time ago, if you hadn't behaved like this!" She said, "How should I have known that he still had anything? Let him play with it for a while, it won't get away from us." The old man said to himself, "Listen, you impudent one! You won't enjoy this! I thought you'd treat me like a father, as you're supposed to." And he pretended that he was polishing the jewels, and then put everything into a chest. When

17b

he came out of the chamber, the son went to the father, and said, "Dear Papa, you've got to be cold, you go around almost naked. I'll make you a tunic—how would [you like] it?" In the mornings the daughter-in-law would come to him: "Good morning, dear father-in-law. I heard you this past night coughing hard—why don't you drink some brandy every morning? It's very good for you. I have enough good brandy in the house, I just didn't think of it. I have so much to do that I didn't think of you." And then she became angry with the cook: "Why don't you prepare my father-in-law a good beer soup every morning? Go bring him some of the preserves!" Later she came back: "Dear father-in-law, you're definitely cold in this room. Why don't you come in our room? Are you angry with someone?" And she let him sit at his own table again, and let him eat with them.

After all this, the boy went to the people and brought back everything that they lent him. The old man put large locks on his chest. The old man once again had it good until the time came for him to die. He called his son to him, and gave him his last will and testament in front of other people, as the custom is. He asked him to say Kaddish diligently for him, and to light a candle for him. "I will leave enough to you, that it will help your children and your grandchildren. I just ask you to do what I tell you. If you do it, things will go well for you. But if you don't do it, things will, God forbid, go poorly for you. You may not approach the chest until a year has passed. When you open it after the year, you should do so with the rabbi of the city, the cantor, the beadle, and the other community leaders, so that they should see the large inheritance that I'll leave to you." And the old man died. The son obeyed the will, and said Kaddish very diligently for his father, and burned his candle.

When the year—which seemed very long until he could receive his inheritance—had passed, he immediately sent for the rabbi, cantor, and beadle, and the community leader, and went with them to the chest. Inside they found a big club, and written on it was: "Whoever gives away everything he has while he lives, will be beaten to death with a club."

17b

9   *Tunic.* (שויב 2:). Yiddish *svib*; see Middle High German *swibel-swanz*—dress with a train; cf. Lexer, *Handwörterbuch* (Dictionary), p. 222.

21   *Custom.* (סדר 14:). The establishment of a testament depended on the local custom (*minhag*), cf. Shulḥan Arukh, *Ḥoshen Mishpat*, 110:9.

18a

The son was disgraced, and did not know what to say out of great shame that the people saw (what had happened). Afterwards the grandson said to (his) father, "Dear Papa, please give me grandpa's blanket." He got angry and said, "What do you need it for?" (The grandson) replied, "I want to keep it for you for when you also get old. Then I'll also wrap
5   you in the blanket the way you did your father."

Our sages said,[20] "With the measurement a person measures, he will be measured." This means in Yiddish, how a person measures another, so too he will be measured. The way he treated his father, he will be treated. This is why every pious person should be warned not to abuse and disrespect her or his parents.

10   One should tell this to young women in particular. A poor mother does her part: When her daughter has a rough time she gives her the shirt off her back. Afterwards, when the daughter has a husband, she doesn't think of making a living decently with God's (help), but relies once again on her father and mother. But a God-fearing woman remembers, "My father and mother have always done enough for me. If I were fortunate enough to be able
15   to fulfill (the commandment) of honoring father and mother, I would gladly do it with all my heart." And if she cannot do so with her money, she should do so with her body, and should say, "My dear mother, let me do that, I am young and strong, and you are now old and worn out." But we see, due to our many transgressions, some undutiful daughters who watch while their mothers work until they're ready to keel over. Our Gemara[21] said about
20   that, "Happy is he who did not [see] his mother and father." This means in Yiddish, happy is he who did not see his mother and father.

We also see some who eat delicacies, and let their father and mother starve. She says, "I'm not permitted, because of my husband." But a pious wife can pacify her husband easily,

---

18a

6   ***Sages.*** (חכמים 6:). S. B. Sanhedrin 100a: "At sunset, Raba bar Mari said: The Holy One, blessed be He, will give every righteous 310 worlds, as it is written, 'I endow those who love me with substance; I will fill their treasuries' (Prov. 8:21). *Yesh*—substance—is in *gematria* 310. A teaching: Rabbi Meir said: With the measurement a person measures, he will be measured." Similar in B. Sotah 8b.

16   ***Body.*** (גוף 16:). Regarding the demand that the daughter support her parents, if required, in a non-material manner, by the labor of her hands, see also the commentary on p. 195/8 ("money").

19   ***Gemara.*** (גמרא 19:). S. B. Kiddushin 31b: "Fortunate is he, who did not see them. Rabbi Yohanan's father died, when his mother conceived him, and his mother died, when she delivered him."

23   ***Because of my husband.*** (פר מיין מאן 22:). A married woman is exempt from the obligation of providing her parents with material support, because her husband's authority takes priority over the parents' authority; cf. Shulhan Arukh, *Yore De'ah*, 240:16f. However, with her husband's consent she is permitted to support her parents; this is why she should ask her husband and convince him with all kinds of arguments (fols. 18a–18b).

and say to him, "My dear husband, how can I savor my food when my poor father and mother are suffering under great deprivation?" The same applies to clothing. She should say: "What good is this unnecessary sumptuousness to me—my poor father and mother are bare-naked! I would prefer to invest in them, and it would help my soul (to have a share) in

18b

5   the world to come."

And so, dear women, please do not take amiss what I have written or that I have admonished you. I mean this by no means negatively, since my intention is purely good. I do not want to generalize, God forbid, because most women are truly righteous, and are punctilious about their good deeds. One does not need to rebuke them or even tell them

10   anything. They know everything themselves ten times better than what I have written; rather, my intention is to find the one among these thousands who does not. I hope to God, may His name be blessed, that my words enter her ears, and that she follows me. My effort will then have been worthwhile, and I might also gain some merit for it. Amen.

Chapter Four

15   About the father-in-law and mother-in-law: how a wife should honor her parents-in-law out of respect for her husband. And for the sake of her merit God, blessed be His name, will hear her prayers, wherever she may turn.

Similar in *Brantshpigl*, p. 227; there, however, the woman is strongly warned against supporting her parents without her husband's consent: "If a woman cannot, because of her husband, support (her parents) in all matters as I described, she should ask the man amicably to allow her. If she does it without her husband's knowledge or consent, she does not perform a mitzvah, but rather commits a great sin." See the commentary on p. 136/4.

18b

15   *Father-in-law and mother-in-law.* (שוער אונ׳ שוויגר :11). The moral literature hardly refers to the woman's conduct toward her in-laws. *Brantshpigl*, too, which is relatively comprehensive in dealing with daily situations, does not deal with the issues arising from this relationship; it says there, in short, in the context with generally improper conduct, ibid., p. 16: "Rabbi Nehorai taught: In the days of the Messiah, the people will be such: they shame the elderly, the elderly must rise before the young, the daughter of the house must rise before the maid, the daughter-in-law yells at her mother-in-law. People will be as shameless as dogs. A son will not feel shame toward his father."

(לכבוד :12). The word is probably a duplicate of the same word in line 11 (Yiddish text); it is redundant because of the subsequent Yiddish word *eren* (honor) and was consequently not translated. The krakow print reads accordingly.

16   *For the sake of.* (אין :12). The syntactic reference is unclear both for the case in which *in* is perceived as the preposition "in" and as personal pronoun "him." It may need to be emended to the conjunction *um*—for the sake of; it has been translated accordingly.

"Property and riches are bequeathed by fathers, but an efficient wife comes from the LORD."[1] This means in Yiddish, one can inherit a house and possessions from one's parents, but a prudent woman must be earned from God, blessed be His name. King Solomon, peace be upon him, spoke this verse about a woman who is prudent, and so thinks of her

5 purpose; and who merits from God, blessed be His name, that when she gets parents-in-law, she knows how she should respect them. One does not need to write much about a God-fearing woman. A pious woman thinks as follows: "Since my husband is obligated to honor his father and mother, I must also honor them, in honor of my husband. And I'll consider them as father and mother." As we also find regarding King Saul, that his son-

10 in-law King David, peace be upon him, called him "my father," as the verse says, "Please, my father, look."[2] And he respected him greatly, even though he was [seeking] his life, and said to him, "Let my life be precious in God's eyes."[3] This means in Yiddish, my body

19a

should be as worthy in God's eyes as you are in my eyes. We also learn this from Ruth, the Moabite woman. She had so much merit that the kingship of the House of David came

15 from her, and the Messiah will come from her. She merited all this because she was charitable toward her mother-in-law.

The Gemara[4] interprets the following verse, "The righteous man eats to sate his soul."[5] This means in Yiddish, a righteous man eats, and even if he eats only a little, he is full and satisfied. There is a verse that relates this to Ruth the Moabite woman; the verse says as

20 follows, "And she ate her fill and had some left over."[6] That means that she ate but she was frugal, and she also brought something to her mother-in-law. She went out of her way and helped her. She spared her parents and let them sit at home. The righteous woman said to her mother-in-law, "It is so hot." And Boaz said to her, "I have been told of all that you did for your mother-in-law."[7] This means, the kindness you showed to your mother-in-law was

25 told to me through divine inspiration. For this reason you are fitting for me to bring you

---

12   *Precious.* (תיקר :24). S. II Kings 1:14 (King Ahaziah and Elijah); however, the intended reference is probably I Sam. 26:24 (David and King Saul); cf. I Sam. 26:21.

19a

17   *Gemara.* (גמרא :4). See, e.g., Ba-midbar Rabbah 21.20: "'The righteous man eats to his heart's content' (Prov. 13:25), that is Ruth the Moabite, for which it is written, 'She ate her fill and had some left over' (Ruth 2:14). The blessing was still in the mouth of this righteous woman." Same in Yalkut, §950.

        The talmudic attribution is possibly influenced by the interpretation of Prov. 9:9 in B. Shabbat 113b and of I Chron. 4:22 in B. Bava Batra 91b: both interpret as "This is Ruth the Moabite."

23   *It is so hot.* (היץ :11). Play on words based on the similarity in sound of *ḥamot*—mother-in-law—and *ḥammut*—heat—which are pronounced identically in Yiddish.

into my house. Since you have so many good qualities and have done so many deeds, I have no doubt that much good will come from you.

From that we can learn something: If Ruth even followed her mother-in-law—which seemed to be [reprehensible] and appeared to be shameful—and even thought, "My mother-in-law is a righteous woman, and is good to me," all the more so should another woman think, "My mother-in-law only criticizes me for my own good. She loves her son so much and she would like to see only good from my husband and my children."

All this speaks of an efficient and prudent woman. (She) remembers this all and honors her mother- and father-in-law. She accepts their criticisms, adheres to their admonitions, and thinks, "They do this all for my own good." But a foolish woman is just the opposite— she doesn't adhere to any admonition, and she thinks that they do everything to anger her. She directs hatred toward them, and lets loose with rage. She thinks it's a great accomplishment when she convinces her husband to follow her and to repudiate his father and mother. She destroys his soul and causes him to become sinful. She doesn't think of any of this—she only asserts her maliciousness.

Who can write of all the bad things and anger that come from this, as are written in

19b

Sefer Middot[8] in (the chapter) "Quality of Anger"? And she also rewards good with bad, since the prayer that every father and mother direct toward the Holy One, blessed be He,

---

4   **Reprehensible. ([כמכוער]** :16**).** As opposed to most of the Hebrew words, this word is explained with a Yiddish word, *nivzig* (Krakow 1618: *nivzik*), which is based on the Hebrew adjective *nivzeh*—despicable, disparaging, disdainful. Cf. *Sefer Middot*, fol. 48b, where laziness is described as *ayn nivze midde*—a despicable trait.

8   **Efficient. (המשכלת** :20**).** By mention of the word from Prov. 19:14, the preceding remarks refer to Prov. 19:14 on fol. 18b.

17   **Sefer Middot. (ספר מדת** :28**).** Yiddish spelling of *Sefer Middot*; cf. the spelling *Orḥot Ẓaddikim* on fol. 12a/17 and 24a/12 (Yiddish text).

     S. *Sefer Middot*, fol. 42a: ווער קאן עש אלש שרייבן וואש אונהאייל בון צורן קומט עש"
הוט קיין ענדא. האדר אונ' צאנק אונ' קריג. אונ' קנאה אונ' שנאה. דש זיין אייטיל בויזי מדות די
קומן אל בון צורן."—"Who can describe all the disasters that result from anger, there is no end to it. Discord, quarrel, dispute, jealousy, and hatred—these are completely bad traits that all result from anger."

19b

17   **Quality. (מדות** :1**).** The spelling is based on the Yiddish pronunciation of the *constructus* form in the singular (*middat*). Possibly this form was switched with the one on fol. 19a/28 (Yiddish text); cf. see commentary above.

18   **Prayer. (גבעט** :2**).** The contents are only indicated; see also, on the other hand, the detailed prayer for children to turn out well, in *Brantshpigl*, p. 300f.: The sons may be God-fearing, and practice *talmud Torah* and good deeds; may they earn their living honestly, and associate only with pious, learned people; may they conquer their evil desires all

and into which they put all their hope is entirely for their children—that they should be privileged to spend their time in the service of God, the study of Torah, and the pursuit of good deeds. A God-fearing woman remembers this. About a foolish woman who doesn't remember this, however, King Solomon, peace be upon him, said, "The stupid woman bustles about, she is simple and knows nothing."[9] In Yiddish that means, a foolish woman always moans and grumbles, but she knows nothing. This means that she does not know how far it will reach.

Some women or men are so foolish that they direct all their thoughts and hopes toward their mother- and father-in-law and want only to reap benefits from them. And when they don't receive them, they become angry at them, and become jealous and full of hatred: "They do more for the other children than for us." Much evil comes from that, God protect us. As we learn from Joseph the Righteous, peace be upon him—the brothers should not have been jealous of him.

Every person should have trust in God, may His name be blessed, as the verse says, "Blessed is he who trusts in the LORD, whose trust is the LORD alone."[10] This means in Yiddish, blessed is the person who places his trust in God, blessed be He, and God, may He be blessed, will inspire him with trust. As King David also said, "It is better to take refuge in the LORD than to trust in mortals."[11] This means in Yiddish, it is better to seek God's shelter, may He be blessed, than to trust in a person. One could ask about this verse, why is the word "to take refuge" used referring to God, blessed be He, and referring to persons the verse speaks of "trust?" It means the following: when a person offers you trust and promises, (and says): "You never again need to worry about anything, I'll make sure you're satisfied," but God, blessed be He, promises him [nothing], you should nevertheless rather rely on God's kindness. This is why the verse says, "It is better to take

their lives, and die only in old age, highly respected, and blessed with grandchildren. Daughters may be modest, and perform good deeds; may they not talk useless talk, not gossip, and not slander; may they marry pious, God-fearing scholars, and may they not strive to dominate their husbands; may they serve their husbands modestly and honestly, and urge them to perform good deeds; may they go to prayer service diligently, and be domestic and diligent; may they instruct and supervise the servants, be hospitable and charitable, and generous toward the poor, and may they be blessed with grandchildren.

7   **Reach.** (גרייכט :8). Regarding criticism of thoughtless conduct of the woman, see Ibn Ezra on Prov. 9:13: "'The stupid woman bustles about' (Prov. 9:13), but without knowledge, that means 'And knows nothing' (ibid.). This meant that she has no knowledge, she lacks (it), like in 'Come what may upon me' (Job 13:13), which is interpreted as 'something,' as in 'Wisdom amounts to nothing' (Jer. 8:9) 'over emptiness' (Job 26:7). If she is told something, or if she knows it herself, she may perhaps be careful and stop her bustling."

11   **They do.** (זיא טואן :11). Preceding text *un' zogen* (and say) was perhaps dropped.

13   **Jealous.** (מקנה :12). Cf. Gen. 37:11.

24   **Rather.** (ליבר :20). Cf. Ps. 118:9.

refuge in the LORD"[12]—it is better that he seeks God's shelter, blessed be He, and not a person's, even if he promised him a lot. As another verse says, "Put not your trust in the great, in mortal man who cannot save."[13] This means, do not trust in persons, who cannot help. As Jeremiah the Prophet also said, "Cursed is he who trusts in man, who makes mere flesh his strength."[14] This means, cursed is the person who relies on another and seeks trust

20a

in a person of flesh and blood. The midrash[15] explains the verses in relation to Joseph the Righteous who sinned in that he relied on the cupbearer to release him from captivity, and so he had to stay two years longer in jail.

And further, a daughter-in-law should accept her mother-in-law's criticism agreeably, and should remember, "She does it for my own good," as the verse says, "Wounds by a loved one are long lasting; the kisses of an enemy are profuse."[16] In Yiddish this means, the [wounds] of a friend are genuine, and should be preferred by you over the kisses of an enemy. The midrash[17] says, explaining the verse in relation to Moses, our teacher, peace be upon him, and to Balaam the Wicked, that it would have been more appropriate for Moses to have spoken the blessings that Balaam gave to Israel, and for Balaam to have spoken the curses that Moses uttered in the biblical rebuke. Our sages[18] explain this as follows: If Moses, our teacher, had given the blessings that Balaam did, the nations of the world would have said, "What's so new, that a friend says what he'd like to hear?" So the Holy One, blessed be He, let the prophecy of the blessing be said by an enemy, who had to say it against his preference.

20a

6   *Midrash.* (מדרש: 1). S. Bereshit Rabbah 89.3: "'Happy is the man who makes the LORD his trust' (Ps. 40:5). This refers to Joseph, 'Who turns not to the arrogant' (ibid.), by saying to the chief cupbearer: 'But think of me' (Gen. 40:14), 'Mentioning me' (ibid.), for what reason he was given two more years (in the dungeon)." Similar in Yalkut, §147 and Rashi on Gen. 40:23.

6   *Verses.* (פסוקים: 1). S. Gen. 40:14ff.

13   *Midrash.* (מדרש: 7). See the commentary on line 16 below.

15   *Blessings.* (ברכות: 8). Blessings of Balaam, cf. Num. 23:20ff.

16   *Curses.* (קללות: 9). Moses' curses, cf. Deut. 28:15ff.

16   *Sages.* (חכמים: 10). S. Devarim Rabbah 1.4: "'These are the words' (Deut. 1:1). Rabbi Aḥa ben Rabbi Ḥanina said: The sayings were rebukes, i.e., they came from the mouth of Balaam, and the blessings came from the mouth of Moses. Had it been that Balaam rebuked them, Israel would have said, 'He who hates, rebukes.' Had Moses blessed them, the nations of the world would have said, 'He who loves them, blesses them.' Therefore the Holy One, blessed be He, said that Moses, that he who loved them, should rebuke them, and that Balaam, who hated them, should bless them, so that both the blessings and the rebukes of Israel shall be fulfilled."

I could also explain the meaning of the verse as follows: Moses, our teacher, acted as a father toward his much-loved child and showed the rod—"If you do such and such, I'll hit you with the rod."

5 When Balaam praised Israel highly and blessed them, his intention was such that he said, "No harm is in sight for Jacob, no woe in view for Israel, and their King's acclaim is in their midst."[19] In Yiddish this means, nothing improper will be seen among Jacob, and no falsehood will be seen among Israel, because God is with them and their community. This means to say that if they coexist in unity, the King, the Holy One, blessed be He, will help them. This is what is meant: If, however, they behave conversely and

10 engage in deceit and improper behavior, and do not support one another, he would have said *kalem* instead of *melekh* which is *kalem* backwards, meaning in Yiddish "annihilate them." So the Holy One, blessed be He, turned the word around in his mouth so that he had to say *melekh*—king—, as the verse says, "The LORD your God turned the curse into a blessing, for the LORD your God loves you."[20] This means, God, blessed is He,

15 reversed his curses into a blessing, because God loves you. This is why King Solomon said, "Wounds by a loved one are long lasting."[21] This refers to Moses, our teacher, and "The kisses of an enemy"[22] refers to Balaam. The friend intended good and the enemy intended bad. And that is how (Balaam) intended all his blessings—toward bad ends, again when he said, "There is a people that dwells apart, not settled among the nations."[23] This means

20b

20 in [Yiddish], the people should rest alone, and should not mix with the nations in food, drink, and manner of dress. They should not marry them, and should not intermingle with them unless it is for a necessary end. As is also written in the Torah, "I have set you apart from other peoples."[24] This was also an evil intention on his part: if Israel holds to all of this, it will live alone, meaning they will be the only ones in *Gan Eden*.

11   *Kalem...melekh.* (כלם ומלך: 23). The interpretation goes back to Va-yikra Rabbah 27.6 and is based on the literal understanding of Num. 23:6 ("God turned") and it shuffles *melekh*—king—from Num. 23:21 (s. above) into its palindrome *kelem*—destruction. Same in *Ze'enah u-Re'enah* on Num. 22:9, p. 765.

15   *Curses.* (קללת: 26). Spelling based on Yiddish pronunciation *klalles*.

19   *Settled.* (יתישב: 29). Num. 23:9 reads instead "not reckoned among."

20b

21   *Dress.* (מלבושים: 2). Regarding the interpretation of Num. 23:9 in respect to social differentiation by way of life, see Yalkut, §768: "'There is a people that dwells apart' (Num. 23:9). They differ from idolaters in every aspect: their clothing, their food, their bodies, and their houses. Then he shall not judge them as idolaters." Rashi on Num. 23:9 emphasizes the marriage prohibition.

    A similar interpretation with marriage prohibition and restricted social association is brought in *Ze'enah u-Re'enah* on Lev. 20:26, p. 610.

But if not, it will be the opposite. When he said, Israel is like "cedars,"[25] like the pine tree, he also meant this negatively—they act with haughtiness and arrogance because they are descendents of Abraham, Isaac, and Jacob, and cannot tolerate the exile. The midrash[26] says about this, "The curses of Ahijah of Shiloh are better than the blessings of Balaam." (This means in Yiddish), the curse of Ahijah of Shiloh was better for Israel than the blessing of Balaam. Why did Ahijah of Shiloh[27] say that Israel should be in exile like a reed in a pond that always waves back and forth? Israel should be constantly worried, and should always be subjugated in exile, until God, blessed be He, will have mercy on them. Just like when the wind blows and threatens to uproot it, the reed bends low until it is gone, and afterwards rights itself again. The midrash goes on to say that the pine tree says to the reed: "How is it that you are so pliable, but the wind can not uproot you? I am so strong and tall, but the wind uprooted me!" The reed answers him, "If you would do as I do, and bend yourself as I bend myself, and lie low, then it could also do nothing to you." And so we see well that the curse of Ahijah of Shiloh was a blessing and good advice to Israel in exile, and Balaam's intention was wicked.

We see the same thing every day in front of our own eyes—wicked people who have no fear of God, as are common due to our many transgressions, and who provoke disputes between people, including between daughter-in-law and mother-in-law. They say, "Do not let her become accustomed to treating you or your husband poorly." And they provoke one another, from which nothing good comes—only disputing and quarreling. Who can

---

3   *Midrash.* (מדרש‎ 9:). S. Yalkut, § 203: "What is written: 'Wounds by a loved one are long lasting; the kisses of an enemy are profuse' (Prov. 27:6). The curse of Ahijah of Shiloh, with which he cursed Israel, was better than the blessing of Balaam the Wicked. Ahijah of Shiloh cursed Israel, that it may be a cane of reed. What is a cane? It stands by the water, its sprout is flexible, and it has many roots. Even when all the winds of the worlds were to blow, it will move with them, back and forth, and when the wind would quiet down, it would return to its position. Balaam blessed (Israel) as being like a cedar, 'Like cedars beside the water' (Num. 24:6). What is a cedar? It does not stand by the water, its trunk does not sway, and it does not have many roots. Even if all the winds of the world were to blow, (its trunk) would not move from its place. A southern wind would tear them out and topple them. Rabbi Shimon ben Eliezer taught: A man shall always be soft as a cane, but never rigid as a cedar. Therefore, the cane was worthy of becoming the quill for writing (the Torah).' Same in B. Ta'anit 20a and B. Sanhedrin 105b–106a; Similar in *Avot de-Rabbi Natan*, A, chap. 41.

      Different in *Panim Aḥerim*, B, 6, which has an even more overt reference to the situation of exile. The parable has been significantly abridged; the reference to blessing and curses is missing, as is the quote from Lev. 20:26: "The Holy One, blessed be He, said to him: The grass symbolizes Israel as a cane of reed, standing in water and moving with every changing wind. And although the water has great strength, the cane remains in its position. Such also is Israel. It goes along with every nation, as it is written, 'Until it sways like a reed in water (I Kings 14:15), and yet it remains standing in its place."

4   *Ahijah of Shiloh.* (אחיה השלוני‎ 11:). Cf. I Kings 14:15. The Hebrew quote has possibly been dropped.

measure the evil that comes from that, God protect us. On the contrary, a pious person should rebuke them, and make peace between them, and say, "Don't take it so hard."

21a

It will be better if they speak like that and make peace among people. Then they will [also] merit having peace in their own households, proportionally to their actions. Peace is the goal of everything, and so all our prayers end with *shalom*. If it were only so, that peace would exist among all people, then all the blessings with which God, may His name be blessed, blessed Israel would be fulfilled for us, and we would merit the redemption that will create peace in the entire world. Amen.

Chapter Five

Of the matter of raising children: How a woman should diligently endeavor to raise her children to observe the Torah and act righteously—thus will people bless her, "Fortunate is the tree that gave bloom to such fruit."

The verse in Proverbs says, "Her children declare her happy, her husband praises her.[1] Many women have done well, but [you surpass] them all."[2] King Solomon, peace be upon him, spoke these verses regarding a respectable woman who raised children who say, "My dear mother brought me up such that I have learned what is pleasing to God, blessed be His name, and what is pleasing to people." If her child sees something improper done, he says, "My mother did not permit me to do something like that." Her husband, too, when he sees another man doing something improper, says, "I won't do that—my wife also

---

21a

5   *Prayers.* (תפילת :3). Spelling based on Yiddish pronunciation.

Regarding the word "peace" in the prayers, see Va-yikra Rabbah 9.9: "Rabbi Shimon ben Yoḥai said: Peace is the most important, because all blessings are contained in it: 'May the LORD grant strength to His people; may the LORD bestow on His people peace' (Ps. 29:11)."

The benediction *sim shalom* or *shalom rav* takes on an outstanding position as the last blessing of the *Shemoneh Esrei* (*Amidah*); the priestly blessing preceding it also contains a reference to peace. The benedictions mentioned below enhance the liturgic reference. This is also the context in which the mention of redemption (see below) should be seen, appearing immediately before the *Shemoneh Esrei*.

Cf. Va-yikra Rabbah 9.9: "Peace is the most important, for all blessings, all good deeds and charities, which the Holy One, blessed be He, brings to Israel, are sealed with peace. In 'Shema Yisrael,' in the 'Proclaim a house of peace,' in the prayer 'He, who creates peace,' and in the priestly blessing 'And grant you peace' (Num. 6:26)."

13   *Declare.* (ראוה :12). Conflation of Prov. 31:28–29 and Songs 6:9.

wouldn't permit me to do it." This is what King Solomon, peace be upon him, meant by the verse. And as he goes on to say, "Many women"[3] etc. This is to be understood as follows: There are many daughters of Israel who perform good deeds, or do much good otherwise, but she who raises upright children is to be praised above the rest. King Solomon, peace be upon him, wrote many verses about this, and they are explained as I've written here, and as I've explicated them, one after the other. God, blessed be His name, spoke through Jeremiah the Prophet also about a woman, who wishes to have pious, upright children,

21b

[and] the verse is as follows: "Before I created you in the womb, I selected you."[4] This means in Yiddish, before I created you from the womb, I knew you. This means, I knew your mother's good thoughts, and so I love you. But when it is, God forbid, the opposite, King David, peace be upon him, said, "The wicked are defiant from birth, the liars go astray from the womb."[5] This means in Yiddish, the wicked ones are distanced in their mother's bellies because she [told lies]. Therefore every pious woman should take care to follow what I wrote in the first chapter.

Now we would like to speak more about those things that *Reshit Ḥokhmah*[6] writes: How an upright woman who wants to raise her children to observe the Torah and to perform good deeds should exert herself. Pregnancy and giving birth are the simplest—even an animal becomes pregnant and gives birth. And this is how the Gemara[7] explains the verse

1   ***Permit.*** (גשטטין 19:). In *Brantshpigl* the word marks the woman's extremely negatively connoted claim on authority; see ibid., p. 46: "She does not want to permit him to be charitable, or to take in guests. She manipulates him, she wants to control him, and she wants him to serve her completely. She says to him: This is how I want it, this is how you must do it, and not any other way."

21b

8   ***Created you.*** (יצרתיך 1:). Jer. 1:5 reads literally, "I created you." Jer. 1:5 and the ensuing Ps. 58:4 are often passed on together in rabbinic literature, as a description of the naturally righteous (Jer. 1:5) or evil (Ps. 58:4), among others in Devarim Rabbah 10.5; Midrash Tehillim 58:2. Regarding the tradition, according to which Jacob (Jer. 1:5) and Esau (Ps. 58:8) were influenced by Rebekah's actions, see the commentary on p. 94/2.

14   ***First chapter.*** (ערשטן שער 6:). Reference to the request to conduct oneself correctly, particularly during pregnancy, in fol. 4b.

15   ***Reshit Ḥokhmah.*** (ראשית חכמה 8-7:). S. *Reshit Ḥokhmah*, III, p. 80, §42: "The woman bears the greatest part of the pain of child upbringing. Therefore her merit is great, when she brings the children onto the correct path." See ibid., p. 197, §2: The mother's task is the education of the sons to *talmud Torah* and to compliance with the obligations. Pregnancy and birth as the easiest part of child raising are not mentioned there.

18   ***Gemara.*** (גמרא 10:). S. B. Eruvin 100b: "Eve was cursed with ten curses, as it is written, 'And to the woman He said: I will make most severe' (Gen. 3:16). The (words 'most severe'—*harbeh arbeh*) are the two drops of blood: one, the drop of menstruation, the other the blood of virginity. 'Your pangs' is the pain of child raising, 'childbearing' is the pain of pregnancy, 'In pain shall you bear children' (ibid.) is conforming to the literal meaning." Despite the detailed explanation, the word "blood" is not mentioned there.

that our dear Lord God said to Eve when she ate the apple: "I will make most severe your pangs."[8] This means, I will increase your pains. This refers to the raising of children, because raising children is essential, and much depends on it, as I will write here. "Your pregnancy"[9] means in Yiddish, your pregnancy and refers to the arduousness of pregnancy. "In pain shall you [bear] children,"[10] in Yiddish this means, you shall bear your children with pain.

I could also explain the verse as follows: "Your pangs,"[11] (which means in Yiddish) your pain. This means that her menstruation causes her distress, before she can dress herself in white and afterwards immerse herself. This is the greatest distress, because some women would rather become pregnant and have children, if it were God's will. But we do not want to talk of this—"One does not question God's judgments," we cannot understand it (anyway).

Now I would like to further explain the verse "Your pregnancy,"[12] which refers to pregnancy as I already said above. "In pain"[13] could be translated as with work, as the verse

8   **Menstruation. (וסתה** :16). The interpretation of "Your pangs" as menstruation has no basis in rabbinic literature. Perhaps it is a result of the influence of *Avot de-Rabbi Natan*, A, chap. 1: "'Severe': When the woman sees her menstruation blood at the beginning of her period, it is painful to her."

Here, however, not the monthly menstruation pain or the effort of the *tevilah* are considered as greatest pain, but the lack of pregnancy. *Reshit Ḥokhmah*, III, p. 79, §41, emphasizes the significance of the fatherly effort, thus explicitly distancing itself from the interpretation in Bereshit Rabbah 20.2, where pregnancy and birth are central, whereas children only range as one task among others. Bereshit Rabbah 20.2 and *Reshit Ḥokhmah* each interpret "Your pangs" as pain of conception—*ẓa'ar ha-ubbar*; "Your childbearing" as pain of menstruation—*ẓa'ar ha-niddah*, or in Bereshit Rabbah 20.2, as pain of pregnancy—*ẓa'ar ha-iddui*; "In pain" as the pain of miscarriage—*ẓa'ar ha-nefelim*; "Shall you bear children" as pain of birth—*ẓa'ar ha-ledah*; "Children" as pain of child raising—*ẓa'ar giddul banim*.

In her interpretation, the author is guided more by B. Eruvin 100b than by *Reshit Ḥokhmah*, or by Bereshit Rabbah 20.2, but at the same time she deviates from the talmudic interpretation also in matters of contents: She interprets "Your pangs" (B. Eruvin 100b: pain of child raising) as an unfulfilled wish for children, or the work of birth and raising; "Your childbearing" (B. Eruvin 100b: pain of pregnancy) as pregnancy as a natural process; and "In pain" (B. Eruvin 100b: pain of pregnancy and birth) as labor of birth and education. Particularly the last interpretation deviates from the talmudic interpretation in that she translates, with the help of Prov. 14:23, "pain" as "work," which bears a stronger implication for future merit.

S. Brantshpigl, p. 343: "'In pain shall you bear children' (Gen. 3:16). This means in Yiddish that you shall bear your children with pain. The sages interpret this that you shall raise your children that you bring forth, with great pain, i.e., with great efforts."

11   **One does not. (אין** :19). S. Yalkut, §942: "One does not question one's terms." S. Sifrei Devarim, §307: "One may not question one's work."

13   **Work. (ערבט** :24). Possibly an allusion to the curse of Adam in Gen. 3:17 or Gen. 3:19. However, the author does not continue the idea of the conformity between the curses of Adam and Eve, based on the common Hebrew root *ayin-zadik-bet* for the expressions "Your pangs," "In pain," and "by toil." S. Bereshit Rabbah 20.9: "'By toil

says, "From all toil there is some gain, but idle chatter is pure loss."[14] This means, for all the work that a person does he gets correspondingly more; for talking too much he gets correspondingly less. Now we can clearly see that "pain" means work. This is what the verse here could also mean: With great effort and work, you will bear and raise your children. Both of these can be read in the verse.

Or the verse means this: [The] children that you will bear should be raised with pain.

22a

The verse is here referring to the fact that the distress of raising children is contained in "Your pangs."[15] And it alludes to it again, because the distress of raising children is greater than all others.

I should ask another question [on] the verse: The Holy One, blessed be He, said, "I will make most severe your pangs."[16] This means, (I will) increase your pain. But we find nowhere that the Holy One, blessed be He, used His own name regarding retaliation. As we

(*be-iẓavon*) shall you eat of it' (Gen. 3:17). Rav Assi said: Providing livelihood is twice as hard as giving birth. About birth it is written, 'In pain (*be-ezev*) shall you bear children' (Gen. 3:16), and about livelihood it is written, 'By toil shall you eat of it' (Gen. 3:17)." Applying a linguistic approach (referring to the longer and more ponderous noun *be-iẓavon*), the Midrash interprets Adam's curse as more severe.

Cf. *Ẓe'enah u-Re'enah* on Gen. 3:16, p. 65, which discusses the relationship between the curse of Adam and that of Eve: Woman can assume Adam's curse (work), which is why hardworking women have comparatively easier births. This also alleviates the female pain-centered curse, but it does not equalize it with the male action-oriented curse.

22a

11-12   **Nowhere. (נירגנץ 4:).** Regarding the rabbinic discussion that divine curses are not uttered in the first person, cf. Ba-midbar Rabbah 20.19.

12   **Retaliation. (פורענות 4:).** The word is used for Eve's punishment instead of "curse" (same below) and has been handed down in various traditions in the context of the curse of Adam and Eve, e.g., B. Berakhot 61a: "Cursing, one begins with the smallest: first the snake was cursed, then Eve was cursed, then Adam was cursed. However, on the retribution by the Flood it is written, 'All existence on earth was blotted out—man, cattle' (Gen. 7:23). First humans, then cattle."

The author's interpretation also deviates from that presented in other moral books, which understand the traditional interpretation of Gen. 3:16 perhaps not as curse, but as extreme punishment; see *Eyn shoyn Froyenbuykhleyn*, fol. 4a: דרום הוט אויך די ורויא וואל"

מרטיר אונ' אונגליק. דו זיא לייט אונ' ליידן מוז. אונ' דרום מוז זי אויך איר צייט האבן אלי חודש אונ' מוז איין מאל אודר צווייא פסטין. אין דער וואַרטין דז זי זול אימר דרום אן איר זינד גידענקן אונ' זאל אימר דרום אין דער תשובה בלייבן. אונ' אן הלטן אז איין מערדר טוט. דר מוז אל זיין טאג אלי חודש איין מאל צווייא אויף זיין זינד. אין דר וואַרטין דז ער זאל אן דר תשובה גידענקן. אונ' דז ער זאל חרטה האבין אויף זיין זינד. אזו מוז דיא ורויא אויך טון. אלי מאניט איין מאל צו טבילה גין אין דער וואַרטן דז זי זאל אן אירי זינד גידענקן [...] וועז זי פירציג יאר הוט תשובה געטון זו ".הוט זי זיך נון גיווינט אין דער ורמקיי"—"Therefore the woman, too, suffers such agony and misfortune, she suffers, and she must suffer. Therefore, also, she has her monthly

see in our Holy Torah, in the passage of admonition: For the blessing, He says, "I will grant your rains in their season, and I will grant peace in your land."[17] This means in Yiddish, I will give rain in its time, and later also says, I will give peace in your land. But for the curse He does not say, "I will bring [it] upon you." It says, rather, "it will be brought

5 upon." As the Holy One, blessed be He, also said regarding Eli the Priest's sons [Hophni and Phinehas], "I honor those who honor Me, but those who spurn Me shall be dishonored."[18] In Yiddish this means, those who honor Me, I will honor in return, (and) those who despise Me will be disdained. It does not say, "I will despise them."

We find in many similar cases that the Holy One, blessed be He, does not use his

10 holy name regarding any retaliation. So why did the Holy One, blessed be He, write here, "I will increase your pangs"? He meant it, rather, as follows: The more distress you have raising your children, the more reward I will give you. The Gemara[19] also explains that our Patriarch Jacob had more merit than Abraham and Isaac, because he had distress in raising his children.

15 Now I would like to begin writing again how a woman should educate her children in two paths. The first path relates to the body and the other to the soul. And so every woman must apply great diligence and effort in raising her children. First, as soon as the child is born, she must watch over the child, and be careful not to give the child to anyone else for

period, and must fast once or twice a month, so that she may always remember her sin, and repent constantly. She must conduct herself like a murderer, who during his entire life fasts once (or) twice per month, so that he may think of repentence, and regret his sin. Such must also the woman conduct herself: to go to the *tevilah* once a month, so that she may remember her sin. . . . After having repented for forty years, she will have accustomed herself to piety."

Numerous mentions of Eve's curse can also be found in *Brantshpigl*, as indication to her guilt of having brought death to the world; see ibid., p. 251: "The blood, poisoned by the snake, comes from Eve. Everybody knows that blood is pure poison. There are books that write that no man will be forgiven for having to die. (Therefore) women spend the time of their menstruation with headaches, and she bears her children in pain. All this comes from Eve." Cf. ibid., pp. 75, 253, 263.

1   *Admonition.* (תוכחה: 5).   See Lev. 26:3–46, where various threats of punishment and blessings are listed; cf. Deut. 28:1ff.

1-2   *I will grant.* (ונתתי: 6).   Conflation of Lev. 26:4 and Lev. 26:6.

11   *Distress.* (צער: 14).   S. *Ozar Midrashim*, p. 78, chap. 11: "Great is the reward for having brought children on the right and upright path. But if the pain of child raising is especially great, so is (the reward)." Similar in *Reshit Hokhmah*, III, p. 80, §42.

12   *Gemara.* (גמרא: 16).   S. B. Shabbat 89b: "In the future, the Holy One, blessed be He, will say to Abraham, 'Your children have sinned against me.' He will reply, 'Master of the World, may you eradicate them, for the sanctity of your name.' Then he will say to Jacob, who has experienced the pain of child upbringing, 'Perhaps he will have mercy on them.'"

16   *Two paths.* (צוויא דרכים: 18).   Regarding the discussion of the "paths" of "wisdom of the body" and "wisdom of the soul," see the commentary on pp. 87/7; 90/11; 122/6.

nursing. She herself should begin the next day, since as soon as the child tastes another, it will not want to suckle from the mother again. And then her milk will flow all of a sudden. There is no cure for that but to exercise (nursing) often.

Some are so undutiful that they do not want to suffer any pain, and let the child be nursed by another woman. In the meantime, her milk goes bad and becomes bitter, and then she no longer wants to nurse the child at all. A woman who does this will never nurse

22b

well. Her milk is no good but watery and bitter. In short, what is there to write about this? Every woman who behaves this way or nurses with one breast—whoever it may be, she is held to be uncapable. She squanders (her reputation) and she will suffer from this her whole life. Later she will have to work hard and withstand a lot, and she'll wish she could buy it back for any amount of money.

But a woman who is upright and smart, thinks of the goal of it all, and puts all her effort into it, even if she is rich—one never knows what the future holds. King Solomon, peace be upon him, said, "Every prudent man acts knowledgeably, but a dullard exposes his stupidity."[20] This means in Yiddish, every smart person does everything with sense and wisdom, but the fool separates out foolishness. That is to say, a smart person remembers his goal—if a person tells him something, he listens and follows the good things he was taught. But a fool separates himself from a wise man. That is to say, he is the opposite of a wise man—he thinks that his opinion is always the best. And so he can never reach any goal. This is why a youth should learn from and follow his parents, because they are experienced.

Now, I would like to speak about the things that I learned from the venerable doctor, our teacher and master, Rabbi Samuel, namely how one should bathe a child. One should

1   *Nursing.* (זוֹיגן :22). The author substantiates the rejection of strangers as wet nurses with the negative consequences for the mother; she does not mention the existence of Christian wet nurses. See on the other hand *Brantshpigl*, p. 137, which discusses the non-*kashrut* of the wet nurse's milk as a quasi halakhic problem: "And those, who have gentile wet nurses commit a great injustice, if they could have a Jewish (wet nurse). The milk of a gentile wet nurse comes from the food she eats, which is *trefe*, she blocks the heart of the child that drinks of her."

S. ibid., p. 138: "Our sages write that a daughter of Israel should not nurse the child of a gentile, but that a gentile can, with her consent, nurse a Jewish child. She explains that the nurse should also receive food, so that she should not eat *trefes*, and pay attention that she does not speak idolatrous in front of the child."

Other moral books mention in connection with nursing only that the woman should not, for reasons of modesty, expose her breast in public in order to nurse a child; such in *Eyn shoyn Froyenbuykhleyn*, fol. 47b; also *Brantshpigl*, p. 122.

22b

21-22   *Doctor* [...] *Samuel.* (שמואל [...] דאקטר :14). Kisch, "Jewish Pharmacists," p. 157, notes that until the middle of the 17th century, the professions of the pharmacist or medical doctor in Prague were not distinct; members of the Jewish Lekarz (pharmacist)

not bathe the child in water that is too hot, since it makes the child weak and sluggish. And one should not wet its head at all, because its brain is soft, and much bad, God forbid, comes of it, so that I will not write here what, God protect us, comes of it. When one takes it out of the bath, one may wash it carefully. One should also not leave it in the bath for too long.

5   It would also be necessary to write and say even more to the young people, because no matter how much one writes or speaks about it, it is never enough. Namely, she should not allow the child to become too attached to her. It all depends on an upright mother, because as soon as she takes the child to her, even once, its process has already started, and it will be difficult later to deacclimate the baby. One could write a lot about this subject. But one

10 does not need to forbid a God-fearing woman, because she is herself smart enough. As King Solomon, peace be upon him, said, "A rebuke [works on a wise man] more than one hundred blows on a fool."[21] In Yiddish this means, the rebuking and screaming of a wise person—that is to say, less serves a wise person more than giving a fool one hundred strokes.

23a

    It is also very necessary to tell a young woman to take care of a child like the shell of an

15 [egg], because one can, God forbid, harm the child very quickly. And then afterwards they say, it has grown on him, or they say someone cast an evil eye on it. Then they bring an old

family were represented in Prague already in the middle of the 16th century, but none by the name of Samuel; cf. Wolf, *Geschichte* (History), p. 178ff. It could also be a fictitious person, because the argumentation here emphasizes the recognition of persons of authority (who "tells him something"; see above). Shemuel bar Abba Kohen (Mar Shemuel) comes to mind as a historic example, the most important medical doctor in talmudic literature.

2   **Brain. (גיהירין**‎ :16). The idea of the "soft brain" most probably results from the newborn's soft skullcap. Thus the brain was all the more endangered, as in the early modern era the skin was perceived as permeable film which did not constitute an absolute barrier between the body and its environment; cf. Benthien, *Haut* (Skin), p. 51f.

8   **Takes the child to her. (צו זיך נעמט**‎ :22). What is probably meant is that the mother takes the child into bed with her at night. The reference to the knowledge of the God-fearing women allows the assumption that the author hints to the rabbinic warning of "the illness that one must not mention" (B. Pesaḥim 117b), interpreted as epilepsy.

    S. *Brantshpigl*, p. 65: "She shall keep clean the bed, in which (her husband) lies.... She should also not get the child accustomed to it, so that it will want to lie in it always. There is a danger, when they fall asleep, that they crush it to death, as has happened many times. It is written in the tractate Pesaḥim, that when man and woman perform intercourse while the child lies next to them, the child will have the illness that one must not mention."

23a

16   **Grown on. (אן גיוואקשין**‎ :2). Possibly a magical binding spell is meant; in that sense, "grown" could be understood in the sense of "tied," cf. Trachtenberg, *Magic*, p. 127. The sixty-eighth chapter of *Brantshpigl* deals with the prohibition of magic, which is understood to mean mainly divinatory practices like foretelling.

16   **Evil eye. (ביז אויג**‎ :3). The idea of the evil eye (the negative power of envy and jealousy) is popular also in other moral books; see *Brantshpigl*, p. 243: "One should also

Gentile woman, and have her cast a spell on it. This is a major sin, and I would like to keep far apart from [such] (things). Our Holy Torah forbade it to us numerous times, as the verse says, "Let there not be among you a diviner or a sorcerer."[22] This means in Yiddish, there should be no soothsayers or sorcerers among you. As we find regarding Ahijah of Shiloh, the Prophet, who said to the king: "Is there no God in Israel? Assuredly you shall not rise from the bed which you are lying on; but the boy shall die."[23] In Yiddish this means, is there (no) [God] in Israel? Therefore the sick boy will never rise from the bed on which he lies. The boy must die.

Sefer Ḥasidim[24] writes, one may not speak of or believe things such as: One should not take fire from (a place where) a woman is lying in childbed; or one may not perform a (circumcision)

not boast in front of gentile men or women with one's jewelry or expensive clothing. Much evil arises from it. They begrudge it the Jews, and cast an evil eye upon it." Similar in *Ze'enah u-Re'enah* on Num. 12:1, p. 702, and on Deut. 5:21, p. 824; cf. Trachtenberg, *Magic*, p. 54ff.

1   *Cast a spell.* (אן שפרעכן: 4-3). Incantation with powerful names was a widespread healing practice also in the early modern era; cf. Trachtenberg, *Magic*, p. 200ff.; regarding the respective practice in the Talmud, cf. Veltri, *Magie* (Magic), p. 230ff.

3   *Not.* (לא: 5). The masoretic text of Deut. 18:10 differs significantly.

5   *Is there no.* (המבלי: 7). The quote deviates from II Kings 1:16 (an angel speaks with Elijah about the questionable recovery of King Ahaziah); similar in II Kings 1:3.6. The author probably confused the names of the prophets, because Ahijah of Shiloh, as opposed to King Jeroboam, condemns idolatry (I Kings 11:33f.).

7   *(No).* (ניט]: 8). The Prague 1609 printing cites the subjunctive form *zay*—be, which corresponds with the absence of negation in the preceding Hebrew quote. The translation here is rather a word-by-word transfer, as can be found frequently up to fol. 24a.

9   *Sefer Ḥasidim.* (ספר חסידים: 10). S. *Sefer Ḥasidim*, §59: "ובעונותינו שרבו כיום הזה מנחשים בישראל [...] שלא לקחת אש שתי פעמים כשיש חולה בבית או יולדת תוך תשעה ימים וכמה דברים שאין הפה יכול לדברם ועוברים על מצות מלכנו. [...] ראין אש וגחלות בוערות מעומד אומרים יהי' לנו אורח אם תכבהו במים מים האורח יפול במים ואין לך ניחוש גדול מזה, ואמת מייצב הדבר כמה בני אדם ניסוהו אך הוא השטן הוא המתעה אותם כשרואה השטן שזה מנחש ואומר יפול האורח במים אז אומר השטן אלך ואפיל האורח במים להטעות להיות זה בידי לנחש לעולם. לסימן"—"In our days there are many among Israel, who tell fortune:... that one must not take fire twice (from the hearth) of a sick person's house or of a woman in childbed during the nine days. And other things that one cannot even utter, and which ignore our King's mitzvot:... When one sees a flaring coal fire, so they say, we will have a guest coming. If it is extinguished with water: the guest will fall into water. Although you are not a believer in great fortune telling, these things are true and fixed for some people, who will try them out. Satan leads them astray: When Satan hears somebody telling fortune, saying that the guest will fall into the water, Satan says (to himself): I will go and push the guest into the water, in order to lead the other one astray. He will take it as a sign, and will forever tell fortune."

10   *Circumcision.* (צו שניידין: 12). This may possibly mean the postponement of the circumcision from the eighth day to a later time, which bears not magical but halakhic implications; perhaps it is only mentioned here by mistake because of the preceding men-

on any particular day. Or (one must not say), "The magpie is crowing—we'll have guests"; or, "The fire lit up and can not be extinguished—the guest who is coming will drown." Some who believe in these things attempt to test whether they are true, and then Satan quickly comes, God protect us, and makes it happen, so that they will believe in it again the next time.

We often see that some people allow enchantresses to tell their fortunes or cast spells, and thus make mention of impure and false gods. This is a major sin—our Holy Torah forbade it. As the verse says, "Make no [mention] of the names of other gods; they shall not be heard on your lips."[25] In Yiddish this means, you shall not recall the names of foreign gods—that is to say, you cause them to recall them—and it should not be heard from your mouth—one may not mention their festivals. But one does not need to forbid these things to a God-fearing woman.

Therefore every pious mother should watch over her child and should not [entrust] it to a young girl. At times one finds a woman who goes to weddings or memorials, and forgets

tion of the woman in childbed; the statements here deviate in contents completely from the passage in the *Sefer Ḥasidim*.

1   *Magpie.* (אגלשטר: 12). The word appears here instead of אש וגחלות, with which it shares a certain visual similarity. Popular belief in divinatory abilities of the magpie was widespread in Poland of the 17th and 18th centuries. See a contemporary aphorism: "The virgins ask the magpie, whether they can tell that guests will come, if they behave well"; cf. Wyczanski, *Polen* (Poland), p. 399. Cf. the German proverb "I have heard the magpie, a guest is on his way" Wander, *Sprichwörterlexikon* (Lexicon of Proverbs), p. 810.

11   *Festivals.* (חגאות: 21). Aramaism, literally "scare," "shiver"; used in the rabbinic literature also as pejorative designation for pagan feasts and celebrations; cf. Isa. 19, 17.

14   *Weddings.* (חתונת: 25). Spelling here reflects the Yiddish pronunciation. Weddings, memorials, and *brit milah* celebrations offered some of the few opportunities for social get-togethers or exuberant celebrations, which receive only rare attention in the moral literature; see *Brantshpigl*, p. 435: "The sages of virtue (*Reshit Hokhmah*, II, p. 388) write: When someone goes to the wedding of a scholar with the daughter of a scholar, or where an orphan marries another orphan, or to a circumcision, or when scholars finish reading a book and invite to a feast, and he sits there modestly, or pleases bride and groom . . . , then all of this is better than to fast."

Common are warnings of exaggerated exuberance, see *Brantshpigl*, p. 244: "On a wedding women should be careful not to mix with the men."

There is also the warning of inviting Christians, ibid., p. 243: "It must also be urgently warned before inviting the uncircumcized to a wedding."

In addition there is criticism against weddings that serve to demonstrate or improve the social status; see ibid., p. 324: "There are people, who celebrate real (large) weddings, *brit milah* celebrations, and bar mitzvah celebrations, or when important representatives of the community arrive, they are asked into the house. They act as if it is their obligation to give a large dinner, and as if they are joyful, but in their hearts they only think about the cost of feeding strangers, and serving them with their crockery and servants. They look at them with an evil eye and begrudge them the food and the drink. These are all plain meals, and do not count as mitzvah."

that she has a child at home. I once saw that a memorial was held just after the end of Yom Kippur. On the preceding night—*Kol Nidrei* night—they ran out of the synagogue immediately after *Barkhu*, saying, "I have to go home to my child." And the next night at the

23b

memorial, they stayed half the night and didn't think at all about the children. It is certainly
5   preferable for one to stay with her children and not go to synagogue if she has no one else. As it is said, it is better for her to stay at home and think of the synagogue [than] to go to synagogue and think of home.

As King David, peace be upon him, said, "Give ear to my speech, O LORD; consider my utterance."[26] This means in Yiddish, listen to what I say—in other words, listen to the
10   prayer that I make to you. If I cannot (pray), you should examine the thoughts in my heart. King Solomon, peace be upon him, said, "The one no less than the other was God's doing."[27] This means in Yiddish as follows: God, blessed be His name, created one just as the other. That is to say, this means that a woman should think, "I cannot, at the moment, go to synagogue, and I must miss the prayers, but I hope to God, blessed be His name,
15   that if I raise the child to serve Him and praise Him, and to follow the Torah and commandments, it will be considered equivalent." King David, peace be upon him, said, "It is a time to act for the LORD, for they have violated your teaching."[28] This means, there will be a time to act for God, even if one abrogates a commandment (now). It often happens that one is in the middle of the greatest prayer and must leave urgently, such as when a
20   woman goes to her child or the like. She should not think then, "I want to listen." So too when she has a small child and wants to leave it alone—it is better for her to stay with her children, since all kinds of accidents have happened, God protect us, when a women left her children, one cannot even mention them all.

3   ***Barkhu.*** (ברכו :27). Prayer which immediately follows the *Kol Nidrei* on the eve of Yom Kippur.

23b

10   ***Prayer.*** (תפילה :6). S. *Yalkut*, §630: "'Give ear to my speech (Ps 5:2), said David to the Holy One, blessed be He. When I am strong enough to stand before you and say my prayer, (it is said in respect to that): 'Give ear to my speech' (ibid.). But if I am not strong enough, then ponder over what is in my heart, (as it is written): 'Consider my utterance' (ibid.)." Same in Rashi on Ps. 5:2.

22   ***Children.*** (קינדר :17). S. *Brantshpigl*, p. 290: "When the woman goes to the synagogue, she should put everything into order at home, and she should have instructed the children and the servants accordingly, so that she doesn't need to worry about anything, and can deliver her prayer with dedication. Our sages had a sign installed in all synagogues, 'A prayer without dedication is like a body without a soul.'...Children that still wet the bed should not be taken into the synagogue. If the child does something, it will receive gifts from the malevolent demons, which only wait for such an opportunity. However, if it is dressed dry and clean, it shall be accustomed to the synagogue, and that

Therefore every upright woman should remain with her child, and should not go to the holy synagogue. Just as when she wants to go for a walk, or to sit in front of the door, nothing good can result. But if she sits beside the cradle, she can keep the child asleep and also do her work. If she is privileged with more children, and they are grown up, she should sit and listen to their praying and their blessings, and not rely on the teacher. It is said, "There is no work as good as that one does oneself." So too, the studying that a mother does with her child is much more successful than with someone else, as we learn

5

it should be quiet there, and not scream. . . . One should not kiss the child inside the synagogue, and express love only to God, blessed be He."

See ibid., p. 302: Domestic chores should not be neglected because of the service, in order to avoid arousing the husband's anger. On the other hand, women are often called to perform *tehinnot* (*tkhines*, Yiddish prayers) at home, e.g., ibid., p. 301.

S. *Eyn shoyn Froyenbuykhleyn*, fol. 5a: ‏"אונ׳ ניט גיא מיט דיינים בעזם [!] אין דיינר הנט אונ׳‎ ‏דו טושט אורן אדר בענשן. אז די נערישן ורויען פפלעגין צו טון. אדר נעמן אירי קינדר אויף אירי‎ ‏שושא אונ׳ אורן דער בייא. אלש אין אין מולט. אונ׳ די קינדר זיין ביפישט אדר בישמישן. אונ׳‎ ‏ועען די קינדר זיין ואול שין אויז גיוואישט. זו זיין אירי קליידר ניט ריין. דרום גיביט איך דיר‎ ‏ווילשטו אורן זא טוא דו נישט ביז דוא אורשט. אונ׳ האב דיין כונה צו גוט יתברך שמו. אונ׳ ניט‎ ‏גידענק וואז דוא טון האשט"‎.—"Don't walk with a broom in your hand while you are praying or saying blessings, as foolish use to women do. They sit their child on their lap while they are praying, all at the same time. But the children have wet or soiled themselves. Even when the children are nicely washed, their clothes are still not clean anymore. We therefore recommend, if you wish to pray, do not pray until you (actually) pray. Dedicate yourself completely to God, blessed be His Name, and don't think about the things you still need to do."

See ibid., fol. 48a: A good housewife should go to service; on the other hand, on fol. 48b, she is told that when her husband comes home from the synagogue, she should be pretty in appearance and friendly to him.

2-3   *In front of the door.* (‏פר דיא טיר‎ :21). *Brantshpigl* mentions "sitting in front of the door" as a very common *topos* for idleness and the woman's "inconsequential talk"; see ibid., p. 92: "The woman's greatest virtue is modesty. She should be shy to step out of the door, unless it is truly necessary. She should certainly not stand or sit in front of the door. People might sin and cause her a bad reputation."

S. ibid., p. 129f.: "Women or men sitting like this in front of the door talk about inconsequential things, tell each other stories about strangers, or about what is happening with other people. They take young women or men into their midst and arrange where they should meet and enjoy themselves. That is a great sin."

Similar in *Sefer ha-Gan*, fol. 7b: ‏"אונ׳ ווען איין מענש פון זיין משא אונ׳ מתן איין היים‎ ‏גיט אונ׳ לערנט ניט דא היישט זיין היוז קריג אדר ועון ער זיצט אין דער גסין אונ׳ רעט אוניצין ריד‎ ‏אונ׳ לערנט ניט זיין זינט דיא איז גרוש"‎.—"If one comes home from negotiations, and does not study, then his house will be called quarrel. Or, if he then sits on the street and talks useless talk instead of learning, he commits a great sin."

5   *Praying.* (‏דבנין‎ :24). Regarding this Eastern Yiddish word *davenen* (also Yiddish text 27b/23), cf. Weinreich, *History*, p. 726, and cf. the commentary on p. 138/12, as well as the section "Origin and Family" in the Introduction. *Brantshpigl* only uses *tefille tun*—to perform a prayer—and *beten*—pray, request; *Eyn shoyn Froyenbuykhleyn* and *Sefer Middot* only cite the Western Yiddish word *oren*—pray. *Sefer ha-Gan* cites both *oren* and *davenen*.

from the verse, "My son, heed the discipline of your father, and do not forsake the instruction of your mother."[29] This means in Yiddish, my son, follow the admonition

24a

of your father and you shall not leave the teaching of your mother. As the Gemara explains: Why does the verse say regarding the mother, "the teaching of your mother," and regarding the father says as above? This is because the father must obtain his livelihood, and is not always at home. So he sees only occasionally that (the child) is misbehaving and then he speaks to him. But the mother is always at home and watches over her children. She can teach them many good deeds, and should pay close attention to every [step] and every word. As it is written in our beloved Torah, "Impress them upon your children, recite them when you are at home,"[30] etc. We say this in our prayers morning and night. It means in

---

24a

3   *Gemara.* (גמרא 2:). It is unclear whether this is a talmudic source; possibly a different interpretation of Prov. 6:20.

6   *At home.* (דער היים 5:). Regarding the mother's prime responsibility for the children's education, see *Eyn shoyn Froyenbuykhleyn*, fol. 6a: "אונ׳ הלט זיא אן צו תורה אונ׳
צו מעשים טובים וועז דאש טריפט נימנץ מין אן אז די ורויאן. אז דער פסוק שפריכט שמע בני
מוסר אביך ואל תטוש תורת אמך דאז מיינט הויר מיין זון שטראפֿונג דיין ואטיר. אונ׳ ניט דוא
זאלשט ור לאשין לערנונג דיינר מוטר. דען דער ואטר איז דען גנצן טאג ניט אין דען הויז דרהיים.
אונ׳ קאן זי ניט שטראפֿין. ניירארט צו צייטן זעלטין. [...] אבר דיא מוטר איז אימר דארין דער
היים.—אונ׳ זיכט אלז אונ׳ הוירט אלז וואז דיא קינדר טואן." —"(She) urges them to study Torah and to perform good deeds, because this applies to nobody as much as to the women. Thus says the verse, 'My son, heed the discipline of your father, And do not forsake the instruction of your mother' (Prov. 1:8). This means, hear, my son, the admonition of your father, and do not forsake the instruction of your mother. Because the father is absent from home all day long, and he can only rarely admonish them. But the mother is always at home, and she sees and hears everything that the children do." Similar on fol. 46a.

     S. *Brantshpigl*, p. 172: "Rav said to his son Rabbi Ḥiyya: How do women earn their share in eternal life? He answered: By bringing the children into the synagogue and the study house, and taking them back from there, and by waiting with the meal for their husbands, until they come home from the yeshivah, or from their business."

     Similar in *Ze'enah u-Re'enah* on Exod. 16:16, p. 414: "She must remain completely in the house, and should not run around outside. Thus every man is urged to provide all the needs of his wife and of his small children." The woman's domestic chores include (ibid., on Exod. 19:3, p. 427) always to be at home, and therefore it is she, who raises the children, brings the sons to the Rabbis, and only speaks pious and gentle words.

     Cf. *Sefer Middot*, 98a: Since the woman is at home, she raises the children, and performs domestic chores such as cooking and laundering; similar in ibid., 7b and 22b. Regarding the fatherly educational tasks see also the commentary on p. 103/3–4.

10   *Prayers.* (תפילה 8:). Deut. 6:7 is part of the *Shema*, which is prayed during the *Shaḥarit* and *Ma'ariv* services.

Yiddish, you shall teach them to your children and you shall speak about them when you are sitting. That is to say, you should sit with your children and speak to them of Torah-related things, and not inconsequential matters. This is why the Torah says, "(recite) them," meaning "to them." But one should not speak of inconsequential things with them, as *Orḥot Ẓaddikim*[31] writes: When one speaks with a child about inconsequential things, it is like when one has a board, and wants to write on it something useful. Along comes someone else and fouls the board so that he cannot write on it. This is also similar: The Holy One, blessed be He, created a human and gave him a heart in order to think about His holy name and His holy Torah. As the verse says, "Write them on the tablet of your mind."[32] This means in [Yiddish], and you shall write on the board of your heart. Now, when a person talks about trivialities or other inconsequential things with a child, his heart will also be fouled. (The child) will be spoiled and blemished, and one can only bring it out with difficulty.

And the verse says, "When you lie down."[33] This means, when one lies down, one should speak with him about fear of God and say, "I want to tell you nice stories from

---

5   *Orḥot Ẓaddikim.* (אורחת צדיקים :12). For the Yiddish spelling, see the commentary on p. 124/7. S. *Orḥot Ẓaddikim*, fol. 3b: אך לבו דומה ללוח שהוא מוכן לכתוב עליו" אם הלוח הזה ביד טיפש ושרטט עליו שרטוט הבלים עד שיתקלקל ולא יהיה בו תועלת עוד [...] כך לב האדם הכסילי׳ יצייירו בו ציוורי הבל ושקר ויכתבו עליו חקקי הבל ואון וימלאו לבם מחשבות הבל וריק והמשכילים יכתבו על לבם מכתב אלהים שהוא יסוד התור׳ והמצות וחכמות המידות."—"But the heart resembles a writing board. When this board is in the hands of a fool, he will scribble all kinds of nonsense on it, until it becomes spoilt and useless.... Such is the heart of the foolish man, into which nonsensical or mendacious signs have been inscribed, and into which empty and vain symbols have been written: His heart is filled with vain and empty thoughts. But those who understand write into their heart the writings of God, which form the foundation of the Torah, and the mitzvot, and the wisdom of virtues."

A Yiddish version that comes closer to the formulation of Rivkah bat Meir, because of the explicit reference to childhood, can be found in *Sefer Middot*, fol. 5b–6a: אבר דעש" מענשן הערצן דש איז צום ערשטן גלייך אז איין הויפשי טאביל אודר גלייך אלז איין נוייא פאפייער דא מן וואל אויף קאן שרייבן וען נאר דיא טאביל אודר דש פאפייער צו גימאלט הוט זא קראצט ער דרויף אונ׳ מולט דרויף נארהיט אונ׳ ונטיזייא. דש דאש פפייער אודר דיא טאביל דרונך ניט טויג עצוואש גוטש דארויף צו מולן אודר צו שרייבן. [...] אזו איז אויך דער מענשן הערץ דיא טוריכט זיין. דיא שרייבן אויף איר הערץ אין אירר יוגנט נארהייט אונ׳ שמועות אונ׳ דברים בטלים [...] דש מן דרונך ניט צו ברענגן קאן אין איר הערץ קיין תורה אודר קיינרלייא וויזהייט אודר גוטי ווערק."—"But the human heart is initially a pretty board, or a new sheet of paper, which can well be written upon. If a fool fills the paper with his scribbles, he will smear and paint on it all kinds of foolishness and fantasies, so that after that the paper can no more be used in order to be painted or written upon.... Such is the heart of the foolish people. They fill their heart of youth with foolishness and tales, and all kinds of inconsequential matters... so that one cannot bring into their hearts any Torah, wisdom, or good deeds."

9   *Write.* (וכתבתם :16). The masoretic text of Prov. 3:3 differs slightly.

15   *Nice stories.* (שיני שמועות :21). S. Rashi on II Chron. 7:20: "'And make it a proverb and a byword': This means, when something is clarified with a proverb about

the Torah, and tales from the Gemara." One should tell him how many people let themselves to be killed for His holy name. One should tell him as well how our Patriarch Isaac, peace be upon him, wanted to let himself be slaughtered, because God, blessed be His name, commanded it, and also because he did not want to go against his father. He also asked him to tie him up well, so that he would not hit him. One should also tell him about

24b

Chenaniah, Mishael, and Azariah—how the king took youths captive. Those who were evil and greedy ate nonkosher food and drank forbidden wine, and they turned yellow and green from their portion. But those who were pious and upright had a pure mouth, and were not greedy—they did not want to eat nonkosher food, and ate and drank nothing but bread and water. Nevertheless they were strong and healthy and fair like milk and blood. And then our dear Lord God sent an angel to them, who studied with them. Afterwards the king had an idol made. The bad youths did not want to disobey the king's command, and bowed before the idol because they were afraid that they would be thrown into a furnace. But the three pious youths did not want to bow to the idol, and let themselves to be thrown into the furnace. Thereupon God, blessed be His name, sent them an angel who protected them from the fire. They came out of the furnace strong and healthy without injury. But [the king] slew the evil youths who bowed to the idol, (after) he had said [...], "You have

somebody, who has met with an accident. 'A byword': as in 'Impress them upon your children' (Deut. 6:7): repeat it in the language of a simple story. The translation of 'Recite' (ibid.) is thus he told an entertaining story."

1   *Torah.* (חומש :22). Spelling based on Yiddish pronunciation.

3   *Let himself be slaughtered.* (וועלן לאזין שעכטין :24). Similar statements regarding the sacrifice of Isaac (Gen. 22:9) can be found, among others, in *Ozar Midrashim*, p. 146: "And Isaac said to his father, 'Father, hurry and expose your arm, bind my hands and feet nice and tight. Because I am a young man of thirty seven, and you are old. When I will see the knife, I might kick you, for fear of the knife.'"

     Shorter in Yalkut, §101.

24b

6   *Chenaniah, Mishael, and Azariah.* (חנניה מישאל ועזריה :1). The subsequent story is a conflation of Dan. 1:6–21 (Daniel is promoted to royal advisor), Dan. 3:1–30 (the youths in the furnace), and Dan. 6:1–28 (Daniel in the lions' den), for the version of which the author may possibly have had a sample. Here, in comparison to Dan. 1:6–21, the element of the distinction and elevation of the Jews by the gentile ruler is missing; here, as opposed to Dan. 3:1–30, the element of punishment is missing. The structure of Dan. 6:1–28 and the preceding version is generally identical.

     The story of the three youths is very popular in Yiddish literature; cf. *Ze'enah u-Re'enah* on Gen. 49:9, p. 329; on Exod. 13:17, p. 394; on Lev. 4:2, p. 548; *Brantshpigl*, pp. 158f., 374; another version in *Maysse Bukh* (Gaster), no. 193. Regarding the rabbinic version, cf. B. Sanhedrin 93a.

such a powerful God, (yet you bowed to the idol). You have corrupted your land with sin and will corrupt my land with sin." One should tell such stories to children. This is what the Torah means by saying, "Impress them upon your children, recite them."[34]

And one should also teach the children Hebrew.

4   *Teach the children Hebrew.* (קינדר לערנן לשון הקדש) :18-17). The non-gender specific pedagogic context may imply that the request to teach "children" (*kinder*) Hebrew includes girls as well. Other sources often use the term *banim*, which means both "sons" and "children," and so are ambiguous as to whether only sons or daughters as well should be taught the Hebrew language.

S. *Brantshpigl*, p. 338: "It is good to teach children (*kinder*) the Hebrew names of the body parts and all devices in the house, so that they might become accustomed to the holy language."

Ibid., p. 340: "And when the child (*kind*) is a little bigger, and it has already been taught verses, one should teach it the Hebrew alphabet."

Ibid., p. 26, where the reference is probably limited to boys: "If they get the children (*kinder*) accustomed from an early age to learn the Torah, and they are brought to the Rabbi; if they take care of the children (*kinder*), and tell them God's word, (this) awakens their hearts, then they will find joy in learning, they will perform the mitzvot, and fear their Rabbi."

See the comparison between boys' and girls' education in ibid., p. 305: "When (the mother) comes home, and she has male children (*kinder mans namen*), she will give them to eat, after she recited to them the benedictions and the short benediction *barukh raḥmana*. Then she takes them to the Rabbi and lets them run inside. If she has girls (*maydlekh*), she should dress them nicely and plait their hair. She will give them a good, warm meal, not only sweets, and will get them accustomed to staying at home, and not to run around outside. In time she will get them accustomed to working a little, so that they can manufacture their own linens, and do not have to pay anything for this work."

S. *Sefer Middot*, fols. 97b–98a: אויך זול איינר זיין קינדר לערנן לשון הקדש רידן אונ' זול "מיט אינן רידן דברי תורה אונ' שמועות אויז דער תורה אונ' צו בור איוז אויבר טיש וען מן אישט אונ'—זוינשט אויך וען מן ער מוישיג איז." —"One should also teach one's children (*kinder*) to speak Hebrew. One should tell them words of the Torah, and stories from the Torah. Even before that, one should (speak Hebrew) (also) around the table, during the meals, and also otherwise, during leisure."

Here, as generally in Yiddish moral literature, there is no reference to the limitations on education of girls if the subject is mentioned at all; see *Sefer Middot*, fol. 97b: אונ' וויא" וואל דיא גמרא גיט ורויא דורפן ניט לערנן. דש מאיינט זיא דורפן ניט תלמוד לערנן. אבר עשרים וארבע אונ' איסור והיתר זול מן זיא לערנן דש איז מצוה אונ' דיא ורויאן זולן איר מאנן אונ' איר "קינדר תורה לושן לערנן אונ' זולן זיא ניט מבטל זיין.—"It also says in the Gemara that women are not permitted to study. This means, they are not permitted to study Talmud. But they should be taught the Bible, and the 'Permitted and Prohibited.' That is an obligation. The women should let their husbands and children study Torah, and they should not allow them to be idle."

Eyn shoyn Froyenbuykhleyn only indicates on a number of occasions that women should read and study the *Froyenbuykhleyn* or other moral books and teach other women; see ibid., fols. 24b; 37a; 39a; 49b.

The rabbinic foundation for the discussion of female education is laid out in Y. Sotah 3d; B. Sotah 20a and 21b; B. Kiddushin 29a. Regarding the ambivalent stand of the rabbinic literature on Torah studies by women, and its rather negative assessment by the Shulḥan Arukh, *Talmud Torah*, 246:6, cf. Biale, *Women and Jewish Law*, pp. 29–37.

The mother should also familiarize the child with respecting its father. The mother should give the child a treat or an apple, and should say to him, "Dear child, give this to your father so that you can honor him, and God, blessed be He, will lengthen your life." The father should do the same, and should tell the child, "Dear child, honor your mother however you can." If a child has a grandfather or grandmother, he should honor them all the more.

But one sees some fathers or mothers who laugh when they hear a child curse or swear—they enjoy it very much, and say, "What a clever child this is!" But it should not be so—it is a (bad) habit. When a child is able to reach for something, one should teach it: When it wants to take a knife, one should hit its hand to give it a fright. No pious woman

25a

should spare the rod, as King Solomon, peace be upon him, writes in Proverbs, "Beat him with a rod and you will save him from death."[35] This means in Yiddish, you shall beat your

25a

From death. (ממות :1).   Prov. 23:14 reads instead "from the grave." Regarding the formulation "save him from death," cf. Prov. 10:2 and 11:4.

Beat. (שלאגין :2).   The beating of children as an appropriate educational method is substantiated in many moral texts; at the same time there are warnings of excess permissiveness or pity; see *Brantshpigl*, p. 334: "If the child ignores the gentle words, one must become angry. If this doesn't help, one should beat the child with a small rod. If the child is already bigger, one should take a bigger (rod). King Solomon says in Proverbs, 'He who spares the rod hates his son' (Prov. 13:24).... This means, if he does not want to beat him with the rod, it means that he hates him, and that he does (not) want him to be well behaved."

S. *Sefer Middot*, fols. 27b–28a: דש זיך אייז ואטר דר באָרמט אויבר זיין קינדר דש איז דער קיין"
וואונדר דעז עז איז דיא דיא נטויאר. דש ויך אונ׳ דיא הונט האבז איר קינדר אויך ליבא. וועז אבר אייז
מענש זיך דרבאָרמט אויבר זיין קינדר דש ער זיא ניט שלאגז מאג אודר ניט רעכט צידן מאג. דז
איז ניט אייז גוטי ער דר באָרמונג. אונ׳ מיט דער זעלבז דרבאַרמיקייט מאכט ער דאש ער אונ׳ דיא
קינדר ור לירן דעז עולם הבא. [...] אבר דאש בעשטע רחמנית דש מז וינט דש איז דש איינר זיין
קינדר ציכט צו גוט ית׳ דינשט אונ׳ זיא שלאגט וועז זיא אים ניט באלגז וועלן צום בעשטן. אונ׳ זיך
ניט אויבר זיא דר באָרמט. ער זול זיך דר באָרמן אויף זיינר קינדר נשמה מער דעז אויף ארין
 לייבא.—אונ׳ זול זיא שלאגן מיט רוטן אונ׳ מיט גאייזלן." —"It is no wonder that a father has pity on his children, because it is natural. Even the cattle and the dogs love their young. But if a person has pity with his children, and does not want to beat them, or to educate them appropriately, then this is not a good kind of pity. This kind of pity leads to him, and his children, losing the world to come.... But the best kind of pity to be found is to educate one's children to serve God, blessed be His Name, and to beat them. If they don't want to follow him, to their benefit, he should not have pity on them. He should have more pity on his children's souls than on their bodies. He should beat them with rods and with whips."

S. ibid., fol. 28a: דענוך איז עז מצוה דש מן דיא יתומים שלאגט וועז מן זיא ציכט צו"
מעשים טובים. אבר דוך זול מן הויפשליכר טוז דעז מיט אנדרז זיינן קינדרן אודר מיט אנדרז
קינדרן דיא אויך ואטר אונ׳ מוטר האבן. אבר כלל וכלל זול מן דענוך אייז יתום ניט און גישלאגן
לאשן." —"Yet it is an obligation to beat the orphans, if one wishes to educate them to do

child with the rod, and you will thereby protect his life from death. That is to say that he will not incur the death penalty, as our Torah requires, "He who insults his father or his mother shall die a [death]."[36] This means, he who disrespects his father and mother and defies them and causes them worry should be killed. Therefore, it is written twice: "Shall die a death,"[37] that is to say, if the earthly court does not deal with him, he will not be overlooked in the world to come.

Therefore, one should be cautioned to [educate] the child in [good] behavior in good time. As King Solomon, peace be upon him, said, "Train a lad in the way he ought to go; he will not swerve from it even in old age."[38] This means in Yiddish, familiarize a child to go on the right path, and when he is old he will not turn from it. That is to say, he will remain on the right path. But *Reshit Hokhmah*[39] explains the meaning as follows: If you want to raise a youth, but he takes as his example what he sees from other disrespectful boys, he will not be able to change himself when he is old. (*Reshit Hokhmah*) tells a parable about this:

There was once a thief who did a lot of mischief. His father admonished him, "My son, think of what will become of you." The son answered his father, "My dear father, you are right, I want to follow you. Come on a walk with me." He led him into a forest in which small trees stood, whereupon the son said to the father, "Take this small tree and bend it to the side all the way to the ground, and then again to the other (side)." The father did it—he bent it in every direction that he wanted to. Then they went further to a larger, thicker [tree]. The son said to his father, "Take this tree and bend it to the ground too, the way you bent the other one." The father said, "I cannot reach this tree, it is too high and thick." The son said, "Listen to yourself—do you want to admonish me or educate me now?

good deeds. One should treat them more politely than one's other children, or children, who still have mother and father. But under no circumstances should one raise an orphan without beatings."

9   ***Swerve from it.*** (יסיר ממנו :9).   The masoretic text of Prov. 22:6 differs slightly.

11   ***Reshit Hokhmah.*** (ראשית חכמה :11).   S. *Reshit Hokhmah*, III, p. 59, §9: "One who uses the rod sparingly to beat his son, as long as he is young, hates his son. The son will eventually go astray, because his father did not punish him when he was young. Eventually he will kill his son because of his bad deeds." Immediately preceding the text above (ibid., p. 56, §4) there is a story of the son of Rabbi Hanina ben Teradyon, who joined a band of robbers. Later, however, he gave the robbers away, who then killed him because of that. Now the father bitterly accuses himself for having neglected his son's upbringing.

13   ***Tells a parable.*** (ברענגט איין משל :14).   This formulation suggests that the author took the parable from *Reshit Hokhmah*; however, there it is not substantiated.

See Perush Rabbenu Yonah Gerondi on Avot 1:14: "'Train a lad in the way he ought to go; He will not swerve from it even in old age' (Prov. 22:6), and it is written: 'Are trees of the field human' (Deut. 20:19). During (the time of youth) there is repentance, but at old age there is no more complete repentance. At that time, the urge is not strong, and the wish is pure. It does not mix with the soul, and it does not long for sinful pleasures."

You should have admonished me when it was possible to educate me when I was young—then it would never have [come] to this!" And he pulled out a sword and chopped off his father's head.

But some undutiful mothers do not think of this when a father wants to rebuke or hit a

25b

child. They will not tolerate it, or conversely, when she wants to hit the child, the father will not tolerate it. This is where [bad] children come from, God protect us.

It is the same when a child says, "Look what I found!" They say, "What a lucky child!" and do not think that the child must have taken it from somewhere, and got his hands on it that way, God protect us. [Or] also when a child sees something that someone else has, and wants to take it away with force, and the father or mother goes and takes it away from the other (child). Nothing good is [taught] to the children this way, it should not be like this. One should talk the child out of it, and say, "You may not take what is not yours, even if, God forbid, someone dies. Our dear God prohibited it." One should hit the child and say, "Don't let [me] hear that from you again!" King Solomon, peace be upon him, also said this: "He who spares the rod hates his son, but he who loves him disciplines him early."[40] This means, whoever spares his child the rod hates his child; however, he who loves his child inquires after him. That is to say, how he behaves around his teacher, and is appropriately admonished.

The Gemara[41] explains that Ishmael went astray because our Patriarch Abraham spoiled him. Similarly, Esau went astray because our Patriarch Isaac spoiled him. *Reshit Ḥokhmah*[42] explains the verse as follows: If a man spares his son the rod, you can rest assured that that same child will hate his father. However, if you see that a father or mother chastises their

25b

17   *Inquires.* (פארשט :12). This formulation does not exclude the possibility of the mother consulting the Rabbi herself; see, on the other hand, *Brantshpigl*, p. 345: "If the mother brings the child to the Rabbi, she should let it run inside and not enter herself, so that the Rabbi should not sin in his thoughts and bring impurity upon himself."

19   *Gemara.* (גמרא :13). S. Shemot Rabbah 1.1: "Such we also find with Ishmael, who rebelled against his father. The father did not punish him, which is why (Ishmael) was led astray. (Finally) he hated him, and expelled him from his home."

19   *Astray.* (לתרבית רעה :14). Spelling based on Yiddish pronunciation; same in 25b/15 (Yiddish text).

20   *Reshit Ḥokhmah.* (ראשית חכמה :15). See the commentary on p. 166/11. S. also *Reshit Ḥokhmah*, III, p. 57, §5: "If you bring up the lad according to his manner—but what is the manner of a lad? Not to learn, and not to pray! Instead, he sits around idle, and follows his pleasures. If you leave him to his manner and nature in his youth, it will not be possible to drive it out of him, and to lead him back to the right path. Even when he is old, he will not let go, because it will have become his nature."

child, you can rest assured that that same child will love his father and mother, and will obey their will. We also find this regarding King David, peace be upon him. Because he did not chastise Absalom, he ultimately sought his life, and caused a great sin to be committed by the people of Israel, and caused thousands of the people of Israel to die by the sword.

5 And so it is also written regarding Adonijah, "His father had never scolded him."[43] This means in Yiddish, his father did not cause him to be sad. And the verse also says, "He was the one born after Absalom."[44] If he did indeed have a different mother, why does the verse say that he was born after Absalom? Rather, the verse is saying to me that he took after Absalom, and broke with his father and had himself anointed king during his father's

10 lifetime. [Ultimately] he wanted to take his father's wife, which is why he came to a bad

26a

end. Nevertheless, King Solomon said, "Discipline your son while there is still hope, and do not set your heart on his destruction."[45] This means, chastise your child, because there is [hope] that (he) can become good; but you should not harbor a desire to kill him. That is to say, it means as follows: You should not think, "If I were to hit my child, he is badly off,

15 and he could become sick." You should not think that. King Solomon, peace be upon him, also [said], "If folly settles in the heart of a lad, the rod of discipline will remove it."[46] This means in Yiddish, foolishness is bound to the heart of a youth—which is to say, "Wisdom comes with age"—(and) the rod with which one punishes a child knocks it out of him.

Reshit Ḥokhmah[47] writes that parents should not think, "Why should I punish him? It's

---

2   ***Regarding King David.*** (בייא דוד 19:). S. II Sam. 13:39, 14:11; 18:5.

7   ***After Absalom.*** (נאך אבשלום 25:). S. Shemot Rabbah 1.1: "'He was the one born after Absalom' (I Kings 1:6). Is Absalom not the son of Maacah and of Adonijah, son of Haggith? What, then, does it mean, 'He was the one born after Absalom?' It means that he was led astray, and his father did not punish him, as is written for Adonijah, 'His father had never scolded him' (ibid.). But he was led astray, and therefore it is written, 'He was the one born after Absalom' (ibid.)."

     Similar in B. Bava Batra 109b. It is unusual that the author presents the rabbinic interpretation as her own—"the verse is saying to me."

26a

13   [*Hope*]. (האפונג 2:). Regarding the emendation see also 19b/2, 9 (Yiddish text).

14   ***Badly off.*** (דר ביזרין 5-4:). Krakow 1618 reads *der bozern.* Cf. the traditional interpretation, that the child should not be given a deadly blow, e.g., in Rashi on Prov. 19:18.

17   ***Wisdom.*** (וויץ 7:). The German proverb is substantiated since the 16th century; cf. Grimm, *Wörterbuch,* vol. 30, p. 863; also on fol. 30a.

19   ***Reshit Ḥokhmah.*** (ראשית חכמה 8:). S. *Reshit Ḥokhmah,* III, p. 55, §2: "'While there is still hope' (Prov. 19:18). When it seems that your son is stupid, do not say: What use is a beating to him. It will be useful to him, even if he does not have the intelligence to understand, therefore you must give him (the beating). Even if he is stupid, there is still hope in studying and in beating."

a lost cause anyway—punishing him won't help." It gives a parable: A drop of water that continuously drips onto a stone will ultimately make a hole in the stone. How similar, then—a stone is a hard thing, and a drop of water is a soft thing. It takes much [wisdom] and righteousness for (education).

5 　There are, due to our many transgressions, some children orphaned at a young age, whose stepmother does not want to discipline them, and says, "I don't want people to talk about me." But [it] should not be so. She should admonish (the orphans) with [gentle] words, for which she will be repaid by God, blessed be He. As the verse says, "Happy are those who act justly, who do right at all times."[48] This means in Yiddish, happy are they

10 who watch over judgment, that is to say, who fear the judgment that God, blessed be He, will bring, and who act righteously at all times.

　The Gemara[49] explains: How is it possible for people to act righteously at all times? Rather, this refers to people who purchase religious books and lend them to [people] to learn from—thus many may benefit from them. Or it refers to people who take orphans into

15 their homes, and raise them to practice good deeds. The Gemara[50] explains the verse, "And the persons that they had acquired in Haran."[51] The verse refers to our Patriarch Abraham, peace be upon him, and Sarah, peace be upon her, and it means in Yiddish, they took along

1　*Parable.* (משל :10). The parable derives from the German-Yiddish proverb "Constant dripping wears the stone."

7　*Admonish.* (שטראפין :16). See, on the other hand, the request for physical beating in *Sefer Middot*; see the commentary on p. 165/12.

12　*Gemara.* (גמרא :19). See B. Ketubbot 50a: "How is it possible to perform justice at all times? Our teachers in Yavne interpreted, and some say that it was Rabbi Eliezer, (who interpreted Ps. 106:3): One who provides for his sons and daughters, for as long as they are underaged. Rabbi Shemuel bar Naḥmani said: One who raises an orphaned boy or girl in his house, and marries them off. 'Wealth and riches are in his house, and his beneficence lasts forever' (Ps. 112:3). Rav Huna and Rav Ḥisda (said): The one said, 'One who studies and teaches Torah'; the other said, 'One who writes the Torah, the prophets and the hagiographic writings, and lends them out to others.'"

　See the formulation in Midrash Tehillim 106:3: "His pupils asked Rabbi Tarfon: Who performs justice at all times? He said to them: He who writes books and lends them to others." Accordingly *Brantshpigl*, p. 213.

15　*Gemara.* (גמרא :23). Gen. 12:5 is used in B. Avodah Zarah 9a and in B. Sanhedrin 99b in a different context (Abraham's age). The interpretation is congruent with that in various Midrashim, most detailed in Bereshit Rabbah 84.4: "'And the persons that they had acquired in Haran' (Gen. 12:5). However, it is not written 'that he had acquired,' and instead, 'That they had acquired' (ibid.). Rabbi Hunaya said, Abraham converted the men, and Sarah (converted) the women to Judaism. What does the teaching mean with 'That they had acquired'? It teaches that Abraham led them into his house, gave them to eat and to drink, and led them under the wings of the *Shekhinah*."

　Same in Yalkut, §§ 66, 140, 837; similar in *Avot de-Rabbi Natan*, B, chap. 26.

the bodies which they had created. The Gemara[52] goes on: If the whole world would come together, they could not create a midge, which is a tiny thing—all the more they could not have created people. [...]

26b

(The Gemara says: "create": this means that) they took them under the wings of the *Shekhinah*, and taught them so [they] would truly recognize the Creator, blessed be His name. And so the verse says that it is as if they [had] created them.

The midrash[53] says, when our Patriarch Abraham had guests and they were preparing to leave and thanked him, he said to them, "Why are you thanking me? Thank the One who created everything." And he said, "Let us bless Him from whose possessions we have eaten." This means in Yiddish, let us praise, since we have eaten from his possessions. Whereupon they asked, "Who or what is he?" And so he taught them of His holy name, and converted them. These were proselytes who recognized the Creator, blessed be His name.

All the more so should one lead poor orphans—left, pitifully, without parents, who had been respected and pious—on the righteous path. But it requires great wisdom and fear of God. One should admonish them with friendly and kind words: "Dear child, just obey me, and do everything that is pleasing to [God], blessed be His name, as well as to all people. I hope to [God], blessed be His name, that I will earn *Gan Eden* through you. I beg of you, do not disgrace your parents—they worry for you from the grave, since they know everything that happens in this world. When things go poorly for their children in this world, they cry to the Holy One, blessed be He, and pray for them."

1   *Gemara.* (גמרא :25).   S. Bereshit Rabbah 39.14: "'And the persons that they had created in Haran.' Rabbi Eleazar ben Zimra said: Even when all the people of the world would come together in order to create something; they could not breathe a soul even into a midge. When it is written, 'And the persons that they had created in Haran' (Gen. 12:5), this only refers to the proselytes, who were converted to Judaism." A little shorter in Bereshit Rabbah 84.4, also in Yalkut, §§ 66, 140, 837.

3   [...]. (גיט...אננדר :28-27).   Duplicate from lines 25–26 (Yiddish text); the printer realized the mistake at the beginning of fol. 26b and for this reason did not employ the catchword *anander*—together (line 28; Yiddish text)—but continued with the correct text. The missing original reading could have been instead: *get di gemore beshafen doz maynt daz*—The Gemara says, "create": this means that—; cf. the commentary above. The translation reads accordingly.

26b

7   *Midrash.* (מדרש :3).   S. Bereshit Rabbah 49.4: "How did Abraham receive the passersby? When they had eaten and drunk he told them, "'Say the blessing.' They asked him, 'What does that mean?' He said to them: Say 'Blessed be the Lord of the world, from whose possession we have eaten.'" Same in Bereshit Rabbah 54.6 and Yalkut, § 82.

9   *Let us bless.* (נברך :5).   The formulation is substantiated in B. Berakhot 50a, there in a different context.

Reshit Ḥokhmah[54] writes: When someone leaves pious children behind him in the world—whenever the child does good deeds, or studies with pleasure, or goes willingly to synagogue, and prays with proper intention—each time his father or mother is raised higher in *Gan Eden*. The angels bring everything before His throne of glory, and pray for
5   the souls that brought such offspring to the world. If, God forbid, the opposite occurs, the child does not do what pleases God, blessed be His name, and does not obey the people who admonish him for his own good, and is disrespectful. One who does not obey the people, and does not do what would please them, that one does not do what would please the Holy One, blessed be He, either. One instance of evil brings more (evil) with it, as we
10   see every day, due to our many transgressions. Such a person causes distress to his father and mother that they brought such offspring to the world. But he who is modest in personality and is pious accepts the criticism when he is rebuked. He enjoys studying, and prays

27a

with proper intention. He has a clean mouth and eats what he is given. He is well mannered, and acts as if even what he is given is far too much. But if one is disrespectful, and is

1   **Reshit Ḥokhmah. (ראשית חכמה** :15). S. *Reshit Ḥokhmah*, III, p. 55, §2: "Teach your son Torah, so that he may save you before judgment to *Geihinnom*. 'He will gratify you with dainties' (Prov. 29:17), so that he brings you to *Gan Eden*, with the righteous."

        S. *Ozar Midrashim*, p. 262: "He who is evil, and has a righteous father, or he who is righteous and has an evil father, receives from the Holy One, blessed be He, a (share) in *Gan Eden*, because of his son."

        See in that matter *Brantshpigl*, p. 349f.: "The sages write, a pious son brings his father and his mother to *Gan Eden*."

27a

13   **Well mannered. (בתרבית** :1). The author does not discuss table manners, she only mentions that one should "eat(s) what he is given"; see *Brantshpigl*, p. 339: "They should sit at the meal well mannered (*be-tarbut*), with consideration, and properly. (They shall) not take large bites or big gulps. They shall not always demand meat, like wild animals. When they eat, they should share with others, then they will be accustomed to receiving guests. They should like everything they are given to eat, and not say, 'I don't want that,' or 'I don't like to eat that.' That is a very bad habit."

        S. also ibid., p. 318: "Every woman who has been well educated from an early age, and eats what she is given.... She also does not pick things out of her food."

14   **Too much. (צו פיל** :1). The demand for moderate eating is widespread in the moral literature; see *Sefer Middot*, fol. 51a: דש איינר זיינם גילושט ניט זול איין גינויגן טון מיט" אלן דינגן מיט עש עשן אונ' מיט טרינקן ער זול ניט עשן זיין בויך בול וזש אים וואל שמעקט ער זול לושן איין טאייל אויבר בלייבן אונ' זול ניט זיינם גילושט אן גינויגן טון." —"When someone is eating and drinking he should not give in to his lust for all kinds of things. One should not fill one's stomach to the brim, just because it tastes good, but instead leave something, and not give in to one's lust completely." Same in *Brantshpigl*, p. 316.

        See *Ze'enah u-Re'enah* on Exod. 23:19, p. 459f.: Eating for pure pleasure is forbidden; ibid. on Exod. 23:25, p. 460: illnesses are the result of exaggerated eating and drinking; see

irreverent toward [God] as well as humanity—when one admonishes him, he says, "What is it to you?" And he is greedy—if you feed him, you will not be able to give him enough. He even has to steal, so that he can satisfy himself. This is all a result of a sinful mother who spoils her child when she feeds him: If the child [says], "I don't want this," she says, "Listen, I'll give you something else." But it should not be so. One never knows what will be, and one should not assume that one will always have the same amount of money. One doesn't need to bring many examples to prove this—one sees [every day] how some mothers, who did not remember their goal, spoiled their children.

But one must instruct a child, as *Reshit Ḥokhmah*[55] writes: As soon as a child is able to understand, one should speak with him and inculcate him. When you leave the house with him, one should allow the child to touch the *mezuzah*; if religious books or phylacteries are lying on the table, one should let the child kiss them; when one makes a blessing, one should instruct the child to respond, "Amen." When a child begins to study (Torah), one should make sure that he enjoys studying—one should give him some sugar one time, another time nuts, or honey spread on bread, so that he will study with joy. As the

---

ibid. on Lev. 11:44, p. 573: If a person eats and drinks much, following his evil inclination, his body will soon be destroyed. See *Sefer Ḥayyei Olam*, fol. 2b: "להיות צנוע באכילתו." "One should be moderate in eating."

9   ***Reshit Ḥokhmah.*** (ראשי' חכמ') (:11).   Only similar in *Reshit Ḥokhmah*, I, p. 838, §28: "When the child begins to speak, its father speaks with him the holy language and teaches it Torah."

See Shulḥan Arukh, *Yore De'ah*, 291:3: "Everybody must attach a mezuzah (to their doors), even women and servants. One must teach the little ones to pay attention to *mezuzot* on the doors."

15   ***Nuts, or honey.*** (ניס אדור הונג) (:15).   The ritual at the beginning of the Torah lesson has already been described in *Sefer ha-Rokeaḥ* by Eleazar of Worms (13th century), in the *Maḥzor Vitry*, and the *Sefer Orḥot Ḥayyim* by Aaron ben Jacob ha-Kohen of Lunel (14th century); cf. Marcus, *Rituals*, p. 26f.; 33. M. Avot, 5:21 demands that school begins for boys at the age of five; in the early modern era, depending on time and place, different ages, ranging between three and six, must be assumed; cf. Hundert, "Jewish Children," p. 87.

See *Brantshpigl*, p. 341, "The *Shevilei Emunah* (14th century) says, when the child is brought to the Rabbi the first time, one should bake for him cookies with sugar and honey, in order to strengthen his heart for the Torah."

See *Sefer Oraḥ Ḥayyim*, fol. 15a: "אונ' ואר צייטן וואז דער מנהג אזו וועז איינר זיין קינד וואלט לערנן לעזן דא הוט מן גשריבן אותיות אויף איין פערמיט אודר איין טעבלן אונ' מן הוט דאז קינד גיבאדט אדר גיוועשן. [...] אונ' האט אים אים איין קיבליין אין הינק אונ' אין מילך גיב[ר]אכן אונ' מן האט אים ור גישטעלט קעשטעליכי פירות אונ' אויך גוטי שפייז אונ' איין קעשטעליכר רב הוט עז גפירט אין דאז בית המדרש אונ' ער הוט עש צו גידעקט מיט זיינם מנטיל. אונ' מן הט אים דאז קיכל מיט הינק אונ' מילך צו עשן געבן אונ' אויך די פירות אונ' די גוטי שפייז אונ' עש הוט די אותיות גילייאט די מן אים האט אויף גישריבן אונ' דר נאך האט מן אים הונינג גישמירט אויף די אותיות אונ' דאז קינד דין הוניק פון דען אתיות גילעקט." —"A long time ago there was a custom that one who wanted to have his child learn how to read would write letters on parchment or on a board. One would bathe or wash the child.... One would break cookies into honey and milk, and would put before him delicious fruit

Gemara[56] says, "Prophecy does not reside in sadness, rather in joy." This means, prophecy does not rest on a person when he is sad, only when he is happy. This is learned from a [verse] regarding [Elisha] the Prophet, "'Now then, get me a musician.' As the musician played, the hand of the LORD came upon him."[57] This means in Yiddish, and when he played the instrument, the [divine] prophecy rested upon him.

Additionally, when a child is able to understand a little more, one should say to him, "Dear child, be pious and study, and I will make nice clothes for you." When he becomes even smarter, one should say to him, "If you study enthusiastically, you will, God willing, be a well-respected young scholar, and you will be given the daughter of a Torah scholar with a lot of money, and you will become a *Rosh Yeshivah*." When he gains full understanding, one should say to him, "Dear son, study for the sake of Heaven—you can gain this world as well as the world to come." One should give him an example: "See what

27b

happens to those who did not choose well, and on the other hand, see what happens to those who study day and night—what a big difference between the two."

One should also instruct [a] child, and tell him about the kindness that the Holy One, blessed be He, did for him. As King David, peace be upon him, said, "So that a future generation might know, even the children which should be born, and declare them to their children."[58] This means, you shall therefore relate it to your offspring, and the children shall relate it to their children, and not forget His kindness. It is a very bad thing when one disclaims a favor—when one forgets about a favor that someone did for him, even if it is a sinful person, all the more so when it is the Holy One, blessed be He. One should not forget the kindness that He shows day after day.

One should tell him all of this: "Dear child, how much trouble and pain have I had from you, before I even started to raise you! On your behalf I often repented, prayed, and

---

and good food. A respected Rabbi would take him into the study house and wrap him in his coat. One would have him eat the honey-milk cookie, the fruit, and the delicious food, and then he would read the letters that one had written for him. After that one would spread honey over the letters, which the child would lick off the letters."

1   *Prophecy does not.* (אין הנבואה 16-17:). S. B. Shabbat 30b: "In order to teach you that the *Shekhinah* does not linger with sadness, or with laziness, not with play, not with carelessness, not with talk, and not with gossip, but instead with the joy of obligation, as it is written, 'Now then, get me a musician. As the musician played, the hand of the LORD came upon him' (II Kings 3:15). Similar in B. Pesaḥim 117a.

5   *Prophecy.* (נבואה 21:). The translation is influenced by Ezek. 33:32–33.

10   *A lot of money.* (פיל געלט 25:). There is various evidence for the endeavor during the early modern era to create or strengthen social connections between the educational and economic elite through marriage; cf. Katz, *Tradition*, p. 118ff. Regarding the ideal of belonging to an educated family, see the commentary on p. 191/15.

gave to charity. When you were sick, I prayed to the Holy One, blessed be He, to allow you to live to serve Him with Torah and good [deeds]." We also find in a verse that Bathsheba, the mother of King Solomon, said to him: "No, my son! No, O son of my womb! No, O son of my vows!"[59] This means, what difference does it make that I made vows on your

5   behalf, if all you want is to follow your bodily desires?

A mother should also tell her child: "Dear child, I had very little that is good in the world. I hope to God, blessed be He, that you will comfort me and make me joyful by doing what pleases God and people." Because he who finds favor in the [eyes] of God, blessed be He, also finds favor in the eyes of humankind, as the verse says, "And you will

10   find favor and approbation in the eyes of God and man."[60]

A pious mother should also forbid her child from calling people with derisive nicknames. (She should) say, "I don't want to hear that from you. If other people call you names, you should still not do it, because it is a big and major sin." All the more so when the mother hears him curse someone, God protect us, or talk back to an elder.

27b

5   **Bodily desires.** (לייב לושט :15). Regarding the interpretation of Prov. 31:2, see Tanḥuma (Warsaw), Shemot 1: "'No, O son of my vows' (Prov. 31:2). All of your father's wives made vows, and say, 'When I have a son, who is capable of kingdom.' But I vowed, 'When I have a son, who is filled with teaching, capable of prophecy.' She hit and beat him, and said, 'Not like the kings, Lemuel, not like the kings, who drink wine.'"

9-10   **You will find.** (ונמצא :19). The masoretic text of Prov. 3:4 differs slightly.

12   **Nicknames.** (צו נאמן :20). This refers to insulting names intended to ridicule, which rabbinic literature denounces; see B. Bava Metzi'a 58b: "All but three will descend into *Geihinnom*, and never come back up: Those that go down, and never come up are the adulterer, the one who shames his comrade in public, and the one who calls his comrade with nicknames. 'Calls' means 'insults.'"

Moral literature, too, condemns this explicitly; see *Brantshpigl*, p. 126: "If one has a derisive nickname, one must not call him by that name. One should avoid, as far as possible, soiling one's mouth. One should also not give a child an impure nickname, even if it is meant lovingly, such as piggy, scoundrel, or rascal. The sages write that these children will become just that, before they die." Similar in ibid., p. 375.

S. *Den Muser un' Hanhoge*, fol. 5b, no. 9: שלא יכנה שם לחברו ושלא יקראנו בכנוי" שכנוהו אחרים אם לא יהא נזכר ונכבד בשמו. דש ניט ער זול צו נאמן זיין חבר אונ' זול אין אפי' ניט רופן מיט אויין צו נאם דא אין אנדרי מיט צו נאמן עש זיי דען עש וער אויין אירליכר צו נאם."—"One should not give one's companion a nickname, and not call him by the nickname given to him by others, unless the name has the purpose of giving him honor.—One should not give one's companion a nickname given to him by others, unless it is an honorable nickname."

S. *Sefer Middot*, fol. 91a: הוט איינר זיינם חבר איין צו נאמן געבן זא מוש ער אין מחילה" ביטן בור דען לוייטן אונ' זול זיך מלקות שלאגן אל זיין טאג אונ' זיין זוינדא ביקענן."—"If one gave his companion a nickname, he must ask his forgiveness publicly. He must beat himself with a whip (because of that) and admit his sin daily."

13   **Major sin.** (הייפט עברה :22). See *Brantshpigl*, p. 371: "All this happened because they slandered, therefore they were lost. One who gossips, or slanders, is like one who

She should also be careful that he should keep himself clean when he prays. One should also not let a child under three into a synagogue. We learn this from the verse[61] regarding a tree that is *arel*. For the first three years that is was planted, it is hled to be *arel* and one may (not) eat the fruit from it, but in the fourth year it is holy and sanctified. So too a child—after

28a

three years it has intelligence, and knows how to contain himself, and can say "Amen" nicely. The Gemara[62] explains the verse, "From the mouths of infants and sucklings You have founded strength."[63] [This] means, the world remains in existence because of the [small] children who say, "Amen, may His great name." This is why a child should be raised in purity.

Another reason why children under three years should not be brought to synagogue is that they cannot yet speak, and distract their parents from praying. Our books have forbidden taking a child in one's arms during prayer, because the prayers require great devotion.

commits one of the three major sins—idolatry, adultery, and bloodshed." Regarding social condemnation of gossip and slander, see the commentary on p. 93/7–8.

1   *Prays.* (דבנט :23).   See the commentary on p. 160/5.

2   *Child.* (קינד :24).   Regarding the accompaniment of children, see the commentary on p. 159/22.

3   *Arel.* (ערל :25).   Literally "uncircumcised," s. Lev. 19:23f. Cf. Yalkut, §615: "'And plant any tree for food, you shall regard its fruit as forbidden' (Lev. 19:23). This means a small child. 'Three years it shall be forbidden' (ibid.). This means that it cannot converse, and not talk. 'In the fourth year all its fruit shall be set aside for jubilation before the LORD' (Lev. 19:24). Because his father dedicates it to the Torah, in a celebration that celebrates the Holy One, blessed be He."

28a

6   *Gemara.* (גמרא :1).   Mixture of various rabbinic sources. The author possibly uses an appropriate sample; see B. Shabbat 119b: "The world endures only for the sake of the breath of school children."

Similar in *Ozar Midrashim*, p. 51: "Rabbi Ḥelbo said: From the day of destruction of the temple, the world only prevails by virtue of the breath of the school children, as it is written, 'From the mouths of infants and sucklings' (Ps. 8:3) etc."

See B. Sotah 49a: "But how does the world endure? It is sanctified by the reading of the weekly Torah reading, and when they say, 'may His great name' in the *Kaddish* after the reading of the weekly Torah reading, as it is written, 'A land whose light is darkness, All gloom and disarray' (Job 10:22)."

10   *Synagogue.* (שולן :4).   Regarding children in the synagogue, see the commentary on p. 159/22.

11   *Books.* (ספרם :6).   Cf. Shulḥan Arukh, *Oraḥ Ḥayyim*, 98:1; there it says that one should not kiss little children in the synagogue; same in *Sefer Ḥasidim*, §255.

They should also make sure that the child does not lie. They should say to him, "Dear child, lying is not allowed—whoever lies cannot enter *Gan Eden*."

There are also some sinful mothers who teach their child to tell them, "Such-and-such was said about you." She listens to him, and accustoms the child to spread gossip and tattle,

5 and it takes root in him. But it should not be so. When a child comes to his mother and wants to say, "Such-and-such was said about you," she should yell at him and say, "You may not tell me this! He is right, since I told him something that he didn't like." And she should convince the child not to do it anymore, as the *Sefer Ḥasidim* writes, presenting a story:

Once someone argued with a pious man. He spoke ill of him, and slandered him. The

10 son of the pious man was standing nearby and heard this. He wanted to assist his father and to seek vengeance, but the pious man said to his son: "My dear son, be silent, let it be. No matter the situation when you look at it, what he said about me is true. If I did those bad things, then it is fitting that I remain silent. But if it is not true, and he is doing me an injustice, I'll still be silent—maybe it will be a penance for my sins."

15 This we learn from King David, peace be upon him, who suffered tremendous abuse and disgraceful curses from [Shimei] son of Gera. "Disgraceful" is (in Hebrew) *NiMRaẒoT,* the acrostic for "adulterer, bastard, murderer, strangler, abomination."[64] King David, peace be upon him, had many people with him, and could certainly have avenged himself, but did not do it. He thought to himself, "Let it be (an atonement) for my sins. Perhaps he will

20 acquire my sins from me, and in the merit of that God, blessed be He, will have mercy on me, and will accept me mercifully."

---

4   *Gossip.* (רכילות 11:).   Regarding the prohibition of gossip, see the commentary on p. 93/7–8.

8   *Sefer Ḥasidim.* (ספר חסידים 15:).   It is unclear which place this refers to. The story can be related to the motif of the "pious sinner," who, because of his piety, accepts the inadvertent and humiliating accusations; cf. Alexander-Frizer, *Pious Sinner*, p. 112f. Similar versions can be found in *Reshit Ḥokhmah*, III, p. 86, § 53: a "story of a pious man" who quarrels with someone and whose son wishes to avenge him; same in *Brantshpigl*, p. 343.

12   *No matter the situation.* (ממה נפשך 20:).   Term from the rabbinic discussion, e.g. B. Shabbat 35b; same on fol. 11b.

16   *[Shimei] son of Gera.* (שמעון בן גרא 23:).   Cf. I Kings 2:8.

16   *Disgraceful.* (נמרצת 24:).   Spelling based on Yiddish pronunciation.

17   *Acrostic.* (ראשי תיבות 24:).   What is meant is a *notarikon*, to be found in various rabbinic interpretations; see Yalkut, § 170: "'He insulted me outrageously' (I Kings 2:8). Rabbi Aha bar Jacob said: 'he is an adulterer, he is a Moabite, he is a murderer, he is a strangler, he is a monster.'" Same in B. Shabbat 105a.

S. Ba-midbar Rabbah 9.7: "What does 'disgraceful' mean? Adulterer, bastard, evil-doer, strangler."

28b

The Gemara[65] teaches (concerning) what Deborah the Prophetess said, "But may His friends be as the sun rising in might!"[66] This means in Yiddish, the lovers of the Holy One, blessed be He, will shine like the sun when it is at its highest and burns at its brightest. So will be those who allow themselves to be embarrassed and abused. They do not respond to those who disgrace them. This is what the Gemara[67] means by saying: "A person should always be among the disgraced, and not among those who disgrace." This means in Yiddish, a person should always be one of those who allow themselves to be humiliated, and not one of those people who humiliate others. One should relate all of this to a child. The Gemara[68] also says about this: "Who is a hero? He who conquers his inclination." This means in Yiddish, who is called a hero?—He who overcomes his evil inclination, and does not allow his anger to precede his honor. This is also what is meant by the verse, "But may His friends be as the sun rising in might!"[69]

Now I would like to explain the meaning of the verse that says, regarding Deborah the Prophetess, "The stars fought from heaven."[70] This means in Yiddish, the stars fought from heavens. I have the following problem with this: How did the stars fight? Rather, it means that the merit of our forebears fought with our enemies. We see every day how we benefit from the merit of our forebears, as the verse says, "And the knowledgeable will be radiant like the bright expanse of sky."[71] This means in Yiddish, the wise ones will shine like the brightness of the heavens. "And those who lead the many to righteousness will be

---

1 *Gemara.* (גמרא 28:). S. B. Gittin 36b: "The sages taught: The disgraced, not those who cause disgrace, who hears his disgrace, and does not respond, who performs (mitzvot) out of love, and he rejoices in chastisement. About those the Scripture says, 'But may His friends be as the sun rising in might' (Judg. 5:31)." Same in B. Yoma 23b; Derekh Erez, 13; Yalkut, §613; and *Brantshpigl*, p. 8.

28b

2 *Rising.* (בצאתו 1:). Judg. 5:31 reads slighty different.

5 *Gemara.* (גמרא 4:). The author uses the expression *le-olam yehei adam*—a person should always be (among those)—a phrase common for ethical standards in rabbinic literature, but which is not substantiated for the quote used here; see the commentary on the line above.

See, on the other hand, the respective expression in *Orḥot Ẓaddikim*, fol. 10a: "לעולם יהיה אדם מן הנעלבין ולא מן העולבין. ומן השומעין את חרפתם ואינם משיבין." "A person should always be among the disgraced, not among those who cause disgrace."

9 *Gemara.* (גמרא 7:). S. B. Tamid 32a: "Who is a hero? He who conquers his evil inclination." Same in M. Avot 4:1; B. Yoma 69b; Yalkut, §86 and in other places.

15 *I have the following problem.* (איז מיר קשה 11:). The following interpretation has no model in the rabbinic literature, where the heavenly bodies are considered symbols for human behavior. S. *Ẓe'enah u-Re'enah* on Gen. 47:28, p. 315, "Life is obviously dependent on the planets and the heavenly bodies. If a person has a lucky star, he will live long. In the opposite case, however, his life will be short."

like the stars forever and ever"[72]—this means, those who cause many people to be pious will shine like the stars in heaven forever and always. The Holy One, blessed be He, also blessed our Patriarch Abraham with the blessing, "And your descendants will be as numerous as the stars of heaven."[73] This means in Yiddish, your seed will be like the stars in the heavens.

5   The verse goes on, "Curse Meroz!"[74] This means in Yiddish, cursed is the star called Meroz. This means: The chieftain of Esau the Wicked did not want to help the children of Israel, who had the virtue of strength (*gevurah*). *GaVaR* is the acrostic of charitable, humble, merciful. Regarding this, King David said, "Praise the LORD, all you nations; extol Him, all you peoples, for great is His steadfast love toward us."[75] This means in Yiddish, all
10   peoples will praise God, because he has strengthened us with his benevolence. This is referring to the future, when the nations (of the world) will praise the Holy One, blessed be He, for helping Israel, which possesses the virtue of a hero, and suppressed its (evil) inclination, and suffered the exile with good will.

Until now we have spoken about how children should be raised, as we are reminded

29a

15   morning and night in our prayers—as it is written in our Torah, "Impress them upon your children, and recite them."[76] The verse also states, "And teach them to your children, reciting them."[77] In Yiddish this means, you shall teach your children Torah.

We have spoken so far about how sons should be raised to Torah and good deeds. Now I will also speak about how one should raise daughters. As our sages[78] write, it is a

1   *Pious.* (ורום 16:). See similar idea in B. Bava Batra 8b: "'And the knowledgeable will be radiant like the bright expanse of sky' (Dan. 12:3)—that is a judge who hands down truthful judgments, and the collector of a charity. 'And those who lead the many to righteousness will be like the stars forever and ever' (ibid.)—these are the teachers of the smallest children."

5   *Star.* (שטערן 19:). Regarding the interpretation of Meroz as "star" or as warriors that did not rush to help God (cf. Esau, who is, however, not mentioned), cf. B. Moed Katan 16a; Rashi on Judg. 5:23; Yalkut, § 54.

7   *Acrostic.* (ראשי תבת 21:). Spelling based on Yiddish pronunciation. What is meant is a *notarikon*; same on fol. 34b.

7-8   *Charitable, humble, merciful.* (גומלי חסדים בישנים רחמנים 22-21:). In rabbinic literature these are known as the three virtuous characteristics of Israel; cf. B. Yevamot 79a; Yalkut, §§154, 276; Devarim Rabbah 3.4; Midrash Tehillim 1:10; Y. Sanhedrin 6d, however without derivation from Ps. 117:2. None of the rabbinic traditions lists the required sequence of the three signs. The respective context is not appropriate either. Cf., however, the context with Abraham's hospitality (as on fol. 34b) as mentioned in the commentary on p. 170/6.

29a

15   *Prayers.* (תפילה 1:). See the commentary on page 161/10.

sign of blessing to have a daughter as firstborn, since she can help her mother raise the rest of the children she will have. This is why every woman should make sure that she herself guides her daughter to perform good deeds. Regarding this, a verse from the Giving of the Torah says, "Thus you shall say to the house of Jacob and declare to the children of Israel."[79] ("House of Jacob") means "the daughter of Jacob," as the Gemara[80] explains: "Do not read 'le-veit Ya'akov' (the house of Jacob), rather 'le-vat Ya'akov' (the daughter of Jacob)."

She should remember that she can easily give away her child when it can be said, "Happy is the mother who raised this child." This is so even if she is rich—one never knows what will happen, as we see every day with our own eyes—she should not think, "Why does my child need to work? I have plenty of money!" We learn this from the Torah: about the uprightness of our mother Rebekah, peace be upon her—the Torah praises her for being an industrious woman. As the verse says, "Quickly, she ran."[81] This means in Yiddish, she hurried and ran [to] the spring, swiftly drew the water, and watered all of his camels. This

1   ***Sign of blessing.*** (סימן ברכה 5:). S. B. Bava Batra 141a: "Regarding the inheritance, a son is better for him. Regarding livelihood, a daughter is better for him. Shemuel spoke: We have here (the case) of one, who gave birth first (to a daughter), according to Rav Ḥisda, because Rav Ḥisda said: To have a daughter first is a good boding for children. Some say: This is because she will raise the brother; others say: Because the evil eye does not affect him (because she attracts it). Rav Ḥisda said: I prefer daughters to sons." Similar in B. Ketubbot 43a.

2   ***Herself.*** (זעלברט 7:). Regarding child upbringing by the mother, see the commentary on p. 161/6 and the commentary on p. 103/3–4, regarding the educational tasks of the father or of the parents.

5   ***Gemara.*** (גמרא 10:). S. Mekhilta de-Rabbi Yishmael, *Yitro* 2: "'Thus shall you say to the house of Jacob' (Exod. 19:3). These are the women. 'And declare to the children of Israel' (ibid.) These are the men. . . . Another interpretation: 'Thus shall you say to the house of Jacob.' Speak with gentle words, discuss (only) the most important matters with the women. 'And declare to the children of Israel' (ibid.). (But) explain it in precisely (to the men), and tell them." Same in Yalkut, §276; similar in Shemot Rabbah 28.2.

See *Ze'enah u-Re'enah* on Exod. 19:3, p. 427: "Why did the Holy One, blessed be He, command to reveal (the commandments) to the women first? Because they have a less receptive mind for the Torah. . . . They do not have as much understanding as the men for studying the Torah and all the commandments at once."

5-6   ***Do not read [...] rather.*** (אלא [...] אל תקרא 10:). The application of this hermeneutic rule is not substantiated in rabbinic literature in regard to Exod. 19:3; see, however, *Oẓar Midrashim*, p. 51: "'He was foster father to Hadassah; and when her father and mother died, Mordecai adopted her as his own daughter' (Esther 2:7). Do not read *le-vat*—as daughter, but instead *le-vet*—into the house, because the house is the wife of a man."

8   ***Rich.*** (עשירה 12:). S. *Brantshpigl*, p. 347: "And one shall accustom (the daughter) to work. Who knows what is going to happen, and how it will be useful for her. Even if she should be rich, she can still be charitable with her own hands."

12   ***Quickly, she ran.*** (ותמהר ותרוץ 16:). Combination of two words from Gen. 24:20.

is to be understood as follows: The holy Torah[82] writes this because it was a sign for Eliezer who saw that she was an industrious woman with good qualities, and saw that she was charitable. As King Solomon, peace be upon him, writes about a woman who is industrious, "She girds herself with strength, and exerts her arms."[83] This means: She girds her loins and girds her arms. We also learn of our mother Rebekah that Eliezer saw in her many good deeds that he did not see in the other young women. He praised God, blessed be His name, that He led him on the right path, and sent him a good match who had the virtues of our Patriarch Abraham, among them, charity and hospitality. He saw her dedicated heart, and

29b

she said, "We are very used to having guests." He only sought lodging for one night, but she said, "If you would like to stay many nights, we are, praise God, accustomed to having guests."

We can learn from this how one should raise a daughter—not to laziness and idleness. Nothing good comes from that—one bad quality brings, God forbid, others, and she will later speak of inconsequential things. These are very bad, as the Gemara[84] writes: "Whoever is lazy becomes crazy, God protect us." Regarding this, King Solomon, peace be upon him, said, "Laziness induces sleep."[85] This means, a woman who is lazy and sleeps will wind up in the end in torn clothing. But about a woman who is industrious and does not sleep away all her time in laziness, the verse says, "Never eats the bread of idleness."[86] This means, she does not eat her bread unless she earned it herself. Regarding this, the verse says, "You shall

---

1   *Sign.* (סימן טוב :19).   Cf. Gen. 24:14.

5   *We* [...] *learn.* (לערנן מיר :23).   Cf. Gen. 24:18–27.

29b

9   *Said.* (גשפראכן :1).   Cf. Gen. 24:25.

9   *One night.* (איין נכט :1).   See Bereshit Rabbah 60.6: "'Pray tell me,' he said, 'whose daughter are you?' (Gen. 24:23) etc. (This means): one overnight stay. She replied, 'I am the daughter of Bethuel the son of Milcah' (Gen. 24:24), '(there is) also room to spend the night' (Gen. 24:25). (This means): many overnight stays." Cf. also Gen. 24:54f.

14   *Gemara.* (גמרא :6).   S. B. Ketubbot 59b: "Even if she brings one hundred maids into the house for him—she must process the wool, because idleness leads to disgrace. Rabban Shimon ben Gamliel says: Even if the man swears to his wife that she need not perform any work—(in the end) he will send her away, and give her the *ketubah*, because idleness leads to insanity."

S. *Brantshpigl*, p. 123: "They shall not be idle, and not speak of inconsequential matters, then they will not need to walk barefoot, nor suffer thirst. If they spend their time with inconsequential matters, they will have nothing to buy with. In tractate Ketubbot it is said: 'Idleness leads to insanity.' Rabbi Eliezer interprets (insanity) as restlessness. Rabban Shimon ben Gamliel interprets it as nonsense. Both are very bad."

18   *Idleness.* (עצלית :10).   Spelling based on Yiddish pronunciation.

enjoy the fruit of your labors; you shall be happy and you shall prosper."[87] The Gemara[88] explains the verse as follows: There is more merit for him who eats the fruits of his own labor than in fear of God. Therefore every pious and wise woman should be careful, and should think of the goal, since she can provide for everything with her wisdom.

5   When she sees that she has well-brought-up children, whether sons or daughters, she is happy in her heart (because) it will help her in this world, and even more in the world to come. All the work and effort that a father and mother put into their children is all on behalf of the children. As the verse says, "But for his sons after him."[89] Therefore they should make sure that their effort is well spent. In the merit of this, we should all merit
10 such happiness, and the happiness of the redemption. Amen.

Chapter Six

How a mother-in-law should behave toward her daughter-in-law and her [son-in-law], and should avoid quarrelling and fighting in her house, and God, blessed be He, will bestow His blessing on her house, on both of them.

15   The verse says, "A graceful woman obtains honor; ruthless men obtain wealth."[1] This means that a woman who wants to find favor in the eyes of God, blessed be His name, and in the eyes of people should think only of her honor. But if she does the opposite, and does not seek honor, but merely money, then she relies on her money, and desires neither favor nor honor. In that verse, King Solomon, peace be upon him, referred to a God-fearing woman
20 who desires honor.

1   *Gemara.* (גמרא 12:). S. B. Ḥullin 44b: "Mar Zutra taught on behalf of Rav Ḥisda: Of every one, who studies and teaches, who seeks to provide his own livelihood, and who serves scholars, the scriptures say: 'You shall enjoy the fruit of your labors; you shall be happy and you shall prosper' (Ps. 128:2). Rav Zevid says: He deserves to acquire two worlds—this world, and the world to come. 'You shall be happy' (means) in this world, 'You shall prosper (means) in the world to come.'" Similar in Midrash Tehillim 128:2, see the commentary on p. 195/3.
    Cf. Midrash Tehillim, 128:1: "'Happy are all who fear the LORD' (Ps. 128:1). Rabbi Ḥiyya bar Abba said on behalf of Ula: He is more important, who enjoys his work, than he, who fears God." Regarding the work ideal, see the commentary on p. 194/2.

8   *But.* (כי אם 19:). Exod. 29:29 does not contain the words *ki im* ("but") that may have been integrated by association with I Kings 8:19: "However, you shall not build the House yourself; instead, your son, the issue of your loins, shall build the House for My name."

15   *Obtains.* (יתמוך 24:). The masoretic text of Prov. 11:16 differs slightly.

15   *Honor.* (כבד 26:). Spelling based on Yiddish pronunciation; same in line 27 (Yiddish text).

    (אויף 27:). The first word in the line is a duplicate.

18   *Honor.* (כובד 28:). Spelling based on Yiddish pronunciation; same in line 29 (Yiddish text).

30a

Such a woman, who merited raising her children in her household to Torah and good deeds, and proper conduct, and who wishes to fulfill her obligations to God, blessed be His name, and to all people—such a woman requires fear of God and wisdom.

Just as I wrote above about how a woman should behave toward her mother-in-law and father-in-law, it is now worth remembering the opposite: That the mother- or father-in-law should behave in the proper manner toward her. I would like to write here a special lesson about this, and want to consider many things that I did not bring up earlier. Even though I could have recalled them earlier, I preferred to write them here.

Now, every woman should be aware and make sure that she does not sin against her son- or daughter-in-law, God forbid. As we see regarding King Saul, peace be upon him, who hated his son-in-law, King David, peace be upon him, much bad came from that—he caused himself and his children to sin. Nothing good comes from conflict, only jealousy and hatred. Even if a daughter- or son-in-law does not always do the right thing, one should judge them favorably. One should also remember, it is because of their [youth]— we were also once young, and "Wisdom comes with age." If they had as much experience as we do, they would probably change. One should admonish them kindly, and alone— not in front of others. The verse says, "Do not rebuke a scoffer, for he will hate you; Reprove a wise man, and he will [love you]."[2] This means in [Yiddish], you should not rebuke a fool, because he will hate you; rebuke a wise person, and he will love you. This raises a question: If I'm not supposed to admonish a fool, whom should I admonish? I don't need to admonish a wise and pious person! Rather, the meaning of the verse must be as follows: When it says that one should not admonish a fool, it means that you should not admonish the way you would admonish a true fool who is completely evil. And if you want to say to him, "You *goy*, you apostate, why did you do this?" the way one would to a truly evil person, you shouldn't. If you were to speak angrily to him, he would not accept your criticism, and would become even worse and even more stubborn. As the verse says, "A harsh word provokes anger."[3] This means, a saddening word brings rage and makes

---

30a

4   *Above.* (אבין :4).   See fols. 18b ff.

10   *King Saul.* (שאול המלך :10).   Cf. I Sam. 18:8f. and 18:28f.

15   *Wisdom.* (וויץ :14).   See the commentary on p. 168/17.

23   *Completely evil.* (רשע גמור :22).   S. *Derekh Erez*, 9: "Wisdom without piety is contemptible. He who has no wisdom and no piety is a complete evildoer. He who has wisdom and piety is completely righteous."

25   *Truly.* (גאמר :24).   Spelling based on Yiddish pronunciation; same also in lines 22 and 29 (Yiddish text).

him angry. He should be rebuked the way a wise person should be rebuked. Meaning, he is not, so to speak, a completely evil person because he acted in an improper manner—

30b

he is still called a wise person. The Gemara[4] explains "Reprove, you shall reprove."[5] How do we know that a student must rebuke his teacher, if he sees him do something improper? We know it from the verse, "Reprove, you shall reprove, which implies under all circumstances." The verse also means that he should go to him and say, "Dear child, you have done wrong. I am surprised that you've done something like this—you are so pious and smart enough. It's also not inborn. It must have been bad people who attracted you to it and talked you into it. Follow me, and never do it again." On this matter the verse says, "A gentle response allays wrath."[6] This means in Yiddish, gentle talk deters anger. This is what the verse means, "Reprove a wise man, and he will love you."[7] If you criticize someone like a wise person, he will love you, [and] will accept the criticism with [affection].

But some (women) who do not fear God don't remember this, and let their anger surpass their honor. As King Solomon, peace be upon him, said, "The (stupid) woman (bustles about; she is simple and) knows nothing."[8] This means, a woman who is a fool and moans and grumbles doesn't know how it started or why. She also doesn't realize what kind of a result it will have, and what kind of bad can come of quarreling and conflict.

Some (women) who have a son- or daughter-in-law, and who hate them—they eat too much, or they drink too much—about this, King Solomon said, "Do not eat of a stingy man's food."[9] This means in Yiddish, you should not eat with someone who will begrudge it to you. But one who is wise and God-fearing should speak pleasantly to them: "My dear son-in-law," or "my dear daughter-in-law, bear with me—I would gladly give you better if

---

30b

3   *Gemara.* (גמרא 1:). S. B. Bava Metzi'a 31a: "And what does 'Reprove' (Lev. 19:17) mean, the first time, and 'You shall reprove' (ibid.), the second time? He said to him: 'Reprove': this should mean even a hundred times. 'You shall reprove': not only (must) the teacher (rebuke) the student, but also the student (must rebuke) the teacher. Where do we find evidence to this? The Torah says, 'Reprove, you shall reprove' under all circumstances." Same in Yalkut, § 613. The author quotes here only the second part of the interpretation (a pupil reproves the Rabbi), although the context is aimed at the rebuke of a young person (see below, "Dear Child").

3   *Reprove, you shall reprove.* (הוכיח תכיח 1:). The masoretic text of Lev. 19:17 differs slightly.

10   *Allays.* (משיב 7:). Prov. 15:1; see the commentary on p. 130/1.

11   *Reprove.* (הוכיח 8:). The masoretic text of Prov. 9:8 differs slightly.

14   *(Stupid).* (כסילות 12:). The Hebrew quote lacks the word; it is included, however, in the author's translation—*nerin* ("fool").

I were able." About this the verse says, "Better a dry crust with peace than a house full of feasting with strife."[10] This means, a piece of bread with peace is better than a house full of meat with conflict. Another verse says, "Better a meal of vegetables where there is love than a fattened ox where there is hate."[11] This means, it is far better to eat a meal of vegetables with someone, who gives it to him with love, than to eat only fattened oxen with a person one hates, and to whom one begrudges it.

31a

We also learn much from Naomi, who was kind to her daughter-in-law Ruth. She was concerned with her well-being, as the verse says, "Daughter, I must seek a home for you."[12] And she swore to her, "Truly, my dear daughter, I pray to God, blessed be He, that He will show you a good path and grant you true rest." When they were about to get separated, God protect us, she also prayed for her welfare, as the verse says, "Go down to the threshing floor."[13] Rashi[14] explains the meaning as follows: My virtue will support you. Later, when she had a son with Boaz, the neighbors consoled her and said to her, "You've been compensated for your pain," and she raised the child as her very own.

Every pious mother-in-law should learn from that how she should interact with her daughter-in-law—with love and with affection, for the sake of heaven. And she should hope to God, blessed be He, that her grandchildren should be raised to Torah and good deeds. One does not need to write too much about this—every woman who is God-fearing knows this well herself.

Yet one finds some (women) who put their anger above their honor. About such a (woman), the verse says, "Folly tears it down with its own hands"[15]—she listens to gossip which is destructive, and nothing good comes of it. As we see regarding King Saul, peace be upon him, much misfortune came from the fact that he commanded his servants to

---

5   ***With love.*** (באהבה 25:). See *Ẓe'enah u-Re'enah* on Exod. 38:21, p. 535f., referring to a literal interpretation of the loving wife, whose mere presence makes a simple dish taste better.

31a

12   ***Rashi.*** (רש"י 6:). S. Rashi on Ruth 3:3: "'Go down to the threshing floor'— however it is written there: And I go down—(this means), my merit will go down with you." Similar in Yalkut, § 604.

13   ***Said to her.*** (צו איר גזאגט 7:). Cf. Ruth 4:14–17.

14   ***Compensated.*** (דר געצט 8:). Cf. Ruth 4:14.

14   ***Her very own.*** (שוס 8:). Cf. Ruth 4:16.

21   ***Folly.*** (איוולת 13:). See the interpretation of Prov. 14:1 on fols. 3b; 4a; 5a; 7b. The verse serves as interpretation template for various female ideals and behavioral requirements. The interpretation of folly as gossip here is new.

convey gossip about his son-in-law King David, peace be upon him. As the verse says, "And the Ziphites said to Saul, 'Know, David is in hiding [among us].'"[16] This means, the pitch-makers came to Saul (and said), "You'll find David there!" Because of that, Doeg the Edomite sinned—he is one of the three who do not have a share in the world to come, because he slandered David, and caused much bloodshed due to that, and killed all the priests of Nov. All of that happened because he (Saul) hated his son-in-law King David. Even though he regretted it in the end, and owned up to it, he still had to pay dearly for it in flesh and blood.

Every pious woman should think about this. This is also meant by the verse, "A graceful woman obtains honor."[17] It means, a woman who is interested only in honor, and thinks she wants to find favor in God's eyes and in people's eyes. This means that she wants people

31b

to want to marry her, and to gladly give their children over to her, in her house. King Solomon, peace be upon him, may have spoken about this, and may have meant this with the verse, "She is like a merchant fleet, bringing her food from afar."[18] In Yiddish this means, a woman of valor is similar to a merchant who brings his goods [from] distant lands on a ship. That is to say, one brings children from a distant land to her in her house, since one says that one would like to put a child into the house of such a respectable woman. And she can achieve this with her good name.

2   *Said.* (ויאמרו 17:). Cf. I Sam. 23:19 and 26:1.

3   *Pitch-makers.* (פעך מכיר 18:).   The translation of *zifim*—"Ziphites"—as "pitch-maker" is based on the Hebrew *zefet*—"pitch." See *Shmuel Bukh*, fol. 34a: נון וארן עש ".מאנן דיא קונטן מאכן בעך —"So these were men, who could make pitch." The translation is more of an interpretation, and follows I Sam. 23:7, 13, 19, and 26:1.

3   *Doeg.* (דואג 19:). Cf. I Sam. 22:9ff.

4   *One.* (איינר 19:). S. *Avot de-Rabbi Natan*, A, chap. 36: "Three kings and four men of the people do not have a share in the world to come: the three kings are Jeroboam, Ahab and Menashe. The four men of the people are Balaam, Doeg, Ahitophel, and Gehazi." Similar in B. Sanhedrin 90a and Midrash Tehillim 5:9.

5   *Slandered.* (רכילות 20:). S. Devarim Rabbah 5.6: "'When Doeg the Edomite came' (Ps. 52:2) etc. 'When the Ziphites came and told Saul' (Ps. 54:2): Therefore they fell in the war. Another interpretation: Rav Muna said: Every person that slanders drives away the *Shekhinah* from down here upward."
S. Midrash Tehillim 52:2: "Slander is worse than bloodshed. He who kills a man, kills only one, but he who slanders, kills three: himself, because he tells (the bad things), the person, who listens to it, and the person he is talking about. Where can you learn that? From Doeg, who spoke badly before Saul about Ahimelech, and all three—Saul, Ahimelech, and Doeg—were killed. About Ahimelech it is written, 'You shall die, Ahimelech' (I Sam. 22:16). About Saul it is written, 'Saul died for the trespass that he had committed' (I Chron. 10:13). About Doeg, who was driven from the world, it is written, 'So God will tear you down for good' (Ps. 52:7) from the world to come."

But about where it is the opposite, the verse says, "Ruthless men obtain wealth and honor."[19] This refers to a woman who is only interested in money, and not in honor. And so every smart and pious woman should choose the better of the two ways, because God, blessed be His name, prepared two ways for all people—one good, and one bad. As the

5 verse says, "See, I set before you this day life and death, prosperity and adversity."[20] A human being has the choice—he may choose whichever he wishes. But God, blessed be His name, gave good advice to his beloved nation of Israel in our Holy Torah. He wrote, "Choose life."[21] He gave every human being a good inclination and an evil inclination; correspondingly, he created *Gan Eden* and *Geihinnom* in order to give everyone his due according to

10 his actions. And so God, blessed be His name, gave his beloved nation Israel the Holy Torah, and commanded them with its precepts for them to observe. He courted and reprimanded often, the way a father reprimands his beloved child, because he would like to see him (choose) properly. So too, God, blessed be He, did everything for his beloved children of Israel, so that they should merit therewith the world to come in eternal life.

15 Amen, so may it be His will.

Chapter Seven

This will speak of how a woman should supervise her household staff.

"Many women [have done] well, but you surpass them all."[1] This means, many daughters of Israel (own) much money and property, but you are praised above them all. King

20 Solomon, peace be upon him, spoke the verse about an unflawed woman who is not only concerned for herself and her children, (but) thinks of and is concerned even for others who

31b

1-2   *And honor.* (וכבוד :7). The word is not contained in Prov. 11:16; the correct quote is in 29b/24 (Yiddish text); here possibly influenced by *osher ve-kavod*—"riches and honor"— in Prov. 3:16; 8:18 and 22:4.

5   *See.* (ראה :11). S. Yalkut, § 919: "And what does 'I set before you the way of life and the way of death' (Jer. 21:8) mean? The Holy One, blessed be He, said: But I gave Israel two paths, the path of good and the path of evil, one of justice, and one of mercy."

8   *Inclination.* (יצר :15). S. *Brantshpigl*, p. 52: "'I have put before you life and death, blessing and curse. Choose life' (Deut. 30:19)....Our sages write that the Holy One, blessed be He, gave man good advice, namely, 'I have put before you life'—that is the good inclination. 'And death'—that is the evil inclination. 'Blessing'—that is the reward in the world to come. 'And curse'—that is the punishment in *Geihinnom*."

    See *Orḥot Ẓaddikim*, 50a: "וזהרי זה דרך יצר הרע ועצתו שמסיתו מדרך החיים אל דרך המות."—"This is the path and the counsel of the evil inclination, leading him astray from the path of life, to the path of death."

    [Have done]. ([עשׂו] :24). The word was emended according to the masoretic text of Prov. 31:29.

32a

are not related to her. I will, God willing, write about this. Until now we have spoken
about how a woman should conduct herself, and how she should relate to her husband, and
father, and mother, and mother-in-law, and father-in-law, and her children, and son-in-law,
and daughter-in-law. She could then think to herself, "I do not need to concern myself with
5 anything else." We find such attitudes often, "may the Merciful One save us from such a
view!" This means in Yiddish, God, blessed be His name, should protect us from such
views. We see clearly in our Holy Torah that God, blessed be He, warned many times
[about] this, and said, "Love your fellow as yourself."[2] This means in Yiddish, you should
love your companion as yourself. The Gemara[3] says about this, "Rabbi Akiva said, the
10 greatest principle of the Torah is, "Love your fellow as yourself."[4] And says additionally,
"What is hateful to you, do not do to your neighbor."[5] This means in Yiddish, everything
that you do not like, you should not do to your friend.

About this, another verse says, "Her lamp never goes out at night."[6] This means in
Yiddish, her light will not be extinguished at night. That is to say, it means that she gives
15 the young scholars enough light so that they can learn. She should not do like some who

---

32a

5   ***The Merciful One.*** (רחמנא **:4**). Rabbinic apotropaic call of protection; e.g.,
B. Shabbat 84b; Yalkut, § 667.

9   ***Gemara.*** (גמרא **:8**). S. Y. Nedarim 41c: "'Love your fellow as yourself' (Lev.
19:18). Rabbi Akiva says: This is the most important commandment in the Torah." Same
in Bereshit Rabbah 24.7 and Yalkut, § 40.

10   ***Yourself.*** (כמוכה **:9**). The masoretic text of Lev. 19:18 slightly differs; cf. the
spelling in Exod. 15:11.

10   ***Additionally.*** (וייטר **:9**). The following is brought as interpretation of Lev.
19:18, it is, however, based on a different tradition; see *Avot de-Rabbi Natan*, A, chap. 26:
"A story of one, who came to Rabbi Akiva. He said to him: Rabbi, teach me the entire
Torah in one lesson. The Rabbi said to him: My son, even our teacher Moses, may he rest
in peace, remained forty days and nights on the mountain, until he learned the entire
Torah, and you say, teach me the entire Torah in one lesson! Well, my son, the Torah, as a
whole, says: do not do to others what you do not want to have done to you!" Similar in
B. Shabbat 31a and in other places, there Hillel instead of Akiva.

13   ***At night.*** (בלילה **:11**). The masoretic text of Prov. 31:18 differs slightly.

15   ***Young scholars.*** (בחורים **:12**). Regarding the obligation to take on Torah pupils,
and to provide for them, see *Brantshpigl*, p. 208: "The scholars must be given a table, a
bench, a lamp, and light.... The sages write, he who provided light to study, deserves
children that shine in matters of Torah."
S. ibid., p. 212f.: "If one is not a scholar, and has no scholarly son or son-in-law, he
should provide for a scholar to study in his house, and shall give him light to learn.... The
people who say, 'I built my house for myself, not for other people,' say also, 'If I bring a
scholar into my house, he has pupils, who will mess everything up, and I will have no

have no fear of God, and not ask after a boy who has not gone to a teacher for an entire week and does not want to learn a single word. She won't ask a thing if he just carries out everything for her, and has a servant with him. She requires nothing more than that he earns his Shabbat meals from her. But it should not be so. She should remember that she has no license that her children will not also come into foreign hands.

As the midrash[7] explains the verse, "For in return the LORD your God will bless you."[8] This means in Yiddish, because of this, God, blessed be His name, will bless you in all that you do. And the language used is not "for the sake of" or "for the benefit of," as it says elsewhere. The language used is "in return" (*galal*). The Gemara[9] explains here: "The world is a wheel (*galgal*) which revolves." The wheel turns in the world such that it is not so that one who is rich today is rich tomorrow. Therefore every God-fearing woman should

peace in my own home. I cannot keep anything for myself, they do damage, and I will feel cramped.' The sages write that the Holy One, blessed be He, sends leprosy to such a house owner."

Regarding the concept of ideal conduct of taking in pupils and scholars as guests into homes, cf. B. Berakhot 10b; 63b; B. Kiddushin 76b; *Sefer Middot*, fol. 14a; *Sefer Orah Ḥayyim*, fol. 4b; *Den Muser un' Hanhoge*; fol. 4b; *Sefer ha-Gan*, fol. 7a; *Sefer Mishlei*, fol. 26b; *Iggeret Derekh ha-Shem*, fol. 8a; *Eyn shoyn Froyenbuykhleyn*, fol. 6b.

3　　　*Servant.* (עבד כנעני :16). Literally "Canaanite slave" (*eved kenaani*), which is a halakhic term for a slave who is purchased for an unlimited time (Lev. 25:46; cf. B. Kiddushin 22b), as opposed to "Hebrew slave" (*eved ivri*), who must be set free in the seventh year (Exod. 21:2; Deut. 15:12; cf. B. Kiddushin 69a). In a nonhalakhic context, the term describes a slave who depends indefinitely on his master.

5　　　*License.* (בריב :17). See the Middle High German *briev*—document, certificate, report, evidence—; cf. Lexer, *Wörterbuch* (Dictionary), pp. 26 and 377. In *Brantshpigl*, *briv* or *brif* appears several times, meaning an official, legal document; see ibid., pp. 37, 231, 235, 325.

6　　　*Midrash.* (מדרש :18). The interpretation of Deut. 15:10 is based on the common root g-l-l of the words *biglal*—in return, because of—and *galgal*—wheel, cycle; see Tanḥuma, Mishpatim 15: "Look, what is written: 'Give to him readily and have no regrets when you do so, for in return' (Deut. 15:10). It does not say, 'because of this,' or 'to the benefit of,' or 'for,' or 'instead of,' but 'in return': I will make you rich, and him I will make poor. If you don't give him, I will turn the wheel around, and I will make you poor and him rich." Similar in Yalkut, §350.

9　　　*Gemara.* (גמרא :22). S. B. Shabbat 151b: "Rabbi Eleazar ha-Kappar says: One should always ask for mercy before the fate (of poverty). If it does not hit him, then it will hit his son, and if not his son, then his son's son, as it is written, 'For in return' (Deut. 15:10). A teaching from the school of Rabbi Yishmael: 'The world is a wheel which revolves.'" Same in Yalkut, §898. The homiletic connection between *Avot de-Rabbi Natan*, Tanḥuma, and B. Shabbat, results in the interpretation that the woman's conduct toward the Torah pupils will repeat itself in her own boys see line 5 above.

11　　　*Rich today.* (הייט רייך :23). S. Shemot Rabbah 31.14: "Why does the world resemble a wheel (for irrigation) in a garden, of which the lower clay ladles rise full, and the upper ones come down empty? Because not everybody, who is rich today, will also still be rich tomorrow, and not everybody, who is poor today, will still be poor tomorrow."

remember this, and should admonish him to learn day and night, and to go to synagogue, as if he were her own child. She should say to him, "If you do not do this, I will not let you stay in my house. Your father and mother sent you away in order to learn and pursue good deeds. They hope to have happiness from you and to earn *Gan Eden*. As it is written, "A
5   stairway was set"[10] and so forth. This means in Yiddish, a ladder stands on the ground, and

32b

its top reaches up to heaven. That is to say, the word *sullam* (ladder) has the same numerical value as *mamon* (money). This means that God, blessed be He, allotted money on earth so that with it one could earn the kingdom of heaven. But whoever does not have money can fulfill other commandments without money—for example, some can learn with orphans,
10   and so forth. There are so many commandments relating to loving-kindness, that I cannot write them all down.

Even a cook should remember that she too can earn *Gan Eden* through a young scholar. Her mistress will surely not prevent her from washing his shirt or taking his bedding so that it doesn't become bug-ridden. One sometimes finds (people) who let the boys go four

---

Why (is it so)? Because the world is a wheel, (as it is written,) 'For in return' (Deut. 15:10)."

The metaphor of the way of the world, or fate, as a wheel was very popular in moral literature; see *Brantshpigl*, p. 193: "'*Biglal*'—in return—means poverty. 'The world is a wheel which revolves.' This means, the wheel of poverty revolves in the world. One cannot know who is to be poor or rich, as one can see again and again. The Holy One, blessed be He, tests the poor, whether he loses courage as a result of his poverty. If he remains pious, surrendering to it as something that comes from God, and suffering it, the Holy One, blessed be He, will give him twice in return." Similar in *Sefer Oraḥ Ḥayyim*, fol. 10b.

S. on Deut. 15:10f., p. 853: "A wheel revolves in heaven, and orders the fate of mankind. One day, one is rich, the next day another one. People must therefore be careful to be charitable, because wealth and disaster are connected to each other. . . . One must give to the poor before he falls even deeper (from the wheel)."

S. *Mishlei Ḥakhamim*, fol. 3a–b: ‏דער נײנצעהנט שפּראך גידענק אונ׳ דארויף טראכט, דען לייטן ועד געלט גינאד בייא טאג אונ׳ בייא נאכט. דארויף זייא גאך אונ׳ זייא דיך אײלן, וען דיא צײַט ועד קערט זיך אונטר ווײַלן. עז גיט ניט איביג גלײַך, דער ארם בלײַבט ניט אימנדר ארם אונ׳ דער עשר רײַך. דאש גלגל איז זיך אפט אום קערן, דער ארם ווערט רײַך אונ׳ דער רײַך טוט ארם ווערן.‏"—The nineteenth spoke: Consider and strive to grant people grace, by day and by night. But be nimble and hurry, because times can change. It will not always be the same, the poor do not always remain poor, and the rich (do not remain) rich. The wheel turns often: the poor becomes rich, and the rich becomes poor."

32b

6   **Ladder.** (‏סולם‏ :1). Regarding the common tradition of the "wheel" and the Gematria of "ladder," see the commentary on p. 122/8.

12   **Cook.** (‏קעכין‏ :5). Regarding female cooks, see the commentary on p. 105/2 (Christian maids).

weeks in the same shirt, and don't remember that he too is descended from our Patriarch Abraham. "He who has mercy on creatures is treated mercifully in heaven."[11] This means in Yiddish, he who takes pity on people will have pity taken on him in heaven. The Gemara also explains the verse, "Send your bread forth upon the waters; for after many days you

5 will find it."[12] In Yiddish this means, send your bread on the water, for you will find it in many days. It does not say, "at the end of days," but says "many days." This means the eternal life in the world to come, which will be many days. Or it could mean that you will enjoy it many times. And the meaning of the verse is that it is talking about the Torah, which is compared to bread and water. As the verse says, "Come eat my food,"[13] and

10 "Ho, all who are thirsty, come for water."[14] That is to say, those who help strengthen Torah students. Because we have nowadays, due to our many transgressions, no Temple, or sacrifices—[only] the Holy Torah is left for us. All of our belief, and this world, and the

2   *He who has mercy.* (כל המרחם 9:). S. B. Shabbat 151b: "Rabban Gamliel says on behalf of Rabbi: 'Show you compassion, and in His compassion increase you' (Deut. 13:18). The heaven will have mercy with those, who have mercy with the creatures, and the heaven will not have mercy with those, who do not have mercy with the creatures."

    S. the formulation in B. Beẓa 32b: "'Show you compassion, and in His compassion increase you' (Deut. 13:18). Of everyone, who has mercy with the creatures—he knows that he is a descendent of our father Abraham; and of someone, who does not have mercy with the creatures—he knows that he is not a descendent of our Patriarch Abraham."

3   *Gemara.* (גמרא 11:). Regarding the interpretation of "many days" as "eternal life in the world to come," see *Avot de-Rabbi Natan*, A, chap. 3: "At the same time, Rabbi Akiva taught and said: 'Blessed be God, the God of Israel, for having made his decision for the words of the Torah and the words of the sages, because the words of the Torah, and the words of the sages, shall exist for ever and ever, as it is written, "Send your bread forth upon the waters; for after many days you will find it"' (Eccles. 11:1). And further it is written, 'But righteousness saves from death' (Prov. 10:2)."

    S. Midrash Tannaim, chap. 6:9: "'For our lasting good' (Deut. 6:24)—that is the world to come, because it is completely good. 'For our survival, as is now the case' (ibid.)—that is this world."

9   *Bread and water.* (לחם אונ' מים 15:). The interpretation of the Torah as water and bread is often found in the Midrash literature, among others in Bereshit Rabbah 52.1; 54.21; 70.5; Shemot Rabbah 25.8; Yalkut, §§123, 406.

11   *Torah students.* (לומדי תורה 17:). S. B. Berakhot 57a: "'Give strong drink to the hapless and wine to the embittered' (Prov. 31:6). Rabbi Yoḥanan said to the Tanna: Teach this—the scholar will be well forever, as it is written, 'Come, eat my food and drink the wine that I have mixed' (Prov. 9:5)."

12   *Sacrifices.* (קורבנות 18:). S. B. Ketubbot 105b: "Everyone who brings a gift to a scholar is like one who sacrifices his first fruits (in the Temple)."

12   *This world.* (עולם הזה 19:). Regarding the interpretation of Deut. 30:20 see *Avot de-Rabbi Natan*, B, chap. 31: "The creatures were not created by idle talk, but by the words of the Torah, as it is written, 'For thereby you shall have life and shall long endure' (Deut. 30:20): 'Life' (means) this world, 'Shall long endure' (means) the world to come."

world to come depend on the Holy Torah, as the verse says, "For thereby you shall have life and shall long endure."[15] This means in Yiddish, it is your life and will lengthen your years.

Due to our many transgressions, there are some people nowadays who distance themselves from Torah students. They are happy when they have a nice room, and don't let any young scholar or boy learn there. And if one wants to give him a noteworthy young scholar, he gives money as payment in order to get [a] boy who can be his servant, and will not let him learn with (other) boys in his house.

There are also some [undutiful] cooks who do not fear God, and become angry if a

33a

religious book is lying on the table, and say, "I've cleaned up here, and now you're putting books on the table!" But if she puts the children bare-naked on the table and they urinate on it, this filth means nothing to her. It is a great sin, and is a danger to the child, as we find in a story in *Sefer Ḥasidim*:[16] One day a child broke its feet, and the pious man said, "It was a sin that she put the child on the table, because the table is compared to the altar."

But those who are pious and God-fearing will think, "What a merit my children will have!" as our sages[17] said: "He who loves the scholars will have sons who are scholars." In Yiddish this means, whoever loves Torah students and supports them will merit having

---

1   ***Thereby.*** (היא :20). This spelling, which deviates from the Masorah, is also substantiated in rabbinic literature, as a result of the equalization of the Tetragrammaton with the Torah; see Yalkut, § 65: "One who is given a Torah to read, but he does not read it—(to him applies) as it is written, 'For thereby you shall have life and shall long endure' (Deut. 30:20)."

4   ***Torah students.*** (לומדי תורה :22). Regarding the obligation to take in Torah students, see the commentary on p. 187/15.

33a

11   ***Sin.*** (עברה :3). S. B. Menaḥot 97a: "At the time when the Temple existed, the altar atoned for every person. Now that the Temple exists no more, the person's table atones for him." Cf. B. Ḥagigah 27a.

     S. *Brantshpigl*, p. 113: "The (table) is holy, because one studies on it, blesses, and speaks benedictions. Therefore it is compared with the altar, on which one brings sacrifice. . . . It sometimes happens that a woman is impure, and yet sits on the table with her behind. Woe to her soul! Some lay some cloth underneath, but that is hardly of any help. One who sits his child on the table, and it dies early, is blamed for it: . . . They have sat themselves and their children on it, or laid some trivial things on it, like a brush or a comb."

12   ***Sefer Ḥasidim.*** (ספר חסידים :4). *Sefer Ḥasidim*, § 920: "A child stepped onto a table, upon which its father would often lay his books, however, not while it was with him, only alone. Every day, books were lying on the table. Only when he wanted to eat bread did he remove the books, until he finished his meal. Now the child stood on the table, and as it wanted to climb down, it cut its foot with a knife. The father said, 'My sin led me to allowing you to stand on the table.'"

15   ***He.*** (מאן :8). S. B. Shabbat 23b: "Raba said: He who loves the scholars will have sons who are scholars. He who respects scholars will marry off his children to

children who will be Torah scholars." The Gemara[18] says, "He who respects the scholars will have sons-in-law who are scholars." In Yiddish this means, he who esteems the Rabbis will merit having sons-in-law who will be Rabbis. The Gemara[19] goes on, "He who reveres the scholars will bear the mark of a scholar, and if he is not suited for this, his words will be listened to as if he bore the mark of a scholar." In Yiddish this means, if he fears Torah scholars, he will himself become a Torah scholar, but if he is not a learner, his words will be as important as if he were a Torah scholar. About this the Gemara says, "All the Prophets prophesied only for he who allows a Torah scholar to benefit from his property."[20] In Yiddish this means, [all] the words of blessing and comfort from our Prophets were said only for those who support Torah students from their money. We also learn this from the verse about the [Shunammite] woman—she gave a room to the Prophet Elisha in which he learned, and a table on which he put his books, and enough light. Therefore, she merited having an admirable son, who was Jonah the Prophet, and through whom God, blessed be His name, displayed miracles from which there is much to be learned. Why is it written there that the child died, and that he brought it back to life? The verse [shows] that, through the commandment to support Torah students that she fulfilled, people who do thus will merit the resurrection of the dead. The Gemara[21] teaches from that, that this (commandment) is equivalent to bringing a daily sacrifice. Concerning a sacrifice, it is written,

scholars. He who shows mercy for scholars, his body will bear the mark of the scholars. If he is not suited for it, his words will be heard like those of a scholar."

S. *Brantshpigl*, p. 208: "In tractate Shabbat it is written: He who respects scholars will marry off his children to scholars. In Yiddish this means, he who admires and dignifies Torah scholars, he will have learned sons-in-law."

6   *Learner.* (למדין 16:).   Yiddish spelling of *lamdan*.

7   *Torah scholar.* (תלמד 16:).   Yiddish spelling of *talmid*.

7   *Gemara.* (גמרא 17:).   S. B. Berakhot 34b: "Rabbi Ḥiyya bar Abba said, Rabbi Yoḥanan said: A prophet only prophesies in order to marry off his daughter to a scholar, to provide a scholar with a deal, and to support a scholar from his income."

11   *[Shunammite].* (שונמית 20:).   Regarding the Shunammite and Elisha, cf. II Kings 4:8ff.

13   *Jonah the Prophet.* (יונה הנביא 22-23:).   S. Midrash Tehillim 26:7: "And who was the son of the Shunammite? As it is written, 'The child grew up. One day, he went out to his father among the reapers' (II Kings 4:18.) After his death he was laid into his grave a second time, so that Elisha may bring him back to life—he came back to life, stood up, but he died (again). The third time they buried him in a different location. Why did he die? He was evil, but the son of the widow of Zarephath (cf. I Kings 17:17ff.) was (the prophet) Jonah ben Amitai; he was completely righteous."

17   *Resurrection of the dead.* (תחיית המתים 26:).   S. Shir ha-Shirim Rabbah 2.2: "Yoḥanan said on behalf of Rabbi Shimon ben Yoḥai: Support for livelihood is the most important, it leads to resurrection of the dead prior to the determined time: The woman from Zarephath deserved the resurrection of her son, because she had fed Elijah. The Shunammite deserved the resurrection of her son, because she had fed Elisha."

17   *Gemara.* (גמרא 26:).   S. B. Berakhot 10b: "'Who comes this way regularly'

33b

"The regular burnt offering,"[22] and concerning Elisha also, "He comes this way regularly."[23]

Now, as we spoke above about the verse, "She supplies provisions for her household"[24]—and she gives food to her house—we would like to explain the verses from *eshet ḥayil* further. As the verse says, "She is not worried for her household because of snow."[25] This means in Yiddish, she does not fear snow in her house. As *Reshit Ḥokhmah*[26] writes, quoting the Gemara[27] (where it is said that snow) means *Geihinnom*, as the verse says, "It seemed like a snowstorm in Zalmon."[28] This means that a woman of valor who makes sure that everything carries on in a Jewish manner in her household does not need to fear *Geihinnom*.

Now we would like to explain these verses further, as he praises the woman of valor and says, "She gives open-handed to the poor; her hands are stretched out to the needy."[29] This means, her hand is open to the poor, and she reaches out to the needy. There is an objection to raise here—why does he use a pleonasm? The verse must mean it as follows: When he says, "Her hand is open to the poor," he means someone who is a beggar, who holds out his hand and she does not let him leave empty-handed. When he then says, "Her hands are stretched out to the needy,"[30] he means a poor householder who is ashamed to ask for something, but is suffering under great need. She sends [such a person] into her house.

(II Kings 4:9). Rabbi Yosse said on behalf of Rabbi Ḥanina on behalf of Rabbi Eliezer ben Ya'akov, 'The scripture says of him: He who takes in a scholar as a guest into his house, and supports him with his possessions—he is like one who brings his daily sacrifice.'"

33b

2   *Above.* (אובן 1:).   Prov. 31:15 has not yet been interpreted; it probably refers to the interpretation of Prov. 31:14 on fol. 31b.

3   *Verses.* (פסוקים 3:).   Prov. 31:10–31.

4   *Not.* (לא 3:).   Regarding the interpretation of Prov. 31:21, see p. 100/1 and the respective commentary.

5   *Reshit Ḥokhmah.* (ראשית חכמה 4:).   This interpretation is not contained in *Reshit Ḥokhmah*; see the commentary on p. 100/2.

6   *Gemara.* (גמרא 5:).   S. B. Berakhot 16a: "Rabbi Ḥama said on behalf of Rabbi Ḥanina: Everyone who says the *Shema* and observes every one of its letters will be cooled in *Geihinnom*, as it is written, 'When Shaddai scattered the kings, it seemed like a snowstorm in Zalmon' (Ps. 68:15). Do not read *be-fares*—scattered—but instead *be-faresh*—interpreted; do not read *Zalmon*, but instead *zalmavet*—shadow of death." Same in Yalkut, §795.

12   *Objection.* (קשיא 10:).   See the commentary on p. 126/1.

15   *Poor householder.* (הויז עני 14:).   One who has a roof over his head, yet is suffering from poverty, as opposed to the "poor" (see above), being a begging homeless.

16   [*Such a person*]. (דןען זעלבגנן 14:).   The writing is rubbed off at the end of the line.

I could also explain the meaning of the verse as follows: "[She gives open-handed] to the poor"[31]—she should work with her hands in order to be able to give to the poor, as we also

1   *[She gives open-handed]*. ([כפיה פרשה] :15). The writing is rubbed off at the end of the line.

2   *Work.* (ערבטן :16). Regarding the ideal conduct derived from Prov. 31:20 (a woman should work and earn money, so that she may be charitable), see also the commentary on pp. 179/2 and 180/14. *Brantshpigl*, p. 306, particularly points out the morally supporting effect of housework that protects from idleness: "After she finished all her chores in the house, she should still work, so that she does not remain idle, because idleness is the source of much evil. If she earns a little, and it is all honorable, it will be blessed (i.e., the house)."

This applies also to cases, where the husband is financially capable of supporting wife and family by himself; see ibid., p. 123: "Particularly, when women see how others go idle and talk useless talk, they should not develop an urge to go idle or to tell stories, as well... and think: Why should I worry, after all, my husband must provide for me and feed me. Of this people say, 'Many words lead to much nonsense.'...Therefore the wise women say that every woman should stay in her house and not be idle."

As positively as *Brantshpigl* judges the woman who earns "a little" through work at home in order to use the money for charity, it regards quite negatively work she performs outside the house, because it leads to the woman's independence, to dominant behavior, and finally to an inversion of the power structure in the home; see ibid., p. 95: "Women who are involved in commerce, and provide for their home, take their husbands to the market, to the merchant, or to the shop. If something needs to be debated before a Rabbi or a judge, she will be in the back and in the front, and will constantly interrupt her husband. If she does not agree with her husband's speech, she begins to scream aloud. She screams at her husband, thinks she knows everything better, and forces him to do whatever she wants."

Similar in ibid., p. 305: "When women want to provide for the men, the men rely on them, and do nothing.... Or she wants to rule over him, and does whatever she wants. He is not allowed to move, in order to be charitable to the poor and to honor the guests. But when her friends come for a visit, she allows him (to be hospitable). If the man says something, she says, 'Why don't you arrange everything?' She makes the man sad—all this is contrary to the Torah."

Although these descriptions arise from Moses Henokhs Altshul's rigorous ideal of modesty and domesticity, they still need to be aligned with reality (women traveling, e.g., female merchants going to fairs); see ibid., p. 101: "The fact that they (the women) buy and sell amongst men is wrong, because the women have an insufficient understanding; they always think they are mistreated and begin to quarrel.... She should not be together with a stranger, whether Jew or gentile. When she travels, she must have a guardian with her. Whether boy or girl—it must be an adolescent who has understanding, not a little child that knows of nothing."

The concept of women working is generally received favorably, as long as the work helps to support men's efforts toward erudition in Torah learning; nevertheless, women's work is still considered subordinate to men's activities. See *Meshiv Ḥema—Minhagim Eshet Ḥayil*, 8a, in connection with the interpretation of Prov. 31:18: דיא אשת חיל הט פר" זוכט אונ' גשמעקט דש איר דער האנדיל גאר גוט איז אונ' טראגט גרושה רווחים. אזו טוט זי זיך נאך מער פרוישן צו דער ערבט דש זיא איז לאוט ליכט ברענה דיא גאנצי נכט. [...] די אשת חיל זעהט דש "דער—מאן טוט טוט לערנה. אונ' דיא סחורה פון דיא תורה איז בעשר אז אל דיא סחורה. The capable woman tried and experienced that her trading is successful and provides high

learn from the verse, "You shall enjoy the fruit of your labors."[32] The verse means that you should eat and also give to the poor from the work of your hands—all will be good for you in this world and in the world to come.

It is also written in the Torah, "All the skilled women spun with their own hands."[33] Every prudent woman spun with her own hands for the construction of the Tabernacle. We can learn from that, that what a woman makes with her own hands is more acceptable to the Holy One, blessed be He. Even the charity that she gives from it is worth more than when she gives with her money. The Gemara[34] explains (the verse), "Happy is he who is thoughtful of the wretched."[35] This means, happy is he who understands the poor. The verse does not say, "who gives to the poor," by which it means that one should deal with the poor with wisdom. If one sees that he is needy and is also ashamed, one should not embarrass him. One can also help him and give him advice, with the help of God, may He

34a

be blessed. If one does not give to him, or has nothing to give, he should grant him a pawn,

revenues. Therefore she tries to make an even greater effort at her work, and her light burns all night long....The capable woman sees to it that her husband studies (also at night). The merchandise of the Torah is better than all the merchandise of the trading."

3   *This world.* (עולם הזה: 19).   Such is the interpretation on Ps. 128:2 in M. Avot 4:1: "Who is rich? He who is happy with his share, as it is written, 'You shall enjoy the fruit of your labors; you shall be happy and you shall prosper.' 'You shall be happy' (means): in this world, 'You shall prosper' (means): in the world to come." Same in B. Ḥullin 44b and Yalkut, §96. See the commentary on p. 181/1.

8   *Money.* (געלט: 23).   The indication that the woman can exercise charity in a non-material manner, by giving "helpful advice" (cf. 34a) or by extending an interest-free loan against a pawn (34a), must be understood in the context in which women often did not have (their own) cash; see also the mentioning that the daughter should support her parents with her work, in case of lack of money; see fol. 18a.

8   *Gemara.* (גמרא: 23).   S. B. Nedarim 40a: "Rav said: He who visits the sick will be saved from *Geihinnom*, as it is written, 'Happy is he who is thoughtful of the wretched; in bad times may the LORD keep him from harm' (Ps. 41:2). This does not refer to the sick but to the needy."

10   *Gives.* (נותן: 25).   S. Va-yikra Rabbah 34.1: "Rabbi Yonah said: It is not written, 'Happy is he who gives to the wretched,' but 'Happy is he, who is thoughtful of the wretched' (Ps. 41:2). This means, who looks at him to see, how he can help him. Rabbi Yonah did this when he saw a wealthy and respected person who had lost his fortune and was ashamed to accept (help)." Similar in Yalkut, §665.

34a

13   *Pawn.* (משכון: 1).   This probably refers to an interest-free loan against a pawn as a form of charity. See *Brantshpigl*, p. 326f.: "When they are needy we shall help them to the best of our ability. If they do not want to accept gifts, we shall lend them something, or sell it so cheap, that they have a gain from it. Then they will not be ashamed."

"אונ' דרום אויך זאל אײן אײקליכר רידן מיט דען עני :Similar in *Sefer ha-Gan*, fol. 9b

גיטליך [...] אונ' אירן אויך אישט ער שולדיג אז ער אין זאל לײאן אונ' געבן וועז ער נארט (!)

or give him good advice so that he can support himself. This is a case of "One benefits, and the other has lost nothing." This is what the verse, "Happy is he who is thoughtful of the wretched,"[36] is referring to. Or the verse could be explained like this: One should give to one in whom it is well invested. Or the meaning could be that one should support a poor

5 person, and should give him work that he can benefit from. As it is written in the Torah, "By your side as your brother."[37] This means, make sure that your brother can find sustenance with you. Not like some, who are not God-fearing, and give work to gentiles, neglecting poor (Jewish) people. Even when the gentile steals, he does not care.

Now we would like to start again from the verse, "She gives [open-handed] to the

10 poor."[38] I could explain the meaning of the verse as follows: If he sees a comrade in a time of need. This means a poor person, as King David, peace be upon him, often said, "For [I] am poor and needy."[39] This means in Yiddish, for I am poor and needy. That is to say, this is what he meant: I am poor in (the fulfillment of) commandments, and need your great grace. The verse also means the [following]: When she sees a needy person, she should raise

15 her hands to God, blessed be His name, and should pray to Him. As King David, peace be upon him, also said, "Yet, when they were ill, my dress was sackcloth; and my prayer returns upon my bosom."[40] This means in Yiddish, when I saw that someone was sick, I prayed on his behalf, and this same prayer came into my bosom. That is to say, it benefited me. As our sages write,[41] "Everyone who [prays] for his friend, and requires the same thing,

20 will be answered first." The Gemara[42] says about this that a captive cannot take himself out of captivity—someone else must support him. Therefore someone else must also pray on his behalf.

Now we would like to continue explaining the verse. The verse goes on: "Her mouth is full of wisdom, her tongue with kindly teaching."[43] This means as follows in Yiddish, she

25 opens her mouth only with wisdom, and only the teachings of kindness are on her tongue. This refers to an unflawed, hospitable woman. In this regard, *Reshit Ḥokhmah*[44] describes

---

האט אונ׳ וועו עש איינר ניט ור מאג דא זאל ער אנדרי לייאן ראטן אונ׳ דער צו הלטן אז זיא עש טונן.—"Therefore one should speak amicably with the poor . . . and respect him. One should also lend or give him something. However, if one suffers hardship, and cannot help, one should ask others to lend (to the poor), and see to it that they do it."

1   *One benefits.* (זה נהנה 2:).   Cf. B. Berakhot 20a–b.

19   *Everyone.* (כל 18:).   S. B. Bava Kamma 92a: "From where is the teaching derived, which a Rabbi said: Everyone, who asks for mercy for his fellow man even though he himself needs it, too, will be answered first? He said to him: As it is written, 'The LORD restored Job's fortunes when he prayed on behalf of his friends' (Job 42:10)." Similar in Yalkut, §§ 91 and 928.

20   *Gemara.* (גמרא 19:).   See above.

26   *Reshit Ḥokhmah.* (ראשית חכמה 25:).   S. *Reshit Ḥokhmah,* III, p. 208, § 23: "If guests come into one's house, one shall honor them in accordance with one's ability, and even beyond one's capability. One does not present oneself to them as a poor person, but

how she should welcome a guest in a friendly and agreeable manner and be hospitable to him. And she should say to him: "My dear friend, we are very used to guests here. Please

34b

accept what God, blessed be He, has allotted us, so that we can honor guests." If, however, she has a husband who does not like to mingle with people, as one sometimes finds, she should reassure the guest and say to him, "Pay no attention to him, that is just how he is—he has other things on his mind." This is what the verse "Her tongue with kindly teaching"[45] means. This is the virtue of our Patriarch Abraham, peace be upon him, who showed grace to guests. Therefore, someone who adopts the virtue of hospitality shows that he is a descendant of our Patriarch Abraham. As I wrote above, "For great is His steadfast love toward us."[46] (*GaVaR*—great—) is the acrostic for *gomlei ḥasadim, bayshanim, raḥmanim*—those who are charitable, bashful, compassionate.

And about poor people: Of poor people, the Holy Torah wrote, "You shall open."[47] This means in Yiddish, open, you should open your hand to the poor and needy. It uses a pleonasm because the Torah is particularly vigilant regarding poverty. The verse goes on,

> as a rich person, even if one is poor. One should never receive them in an unfriendly manner, but with a friendly expression. One takes them in, even if one is wretched."
>
> Regarding the ideal of hospitality, see *Brantshpigl*, chap. 31 on hospitality, pp. 207–221; *Sefer Middot*, fol. 43a: One should particularly not become angry with guests; *Sefer Hayyei Olam*, fol. 3b: One should receive guests in a friendly manner, serve them immediately, and comfort the depressed among them. *Eyn shoyn Froyenbuykhleyn*, fol. 6b: One should not be miserly toward guests. *Sefer Oraḥ Ḥayyim*, fol. 5b: One should receive guests in a friendly manner, and not cause them sorrow (fol. 6b). See the commentary on p. 202/4.

34b

7   *Abraham.* (אברהם :5).   In the rabbinic literature, Abraham (cf. Gen. 18:2ff.) is considered an example of hospitality; see *Avot de-Rabbi Natan*, A, chap. 9: "You sit quietly in your house, suddenly guests come by. As you would eat wheat, so you serve him wheat. As you would eat meat, so you serve him meat. As you would drink wine, so you serve him wine. But Abraham did not act like this. He prepared everything and went out on the road, until he found guests and could bring them into his home."

S. Tanhuma, Ḥayyei Sarah 2: "All of the Lord's hospitality is grace and truthfulness. Abraham strongly observed the virtue of grace. Then the Holy One, blessed be He, told him: 'This is my virtue, and you have taken it on.'"

9   *Above.* (אובן :7).   See 28b. However, the exegetic connection to Prov. 31:26 does not lie in "great" (*gavar*), but rather in "steadfast love" (*ḥesed*), referring here to the ideal of grace and kindness.

10   *Acrostic.* (ראשי תיבות :8).   Regarding the *notarikon,* see the commentary on p. 178/7.

14   *Pleonasm.* (כפל לשון :11).   Here, however, the expression is applied to the *figura etymologica* used in biblical Hebrew (lines 9 and 12 in the Yiddish text).

197

"Give readily,"[48] "Furnish him."[49] This means in Yiddish, give, you should give even a hundred times; supply, you should supply even a hundred times from your own possessions. When we had the Land of Israel, we were obligated in the produce of the field, but now we are obligated to give a third of what God, blessed be His name, has allotted us. As the

5 Gemara[50] explains the verse, "Honor the LORD with your wealth."[51] This means in Yiddish, honor God from your [possessions] and from all that God, blessed be His name, has beneficently granted you. One also finds many pious, upright women who, when they cut a cheese, or start a new pot of fat, or whatever else, are careful first to give some of it to the poor. King Solomon, peace be upon Him, said about this: "He who satisfies others shall

10 himself be sated."[52] This means, he who satisfies others will be satisfied by the Holy One, blessed be He. The verse also says, "One man gives generously and ends with more,"[53] after which it says, "Another stints on doing the right thing and incurs a loss."[54] This means, it is common that one gives away a lot to charity, and nevertheless has a lot, but someone who avoids the proper path, and does not do good for God or for any people will come to harm.

15 The midrash[55] tells a story of a pious woman and her husband. He was a great pious man and was extremely needy. So the Holy One, blessed be He, sent him an angel, and had him

---

4   *A third.* (שלשים : 15). Describes the three parts that are set aside as sacrifices from the total harvest, or from the possession: the first part for the Levites (Num. 18:21–24); the second part is eaten in Jerusalem, or redeemed (Deut. 14:22–26); the third part is given to the poor (Deut. 14:28–29; 26:12); cf. Y. Terumah 4c; Y. Maaserot 1a.

5   *Gemara.* (גמרא : 16). S. Y. Peah 15b: "Another said, 'Honor the LORD with all your wealth, with the best of all your income' (Prov. 3:9). (This means) with as much as with the first of every harvest from you."

9   *Satisfies.* (זעט : 21). Regarding the translation see Rashi on Prov. 11:25: "'He who satisfies others' (means): he who feeds the poor to the fill; 'Shall himself be sated' (means): he will be sated with good."

13   *Charity.* (צדקה : 23). S. Yalkut, § 1047: "Rabbi Abbahu said: If you see one who spends his fortune on charity, know that he will receive even more, as it is written, 'One man gives generously and ends with more' (Prov. 11:24). Rabbi Shemuel bar Naḥmani said, if you see one who will not do a thing for charity, know that he will suffer deprivation, as it is written, 'Another stints on doing the right thing and incurs a loss' (ibid.)."

15   *Midrash.* (מדרש : 25). This Midrash is presented with the most detail in Ruth Zuta 4, 11, which differs in several details: instead of appearing as an angel, in the latter it is the prophet Elijah who is dressed as an Arab; instead of carrying clay, the man plows his field; instead of himself, it is his children who find the treasure in the dust at home; instead of taking sacrificial offerings directly from the discovery, the woman in Ruth Zuta recalls the "bond of grace" (cf. B. Ḥagigah 12b), and she alludes to Prov. 11:24; instead of the woman it is her youngest son who writes down all charitable expenses; instead of the angel going to God again, presenting the woman's bill, in Ruth Zuta God listens to her argument and gives them even more. Similar in Yalkut, § 607 and *Maysse Bukh,* no. 148.

35a

ask: "Seven good years have been allotted to you—do you want to have them now, or at the end of your life?" The pious man answered, "I'd like to ask my wife for advice." And so he went to his wife, and told her what had happened. She answered, "I want them now."
Then—to earn money—he went to a field and hauled clay for people, he was so poor. Later
5 he went there again, and found a buried treasure with gold. Together with his wife and children, he carried away a big sum. Afterwards she went and counted it, and put aside the tithe from it. Later, she gave a third to Torah students, and another went to feed the needy. And so the seven years were up. The angel came again to them and said, "Give me back the pledge." The pious man answered him, "Just like I didn't take it without my wife knowing,
10 I also won't give it back without her knowing." And so he went to his wife and told her that (the angel) wanted its pledge back. She said, "Go to him and tell him to give me three days." When the three days were up, he came again: "Give me back my pledge." And she said, "Come—let me [give] you an accounting. I received [such and such] an amount; I gave this as a tithe; and I put this much every week in the charity fund; and I gave [this
15 much] to poor girls; and I gave this much for clothing for poor people. Tell that to your master to whom the pledge belongs and who sent you. If he can find anyone who will manage his pledge better, then let him have it back." So the angel went to the Holy One, blessed be He, and the Holy One, blessed be He, said, "She is right. Let her have the pledge even longer." Thus, the righteous woman kept the riches even longer due to her
20 righteousness. Now, we can understand that the Holy One, blessed be He, gave them blessing and good fortune because of their great charity.

The Gemara[56] expounds on the verse, "And to take the wretched poor into your home."[57] Everyone who has mercy on a poor person will be blessed with 24 blessings. The Yalkut[58] quotes the midrash: Rabbi Yehudah bar Shimon said in the name of Rabbi Yehoshua ben
25 Levi, "The commandment regarding poor people should never be trivial in your eyes." This

---

35a

22   ***Gemara.*** (גמרא :24). S. B. Bava Batra 9b: "He who gives a poor man a coin will be blessed with six blessings, as it is written, 'It is to share' (Isa. 58:7) etc. 'And to take the wretched poor into your home' (ibid.). 'When you see the naked' (ibid.) etc. He who speaks to him in a friendly manner will be blessed with eleven blessings."

23   ***Yalkut.*** (ילקוט :26). S. Yalkut, §665: "Rabbi Yehudah bar Shimon (said) on behalf of Rabbi Yehoshua ben Levi: The obligation of (supporting) the poor shall never be unimportant in your eyes. He who disregards them will suffer 24 curses. He who honors them will receive 24 blessings. He who disregards them will suffer 24 curses: Where (is this substantiated)? As it is written from 'Appoint a wicked man over him' (Ps. 109:6) up to 'The poor and needy man' (Ps. 109:16) (in the psalm), 'Because he was not minded to act kindly' (ibid.). He who honors them, will receive 24 blessings: as it is written, 'It is to share your bread with the hungry' (Isa. 58:7) etc."

35b

means in Yiddish, the commandment regarding poor person should not be small in your eyes. He learns this from the verses, as the verse in Isaiah which is the haftarah for Yom Kippur says, "[It is] to share your bread with the hungry."[59] This means in Yiddish, if you will satisfy the hungry with your own bread, the [24] blessings associated with that will be fulfilled for you. So too with the opposite, God forbid—the 24 curses. These are explained from the verses in Psalm 109, from "Appoint a wicked man over him"[60] etc. (to) "He who abandons a poor man."[61] And the Gemara[62] explains the verse, "Who stops his ears at the cry of the wretched, he too will call and not be answered."[63] This means in Yiddish, he who closes his ears when a poor person comes to him and cries in his time of need, will also not be answered by the Holy One, blessed be He. And the midrash explains the verse, "Because He stands at the right hand of the needy, to save him from those who would condemn him."[64] This means, if a poor person is ashamed, but comes to (somebody) and begs, two angels go with him—one on his right hand and one on his left hand. If he welcomes him, and speaks with him in a friendly manner, [and] fulfills his wish, the good angel comes, and writes the 24 blessings on him. If, however, he embarrasses him, God forbid, the evil angel

35b

3   *[It is].* (הלא] :2).   Regarding the interpretation cf. also fol. 35a.

6   *He.* (ער :5).   Reference to Yalkut, § 665, as above; see also fol. 35a.

7   ***Gemara.*** (גמרא :6).   S. B. Shabbat 55a: "Rav Yehudah once sat in front of Shemuel. Then came (a woman) and screamed at him, but he ignored her. She said to him: 'Don't you know (what is written), "Who stops his ears at the cry of the wretched, He too will call and not be answered"' (Prov. 21:13)."

7   ***Who stops his ears.*** (מסיר אזנו :6).   The formulation has been taken from Prov. 28:9 by mistake.
S. Midrash Mishlei, 28:9: "'He who turns a deaf ear to instruction' (Prov. 28:9). Rav Huna said: He who does not love the words of the Torah, 'His prayer is an abomination' (ibid.). Rabbi Ḥanin said: Here it is talking about 'He who turns a deaf ear to instruction' (ibid.), and further it is said, 'Who stops his ears at the cry of the wretched' (Prov. 21:13). What is the (meaning of) further, 'He too will call and not be answered' (ibid.)? Here (it means): 'His prayer is an abomination' (Prov. 28:9)."

10   ***Midrash.*** (מדרש :9).   The source is unclear.
S. Va-yikra Rabbah 34.9: "Rabbi Abin said: This poor man stands outside your door, and the Holy One, blessed be He, stands at his right, as it is written, 'Because He stands at the right hand of the needy' (Ps. 109:31). If you give him, know who stands at his right, and gives you your reward. If you gave him nothing, know who stands at his right. He will retaliate on you, as it is written, 'To save him from those who would condemn him' (Ps. 109:31)."
See also Devarim Rabbah 6.10 on somebody who slanders: "The Holy One, blessed be He, said to him: Know that I will send an angel, who will stand by you, and who will write down everything that you say about your fellow human being." Similar in Tanḥuma, Metsora 2.

comes and writes on him, God protect us, the 24 curses. As the verse says, "Because He stands at the right hand of the needy, to save him from those who would condemn him."[65] This means that Satan stands beside him, and makes sure that he does not fulfill any commandments, so that he should suffer his judgment.

5 This is what Job may have meant when he said the verse, "That a blessing may rest upon your home.[66] You will know that all is well in your tent; when you visit your home you will never fail."[67] The Gemara[68] explains the verse as [regarding] interaction between a husband and wife. But I would like to explain the verse as follows: When it says, "That a blessing may rest upon your home,"[69] it is speaking of an old woman who lives in (their) home. As

10 the Gemara[70] says, "If there is an old woman in the house, there is blessing in the house." In Yiddish this means, an old woman in the house is a blessing. She can make peace in her house with her good deeds, and fear of God, and her prayers, [her] repentance, her charity, and her benevolence. She admonishes her children and her servants so that they don't

---

3   *Him.* (דיר :11). The second person singular is here possibly used by mistake, and is not taken into account in the translation. In line 12 (Yiddish text), the third person singular *er*—he—is used.

5   *May rest.* (להניח :18). Ezek. 44:30 is probably a duplicate; it appears again in line 21 of the Yiddish text.

7   *Gemara.* (גמרא :19). See B. Yevamot 62b: "'Without peace,' as it is written, 'You will know that all is well in your tent; When you visit your wife you will never fail' (Job 5:24). Rabbi Yehoshua ben Levi said: Of him, who knows that his wife is God-fearing, and does not supervise her, it is said, 'Never fails,' as it is written, 'You will know that all is well' (Job 5:24) etc." See the commentary on p. 111/15: this rabbinic teaching joins directly the one quoted there.

9   *Upon your home.* (בביתך :21). The masoretic text of Ezek. 44:30 differs slightly.

10   *Gemara.* (גמרא :22). S. B. Arakhin 19a: "An old man in the house is a trap in the house. An old woman in the house is a treasure in the house."
S. *Ze'enah u-Re'enah* on Lev. 27:2, p. 637: "An old man in the house means quarrels, an old, pious woman in the house means happiness and blessings for the entire house."
S. Rashi on Lev. 27:7: "When a woman has grown old, she is regarded almost like a man. Therefore, a man loses, with age, a third of his standing, while a woman loses nothing, and rather (gains) a third of her standing. This is what the people say: An old man in the house is like a trap. An old woman in the house is a treasure for the house, which is a good sign for the house."
In *Brantshpigl* the old woman is only mentioned as a form of chaperon, assigned to bring charity money to the Gabbai, instead of the young woman (ibid., p. 97), or to receive some instruction from the Rabbi (ibid., p. 247); at one point also as a consultant during pregnancy (ibid., p. 332). The old are criticized, however, where they do not properly fulfill their roles as examples by overly forbearing conduct; instead see ibid., p. 114: "And on the streets, and during banquets the women mix with the men, friends or not. They chat aloud, and talk with one another. If they are reprimanded, they do not care. The young women dress provocatively and look the men in the face, and the old do not stop them from doing it. When asked, the old say, 'They are young, one cannot put an old head on their shoulders.'"

quarrel with each other, and so that no curse or oath leaves their mouths. Thus a respectable woman can, through her piety, ensure that her children benefit from her virtue, and can

36a

bring blessing, success, and long life to her house.

Particularly, when poor people come to her house as guests, she rejoices that God, blessed be He, has given her (the opportunity to fulfill) the commandments. She receives them hospitably, and greets them in a friendly manner, and encourages them: "Please accept what we have." This is what King Solomon said in the verse, "The curse of the Lord is on the house of the wicked, but He blesses the abode of the righteous."[71] In Yiddish this means, the curse of [God] is in the house of a wicked person, and the dwelling of righteous people is blessed with all blessings. This is what Job referred to with "You will know that all is well in your tent."[72]

An old woman who is righteous, and does as I have written, will make peace in her tent, and she will also merit having peace in the world to come. We find that God, blessed be His name, said to the righteous ones: "As for you, you shall go to your fathers with peace."[73]

36a

4   *Guests.* (געשט 1:). Reception of guests is described very similar in *Sefer Oraḥ Ḥayyim,* fol. 5b: אונ׳ מן זאל דיא געסט אנטפפנגן בסבר פנים יפות דאז מיינט ליפליך אונ׳" שוינליך מיט גוטן מוט אונ׳ אזו בלד אז זיא קומן זא טראג אין דאש עשן פור זיא אונ׳ ועז צוא ווילן זיין זיא הונגריג אונ׳ שעמן זיך אן צוא היישן איר בידרפניש אונ׳ ער זאל עש זעלברט טאן ועז ער שון ויל קנעכט אדר מייד האט אונ׳ זאל זיא ערן מיט ווארטן אונ׳ מיט ווערקן." —"One should receive guests hospitably, this means kindly and friendly, and in a good mood. Soon after their arrival you should serve them food, because although sometimes they are hungry, they will be too shy to ask. One should also do it by oneself, even if one has many servants and maids. One shall honor them with words and deeds." See the commentary on p. 196/26.

9   *[God].* (גיוט 5:). In the Krakow edition of 1618, the word *got* (God) is usually printed with a curvature; here, however, it also reads *got* with an *aleph* instead of *vav* and curvature.

10   *You will know.* (וידעת 6:). See also fol. 35b. The exegetic connection between Prov. 3:33 and Job 5:24 lies in the word *naveh*—abode, dwelling place, home—which appears in both verses but is not quoted here.

12   *Peace.* (שלום 8:). See the commentary on p. 201/10. Bringing upon peace is substantiated in other ethical texts as a male ideal of conduct; see *Den Muser un' Hanhoge,* fol. 4b–5a: יב׳ שישתדל להכניס שלום בין איש לאשתו ובין אדם לחבירו. דש ער זול זיך מויאן" צו מכן שלום צווישן מאן אונ׳ וויפא אונ׳ צווישן איין מן אונ׳ זיין חבר." —"12: He shall make an effort to bring peace between a man and his wife, and between a man and his comrade. That he makes an effort to create peace between man and wife, and between a man and his comrade."

S. *Ẓe'enah u-Re'enah* on Num. 21:21, p. 754: "Bringing peace is a basic obligation. A person need not strive to fulfill all commandments, but if he has the opportunity to perform a good deed, he must perform it. In this context, says the Holy One, blessed be He, a person must always strive to bring upon peace."

This means in Yiddish, you will come to your parents in the world to come with peace. As the Gemara[74] says: When a righteous person dies, a delegation of angels approaches him, receives him, and says: "Come with peace, and rest on your couch."[75] This means, the righteous ones should come with peace, and should rest tranquilly on their beds. This means that those who made peace in this world will also merit peace in the world to come. This is why it says, "Come with peace:" the *bet*—with—means that he takes peace with him from this world to the world to come. This is why everyone should pay attention to this, and this is why all of our prayers end with *shalom*.

In recompense of this we will merit the redemption of the [Messiah], who will make peace in the whole world. And we will merit the rebuilding of the Temple, and the *Shekhinah* will once again reside among Israel. The Master of peace will teach us and reveal

2   *Gemara.* (גמרא : 11). S. B. Berakhot 64a: "When somebody dies, one shall not say about the deceased, 'Go in peace' (Exod. 4:18), but instead 'Go with peace' (II Sam. 15:9), as it is also said, 'You shall go to your fathers with peace' (Gen. 15:15)."

S. Ba-midbar Rabbah 11.7: "It says, 'Then I sent messengers from the wilderness of Kedemoth' (Deut. 2:26) etc. And it says, 'Restore it peaceably' (Judg. 11:13). Peace is the most important, because even the dead need peace, as it is written, 'You shall go to your fathers with peace' (Gen. 15:15)." Similar in Yalkut, §711.

S. *Pesikta Rabbati*, 44: "If a man is righteous, his righteousness will be registered. If he was evil, his evil deeds will be registered. Therefore, if a righteous man passes away, the angels sanctify and praise him: 'Yet he shall come to peace, he shall have rest on his couch' (Isa. 57:2)."

Similar in *Eyn shoyn Froyenbuykhleyn*, fol. 3a: אוני' איבר הונדרט יארן וועז דוא ווערט" שטערבן זא ווערן קומן אזו פיל דר הימלישן ענגיל. די דא זיין גיהיישן מלאכי רחמים אוני' זי ווערן דיין זיל אנטפאנגן מיט גרושן פריידן. אוני' זיא ווערן זאגין שלום בואך שלום בואך דז איז אין טויטשן פריד זאל זיין דיין קומן. פריד זאל זיין דיין קומן. אוני' ווערין ווירן אזו בלד וער דען דיין "האמת אוני' דארטין ווערין די ענגיל גוטש אל דיין ויר שפרעכיר זיין.—"And at one hundred, when you will die, just as many celestial angels, the so-called angels of mercy will come. They will welcome your soul with great joy, and say, 'May peace be in your coming, may peace be in your coming' (cf. I Sam. 16:4; I Kings 2:13). This means in Yiddish, 'May peace be in your coming, may peace be in your coming.' They will then lead you to the Judge of Truth, and there the angels of God will be your mediators."

S. Midrash Tehillim 116:7: "When a righteous man dies, three classes of angels come out to meet him. The first class says: 'He shall come to peace' (Isa. 57:2). The second class says, 'He shall have rest on his couch' (ibid.). The third says, 'Who walked straightforward' (ibid.)."

3   *Come.* (יבואו : 12). Come. The masoretic text of Isa. 57:2 differs significantly, but because it is relevant for the interpretation (see above) it was translated literally.

6   *Bet—with.* (ב' : 16). The masoretic text of Isa. 57:2 has in fact no preposition preceding *shalom*.

8   *Prayers.* (תפילו' : 17). Cf. the last benediction in the *Amidah*, *sim shalom* (or *shalom rav*), also quoted after the priestly blessing; see also the commentary to 21a/4.

11   *Master of peace.* (אדון השלום : 20). S. *Oẓar Midrashim*, p. 304: "'Father of truth'—that is our Patriarch Jacob, as it is written, 'I am unworthy of all the kindness and

to us the Torah that is only peace. As the verse says, "All her ways are pleasant ways, and all her paths, peaceful."[76] Amen, so may it be His will.

Finished and completed today, Monday, the 20th of the month of [Elul], 5378 (1618) according to the [lesser] reckoning. By Joseph Samuel bar Mordecai Grozmark, may his memory and that of his house be a blessing.

5

all the truth' (Gen. 32:11). 'Master of peace'—that is our Patriarch Isaac, as it is written, 'And they departed from him in peace' (Gen. 26:31)." Cf. *sar ha-shalom*—"peaceable ruler"—in Isa. 9:5.

1   *Only peace.* (אייטל שלום :21).   S. Yalkut, § 273: "The Holy One, blessed be He, said: 'The entire Torah is peace. Whom do I give it to? To the nation that loves peace, because (it is written) "And all her paths, peaceful"' (Prov. 3:17)."

1   *All.* (כל :21).   According to the Ashkenazic tradition, Prov. 3:17 is said when the Torah is taken from the ark prior to the reading, and when it is brought back to the ark after the reading; cf. Nulman, *Encyclopedia,* pp. 336 and 358.

3   *[Elul].* (אלול] :22).   The reading of the first *lamed* in Krakow 1618 is questionable, but more probable than a possible *dalet*; the *resh* is unequivocal. The 20th of Adar 5378 (17 March 1618) was a Sabbath, therefore it may be assumed that the day of print was the 20th of Elul 5378 (10 September 1618), a Monday. Shmeruk, *Jewish Authoress,* p. 3, reads *aleph-lamed-lamed.*

NOTES TO TRANSLATION OF *MENEKET RIVKAH*

Introduction

1. Gen. 35:8.
2. Deut. 32:13.
3. Exod. 3:7.
4. See Gen. 39:15.
5. Cf. Num. 22:38.
6. See Gen. 26:19.
7. Cf. Gen. 29:2.
8. Cf. Ps. 51:10.
9. Prov. 5:15.
10. Cf. Gen. 27:29; Num. 22:6; 24:9.
11. Cf. Ps. 18:31; 34:23; II Sam. 22:31.
12. Cf. Isa. 59:21.
13. Cf. I Sam. 25:25.
14. Cf. Ps. 115:16.
15. Cf. Ruth 3:9.
16. Cf. Ps. 117:2.
17. I Kings 1:14.
18. Cf. II Chron. 31:3; 35:26.
19. Cf. Ps. 16:2.
20. Songs 1:4.
21. Ps. 119:15.
22. Ps. 119:105.
23. Cf. Ps. 51:6.
24. Cf. Ps. 76:5; 145:18.
25. Cf. Ps. 27:4.

Chapter 1

26. Ps. 45:11.
27. Ps. 45:12.
28. Tanhuma, Lekh Lekha 3.
29. Prov. 10:12.
30. Ps. 45:12.
31. Songs 1:15; 4:1.
32. Ps. 45:14.
33. Ps. 45:17.
34. Songs 8:8.
35. Songs 8:9.
36. Rashi on Songs 8:8.
37. Yalkut, §994.
38. Prov. 7:4.
39. Songs 8:8.
40. Songs 8:9.
41. Songs 8:9.
42. Songs 8:9.
43. Prov. 14:1.
44. Prov. 14:1.
45. Prov. 14:1.
46. Prov. 13:16.
47. B. Ketubbot 63a; B. Nedarim 50a.
48. Prov. 12:10.
49. Maimonides, *Hilkhot De'ot*, 4, 15.
50. Prov. 21:13.
51. Prov. 14:1.
52. Prov. 24:3.
53. Prov. 24:4.
54. Exod. 1:21.
55. Exod. 1:21.
56. See Exod. 35:31.
57. *Reshit Hokhmah*, I, p. 646, §72.
58. *Eyn shoyn Froyenbuykhleyn*, fol. 5a.
59. Devarim Rabbah 3.5.
60. Deut. 28:4.
61. Gen. 25:22.
62. Rashi on Gen. 25:22.
63. B. Avodah Zarah 17a.
64. Prov. 5:8.
65. B. Avodah Zarah 17a.
66. Prov. 14:1.
67. See Gen. 2:22.
68. See Gen. 2:7.
69. Gen. 16:2.
70. See Gen. 30:3.
71. Prov. 9:1.
72. FR Va-yikra Rabbah 23.11.
73. Job 5:19.
74. See Prov. 9:1.
75. See Exod. 25:37.
76. Exod. 25:33; 37:19.
77. Prov. 9:1.
78. Prov. 31:21.
79. Ps. 68:15.
80. *Reshit Hokhmah*, I, p. 267, §75.
81. Ps. 128:3.
82. FR Va-yikra Rabbah 36.2.
83. Ps. 22:11.
84. See Jer. 1:5.
85. Midrash Tehillim 68:14.
86. See Ps. 68:27.
87. See Exod. 15:2.
88. See Ps. 68:27.
89. Prov. 5:18.
90. Judg. 5:9.
91. See Prov. 9:1.
92. See Exod. 25:33; 37:19.
93. Prov. 20:27.
94. Prov. 14:1.
95. Deut. 23:15.
96. See Deut. 23:15.
97. Deut. 23:15.
98. B. Shabbat 55a.
99. Ps. 119:160.
100. B. Niddah 31a.
101. Deut. 23:15.
102. Prov. 24:25.

Chapter 2

1. Prov. 12:4.
2. Ibn Ezra on Prov. 12:4.
3. Bereshit Rabbah 47.1.
4. Prov. 12:4.
5. Bereshit Rabbah 47.1.
6. B. Berakhot 8a.
7. Prov. 18:22.
8. Ps. 32:6.
9. B. Berakhot 8a.
10. Prov. 31:10.
11. Midrash Tehillim 59:2.
12. Gen. 2:18.
13. Ezek. 44:30.
14. Lev. 16:6; 11:17.
15. Job 5:24.
16. Eccles. 9:9.
17. Deut. 14:26.
18. Gen. 2:18.
19. B. Yevamot 63a.
20. See Ps. 32:6.
21. Gen. 2:23.
22. Gen. 1:27.
23. *Alpha-Beta de-Ben Sira* 23a–b.
24. Gen. 29:27.
25. Gen. 29:27.
26. Gen. 29:30.
27. Ps. 77:16.
28. Ruth 2:5.
29. Rashi on Ruth 2:5.
30. Ruth 2:5.
31. Ps. 32:6.
32. See Ruth 4:11.
33. Ruth 4:12.
34. Ruth 4:12.

35. Gen. 49:28.
36. B. Pesaḥim 49a.
37. Ps. 92:7.
38. Deut. 33:1.
39. Lev. 16:3.
40. Deut. 4:44.
41. Deut. 33:7.
42. Rashi on I Chron. 4:21.
43. *Eyn shoyn Froyenbuykhleyn*, fol. 33a.
44. Prov. 19:14.
45. Prov. 14:1.
46. B. Sanhedrin 110a.
47. Avot de-Rabbi Natan, A, 1, 9.
48. Prov. 14:1.
49. *Reshit Hokhmah*, I, p. 9, §18.
50. Prov. 14:1.
51. Reshit Hokhmah, I, p. 9, §18.
52. B. Megillah 14a.
53. Judg. 4:4.
54. Prov. 23:29.
55. Prov. 17:14.
56. Prov. 17:14.
57. See Prov. 26:20.
58. Prov. 20:3.
59. Hab. 2:4.
60. B. Bava Metzi'a 44a.
61. Eccles. 5:5.
62. B. Shabbat 32b.
63. Prov. 22:27.
64. Gen. 28:12.
65. Deut. 4:4.
66. See B. Ketubbot 111b.
67. See Deut. 4:4.
68. See Prov. 28:20; 21:5.
69. *Sefer Middot*, fol. 46a.
70. Tanhuma, Va-yishlaḥ 19.
71. See Eccles. 7:26.
72. Prov. 6:26.
73. See Exod. 20:5; 34:7; Num. 14:18; Deut. 5:8.
74. Gen. 2:18.
75. See B. Yevamot 63a.
76. Shemot Rabbah 52.3.
77. See Eccles. 12:5.
78. B. Ta'anit 25a.
79. See Prov. 15:1.
80. See Eccles. 7:26.
81. Eccles. 7:28.
82. Prov. 18:22.
83. Prov. 18:22.
84. See Eccles. 7:26.
85. Eccles. 7:28.
86. See Va-yikra Rabbah 2.1.
87. Eccles. 7:28.
88. Exod. 32:4, 8.
89. See Exod. 32:3.
90. Prov. 31:23.
91. Gen. 3:16.
92. Gen. 21:12.
93. B. Bava Metzi'a 59a.
94. B. Bava Metzi'a 59a.
95. See Gen. 12:16.
96. Zech. 14:9.

Chapter 3

1. Prov. 31:30.
2. *Sefer Middot,* fol. 4b.
3. Deut. 6:13; 10:20.
4. Lev. 19:3.
5. See Lev. 24:16.
6. Exod. 21:17.
7. Prov. 3:9.
8. Exod. 20:12; Deut. 5:16.
9. See Yalkut, §297.
10. Prov. 3:9.
11. Exod. 20:12; Deut. 5:16.
12. B. Pesaḥim 22b.

13. Deut. 6:13.
14. B. Berakhot 34b.
15. See Exod. 20:12; Deut. 5:16.
16. B. Ketubbot 103a.
17. B. Ketubbot 103a.
18. See Tosafot, Kiddushin 31b.
19. See Tosafot, Kiddushin 31a–b.
20. B. Sanhedrin 100a.
21. B. Kiddushin 31b.

Chapter 4

1. Prov. 19:14.
2. I Sam. 24:12.
3. See II Kings 1:14.
4. Bamidbar Rabbah 21.20.
5. Prov. 13:25.
6. Ruth 2:14.
7. Ruth 2:11.
8. *Sefer Middot*, fol. 42a.
9. Prov. 9:13.
10. Jer. 17:7.
11. Ps. 118:8.
12. Ps. 118:8.
13. Ps. 146:3.
14. Jer. 17:5.
15. Bereshit Rabbah 89.3.
16. Prov. 27:6.
17. Devarim Rabbah 1.4.
18. Devarim Rabbah 1.4.
19. See Num. 23:21.
20. See Deut. 23:6.
21. Prov. 27:6.
22. Prov. 27:6.
23. See Num. 23:9.
24. Lev. 20:26.
25. See Num. 24:6.
26. Yalkut, §203.
27. See I Kings 14:15.

Chapter 5

1. See Prov. 31:28.
2. See Prov. 31:29.
3. Prov. 31:29.
4. See Jer. 1:5.
5. Ps. 58:4.
6. *Reshit Hokhmah*, III, p. 80, §42.
7. B. Eruvin 100b.
8. Gen. 3:16.
9. Gen. 3:16.
10. Gen. 3:16.
11. Gen. 3:16.
12. Gen. 3:16.
13. Gen. 3:16.
14. See Prov. 14:23.
15. Gen. 3:16.
16. Gen. 3:16.
17. See Lev. 26:4, 6.
18. I Sam. 2:30.
19. See B. Shabbat 89b.
20. Prov. 13:16.
21. Prov. 17:10.
22. See Deut. 18:10.
23. See II Kings 1:16.
24. *Sefer Ḥasidim*, §59.
25. Exod. 23:13.
26. Ps. 5:2.
27. See Eccles. 7:14.
28. Ps. 119:126.
29. Prov. 1:8.
30. Deut. 6:7.
31. *Orhot Zaddikim*, fol. 3b.
32. See Prov. 3:3; 7:3.
33. Deut. 6:7.
34. Deut. 6:7.
35. See Prov. 23:14.

36. Exod. 21:17.
37. Exod. 21:17.
38. See Prov. 22:6.
39. *Reshit Ḥokhmah*, III, p. 59, §9.
40. See Prov. 13:24.
41. Shemot Rabbah 1.1.
42. *Reshit Ḥokhmah*, III, p. 59, §§9–13.
43. I Kings 1:6.
44. I Kings 1:6.
45. Prov. 19:18.
46. Prov. 22:15.
47. *Reshit Ḥokhmah*, III, p. 55, §2.
48. See Ps. 106:3.
49. B. Ketubbot 50a.
50. Bereshit Rabbah 84.4.
51. Gen. 12:5.
52. Bereshit Rabbah 39.14.
53. Bereshit Rabbah 49.4.
54. *Reshit Ḥokhmah*, III, p. 55, §2.
55. *Reshit Ḥokhmah*, I, p. 838, §28.
56. See B. Shabbat 30b.
57. II Kings 3:15.
58. See Ps. 78:6.
59. Prov. 31:2.
60. See Prov. 3:4.
61. See Lev. 19:23–24.
62. See B. Shabbat 119b.
63. Ps. 8:3.
64. See Yalkut, §170.
65. B. Gittin 36b.
66. See Judg. 5:31.
67. B. Yoma 23b.
68. B. Tamid 32a.
69. Judg. 5:31.
70. Judg. 5:20.
71. Dan. 12:3.
72. See Dan. 12:3.
73. See Gen. 22:17; 26:4.
74. Judg. 5:23.
75. See Ps. 117:1–2.
76. Deut. 6:7.
77. Deut. 11:19.
78. B. Bava Batra 141a.
79. Exod. 19:3.
80. Mekhilta de-Rabbi Yishmael, *Yitro* 2.
81. See Gen. 24:20.
82. See Gen. 24:14.
83. See Prov. 31:17.
84. B. Ketubbot 59b.
85. Prov. 19:15.
86. Prov. 31:27.
87. Ps. 128:2.
88. B. Ḥullin 44b.
89. See Exod. 29:29.

Chapter 6

1. See Prov. 11:16.
2. Prov. 9:8.
3. Prov. 15:1.
4. B. Bava Metzi'a 31a.
5. See Lev. 19:17.
6. Prov. 15:1.
7. See Prov. 9:8.
8. Prov. 9:13.
9. See Prov. 23:6.
10. Prov. 17:1.
11. See Prov. 15:17.
12. See Ruth 3:1.
13. Ruth 3:3.
14. Rashi on Ruth 3:3.
15. See Prov. 14:1.
16. See Ps. 54:2.
17. Prov. 11:16.
18. Prov. 31:14.
19. See Prov. 11:16.
20. See Deut. 30:15.
21. Deut. 30:19.

Chapter 7

1. Prov. 31:29.
2. Lev. 19:18.
3. Y. Nedarim 9 (41c).
4. Lev. 19:18.
5. See Avot de-Rabbi Natan, A, 26; see B. Shabbat 31a.
6. Prov. 31:18.
7. Tanḥuma, Mishpatim 15.
8. Deut. 15:10.
9. B. Shabbat 151b.
10. Gen. 28:12.
11. B. Shabbat 151b.
12. See Eccles. 11:1.
13. See Prov. 9:5.
14. See Isa. 55:1.
15. See Deut. 30:20.
16. *Sefer Ḥasidim*, §920.
17. B. Shabbat 23b.
18. B. Shabbat 23b.
19. B. Shabbat 23b.
20. See B. Berakhot 34b.
21. See B. Berakhot 10b.
22. See Exod. 29:42; Num. 28:6.
23. II Kings 4:9.
24. Prov. 31:15.
25. Prov. 31:21.
26. *Reshit Ḥokhmah*, I, p. 267, §75.
27. B. Berakhot 16a.
28. Ps. 68:15.
29. See Prov. 31:20.
30. Prov. 31:20.
31. See Prov. 31:20.
32. Ps. 128:2.
33. See Exod. 35:25.
34. B. Nedarim 40a.
35. Ps. 41:2.
36. Ps. 41:2.
37. Lev. 25:36.
38. Prov. 31:20.
39. Ps. 86:1.
40. See Ps. 35:13.
41. B. Bava Kamma 92a.
42. B. Bava Kamma 92a.
43. Prov. 31:26.
44. *Reshit Ḥokhmah*, III, p. 208, §23.
45. Prov. 31:26.
46. Ps. 117:2.
47. Deut. 15:8, 11.
48. Deut. 15:10.
49. See Deut. 15:14.
50. Y. Peah 1 (15b).
51. Prov. 3:9.
52. Prov. 11:25.
53. Prov. 11:24.
54. Prov. 11:24.
55. Ruth Zuta 4, 11.
56. See B. Bava Batra 9b.
57. Isa. 58:7.
58. Yalkut, §665.
59. See Isa. 58:7.
60. Ps. 109:6.
61. See Ps. 109:16.
62. B. Shabbat 55a.
63. See Prov. 21:13.
64. See Ps. 109:31.
65. See Ps. 109:31.
66. See Ezek. 44:30.
67. Job 5:24.
68. B. Yevamot 62b.
69. See Ezek. 44:30.
70. B. Arakhin 19a.
71. Prov. 3:33.
72. Job 5:24.
73. See Gen. 15:15.
74. See B. Berakhot 64a.
75. See Isa. 57:2.
76. See Prov. 3:17.

מנקת רבקה

הערט צו מיר ליבן קעטצליכה פרואה פרומן . מיר וועלט דרש
טייטש ספר וואל מיר ליבר לייאכן מול און טוימן . דז אן צו וועלין
ערגן מלאועכטיגן זיין טוריאן . מול מיר מל מיט וורקן מון מין
מיאן . ווייל מיר המט דר קעגנט דיט מטה דהשובה הרבנית
הדרשנית ארת רבקה ז"ל בת הגאון אהירר אמר טיקטינר נ"ל
ד' דמש ספר המט גיטורלט . מול גיאלט . אול מיר כונה מון
מיטול ירמת שמיק גיווטשט טון מול כלט . מול מיר אחשבה
צארי ניט גיווגן מון פרכט . מודר מער חמט דמט חידוש אין
גיהערט מודר גיזגהן . דז מן מיביגן ימרן מיז אין גישעהן . דז
מין מטה העט טוים מירן קמם וטט אחבר גיווגן . מול העט
פסזיקיק מול ארדטיק צו הוון גילטגן . דרוק המב מיך עש לאמין
דריקן . דז מין מיקליכה פרוא ריא דערינן ווערט לייאכן ווערט
מיכש קיפן מול צוקן . מול המט דמט ספר גיהייטן
אנקת רבקה (מיר צו מין גירעלטניט מול זכבוד מלי נטיק ·
דז מין מטה מוך מוך קמן איחבר זיין דברי אוסר מול גוטה
פסטיק מזו וואל מו אענכי מנטיק . מול המטט
גיטיילט מוך מין טבעה טעריק . גמר קורן
מול ניט אמריך גיווגן בד'נריק בצלות
זה ווערט מיר זכה זיין נודר
גמולה מון אטח הזריט
שכינה ווערט זיך מונטר ישרמל וודר דר איימן מן וכן יהי רצון
פה פראג לפ"ק
עי ירשם בן מהרר בצלאל כץ זצל מחוקק

Meneket Rivkah, Prague 1609, title page. Courtesy of the Alte Universitätsbibliothek Erlangen.

APPENDIX I

MENEKET RIVKAH:
YIDDISH TEXT (Prague 1609)

[מנקת רבקה]

הערט צו איר ליבן קעשטליכה פֿרומה פֿרויאן. איר מעלבֿת דאש
טייטש ספֿר וואל איבר לייאנן אונ׳ אן שויאן. דז מן זאל זעצין צו
גו* דען אלמעכטיגן זיין טרויאן. אונ׳ אין אל זייני ווערקן אויף אין
בויאן. ווייל איר האט דר קענט דיא אשה החשובֿה הרבנית
הדרשנית מרת רבקה ז״ל בת הגאון מהר״ר מאיר טיקטינר ז״ל
די דאש ספֿר האט גיטרבֿט. אונ׳ גימלט. אונ׳ איר כוונה אויף
אייטל יראת שמים גיוועשט טאג אונ׳ נכֿט. אונ׳ איר מחשבֿה
לגמרי ניט גיוועזן אויף פרכֿת. אודר ווער האט דאש חידוש מין
גיהערט אודר גיזעהן. דז אין איביגן יארן איז מין גישעהן. דז
איין אשה העט גיטאן אויש אירן קאפֿ וואש מחבר גיוועזן. אונ׳ העט
פֿסוקים אונ׳ מדרשים צו הויף גילעזן. דרום האב איך עש לאזין
דרוקן. דז איין אייקליכֿה פֿרויא דיא דארינן ווערט לייאנן ווערט
איינש קויפֿן אונ׳ צוק. אונ׳ האט דאש ספֿר גיהיישן
מנקת רבקה) איר צו איין גידעלטניש אונ׳ לכֿבֿוד אלי נשים.
דז איין אשה אויך קאן מחבר זיין דבֿרי מוסר אונ׳ גוטה
פשטים אזו וואל אז מענכֿי אנשים. אונ׳ האטש
גיטיילט אויף שבֿעה שערים. גאר קורץ
אונ׳ ניט מאריך גיוועזן בדברים. בזכֿות
זה ווערט איר זוכֿה זיין צו דר
גאולה פֿון משיח דז דיא
שכֿינה ווערט זיך אונטר ישראל ווידר דר מייאן אמן וכֿן ויהי רצון

פֿה פֿראג לפ״ק
ע״י גרשם בן מהר״ר בצלאל כץ זצ״ל מחוקק

ספר
הקדמת הרבנית
מנקת רבקה[1] ויניקהו דבש מסלע[2]

ראה ראיתי[3]. בלבבי הגיתי. קולי הרימותי וקראתי[4]. הנה עתה באתי[5]:
והיום יצאתי. ובאר מים מצאתי[6]. והאבן הגדולה מן הבאר גליתי[7]:
וממנו שתיתי. ועוד צמיתי: ואמרתי בלבבי. אלכה ואביא. לקרובי
וקרובתי. ותגלני עצמותי[8]: שישתו לימים אורך. לקיים מה שנאמר שתה מים
מבורך[9]. ומברכך מבורך[10]. וכל החוסים בצילך[11]. שכן הבטחתני על ידי נביאך.
לא ימושו מפי זרע זרעך[12]. וגם אני אמתיך[13]. בת עבדיך[14]. ופרשת עלי כנפיך[15].
שלא אבוש בפיקודיך. כי גברו עלי חסדיך[16]. לקיים אמרתיך. וגם אני אבא
אחריך. ומלאתי את דברך[17]. [ככתו'] בתורתך[18]. כי כל טובתי בל עליך[19].
ומשכיני אחריך[20]. ואביטה אורחותיך[21]. כי נר לרגלי דבריך[22].
למען תצדק בשופטיך[23]. כי אתה קרוב לכל
קוראיך[24]. ולכל חפצים ליראתיך.

יזכו לחזות בנועם

פניך[25]:

ואפריון נמטי להנעלה ר׳ עזריא נקר׳ זיסקינד בן הר״ר שמואל המכונה ר׳ זנוויל טיימר מק״ק
פוזנן אשר שם נפשו בכפו והזיל כסף מכיסו עד אשר הוציא הספר הזה לאורו כדי
לזכות בו רבים:

---

[1]Gen. 35:8.   [2]Deut. 32:13.   [3]Exod. 3:7.   [4]Cf. Gen. 39:15.   [5]Cf. Num. 22:38.   [6]Cf. Gen. 26:19.   [7]Cf. Gen. 29:2.   [8]Cf. Ps.
51:10.   [9]Prov. 5:15.   [10]Cf. Gen. 27:29; Num. 22:6; 24:9.   [11]Cf. Ps. 18:31, 34:23; II Sam. 22:31.   [12]Cf. Isa. 59:21.   [13]Cf. I
Sam. 25:25.   [14]Cf. Ps. 115:16.   [15]Cf. Ruth 3:9.   [16]Cf. Ps. 117:2.   [17]I Kings 1:14.   [18]Cf. II Chron. 31:3; 35:26.   [19]Cf. Ps.
16:2.   [20]Songs 1:4.   [21]Ps. 119:15.   [22]Ps. 119:105.   [23]Cf. Ps. 51:6.   [24]Cf. Ps. 76:5; 145:18.   [25]Cf. Ps. 27:4.

11 בכתו K 1618;   P 1609 כתהו

דאש ווערט רידן וויא זיך איין אשה זאל פירן. וויא זיא אירן גוף זאל
צירן. די אירי נשמה ניט וויל פר לירן:

דוד המלך ע״ה) האט גשריבן אין (תהילים) דען פסוק (
שמעי בת וראי [והטי] אזניך ושכחי עמך ובית אביך¹ ויתאו המלך יפיך כי [הוא] אדוניך
5   והשתחוי לו²) דאש איז טייטש היר מיר צו מיין טאכטר אונ׳ זיך נייג דיין אורן אונ׳
פר געש דיין פאלק אונ׳ הויז דיין פאטר דא ווערט דער קיניג הקב״ה דיין
שונהייט גילושטן דען ער איז דיין הער אונ׳ נייג דיך צו אים דאש מדרש³ גיט
אזו אין פרשת לך לך עש גיט אויף אברהם אונ׳ שרה דא זיא (הקב״ה) האט
היישן אויש אירן לנד גין דא האט ער צו זיא גיזאגט זיא זאלין פר געשן איר פאטר
10 אונ׳ מוטר אונ׳ איר משפחה (רצה לומר) זיא זאלין זיך מרחיק זיין פון
אירן עלטרין מעשים דא ווערט הקב״ה גילוסטן אירי שונהייט דאש מיינט אירי
מעשים טובים) אויך מאג איך דען פסוק אזו אויש ליגן אונ׳ אזו דרשן דז
דוד המלך ע״ה) דען פסוק גיזאגט האט אויף איין בת ישראל דיא איין מאן
האט גינומן דיא זאל זיך אזו אין איין דרך פיר נעמן אונ׳ אויף איין תכלית)
15 גידענקין דאש מיינט אזו דאש זיא זאל פר געשן דיא (מעשים) אונ׳ וואל טאגין
דיא זיא בייא איר עלטרין האבין גיהט צו מיר זעהן אלי טאג אז איין פאטר אונ׳
מוטר איר קינד פר ענטפרין וועז עש שון גלייך ניט רעכט טוט (מכח אהבה)
אז דער פסוק גיט (על כל פשעים תכסה אהבה)⁴ דרום גיט דער מזמור זיא
זאלין דיא זעלביגן שיבושים פר געשין אונ׳ זאלין זיך גוטה (מעשים טובים)
20 אן נעמין דרויף גיט דער פסוק (ויתאו המלך יפיך⁵) דאש מיינט הקב״ה ווערט
לושט האבין צו דייני מעשים טובים אז דר פסוק אויך גיט (הנך יפה רעיתי⁶)
דאש איז טייטש דו בישט שין מיין גיזעלין מיט (מעשים טובים) אז דער פסוק
אויך וויטר גיט כל כבודה בת מלך פנימה ממשבצות זהוב לבושה⁷) דש איז טייטש
וען איין אשה איין צנועה איז אונ׳ בלייבט אין אירן הויז דא רעכנט זיא
25 הקב״ה פר איין טאכטר מיר אז דיא זיך צירט מיט אייטל גים גאלד דרויף גיט דר
מזמור וויטר (תחת אבותיך יהיו בניך⁸.) דאש איז טייטש דו ווערשט פרומה
קינדר האבן די דא ווערין (ממלא מקום אבותהם) זיין מיט אירי מעשים טובים
נון/

¹Ps. 45:11.   ²Ps. 45:12.   ³Tanhuma, Lekh Lekha 3.   ⁴Prov. 10:12.   ⁵Ps. 45:12.   ⁶Songs 1:15; 4:1.   ⁷Ps. 45:14.   ⁸Ps. 45:17.

4 והט P1609 K1618 | הו P1609 K1618

[3a] נון זעהן מיר וואל דז (דוד המלך ע״ה) האט גירעט אויף איין (בת ישראל דיא
זיך אין גוט דרך גיווינן זאל דארויף האט שלמה המלך ע״ה אין שיר השירים
גיזאגט (אחות לנו קטנה ושדים אין לה מה נעשה לאחותינו ביום שידובר בה⁹ אם
חומה היא נבנה עליה טירת כסף ואם דלת היא נצור עליה לוח ארז¹⁰ רש״י¹¹ מלט

5   דען פשט עש גיט אויף דיא (אומה הישראלית) דיא אין דען גלות זיין וועז שון
די (אומות העולם) אויף ישראל טרבלטן עלילות וועז אבר ישראל בישטין וויא איין
מויאר קעניין זיא אין נישט טון אבר דר (ילקוט¹²) שרייבט עש גיט אויף די תורה
די איז גליבט צו איין אשה אז דער פסוק גיט (אמרי לחכמה אחותי את¹³) דז איז
טייטש זאג צו דר חכמה דוא בישט מיין שוועשטער אוני היישט זיא קטנה דאז מיינט

10 אזו די תורה איז קליין אן צו זעהן אוני איז גרוש מיט מצות אויף מאג איך דען פשט
אזו זאגין דז שלמה המלך ע״ה האט גירעט אויף איין בת ישראל דיא דא נאך יונג
איז וואש זאלין מיר טון מיט אונזרי שוועשטער אן דען טאג אז מיר מיט איר רידן זאלן
ווערט זיא זיך הלטן אז איין מויאר דיא זיך מיינט דז זיא זיך וערט בכשרות הלטן אין
אל אירי מעשים וויא אש איין בת ישראל צו שטיט דא ווערט זיא זולה זיין דז זיא

15 ווערט קינדר האבן תלמידי חלכמים דיא דא ווערין אזו חשוב זיין אז איין גיביא מיט
זילבר אודר אז ער שפריכט (שדים אין לה¹⁴) דא מיינט דער פסוק איינ׳
דיא דא איז יונג פר וויישט איז גיווארין איין יתומה די דא קיין פאטר נאך מוטר
האט שדים דיא טייטש פאטר דיא מוז מן מין שטראפין אז איין אנדרה
אודר איינה דיא דא אין פרעמדן לנדן קומט איין וועק פון אירן עלטרן אוני׳ גיט

20 אונ׳ אונגיצוגן דיא איז גלייך וויא איין יתומה דארויף ווערט דר פסוק אזו רידן)
אם חומה היא¹⁵ ווערט זיא זיין אז איין מויאר דיא דא בישטיט וועז מן גלייך
אויף איר שיסט (כלומר) עש מיינט זיא ווערט מקבל מוסר זיין אונ׳
ווערט זיך לאזין שטראפין אונ׳ ציאין צו אירין גוטן דא גיט דר פסוק וייטר נבנה
עליה טירת כסף¹⁶ דא ווערט איוף איר גיבוט ווערין פאלש מיט אייטל זילבר

25 (כלומר) זיא ווערט אזו הוך גיהלטן ווערין דא גיט דער פסוק וייטר אם
דלת היא¹⁷ דאש מיינט ווערט זיא ניט (מקבל מוסר) זיין אונ׳ ווערט ניט
פאלגין אונ׳ ווערט איין יוצאנית זיין איין אויש לויפרן דא וועלין מיר זי גלייכן
צו איין /

⁹Songs 8:8.   ¹⁰Songs 8:9.   ¹¹Rashi on Songs 8:8.   ¹²Yalkut, § 994.   ¹³Prov. 7:4.   ¹⁴Songs 8:8.   ¹⁵Songs 8:9.   ¹⁶Songs 8:9.
¹⁷Songs 8:9.

[3b] צו איין טאבֿיל פֿון טעני האלץ דיא דא דיא ווירום אויף עשן (כלומר) זיא ווערט

קיין קיום האבן אויף דעם ווערט שלמה המלך ע״ה אויך גירעט האבן דען פסוק

חכמת נשים בנתה ביתה [אֵיולֵת]¹⁸ בידה תהרסנה דאז איז טייטש די קלוקייט דר

ווייבר בויט איר הויז אבר איין נערין צו פֿירט איר הויז מוט ווילוג איז מיר קשה אויף

5 דען פסוק ער רעט (חכמת לשון רבים) דר נאך רעט ער זיא בויט איר הויז

(לשון יחיד) דא מאג איך דען פסוק אויך אזו אויש ליגן ער האט אויף צווייא

ענינים גרעט פֿון איין אשה. ערשטליך חכמת הגוף דז איין אשה חכמה מוז

ברוכֿין אויף אירן גוף אז איך אי״ה ווער שרייבן. דער נאך אויף חכמת הנשמה

אז איך אי״ה אלש וויל שרייבן איטלבֿז אין זיינם עניין: נון וויל איך דיא פסוקים נאך

10 קומן אונ׳ וויל אויך רידן דער פֿון מיט איינר בת ישראל אונ׳ בפֿרט מיט איינר יוגנט

די זיך נאך ניט פֿיל גוטן האט אונ׳ וויא זיא זיך זול הלטין וואו אן בלנגן איז אירן גוף דר צו

גיהארט גרושי חכמה וויא דר פסוק שפריבֿט (חכמת נשים בנתה ביתה¹⁹)

דאז מיינט דען גוף דען הייושט ער (ביתה) אויך גפֿינדן מיר אין (פֿיט)

פֿון יום כפור דז ער שפריבֿט וויא דען בעל הבית דער זיין הויז פֿר וואושט דז מיינט

15 אויף דען גוף דרום שפריבֿט ער אויף איין אשה דאש זיא מוז גרושי חלמה ברוכֿן וואו אן

בלנגן איז אירן (גוף מה שאין כן) ביא איינם מאן דערף עש ניט אזו זיין דען

איין אשה מוז איין צייט פֿר אנדר הלטין דר נאך דיא צייט איז פֿון דעם דערף

איך ניט פֿיל שרייבן דען איין איטלבֿי אשה ווייש עז זעלברט וואל וויא זי זיך זאל הלטן

זיא זאל זונשט קרג זיין אונ׳ שפֿארין אבר אין דער צייט זאל זיא זיך פֿר זעהן דז זיא

20 אירין גוף ניט פֿר דערבט דער נאך קענט זיא זיך ניט כשרן דרויף האט שלמה מלך

ע״ה גזאגט איולת בידה תהרסנה²⁰ דאש מיינט אזו די נרהייט צו פֿירט איר הויז

מוטוויליג אויף דאש גיט דער פסוק (כל ערום יעשה בדעת)²¹ דאז איז טייטש

איין איטליכר קלוגר טוט אלש מיט זין אונ׳ וויץ. אויך דרשת דיא גמרא²² (יודע

צדיק נפֿש בהמתו)²³ דאז מיינט איין איטליבֿר פֿרומר יוד דער ווייש וואז

25 זיינר בהמה נוט טוט מכל שכן זיין וויב אויך שרייבֿן [אונזרין] חלמים ז״ל פֿיל פֿון דען

זלין דז דר בן אדם זאל גוואָרנט זיין דז ער זיין גוף זאל שונן דז ער נישט אונגזונדש

עשט דען וואו ער חס ושלום קרנק ווער קענט ער פֿיל מצות ניט הלטין דיא ער טון

קאן /

---

¹⁸Prov. 14:1.   ¹⁹Prov. 14:1.   ²⁰Prov. 14:1.   ²¹Prov. 13:16.   ²²B. Ketubbot 63a; B. Nedarim 50a.   ²³Prov. 12:10.

3 אֵיולֵת P1609 K1618 | 25 K1618; אוזרי P1609

[4a] קאן ווען ער גיזונט איז אויך שרייבט דער (מיימוני[24]) אויף דען פסוק (שומר
פיו ולשונו שומר מצרות נפשו[25] דז מיינט אזו דער זיין צונג היט פר לשון הרע. און'
זיין מויל פון אונגזונט' אכילות דז פיל חליות חס ושלום דער פון קומן דרום רעט דר
פסוק (כפל לשון פיו ולשונו) מכל שכן איין אשה דרויף האט שלמה [המלך] ע'ה

5   גזאגט (איולת בידה תהרסנה[26]) דאז מיינט דיא נרהייט צו פירט איר הויז מוט
וויליג אויף אויף דעם האט שלמה המלך ע'ה אויך גיזאגט (בחכמה יבנה הבית
ובתבונה יתכונן[27] ובדעת חדרים ימלאו כל הון יקר ונעים[28])
דאז איז טייטש מיט דער קלוגהייט ווערט גיבוט דאז הויז (רצה לומר)
דאז מיינט אויך חכמת הגוף דז דא גלייך איז צו איינם בית אז אויך פארט גשריבן

10   האב און' מיט דער פר שטעגנדיג קייט ווערט דאז אן גיבריית דאז מיינט (חכמת
הנפש) דאז איז דיא נשמה וויא דיא אשה איר נשמה זאל ביווארנן און' מיט דען
גוטין זין ווערן אן גפילט אירי קאמרין מיט אייטל קעשטליכי און' ווירדגי תלבשטים
(רצה לומר) ווען זיא אירן גוף און' נשמה ווערט אין דען גוטן דרכים פירין דוא
ווערט זיא זולכה זיין קינדר צו האבן דיא דא ווערן ווירדיג און' קעשטליך גיהלטין

15   זיין מין אז דאש גים גאלד אויף אויך דאז דערף מן ניט פיל (ראיות) צו ברעגגן אויך
לערנון מירש אויף דען פסוק (ויעש להם בתים[29] דאז איז טייטש און' ער מכט
זיא היזר דאז שטיט בייא דיא יולבבד און' מרים (ויהי כי יראו המילדות את האלהים[30]
דאז איז טייטש דרום דז זיא יראת שמים אין זיך גיהט דא האט אין השם
יתברך זעלכי היזר גבויט [גבויט] דז זיא האבן זולכה גיווענזין דז פון אין קומן איז כהנים לויים

20   און' מלכים דרום שטיט אויך בייא בצלאל דער פון מרים קומן איז (וימלא אותו רוח
אלהים בדעת ובתבונה ובחכמה[31]) דאז איז טייטש און' ער דער פילט אין
דען גמיט גו*טש מיט זין און' פר שטעגדיקייט און' קלוקייט אויף דאז שרייבט (
ראשית חכמה[32]) עש זייא איין איש אדר איין אשה דיא דא (יראת שמים)
אין זיך האט דיא איז זולכה דז דער (רוח הקודש) זאל אויף איר רואן. דרום זאל

25   זיך איין איטליבי אשה הלטין (בקדשה ובטהרה) אז אונזרי חכמים שרייבן
אז אלש אן דער אשה גלעגין איז אז מירש אויך גפינדן אין דר פרואן בוך[33] דז פיל אן
דר אשה מחשבה גלעגן איז אז דז מדרש[34] גיט אין (כי תבא ברוך פרי בטנך
ופרי אדמתך.[35]) דאז איז /טייטש

[24]Maimonides, *Hilkhot De'ot*, 4, 15. [25]Prov. 21:13. [26]Prov. 14:1. [27]Prov. 24:3. [28]Prov. 24:4. [29]Exod. 1:21. [30]Exod. 1:21. [31]See Exod. 35:31. [32]*Reshit Hokhmah*, I, p. 646, § 72. [33]*Eyn shoyn Froyenbuykhleyn*, fol. 5a. [34]Devarim Rabbah 3.5. [35]Deut. 28:4.

4 K1618; המלט P1609 | 19 גבוט P1609 K1618

[4b] טייטש דיא פרולט פון דיינם בויך ווערט גיבענשט זיין און' דיא פרולט פון דיינר
ערדן הקיש פרי [בטן] לפרי האדמה דר פסוק גלייכט דיא פרולט פון דען בויך
צו דען פרולט צו דער ערדן צו דער ערדן דאש מיינט אזו ווען איין גערטנר וויל האבן דאש זיין
גארטן זאל גוטי גוטי פירות טראגן אודר גוטי וואל גישמקה קרייטר זאלין וקשן דא מוז
5 ער זיך גאר גאר וואל מיאן און' גרושן פלייש אן ליגן און' מוז דיא קרקע גאר וואל אויש
אקרון און' מוז דיא ביזה וואורצלן אלי אויש גראבן דז גאר קיני דא בלייבט ווען נוא
דיא קרקע גנץ ריין איז ריין מוז ער דען זאמן גאר ריין אזו זאמן גאר ריין אזו איין אשה
ווען זיא וויל פרומה זעליגה קינדר האבן דיא איין גו*טש דינשט און' פארלט זאלין
10 גיראטן דא מוז זיא זיך גאר וואל מתקן זיין מיט אירי מעשים טובים און' זאל זיך פון
ביזה מעשים מרחיק זיין וויא וואל זיא אלי ווען מחויב איז דאך אין דער צייט אזו
בלד אז זיא היבט אן צו טראגין זאל זיא זיא נזהר זיין מער אז איין אנדר מאל דז זיא קיין
ליגן זאל זאגן אודר רכילות טרייבן אויך זאל זיא נישט בגניבה נעמן ווען עש גלייך
איין דבר מועט איז דען דאש קינד מעלט ח"ו דר דאך גיראטן איין זעליכה אשה זאל
15 זיך אייטל מעשים טובים אן נעמן און' זאל גערן הערן צו לערנן און' צו דרשות גין
דא ווערין דיא קינדר אזו גיראטן אז מיר גיפינדן אין אונזר הייליגה תורה כתיב
אונזר מוטר רבקה דאר בייא שטיט גישריבן (ויתרוצצו הבנים בקרבה[36]) דא מלט
(רש"י[37]) דען פשט ווען זיא גינג פר (ע"ז) דא האט עשו ארויש גיוואלט ווען זיא
איז גנגן פר בתי כנסיות און' בתי מדרשות דא האט יעקב ארויש גיוואלט נוא
20 ווערט מתורץ ווערין וואו עשו עש האט קומן איז דז יעקב פרום איז גיוועזן דרום דאש
איר כוונה איז גיוועזן אויף אויף דער תורה און' מעשים טובים און' אז עשו איז גיראטין
איז האט עש עש די וויא צדקות פר זינט דז זיא פר (ע"ז) פיר גנגן איז און וויא וואל קיין
כוונה דרוף האט גיהט נאך האט זיא זיא ניט זעלין דר פיר פר איבר גין דוראן האטש
דיא צדקות וואש פר זינדיקט אז דיא גמרא[38] אויך גיט איינר זאל איהר זאל פר איין
25 בית זונות) און' זאל ניט גין פר (בית ע"ז) מיר לערנן עש אויש דען פסוק
אל תקרב אל פתח ביתה[39] דא דרשת דיא גמרא[40] אויף ע"ז אויף לערנן עש טייטש ניט
דוא זאלשט גינעהן צו דר טיר פון דר ע"ז וויא וואל אונזרי (מפרשים) מאכן
פיל/

[36]Gen. 25:22.   [37]Rashi on Gen. 25:22.   [38]B. Avodah Zarah 17a.   [39]Prov. 5:8.   [40]B. Avodah Zarah 17a.

2 K1618; בטו P1609

[5a] פיל תירוצים דרויף דיא איך דא הער דערף ניט צו שרייבן. נוא מכ״ש ש איין אנדרי
אשה דז זיא זיך זאל מרחיק זיין פון אלין דז דא ניט גוט איז. אויף דאז ווערט דר
פסוק גרעט [האבן] חכמת נשים בנתה ביתה [איולת] בידה תהרסנה⁴¹ אויך לערנן
מירש אויש דען (פסוק ויבן ה׳ את הצלע⁴²) דאש איז טייטש אונ׳ ער בויאי דיא
5   ריפא דיא ער האט גנומן פון דען מענשין דא איז מיר קשה ווארום ער רעט בייא
דר אשה דאש (לשון) פון (בניין) דאש איז טייטש בויאן אונ׳ בייא דען מאן רעט
ער (לשון ויצר⁴³) אונ׳ ער בשוף אלא מיך דונקט אזו זיין דז דר עיקר בניין אן דר אשה
הענקט אז איך אובן גשריבן האב אויך לערנן מירש פון [אונזרי] מוטר שרה דז זיא צו
אברהם האט גשפראכין דוא זיא אים הגר האט גיגעבן (אולי איבנה ממנה⁴⁴
10 דאש איז טייטש לייכט איך ווער גבויט פון איר דא האט זיא אויך דאש (לשון פון
בניין) גרעט. דרום דז זיא אויך האט וועלין דען עולם בויאן דרום האט רחל אויך
דאש (לשון) גרעט אולי אבנה גם אנכי⁴⁵ אזו ואול אז שרה איז זולה גיוועזין.
דרום אויך זאגין מיר אין דיא שבע ברכות והתקין לו ממנו בניין עדי עד דאש איז
טייטש דז הש״י וויל האבן דז דר אדם זאל זיין כוונה. האבן אויף איין בניין
15 דאש מיינט דיא קינדר איינר פון דען אנדרן אדור מיינט דיא (נשמה) דז איר
בניין איז אין עולם הבא אויף איבג נוא מאג דר פסוק דז שלמה המלך ע״ה האט
גזאגט חכמת נשים בנתה ביתה וחצבה עמודיה שבעה⁴⁶ מאג אויך אויף דען דרך גין
אז איך אובן גשריבן האב דרום פון דען גוף אונ׳ (נשמה) דז די אשה זאל איר מחשבה אויף
אלי בידן האבן דא איז נוא טייטש פון דען פסוק דיא קלוגי בוט איר הויז ציבן
20 זיילין וואש האט דר פסוק גמיינט דז ער רעט דווקא זיבן זיילין נוא דולט מיך זיין
דיא כוונה פון דען פסוק אזו וויל ער רעט דווקא זיבן דאש איז אונש ווישקליך
דז אונזרי (מפרשים⁴⁷) שרייבן אויף דיא שבעיות דז זיא אונורם ליבן גו*ט יתברך
שמו ליב זיין אז בייא (מעשה בראשית) האט דער (בורא יתברך שמו) אין זעקש
טאגין דיא וועלט בשפין אונ׳ האט דען זיבטין טאג גהיילגט דר נאך האט ער אונש
25 דיא (ימים טובים) גיבאטין זיבן טאג (פסח סוכות) דאש זיבנט יאר (שמיטה)
[זיבן] (שמיטה) דר נאך (יובל זיבן ספרים אין דר תורה (חודש השביעי ראש
השנה) זיבן מדברות זיין האט הקב״ה (מדבר סיני) אויז דער וואלט זיבן
[לעגדרן]

---

⁴¹Prov. 14:1.   ⁴²See Gen. 2:22.   ⁴³See Gen. 2:7.   ⁴⁴Gen. 16:2.   ⁴⁵See Gen. 30:3.   ⁴⁶Prov. 9:1.   ⁴⁷Va-yikra Rabbah 23.11.

3 האט P1609 K1618 | אוילת P1609 K1618 | 8 K1618; אחרי P1609 | 26 K1618; זבין P1609 | 28 K1618; לערדר P1609

[5b] לעגנדר האט ער זיך (ארץ ישראל) גנומן אויך איז משה רבינו דר זיבנט פון דען

אבות דער זולה איז גוועזין צו (מתן תורה) אויך איז דוד המלך דר זיבנט פון דען

ברידר גוועזין דז ער האט זולה צום (מלכות) גיוועזן אויך האט (הקדוש ברוך

הוא) זיבן הימל בשפין אונ' האט דען זיבטין צו זיינם גזעש אויז דר וילט אויך האט

5 (השם יתברך יוסף הצדיק) דען חלום פון שבע פרות אונ' שבע שבלם לאזין ווישין

אונ' נאך פיל שביעיות דיא איך ניט אל שרייבן וויל דען זיא האבן אל איין כונה אונ'

איר (כוונה) איז זיר טיף אונ' וויט גרייכט דז מיר ניט פיל דר פון רידן קעניין אונ'

אויך דרום זיין מיר דען חלום מטיב זיבן מאלט אונ' אויך אן יום כיפור זאגין מיר זיבן

מאלט ה' הוא האלהים אונ' אויך אויף דען טעם האט אויך בלעם הרשע זיין כוונה

10 גיהט דז ער האט זיבן מזבחות גיבויט דז ער האט וועלין דיא אומה פון ישראל מבטל

זיין דיא איר כוונה אלש אויף דען (שביעיות) האבן אונ' איר בניין אויף דען עולם

(השביעי) האבן דער אייטל שבת איז אויף עולם הבא דאש איז דער אלף השביעי

אויף דען האט איוב אויך גרעט בשש צרה יצילך ובשבע לא יגע בך רע[48] דאש איז

טייטש פון זעקש צרה ווערט דיך הש״י מציל זיין דז מיינט אין די זעקש טויזינט יאר

15 אז די וועלט זאל שטין אונ' אין דען זיבטין טוזנט ווערשטו ווייטר פון קיין ביזין

ווישין צו זאגין אויף דען האט שלמה המלך ע״ה אויך מרמז גוועזן חכמת נשי' בנת' ביתה

חצבה עמודיה שבעה[49] אויך האט ער דרום גרעט (בלשון נקיבה) דז דיא אשה

כשרה די איר שבעה נקים רעכט הלט דא ווערט זיא זולה זיין דז זיא ווערט קינדר

האבן דיא דא דאש ווערן (משיג) זיין אונ' ווערין איין אמונה האבין אן דען (יחוד

20 יתברך) דער דא איז איין הער איבר די [שש (קצוות)] אונ' דאז איז אויך דער רמז

פון דען שביעות אונ' אזו איז אויך דיא כוונה פון דער (מנורה השם יתברך שמו)

האט משה רבינו גיהיישין מכין אונ' האט אים גיבאטין העלה שבעה נרותיה[50] אבור

דז ער האט גזאגט כן לששת הקנים היוצאים מן המנורה[51] דיא כוונה מוז אויך אזו

זיין דר גוף פון דער מנורה דאז איז מרמז אויף דיא אשה דיא דיא זעקש צנקין זיין די ו'

25 שערים דיא איך הינטן נאך דען שער שרייבן וויל אי״ה דיא אל אן איר העניגין ר״ל

ווען זיא הלט די זעקש שערים מיט דען ערשטן שער דער דא איז איין גוף צו דען

אנדרין זעקש שערים. דרום זאל אויך איין איטלכי אשה איר כוונה האבן דז זיא

זאל /

[48]Job 5:19.   [49]See Prov. 9:1.   [50]See Exod. 25:37.   [51]Exod. 25:33; 37:19.

20 ששה (קצוות) P1609 K1618

[6a] זאל זולּה זיין צו קינדר צו קינדר האבן דיא צו דען ז׳ מעלוֹת קענען קומן דאש מיינט דר פסוק

וחצבה עמדיה שבעה[52] אויף איין זילּי אשה גיט אויך דר פסוק לא תירא

לביתה משלג כי כל ביתה לבוש שני[53] דאש איז טייטש זי דערף זיך ניט צו פערלטין

פר דען גיהנם אז דר פסוק גיט תשלג כצלמון[54] אז דר ראשית חכמה[55] דרשת אונ׳

5 אזו האט דוד המלך ע״ה אויך גיזאגט אשתך כגפן פוריה בירכתי ביתך[56] דאש איז

טייטש דיין וייב ווערט זיין אז איין ווין שטיאק דער דא שטיט אן דר זיט פון דיין

הויז דא דרשת דיא גמרא[57] דען פסוק (מה גפן פריה לברכה אף אשה פריה לברכה

) ווען מן איין זעליג קינד זיכט דא שפרילּט מן וואל דער מוטר דיא דאש קינד

גיטראגן האט אויף דאש האט דוד המלך ע״ה גירעט עליך השלכתי מרחם מבטן

10 אמי אלי אתה[58] דאש איז טייטש דוא איך נאך אין מיין מוטר לייב בין גווען האב

איך דיך דר קענט דז דוא מיין גו*ט בישט פון וועגן מיינר מוטר מחשבה טובה אויף

דאש האט (השם יתברך) גשפראכלין צו (ירמיה הנביא ע״ה בטרם יצרתיך מבטן

ידעתיך[59] דאן איז טייטש אי איך דיך האב בשפין אויז דיין מוטר בוייך האב איך דיך ליב

גיהט אויך דרשת דאש מדרש[60] דען פסוק (ברכו ה׳ אלהים ממקור ישראל[61] דאש איז

15 טייטש גלובט זייא גו*ט יתברך שמו אויז דען אורשפרונג ישראל דאז מיינט דיא

קינדר אין דר מוטר לייב דרום לובן גו*ט יתברך שמו דאש דא מיינט דוא [ישראל] זיין דורך דעם

ים גגין דא האבן דיא קינדר גזונגין (זה אלי ואנויהו[62] דאן איז

טייטש דאש איז מיין גו*ט אונ׳ איך וויל בשיין אין דאש קינד האט די ברוסט אויז דען

מויל לאזין גין אונ׳ האט שירה גזונגין דאז לערנן מיר אלש אויך דען פסוק (אלהים

20 ממקור ישראל[63] אפילו דאש קינד אין דר מוטר לייב האט גיזונגין שירה אויף דש הט

שלמה המלך ע״ה גזאגט יהי מקורך ברוך ושמח באשת נעורייך[64] דז איז טייטש דיין

אורשפרונג ווערט גבענשט זיין ווען דוא דיך ווערשט משמח מיט דיין וייב דאז

מיינט איין אשה אשה חשובה דיא איר מחשבה אויף אייטל גוטים איז אונ׳ אזו איין אשה די

זאל זיך הלטין צו אייטל פרומן לייטן אונ׳ זאל זיך גוויין דריין דז זי אין טייטשי ספרי׳

25 לייאט קאן דען זי ניט לייאן דא זאל זיא צו היארן לייאן אדור צו הערן דרשות אז

מיר גפין בי דבורה הנבי׳ דז זי הט גזאגט ליבי לחוקקי ישראל[65] דז איז טייטש מיין

הערץ הענקט מיר צו דן לערנר ישראל דרום איז זי זולּה גוועזן דז די גרוש ישועה

צו ישראל דורך איר איז גשען ווייל זי די לערנר הט גינשטג גיהט /אויך

[52]Prov. 9:1. [53]Prov. 31:21. [54]Ps. 68:15. [55]*Reshit Hokhmah*, I, p. 267, § 75. [56]Ps. 128:3. [57]Va-yikra Rabbah 36.2. [58]Ps. 22:11. [59]See Jer. 1:5. [60]Midrash Tehillim 68:14. [61]See Ps. 68:27. [62]See Exod. 15:2. [63]See Ps. 68:27. [64]Prov. 5:18. [65]Judg. 5:9.

16 K 1618; ישראל P 1609

[6b] אויך מאג דיא כוונה פון דער מנורה אויך אזו זיין דז איין אשה טובה דער צו גלייך
איז אזו וואל אז ער גלייכט איין אשה טובה צו אונזרי תורה דען מיר לערנן פון דען
פסוקים חכמת בנתה ביתה66) גיט אויף דיא תורה אונ' אויף איין אשה טובה
דען (שלמה המלך ע"ה) האט משלי אוי גלאשן מיט (אשת חיל) אונ' האטש

5   אויך דרום דען אלף בית נאך גימאכט אונ' האטש זונשט אין (משלי]) ניט מין
גטאן דז מן זאל וויישן דז איין אשה טובה איז גיוואגן קיגן דער גנצי תורה אונ' אזו
וואול אז אונזרי תורה אן איין (אות) ניט קאן זיין אזו אויך איז איין אשה טובה
זאל גנץ זיין מיט אלי (מעשים טובים) קיגן גו*ט יתברך שמו אונ' קיגן דען לייטן
אונ' אזו וואול אז אונזרי ליבי תורה וויל דען האבן דז מיר אירי מצות זאלין הלטין דרום דז

10 זיא אונש אונזרין לון וויל געבן אזו אויך איז איין אשה טובה די זעך גערין דז אירי
קינדר זעליג ווערן דרום איז זיא אויך גלייך צו דער מנורה הטהורה דא איז טייטש
צו דעם ריינין לייכטר דען השם יתברך האט (משה רבינו גוויזן אין הימל וויא ער
זיין זאל אונ' האט אים אין ביפולין ער זאל זיא מאכן אין איין שטיק פון לויטרים
ריין גאלד נון וויל זי גימאלט איז גיוועזן אין איין שטיק אונ' פון לויטרים ריין גאלד

15 דא מן איינרלייא גאלד זיין דער צו גיוועזט אונ' דאש אלדר בעשטי דען מן גפינד
פילר ליי גאלד אונגרש גאלד קרונן גאלד ריינש גאלד דז איך וואלט זאגן די קנעפ
אדור דיא בעכיר אדור דיא בלומן דיא דראן זיין גימלט גיוועזין דז איך וואלט צו
איין איטליכן ביזונדר גאלד האבן גינומן דאז האט נינט קעניין גזין וויל עש אין איין
שטיק איז גיערבט גיוואַרדן אזו אויך איז דיא כוונה פון דר אשה וון איר מחשבה

20 לטובה איז אונ' דען מאנש מחשבה אויך לטובה דא ווערין אויך פון אין קומן קינדר
דיא דא ווערין אויך לויטר אונ' ריין זיין מיט איר פרומקייט דרום רעט דער פסוק
כן לששת הקנים היצאים מן המנורה67) דאז איז איין רמז אויף דיא קינדר דיא דא
פון דער אשה קומן דז זי כשרים ווערן זיין. אויך מאג איך דיא כוונה זאגין זונדר
גלייך אז די די מנורה דיא האט מען מיט בום איל גלייכט דאז איז איין דבר ידוע איין

25 זך די ווישיגליך איז כל זמן אלי צייט דז דיא ליכט שערבן פון דער מנורה וואו מען
דא איל דריין גיגאשין האט דאז האט מוזין ריין זיין אונ' אויך דאז בום איל אונ'
אויך דיא צוכין ווען עז אלש איז אזו גיוועשט דז אלש ריין איז גיוועשט דא האט דז /ליכט

66See Prov. 9:1.   67See Exod. 25:33; 37:19.

5 K1618; P1609 מישלי

[7a] ליכט אויך לויטר אונ' ריין גיברענט וויל איין טראפֿן דרינן גיוועזט אבר ווען איינש
ניט ריין ווער גוועשט עש זיא דיא שערבן וואו מען דאז איל דריין גיגאשין האט
אדר דז בוים איל אדר דיא צולין דא האט דאש ליכט שון טונקל גברענט אונ' לעשט
אויך בלד אויף פֿר די צייט. אזו אויך די אשה ווען זי פֿרום אונ' זעליג איז מיט מעשים
5 טובים אונ' אויך דער מאן אזו האבן זיא אויך זעליגי קינדר גיהט ער אויך (מעשים
טובים) אן זיך האבן אונ' לייכטן אין דער תורה דיא דא גגליכן איז צו איינם ליכט
אונ' דער פֿלם פֿון דען ליכט איז גיגליכן צו דער נשמה אז דער פסוק גיט נר אלהים
נשמת אדם[68] אויך גפֿינט מען צו צייטן ווען שון די לאמפ גאר ריין איז אונ' אויך
דאז איל אונ' אויך דיא צולין דא גיט עז דענוך אויז אז ווען איין ווינט קומט דורך
10 איין פֿענשטר אונ' לעשט דאז ליכט אויז אונ' העטש וואל קענן ביווארן. אזו אויך
ווען שון פֿאטר אדר מוטר פֿרום זיין אונ' דאז קינד אויך איין תלמיד איז דא קומט
השם ישמרינו) איין ווינט דורך איין פֿענשטר אונ' לעשט דאז ליכט אויז (כלומר)
[מן] פֿר זינט זך אן הצד דער זיך אבר פֿיר זעהן דער קאן עש עש וואל ביוואורן דז
קיין ווינט קאן דר [צו] קומן צו דעם ליכט אזו אויך דיא אשה מוז גיווארנט זיין דז זיא
15 אכטונג מוז האבן אויף איר הויז גזינד דז ניט ח"ו עבירות גשעהן אין אירן הויז
ווען זי שון קיין טייל דרן הט דז ניט דר אונשולדג מוז ח"ו אנטגעלטן אז ספר חסדי'
שרייבט ווען ח"ו איין עברה אין זיינם הויז גשילט אונ' איינר איז אין איר הויז דער עש
ווערן קאן אונ' טוט עז ניט דא מוז ער (השם ישמרינו) דאז באד אויז גיסין גשעהן
דען עבירות אין איין שטאט דער זעלביג דער עש ווערן קאן אונ' טוט עש ניט
20 אזו מוז דער זעלביג ח"ו דאש אנגעלטן גשילט דען איין עבירה אים לנד דא מוז דר
זעלביג גדול הדור דער עש ווערן קאן בעו"ה אנטגעלט דז מיר בעו"ה זעהן דז אין
קורצין צייטן זעלכי גדולי הדור אונ' גרושי חסידים אין אירן יונגין יארן בעו"ה זיין
איין ועק גגנן (ה"י יסיר מעלינו שבטו) ער זאל אב טאן פֿון אונש זיין צארן
דאך מוז איך שרייבן פֿון וואז איך גזעהן האב דען גרושן חילול השם בעו"ה דער דא
25 גשילט מיט אויך דען שקצות אין רייסר לנד דאש גרוש טריפֿות האב איך גזעהן דז זיא
אן פֿרייטאג צו נכט דא אידר מאן האט גישלאפֿן דא האט זי דאז גפֿעס אב גיוושין
אונ' האט גנומן דאז מילכיג שעפֿל דיא זעלבגי (בעל ביתה) האט אויך קי גיהלטן
האט/

[68]Prov. 20:27.

13 אן P 1609 K 1618 | 14 K 1618; נו P 1609

[7b] אונ' האט דאז גיפֿעס אויז דען מילך שעפֿיל אב גשוועגקט דר נאך האב איך ווידר
גזעהן דז זיא האבן גענן גשעבֿט דא האט דיא שיקצה דיא קעפ גנומן אונ' האט זי
אין דען מילבֿגין שעפֿל גטאן אונ' האט זידנדיג וושיר דריבר גיגאשין אזו האב איך
עש דר בעל ביתה גזאגט האט זיא מיר גענטווערט איך גלויב עש ניט עש האט זיא פֿיל
5 יאר בייא מיר גדינט. דר נאך איז ווידר איין מעשׂה גישעהן בייא איין אנדרי יודין
האט אם יום כיפֿור צו מנחה לאזין דען אובֿן איין הייצן אונ' האט לאזין דיא שקצה
דיא פֿילין הינר אויף דר שׁול קומן איז דא איז נוא אלש אלש פֿערטיג גיוועזן אונ' איז
זעלברט מתחילה דר בייא גשטנדן אונ' האט גישפֿט מלש אזו אונ' אזו האב איך איך
גפֿרעגט ווארום האשׁטו דאשׁ גטאן איז עז דאך איין עבֿרה האט זיא מיר גענטווערט
10 איך האב עש אזו גזעהן אונ' אל מיין טאג האב איך אזו גיטאן. איך העט דאשׁ ניט
אן גשריבין אבר איין עונשין אלא אם כן מזהירין דש איז טייטש מן שעדיגט קיין דן מן
ווארניט אין פֿאר דרום דז עז נימר זאל גשעהן דרויף ווערט איך דר פֿסוק גין חכמת
נשׁים בנתה ביתה ואיולת בידה תהרסנה[69] דאש מיינט זיא צו פֿירט איר הוין
מוט וויליג דרום מוז איטלבֿי אשה גווארט זיין אונ' אויף איר הוין גינד אכטונג
15 האבין מיט איר זלין אונ' מיט אירין מאן אונ' מיט אירין קינדרן אונ' מיט אירין גזינד
עש איז אלש אן איר גלעגין אונ' בפֿרט שבֿועות אדור גו*ט בהיט דיא קללות דיא זאל
זיא ניט ליידין אין אירין הוין דען דיא [דעות] זיין ניט אל גלייך השם ישמרינו דא
לערנן מיר פֿון יעקב אבֿינו דז רחל איז דרום גשטארבין דער צדיק האט פֿון
נישׁט גוויישׁט נאך איז זיא זיא (נעגוש) גווארדין מכ״ש איין אנדרר דז ער זיך דר פֿיר
20 היטן זאל אויך האב איך האב גזעהן דז איינו האט פֿר לארין קעלניש צו איין העמד האט
זיא אן גהובין מקלל צו זיין דז מן דר אין גנומן האט זאל מן תכֿליכים דרויף מכין
דר נאך האט זיא דען קעלניש ווידור גפֿונדן אונ' האט איין העמד דרויף גמכֿט עש
איז בעו"ה ניט שׁלשׁים אן גשטנדן דא האט מן דעם מיט דען העמד אין דר ערד
גליגט דרום זאל מן [גיווארנט] זיין אן דען קללות אויך זאל איין אשה גיווארנט זיין אונ'
25 אכֿטונג אויף אירן הוין האבן דז עש ריינטליך זאל זיין אונ' בפֿרט ווא מן תפֿלה טוט
אדור ספֿרים זיין אדור בייא דר מזוזה אויך מיט אירם גנג מיט דען הארין אויך
אנדר צניעות דיא איך ניט דערפֿ גאר שרייבן אונ' טואן זיער נוט אויך האט אונזרי
תורה/

[8a] תורה אז גשריבן (לא יראה בך ערות דבר[70]) דאש איז טייטש עש זאל קיין שעניטליכי

זלין אז דיר גזען גווערדין אז דר פסוק גיט כי ה' אלהיך מתהלך בקרב מחניך והיה

מחניך קדוש[71] דא איז טייטש וון [גו*ט] דר מייאט זיך צווישן דיין שאר דרום זאל דיין

שאר הייליג זיין אויף דען גיט דר פסוק ווייטר ולא יראה בך ערות דבר ושב מאחרך[72]

5 ווען איר ח'ו איהר שאר ניט ריינטליך הלט אדר בצניעות מיט אייהרן גנג דא ווערט

זיך דיא שלינה ח'ו פון אייך אב טון אבר וואו איר אייך יוא ווערט בקדושה ובטהרה

הלטין דא ווערט דיא שלינה רואן אונטר ישראל. אויף דען עניין ווערט זיך אויך

רידן אז דיא גמרא[73] גיט חותמו של (הקב'ה אמת דא מיינט דאז אירשטי אות פון

א'ב אונ' דאש מיטלשטי די מ' אונ' דאש הינטרשטי די ת' דאז מיינט דז (השם יתברך

10 היה הוה ויהיה איז אונ' דר פסוק גיט אויך ראש דברך אמת[74] דאש מיינט דיא א' פון

אנכי ווען דר מענש ח'ו ניט אין רעכטין וועג גיט אונ' ברעלבט אן אנכי דא [נעמט]

(הקדוש ב'ה) אויך דיא א' פון אמת די וועק דא בלייבט איבר מת אז דיא גמרא[75]

גיט שלשה שותפין באדם אביו ואמו וקב'ה דאש איז טייטש דרייא האבן חברותה

אן דען מענשן קב'ה אונ' פאטר אונ' מוטר וון השי'י זיין חלק איין וועק נעמט דאז

15 איז דיא נשמה דא בלייבט ער מת אויף דעם האט דר פסוק גרעט ושב מאחרך[76]

דרום זאל איטלבי ורומו ורוא אונ' מאן מדקדק זיין אויף אל אירי מעשים אויף איטלכן

דיבר אונ' איטלכין טריט. ומי יתן דאש דיא זיא זיך זאלטין אן מיין זאגן קערן אולי ווער

איך אויף איין זלות דר פון האבן אז איך הב פארט גשריבן אז דיא זיך לאזין שטראפין זיא ווערן זיין גזיסט

תבא ברכת טוב[77] דאש איז טייטש אונ' דיא זיך לאזין שטראפין זיא ווערן זיין גזיסט

20 אונ' אויף זיא ווערין ברכות גוטי קומן. דאש אלש ריד איך מיט דען יונגן ווייברליך

אבור קיגן דען נשים צדקניות חלילה דז איך וואלט נוגע בכבודם זיין מי יתן דז איך

זאלט זולבה זיין מייני קינדש קינדר אין זעלבי מעשים טובים צו זעהן מיט אירן שול

גנג אונ' תפילית אונ' וואש זיא טואן מיט לומדי תורה גו*ט ית'ש זאל עש געבן דז עש

זאל לנג מיט ליב גווערין עד ביאות גואלינו אמן:

---

[70]Deut. 23:15. [71]See Deut. 23:15. [72]Deut. 23:15. [73]B. Shabbat 55a. [74]Ps. 119:160. [75]B. Niddah 31a. [76]Deut. 23:15.
[77]Prov. 24:25.

3 K1618; גו*ט P1609 | 11 K1618; נעמט P1609

[שער שני]

דאז איז דער אנדר שער. דאן ווערט רידן וויא זיך איין אשה קיגן אירן מאן זאל
הלטן. דיא מיט אננדר אין אירן ווֿעלין אלטין:

שלמה המלך ע״ה) זאגט אין (משלי אשת חיל עטרת בעלה ולֿרקֿב בעצמותֿיו
מבֿישֿה[1] דאז איז אזו טייטש איין פֿרויא דיא איז איין בידר וויב
5   איז דיא איז איין קרון פֿון אירן מאן אבר איין פֿר שעמט וויב דז מיינט דז זיך
אירר מאן מוז שעמן דיא איז איין פֿוילונג אין זיין בֿיין דיא דיא מפֿרשים[2] שרייבן אזו
וואל (השם ישמרינו קיין רפֿואה איז זיינם דיא איז בֿיין פֿולין אזו אויך האט דער
מאן קיין תקנה דער איין מאן זעלין אונ׳ זעלֿיג וויב דיא גמרא[3] דרשת דען פֿסוק אשת
חיל עטרת בעלה[4] דאז זעלֿבֿיג איז שרה דא הש״י האט דיא יוד פֿון שרה
10   גנומן אונ׳ האט זיא גטיילט מיט אברהם אונ׳ הט אברהם אין ה׳ גבֿן אונ׳ שרה איין
ה׳ הינטן אונ׳ דיא גמרא[5] זאגט ווייטר בעלה נתֿעטר בֿאשתו דאז איז טייטש עש
ווערט דער קעננט אין טור איר דאש מיינט וועין ער זיצט אונטר דען תלמידי
חלכֿים דיא דא היישין [זקֿנין] שער ערו דא ווערט ער דר קעננט דאז מיינט אזו איין
אשה כשרה דיא אירין מאן אן הלט צו זיינם לערנן אז מיר גֿפֿינדן אין דר גמרא[6] איין
15   תלמיד חכֿם האט זיינם זון איין וויב געבֿן צו מארגֿנש האט ער אין גֿפֿראגֿט וואש
האשטו פֿר איין [וויב]ן בקומין מצא או מוצא דא האט ער גֿעטוורט מצא דאש האט
ער אזו גמיינט דר פֿסוק זאגֿט מצא אשה מצא טוב ויפֿק רצון מה[7] דאש איז טייטש
דר דא גֿפֿינט איין אשה דיא דא פֿרום איז דר גֿפֿינט אלש גוט ער ציֿלֿט אויז דען
גוטין ווילין פֿון (הקדוש ברוך הוא) דאז מיינט השם יתֿברך טוט אל אירין רצון דא
20   האט ער אים וידר גֿפֿרעגֿט וויא וויישטא עש דז זיא פֿרום איז דא האט ער גֿעננטוורט
איך האבֿ גלערנט איין גוצי נלֿט דא האט זיא מיר גֿלֿייֿלֿט אויף דאש האט דוד המלך
ע״ה גרעט על זאת יתֿפלל כל חסיד אלֿיך לעת מצוא[8] דיא גמרא[9] דרשת פֿיל אויף
דען פֿסוק אבור איך ווילֿש ניט דא הער שרייבן אונ׳ זאג לעת מצוא זו אשה זו שלמה
המלך ע״ה הינטן אין משלי האט גשריבן אשת חיל מי ימצא וֿרחוק מפֿנינים מכֿרה[10]
25   דאש איז טייטש איין פֿרויא איין העלדין ווער קאן זיא גֿפֿינדן אונ׳ איז פֿער מער
ווען גים גאלד איז איר קויף שֿן דען אן איינר סחורה קאן איינר גווינן אדור פֿר
/לירין

---

[1]Prov. 12:4.   [2]Ibn Ezra on Prov. 12:4.   [3]Bereshit Rabbah 47.1.   [4]Prov. 12:4.   [5]Bereshit Rabbah 47.1.   [6]B. Berakhot 8a.
[7]Prov. 18:22.   [8]Ps. 32:6.   [9]B. Berakhot 8a.   [10]Prov. 31:10.

13 זקֿנו P1609 K1618 | 16 K1618: וויב P1609

[9a] לירין אדור איין אשה טובה ווער קאן זיא שצין וואש גוטש פון איר קאן קומין. אויך
דרשת די גמרא[11] השרוי בלא אשה שרוי בלא טובה בלי ברכה בלי כפרה בלי שלום בלי
חיים בלי עזר בלי שמחה) דאש איז טייטש דער דא איז אן וו״יב דער איז אן
טובה אן גוטש אן דר פסוק גיט לא טוב היות אדם לבדו[12] עש איז ניט גוט דז
5 דער מענש אליין זאל זיין בלי ברכה שנאמר להניח ברכה בביתך[13] דו זאלשט ברכה
אין דיין הוז לאזין בלי כפרה שנאמר וכפר בעדו ובעד ביתו[14] דר כהן זאל
פאר אום זיך אונ׳ זיין וו״יב אונ׳ קינדר פר געבן. (בלי שלום שנאמר וידעת כי
שלום אהליך[15]) דוא זאלשט וושין דז שלום איז אין דיין דאז מיינט ווען איין
אשה איז אין גצעלט איז שלום דא. בלי חיים שנאמר ראה חיים עם האשה[16] זיך
10 דאש לעבן מיט דיינם וו״יב. בלי שמחה שנאמר ושמחת אתה וביתך[17] וגו׳ דאש מיינט
דאש וו״יב דוא זאלשט דיך וריין אן דיין ימים טובים דוא אונ׳ דיין וו״יב)
בלי עזר שנאמר אעשה לו עזר כנגדו[18]) איך וויל אים איין וו״יב בשאפין דיא איא זאל
העלפין דא דרשת דיא גמרא[19] (זלה עזר לא זלה כנגדו) דאש]איזן[טייטש איז
איינר זולה דא איז אים איין הילף. איז ער ניט זולה איז זיא אימדאר ווידור
15 אים אונ׳ דרום שפרעלבט דר פסוק (על כל זאת יתפלל כל חסיד[20]) אונ׳ דרום האט
אדם הראשון גזאגט דא אים גו*ט יתברך האט חוה בשפין זאת הפעם עצם מעצמי
ובשר מבשרי לזאת יקרא אשה[21]) אונ׳ ניט לילות דען דר פיר שטיט גשריבן
(זכר ונקבה ברא אותם[22]) אזו האט ער גזעהן דז זיא איז ניט גוט גוועזין דא
האט ער זיא ניט וועלין האבן וויא דאש מדרש[23] גיט. דרום אויך שרייבט דר פסוק
20 בייא יעקב אבינו (מלא שבע זאת[24]) כלומר דוא מיינשט רחל איז אליין איין צדקות
לאה איז גלייך אזו איין צדקות אונ׳ דרום שפרילבט דר פסוק (גם את זאת[25]) איז
ר״ת מיט גוף אונ׳ ממון איז זיא אזו פרום אז רחל אונ׳ דרום גיט דר פסוק ווייטר)
(ויאהב גם את רחל[26]) אונ׳ ער האט רחל אויך ליב מיט דעז לאשט ער אונש ווישן
דז ער האט ליאה ליב גיהט אונ׳ רחל האט ער נאך ליבר גיהט דז ווייל זיא איז זיינר
25 מחשבה דיא אירשטי איז גוועשט דרום שפרעלבט דר פסוק גאלת בזרוע עמך בני
יעקב יוסף סלה[27]) דאש איז טייטש דוא האשט דר ליזט מיט דיינם ארם דיין
פאלק דיא קינדר יעקב יוסף אלי וועגן דא נענט ער יוסף אליין דרום ווייל ער פון
/רחל קומן

[11]Midrash Tehillim 59:2. [12]Gen. 2:18. [13]Ezek. 44:30. [14]Lev. 16:6; 11:17. [15]Job 5:24. [16]Eccles. 9:9. [17]Deut. 14:26.
[18]Gen. 2:18. [19]B. Yevamot 63a. [20]See Ps. 32:6. [21]Gen. 2:23. [22]Gen. 1:27. [23]Alpha-Beta de-Ben Sira 23a–b. [24]Gen.
29:27. [25]Gen. 29:27. [26]Gen. 29:30. [27]Ps. 77:16.

13 איו P 1609

[9b] רחל קומן איז דא איז זיא עיקר גוועזין. אויך גפֿינדן מיר בייא רות דוא בועז האט
גפֿרעגט למי הנערה הזאת[28] דא מלט רש״י[29] איז דען דר סדר אז איין מאן אז ער וואר
איין צדיק דז ער זאל נאך נשים זעהן אלא ער האט דרום אויף איר גפֿרעגט דען ער
האט פֿיל צניעות פֿון איר גזעהן וויא רש״י מלט און׳ דרום האט ער גשפֿראלכֿן)
5   הנערה הזאת[30] כלומר על זאת יתפֿלל[31] דרום שפּריכֿט דר פּסוק אויך הינטן)
ויאמרו כל העם אשר בשער הזקנים יתן ה׳ את האשה הבאה אל ביתֿךֿ כרחל וכֿלאה
אשר בנו שתיהם את בית ישראל[32] ויהי ביתֿךֿ כבית פֿרץ אשר ילדה תמר ליהודה מן
הזרע אשר יתן ה׳ לֿ מן הנערה הזאת[33] דאז איז טייטש אזו דא בועז האט רות
גנומן דא האבן אים דאש פֿאלק און׳ אלי דיא סנהדרין דיא ברכֿה געבן און׳ האבן
10   אזו גשפֿראלכֿין גו*ט זאל געבן דז דיא דאזיגי אשה דיא דא איין דיין הויז קומט דיא
זאל זיין אז רחל און׳ לאה דיא דו האבן גבויט דאז הויז ישראל און׳ זעצט רחל פֿר
לאה דרום דז זיא איז דיא ערשטע גוועזין אין זיינר מחשבה און׳ זאגט דרום רחל און׳
לאה און׳ ניט שרה אדור רבקה וייל עשו עשו איז פֿון זיא אין קומן און׳ פֿון רחל און׳ לאה איז
קיין פּסול קומן און׳ דרום זאל זיין הויז אזו דז דאז הויז פֿון פֿרץ אז זיא האט גוואונן תמר צו
15   יהודה פֿון דען זאמן דז ער וואֶרט געבן גו*ט צו דיר פֿון דר יונג ורויא די דאזיג
און׳ דרום שטיט בייא יעקב אבינו דא ער זיין קינדר האט צוואֶה גטאן (וזאת אשר
דיבר להם אביהם[35] האט ער אויך מרמז גוועזין דז זיא זאלֿין איר כוונה האבן אויף
פֿרומי ווייבר אז דיא גמרא אויך (דרשעת[36] לעולם ימכור אדם כל מה שיש
20   לו וישא בת ת״ח) דאז איז טייטש אייבֿג זאל איין מענש ור קופֿן אלש וואש
ער האט און׳ זאל זעהן אז ער איין בתֿולה נעמט דיא איין ת״ח טאכֿטער איז ווי וואל
דז בעו״ה איז דען דורות זעהן נאך אייטל גלֿט וועון שון דוא איין בת ת״ח איז ווען זי
קיין גלֿט האט זאל זיא מן זיא דוחה מיט בידי העני דרויף האט דוד המלך גרעט
(איש בער לא ידע וכֿסיל לא יבין אֶת זאתֿ[37]) דאז איז אזו טייטש דר נר
25   וויל ניט וויישן איין בת ת״ח אבֿור ער וועֶרֿט ניט זולֿה זיין דז ער וועֶרֿט קינדר
/האבן

[28]Ruth 2:5. [29]Rashi on Ruth 2:5. [30]Ruth 2:5. [31]Ps. 32:6. [32]See Ruth 4:11. [33]Ruth 4:12. [34]Ruth 4:12. [35]Gen. 49:28.
[36]B. Pesaḥim 49a. [37]Ps. 92:7.

[10a] האבן דיא דא ווערין פֿר שטין דיא תורה דיא היישט (זאת) אזו אויך

האט משה רבינו עליו השלום ישראל גיבענשט מיט (זאת הברכה[38]) אויך

[שטיט] בייא אהרן הכהן בזאת יבֹא אהרן[39]) בזכות התורה דיא דא היישט זאת

אונ׳ דרום מיט דעם דאזיגין איז אהרן אונ׳ משה אויך זכֹה גֹוועזט דז זיא צו דער

5 גדולה זיין קומן ווייא זיא אזו איין קעשטליכֿי מוטר האבן דיא תורה אויך גהט אויף משה רבינו

דרום זכֹה גֹוועזט דז ער האט דיא תורה מקבל גֹוועזט אונ׳ שפריבֿלט דר פסוק

וזאת התורה אשר שם משה[40] אונ׳ דרום האט משה רבינו ע׳׳ה יהודה פֿר זיין טוט

גבענשט (וזאת ליהודה[41] דז דאז מלכֹות בית דוד זאל פֿון תמר קומן ווייא דיא

(פרשנים[42]) מלֹין אויך דערף איך ניט אלֹש דא הער צו שרייבן דען עש שטיט אין

10 ורויאו ביכֹל[43] ווייא עש איז דער אשה איז גלעגין אונ׳ ברעֹנגט פיל ראיית דרויף

אויך גיט דר [פסוק] (בית והון נחלת אבות ומֹה׳ אשה משכֹלת[44] דאז איז

טייטש איין הויז אונ׳ [גוט] קאן איינר וואול פֿון עלֹטרין ירשין אבור איין קלוג וייב דא

מוז איינר פֿון גו*ט ית׳׳ש פֿר דינן אז אויך פֿארט האב גשריבן דז איין אשה מיט

אירי חכֹמה פיל קאן בוואורנן צום אירשטן וואז דו בלונגין איז אירן גוף דז זיא

15 [איטלכֹר] צייט איר רעלֹט טוט אויך מוז זיא איר נשמה בדענקין אונ׳ זאל

גדענקין דז דר העולם הזה ניט דר עיקר איז נייארט עולם הבא אויף דאז האט שלמה

המלך ע׳׳ה גזאגט חכֹמת נשים בנֹתֹה ביתֹה ואיוולתֹ בידה תהרסנה[45]) דיא גמרא[46]

דרשת דען פסוק (חכֹמת נשים) דאז גיט אויף און בן פלֹת וייב ואיוולתֹ דאז

איז קורח וייב דרום זאל איין איטלכֹי ורמוֹ ורויא אירין מאן אף רידן דז ער מיט

20 קיינם ביזן חבר זאל חברותֹה מכֹן אז אונזרי חכֹמים[47] גזאגט האבן (הרחק משכֹן רע

ואל תתחבר לרשע) אזו אויך איז קורח וייב גשעהן זיא האט אירין

מאן אן גרייצט אונ׳ גהעצט דז ער אויף משה [רבינו] ע׳׳ה קריגט האט אזו האט זיא

אויך אירין לון איין גנומן אבור און בן פלֹת וייב דיא האט להיפֿך גטאן האט אירין

מאן ניט וועלין גשטטין דז ער זיך זאל קריגן ווען קורח איז קומן אונ׳ האט אירין

25 מאן וועלין רופֿין דא האט זיא זיך

אין/

---

[38]Deut. 33:1. [39]Lev. 16:3. [40]Deut. 4:44. [41]Deut. 33:7. [42]Rashi on I Chron. 4:21. [43]*Eyn shoyn Froyenbuykhleyn*, fol. 33a.
[44]Prov. 19:14. [45]Prov. 14:1. [46]B. Sanhedrin 110a. [47]Avot de-Rabbi Natan, A, 1, 9.

3 שטיש P1609 | 11 פֿטוק P1609 | 12 גו*ט P1609 | 15 איטלנר P1609 | 22 רבינ P1609

[10b] אין איריך הארין גשטעלט וויא זיא זיך קעמין וואלט דר וואַרטן דז ער זאל וועק לויפן
דר מיט האט זי איריך מאן מציל גיוועזט. אדור דר פסוק איוולת [48] וגו׳) מיינט איזבל
אחאבש ווייב דיא איריך מאן אויך צו אלין ביזין אן גיהלטין האט דרום איז זיא אויך
אין בֿיז ענד גינומן אונ׳ איר מאן אונ׳ אירי קינדר אביר (ראשית חכמה [49]) שרייבט
5 (חכמת נשים [50]) דאז איז דבורה הנבֿיאה דאז איז אונזרי חכמים אין גרושי תמיה
זיא וואונדרן זיך דריבר דען פנחס הכהן איז אין דיא זעלבֿיגן צייטן גוועזן דז השם
יתברך אין גרושה אהבה האט צו אים גיהט אונ׳ האט זיין נבֿואה אויף אין אשה
לאזין רוען אונ׳ פנחס לאזין בלייבן אביר ער [51] שרייבט ווייטר אזו יעד עלי שמים וארץ
הימל אונ׳ ערד דיא זאלין מיין עידות זיין דז עש קיין חילוק איז בין איש ובֿין אשה בין
10 עבֿד ושפֿחה עש זיא איין אדור ווייב קנעכט אדור מייד דז דא זעליג איז דר
איז זולבֿה צו דען (רוח הקדש) אז מיר עש מאלט זעהן אונ׳ אויך ביא פרעה
טאכטר בתיה וואש זיא זולבֿה איז גיוועזן דרום אז זיא משה רבינו ע״ה האט דר צוגין
דא האט [גו*ט] יתברך שמו זעלברט דען נאמן גבֿן בֿתיה דאש איז דיא טאכטר
גו*טש אונ׳ איז זולכֿה גיוועזן דז זיא זיא לעבֿדיג אין דאש גן עדן קומן איז אונ׳ פֿיל דר
15 גלייכֿין דז איך ניט אלש וויל דא הער שרייבן דען עש גהערט אלש אויף זיין שטאט.
נון וועלין מיר ווייטר שרייבין וויא אונזרי חכמים [52] זאגן ווארום האט דיא דבֿורה אשת
לפֿידית [53] גיהיישין ווער איז דער לפֿידית גיוועזן דא זאגן אונזרי חכמים זכֿר לברכֿה
לפֿידית איז ברק גוועזן ווארום האט ער לפֿידית גיהיישין דרום דז דבֿורה האט צולך
אין בית המקדש גימכֿט אונ׳ האט זיא איריך מאן געבֿן דז ער זיא האט אן גיצונדן
20 אונ׳ אין דר צו אן גהלטין דז ער די תורה האט יום ולילה גלערנט דיא דא איז גיגעבֿן
וואַרדין אין דוניר אונ׳ אין בליץ דאש איז (לפֿידית וברקים) נוא איז צו פֿרעגן
ווען ער איר מאן אין גיוועזן ווארום האט זיא צו אים גשיקט דז ער זאל איבֿר סיסרא
ציהן דאז איז משמע אז ווער ער ניט איר מאן דרום דז דיא נבֿואה אויף איר קומן
איז דא האט זיא זיך פֿורש פֿון אים דרום האט זיא צו אים גשיקט אונ׳ דרום
25 האט ער אויך גזאגט וויילשטו מיט מיר גין דא וויל איך גין וואו אדר ניט זא וויל
איך אויך ניט גין גין דיא וואלט זיך אן הֿיבֿן דז ער מיט אן אין אנדרי אשה וואלט ציהן אלא
זיא איז זיין ווייב גוועזן נייארט זיא האט זיך פֿון אים פֿורש גוועזין דען ער האט
וואל/

---

[48] Prov. 14:1. [49] *Reshit Hokhmah*, I, p. 9, § 18. [50] Prov. 14:1. [51] *Reshit Hokhmah*, I, p. 9, § 18. [52] B. Megillah 14a. [53] Judg. 4:4.

[11a] וואל גוווישט דז זיא איין צדקות איז אולי וואר איך אירין זכות גנישין נוא פון אל

עניינים אז איך דא גשריבן האב דר פון קאן איין איטלי׳כי פרומה אשה לערנן דז זי

אירן מאן זאל צו גוטי מעשים אן הלטין אונ׳ פון בזן אפ רידן אונ׳ זאל אים פון אל

דינג ניט זאגין ווע שון היא הוֹיז ניט גליך דר אר גלייך צו גיט זאל זי אימש אויז רידן

5 דען עש קומט נישט גוטצ פון קריג אז דר פסוק גיט למי אוי למי אבוי למי מדנים⁵⁴

דאש איז טייטש וער איז וויא וער זאל קלאגין דר דא קריגט. אויך האט שלמה

המלך ע׳ה גזאגט פוטר [מים] ראשית מדון⁵⁵ דאש איז טייטש אז וועז מן איין ברוין

גראבט היבט דאש וושיר לנצים אן צו רינן דר נוך קומט עש מיט גרושר מלט צו שיסן

אזו איז אויך דש השם ישמרינו איין קריג צום אירשטן היבט זיך מיט מיט איינם קליינן ווארט

10 אן צו קריגן דר נאך וערט איין גרושר קריג דרויש דרום זגט דר פסוק לפני התגלע

הריב נטוש⁵⁶ דאז איז טייטש אי זיך אנפלעקט דר קריג פר לאז אין דאז מיינט מן

זאל בלד אפ שניידן אויך שפריכלט דר פסוק ווייטר באפס עצים ישקיט אש ובאפס

נרגן ישקיט ריב⁵⁷ דש איז טייטש וועז מן ניט האלץ אויף אין פייאר ליגט דא גיט דז

פייאר אפ אונ׳ פר לעשט אזו אויך וועז קיין רכילת טרייבר דא איז דר הין [אונ׳] הער

15 גיט דא ווערט דר קריג גשטילט אויף דז גיט דר פסוק ווייטר כבוד לאיש שבת מריב⁵⁸

דאז איז טייטש ועלי׳כר דר דא כבוד וויל האבן דר זאל אפ לאזין פון קריג אונ׳

זאל אויך אייטל שלום אוישין זיין דר פון וער פיל וער צו שרייבן וואש גוטש פון שלום קאן

קומן. נוא וועלין מיר ווייטר רידן וויא וויא איין פרום זעלי׳ג ווייב אירן מאן זאל אן הלטין

צו גוטין דז ער זאל אין באמונה [זאל] הנדלין אז דר פסוק גיט צדיק באמונתו יחיה⁵⁹ דאש איז

20 טייטש דר צדיק דר באמונה דר הנדילט דער ווערט לעבן אין עולם הבא ולכן להיפך דר

ניט ח׳ו באמונה הנדלט דא גיט די גמרא⁶⁰ מי שפרע מאנשי דור המבול ודור הפלגה

הוא יפרע מי שאינו עומד בדיבורו דאש איז טייטש דר דא האט גשטראפֿט דור

המבול ודור הפלגה דר ווערט שטראפֿין דער ניט הלט זיין פֿר פר זינדיקט זיין וויב

וועז איינר ח׳ו שבועת שוא טוט אונ׳ ניט רעכט הנדילט דער דער פֿר זינדיקט זיין ווייב

25 אונ׳ קינדר אז דר פסוק גיט אל תתן את פיך [לחטיא] את בשרך⁶¹ עש איז אזו טייטש

דוא זאלשט מיט דיינם מויל ניט זינדגן דז דו דיין בלוט אונ׳ פֿלייש ניט פר זינדגשט

אויך דרשת דיא גמרא⁶² דען פסוק למה יקח משכבך מתחתיך⁶³ דאש איז טייטש .

ווארום/

---

⁵⁴Prov. 23:29. ⁵⁵Prov. 17:14. ⁵⁶Prov. 17:14. ⁵⁷See Prov. 26:20. ⁵⁸Prov. 20:3. ⁵⁹Hab. 2:4. ⁶⁰B. Bava Metzi`a 44a.
⁶¹Eccles. 5:5. ⁶²B. Shabbat 32b. ⁶³Prov. 22:27.

7 מיס P1609 | 14 אזנ׳ P1609 | 19 ואל P1609 | 25 לחטוא P1609

[11b] ווארום זאל דיין גלעגיר פֿון דיר גנומן ווערין דאז זאל איין איטלכי ורומי אשה

גדענקין אונ׳ אירין מאן צוא אייטיל גוטין מעשים אן הלטין אויף דאז גיט דיא

גמרא עולם הזה אונ׳ עולם הבא איז גלייך אז איינר דער ב׳ נשים האט וען ער איינר

איר רצון טוט דא צירנט דיא אנדר אזו איז אויך עולם הזה אונ׳ וען איין מענש דען עולם

5 מעלט גנוגין טון אלש וואש דער בן אדם בדערף אז אכילה ושתייה אונ׳ קליידר אונ׳

בניינים אונ׳ פֿיל געלט אונ׳ זייני קינדר אלש גנוגין טון דא מוז ער פֿיל האבן אונ׳

ווען ער יוא דאש ראש מיגן ניט האט דא מוז ער ח״ו ניט רעכט הנדלן אונ׳ מושט זיין

חבֿר בטריגן אונ׳ אים דא זיין אף לייקנן אדור אפ שווערין אדור מעלט זיין חבֿר צו

איין שבֿועה דרינגן דאז מעלט טון ח״ו אין עונש ברענגן (ממה נפשך)

10 איז ער גירעלט דא טוט ער ניט רעכט דז ער זיין חבֿר לאשט איין פֿלשי שבֿועה טון

איז ער אדור און גרעכט דא האט ער אבור איין עונש דער פֿון דז ער אים אום .

זונשט לאשט שווערין דער אבור עולם הבא וויל בדענקין דער קאן עש עש וואל בוואָרן

דא איז איין משל אז איין אונ׳ וואג שאל וען איין איינר מיר ליגט אז איין דר אנדר דו אביר

וועגט זיא דיא אנדר אזו אויך אז איינר דעם גוף וויל מיר טון אז דר נשמה דא מוז

15 ער דאן גן עדן לאזין פֿארין אונ׳ הלט זיך דז דאן גיהנם השם ישמרינו אויך גיט דאז

(מדרש סולם מוצב ארצה וראשו מגיע השמימה[64] סולם איז בגמטרא ממון דאז

ווארט פֿון סולם האט אזו פֿיל אין דר צאל אז דאז ווארט פֿון ממון כלומר דאז ממון

האט הקב״ה אויף דיא ערד דיא מן דר דורך אין דען הימל קאן קומן וועם הקב״ה

דיא ברכה גיבט דז ער איין גוטי דיעה האט דז ער עש וואול אן ליגט מיט צדקה

20 אונ׳ גמילות חסדים אז עש אונזרי ליבי תורה האבן וויל אז מירש תהילה לאל קלאר

בשיידליך אונ׳ אפֿין ווֹאר האבן וואל מירש נייארט טון וועליין אונ׳ רעכט וואלטין

בדענקין דא קענטן מיר וואל וואל (עולם הזה) אונ׳ (עולם הבא) האבן

אז משה רבינו עליו השלום האט גיזאגט (ואתם הדבֿקים בה׳ אלהיכם חיים

כלכם היום[65]) דא דרשת דיא גמרא (ולי אפֿשר לדבֿק בשכינה אלא

25 מה (הקדוש ברוך הוא) צדיק אף אתה צדיק מה הקדוש ברוך הוא
/רחמן

[64]Gen. 28:12.   [65]Deut. 4:4.   [66]See B. Ketubbot 111b.

[12a] רחמן אף אתה תהא רחמון מה הוא גואל חסדים אף אתה תהא כן מכאן תחיית

המתים מן התורה שנאמר חיים וכלבם היום[67]) אויך נאך איין פשט וויא איז

איין לייטר דיא מן אויף אונ' אפ גיט אזו איז אויך דאז ממון איינר קאן בלד רייך אדור

ארום ווערין וויא ערש זולה איז אונ' אים פֿון גו*ט ית"ש נגזר איז אויך גפֿינט מן לייט

5 צו צייטין דיא מיט גוולט וועלין אויף דיא לייטר שטייגן העבליר אז אים צו גהארט דא

גיבט מן אים איין שטוס דז ער גען הינדר פֿלט אזו אויך דר דא מיט גוולט וויל רייך

ווערין אונ' הנדלט ניט רעדליך אונ' שטוסט זיך אין איין סכנה אונ' קומפֿט גניבֿות

אונ' דעש גלייכן פֿיל דא איז עש בלד גישעהן דז ער אפֿילו אום זיין קומט

אפֿילו וואש ער פֿאר האט גיהט אז דר פסוק גיט (ואץ להעשיר אך למחסור[68]

10) דאש איז טייטש דער זיך אײלט רייך צו ווערין האט ער זונשטר ווינוגר אויך

איז מעגבֿלר דר האט איין גוטי (מחיה) אונ' זילֿט דז זיין חבֿר נעבוך

אויך איין אנדרה (מחיה) פֿיר האט דז ער זיך אויך (מחיה)

וויל זיין דא האט ער איין קנאה אויף אים אונ' פֿלט אים אין זיני נארונג אונ' לאזט

זיני פֿארגי נארונג פֿלין ער מיינט דיא איז בעשר אונ' ברענקט נעבוך זיין חבֿר

15 אום זייני נארונג דא שטראפֿט אים (הקדוש ברוך הוא)

דז ער אום אלש קומט אפֿילו וואש ער מיט דר אירשטי נארונג האט גיוואונן

אזו איין משל שרייבט (אורחת צדיקים[69]) אז מן אין דער

(מדבר) גפֿינט פֿיל ארלייא פֿיגל איין טייל זיין געל אונ'

איין טייל זיין גרין איין טייל זיין רוט אלר לייא פֿערבן דער ראב איז דיא פֿיגל מקנא

20 אום אירי שיני פֿערבן אונ' רייסט זיך אירי שוואראצי פֿעדרן אל אויז אונ' קלויבט דיא

שיני פֿעדרן אויף דיא יעני פֿיגל האבן לאזין פֿלן אונ' שטעקט זיא זיך אין דר נאך

קומן דיא פֿיגל איטלֿבר דער קענט זיין פֿעדר אונ' פֿלוקין אים דיא פֿעדרין אל

אויז איטליכר נעמט זיין פֿעדר אזו בלייבט ער גאר בלוש אונ' נקיט דרום זאל איטליכי

פֿרומי אשה גוואַרנט זיין אונ' זאל אירן מאן צו גוטין אן הלטין אונ' מיט גוטן

25 רידן דען עש איז פֿיל אן דער אשה טובה

/גלעגין

---

[67]See Deut. 4:4.   [68]See Prov. 28:20; 21:5.   [69]*Seyfer Middes*, fol. 46a.

[12b] גילעגן אז דאש שפריך וואָרט גיט איין פֿרום ווייב ציבֿט איין פֿרומן מאן אז דער
מדרש[70] גיט יעקב אבֿינו האט ער זינדיגט זיין טאָבֿטר דינה איז דרום פֿר
אונרייניגט גיוואָרדן ווייל ער זיא עשו האט ניט וועלין געבן דרום זיא העט איין
פֿרום גימאכֿט אונ׳ אויך כן להיפֿך איין אשה רעה גידענקט ניט דז שלמה המלך
5 ע׳׳ה האט גיזאגט (אשה רעה מר ממות[71]) איז איין קשיא צו פֿראגן וואו קאן
זיין ביטרירר אז דער טוט דז מיינט דז איין אשה רעה די אירין מאן דער צו ברענגט
דז ער מוז (גוזל וחומס) זיין אונ׳ דען לייטן דאז אירי אבֿ שווערט אונ׳ לייקנט
אונ׳ דאז גלייכֿן פֿיל מיר דז איך אליש ניט שרייבן מאג דיא זעלביגי אשה ברענגט
אירין מאן אין דאז גיהנם אויף דאז גיט דער פסוק (נפֿש יקרה תצוד[72]) דאז
10 איז טייטש וועַן ער שון גאר קעשטליך איז טוט זיא אים יאגן אין דאש גיהנם וועַן
אבֿר איין אשה טובֿה איז בֿדעַנקט דאש אלש זעלברט אויף איין תכלית וועַן איך אלז
וועַר האבן וויא עש מיר וואל גיפֿעלט אונ׳ מיין לושט אונ׳ ווילין ווער האבֿן מיין מאן ניט
רעכֿט הנדלין ווערט דו ווערנש מייני קינדר חס ושלום מוזין אנטגעלטין אז דר פסוק
גיט (פּוקד [עוון] אבֿות על בנים[73]) דאז איז טייטש וושם יתברך גדענקט דיא זינד
15 פֿון דעַן עלטרין אויף דיא קינדר מן גֿינט מעַנכֿה אשה איר ליגט נישט דראן וועַן
מן גלייך דעַן מאן אין אלי חרמות רופֿט וועַן זיא נייעַרט גנוק הוט השם ישמרינו פֿר
זעלבֿי דעות זאלט זיא אבֿר ווישן וויא ווייט דער עונש גרייכֿט וועַן מעַן איינם מחרים
איז דער מוז מעַן קריעה רייסין השם ישמרינו אונ׳ מוז וויא איין איין אבֿל אויף ערדן זיצן
אויך גיט דאש מדרש איינר אין דר הש׳׳י איין טאג אין חרם איז דער איז אין הימל דריי
20 טאג אין חרם אונ׳ דער דרייא טאג אין חרם איז דער מוז אים אין הימל וואוך אים
חרם זיין אונ׳ ווער דא איין וואוך אים חרם איז דער מוז אים אים הימל (שלשים יום)
אים חרם זיין אונ׳ ווער דא איז שלושים יום אין חרם איז דער מוז אים אים הימל גנץ יאר
אים חרם זיין אונ׳ ווער דא איין גנץ יאר אים חרם איז ( ) ( )
דער מוז אין (עולם הבא עולמות) אים חרם זיין דרום זאל איין איטלבי פֿרומי
25 אשה אירן מאן דער פֿיר בֿהיטן אונ׳ זיא זאל אים אין אלי זלין בֿהילפֿיג זיין אז דער
פסוק גיט אעשה לו עזר כנגדו[74] זכֿה נעשה לו עזר [לאַ] זכֿה כנגדו[75]
דאז מיינט אזו וועַן זיא וויל העלפֿט זיא אים אין גן עדן וועַן זיא אבֿור ניט וויל דא
העלפֿט/

---

[70]Tanhuma, Va-yishlah 19. [71]See Eccles. 7:26. [72]Prov. 6:26. [73]See Exod. 20:5; 34:7; Num. 14:18; Deut. 5:8. [74]Gen. 2:18.
[75]See B. Yevamot 63a.

14 fehlt P1609 | 26 לו P1609

[13a] העלפֿט זיא אים אין גיהנם אז דיא גמרא⁷⁶ גיט אין מעשה פֿון רבי יוסי בר חלפתה

דער האט איין פֿרום וייב גיהט ער איז אין גרושר עני גיוועזן האט ניט חיי שעה

גיהט איין מאל אן ערב שבת האבן זיא נישט גיהט דז זי שבת העטן גימלט אזו

גרושי עניים זיין זיא גוועזין דר חסיד האט זיך מצער גיוועזין אונ׳ איז אויף דאש

5 פֿעלד גגין אונ׳ האט תפֿילה גיטאן דז הש״י זאל אים בשערין דז ער זיין וייב אונ׳

קינדרליך אן דר לייט גאב קאן דר נערין (זו בלד האט הש״י זיין תפֿילה דר הערט

אונ׳ האט אים אים] | איין אבֿן טוב הראב גיוואורפֿין אזו אים איז ער צו זיין רבי ר׳ שמעון בן

יוחי גגין אונ׳ האט אים גזאגט וויא אים גשעהן איז דא האט ער גזאגט ער איז

פֿיל ווערט דוא קאנשט אין ניט גער צו קופֿן לייא דרויף אויש וואש דוא אויף

10 שבת בידרפֿשט אזו האט ער גיטאן אונ׳ האט אויף שבת גיקופֿט וואז ער האט

בידרפֿט דוא זיא נוא האבן זעלין עשן האט זיין וייב גפֿראגט אים וואו ערש גנומן

האט אונ׳ האט ניט וועלן עשין עש זייא דען ער זאלט איר זאגן וואו ערש גנומן האט

עש קעם אים ניט מיט רעכטן הער דא ער איר נוא גזאגט האט דז האט זיא אן

גיהובין זיא וואלט נישט עשין פֿון עשין דר זעלט איר צו זאגין אז ער דען אבֿן טובֿ

15 וואלט אויף ליזן אונ׳ זאל אין ווידר געבן דען מן האט אים פֿון זיין חלק לעולם הבא

געבן זיין שכֿר ווערט ניט צו גנץ זיין אין עולם הבא דא איז ער צו זיין רבי גגין אונ׳

האט ער גיזאגט אזו האט מיין וייב גרעט דא האט ער גזאגט זאג דיין וייב וואו

דיר ווערט אפֿ גין וויל איך דיר דער ממלא זיין דא האט זיא אן גיהובין דר פֿסוק גיט

כי הולך אדם לבית עולמו⁷⁷ דאז איז ער טייטש ווען דער מענש גיט צו זיינם עולם איטלכר

20 צדיק האט איין בזונדרין עולם פֿר זיך דו האבן זי איר מודה גוועזן אונ׳ ער איז ווידר

גגין אויף דאז זעלביג אורט אונ׳ האט [תפֿילה] גיטאן דא איז איין הנט קומן אונ׳

האט דען אבֿן טובֿ ווידר איין וועק גינומן. אונזרי חכֿמים⁷⁸ ז״ל האבן גזאגט דאש

הינטרשט נס איז גרעשר גיוועשט אז דאש ערשטי דען מן האט ניט גיהערט דז

הקדוש ברוך הוא פֿלעגט צו געבן אדור מן האט גהערט דז ער האט ווידר

25 גנומן. אזו אויך זאל זיך איין איטלכֿי פֿרומי פֿרויא טון עש זיין אדור בעו״ה וינוק

דיא אזו איין דיעה אבֿן האבן אונ׳ פֿרעגן ווינק דר נאך וואו עש דער מאן נעמט ווען

זיא עש נייארט האט דרום איר ליבן ורומין ווייבר ביט איך אייך דז איר מיך זעלט

/דן לכף

⁷⁶Shemot Rabbah 52.3.   ⁷⁷See Eccles. 12:5.   ⁷⁸B. Ta'anit 25a.

7 אים P1609 | 21 הפלה P1609

[13b] דן לכף זכות זיין דען מיין כוונה איז דז אנדרי זאלין (לוקח מוסר) זיין און'
זאלין זיך דראן שטושין דז איין איטלכי זאל מיט אירין מאן פר גוט נעמין און' ניט
מער פון אים בגערין דז [גו*ט] י"ש טוט אין בשערין אז שפריך וורט גיט כל המפזר
יותר ממה שהשם גוזר אין זה פלאות. שילך בבלאות) און' דאז טייטש איז

5 אויך אזו דר דא מער טוט ור צערין אז גו*ט ית"ש טוט אין בשערין דז איז קין וואונדר
דז ער גיט אין פלונדר דרום זאל איין איטלכי ורויא אירין מאן דר צו הלטין דז ער
ניט טוט פר פרסין און' מער פר צערין אז זיין פר מיגן איז דאך ניט מיט בושיקיט
און' צארין נייארט ווען זיא זילט דז ער גוט וויליג איז אז שלמה המלך ע"ה האט
גזאגט (מענה רך משיב חימה ודבר עצב יעלה אף⁷⁹) דאז איז טייטש

10 איין דעמהפטיגי ריד ווידור קערט דען צארין אדור איין ריד דיא איין טרויאריג
מכט דאז ברענגט אויף צארין מכל שכן דז איין אשה אירין מאן וואל גטרייא זיין און'
דא זיין צו הויף הלטן זאל וואז זי קאן אדור מאג דען ווען דיא הנט איין דיא אנדר וושט
דא ווערין זיא ביידי ריין אויף דיא עניינים אז איך גשריבן האב דז מן גפינט דעות
דיא ניט גלייך זיין דרויף האט שלמה המלך ע"ה אויף גזאגט (מוציא אני מר ממות

15 האשה⁸⁰) און' איין מאלט שטיט ואשה בכל אלה לא מצאתי⁸¹ און' איין מאלט האט ער
גזאגט מצא אשה מצא טוב⁸² דא איז דר פשט אויף דיא דרייא פסוקים דער פסוק
(מצא אשה מצא טוב⁸³) דא איז דאן וורט פון אשה דאז האט ווניגר אין דר
צאל אז דאן וורט פון איש כלומר דאז מיינט ווען ער טרופט אויף איני דיא דא
אירין מאן אונטר טעניק איז און' איז וויניגיר אין אירי דיעה אז איר מאן

20 און' פאלקט אים און' גדענקט ניט ער איז מיר צו שפל דער זעלביג מאן האט גוטש
פון גו*ט יתברך שמו גיפונדין און' דר נאך שפרעלט דער פסוק (מוציא אני מר
ממות את האשה⁸⁴) דאז איז טייטש דר דא גפינט איין וויב דיא דא אזו פיל
וויל זיין אז דר מאן און' וויל אים נישט נאך געבן דאז מיינט דז האשה האט אזו פיל
אין דר צאל אז איש אזו אין דר צאל האט דאז זעלביג וויב ביטרר אז דר טוט אבור

25 ואשה בכל אלה לא מצאתי⁸⁵) וועט איין וויב וויל מיר זיין אז דר מאן כלומר ואשה
האט איינש מיר אין דר צאל אז איש אזו איין אשה איז גאר אויך דר וויז ווייא ווא ואול
דאך אונזרי חלמים⁸⁶ האבן דען פסוק אונש צו גוטין אויז גליגט אז דר פסוק
שפריליט ואשה בכל אלה לא מצאתי⁸⁷ דז מיינט דוא ישראל האבן דאז עגל גמלט און'
האבן/

---

⁷⁹See Prov. 15:1. ⁸⁰See Eccles. 7:26. ⁸¹Eccles. 7:28. ⁸²Prov. 18:22. ⁸³Prov. 18:22. ⁸⁴See Eccles. 7:26. ⁸⁵Eccles. 7:28.
⁸⁶See Va-yikra Rabbah 2.1. ⁸⁷Eccles. 7:28.

3 גוט P 1609

[14a] האבן גשפראכין (אלה אלהיך ישראל[88]) דאז איז טייטש דאז איז דיין גו*ט ישראל
דאראן האט קיין קיין אשה געהט חלק גיהט דען זיא האבן אירין רצון ניט גוועלט דר צו
געבן אז דר פסוק גיט (ויתפרקו הנזמים אשר באזניהם[89]) דאז איז טייטש זיא
האבן איר אור רינג געבן אביר דיא וייביר וואלטין איר אור רינג ניט דר צו געבן
5 דרום גפינדן מיר ניט ביא דיא (מתי המדבר) דז איין אשה ווער דרונטר
גיוועזין אויך גיט דר פסוק אויף דיא עניינים דיא איך אובין גשריבן האב (נודע
בשערים בעלה[90]) דאז איז טייטש דען מן דר קענט דען מן אן דעם וייב דר איין
זעליג וייב האט דיא קרינט מאן מיט אירי מעשים טובים אונ׳ זיא זאל אים
אירלך האלטן אז דש שפריכט וורט גיט וורשטו דיין מאן אירלך האלטן [ווערשטון] אויך
10 ביא איר אים אז איין מלכה אלטין דען איין אשה זאל גדענקין וויא אין אונזרי היילגי
תורה שטיט גשריבן (והוא ימשול בך[91]) אונ׳ אויך לערנן מיר פון זארה מוטר שרה
דז זיא אירין מאן האט גהיישן מיין הער וויא וויא איז אים מיר אין דר נבואה
[גוועזין] אז ער אז דר [פסוק] גיט (כל אשר תאמר אליך שרה שמע בקולה[92])
דאז איז טייטש אלז וואז זיא צו דיר זאגט שרה הער צו איר שטים אונזרי חכמים[93]
15 האבן אויך גשריבן (לעולם יהא אדם נזהר בכבוד אשתו) דאז איז טייטש
איביג זאל איין מענש גוורנט זיין אן דען ווייבש לבוד דען דיא גמרא[94] גיט
וייטר שאין ברכה מצויה בתוך ביתו של אדם אלא בשביל אשתו שנאמר ולאברהם
הטיב בעבורה[95]) דאז איז טייטש דיא ברכה איז ביא איין מענשין אין הויז פון
זין וייב זלות וועגין אז ביא אברהם גיט זיין ברכה גשריבן דז ער האט זולכה
20 גוועזין צום עושר פון שרה זלות וועגין אז בור דז איז איין כ״ש זי אן זיין לבוד זאל מן
נזהר זיין אונ׳ איטליכי פרומי ורוי זאל גוורנט זיין דז זי אירין מאן ח״ו ניט מקלל איז
אז מן עש גש גפינט ביא עטלכי דען זיא קאן זיך ח״ו ור זינדגין דז מיר גפינדן ביי מיכל
בת שאול דז זיא זיך האט פר זינדגט אן אירין מאן דוד המלך ע״ה אז זיא ביז
אירין ענד קיין קינד קונט האבין דרום זאל זיך איין איטלכי ורויא היטין דר פיר דז
25 זי זיך ניט זאל פר זינדגין אן אירין מאן מכל שכן אן אנדרין לייטין דאך זיא זאל אים
ניט גשטטין וען זי פון אים זעך אז וואז ניט רעלט איז דען אין ורום וייב ציבט איין
ורומין מאן אונ׳ זיא זאל מיט גיטין מיט אים אויז רידן דא ווערט ער איר גוויש
פאלגין אונ׳ ווען עש אזו ווערט זיין דז ער איר ווערט פאלגן אונ׳ זי אים אונ׳ שלום אונ׳
לב/

---

[88]Exod. 32:4, 8. [89]See Exod. 32:3. [90]Prov. 31:23. [91]Gen. 3:16. [92]Gen. 21:12. [93]B. Bava Metzi'a 59a. [94]B. Bava
Metzi'a 59a. [95]See Gen. 12:16.

9 ווערשטו P1609 | 13 גוועגין P1609 | פטוק P1609

[14b] לב אחד האבן דא ווערין זיא מיט אננדר זולכה זיין דז זיא ווערן מזל וברכה אונ'
הצלחה האבן אין אל איירי עסקים לאורך ימים אונ' ווערן זולכה זיין דז זיא ווערן מיט
אננדר קינדר האבן דיא דא תלמידי חכמים ווערין זיין דאז איז דר גרעשטי עושר
אונ' שמחה אונ' איז הקב"ה ליב ווען דער זיווג באהבה ובחיבה איז אונ' אין זיינם
5 דינשט צו הלטין זייני הייליגה תורה דאז איז דר תכלית פון דר בריאה דא ווערט
אלש גשעהן במהרה בימינו אמן דא ווערט אויך מקום דר פסוק זיין (ביום ההוא
יהיה ה' אחד ושמו אחד)[96]: ( )

שער שלישי

וויא איין אשה מיט איריו מאן מיט איר אונ' ואטר אונ' מוטר איר צייט זאל פר ברענגן.
10 דא ווערט גו*ט יתברך שמו איר יאר בעולם הזה ובעולם הבא דר לענגין:

דער פסוק גיט אין משלי אשה יראת ה' היא תתהלל[1] דאש [איז] טייטש איין
ורויא דיא גו*טש פארכט אין זיך האט דיא דיא זאל מן לובין דאש איז אונש
ווישגליך דז יראת ה' דאש איז גו*טש פארכט דער עיקר פון מעגשין איז אז ספר
מדות[2] שרייבט גלייך אז איין שנור פערליך אל דר וויל דז דר קנאפ דראן איז דא
15 בלייבן דיא פערליך בייא אננדר אזו אויך ווען איין מענש גלייך אלש חפצות אן אים
איז אונ ווען יראת שמים אן אים ניט דא איז דא עש אלש אלש פר לאריך ווען אבור יראת
שמים אן אים איז דא זיין גוויש אלי מדות טובות אן אים אונ' אזו האט אונזרי ליבי
תורה אן גשריבן את ה' אלהך תרא[3] דש איז טייטש פר גו*ט דיין גו*ט דוא זאלשט דיך
פערכטין. אונ' אויך גיט דר פסוק (איש אמו ואביו תראו[4]) דאש איז טייטש איין
20 מאן זיין מוטר אונ' פאטר זאל פערכטן דא האט דיא תורה מזהיר גוועזט אויף
פאטר אונ' מוטרש מורא אזו וואל אז אויף זיין מורא אונ' בייא דעו ענוש האט דיא
תורה זיא אויך צו הויף גגליכן אונ' האט אן גשריבן (בנוקבו שם ה' מות יומת[5]
דאש איז טייטש דער דעו שם בשייד מיט זיין אותיות דער איז חייב מיתה אזו אויך
גיט דר פסוק (מקלל אביו ואמו מות יומת[6]) דאש איז טייטש דר דא פלוכט
25 פאטר/

---

[96]Zech. 14:9.　[1]Prov. 31:30.　[2]*Seyfer Middes*, fol. 4b.　[3]Deut. 6:13; 10:20.　[4]Lev. 19:3.　[5]See Lev. 24:16.　[6]Exod. 21:17.

[15a] פֿאטר אדר מוטר גטיט ער זאל ווערן גיטיט. אויך בייא דען כיבוד האט די תורה

אויך אן גשריבן (כבד את ה׳ מהונך[7]) דאש איז טייטש איר גו*ט פֿון דיין גוט

און בייא פֿאטר אונ׳ מוטר האט ער אן גשריבן (כבד את אביך ואת אמך[8])

דאש איז טייטש דוא זאלשט אירן דיין פֿאטר אונ׳ מוטר דא האט הקב״ה דרייא מאל

5 מזהיר גיוועשט אויף פֿאטר אונ׳ מוטר אזו וואל אז אויף זיך זעלברט מיט דר מורא

אונ׳ מיט דען עונש אונ׳ מיט דען כיבוד אז איך אלש דא גשריבן האב אויך דרשת

דיא גמרא[9] גדול כבוד אב ואם יותר משל קב״ה) עש איז גרעשר דער כיבוד בייא

פֿאטר אונ׳ מוטר דען הקב״ה הט דען מיר דרויף מזהיר גיוועזן אז אויף זיין כיבוד ברוך

הוא שטיט גשריבן (כבד את ה׳ מהונך[10]) דאש איז טייטש ווען דוא פֿיל

10 האשט בישטו מחוייב פֿיל צו גַעבן אז מיר גפֿינדן בייא דען קרבנות אונ׳ תרומות

אונ׳ מעשרות אבר בייא כבוד אב ואם זאגט כבד את אביך ואת אמך[11] עש זייא דו

האשט אדר האשט ניט דא בישטו מחוייב צו טון (אפֿילו חוזר על הפתחים)

דז איינר מוז בעטלין גין אונ׳ מוז זיין פֿאטר אונ׳ מוטר דר הלטין. אויך דרשת דיא

גמרא[12] (את ה׳ אלהיך תירא[13]) את) איז מרבה תלמידי חלמים דז מן זאל זיך

15 פֿערכטין פֿר איין תלמיד חלם אונ׳ זי מכבד זיין אונ׳ מהנה זיין אז מיר גפֿינדן בייא

יהושפֿט מלך יהודה ווען ער גיזעהן הט איין תלמיד חלם קומן איז ער פֿון זיין שטול

אויף גישטונדן אונ׳ איז אים קיגן גלאפֿין אונ׳ האט איר גהלשט אונ׳ גקושט. אויך גיט

דיא גמרא[14] כל הנבֿיאים לא נתנבא אלא על המהנה תלמיד חלם ומנכסיו דאש

איז טייטש אל די טובֿות דיא אומרי נביאים האבן אויף ישראל גזאגט אונ׳ אלי דיא

20 טרושט דז זיא גטרישט האבן דא האבן זיא גרעט אויף איין זילכין דר דיא לומדי

תורה מהנה איז פֿון זיין גוט וואש אים ([גו*ט] יתברך שמו) בשערט

האט. אונ׳ דאש את דז בייא (כבוד אב ואם[15] שטיט) דרשת

דיא גמרא[16] (את לרבות אשת אביך) דאש טייטש דיא שטיף מוטר

אדר איין שטיף פֿאטר זאל מן אויך מכבד זיין פֿון וועגן כבוד פֿאטר אונ׳ מוטר. אונ׳

25 דאש אנדר ואת איז (מרבה אחיך הגדול[17]) דען [עלצטן] ברודר זאל

מן אויך מכבד זיין צו דען זלין גהירט אלש יראת שמים דער יראת שמים אין זיך

האט/

[7]Prov. 3:9.   [8]Exod. 20:12; Deut. 5:16.   [9]See Yalkut, § 297.   [10]Prov. 3:9.   [11]Exod. 20:12; Deut. 5:16.   [12]B. Pesahim 22b.
[13]Deut. 6:13.   [14]B. Berakhot 34b.   [15]See Exod. 20:12; Deut. 5:16.   [16]B. Ketubbot 103a.   [17]B. Ketubbot 103a.

21 גוט P1609 | 25 טלצטן P1609

[15b] האט דערף מן ניט פיל פון דר פון צו שרייבן דן איטלכר פרומר וייש זעלברט ואל דען
שכר פון כיבוד אב ואם אונ׳ ואש דר צו גיהערט אונ׳ ויא מן ויא זאל מלבד זיין וכן
להיפך השם ישמרנו דען גרושן עונש פון דרום איז עש עש ניט דז מן פיל דר פון
שרייבן זאל דז מן ניט זאל נוהג קלות אן זיא זיין אז מיר אויך גפינדן אין דר גמרא[18]

5   איינר האט זיין פאטר מעדנים צו עשין גיגבן אונ׳ האט זיך אן אים פר זינדגט דז
     ער אין גיהנם איז קומן אונ׳ איינר האט זיין פאטר אין דר מיל לאזין מאלן אין
     שווערי מלאכה דז ער האט אין מיל שטיין גצוגין אונ׳ איז אין גן עדן קומן דאש איז
     אזו צו גגין דער אים האט מעדנים צו עשין גיגבן ווען ער האט וואז גקויפט פיש
     אדר פלייש האט אים דער פאטר גפרעגט ויא טייר האשטו דאש גקויפט דא

10   האט ער אין אן גשריאן וואש פרעגשטו דר נאך זארגשטו דאך ניט דר פיר
     אויך גיבשטו מיר נישט דר צו אונ׳ ווען ער גושין האט גיבער דען טיש האט ער צו
     אים גזאגט אנדרי לייט האבן אירין קינדרן פיל גטאן אונ׳ גהאלפין אונ׳ איך האב
     אל מין טאג פון דיר נישט גיהט דא איז דר אים דר בישין אין הלז דר שטערט זילכי
     אונאות דברים דז מן דען עלטרן גיבט וער קאן זיא אל דר ציילן אבור איינר האט

15   זיין פאטר אין דר מילין מלין ערבטן דאש איז גאר איין שווערי ערבטן גוועזין אונ׳
     איז דאך אין גן עדן קומן דען ער הט זיין פאטר גטרישט אונ׳ הט גזאגט מיין ליבר
     פאטר איך קלאגש גו*ט דען הערין דז איך דיר ניט פר מאג צו טון אז איך מחוייב
     בין צו טון אונ׳ ווען איך מעלט זולה זיין דז מיר השם יתברך זעלט בשערין אין קליין
     נארונג וואלט וואלט איך דיך ניט לאזין אזו שווער ערבטן דרום איז ער זולה גיוועזן דז

20   ער עולם הבא האט גיהט. אויך גפינדן[19] מיר אז רבי טרפון זיין מוטר האט דיא
     תלמידי חכמי׳ איבר אים גקלאגט דז ער ניט איר וויל טון די תלמידי חכמי׳ האבן
     זיך מתמיה דרויף גיוועשט אזו אייך קעשטליכר תלמיד חכם אז רבי טרפון איז דער
     זאל ווידור זיין מוטר טון אונ׳ זיין גגין אונ׳ האבן אים גפרעגט איז דאש ואר אז דו
     דיין מוטר ניט מלבד בישט דא האט ער גיענטוורט פרעגט זיא מיט ואש איך איר

25   ווילן ניט טוא אזו האבן דיא חכמים זיא גפרעגט וואש איז דיא קלאג דיא דוא איבר
     דיין זון קלאגשט דא האט זיא אין גיהובין מיט דעם טוט ער ניט מיין ווילין ווען ער
     אויש דען בית המדרש קומט אונ׳ וושט זיך דיא פיש דיא גלושט מיך דאש ושיר צו
     טרינקן /

[16a] טרינקן דא האבן דיא חכמים גזאגט אפילו הבי דיא וייל דז עש זיא גלושט זאלשט
דוא אירש ניט פר זאגין מכל שכן זאז זד אז פאטר און' מוטר איין טובה איז דן מן
אינש ניט פר זאגין זאל אבור עש איז בעו"ה שכיח אל צו פיל דז מן נוהג קלות איז
אן דיא עלטרין אז דאש שפריבלט וארט גיט איין מוטר קאן דר ציהן צעהן קינדר
5 אבר ציהן קינדר קענין איין מוטר ניט דר נערן און' איז אלש צו פיל וואש זיא אין
טאון אדור וואש זיא עשין אדר רידן איז אין אלש אומער און' לבין און' שפאטין אירר
און' גדענקין ניט וען זי וערן אויך אלט וערן וערט מן זיא אויך מיט דער מאש
מעשין אז זיא איר עלטרין האבן גימעשין. איין שין מעשה האב איך גהערין זאגן
ווא קומט דאש שפריבלט וארט דער בייא זיין לעבן אלש גיבט איין וועק וואש
10 ער האט. דא זאל מן אים מיט קיילין שלאגין טוט. דאש איז אזו גוועזין
איין מאל איז איינר איין גרושר עושר גיוועזט און' האט איין אייציגן זון גהט דען
אלטן פאטר איז דאש וייב גשטארבן דיא שנור האט דען שוער אלש גוטש גטאן
אז ביליך איז צו טון דער אלטי האט גזעהן דז אים נישט אף גיט ער האט ער צום זון
און גיהובין ליבר זון איך זיך דז איבלש ת"ל זיאר גוט האב בייא דיר ווי איבש
15 האבן וויל וואש זאל מיר נוא דיא זארג מיט מיין געלט און' גוט און' דען הנדיל און'
מייני הייזר איך דיריש נוא אלש איבר געבן און' אל מייני תכשיטים און' חובות
און' האט אים דיא שליסל פון אלים געבן און' כל אשר לו במתנה געבן ניט לנג דר
נאך דוא דיא שנור האט גזעהן דז ער נוא נישט מיר האט און' אלש אויז גנרט מיט
איר חניפות און' זייפניית דא האט דיא אשה רעה אן גהובן צו קיפלין צו אירין מאן
20 און' האט אן גהובין זיא קענט ניט ליידן דז דר אלטי איבר דען טיש אזו הושט דאש
הערץ ווידלט איר עש איז איר מיאוס צו עשין פר אים ריד מיט אים דז ער אן דען
אנדרן טיש זאל עשן איך עשן דש בעשט און' דאש [שעושטן] הין געבן דער אלטי
נעבוך האט דאז וואל מוזין טון וען עש גרען גלייך ניט גארן האט גטאן איין וייל האט
עש גוועורט דז מן אים די האט גנוק געבן דר נאך האט זיא איין מאלט געשין און'
25 האבן דען אלטין נישט געבן דא האט דער זון אן גיהובין צו זיין וייב וארום גיבשט
דוא מיין פאטר ניט אויך צו עשין דא האט דיא אשה רעה אן גיהובן ער קאן וואל
הרין ביז מיר האבן אפ געשן ער עשט ער וערט ניט ( ) ( ) ( ) ( ) ( )
/ דר הונגרין

[16b] דר הונגרין דא האט ער נעבוך מוזין הרין ביז דאז עשין איז קלט גווארדין דא האט

מן אים די ביין גיבן אפ צו נאגין דר נאך איז דר זון ראש הקהל גיווארדין דא זיין

לייט צו אים אויך אונ' איין גיגנגן וואו איין עסק איז גוועזין דא האט דער אלטי אויך

דרייין גרעט צו צייטין אזו איז ער פר צייטין גשעהן דר זון האט דאז ניט גוועלט ליידין

5 אונ' האט צו אים גזאגט ליבר פאטער ניט ריד אין אל דינג דר עולם האטש ניט

גערין דז מן אין אל דינג רעט נאך דעם האט ער גרעט ליבר פאטער דוא בישט נוא

עבר ובטל איך שעם מיך דיינר פר לייטין ביט דיך טואן מיר עש צו ליב בלייב אין

יענר שטוב וואו דאז גזינד איז איך דיר גונגין אניין גיבן צו עשין אונ' טרינקין

דר אביון האטש וואול מוזין טון וואן ערש גלייך ניט גערין האט גטאן אונ' איז

10 אין דר אנדר שטוב גנגין וואו דיא קנעכט אונ' מיידן זיין גוועזין איין ווייל האטש אן

גשטנדין דז מן אים האט גיבראכט צו עשין אונ' טרינקין אונ' דר נאך זיין זיא מיד

גווארדין אונ' האבן אים פר געשין צו צייטין דר אביון האטש מוזין פר גוט נעמן

האט נישט [גדערפֿט] ריידן דרום אונ' האט געשין וואו עש אים צו קומן נאך האט

דר אלטי איין קליין שטיבכן גיהט וואו ער דרינן גלעגין איז דא האט דר זון אן

15 גהובין ליבר פאטער איך בדערף דאז קלייני שטיבל דען עש קומן לייט צו מיר איך מוז

איין אייגין גמך האבן איך וויל דיר אין אייגני קמיר גיבן ער האט ניט לנג אן

[גשטנדין] דא האט דאז ביזי ווייב אן גיהובין דען מאן אן צו קיפלין זיא קענט דיא

קמיר ניט אנטפֿערין זיא מוז דיא קמיר האבן דז זיא אל דינג מוז דרייין טון האט

ער דאך ניט מער אז דאש בעט דאז קאן וואול שטין אין דען קליני קעמרל אונטר

20 דר שטיגן אזו האט מן אים דא בעט אין דען קליני קעמרל אונטר דר שטיגן

קעשטעלט וען ער האט גזאלט ליגן גין איז זיין בעט אייטל שטיב גיוועזין האט

דאז בעט מוזין פֿארט אפ שיטלין אונ' וען ער דרינן גלעגין איז דא זיין די לייט אויף

אונ' אפ גגנין אונ' האבן אים דיא אויגין פול אן [גשטויבט] נאך דען אלין האט דר

אלטי נעבך זיין קליידר זיין הלז אפ גרישין דא האט דר פאטער אן גהובין

25 צום זון ליבר זון דער ווינטר קומט דא הער איך האב נישט אן צו ציהן מך מיר איין

קלייד האט דר זון וידר צו אים גרעט צו ליבר פאטער וואז זאל איך דיר ערשט

קליידר מכין וואו קומשטו פיל הין דו קאנשט וואול הינטר דען אובין זיצין ווען דיר

קלט/

241

[17a] קלט איז דא וויל איך דיר איין גוטי קאצין געבן דוא קאנשט דיך וואול דריין איין
הילין דער אלטי האט דיא קאץ מוזין פר גוט אן נעמן נון האט דר זון איין יונגין
גיהט איז נו דר ווקשין גוועזט דר האט גזעהן דאז גרוש רחמניּת אונ' דען עלטר
פאטּר וויא זיא אים אל איבול צו גוועלט האבן אפילו קנעלט אונ' מייד דאז גנצי

5 גזינד האבן דאז גשפעט אויז אים גטריבן זיא האבן גזעהן וויא אין דר זון אונ' דיא
שנור האבן אים אים שפל גיהלטין האבן זיא אים אויך אזו גיהלטין נון איז דאז פרום
איניקיל צום עלטר פאטר גגין אונ' האט צו אים גזאגט ליבר זידא איך וויל דיר אויך
אל דיין ניטן העלפּן גוט צו פאר ווען דוא מיר נייארט פאלגין ווילשט אונ' מעלבשט
מיך ניט פר ראטין דער אלטי האט אן גיהובין צו וויינין מיין ליבר זון חס ושלום דז

10 איך דיר דאז טון וואלט דוא דערפשט דיך נישט צו פערכטין דא איז דר פרום יונג
גגין צו זילכּי לייטין דיא יראַת שמים אין זיך האבן גהט אונ' האט אין דיא שמועה
גיזאגט וויא זיין פאטר אונ' מוטר זיין עלטר פאטר מיט פארט אונ' ניט הלט וויא
ער מחויב איז צו טון אין איך בעט אייך טוט אזו וואול לייט מיר גועלט אונ' [תלבשיטם] דז
זיא ווערן זעהן בייא אים דז ער נאך וואז האט וואז דיא פיל לייבט זיא אים בעשיר

15 הלטין אונ' מין חניפוֹת טרייבן דיא לייט האבן זיך פר וואונדרט אויף דען ורומין
יונגין חכמת אונ' האבן אים גליהין פיל געלט טאליר אונ' גאלד גילדין אונ' שיני
תלבשיטם אונ' האט דען אלטין אין איין קמר גזעצט אונ' האט זיך דרינן פר ריגלט
אונ' דאז געלט אונ' תלבשיטם פר זיך גנומן אונ' דער מיט גקלעפרט אזו
איז דער יונג גגין אונ' האט דען פאטר אונ' מוטר גרופין אונ' האט גשפראכליֿן

20 זעלבט וואז דער זידא פיר האט אז ער זיך אין דר קמיר פר ריגלט האט אזו איז גגין
דר זון מיט זיין וויב אונ' האבן דורך איין לאך אניין גזעהן אונ' האבן דאז געלט אונ'
תלבשיטם גזעהן דא האט דר זון צום וויב אן גיהובּן דוא פרוצה דאז האשט דוא
גיטאן איך העט דאז דאז אויך לנג בקומן ווען דו ניט העשט גיטאן דא האט זיא אן
גיהובּן וואז האב אים איך גווישט דז ער נאך וואז האט לאז ער נאך איין וויל דר מיט

25 שפילין עס ווערט דאך אונש ניט אנטגין דער אלטי האט מיט זיך זעלברט גרעט הר
דוא פרעקין דוא זאלשט מירש ניט גנישין איך האב גמיינט דוא ווערשט מיך פר
איין פאטר הלטין אז בילַיך איז אונ' האט גימעלט וויא ער דיא תלבשיטם אויז וויושט
אונ' אלש אין קשטין איין גשלאסין דו ער ווידור אויז דער קמיר קומן איז דו איז דר זון
צום/

13 K 1618; ם }תלבשיט P 1609

[17b] צום פאטר גנגין אונ׳ האט אן גיהובן טעט לעבן דיר איז גיוויש קלט דו גישט גאר
נקט איך וויל דיר איין שויב מלין וויא [ווילשטו] זי האבן צו מארגנש איז די שנור צו אים
קומן גוטין מארגן שווער לעבין איך האב אייך הייט נלט זער גהערט הושטין
וארום טרינקט איר ניט גיברונטן וויין מארגין איז אייך זיר גזונט האב איך דאך
5 גוטין אונ׳ גנוק אים הויז אן דז איך ניט דראן גדענק איך האב אזו פיל צו טון דז איך
אן אייך ניט גדענק אונ׳ האט איבר דיא קעלין אן גיהובן איין רוגז צו מלן וארום
מלשטו דען שווער ניט אלי מארגנש איין גוטי ביר זופא גיא ברעגג אים איין ווינוק
איין גימלטש אריין נאך דעם איז זיא וידור קומן שווער לעבן איז גוויש קלט
אין דר שטוב וארום קומט איר ניט אין אונזרי שטוב וועם אירט איר אונ׳ האט אים
10 וידור אן זיין טיש גזעצט אונ׳ מיט זיך לאזין עשין נאך דעם אלין איז דער יונג הין
גנגין אונ׳ דען לייטין אלש וידער גיבראלט וואז מן אין גליהן האט דר אלטי האט
גרוש שלעשר אן זיין קשטין גליגט דר אלטי האטש וידור גנן גוט גיהט ביז דיא
צייט קומן איז דז ער האט זעלין שטערברן דא האט ער דען זון צו אים גרופין אונ׳
האט אים צוואה גיטאן פר לייטן אז דר סדר איז אונ׳ האט אים גבעטין ער זאל אים
15 פליישיג קדיש נאך זאגין אונ׳ אים ליבט ברענין וער איך דיר דאך גנוק לאזין דז
עש דייני קינדר אונ׳ קינדש קינדר העלפין ווערט אונ׳ איך ביט דיך דוא ווערשט
הלטין וואז איך דיך בעטין ווער אונ׳ ווערשטו עש טון ווערט עש דיר וואול גין ואו
אביר ניט דז דו עש ניט הלטן ווערשט ווערט עש דיר ח״ו ניט וואול גין דז דוא ניט
זאלשט איבר דען קשטין גין ביז דז דאז יאר אויז איז אונ׳ וון דוא ווערשט דריבר גין
20 נאך דעם יאר דא זאלשטו מיט דיר נעמין דען שטאט רב אונ׳ חזן ושמש אונ׳ עיקרי
[הקהל] דען זיא זאלין זעהן דיא גרושי ירושה דיא איך דיר לאזין אזו איז דר
זקן גשטארבן דער זון האט דיא צוואה גיהלטין אונ׳ האט אים גאר וליישיג קדיש
נאך גזאגט אונ׳ זיין ליכט גברענט דוא נוא [דאז] יאר איז אויז גוועשט דעם אין
דיא צייט לונ גוועזט נאך דער ירושה אזו בלד האט ער נאך דעם רב אונ׳ חזן
25 ושמש גשיקט אונ׳ נאך עיקר הקהל אונ׳ איז מיט זי איבר דען קשטין גגנן אזו האבן
זיא גפונדין דרינן איין גרושי קייל איז דרויף גשריבן גשטנדין וור דא אלש איין
וועק גיבט בייא זיינם לעבן וואש ער האט. דען זאל מן מיט קייל שלאגן צו טאט:
/דער

[18a] דער איז בחרפה גיוואורדין הט ניט גוויישט וואז ער ריידן זאל פר גרושי חרפה דז

דיא לייט גזעהן האבן דר נאך הט דאז אינוקיל צום פאטר אן גיהובין ליבר טעט

איך בעט דיך שענק מיר דען זידש קוץ איז ער ברוגז גוווארד וואז זאל זיא דיר דא

האט ער ווידר אן גיהובן איך וויל זיא דיר הלטן ווען דו אויך וואורשט אלט ווערן

5 דא וויל איך דיך אויך דרייַן היל'ן אין דיא קוץ וויא דוא עש דיין פאטר האשט גיטאן

דען אונזרי חכמים20 האבן גזאגט במדה שאדם מודד מודדן לו דאז איז טייטש וויא

דר מענש איינם מעשט דא מעשט מן אים ווידור וויא ער זיין פאטר הט גיטאן

ווערט מן אים ווידור טון דרום זאל איטליכר פרומר [גוווארנט] זיין דז מן ניט זאל די

עלטרין אזו שמעך אונ' גרינג הלטן אונ' בפרט דיא יונגי וויבר ליך מאג מן עש

10 פיר זאגין ווען איין ארמי מוטר דאז אירי הט גטאן אונ' איין טאכטר אויף דען

דרעק דר צוגן אונ' הוט זיך נעבוך נקט אויש גצוגן דר נוך איך וויל זיא נוא איין מן האט

דא גדענקט זיא ניט דראן דז זי זיך מיט גו*ט מיט יתּ"ש אונ' מיט אירן וויל מחיה זיין אונ'

ור לאט זיך ווידר אויף פאטר אונ' מוטר דיא אבר יראת שמים אין זיך האט גדענקט

מיין פאטר אונ' מוטר האבן מיר פארט גנוגין גטאן וווען איך וואר זולה זיין דז איך

15 קענט ווידר מקיים זיין כיבוד אב ואם וואלטש מיט הערצן גערן טון אבר קאן זיא עש

ניט טון מיט אירן ממון זאל זי עש טון מיט אירן גוף אונ' זאל זאגין מיין ליבה מוטר לאז

מיך דאש טון איך בין יונג אונ' שטערק דוא בישט נוא אלט אויך אונ' [האשט] דיך נוא

אף גערבט אבר מן גפינט בעו"ה מענלי אונזעלני טאכטר דיא זילט דער מוטר צו

דז זי ערבט ביז דז זי אויף דאש מויל בלייבט ליגן דרויף האט אונזרי גמרא21 גזאגט)

20 אשרי מי שלא [חמן] אביו ואמו) דאש איז טייטש וואל דעם דר פאטר אונ' מוטר ניט

האט גזעהן אויך גפינט מן מענלי די עשין מעדנים אונ' לאזן פאטר אונ' מוטר פר

שמעכין דר נאך זאגט זי איך טאר פר מיין דען ניט מאן איין פרום וייב קן אירן מן

וואל איבר בעטין אונ' צו אים מיין ליבר מאן וויא זאל מיר מיין עשין בקומן מיין

ארמר פאטר אונ' מוטר ליידן גרוש דוחק דעש גלייכן מיט קליידר זאל זי זאגן וואז זול

25 מיר איברגי האפרט מיין ארמר פאטר אונ' מוטר גיאן נעבוך נקט אונ' בלוס אונ' וויל

עש בעשר אן זי אן ליגן אונ' דש ווערט מיר העלפן אן מייני נשמה אויף עולם

הבא/

20B. Sanhedrin 100a.   21B. Kiddushin 31b.

8 K1618; גוואנרט P1609 | 17 K1618; האטש P1609 | 20 K1618; המי P1609

[18b] הבא דרום איר ליבן ווייבר איר ווערט מיר ניט פר איבל האבן דז איך אזו גשריבן
האב אדר גשטראפֿט האב דען איך האבש אויף קיינם ביזן אן גשריבן דען מיין
כוונה איז אויף אייטל גוטש דען איך בין ניט אויש אויף דען כלל ח״ו דען דיא רוב
נשים זיין צדקניות אונ׳ זיין מדקדק אויף אירי מעשים טובים מאן דערף זיא ניט צו
5 שטראפֿין נאך זאגין זיא ווישין אלש זעלברט פֿארט וואל צעהן מאלט מער אז איך
גשריבן האב נייארט מיין כוונה איז אוב מן איני גפֿענד אונטר טויזינט דיא עש
ניט טעט האף איך צו השם ית״ש דז מיין ריד ווערן אין איר אורן אניין גין אונ׳ ווערט
מיר פֿאלגין דא שטיט עש מיר פֿר מיין מיא אוליי וואר איך אויך אין זכות דער
פֿון האבן אמן:

שער רביעי

10

פֿון שווער אונ׳ שוויגר וויא איין אשה זאל איר שווער אונ׳ שוויגר אירן מאן לכבוד
זאל לכבוד איריך דא ווערט גו*ט ית״ש ווידור אין דען זכות אירי תפלה דר הערן.
ווא זיא זיך ווערט הין וועענדן אדר קערן:

בית והון נחלת אבות מה׳ אשה משכלת¹) דאז איז אזו טייטש איין הוין אונ׳ גוט
15 קאן מן וואל פֿון עלטרין ירשין אבור איין קלוג וייב מוז מן פֿון גו*ט ית״ש פר
דינן שלמה המלך ע״ה האט דען פסוק גרעט אויף איין אשה דיא דא קלוג איז אונ׳
גדענקט אויף [איין] תכלית די פֿון גו*ט ית״ש זולה איז וען זיא איין שווער אונ׳ שוויגר
בקומט וויא זיא זיא זאל אין כבֿוד הלטין דיא יראת שמים אין זיך האט דערף מן ניט
פֿיל דר פֿון צו שרייבן דיא דא ורום איז גדענקט אזו וויל מיין מאן איז מחויב זיין
20 פֿאטער אונ׳ מוטר מכבד צו זיין דא מוז איך אויך מיין מאן לכבֿוד זיא מכבֿד זיין אונ׳
איך וויל זיא הלטין פֿר איין פֿאטער אונ׳ מוטר אז מיר אויך גפֿינדן ביי שאול המלך
אז אין דער דוד המלך ע״ה האט אין גהיישין מיין פֿאטר אז דער פסוק גיט
אבֿי ראה גם ראה² אונ׳ האט אין אין גרושן כבֿוד גיהלטין וויא וואל ער איז אים נאך
זיין לעבן [גשטנדן] אונ׳ האט צו אים גזאגט תיקר נפֿשי בעיני ה׳³ דש איז טייטש
25 /מיין

¹Prov. 19:14.　²I Sam. 24:12.　³See II Kings 1:14.

17 K1618; איין P1609　|　24 K1618; גשטנדן P1609

[19a] מיין לייב זאל איך גו*טש אויגן אזו אוירדיג זיין אז דוא אין מיין אויגן בישט אויך לערנן
מיר פון רות המואביה דז זיא האט פיל זולה גוועזט דז דאש מלכות בית דוד איז
פון איר קומן אונ' מלך המשיח ווערט פון איר קומן דאז האט זיא אלש זולה גיוועזט
דרום דז זיא מיט איךי שוויגר גומל חסד האט גיוועזט אויך דרשת דיא גמרא⁴ דען
5 פסוק (צדיק אוכל לשובע נפשו⁵) דאז איז טייטש דער צדיק עשט ווען ער
שון וועניג עשט איז ער זט אונ' לאט זיך בינוגן דא זאגיט דר פסוק עש גיט אויף
רות המואביה אז דר פסוק גיט ותואכל ותשבע ותותיר⁶ דאז איז אזו טייטש זי האט
געשין אונ' האט זיך בנוגן גלאשן אונ' האט דר שוויגר אויך גבראלט אונ' זיא האט
זיך מטריח גיוועזין אונ' האט איר צו וועגין גיבראלט אונ' האט איר עלטר פר שונט
10 אונ' האט זיא דר היים גלאזין זיצין דיא צדקות האט צו איר שוויגר גשפראלין דיא
היך אין גרוש אז בועז אויך גירעט האט צו איר (היגד היגד לי כל אשר עשית
את חמותך⁷ דאז איז טייטש עש איז מיר ברוח הקודש גזאגט גיווארין וואז
דוא מיט דיינר שוויגר חסד האשט גיטאן דרום בישטו ראוי דז איך דיך זאל אין
מיין הויז ברענגין וויל דוא זילי' גוטי מדות אונ' מעשים אן דיר האשט איז מיר אן
15 צוווייבל דז פיל גוטש פון דיר ווערט קומן פון דען קענן מיר לערנן מה דאך רות די
איךי שוויגר האט גפאלגט דאו זעלביג עניין איז נראה [כמבואר] אין ניבזיג אן צו
זעהן גוועזט נאך דאט עש זיא עש גדולטיג מיין שוויגר איז איין צדקות טוט מיר אלש
לטובה מכל שכן איין אנדרי דיא זאל גדענקן מיין שוויגר דיא דוא שטראפט מיך צו
מיינם גוטין זיא האט איךין זון אזו ליב זיא זעך זער גערין פיל גוטש פון מיינם מאן אונ'
20 מיני קינדר דאז רעט אלש פון דר אשה המשכלת דיא דא קלוג איז בדענק דאז
אלש אונ' איז מלבבד שווער אונ' שוויגר אונ' איז מקבל מוסר פון אין אונ' קערט זיך אן
איךי שטראף אונ' גדענקט זיא טוען מירש אלש צו גוטין אבור איין נערין דיא איז
אלש להיפך אונ' קערט זיך אן קיין שטראף זיא מיינט זיא טוען איךיש אלש שרש להכעיס
אונ' איז מטיל שנאה אויף זיא אונ' לאט איךין צארן פר איר גין זיא מיינט זי האט
25 איין גרושי מציאה ווען זיא איךין מן איבר רעט דז ער איר פאלגט אז ער פאטר אונ'
מוטר פר שטושט אונ' ברענקט אים אויך זיין נשמה אונ' מלט דז ער זיך פר
זינדגט דאש גדענקט זיא אלש ניט אונ' ווען זיא נייארט איר בוזהייט האט פר בראלט
ווער קאן אלש דר שרייבין וואש ביז וייטר דר פון קומט אונ' צארן אז ספר מידת⁸
שרייבט /

---

⁴Ba-midbar Rabbah 21.20.   ⁵Prov. 13:25.   ⁶Ruth 2:14.   ⁷Ruth 2:11.   ⁸Seyfer Middes, fol. 42a.

16 כמבוער P1609 K1618

[19b] שרייבט אין מדות הכעס אונ' איז אויך משלם רעה תחת טובה דען דאש גיבעט

דז איטלכר פאטר אונ' מוטר אל איר האפנוג אונ' גבעט דז זיא טואן צו הק״בה דאש

איז אלש אויף אירי קינדר דז זיא זעלין זולכה זיין איר צייט צו פר ברענגין אין גו*טש

דינשט אין תורה ומעשים טובים איני דיא יראת שמים אין זיך האט בדענקט דאש

5 אלש אבור אין נערין דיא דאש ניט גדענקט האט שלמה המלך ע״ה דרויף גזאגט)

אשת כסילות הומיה פתיות בל ידעה מה⁹) דאש איז טייטש איין נערש וייב דיא

ברומט אונ' מורט אימר דאר דיא נערין וייש ניט וואש דאש מיינט אזו וייש ניט

וויא וייט עש גריילט אויך איז מענלש וייב אדור מאן אזו נערש אונ' האבן אל איר

מחשבה אונ' האפנוג אויף שוער אונ' שוויגר דז זיא אירר אימר דאר וועלן גניישין

10 אונ' ווען זיא עש ניט טואן האבן זיא איין רוגז אויף זיא אונ' האבן קנאה אונ' שנאה

זיא טואן אנדרן קינדרן מין אז אונש דער פון קומט פיל ביז הש״י אז מירש לערנן פון

יוסף הצדיק ע״ה דז דיא ברידר האבן אים זו ניט זעלין מקנה זיין דען איטלכר בן

אדם זאל זיין בטחון אויף הש״י שמו האבן אז דר פסוק גיט ברוך הגבר אשר יבטח

בה׳ והיה ה׳ מבטחו¹⁰) דאש איז טייטש גבענשט איז דר מענש דר זיין פר זילברונג אויף

15 השם יתברך האט אז וערט גו*ט יתברך זיין פר זילכר זיין אז דוד המלך גרעט

האט טוב לחסות בה׳ מבטוח באדם¹¹) דאש איז טייטש עש איז בעשר דז איך מיר זאלין

זיך בשיצין אן גו*ט יתברך מיר אז דיא פר זילכרונג פון איינם מענשין דו איז צו ורענגן

אויף דען פסוק וארום רעט ער בייא השם יתברך דאש לשון לחסות אונ' בייא דען

בן אדם רעט דאש לשון פון בטחון דאש מיינט אזו ווען איין בן אדם האט דיך פר

20 זילברט אונ' פיל צו גזאגט דז דוא דערפשט אל דיין טאג פר נישט צו זארגין איך וויל

דיר גנוג געבן אונ' השם יתברך הט אים נישט צו גזאגט דו זאל ער דעניך זיך ליבר

אויף השם יתברך חסד בעשר פר לאזין דרום רעט דער פסוק (טוב לחסות בה׳¹²) עש

איז בעשר דז ער זאל זיך בשיצין אויף השם יתברך אונ' ניט אויף דען בן אדם ווען ער

אים האט שון פיל צו גזאגט אז דער פסוק גיט אל תבטחו בנדיבים בבן אדם

25 שאין לו תשועה¹³) דאש איז טייטש פר זיכרט אייך ניט אן דען מענשין דער קיין

הילף בייא זיך הוט אז אויך ירמיה הנביא גזאגט הוט ארור הגבר אשר יבטח באדם

ושם בשר זרועו¹⁴) דאש איז טייטש פר פלוכט איז דער מענש דער זיך אויף איין

אנדרן מענשן פר לאשט אונ' טוט זיין ור זילברונג אויף איין מענשן דער בשר ודם איז

---

⁹Prov. 9:13.   ¹⁰Jer. 17:7.   ¹¹Ps. 118:8.   ¹²Ps. 118:8.   ¹³Ps. 146:3.   ¹⁴Jer. 17:5.

[20a] דאש מדרש[15] דרשת די פסוקים אויף יוסף הצדיק דז ער זיך ור זינדגט האט דז ער זיך

ור לאזין האט אויף דען שענקן דז ער אין האט ועלן דר תפיסה ברענגין דא

הוט ער צווייא יאר לענגר מוז אין דער תפיסה בלייבן. אויך זאל אין שנור פון איר

שוויגר אירי שטראף ליפליך אן נעמן אונ' זאל גדענקן זיא טאן מירש צו גוטן אז דער

5 פסוק גיט (נאמנים פצעי אוהב ונעתרת נשיקות שונא[16]) דאש איז טייטש זי

זיין ווארהפטיג דיא [וואונדן] פון אין פריינד זאל דיר ליבר זיין אז דאש קושין פון

איינם פיינד דאש מדרש[17] גיט אונ' דרשת דען פסוק אויף משה רבינו ע"ה אונ' אויף

בלעם הרשע עש ווער בילכר גוועזט דיא ברכות דיא בלעם גרעט הוט אויף ישראל דז

משה זעלט גרעט האבן אונ' דיא קללות דיא משה האט גרעט אין דר תוכחה זעלט

10 בלעם האבן גרעט דא איז זיין אונזרי חלכמים[18] אזו מתרץ [זאלט] משה רבינו דיא ברכות

האבן גרעט דיא בלעם האט גרעט דא העטן דיא אומות העולם גשפראכן וואש איז

חדוש דז אין פריינד רעט וואש ער גערן הערט דרום האט הקב"ה דיא נבואה פון

דר ברכה דורך איין שונא לאזין זאגן דז ער האטש מיזן זאגין זאגין איבר זיין דנק אויך

מאג איך דען פשט אזו זאגין אזו זאגין משה רבינו האט אזו גטאן אז אין פאטר זיין ליבן

15 קינד טוט אונ' ווישט אים איין רוט ווערשטו דש אונ' דש טון דא וויל איך דיך מיט דר

רוט שמיצין אונ' דז בלעם האט ישראל זער משבח גיוועזן אונ' זיין כוונה

אזו גוועשט דז ער האט גשפראכן (לא הביט און ביעקב ולא ראה עמל בישראל

ותרועת מלך בו[19]) דאש איז טייטש עש ווערט ניט גלוגט אונטערבלט אונטר יעקב

אונ' ווערט ניט גזעהן פלשיקייט אונטר ישראל דרום אויך איז גו*ט בייא זיא אונ' דיא

20 גזעלשפט ר"ל דז זי מיט אננדר באגודה אחת זיין דא איז דר קינג הקב"ה אין אירי

הילף דו הט ערש אזו גמיינט וען זי אבר ניט ווערן אזו זיין אונ' ווערן מיט פלשרייא

אונ' מיט אונרעכט אום גין אונ' ווערט איינר דען אנדרן ניט בייא שטין דא האט ער

וועלן להיפך רידן כלם אויך מלך איז הינטר זיך כלם דז איז טייטש פר דערב זי דא האט

הקב"ה אים דז ווארט אין מויל פר קערט דז ער הט מיזן רידן מלך אויף אויף דאז גיט דר

25 פסוק (ויהפך ה' אלהיך את הקללה לברכה כי אהבך ה' אלהיך[20]) דז איז טייטש הש"י

הט דיר זיין קללת צו ברכה פר קערט פר דיך גו*ט ליב הט דרום הט שלמה המלך

גרעט נאמנים פצעי אוהב[21] דז מיינט משה רבינו אז נשיקות שונא[22] פון בלעם דר אהב

האטש גוט גמיינט אונ' דר שונא האטש ביז גמיינט אונ' אזו הט ער אל זייני ברכות

אויף ביזן גמיינט אונ' אז ער הט גשפראכן הן עם לבדד ישכון ובגוים לא יתישב[23] דז

---

[15]Bereshit Rabbah 89.3.   [16]Prov. 27:6.   [17]Devarim Rabbah 1.4.   [18]Devarim Rabbah 1.4.   [19]See Num. 23:21.   [20]See Deut. 23:6.   [21]Prov. 27:6.   [22]Prov. 27:6.   [23]See Num. 23:9.

6 K1618; וואונדרן P1609 | 10 K1618; זלאט P1609

[20b] איז [טייטש] דאש פֿאלק זאל אליין רואין און' זאל זיך ניט אונטר די פֿעלקר פֿר מישין

מיט אבֿילה ושתייה און' דן גנג פֿון אירין מלבושים און' ניט מתחתן מיט זי זיין און'

ניט מעורבֿ אונטר זי זיין עש זי דען לצורך וואש ער מוז טון אז איין דער תורה אוך

שטיט גשריבן ואבֿדיל אתֿכם מן העמים²⁴ דאש איז נוא זיין כוונה אוך לרעה גוועזין

5 וען ישראל וערט דאש אלש הלטין דא וערין זי לבדד ישכון זיין דאז מיינט זי וערין

אליין אין גן עדן זיין וואו אבור ניט דא וערין זיא להיפֿך זיין און' דא ער האט גזאגט

ישראל זיין (כארזים²⁵) אז דיא טנין בוים האט ער אוך גימיינט לרעה זיא זאלין

זיך הוך און' האפֿרטיג הלטין וייל זיא מזרע אברהם יצחק ויעקבֿ זיין און' זאלין ניט

דאש גלות ליידן אוך דאש גיט דאש מדרש²⁶ טובֿה קללות אחיה השלוני מברכת בלעם

10 די קללה פֿון אחיה השלוני איז בעשר גיוועזין צו ישראל אז די ברכה פֿון בלעם ווארום

אחיה השלוני²⁷ האט גשפֿראבֿן ישראל זאל זיין אים גלות אז די רור אים טייך דש ווגלט

אימר דאר הין און' הער אזו זאל זיך ישראל אים גלות אימר דאר בזארגין און' זאל זיך

אימר דאר מלבֿיע זיין אים גלות ביז הש"י וערט זיך מרחם זיין איבר זיא אז דאז רור

טוט ווען דר ווינט קומט און' וויל זיא אויש רייסן דא ליגט זיא זיך נידור ביז דר ווינט

15 איין וועק גיט דר נאך ריכֿט זיא זיך וידר אויף דא גיט דאש מדרש ווייטר דער תני

בוים שפֿריבֿט צום רור ווא דו בישט אזו איין ווייך דינג און' דר ווינט קאן

דיך ניט אויש רייסן און' איך בין אזו שטערק און' הוך און' דר ווינט האט מיך אויש

גרישט דא ענטווורט אים דאש רור ווען דוא מעלבֿשט טון ווא איך טוא און' מעלבֿשט

דיך אוך מלבֿיע זיין וויא איך מיך מלבֿיע בין און' מעלבֿשט דיך אויך אנידר ליגן קענט

20 ער דיר אוך איין נישט טון דא זעהן מיר וואל דז דיא קללה פֿון אחיה השילוני איז איין

ברכה און' איין גוטי עצה צו ישראל אין גלות און' בלעם כוונה איז בז גוועזין

דאש גלייבֿך זעהן מיר אלי טאג פֿער אונש דיא ביזן לייט דיא קיין יראת שמים אין זיך

האבן אז שליח איז בעו'ה און' העצין לייט אויף ביזן צוווישן שנור און' שוויגר און'

שפֿרעלין ניט גיווין זיא דרריין דז זיא דיך דיך ניט שפֿל זאל הלטן און' מיט דען זאל

25 אויך אזו און' העצין זיא אויף אנודר דא קומט קיין גוטש דר פֿן קומט אדרבה איין

האדר ווער קאן דאש מעריך זיין וואש בין השם ישמרינו דר פֿן קומט

פֿרומר זאל זיא שטראפֿין און' שלום צוווישן זיא מכין און' שפֿרעלין נעם עש גיטגליך

אויף /

---

²⁴Lev. 20:26.   ²⁵See Num. 24:6.   ²⁶Yalkut, § 203.   ²⁷See I Kings 14:15.

1 K1618; טייטש P1609

[21a] אויף עש ווערט בעשיר ווערין ווען זי אזו רידן ווערן אונ׳ ווערין שלום צווישן דען לייטן

מכין דא ווערין זיא [אויך] זולכה זיין דז זיא שלום ווערן האבן אין אירן הייזרן (מדה

כנגד מדה) דען דר שלום איז דר תכלית פון אלים דרום אויך לאזין אונזרי תפילת

אל אויז מיט שלום. ווען דאז ווערט נוא אזו זיין דז שלום ווערט צווישן דען לייטן זיין

5   דא ווערין אלי דיא ברכות דיא הש״י שמו האט ישראל גבענשט ווערן אל מקיים אן

אונש זיין אונ׳ מיר ווערין זולכה זיין צו דר גאולה דיא דא ווערט שלום מכין אין גנצין

עולם אמן:

שער חמישי

מענין גידול בנים וויא איין אשה זאל זיך פלייישיג מיאן דז זיא איר קינדר זאל צו

10   תורה מעשים טובים דר ציאן דו ווערין זי דיא לייט בענשין וואול דעם בוים דיא זילכי

פרוכט האט מכין בליאין:

דער פסוק גיט איין משלי ראוה בנים ויאשרוה בעלה ויהללוה[1] רבת בנות [עשו] חיל

[ואת עלית] על כלנה[2] שלמה המלך ע״ה הט די פסוקים גזאגט אויף איין אשה חשובה

דיא זילכי קינדר צילט דיא דא שפרעכין מיין ליבה מוטר האט מיך דר צו גיהלטין דז

15   איך דש האב גלערנט וואז גו*ט ית״ש ליב איז אונ׳ דר וועלט ליב איז זילט דען איר קינד

וואש ניט רעכט איז גטאן דא זאגט עש זאגט עש מיר מייני ליבה מוטר ניט גשטט דז

איך דעט דאש גטאן אזו אויך דר מאן אונ׳ ער זילט דז איין אנדרר מאן טוט וואז ניט

רעכט איז גטאן דא שפרילט ער דאז טוא איך ניט אויך מעלט מירש מיין וייב ניט

גשטטין דאז האט שלמה המלך ע״ה מיט דען פסוק גימיינט אונ׳ אז ער וייטר זאגט

20   (רבות בנות[3] וגו׳) דאז איז אזו צו פר שטין עש שטין פיל טעלבטר פון ישראל די דא

זאלן גוטי מעשים אדר אויך פיל גוט נאך ציא די זעלבג מער גלובט איבר די דא

זעלגי קינדר אויף ציט אויף דאש האט שלמה המלך ע״ה דיא פסוקים צו הויף גזעצט

אונ׳ זיין אזו טייטש וויא איך דא גשריבן האב אונ׳ אויש גליגט נאך אנדר אויף דאש

אויך האט הש״י דורך ירמיה הנביא גרעט אויף איין אשה דיא דו פרומי זעלגי קינדר

25   זאל האבן /

---

[1]See Prov. 31:28.   [2]See Prov. 31:29.   [3]Prov. 31:29.

2 K1618; ד [אן] P1609 | 12 עשי P1609 K1618 | 13 ואתה עות P1609; ותה עלית K1618

[21b] זאל האבן [אונ'] דר פסוק גיט טרם יצרתיך מבטן ידעתיך⁴ דאש איז טייטש אי איך
דיך האב בשאפין אויז דר מוטר לייב האב איך דיך דר קענט דאז מיינט איך האב
גוו*שט דיין מוטר מחשבה טובה דרום האב איך דיך ליב וואו עש אבור ח״ו להיפך
איז דרויף האט דוד המלך ע״ה גרעט זורו רשעים מרחם תעו מבטן דברי כזב⁵ דאז
5 איז טייטש זי זיין פר פרעמט די רשעים אים בוך אירר מוטר דרום אז זי ליגן [גזאגט]
הט דרום זול איין איטלכה ורומי ורויא גווארנט זיין אונ' וי איך ערשטן שער גשריבן
האב דז זי זיך דר נאך הלטין זאל. נוא וועלן מיר וייטר פון דען זכין רידן אז ראשית
חכמה⁶ שרייבט ווי זיך איין זעליגי אשה מוז מיאין דיא אירי קינדר צו תורה מעשים
טובים ווי דר ציהן דען דאש טראגין אונ' גוויין איז דאש ווינישטט דען איין בהמה
10 טראגט אונ' גוויינט אויך אונ' אזו דרשת דיא גמרא⁷ דען פסוק דוא אונזר ליבר הער
גו*ט צו חוה האט גזאגט דא זיא דען אפיל האבן געשן הרבה ארבה עצבונך⁸ דאז איז
טייטש איך וויל מערן דיין וויא וואש דאז מיינט דאז אז דער ציהן די
קינדר איז עיקר דען עש איז פיל דראן גלעגין וויא איך אז וויל שרייבין והרונך⁹ דש איז
טייטש דיין טרלט דאז מיינט דאז שווער טראגין בעצב [תלדין] בנים¹⁰ דאז איז טייטש
15 מיט וויא טאג דוא זאלשט גוויין דיין קינדר אויך מאג איך דען פסוק אזו דרשן
עצבונך¹¹ דיין וויא טאג דאז מיינט דז זיא איר וושט מיט צער זאל פר ברענגן אי זיא
זיך קאן וויש אן ליגן אונ' דר נאך דיא טבילה דאז איז דר גרעשט צער עש מעכטין
מענבלין וועז עש גו*טש וויל ווער טראגן אונ' גוויין פון דען וועלן מיר ניט רידן
(אין להרהר אחר מדת ה') דז קענין מיר ניט פר שטין נוא וויל איך דען פסוק
20 וייטר אויש ליגן (והרונך¹²) איז דש טראגין ווי איך פארט גזאגט האב בעצב¹³)
דאש מאג טייטש זיין מיט ערבט אז דר פסוק גיט בכל עצב יהיה מותר אך כדבר
שפתים למחסור¹⁴ דאש איז טייטש אן אליר ערבט דז דר מענש טוט האט ער
זונשטר מער אן דר צו וויל רעט האט ער זונשטר ווינוגר נוא זעהן מיר וואל דז עצב
ערבט טייטש איז אזו מאג דר פסוק היא אויך אזו מיין מיט גרושה מיא אונ' ערבט
25 זאלשטו דיין קינדר גוויין אונ' דר ציהן עש זעהן אלי בייד אויש דען פסוק גיהערט
אדר דר פסוק איז אזו טייטש [דיא קינדר] דיא דוא גוויין וורשט דיא זאלשטו מיט
וויא טאג דער ציאן דא איז דר פסוק אויף דען פסוק אושן וויא וואל דז (צער
/גידול

---

⁴See Jer. 1:5. ⁵Ps. 58:4. ⁶*Reshit Hokhmah*, III, p. 80, § 42. ⁷B. Eruvin 100b. ⁸Gen. 3:16. ⁹Gen. 3:16. ¹⁰Gen. 3:16.
¹¹Gen. 3:16. ¹²Gen. 3:16. ¹³Gen. 3:16. ¹⁴See Prov. 14:23.

1 K1618; אנ' P1609 | 5 K1618; גזאגט P1609 | 14 תלדו P1609 K1618 | 26 דוא קינדר P1609; דאז קינד K1618

[22a] גידול בנים) שטיט אין עצבֿונך [15] אויך אונ׳ [האטש] נאך איין מאלט מרמז גוועזן ווייל
דר צער גידול בנים גרעשיר איז אז די אנדרין אל. אויך איז מיר אויף [דען] פסוק
צו פֿרעגן דז הקב״ה האט גזאגט הרבה ארבה עצבֿונך [16] דאז איז טייטש מערין דיין
וויא טאג דאש גפֿינדן מיר נירגנג דז הקב״ה בייא איינם פורענות זיין נאמן העט
5 גדאבֿט אז מיר עש זעהן אין אומרי היילוגי תורה בייא דער [תוכחה] בייא דר
ברבֿה שפריבֿט ער ונתתי גשמבֿם בעתו ונתתי שלום בארצבֿם [17] דאז איז טייטש איך
וויל געבן דען רעגן אין זיינר צייט אונ׳ דר נאך שפריבֿט אויך אונ׳ איך וויל געבן שלום
אין אייהרין לנד. אבר בייא דר קללה זאגט ער ניט איך וויל [זיא] אויף אייך ברענגן
נייארט זיא ווערן זעלברט קומן אז אויך בייא עלי הכהן קינדר [חפֿני ופֿנחס] האט
10 הקב״ה גזאגט מכבֿדי אכבֿד ובוזי יקלו [18] דאש איז טייטש דיא מיך ערן דיא וויל
איך וווידר אירן דיא מיך פֿר שמעהן דיא זאלין פֿר לייבֿטרט ווערן אונ׳ שפריבֿט ניט
איך וויל זיא פֿר שמעהן אזו גפֿינדן מיר פֿיל מאלט דז הקב״ה זיין היילוגן נאמן בייא
קיינם פורענות ניט לאשט גדענקין וואַרום האט הקב״ה דא אן גשריבן איך אַל וויל
מערן דיין וויא טאג. אלא ער האט דא אזו גמיינט מער צער אז דו האשט מיט
15 דען קינדרן דער ציאן זונשטר מיר שבֿר וויל איך דיר מערין אויך דרשת דיא
גמרא [19] דז יעקבֿ אבינו מער זבֿות האט גיהט אז אברהם אונ׳ יצחק דרום דז ער דען
צער גידול בנים האט גהט נוא וויל איך וווידור אן היבֿן אונ׳ שרייבן וויא איין אשה
איר קינדר אין צוויי דרבֿים זאל גוויונן דר איין דרך וואז אן בלנגין איז דען גוף דר
אנדר דרך וואז אן בלנגין איז דיא נשמה דרום מוז זיך איין איטליבֿה אשה גאר זיר
20 פֿליישין אונ׳ מיאן דז זיא אירין קינדר דר צילבֿט ערשטליך אזו בלד אז דאז קינד
גיבורין ווערט מוז זיא השגחה האבן אונ׳ גווֹרנט זיין דז זיא דאז קינד קיין אנדרה
זאל לאזין זויגן זיא זאל עש זעלברט דעם אנדרן טאג אן ליגן דען אזו בלד אז דאז
קינד איין אנדרי שמעקט דא וויל עש דר נאך דיא מוטר ניט זויגן דר נאן קומט
איר דיא מילך אזו גאך דא האט זיא דען קיין וואורצלין אונ׳ מוז זיך פֿיל גניטין אויך
25 איז מעגבֿי אזו אונזעליג אונ׳ וויל זיך ניט טון אונ׳ לאזט דאז קינד איין אנדרי
זויגן דר וויל שיסט איר דיא מילך אונ׳ ווערט ביטור דר נאך וויל זיא דאש קינד
אבור ניט זויגן דיא איז אזו טוט דיא ווערט איר טאג קיין גוטי עם אונ׳ איר מילך איז
ניט גוט זיא איז איין אז /וושיר

[15]Gen. 3:16.   [16]Gen. 3:16.   [17]See Lev. 26:4, 6.   [18]I Sam. 2:30.   [19]See B. Shabbat 89b.

1 האשט P1609 K1618 | 2 דאן P1609; K1618 | 8 ויא P1609; זי K1618 | 9 K1618; הפֿני ופֿנהס P1609

[22b] ‫וואשיר אונ׳ איז ביטור קורץ ווארט וואו זאל מען פיל פון דער שרייבן איין איטליכי די‬
‫אזו טוט אדר זוגט מיט איינר ברוסט עש זייא וואר זיא וויל זו הלט מן זיא פר איין‬
‫אונטולכט דז זיא זיך לאשט מוט ווייליג פר דערבן דען עש שט איר אל איר טאג דער‬
‫נאך מוז זיא זיך פיל גוטן אונ׳ אוז הלטין דען מעלט זי עש גערין מיט גרושם געלט‬
5 ‫אפא קויפין. אבר איני די דו זעליג אונ׳ קלוג איז די דיא גידענקט אויף איין תכלית‬
‫אונ׳ ליגט אל איר פלייש אן וואז זיא גלייך רייך איז מן וויש ניט ווא וויא איין דינג קאן‬
‫קומן. אויך האט שלמה המלך ע״ה גזאגט כל ערום יעשה בדעת וכסיל יפרוש‬
‫איולת20 דאז איז טייטש איטליכר קלוגר טוט אליש מיט זין אונ׳ וויץ אדור איין נר דר‬
‫שיידט אפא נרהיט כלומר דער קלוג גדענקט אויף איין תכלית אונ וויא מן אים וואז‬
10 ‫זאגט דא הערט ער צו אונ׳ פאלגט וואו מן אים גוטש לערנט אבור איין נר דר שיידט‬
‫זיך אפ פון איין חכם כלומר ער איז דר היפך פון איין חכם אונ׳ אין דולט אלי מולט‬
‫זיין דיעה די בעשט זיין דרום קאן ער צו קיינם תכלית קומן דרום זאל זיך איין יוגנט‬
‫לאזין לערנן אונ׳ פאלגין דען עלטרין דיא זיך גינט האבן. נון וויל איך ווייטר רידן פון‬
‫דען זלין וויא איך פון דען קעשטליכן דאקטור מהר״ר שמואל מקבל האב [גווועזט] וי‬
15 ‫מן דא איין קינד זאל באדין מן זאל דאז קינד ניט צו וורברבן באדן דען עז מלט דאז קינד‬
‫שווך אונ׳ מט אונ׳ זאל אים דען קאפ ניט כלל ניט נעצין דען דז גיהירין איז אים וויך אונ׳‬
‫קומט ח״ו פיל ביז דר פון דז איך עש ניט שרייבן וויל וואז השם ישמרנו דר פון קומט‬
‫ווען מן עש עש אויך דען באד נעמונט מאג מן עש איין וויניק לנצים ווישין אויך זאל מן עש‬
‫ניט לנג אין דען באד לאשין ליגן. אויך ווער פניטן דז מען דען יוגנט ויל אונ׳ אונ׳ פיל‬
20 ‫זאלט שרייבן אונ׳ זאגן דען מן קאן ניט אזו פיל דר פון שרייבן נאך רידן עש איז אלש‬
‫צו וויניק דז זיא דאז קינד ניט זאל צו זיך גוויין דען עז געלט אונ׳ די אז דר מוטר די דא‬
‫זעליג איז דען אזו בלד אז זיא עש איין מאלט צו זיך נעמט דא איז עש נוא גשעהן‬
‫דר נאך קאן מן עש שווערליך דרויז גוויונן פון דער זך דער פיל צו שרייבן אבור איין‬
‫איטליכי דיא דא גוטש פורכט אין זיך האט דערף מן עש ניט פר ביטין דען זיא איז‬
25 ‫זעלברט אזו קלוג אז אויך שלמה המלך ע״ה האט גשריבן תחת [גערה במבין] מהכות‬
‫כסיל מאה21 דאש איז טייטש איין אנגשט אונ׳ אן שרייאן אן איינם קלוגין כלומר ווען‬
‫מן איין קלוגי וויונגט איז מער אז מן איין נרן הונדרט שלעק שלאגט אויך איז וואל ניט‬
‫דז מן‬/

20Prov. 13:16.   21Prov. 17:10.

14 K1618; גווועזט P1609 | 25 גערה במבין P1609; וגערה במבין K1618

[23a] דז מן דען יונגט זאגט דז זיא מוז דאז קינד שונין אז איין שאל דאש [איין] דען עש איז

בלד גשעהן דז מן אים ח״ו וויא טוט דר נאך שפרעכין זיא עש איז אן גיווקשין אדור

זאגין מען האט אים עין ביז אויג געבן אונ׳ ברענגנ דען אלטי גויֹת אונ׳ לאזין זיא אן

שפרעכן דאש איז איין הייפֿט עברה מיין חלק זאל ניט בייא דען [זעלביגן] זיין אומרי

5 היילֹיגֹה תורה האט אונש פֿיל מאלֹט פֿר באטן אז דר פסוק גיט לא יהיה בך מנחש

ומכשף[22] דאש איז טייטש עש זאל ניט זיין אן דיר קיין רעטליר נאך [קיין] ציברר אז

מיר גפֿינדן בייא אחיה השילוני הנביא דער האט צום מלך גשפֿראכֹין המבלֹי [אין] אלהים

בישראל לכן המטה אשר עלה לא יקום מות ימות הנער[23] דאש איז טייטש אוב איז [ניט]

[גוֹ*ט] אונטר ישראל דרום דאש בעט דז דר קרנק יונג דרויפֿ ליגט ער ווערט ניט אויף

10 שטין ער מוז שטערבנ דר יונג אויך שרייבֹט ספֿר חסידים[24] מן טאר ניט רידן נאך

גלויבן זֹילֹבֹי זֹכֹין מן זאל קיין פֿייאר געבן פֿון איין קינד בעטרן אדר דען טאג טאר

מן ניט צו שנידין אדור דער אגֹלֹשטר שרייֹט מיר ווערן גשטהאבן אדר דר ברנט

האט זיך אויפֿ גשטעלֹט ניט לעשטע איין אפֿ דר גשט דער דא קומט ווערט דר טֹרינֹק

עטֹליֹבֹי דיא דא זֹעלֹבֹי זֹכֹין גלוֹיב דיא פֿר זֹולֹין אוב עש וואר איז דר (שטן השם

15 ישמרינו) איז בלֹד דא אונ׳ [מֹכֹטן] דז עש גשיבֹלֹט דר וואֹרֹטן דז אר איין אנדר מאלֹט

ווידר אן אים זאל גלויבן אז מיר פֿיל מאלֹט זעהן דז מעֹנֹבֹי לאֹזין זיך מבֹשֹפֿות

וואש זאגין אדור אן שפֿרעבֹין דז זיא אונֹריֹיֹנֹי (עבודה זרה) דר בייא מזכיר

זיין דז איז איין הייפֿט עברה אומרי הייֹלֹיֹגֹי תורה האט שֹש פֿר באֹטֹין אז דר פֿסוק

גיט ושם אלהים אחרים לא [תזכירו] ולא ישמע על פיך[25] דאש איז טייטש

20 נאמן דש פֿרעמדן געֹטֹיר ניט זאֹלֹט איר גדעֹנֹקֹן כלומר איר מֹלֹט דז זיא

גדעֹנֹקֹין זיא אונ׳ ניט עש זאל ווערין גהערט אויֹף דיינם מויל מן טאר איֹרֹי חגֹאות

ניט נעֹנֹין אבור דיא יראֹת שמים אין זיך דר האט דערף מן דאז אלֹש ניט פֿר ביטֹין

דרום זאל איין איֹטֹלֹיֹבֹי ורומי מוֹטֹר השגחה האבן אויֹף איֹרֹין קינד אונ׳ זאֹלֹש ניט

איֹנֹב קֹלֹיֹנֹין מיֹדֹלֹן [וור] טרֹוֹיֹאֹין אדור מן גפֿינט מעֹנֹבֹי ווייבֹר דיא דא גֹיֹאֹין אויֹף

25 חתֹונת אדור זֹלֹר אונ׳ גֹדֹעֹנֹקֹט ניט דז זֹיֹא איֹיֹן קינד דר היֹם האֹט אויֹך האֹב איֹך

איֹין מאֹלֹט גֹזֹעֹהֹן דז איֹין זֹלֹר מוצאי יום כֹיֹפֿור איֹז גֹוֹעֹזֹין אונֹ׳ דיֹא נֹלֹט דר פֿיֹר אֹן

כל נֹדֹרֹי צֹו נֹלֹט זיֹין זיֹא בֹלֹד נֹאֹךֹ בֹרֹבֹו אויֹש דר שֹול גֹלֹאֹפֹֿין זיֹא האֹבֹן גֹשֹפֹֿראֹכֹין איֹךֹ

מוֹז איֹיֹן היֹם צֹום קיֹנֹד גֹין אֹונֹ׳ דיֹא נֹלֹט דֹר נֹאֹךֹ צֹום זֹלֹר זיֹין זיֹא איֹיֹן הֹלֹבֹי נֹלֹט

דֹא/

---

[22]See Deut. 18:10.   [23]See II Kings 1:16.   [24]*Sefer Ḥasidim*, § 59.   [25]Exod. 23:13.

1 K1618; {}אין P1609 | 4 K1618; זעביג P1609 | 6 K1618; דיין P1609 | 7 fehlt P1609 K1618 | 8 K1618; זיא P1609 |
9 גוט P1609 K1618 | 15 מכח P1609 K1618 | 19 K1618; תזכינו P1609 | 24 זור P1609; ור K1618

[23b] דא גבליבן אונ׳ האבן ניט אן דען קינדרן גדאכלט עש איז וואול איין מיינונג דז

אייני בייא איר קינדר זאל בלייבן די נימען צו אים האט אונ׳ דערף ניט דר שול גין

אז מן זאגט עש איז בעשיר דז זיא דר היים בלייבט אונ׳ גדענקט אין דר שול אז [ווען]

זיא אין דר שול איז אונ׳ גדענקט איין היים אז דוד המלך ע״ה האט גזאגט אמרי

5 האזינה ה׳ בינה הגיגי²⁶ דאז איז טייטש מיין זאג פר נעם עש כלומר דיא

תפילה דיא איך צו דיר טוא פר נעם זיא קאן זיא איך דען זיא ניט טון דוא זאלשט

פרובין מיין גדענק דיא איך אין הערצן האב אויך האט שלמה המלך ע״ה גזאגט

(גם את זה לעומת זה עשה יי׳²⁷) דאז איז אויך אזו טייטש איינש קיגן

דען אנדרן האט גו*ט ית״ש בשפן כלומר דאז מיינט אזו איין אשה זאל גדענקין ווען

10 איך גלייך איצונדר מיין שול ניט גנג קאן ווערטין אונ׳ מוז איין תפילה פר זומן דאך

האף איך צו גו*ט ית״ש ווען איך דאז קינד וואר ציאין צו זיינם דינשט אונ׳ צו זיינם לוב

אונ׳ צו הלטין תורה מצות ווערט עש מיר גלייך זיין אויך זיין האט דוד המלך ע״ה גזאגט

עת לעשות לה׳ הפירו תורתיך²⁸ דאש איז טייטש עש איז ציט צו טון פון

גו*ט וועגין ווען מן שון איין מצוה מבטל איז אז אופט מאלט גשילט דז מן אין דר

15 גרעשטי תפילה הלט אונ׳ מוז גניטג איין וועק גין אז אין איין אשה צו קינד גיט אדור

דעש גלייכן דא זאל זיא ניט גדענקין איך מוז הירן אזו אויך ווען זיא איין קליין קינד

האט אונ׳ וואלט עש אליין לאזין איז בעשר זיא בלייבט בייא אירי קינדר דען עש זיין

השם ישמרינו פיל מכשולת גשעהן ווען איני איר קינד אליין האט גלאזין ווער קאן

אלש דר זאגין דרום זאל איין איטלכי זעלני אשה בייא אירין קינד בלייבן אונ׳ זאל [אין]

20 דיא היילגי שול ניט ווערטין וויא וואלט זיך דען אן היבן דז זיא וואלט שפעצירין גין

אדור פר דיא טיר זיצין דא קאן יוא קיין גוטש דר פון קומן ווען זיא אבור בייא דר

וויגן בלייבט זיצן דא הלט זיא איר קינד אין שלאף אונ׳ קאן איר ערבט אויך דר נעבן

טון איז זיא זולכה דז זיא מיר קינדר האט אונ׳ דר וקשני זאל זיא זיצין אונ׳ זאל צו

הערן דבנין אונ׳ בענשין אונ׳ ניט אויף דען רבי פר לאזין מן שפריכט עש איז קיין

25 ערבט אזו גוט אז זיך דר מענש זעלברט טוט אויך איז דאז לערנן אז איין מוטר מיט

דען קינד לערנט עש פיל מער מוצלח אז פון איין אנדרן אז מיר עש לערנן פון דען פסוק

(שמע בני מוסר אביך ואל תטש תורת אמך²⁹) דאז איז טייטש פאלג

[מיין]/

---

²⁶Ps. 5:2.   ²⁷See Eccles. 7:14.   ²⁸Ps. 119:126.   ²⁹Prov. 1:8.

3 K 1618; ווע P1609 | 19 אי P1609 K 1618 | 28 זיים K 1618; P1609

[24a] מיין זון דיא שטראף דיינם פאטער אונ' ניט דו [זאלשט] ור לאזין לערנין דיינר מוטר

דרשת די גמרא ווארום רעט ער בייא דער מוטר תורת אמך אונ' בייא דען פאטר

רעט ער אזו וויל דר פאטר זיין מחיה מזו ווערטין אונ' איז ניט אלי מאלט דר היים

נייארט צו צייטין וועז ער זילבר דז ער ניט רעבלט טוט דז א שטראפֿט ער אין אבור

5 די מוטר דיא איז אימר דער היים זיא זאל אויף אירי קינדר אכטונג [האבן] אונ' קאן פיל

מעשים טובים מיט זיא לערנן אונ' זאל מדקדק זיין אויף איטלכן [טריטן] אונ' אויף

איטלכֿן ווארט אז אונזרי ליבי תורה האט גשריבין (ושננתם לבניך ודברת בם

בשבֿתך 30 וגו') דז האבן מיר אין אונמרי תפֿילה אבֿנט אונ' מארגנש דז איז טייטש דוא

זאלשט זי לערנן דיין קינדר אונ' דוא זאלשט רידן אן זיא אין דיינם זיצן כלומר דוא

10 זאלשט בייא דיין קינדר זיצין אונ' מיט זיא רידן אויף דר תורה אונ' ניט דבֿרים בטלים

דארום שטיט גשריבין בם אן זיא אין דר תורה אבור אנדרי דבֿרים בטלים זאל מן

מיט זיא ניט רידן אז אורחת צדיקים 31 שרייבֿט ווען מן מיט איינם קינד דברים בטלים

רעט איז גלייך אז איינר אין איינר איין טאבֿל האט אונ' וויל דרוף שרייבֿין וואז אים ניץ איז דא

קומט [איין] אנדרר אונ' פרקלעקט אים דיא טאבֿל דז ער נישט קאן דרוף שרייבין אזו

15 איז דא אויך אויף הקב"ה האט דען מענשין בשפֿין אונ' האט אים אין לב געבן דז ער

זאל אן זיין הייליגן נאמן גדענקין אונ' אן זיין הייליגֿי תורה אז דר פסוק גיט וכתבתם

על לוח לבֿך 32) דאז איז [טייטש] אונ' דוא זאלשט שרייבן אויף דיא טאבֿל

דיין הערצין נוא ווען מן מיט איינם קינד שבֿושים רעט אדר אנדרי דברים בטלים

איז אים אין זיין הערץ אויף ור קלעקט אונ' ור ווינט אונ' פֿר צוגין דא קאן מן דען עש

20 שווער ארווי ברענגין אונ' דר פסוק שרייבֿט (בשלבֿך 33) דאז איז טייטש ווען מן זיך

ליגט זאל מן מיט אים רידן וואז יראת שמים איז אונ' זאגין אך וויל דיר שיני שמועות

אין דען חומש זאגין אונ' מעשים אויז דר גמרא אונ' זאל אים זאגין וויא פֿיל לייט

האבן זיך לאזין [אום] ברענגין פֿון זיין הייליגן נאמן וועגין אונ' זאל אים זאגין וויא

יצחק אבֿינו ע"ה האט זיך וועלן לאזין שעכטין דר וויל דז עש גו*ט ית"ש גיהישין

25 האט אויך האט ער האט ער ווידור זיין פאטר ניט וועלין טון אונ' האט אים געבעטין ער זאל

אים וואול בינדן דז ער אים ניט זאל שטוסין אויך זאל מן אים זאגין פֿון

/מישאל

---

30 Deut. 6:7.   31 Orhot Zaddikim, fol. 3b.   32 See Prov. 3:3; 7:3.   33 Deut. 6:7.

---

1 K1618; זאלשט P1609 | 5 K1618; הבאן P1609 | 6 K1618; טבֿיטן P1609 | 14 אין P1609 K1618 | 17 K1618; טיטש

P1609 | 23 K1618; אים P1609

[24b] חנניה מישאל ועזריה וויא דר מלך האט יונגלין גיפנגי דיא דא זיין ביז גוועזין אונ'

וויַיטי ביזי העלי גיהט דיא האבן טריפֿות געשין אונ' נסך גטרונקֿן דיא זעלבגין זיין איר

חלק גֿעל אונ' גרין גוועזין אבר די דו זיין פֿרום אונ' זעליג גיוועזין דיא האבן איין רֵיין

מונד גיהט אונ' ניט וויַיטי העלי דיא האבן קֵיין טרפֿות געשין וועלין עשין אונ' האבן נישט

5 אנדרש געשין אונ' גטרונקֿן אז וושיר אונ' ברוט אונ' זֵיין דענוך פֿריש אונ' גזונט

גיוועזין אונ' שֵין אז מילך אונ' בלוט גיוועזן דר נאך האט אונזר ליבר הער גו*ט איין

מלאך צו זיא גשיקֿט דער מיט זיא גלערנט האט דר נאך האט דער מלך עבֿודה

זרה לאזין מכֿין דיא ביזין יונגליך האבן דען מלך גבֿוט ניט וועלין ברעליֿן אונ' האבן

זיך צום צלם גֿבוקֿט דען זיא האבן זיך גיפֿערלֿט מן וערט זיא אין קֿלֿך אובֿן וערֿפֿין

10 אבור דיא פֿרומי יונגליך דיא דרֵייא האבן זיך ניט גֿוועלט צום צלם בוקֿין אונ' האבן

זיך לאזין אין קֿלֿך אובֿין וערֿפֿין דוא האט גו*ט יתֿ"ש זיא איין מלאך גשיקֿט דער זיא

האט בשירמֿט פֿר דעם פֿייאר אונ' זֵיין פֿריש אונ' גיזונט אויף גיזונט אויך דעם קֿלֿך קומ אן

שאַדין אבור דיא ביזין יונגליך דיא זיך האבין צון צלם גבֿוגֿט האט [דר מלך] לאזין אל דר

שלאגין ער האט גזאגֿט [   ]

15 איר האט אזו איין מעלֿטיגֿן גו*ט אונ' איר האט אייהר לנד פֿר זֿינט

איר וערֿט מיין לנד אויך פֿר זֿינדֿגין זֿילֿכֿי שמועות זאל מן דען קֿינדֿרֿש פֿיר זאגֿין

דז מיינט אויך די תורה ושננתם לבניך ודברת בם[34] אויך זאל מן די קֿינדֿר לערֿנֿן לשון

הקֿדֿש אויך זאל דיא מוטר דאז קֿינד אזו עש דען פֿאטר זאל מכֿבֿד זיין

דיא מוטר זאל אים איין גוטין בישין געבֿן אדור איין אפֿיל אונ' זאל אים זאגֿין ליביֿש

20 קֿינד הלֿט דאז דיין פֿאטר דז דוא אים דר מיט מכֿבֿד בישט דא וערֿט דיר גו*ט יתֿ'

דיינֿי יאר דר לעניגין אזו אויך זאל דר פֿאטר טון אונ' זאל צו דען קֿינד זאגֿין קֿינד לעב

זֵיא דיין מוטר מכֿבֿד אונ' ווי ער מיט דוא קֿאנֿשֿט מכֿל שלֿן וועֿן עש איין עלֿטֿר פֿאטר

האט אדור איין עלֿטֿר מוטר דז עש זיא זאל מכֿבֿד זיין אבר מיר גֿפֿינדֿן מענֿלֿכֿי

פֿאטֿר אדור מוטֿר דיא דא לֿבֿין וועֿן זיא העריֿן פֿון איין קֿינד קֿללֿות אדור שבֿועות

25 אונ' גֿפֿלֿט אין זיר וואול אונ' שפֿרעכֿן וויא שֵין קֿלֿוג קֿינד איז דאז אבור דאז זאל ניט

זֵיין עש איז אלֿש אום איין גיוואנֿהֵייֿט מן זאל איין קֿינד גיוואֿן אז עש זאל צו גֿרֵייֿפֿֿן קֿאן וועֿן

עש איין מעשֿר וויל נעמין זאל מן אים אויף דאז העֿנֿטֿל שלֿאגֿין אונ' זאל אים איין

מורא מכֿין איין איטֿלֿכֿי פֿרומי פֿרויא זאל איר לאשׁיֿן קֿיֿין רוט אפֿא גֿין אז שׁלֿמה

/המלך

---

[34]Deut. 6:7.

13 דר ניט P1609; ער P1609; fehlt K1618 | 14 גזאגֿט ער האט שלאגֿי ער אל לאזין דר מך האט גבֿוגֿט צלם צום האבן זך די P1609; fehlt K1618

[25a] המלך ע״ש אין משלי שרייבט (אתה בשבֿט תכנו ונפֿשו ממות תֿציל)[35]

דאז איז טייטש דוא זאלשט דיין קינד מיט דר רוטין שלאגין דא ווערשטו זיין לייב

פֿון טוט בשירמן כלומר דז ער ניט חייב מיתה ווערט זיין אז אונזרי תורה וויל האבן

(מקלל אבֿיו ואמו מות יומתֿ)[36] דז איז טייטש דר זיין פֿאטר אונ׳ מוטר פֿר

5 לייכֿטערט דז ער ווידור זי טוט אונ׳ זי מצער איז דר זאל גטיט ווערדן דרום שטיט

צוויי מאלט (מות [יומתֿ])[37] כלומר ווערט אין דר דין אויף דער וועלט אים

נישט טון דא ווערט מן אים אויף יענֿ עולם הבא ניט דר לאזין דרום זאל מן גווארנט זיין

דז מן דאז קינד בצייטן זאל [גווינן] צו [גוטין] אז שלמה המלך ע״ה האט גזאגט חנוך

לנער על פי דרכו גם כי יזקין לא יסיר ממנו[38] דז איז טייטש

10 גווין דען יונגין אויף דען רעכטן וועג וועז ער אלט ווערט דו ווערט ער אויך ניט דר

פֿון אפֿא קערין כלומר ער ווערט אין גוטין וועג בלייבן אבֿור ראשית חכֿמה[39] שרייבט

דען פשט אזו וואן דוא דען יונגין ווילשט גווינן אז זיין סדר איז וויא ווערש פֿר זיך

זילבט פֿון אנדרן עזהתן יונגין וון ער אלט ווערט דא קאן ער שווער ארויז קומן אונ׳

ברענגט אײן משל דרויף אײן גזלן דר האט פֿיל גשטיפֿט דר פֿאטר

15 האט אים גשטראפֿט מיין זון בדענקט דיך וויא ווערט עש מיט דיר גין אויז גין דר זון

ענטוורט ווידור זיין פֿאטר מיין ליבר פֿאטר דוא האשט וואר איך וויל דיר פֿאלגין

קום מיט מיר שפֿצירין אונ׳ פֿירט אין אין אײן וואלד דא איז זיין קלײני ביימליך גשטנדן

דא האט דר זון צום פֿאטר גזאגט נעם דאז ביימכֿן אונ׳ ביגש אויף דר זייט צו דער

ערדן אונ׳ דר נאך אויף דר אנדר זייט אויך אזו דר פֿאטר האטש גיטאן האטש אויף

20 אלי זייטין גבוגין וואו ער האטש גיוואלט דר נאך זיין זיא וויטר גגין דא איז אײן

גרושיר דיקר [בוים] גשטנדן דר זון זאגט אבֿור צום פֿאטר נעם דען בוים אונ׳ ביג

אים אויך צו דר ערדן אז דוא יעגין האשט גיבוגין דר פֿאטר שפֿראך איך קאן דען

בוים ניט גלנגן ער איז צו הוך אונ׳ דיק דר זון שפֿראך הער וואז דו רעטשט ווילשטו מיך

איצונדר שטראפֿין אונ׳ ציאן העשטו מיך ליבר גשטראפֿט דא עש איז מיגלך גוועזט

25 צו ציהן אין דר יוגנט דא וואר עש צו דעם ניט [קומן] אונ׳ נאם דאז שווערט אונ׳ שלוג

דעם פֿאטר דעם קאפֿא אפֿא אבֿור מענלי אונזעלגי מוטר גדענקט ניט דראן ווען

אײן פֿאטר וויל דאז קינד דאז שטראפֿין אדור שלאגין וויל זיא עש ניט ליידין אדור

[להיפֿך]/

[35]See Prov. 23:14.   [36]Exod. 21:17.   [37]Exod. 21:17.   [38]See Prov. 22:6.   [39]*Reshit Hokhmah*, III, p. 59, § 9.

6 ‏יﻣוﺗֿ‎ P1609 ‏|‎ K1618; 8 ‏וﻏינן‎ P1609 ‏|‎ K1618; ‏ﻏו*טיﬥ‎ P1609 ‏|‎ 21 ‏ﺑיום‎ P1609 K1618 ‏|‎ 25 ‏קﻣﬥ‎ P1609 ‏|‎ K1618; ‏להﭘֿﻚ‎ P1609; ‏לﭘֿיﬥﺮ‎ 28 ‏|‎ K1618

[25b] להיפֿך וועז זיא וויל שלאגין דא ווילש דר פֿאטר ניט ליידין דא קומן דיא [אייבל]

גצוגין קינדר הער השם ישמרינו אדור דאז דאז גלייבין וועז איין קינד קומט אוג׳ זאגט

דש האב איך גפֿונדין זאגין זיא וויא איין מזליג קינד איז דאז אוג׳ גדענקין ניט

עש מאגש אירגיץ גנומן האבן אזו קומט עש דריין השם ישמרינו [אדורן] אויך איין

5 קינד עפֿיש זילט בייא איין אנדרין אוג׳ ווילש מיט גוולט האבן אזו גיט פֿאטר

אדור מוטר אוג׳ נעמטש יעניש אויף דר הנט אזו [גוויינט] מן דיא קינדר ניט גוט עש

זאל אבור ניט זיין מן זאלש דען קינד אויז רידן אוג׳ זאגין מן טאר ניט נעמן וואז

ניט דיין איז ח״ו איינר שטערבט אונזר ליבר גו״ט האטש פֿר באטין אוג׳ זאל עש שמיישן

אוג׳ זאגין לאו [מיך] דאז ניט מיר פֿון דיר הירן אזו אויך האט האט שלמה המלך ע״ה גזאגט

10 חושך שבטו שונא את בנו ואוהבו שוחרי מוסר[40] דאז איז טייטש ווער זיין

רוט פֿר מייט פֿון זיין קינד דר האט אויך זיין קינד פֿיינט דר אבור ליב האט זיין

קינד דעם פֿארשט נאך אים קלומר וויא ער זיך בייא דעם רבי הלט אוג׳ שטראפֿט

אים אזו דיא דיא גמרא[41] דרשת דרום אז אברהם אבינו האט ישמעאל פֿר צוגין איז ער

(לתרבית רעה) גגין אזו אויך יצחק אבינו האט עשו פֿר צוגין איז ער אויך גגין

15 (לתרבית רעה) ראשית חכמה[42] דרשת דען פסוק אזו דר זיין רוט פֿר מייט

פֿון זיינם זון דא זאלשטו גושליך ווישן דז דא זעלביג קינד זיין פֿאטר ווערט

פֿיינד האבן זיכשטו אבור אז איין פֿאטר אדור מוטר איר קינד שטראפֿט דא זאלשטו

גווישליך ווישון דאז [דן] דאש זעלביג קינד ווערט זיין פֿאטר אוג׳ מוטר ליב האבן אוג׳

ווערט איר וויל טון אז מירש אויך גפֿינדן בייא דוד המלך ע״ה וויל ער אבשלום ניט

20 האט גשטראפֿט לסוף איז ער אים נאך זיין לעבן גשטנדן אוג׳ האט גמלט דז גרושי

זינד אונטר ישראל זיין גשעהן אוג׳ פֿיל טויזנט אונטר ישראל אין שווערט זיין אום

קומן אזו אויך בייא אדוניה שטיט גשריבן (ולא עצבו אביו)[43] דאז איז טייטש

זיין פֿאטר האט אים ניט טרויאריג גימלט אויך גיט דר פסוק (ואותו ילדה אחר

אבשלום[44]) האט ער דאך איין אנדרי מוטר גיהט וואום שפֿרעכט דר פסוק ער

25 האט אים נאך אבשלום גוואונן אלא דר פסוק זאגט מיר דז ער אויך נאך אבשלום איז

גראטן אוג׳ האט אן זיינם פֿאטר גיבראכין אוג׳ האט זיך בייא זיינם פֿאטר לעבן צו

מלך לאשין זלבין [לסוף] האט ער זיין פֿאטרש וייב וועלין האבין דרום האט ער איין ביז

ענד/

---

[40]See Prov. 13:24.   [41]Shemot Rabbah 1.1.   [42]Reshit Hokhmah, III, p. 59, §§ 9–13.   [43]I Kings 1:6.   [44]I Kings 1:6.

18 דז P1609 | 9 איך P1609 K1618 | 6 K1618; גוויינט P1609 | אדר K1618; אדר P1609; ר]{ר 4 | אום K1618; איב 1 P1609; איב K1618 | 27 K1618; לטוף P1609

[26a] עֶנְד גינומן אך האט שלמה המלך גיזאגט יסר בנך כי יש תִּקְוָה וְאֶל הֲמִיתוֹ

אַל תִּשָּׂא נַפְשֶׁךָ[45] דא איז טייטש שטראף דיין קינד דען דז איז איין [האפֿונג] דז

גוט קאן ווערין אבור צו טיטן אין זאל דיין ווילן ניט טראגין כלומר דאז מיינט אזו דר

דוא זאלשט ניט גדענקן ווען אך דאז קינד שמיישין ווער דא ווערט עש זיך דר

5 בזירין אונ' ווערט קרַנק ווערין דאז זאלשטו ניט גדענקן אוך האט שלמה המלך

ע"ה [גיזאגט] אִיוֶלֶת קְשׁוּרָה בְלֵב נַעַר שֵׁבֶט מוּסַר יַרְחִיקֶנָּה מִמֶּנּוּ[46] דז איז טייטש

די נרהייט איז גקניפֿט אין דען הערצין דז יונגין כלומר ווייל קומט ניט פֿר יארן

רוט דז מן דאז קינד דר מיט שטראפֿט מלט עש פֿערין פֿון אים ראשית חכמה[47]

שרייבט אזו דר איין פֿאטר מוטר זאלין זיך ניט גדענקן ווא זאל איך אים שטראפֿין

10 עש איז דאך פֿר לארין עש העלפֿט קיין שטראף אן אים אונ' ברענגט איין משל איז

איין טראפֿן וושיר דר דא שטעטליך טריפֿט אויף איין שטיין לסוף מלט עש אין גרוב

אין דן שטיין ווי וואל דאך דז איין הערט דינג איז און אום איין שטיין אונ' איין ווייך

דינג אום איין טראפֿין וושיר דא ער צו גיהערט גרושי [חכמה] אונ' צדקות אז מעגלי

קינדר דיא דא [בעו"הן] יונג זיין פֿר ווישט ווארדין אונ' דיא שטיף מוטר וויל זיא ניט

15 שטראפֿין אונ' שפריכט איך וויל ניט מלין דז דיא לייט ווערין פֿון מיר ריד [דאזן] זאל

אבור ניט זיין זיא זאל זיא מיט [גוטין] ווארטין שטראפֿין דא ווערט הש"י אירן לון דרום

געבן אז דר פסוק גיט (אַשְׁרֵי שֹׁמְרֵי מִשְׁפָּט עֹשֵׂה צְדָקָה בְכָל עֵת)[48] דאן איז

טייטש וואול דעם דיא דיא דא ווארטין אויף דאז משפט כלומר דיא זיך פֿערלטין פֿר דען

משפט דז הש"י ווערט ריכטן. אונ' דיא דא צדקה טואן אלי צייט דרשת דיא גמרא[49]

20 וויא איז עש מיגליך דז מען אלי צייט קאן רגע צדקה געבן אלא דאן גיט אויף דן

לייט דיא דא ספרים קויפֿין אונ' לייאן עש [לוייטין] דיא דרויז לערנן דער מיט זיי

מזכה רבים זיין זיין אדור אויף די לייט דיא די יתומים אין אירן הויז האבן אונ' זי מגדל

זיין צו גוטין מעשים אז דיא גמרא[50] דרשת דען פסוק וְאֵת הַנֶּפֶשׁ אֲשֶׁר עָשׂוּ בְחָרֹן[51]

דר פסוק גיט בייא אברהם אבינו ע"ה אונ' שרה ע"ה דאז איז טייטש זיא האבן

25 די לייבר מיט זיך גנומן דיא זיא האבן בשפֿין גיט דיא גמרא[52] ווייטר ווען די גנץ

וועלט בייא אנַנדר ווער קענטין זיא ניט איין מוק בשפֿין דאז איז איין קליין

דינג מכל שלכן דז זיא האבן לייט בשפֿין גיט דיא גמרא דיא גנץ וועלט בייא

/אַנַנדר

---

[45]Prov. 19:18.   [46]Prov. 22:15.   [47]*Reshit Hokhmah*, III, p. 55, § 2.   [48]See Ps. 106:3.   [49]B. Ketubbot 50a.   [50]Bereshit Rabbah 84.4.   [51]Gen. 12:5.   [52]Bereshit Rabbah 39.14.

---

2 האלפֿונג P1609; האופֿן K1618 | 6 גיזאגט P1609; גזאגט K1618 | 13 K1618; חאמה P1609 | 14 K1618; בעווה P1609 | 15 K1618; דאו P1609 | 16 גו*טין P1609 K1618 | 21 לייטין P1609; לוייטן K1618

[26b] זיא האבין זי מלין איין איין אונטר די פליגיל דער שכינה אונ׳ האבן זיא גלערנט דז
[זיא] דען בורא ית״ש דר קענט האבן רעלט דא זאגט דר פסוק גלייך אז זיא [העטן]
זיא בשפין דז מדרש‪53‬ גיט וועאן אברהם אבינו האט געשט גיהט וועאן זיא האבין זעלין
איין וועק גין אונ׳ האבן זיא גדנקט דא האט ער צו זי גזאגט וואז דנקט איר מיר
דנקט דעם דערש בשפין האט אונ׳ האט גזאגט (נברך שאכלנו משלו) דאז
5 איז טייטש מיר וועלין לובין דז מיר געשין האבן פון דען זיין דא זיא גפרעגט
וער איז דער אדור וואו איז ער אזו האט ער זיין הייליגין נאמן צו דר קענן
געבן אונ׳ האט זיא מגייר גוועזט דאז זיין גום גוועזין אונ׳ האבין דען בורא ית׳ש
דער קענט מכל שכן ארמי יתׄומים דיא נעבוך ור ר גווארדין דיא קעשטליכי
10 ורומי עלטרין האבין גיהט דז מן זיא וודור אין גוטין וועג קאן ברעגנגין עש גהערט
אבור גרושי חלכמה דר צו אונ׳ יראֵת שמים מן מוז מיט זיא גיטליך אונ׳ גוטן ווארטין
שטראפין ליבש קינד פאלג דוא מיר נייארט אונ׳ טוא אלש וואו [גוׄ*טן יתׄ] ליב איז
אונ׳ אויך דען לייטין איך האף צו [גוׄ*טן יתׄ״ש איך וויל דאז גן עדן אן דיר פר דינן איך
בעט דיך טוא דיין עלטרין דיא שנד ניט אן דען דיא עלטרין זיין זיך אים קבר מצער
15 דען זיא ווישין אלז וואז אויף דר וועלט גשיבלט וועאן עש איריין קינדרן אין דר וועלט
איבל גיט שרייאן זיא צו הקב״ה אונ׳ בעטין פר זיא ראשית חלכמה‪54‬ שרייבט וועאן איינר
פרומי קינדר הינדר זיך לאטט אויף דר וועלט אזו אפט אז דאז קינד מעשים טובים
טוט אונ׳ לערנט גערין אונ׳ גיט גערין אין דר שול אונ׳ טוט זיין תפילה בכוונה
איטלבז מאלט דר היכט עש זיין פאטר אדור מוטר אין גן עדן דיא מלאכים ברעגנגין
20 אלש ור זיין כסא הכבוד אונ׳ בעטין פר דיא נשמות דיא זילכין ורולט האבן אויף דר
וועלט גבראבלט וואז אבור ח״ו להיפך איז דז דאז קינד טוט ניט וואז גוׄ*ט ית׳ש ליב
איז אונ׳ פאלגט ניט דען לייטין דיא אין שטראפין צו גוטין אונ׳ טרייבט עזות קייט
דען דר דא ניט פאלקט דען לייטין אונ׳ טוט ניט וואז אין ליב איז דר טוט ניט
וואז הקב״ה ליב איז דען איין ביז ברעגגט דאז אנדר אז מירש אלי טאג זעהן בעו׳ה
25 דער זעלביג איז איין פאטר אונ׳ מוטר מצער דז זיא אזו איין פרולט אויף דר וועלט
האבן גבראבלט אבור דער איין בייישין איז דר איז פרום וועאן מן אים שטראפט איז ער
דיא שטראף מקבל אונ׳ לערנט גערין אונ׳ טוט זיין תפילה בכוונה אונ׳ האט איין רייין
מונד /

‪53‬Bereshit Rabbah 49.4.   ‪54‬*Reshit Hokhmah*, III, p. 55, § 2.

2 K 1618; ויא P 1609 | K 1618; רעטן P 1609 | 12 גוט P 1609 K 1618 | 13 גוט P 1609 K 1618

מונד ער עשט וואז מן אים גיבט אונ' איז בתרבית אונ' איז אים אלש צו פיל וואז מן [27a]
אים גיבט וועז וון איינר אבור איין עזות פנים איז דר הט קיין שיא פר [גו*ט] נאך פר
דיא וועלט שטראפֿט מן אים שפֿרילֿט ער וואז ליגט דיר דראן אונ' האט אין בזין
הלז גיבט מן אים צו עשין קאן מן אים ניט גנוגין געבן אויך אז גובן דז ער זיין
הלז גנוגין טוט דאז קומט אלש דז [מעגלין] זינדיגי מוטר איר קינד פֿרציבֿט וועז זיא 5
אים צו עשין גיבט דא [שפרלֿט] דאז קינד איך וויל דאז ניט האבין דא שפֿרילֿט זיא
הר איך וויל דיר איין אנדרש געבן דאז זאל אבור ניט צו זיין מן ווייש ניט וויא איין דינג
קומן קאן מן זאל זיך ניט ניט ור לאזין דיא גלייך פֿיל געלֿט האבן דרויף דערף מן ניט פֿיל
ראיֿת צו ברענגיג דען מן זיבֿט עש אלי [טאגֿן] פֿר זיך וויא מענלֿי מוטר איר קינד פֿר
צוגין הט די ניט אויף איין תכלית הט גידאכט אבר מן מוז איין קינד פֿיר זאגין אז 10
ראשֿי' חכמ'55 שרייבט אזו בלד אז איין קינד ור שטנד הט זאל מן מיט אין רידן אונ' גוויינ
וועז מן מיט אים אום אין דען הויז גיט זאל מן עש אן דר מזוזה לאזין גרייפֿן וועז מן איין
ספֿר אויף דען טיש ליגט זאל מן עש לאזין קושין אדור תפֿילין וועז איינר איין ברכֿה
מלֿט זאל מן עש הייישין אמן זאגין וועז עש היבט אן צו לערנין זאל מן מכֿין דז עש
בשמחה לערנונט מן זאל אים איין מאלֿט צוקיר געבן איין אנדר מאלֿט ניס אדור הונג 15
אויף ברוט שמירין דר ווארטין דז עש בשמחה לערנוט אז דיא גמרא56 גיט (אין
הנבואה שורה לא מתוך עצבות אלא מתוך שמחה דאז איז טייטש דיא נבואה
רוט ניט אויף דען מענשין וועז ער טרויאריג [איז] נייארט וועז ער פֿרילֿך איז אונ'
לערנוט עז זיך פֿון דען [פֿסוק] בייא [אלישע] הנביא (ועתה קחו לי מנגן והיה כנגן
המנגן ותהי עליו יד יי'57) דאז איז טייטש אונ' עש וואר אז ער שלוג 20
אויף דעם כלי זמר דא רואט אויף אים דיא דיא נבואה פֿון [גו*ט] נאך דעם וון דעם דאז קינד
מין שכֿל קריגט זאגט מן צו אים קינד לעבן זיא ורום לערין איך וויל דיר שיני קליידר
מכֿין וועז עש מין נאך קליגר ווערט זאגט מן צו אים וועז דוא ווערשט גערין לערנין דא
ווערשטו גו*טש וויל איין חשוב בחור זיין ווערט מן דיר איין תלמיד חכֿם טאֿכֿטר
געבן מיט עש פֿיל געלֿט דא ווערשט דוא [איין] ראש ישיבה ווערין וועז עש נוא זיין שכֿל 25
קריגט שפֿרעלֿט מן צו אים ליבר זון לערין לשם שמים דא קאנשט דוא עולם הזה אונ'
עולם הבא האבן מן זאל אים איין בייא שפֿיל ברענגין זיך וויא עש גיט דיא ניט
וואול/

55*Reshit Ḥokhmah*, I, p. 838, § 28.   56See B. Shabbat 30b.   57II Kings 3:15.

2 גאט P1609 K1618 | 5 מעגדי P1609 ; K1618 | 6 שפרעט P1609 ; K1618 | 9 טטג P1609 ; K1618 | 18 אז P1609 K1618 | 19 פסוק P1609 ; K1618 | אלשע P1609 K1618 | 21 גוט P1609 K1618 | 25 א'ין P1609 ; K1618

[27b] וואול גוועלט האבן אונ' זיך דר קיגן די דא יום ולילה גלערנט האבן ווא איין גרושר
אונטר שייד איז צווישן דיא ביידֿ אויך זאל מן [איין] קינד פֿיר [זאגין] אונ' דר צילן דען
חסד דאז אים הקב"ה האט גיטאן אז דוד המלך ע"ה האט גזאגט למען ידעו
לדור אחרון בנים אשר יולדו ויספרו לבניהם⁵⁸ דאז איז טייטש דרום זאלשטו דר צילן
5 צו דיין גבירט דיא קינדר זאלין דר צילן צו אירן קינדרן אונ' זאלין ניט ור געשין זיין
גנאד דען עש איז איין גרושי ביזי זך דר דא כופֿה טובֿה איז דר ניט גדענקט אן
איין טובֿה דיא אים איינר גיטאן האט איין זינדיגר מענש מכל שכן הקב"ה דז מן ניט
זאל פֿר געשין זיין גנאד דיא ער בווייזט עלי טאג אויף טאג דאז זאל מן דעם אלש
ויר זאגין ליבש קינד וואז גרושי מיא אונ' ווא טאג וואז האב איך איך דיר האב
10 דר צוגֿין פֿיל מאלט האב איך תשובֿה תפֿילה וצדקה גטאן פֿון דיינט וועגין וועז דוא
בישט קרנק גוועזין דו האב איך הקב"ה גבעטין זאל דיך לאזין לעבן אין זיינם דינשט
צו תורה [ומעשים] טובֿים אויך גפֿינדין מיר אין פסוק דז בת שבֿע שלמה המלך מוטר
האט אים פֿר גזאגט (מה ברי ומה בר בטני ומה בר נדרי⁵⁹)
דאז איז טייטש וואז האט גיהאלפֿין דז איך האב נדרים גטאן פֿון דיינט וועגין וועז
15 דוא דיין לייב לושט וועלט נאך גין אויך זאל איין מוטר אירם קינד פֿור זאגין ליבֿש
קינד איך האב [וורינונג] גוטש אויף דער וועלט גיהט איך הויף צו הש"י דוא ווערשט מיך
דר געצין אונ' דר רייאן וען דו ווערשט טון וואש גו*ט אונ' דר וועלט ליבֿי איז דען דער
אין [גו*טש] יה"ש אויגין חן האט דר האט אויך חן אין דר לייט אויגין אז דר פֿסוק גיט
(ומצא חן ושכל טוב בעיני אלהים ואדם⁶⁰) אויך זאל איין מוטר מוטר איר
20 קינד פֿר וורען דז עש קיין מעגשין צו נאמען אונ' זאגן לאז מיך פֿון דיר דאש פֿון ניט
הערין ווען שון אנדרי לייט אים צו נאמן טוא דוא עש ניט אז דען עש איז איין גרושי
הייפֿט עבֿרה מכל שכן וועז דיא מוטר הערט פֿון אים דז עש איין מקלל איז הש"י
אדיר איין עלטרין ווידור צו רעט אויך זאל מן קיין קינד פֿר דרייא יארין אין דר שול לאזין גין מיר
זאל זיך ריינטלֿט הלטין אויך זאל מן קיין קינד פֿר דרייא יארין אין דר שול לאזין גין מיר
25 לערנן עש וון פֿון דען פסוק⁶¹ פֿון איינם בוים דר ערל איז דען מוז מן דיא עירשטן דרייא
יאר ערל הלטן פֿון דען מאלט אז ער איז גפֿלנצט גווארדין מן טאר דאז אונשניט
דר פֿון עשין אונ' אן פֿירדן יאר איז ער היילֿיג אונ' גלובֿט אונ' אויך איין קינד [נאך]

⁵⁸See Ps. 78:6.   ⁵⁹Prov. 31:2.   ⁶⁰See Prov. 3:4.   ⁶¹See Lev. 19:23–24.

2 K1618; [}אין P1609 | זאגין K1618 ;זאגן P1609 | 12 K1618; ומעשם P1609 | 16 K1618; ווינו P1609 | 18 גוטש P1609
K1618 | 27 K1618; לדדא P1609

[28a] דרייא יארין האט עש שכל אונ׳ וייש זיך צו היטן אונ׳ קאן פיין אמן זאגין דיא גמרא[62]
דרשת דען פסוק (מפי עוללים ויונקים יסדת עוז[63]) [דאן] מיינט דער עולם בלייבט
בשטין פון וועגין דר [קליינן] קינדר דיא אמן יהא שמיה רבא זאגין דרום זאל מן עש
גיווינין ריינקליך אונ׳ נאך איין טעם דז מן די קנדר ניט זאל נעמן אין דר שולן פר דריי
5 יארין דען זיא קענן נישט נאך זאגין אונ׳ זיין אויך דיא עלטרין מבטל אין דר תפילה
דא האבן אונזרי ספרים פר באטין דז מן זאל קיין קינד אין דר הנט נעמן בשעת
התפילה דען דיא תפילה מוז האבן גרושי כוונה אונ׳ זיא זאלן אויך מדקדק זיין דז
עש קיין ליגין זאגט זיא זאל אים זאגין ליבש קינד מן טאר קיין ליגן זאגין דר דא ליגן
זאגט קאן ניט אין גן עדן קומן אויך איז מענגלי זינדגי מוטר דיא דא גווינט איר
10 קינד דר צו דז עש זיר צו טראגט דא אונ׳ דאז האט מן פון דיר גרעט אונ׳ הערט
אים צו אונ׳ גוויינט דאז קינד דז עש רכילות טרייבט אונ׳ צו טראגט אונ׳ דר ווארצלט
דרינן דאז זאל אבור ניט זיין אונ׳ ווען איין קינד צו דר מוטר קומט אונ׳ וויל איר זאגין דאז
אונ׳ דאז האט מן פון דיר גרעט דא זאל זיא עש אן שרייאין אונ׳ זאגין דו דרפשט
מיר נישט צו זאגין ער איז גרעכט דען איך האב אים אויך גרעט וואז אים ניט ליב
15 איז אונ׳ זאל עש דעם קינד אויף ווידן אז דאז ספר חסידים שרייבט ברעגגט איין
מעשה איז גישעהן איינר האט זיך מיט דען חסיד גקריגט אונ׳ האט אים בוזי ריד
געבן אונ׳ שם רעות גרעט זיין זון דאש חסיד איז דר ביי גשטנדין אונ׳ האט דאז
גהערט אונ׳ האט זיך דאז פאטרש אן גנומן אונ׳ האט זיך אן יענם וועלין נוקם זיין
דא האט דר חסיד צו זיינם זון אן גיהובין מיין ליבר זון שווייג שטיל לאז עש בלייבן
20 ממה נפשך איז עש וואר וואז ער מיר גרעט האט אויף מיך דז איך דיא מעשים רעים
גטאן האב דא איז איך בילד דז איך זאל שווייגין איז עש ניט וואר אונ׳ ער מיר
אונרעכט טוט דא וויל איך דענוך שווייגין אולי ווערט עש איין כפרה זיין אויף מייני
עברות דז מיר לערנן פון דוד המלך ע״ה דז ער האט פון גרא גליטין גרושי
זילזולים אונ׳ האט אים קללות נמרצת געבן (נימרצת איז ראשי תיבות נאף
25 ממזר רוצח צורר תועבה[64]) דוד המלך ע״ה האט וויל פאלק ביי זיך גיהט העט זיך וואל
קענן נוקם זיין אונ׳ האט עש ניט גטאן האט זיך גדאכט לאז עש פר מייני עברות זיין
אולי ווערט ער מייני עברות דר מיט אפ נעמין אונ׳ אין דען זכות ווערט זיך הש״י
איבר מיר מרחם זיין אונ׳ ווערט מיך צו גנאדין אן נעמין אויך דרשת די גמרא[65] /אז

[62]See B. Shabbat 119b.   [63]Ps. 8:3.   [64]See Yalkut, § 170.   [65]B. Gittin 36b.

2 דא P1609 K1618 | 3 K1618; קליינו P1609

[28b] אז דבורה הנביאה האט גזאגט ואהביו בצאתו השמש בגבורתו 66 דאש איז טייטש

זייני ליב האבר פֿון הקב"ה ווערן לייכטן אז דיא זון וון זיא אים העלשטן שטיט און'

שטערקשטין שיינט אזו ווערין דיא זיין דיא זיך דיא זיין ור לאזין ור שעמין און' לאזין זיך מזלזל זיין

זיא הערין איר שנד און' ענטוורין נישט דרויף אזו מיינט דיא גמרא 67 לעולם יהא אדם

5 מן הנעלבים ולא מן העולבים דאש איז טייטש מער זאל זיין איין מענש מעטש מן דען

דיא זיך לאזין פֿר שעמין און' ניט פֿון דען לייטן דיא אנדרי פֿר שעמן דאז זאל מן אלש

דען קינד פֿיר זאגן דרויף גיט דיא גמרא 68 אזה גבור הכובש את יצרו דאז איז

טייטש וועלכיר היישט איין גיבור דר זיין יצר הרע קאן בצווינגן און' לאזט זיין צארין

ניט ור זיין גין דז מיינט אויך דר פסו' (ואוהביו כצאת השמש בגבורתו 69) נו מאג

10 איך אויך דען פשט אזו זאגין אז דר פסוק בייא דבורה הנביאה גיט (מן השמים

נלחמו הכוכבים 70 דש איז טייטש פֿון הימל האבן גשטריטן די שטערן דא איז מיר קשה

וויא האבן דיא שטערן גשטריטן אלא עש מיינט דיא זכות אבות האבן גשטריטן מיט

אונזרי שונאים אז מיר עש נאך אלי טאג זעהן דז מיר זכות אבות גניסן אז דר פסוק

גיט והמשכילים יזהירו כזוהר הרקיע 71 דאש איז טייטש דיא קלוגין ווערן לייכטין אז

15 לויטרקייט דאש הימלש ומצדיק הרבים ככוכבים לעולם ועד 72 דש איז טייטש דער דא

מכין פֿיל לייט דז זיא זיך ורום זיין דיא ווערין לייכטן אז די שטערן אים הימל צו אייבג און'

אימר אויך האט הקב"ה אברהם אבינו מיט דר ברכה גבענשט והיה זרעך כלוכבי

השמים 73 דאש איז טייטש דיין זאמן ווערט זיין אז דיא שטערן אים הימל אויף דאן גיט

דר פסוק וייטר (אורו מרוז 74 דאש איז טייטש פֿר פֿלוכט איז דר שטערן דיר דא

20 היישט (מרוז) דאש מיינט דר שר פֿון עשו הרשע האט נוש ניט וועלין העלפֿן דען

בני ישראל דיא דא האבן אן זיך דיא מדה פֿון (גבֿורה גבר איז ראשי תבֿת גומלי

חסדים בישנים רחמנים) אויף דאז האט דוד המלך גזאגט (הללוהו את יי' כל

גוים שבחוהו כל האומים כי גבר עלינו חסדו 75) דאז איז טייטש זיא ווערן לובן גו*ט

אלי פֿעלקר דרום דז זיך האט גשטערקרט אויף אונש זיין גנאד דאז גיט אויף לעתיד

25 לבא ווערן דיא אומות הקב"ה לובן דז ער האט ישראל גהאלפֿין דיא אן זיך האבן

דיא מדות פֿון גבור און' האבן דען יצר הרע כובש גוועזין און' דאש גלות גיטלין גליטין

ווייל מיר ביז אל הער גרעט האבן וויא מן דיא קינדר זאל ציהן אז מיר עש מזכיר זיין

אבנט/

66 See Judg. 5:31.   67 B. Yoma 23b.   68 B. Tamid 32a.   69 Judg. 5:31.   70 Judg. 5:20.   71 Dan. 12:3.   72 See Dan. 12:3.   73 See
Gen. 22:17; 26:4.   74 Judg. 5:23.   75 See Ps. 117:1–2.

אבנט אונ' מארגנש אין אונזרי תפילה אז אין אונזרי תורה שטיט גשריבן (ושננתם [29a]
לבניך ודברת בם[76]) אונ' דר פסוק גיט אויך (ולמדתם אותם את בנכם לדבר בם[77])
דאז איך טייטש דוא זאלשט דיין קינדר לערנר תורה נוא האבן מיר
גרעט וויא מן זאל די דיא זין מגדל זיין צו תורה ומעשים טובים נוא וויל איך אויך רידן
5 וויא מן דיא טעכטר זאל ציהן אז אונזרי חכמים[78] שרייבן עש איז איין סימן ברכה דער
צום אירשטן איין טאכטר האט דז זיא זיך קאן העלפין דר מוטר דיא אנדרן קינדר
די דר נאך קומן דר ציאן דרום מוז איין עטלכי אשה זעהן דז זי די טאכטר זעלברט
פארט וואול ציאט צו אלי מעשים טובים דרויף גיט אויך דר פסוק בייא מתן תורה
כה תאמר לבית יעקב ותגיד לבני ישראל[79]) דז מיינט די טאכטר פון יעקב דרשת
10 דיא גמרא[80] אזו (אל תקרא לבית יעקב אלא לבת יעקב) אונ' זיא
זאל גדענקין דז זיא איר קינד מאג וואול פון זיך געבן דז מן קאן שפרעכין וואול דר
מוטר די דש קינד הט דר צוגן ווען גלייך איין עשירה איז מן וויישט ניט וויא איש איין
זך קאן קומן אז מיר אלי טאג פר אונש זעהן דז זיא ניט זאל גדענקין וש דערף מיין קינד
ערבטין איך האב געלט גנוגין מיר צו לערנן עש אויז אונזרי תורה דרך ארץ פון
15 אונזרי מוטר רבקה ע'ה דז זיא דיא תורה משבח איז וויא זיא איין גברתנית איז
גוועזין אז דר פסוק גיט (ותמהר ותרוץ[81]) דז איז טייטש זיא הט גאיילט אונ' גלאפין
צון] דען ברונין אונ' האט די דיא וושיר גשעפט בזריזות אונ' האט אים אלי זייני קעמליך
גטרענקט דאז איז אזו אזו צו פר שטין דיא היילוגי תורה[82] שרייבט דאז דרום אן דז דר
אליעזר סימן טוב אן איר געזהן האט דז זיא איין גברתנית איז גוועזין אונ' מידות
20 טובות אן איר געזהן דז גמילת חסד בי איר איז גוועזין אז שלמה המלך ע'ה שרייבט
אויף איין אשה די איין גברתנית איז (מתניה ותאמץ חגרה זרועתיה[83]) עש איז
טייטש זיא גיט גט אויף גשירצט מיט אירין לענדין אונ' אויף גשירצט מיט אירן ארם אויך
לערנן מיר פון רבקה אונזרי מוטר דז זיא פיל מעשים טובים אן איר האט גיהט אז
אליעזר אן איר געזהן האט וואז ער אן די אנדרן מיידין ניט גזהן האט אונ'
25 האט גו*ית''ש גלובט דז ער אים האט אין איין רעכטין וועג גפירט אונ' האט אים איין
(זיווג טוב) צו גשיקט דיא דא מידות פון אברהם אבינו אן זיך האט גיהט
מיט דעם גמילות חסד ומכניס אורחים איין גטרייא הערץ אן איר געזהן אונ' האט
גשפראכלין/

---

[76]Deut. 6:7.　　[77]Deut. 11:19.　　[78]B. Bava Batra 141a.　　[79]Exod. 19:3.　　[80]Mekhilta de-Rabbi Yishmael, *Yitro* 2.　　[81]See Gen.
24:20.　　[82]See Gen. 24:14.　　[83]See Prov. 31:17.

17 K1618; לז P1609

[29b] גשפראכן מיר זיין וואול גוואונט געשט צו הלטין ער הט איין נכט בגערט צו הערבר
גין דא האט זיא גשפראכלין וועו איר שון פיל נכט וועלט הרברגין מיר זיין ת״ל
וואול געשט גוואונט צו הלטין דער פון קענן מיר לערנן וויא מן איין טאכטר ציהן
זאל און׳ ניט אין פוליט און׳ מישינג גנג גוויז עש קומט נישט גוטש דר פון דען

5   איין ביזי מדה ברעגנגט ח״ו די אנדרי דז זיא דר נאך דברים בטלים רעט די זיין זיר
ביז אז אויך דיא גמרא⁸⁴ שרייבט איינר דער דא מישיג גיט קומט שיגעון דר פון גו*ט
בהיט דר פיר אויף דעם האט שלמה המלך ע״ה אויך גזאגט (עצלה תפיל תרדמה⁸⁵
דאז איז טייטש אין פוליה דיא שלאפט דר מוז לסוף אין צו רישני קליידר גין אבור
אייני די א איין גברתנית איז און׳ איר צייט ניט פר שלאפט מיט פוליט דא גיט דר

10   פסוק (לחם עצלית לא תאכל⁸⁶) איז טייטש זיא עשט איר ברוט ניט עש זיא דען
זיא האטש פארט פר דינט דרויף גיט דר פסוק (יגע כפך כי תאכל אשריך וטוב
לך⁸⁷) דרשת דיא גמרא⁸⁸ דען פסוק עש איז מיר זלות דר זיך פון זיין ערבט שפייזט
מיר אז בייא יראת שמים דרום זאל איין איטלכי קלוגי ורומי וואול בדאכט זיין און׳
אויף איין תכלית גדענקין דען זיא קאן אלש בווארנן מיט איריי חכמה וועו זיא זיכט

15   נוא דז זיא האט וואול גצוגני קינדר עש זייא דיא זין אדר טעכטר דוא איז זיא זיך
משמח זעלברט אין אירין הערצין דז זיא אזו וואול גצוגני קינדר האט און׳ העלפט
איר אויך אין עולם הזה און׳ נאך מיר אין עולם הבא דען זאל אל דיא ערבט און׳ מיא
אז פאטר און׳ מוטר טואן דו זיין זי אלש אויושין פון דר קינדר וועגין אז דר פסוק גיט
(כי אם לבניו אחריו⁸⁹) דרום זעלין זיא זעהן דז זיא איר מיא וואול אן ליגן בזלות

20   זה וועריו מיר אל אויך זולכה זיין צו דר שמחה און׳ דיא שמחה פון דער גאולה אמן

שער שישי

וויא איין שוויגר זאל זיך נוהג זיין מיט איר שנור און׳ [איידן] און׳ אל דען צנק און׳
הדור אויז אירן הויז פר מיידן ווערט הש״י שיקן ברכה אין אירין הויז אלי ביידין

דר פסוק גיט (אשת חן תתמוך לבוד ועריצים יתמוך עושר¹) דאז איז טייטש

25   אין ורויא דיא דא חן וויל האבן אין גו*ט ית״ש אויגן און׳ אין דר לייט אויגן דיא
גדענקט אויף אייטל כבד אבור דר היפך דר פון וועו זיא אויף
אויף קיין כבד אוישין איז נייארט אויף אייטל געלט די זעלבגי פר לאט זיך אויף
אירין געלט און׳ בגערט קיין חן נאך כובד אביר די יראת שמים אין זיך האט און׳
וויל יוא כובד האבן די זעלבגי הט שלמה המלך ע״ה גמיינט מיט דען פסוק אזו איין

⁸⁴B. Ketubbot 59b.   ⁸⁵Prov. 19:15.   ⁸⁶Prov. 31:27.   ⁸⁷Ps. 128:2.   ⁸⁸B. Hullin 44b.   ⁸⁹See Exod. 29:29.   ¹See Prov. 11:16.

[30a] אשה די דא נוא זולה הט גוועזט דז זי אירי קינדר דר צוגין הט צו תורה ומ' טובים

אין אירין הויז ווי זי זיך זאל נוהג זיין מיט זי בדרך ישרה וועון זי וויל יוצא ידי שמים זיין

קיגן גו*ט ית"ש אונ' אויך קיגן דען לייטין דא ארצו גהערט יראת שמים אונ' חכמה ווי

וואול איך האב אבן גשריבן ווי זיך איין אשה זאל הלטין גיגן אירין שווער אונ' שוויגר

5 דא איז נוא וואול צו גדענקין להיפוך דר זיך פון דר דז דר שווער אדור שוויגר

זיך אויך הלטין זאל קיגן איך דען גוטון וועג נאך גלייך וואול וויל איך איין בזונדרן

שיעור שרייבן דר פון אונ' וויל פיל דרינן גדענקין אז איך אובין ניט גדאלט האב אונ'

עטש קענין גדענקין אונ' ווילש אבור דא הער שרייבן נוא זאל זיך איין איטלכה אשה

גדענקין אונ' זאל זעהן דז זי זיך זאל אן דען איידם אדור שנור ור זינדגן ח'ו אז

10 מירש גפינדן ביא שאול המלך ע"ה אז ער הט מטיל שנאה גוועזט אויף זיין איידם

דוד המלך ע"ה אונ' איז פיל ביז דר דר פון קומין אונ' הט זיך אונ' זייני קינדר פר זינדגט

דען עש קומט קיין גוטש פון קריג נייארט קנאה אונ' שנאה וועון שון איין שנור

אדור איידם ניט אלז אלז מאלט רעלט טואן נאך זאל מן זי דן לכף זכות זיין אונ' זאל אויך

גדענקין עז איז דר יוגנט שולט מיר זיין אויך יונג גוועזין וויץ קומט ניט פר יארין

15 וועון זי זיך ווערין אויך גניטין ווי מיר זיך גניט האבן ווערין זי וואול אנדרש ווערין

אונ' מן זאל זי מיט גיטן גיטן שטראפין אליין ניט פר לייטין אז דר פסוק גיט (אל תכח

לץ פן ישנאך הוכח לחכם [ויאהבך] [2] דאז איז [טייטש] דוא זאלשט איין לץ ניט

שטראפין דען ער ווערט דיך פיינט האבן שטראף אבור איין חכם דא ווערט ער דיך

ליב האבן דא איז איין קשיא ווען איך איין לץ ניט שטראפין זאל וואם זאל

20 איך דען שטראפין דער איין חכם איז אונ' פרום דען דערף איך ניט צו שטראפין אלא

דר פשט מוז אזו זיין דז ער שפרעלבט ער זאל איין לץ ניט שטראפין ווען דר פסוק

מוז מיינן דוא זאלשט איין ניט שטראפין אז מן איין רעכטין לץ דר איין רשע גמור

איז מאג שטראפין אונ' וועלשט צו אים אויך אזו רידין דו גוי דו משומד

וארומ האשטו דאז גטאן אז מן צו איין רעכלטין רשע גאמר רידין דאז מן ניט טון

25 ווען דוא אים מעכשט ביז צו אים רידין דא מעכט ער ניט מקבל מוסר זיין אונ' ווערט

נאך ערגיר אונ' מיר בועט זיין אז דר פסוק גיט (דבר עצב יעלה אף[3] איז טייטש

איין ריד די אין מלט טרויארין ברעעגט איין צארין דז ער ווערט ברוגז

שטראפט ער אין אבור אז מן איין חכם זאל שטראפן דאז מיינט כלומר ער

איז קיין רשע גמור ווען ער שון גטאן הט שלא כהוגן /הייטש

[2]Prov. 9:8.   [3]Prov. 15:1.

17 ויהאבך P1609 K1618 | טייטש P1609; ניש K1618

[30b] הײשט ער דעגוך אײן חכם אז דיא גמרא⁴ דרשת (הוכיח תליח⁵ מנלין) דז אײן
תלמיד מאז זײן רבי שטראפין ווען ער פון אים זעך (שלא כהוגן ןת״ל] הוכיח תוכיח
מכל מקום אזו מײנט דר פסוק אויך דז ער זאל צו אים גין אונ׳ שפרעכין ליבש קינד
דו הושט ניט רעכט גטאן איז מיר אײן חדוש פון דיר דז דו עז זאלשט טון דו בישט אזו
יוא פרום אונ׳ קלוג גנוגין אויך איז עש דיר עש אן גבורין עש מוזין בזי לײט זײן דיא
דיך דוא ארצו האבן אן גיהלטין אונ׳ אן רידון פאלג איז מיר דוא מיר טוא עש נימר אויף דאז
גיט אויך אויף דר פסוק (מענה רך משיב חימה⁶) דאז [אין] טײטש אײן ווײלי ריד מלט
ווידור קערין דען צארין אזו מײנט דר פסוק (הוכיח לחכם ויאהבך⁷) ווען דוא
אין שטראפשט אז אײן חכם ווערט ער דיך ליב האבין אונ׳ ווערט זײן שטראף
5
[באהבה] מקבל זײן אבור מעגלי בדענקט דאש אלש ניט דיא קין יראת שמים אין זיך
האט אונ׳ לאט איר צארין פר איר איר גין אז שלמה המלך ע״ה האט גזאגט
(אשת [כסילות הומיה פתיות ובל] ידעה מה⁸) דאז איז טײטש אײן ווײב דיא איר נערין איז דיא
מורט אונ׳ ברומט אין אירין הויז אונ׳ ווײש ניט אײן צו זעצין אונ׳ ווײש ניט ווארום אונ׳
בדענקט ניט ווי עש ווערט עש אין גנג האבין אויף גנג האבין ווא איז ביר קאן דר פון קומן פון צנק אונ׳
10
הדור אז מעגלי די דו אײן איידם אדור אײן שנור הט אונ׳ איז מטיל שנאה אויף זיא
דא עשט מן איר צו פיל דא טרינקט מן איר צו פיל אויף דאז האט שלמה המלך ע״ה
גזאגט (אל תלחם לחם את רע עין⁹) דאז איז טײטש דוא זאלשט ניט מיט אײנם
עשין דר דירש ניט גינט מיט זיא אײני דיא אבור קלוג איז אונ׳ האט יראת שמים אין זיך
דיא זאל מיט גיטין גיטין זיא רידן מײן ליבר מײן אידום אדור מײן
15
ליבי שנור נעמט פר גוט איך וואלט אײך עש גערין בעשר געבן ווען עש מער פר מיגן
ווער אויף דאז גיט דר פסוק טוב פת (חריבה ושלוה בה מבית מלא זבחי ריב¹⁰)
דז איז טײטש עש איז בעשיר אײן שטיק ברוט מיט שלום אז דאז גנצי הויז פיל
שעלטונג אונ׳ מיט קריג אויף גיט דר פסוק (טוב ארוחת ירק ואהבה בה משור
אבוס ושנאה בו¹¹) דאז איז טײטש פיל בעשר איז דז מן זאל מיט אײנם זאל עשין
20
אײן גריכט קרויט דער אימש באאהבה גיבט מיר אז ווען ער מיט אײנם זאל עשין
אײטל גמעשטי אקשין אונ׳ זאל אויף אים שנאה האבין אונ׳ זאל אימש ניט גינן אויך
לערנן מיר פיל פון נעמי ווי זיא זיא /מיט
25

⁴B. Bava Metzi'a 31a. ⁵See Lev. 19:17. ⁶Prov. 15:1. ⁷See Prov. 9:8. ⁸Prov. 9:13. ⁹See Prov. 23:6. ¹⁰Prov. 17:1.
¹¹See Prov. 15:17.

P1609 K1618 הימיה בל 12 | P1609 באהנה K1618; 10 | P1609 אזו K1618; 9 | P1609 אי K1618; 7 | P1609 K1618 תל 2

[31a] מיט אירי שנור רות האט מטיב גוועזט האט אויף אירי טובה גטרכלט אז דר פסוק
גיט (הלא בתי אבקש לך מנוחה[12]) אונ' האט איר גישוואויך פר וואר מייני
ליבה טאכטר איך בעט השם יתברך דז עש זאל אין גוטין וועג וויזין אונ' זאל
דיר אין ערליכי מנוחה שפֿין דיא דיר זיין דאך נוא גשיידין גוועזין השם ישמרינו נאך
5 האט זי אויף איר טובה מתפלל גיוועזט אז דר פסוק גיט (וירדתי הגורן[13]) דא מכט
רש״י[14] דען פשט מיין זכות ווערט דיר ביא שטין אונ' הינטן נאך דו זי מיט בועז הט
אין זון גיהט דא האבן דיא אבן דיא נאכפֿרינש זיא גטרישט אונ' האבן צו איר גזאגט דוא
בישט דיין לייד דר גצט גיוואורדן אונ' האט דאז קינד אויף איר שוס דר צוגין דוא
ארפֿון זאל איטליכי פֿרומי שוויגר לערנן וויא זיא זיך מיט איר שנור נוהג זיין
10 (באהבה ובחיבה לשם שמים) אונ' זאל האפֿונג האבן צו הש״י דז זי אירי איניקליך
צו תורה ומעשים טובים זאל דר ציהן דוא ארפֿון דערף מן ניט פֿיל צו שרייבן איטליכי
דיא יראת שמים אין זיך האט וויש זעלברט וואול דאך גפֿינט מן מעונכי דיא איר
צארין פֿר איר איר צו לאט גין אויף אן איני האט דר פסוק גרעט (אוולת בידה
תהרסנה[15]) אונ' איז אויך מקבל רכילות אונ' רייסט אין אונ' קומט נישט גוטש דר פֿון
15 אז מיר פֿינדן ביא שאול המלך ע״ה איז פֿיל אונליק דר פֿון קומן דז ער האט זיין
גיזונד גהלטין דז מן אים האט רכילות גטראגין איבר זיין איידם דוד המלך ע״ה
אז דר פסוק גיט (ויאמרו הזיפים אל שאול הלא דוד מסתתר)[16] [עמנו] דאז
אין טייטש דיא פעך מכֿיר זיין קומין צו שאול דא וורשטו דוד גפֿינדן דר פֿון איז
קומן דז מן דז דואג האדומי האט גר זינדיגט אז ער איז איינר פֿון דען דרייאן דיא
20 ניט עולם הבא האבן דרום דז ער רכילות איבר דוד האט גטריבן אונ' האט גימלט
דז פֿיל רציחות דר פֿון קומן איז אונ' האט די כהנים פֿון נוב אל אום גבראכט דאש
איז אלש דרום קומן דז ער האט אין שנאה אויף זיין איידם דוד המלך גיהט וויא
וואול דז אים לסוף גרויאין האט אונ' האט עש מודה גוועזט אונ' האט עש טייאר
מיט זיין בלוט אונ' האט פֿלייש מוזין בישין דרום זאל זיך אין איטליכי ורומי פֿארט
25 בדענקין דאז מיינט אויך דר פסוק (אשת חן תתמוך כבוד[17]) דאז מיינט
אין אשה דיא איז אויף כבוד אוישין איז אונ' גדענקט זיא וויל חן אין גו*ט ית׳ש אויגין
האבין אונ' אויך אין דר לייט דר אויגן דאז מיינט דז זיא וויל מכֿין דז דיא לייט גערין
/מיט

[12]See Ruth 3:1.   [13]Ruth 3:3.   [14]Rashi on Ruth 3:3.   [15]See Prov. 14:1.   [16]See Ps. 54:2.   [17]Prov. 11:16.

17 עמנו P 1609 K 1618

[31b] מיט איר מתחתן זאלין זיין אונ' אירי קינדר גערין צו איר אין אירין הויז אניין געבן

אויף דאז מאג שלמה המלך ע"ה גרעט האבן אונ' מאגש אזו גמיינט האבן מיט דעם

פסוק והיתה כאניות סוחר ממרחק תביא לחמה[18] דאז איז אזו טייטש איין אשת

חיל איז גלייך אז איין סוחר דער צו זיין סחורה אויף איין שיף [אוזן] ווייטן לנד ברענגט

5 כלומר מן ברענגט איר קינדר אויז ווייטן לנד אין איר אירין הויז דן מן שפריכט מן מאג

אזו איין אשה חשובה וואול איין קינד אין איר אירין הויז געבן דאז קאן זיא מלין מיט

אירין שם טוב אבר וואו עש להפך איז דו גיט דער פסוק (ועריצים יתמוך עושר וכבוד[19]

דאז מיינט אזו איינר דיא אויף אייטל געלט אוישין איז אונ' אויף קיין לבוד דרום זאל

זיך איין איטלבי אשה דיא דא קלוג אונ' פרום איז זאל זיך אויש קלויבן דען בעשטן

10 דורך אונטר דען צווייא דרלים דען השם יתברך שמו האט איטלבם מענשין צווייא

דרלים פיר גליגט איין גוטין אונ' איין ביזין אז דר פסוק גיט (ראה נתתי לפניך

היו' את החיי' ואת המות ואת הטוב ואת הרע[20] דר מענש הט די די וואל ער מאג זיך נעמן

ועלכין ער וויל אבר הש"י האט ישראל זיינם ליבן פאלק אין אונזרי היילגי תורה איין

גוט עצה געבן אונ' האט אן גשריבן (ובחרת בחיים[21]) דען איטלבם מענשין האט

15 ער געבן איין יצר טוב אונ' איין יצר הרע דער קיגן האט ער בישפין דאז גן עדן אונ'

גיהנם דז ער איטלבם וויל זיין לון געבן נאך זיני מעשים נאך דרום האט הש"י שמו

זיינם ליבן פאלק ישראל דיא היילגי תורה געבן אונ' מצות גיבאטין אונ' הלטין זעלין

אונ' אופט אום גיחזרת אונ' גשטראפט אז אין פאטער איין ליב קינד שטראפט אונ'

זעך גערין דז עש וואל וואלט אזו האט הש"י אויך פון אלש אלט זיני ליבי קינדר ישראל

20 וועגין גיטאן דז זיא זאלין דר דורך זוכה צו עולם הבא זיין אין דען איבגין לעבן אמן

וכן יהי רצון

שער שביעי

דאז ווערט רידן פון איין אשה וויא זיא איר השגחה אויף איר הויז גזינד זאל געבן.

(רבת בנות [עשו] חיל ואת עלית על כלנה[1]) דר איז טייטש פיל טעבטר

25 פון ישראל די זאלין איין פיל געלט אונ' גוט אבור דו בישט גלובט איבר אלי שלמה

המלך ע"ה הט דו דען פסוק גרעט אויף איין אשה כשרה די דא ניט אליין פר זיך אונ'

אירי קינדר זארגט גדענקט אונ' זארגט אפילו אויף אנדרי די איר נישט צו גהערין

/אי

---

[18]Prov. 31:14. [19]See Prov. 11:16. [20]See Deut. 30:15. [21]Deut. 30:19. [1]Prov. 31:29.

4 אוז P1609; אזו K1618 | 24 עשי P1609 K1618

[32a] איך אי״ה ווער דא שרייבן דער וויל דער פון דער גרעט האבן וויא זיך איין אשה
זיך זעלברט זאל הלטין אונ׳ קיגן אירין מאן אונ׳ פאטר אונ׳ מוטר אונ׳ שווער אונ׳
שוויגר אונ׳ אירי קינדר אונ׳ איידם אונ׳ שנור דא וואלט זיא זיך נוא גדענקין איך
דערף ווייטר נישט צו זארגין אז מיר זילכי דיעות פיל גפינן (רחמנא ליצלן מהאי
5 דעתא) דז איז טייטש גו*ט יֵת׳ ש זאל אונש בהיטן פר זילכי דעות דען מיר זעהן
בשיידליך אין אונזרי היילני תורה דז הש״י פיל מאלט הט מזהר [דרויפן] גוועזט אונ׳
הט גזאגט (ואהבת לריעך כמוך² דז איז טייטש דוא זאלשט ליב האבן דיין גיזעלין
אז דיך זעלברט דא גיט די גמרא³ (אמר ר׳ עקיבא כלל גדול בתורה ואהבת לרעך
כמוכה⁴ אונ׳ זאגט ווייטר (מה דסני לך לחברך לא תעבד⁵) דז איז טייטש אלש וואז
10 דיר ניט ליב איז דאז זאלשטו דיין חבר ניט טון דרויף גיט דער פסוק (לא
יכבה בלילה נרה⁶) דז איז טייטש איר ליכט ווערט בייא נכט ניט אויז גילאשין
ווערין רצה לומר עש מיינט אזו דז זיא דען בחורים גנוק ליכט געבן דז זיא
לערנן זאלן אונ׳ ניט וויא מענליבי טואין דיא קיין יראת שמים אין זיך האבן פרעגן
ירנוק דר נאך שון איין יונגיר איין גוצי וואוך מעלט צו קיינם רבי קומן אונ׳
15 מעלט קיין ווארט לערנן דא ווערגט זיא נישט דר נאך ווען ער נאך זיך בייערט איר אלי גענג
גיט אונ׳ איין עבד כנעני אן אים האט דז ער איר עשן שבתות ואול אב פר דינט דו
בגערט זיא ניט ווייטר דאז זאל אבור ניט זיין זיא זאל גידענקין דז זיא קיין בריב
דר פיר האט דז אירי קינדר אויך איין ורעמדן העגדן קומן ווערין אז דא מדרש⁷
דרשת דען פסוק (כי בגלל הדבר הזה יברכך ה׳⁸) דז איז טייטש פון דעש וועגן
20 ווערט דיך גו*ט יֵת׳ש בעטשן איך אל דיין ווערק אונ׳ רעט ניט דז (לשון בעבור הדבר
אדור (למען הדבר) אז ער אנדרש וואו רעט אונ׳ רעט דאז לשון פון (גלל
דא דרשת די גמרא⁹ גלגל חוזר בעולם דא גלגל גיט אזו אין עולם עש איז ניט איין
איטלכר דר היט רייך איז אויך איז מארגין רייך דרום איין עיטלכה דיא יראת שמים אין
זיך האט זאל אזו גדענקין אונ׳ זאל אין שטראפין אז איר איינין קינד דז ער יום ולילה
25 לערנט אונ׳ אין דר שול גיט אונ׳ צו אים זאגין וורשטו דאז ניט טון וויל איך דיך ניט
אין הויז הלטין דיין פאטר אונ׳ מוטר האבן דיך אויז גשיקט לערנן אונ׳ מעשים טובים צו
טון זיא האפין אויך זיא וועלין שמחה אן דיר זעהן אונ׳ ווערט דז גן עדן ור דיין אז
גשריבן שטיט (סולם מוצב¹⁰ וכו׳) דז איז טייטש איין לייטר איז גשטעלט אויף דער
ערדן אונ׳ זיין הייבט גרייכט אן דעם הימל ר״ל דא ווארט פון /סולם

_____

²Lev. 19:18.   ³Y. Nedarim 9 (41c).   ⁴Lev. 19:18.   ⁵See Avot de-Rabbi Natan, A, 26; see B. Shabbat 31a.   ⁶Prov. 31:18.
⁷Tanḥuma, Mishpatim 15.   ⁸Deut. 15:10.   ⁹B. Shabbat 151b.   ¹⁰Gen. 28:12.

6 דרויף K 1618; P 1609

[32b] סולם האט אזו פיל אין דר צאל אז ממון דאז מיינט אזו הש״ית הט דש דש ממון דרום
גענב אויף דר ערדן דז מן דר דורך קאן דאן הימל רייך דר ווערבן אבור עש ניט
האט דער קאן אנדרי מצות טון אן ממון אז מענגר קאן לערנן מיט יתומים און׳ דר
גלייכין זין דר מצות פיל מיט גמילת חסד דיא איך ניט אל דר שרייבן קאן דאן זאל
5 אויך אין קעכין גידענקן דז זיא אויך ג״ע פר דינן קאן אן אין בחור דא
ווערט איר דיא בעל ביתה גויש ניט ווערין דז זיא אים זיין העמדר לאזט וושין און׳
זיין גלעגיר געבן און׳ ניט לאזין פר לוין אז מן מענלי גפינט די לאזין די יונגין פיר
וואוכין אין אין העמד גין און׳ גדענקט ניט דז ער אויך מזרע אברהם אבינו איז
כל המרחם על הבריות מרחמין עליו מן השמים¹¹ דאז איז טייטש דער זיך
10 דר ברמנט איבר דיא לייט דא דר ברמט מן זיך אין הימל ווידור איבר אים אויך דרשת
דיא גמרא דעם פסוק (שלח לחמיך על פני המים כי ברוב ימם תמצאנה¹²)
דז איז טייטש שיק דיין ברוט אויף דיא וושיר אין פיל דען טאגין ווערשטו עש
פינדן און׳ רעט ניט לסוף ימים און׳ רעט רוב ימים דאז מיינט אין עולם הבא דאז
איבג לעבן דז דארט רוב ימים זיין אדור מאג טייטש זיין דוא ווערשט עש פיל מאל
15 גנישין און׳ דר פשט איז עש זא גיט אויף דיא תורה דיא דא גגליכן איז צו לחם און׳ מים
אז דר פסוק גיט (לכו לחמי בלחמי¹³ הוי כל צמיו לכו למים¹⁴ ר״ל די דא
העלפין שטערקין לומדי תורה דען מיר האבן האבן צו מיר קיין ביּת המקדש
נאך קרבנות (נייארט) דיא היילגי תורה איז אונש איבר גבליבן דען אל אונזר
אמונה און׳ עולם הזה און׳ עולם הבא העניקט אן דר היילגי תורה אז דר פסוק זאגט
20 כי היא חייך ואורך ימיך¹⁵) דאז איז טייטש זיא איז דיין לעבן און׳ ווערט
דיר דיין יאר דער לענגן אדור עש זיין בעו״ה בדורות הללו אין טייל דיא דא
לומדי תורה מרחיק זיין און׳ זיין זיך משמח ווען ער אין שיני שטוב האט און׳ בגערט
קיין בחור נאך יונגין דרינן צו לערנן און׳ ווען מן אים וויל אין חשוב בחור געבן דא
גיט ער געלט צו לון דז מן אים (אייזן) יונגין גיט דער זיין קנעבלט קאן זיין און׳ וויל
25 ניט לאזין מיט יונגין אין זיין הויז לערנן אויך זיין מענכי און׳ זעלגי קעכינש דיא
קיין יראת שמים אין זיך האט זיין ברוגז ווען אין ספר אויף דען טיש ליגט און׳
שפרעלט /

¹¹B. Shabbat 151b.   ¹²See Eccles. 11:1.   ¹³See Prov. 9:5.   ¹⁴See Isa. 55:1.   ¹⁵See Deut. 30:20.

18 אך P1609 K1618 | K1618; נייארט P1609 | 24 אין P1609 K1618

[33a] שפרעכט איך האב עש אויף גירומט אונ' ליגט מיר דיא ספרים אויף דען טיש

וען זיא דיא קינדר זעצט אויף דען טיש נקיט אונ' בלוז אונ' זיין משתן דרויף אבר

מטנף דאז רעבֿניך זיא פר נישט אונ' איז איין גרושי עבֿרה אונ' איז דעם קינד איין

סכנה אז מיר גפֿינדן אין ספֿר חסידים[16] איין מעשה דז איינם קינד זיין איין מאלט

5 דיא פֿיס אפ גברֿאלין דא האט דר חסיד דר האט גזאגט דאז האט מן פֿר זינט דז זיא

דאש קינד אויף דען טיש האט גזעצט דען דר טיש איז גגליכן צום מזבח אבור דיא

זעלבֿגין ורומן דיא יראת שמים אין זיך האבן דיא בדענקין אלש ווֿאז פֿר איין זלות

ווֿערין מיין קינדר אז אונזרי חכמים[17] האבן גזאגט (מאן דרחם רבן הוי ליה

בנון רבנן) דאז איז טײטש ווֿער דיא לומדי תורה ליב האט אונ' איז זיא מהנה דר

10 ווֿערט זולֿכה זיין דז ער ווֿערט קינדר האבן דיא דא תלמידי חכמים ווֿערין זיין גיט

דיא גמרֿא[18] (מן דמוקיר רבנן הווֿי ליה חתֿנותֿי רבנן דאז איז טײטש דר דא ווֿיִרדג

רבנן דער ווֿערט זולֿכה זיין דז ער ווֿערט איידיֵם האבן דיא דא ווֿערין רבנים זיין גיט

דיא גמרֿא[19] ווֿיִטֵר (מן דדחיל מרבנן איהו גופֿיה הוי צורֿבֿי מרבנן ואם לאו בר הכי

הוא משתממעין מיליה כצורבֿא מרבנן) דאז איז טײטש ווֿען ער זיך פֿערכֿט פֿר דיא

15 תלמידי חכמים ווֿערט ער זעלֿברֿט איין תלמיד חכם ווֿערין ואו ער אבור ניט איין

למדן איז ווֿערט זיין ריד אזו חשובֿ זיין אז ווֿער ער איין תלמד חכם דרויף גיט די

גמרֿא[20] (כל הנבֿיאים לא נתֿנבאו אלא למהנה תלמיד חֿלֵם מנכֿסיו) דאז איז טײטש

[אלין] טובֿות אונ' דיא נחמות פֿון אונזרי נבֿיאים האבן זיא אלֵש גרעט אויף דיא דא

לומדי תורה מהנה זיין דז פֿון זיין געלֿט לערנן מיר פֿון דן פסוק פֿון דער

20 [שֿונֵמיתֿ] ת' דז זיא האט אלישע הנבֿיא אין חדר גֵעבן דז ער דרין גלֵערנֿט האט אונ'

איין טיש גֵעבן דז ער זיין ספֿרים האט דרויף גלֵיגט אונ' האט אים ליכֿט גוֿוגין גֵעבן

דרום איז זיא זולֿכה גֿוועזין דז זיא איין קעשטליֵכֿן זון האט גֵיהֿט דער איז יונה

הנבֿיא גיֿוועזין דֿען הש"י שמו זילֵכֵי ניסים בוֿוזין האט אונ' איז פֿיל דֿרוֿיז צו לֵערנן

ואו ארֿצו שרֵייברֿט ער אן דז דאן קינד איז גֿשטֿארֿבן אונ' האֿטֿש ווֿידר לעבֿנֿדֿיג

25 גֵמֿלֿט אלֿא דֿר פּסוק [ווֿיִזֿטֿ] דורֿך דֵר מצוֿה דז זיא מחֿזיק לומדֵי תורה האט גֿוֿועזֿט

דיא אֿזו טֿואן ווֿערין זוֿכֿה צו תֿחיתֿ המֿתֿים זיין אֿונ' דיא גמֿרֿא[21] לֵֿערֿנֿט אֿויך דֿר פֿון

גלֵֿייך אז ער אֵיין קרֿבן אֵלֵי טֿאג בֿרֿעלֿטֿ דֵֿען בֵֿייֿא דֵֿען קרֿבן שֿטֵֿיֿט גֵשֿרֿיבֿן עֿלֿת

/תֿמיד

[16]*Sefer Hasidim*, § 920.   [17]B. Shabbat 23b.   [18]B. Shabbat 23b.   [19]B. Shabbat 23b.   [20]See B. Berakhot 34b.   [21]See B. Berakhot 10b.

18 K 1618; אוי P 1609 | 20 ת{ שמנמן} P 1609; שמנמית K 1618 | 25 ווֿיִזֿטֿ P 1609; יוֿיִזֿטֿ K 1618

[33b] תמיד‎[22] אונ׳ ביי אלישע אויך (עוֹבֵר עלינו תמיד‎[23]) נוא וויא מיר פון אובן דען פסוק
גרעט האבן (ותתן טרף לביתה‎[24]) אונ׳ זיא גיבט שפייז צו אירם הויז וועלן מיר דיא
פסוקים פון אשת חיל וויטר אויז ליגן אז דר פסוק גיט (לא תִירא לביתה משלג‎[25])
דאז איז טייטש זיא דערף זיך ניט פערלרטן אין אירין הויז פר שני אז ראשית חכמה‎[26]
5 שרייבט אונ׳ ברענגט דיא גמרא‎[27] דאז מיינט דאז גיהנם אז דר פסוק גיט (בה
תשלג כצלמון‎[28]) דאז מיינט אין אשת חיל דיא אין אירן הויז איז זילט דז עז
יודשליך צו גיט דיא דערף זיך ניט פר דען גיהנם פערלרטן נוא וועלין מיר דיא
פסוקים וויטר אויז ליגן אז ער זיא אז דיא (אשׁת חיל משבח איז אונ׳ שפרעלט
פרשה לעני וידיה שלחה לאביון‎[29]) דאז איז טייטש אירי הנט איז אפין צו דען
10 ארמן אונ׳ שיקט זיא צו דען בידרפטגין דא איז איין קשיא צו פרעגין וארום זאגט
ער כפל לשון אלא דער פסוק מוז עש עש מיינן אז ער שפריעלט איר דער הנט איז אפין
צו דען ארמן מיינט ער אויף אין דר דא פושט יד דר איז דער זיין הנט אויף הלט דען
לאט זיא ניט לידוג אויז גין אז ער דער נאך רעט (ידיה שלחה לאביון‎[30]) דאז
מיינט ער איין הויז עני דער זיך שעמט אן צו מוטן אונ׳ לייט גרושין דוחק דעֶן זעלבגן
15 שיקט זיא אין איר הויז אניין אדור איך מאג דען פשט אזו זאגין ([כפיה פרשה]
לעני‎[31]) דז זיא זאל מיט איר אירי העדר ערבטן דז זיא עניים קאן געבן אז מיר אויך
לערנן אויז דען פסוק (יגיע כפיך כי תאכל‎[32]) דאש מיינט דער פסוק
פון ארבט דיין טענר דוא זאלשט עשן אונ׳ זאלשט דען עני דער פון גיבן גאוון וואל
דיר בעולם הזה ובעולם הבא אויך שטיט אין דער תורה גשריבן (כל אשה
20 חכמת לב בידיה טווי‎[33]) ביא מלאכת המשכן דז איטליכי קלוגי פרויא האט מיט
אירי אייגנה הנט גישפונין דרויז קעגן מיר לערנן דאז איין אשה מיט איר אייגני
הנט ערבט איז הקב״ה מיר מקובל אויך דיא צדקה דיא זיא דר פון גיבט איז מיר
אז דיא צדקה וועֶן זיא גיבט פון אירן געלט אויך דרשׁת די גמרא‎[34] (אשׁרי משׂכיל
אל דל‎[35]) דאז איז טייטש וואל דעם דער דא קליגט צו דען ארמן אונ׳ דער פסוק
25 שפריעלט ניט (נותן אל דל) דאז מיינט דער פסוק דז מען זאל בחכמה מיט
דען ארמן אום גין וועֶן מען זיכט דז ער נוט לייט אונ׳ איז איין ביישין דז מען אים
ניט זאל מבייש זיין אויך קאן מען אינם העלפֿן אונ׳ ראטין בעזרת האל יתברך וועֶן
[מעֶן]/

[22]See Exod. 29:42; Num. 28:6. [23]II Kings 4:9. [24]Prov. 31:15. [25]Prov. 31:21. [26]*Reshit Hokhmah*, I, p. 267, § 75. [27]B.
Berakhot 16a. [28]Ps. 68:15. [29]See Prov. 31:20. [30]Prov. 31:20. [31]See Prov. 31:20. [32]Ps. 128:2. [33]See Exod. 35:25.
[34]B. Nedarim 40a. [35]Ps. 41:2.

14 K1618; Lakune P1609 | 15 K1618; Lakune P1609 | 28 K1618; מעו P1609

[34a] מען שון אים ניט גיבט אדר האט ניט גיבט ניט צו גיבן זאל מען אים אין איין משכון לייאן
אדור איין עצה טובה געבן דז ער זיך מחייה זיין דאש איז (זה נהנה וזה לא
חסר) אויף דעם מיינט דער פסוק אשרי משכיל אל דל [36] אדור דער פסוק
מאג אזו טייטש זיין דז מן זאל איינם געבן וואו עש וואול אן גליגט איז אדור דער

5 פשט מאג אזו זיין דז מען עני איין זאל מהנה זיין אונ׳ זאל אים צו ארבטין געבן דז
ער זיינר גנישן קאן אז אין דר תורה שטיט גשריבן (אחיך עמך [37]) דא איז
טייטש זיך דז דיין ברודר ביי דיר קאן דר הלטין ניט דז מענגלי טואן די קיין יראת
שמים אין זיך האבן אונ׳ געבן גוים צו ערבטין אונ׳ לאשן עניים שטין ווען שון דער גוי
גנבת ליגט אים נישט דראן נוא וועלין מיר ווידור אן היבן פון דען פסוק [(כפיה]

10 פרשה לעני [38]) מאג איך דען פשט אזו זאגין אונ׳ ווען ער זילט איין חבר בעת צרה דז איז
טייטש איין עני איז אז דוד המלך ע״ה אופט מאלט גרעט האט (כי עני ואביון [אני] [39])
דא איז טייטש דען ארום אונ׳ בדערפטיג בין איך רצה לומר דאז האט ער אזו
געמיינט ארום בין איך פון מצות אונ׳ בדערף דיני גרושי גנאד [אזו] מיינט ער דר
פסוק אויך ווען זיא זילט אין אין ניטן זאל זיא אירי העגד צו גו*ט ית״ש אויף היבן

15 אונ׳ זאל פר אים מתפלל זיין אז דוד המלך ע״ה אויך גזאגט האט (ואני בחלותם
לבושי שק ותפילתי על חקי תשוב [40]) דאז איז טייטש ווען איך האב גזעהן ווען איינר
קרנק איז גוועזין האב איך תפלה פון זיינט וועגן גטאן אונ׳ דיא זעלבגי תפלה איז
מיר אין מין בוזים קומן כלומר איז מיר צו גוטים קומן אז אונזרי חכמים [41] שרייבן (כל
[המתפללן] על חברו והוא צריך לאותו דבר הוא נענה תחילה אויף דז רעט דיא גמרא [42]

20 איין תפוס קאן זיך זעלברט ניט לאז אויז דר תפיסה העלפן איין אנדרר מח אים משתדל
זיין דרום מח אויך איין אנדרר אום אים אויך מתפלל זיין נוא וועלין מיר דען פסוק
ווייטר אויז ליגן דר פסוק גיט ווייטר (פיה פתחה בחכמה ותורת חסד על לשנוה [43])
דאז איז אזו טייטש איר מויל עפנט זיא מיט אייטל חכמה אונ׳ דיא תורה פון אייטל
חסד איז אונטר איר צונגין דאז מיינט איין אשה כשרה דיא דא מכניס אורחים איז

25 דרויף שרייבט ראשית חכמה [44] וויא זיא איין גשט פריינטליך אונ׳ ליפליך אנטפגנין זאל
אונ׳ זאל אים איין פנים יפות ווייזין אונ׳ זאל צו אים זאגין מין ליבר וריינד מיר זיין הין
וואול געשט גוואונט נעמט ור גוט הש״י האטש אונש דרום בשערט דז מיר לייטין
[קענין]
/

[36]Ps. 41:2.　[37]Lev. 25:36.　[38]Prov. 31:20.　[39]Ps. 86:1.　[40]See Ps. 35:13.　[41]B. Bava Kamma 92a.　[42]B. Bava Kamma 92a.
[43]Prov. 31:26.　[44]*Reshit Ḥokhmah*, III, p. 208, § 23.

9 כפרה P1609 K1618　|　11 עני P1609 K1618　|　13 K1618; אז P1609　|　19 K1618; המתפל P1609

[34b] קענון מלבד זיין איז דען דז זיא איין מאן האט דער ניט מעורב עם הבריות איז
אז מען מענבלן גפינט דא זאל זיא דען גשט טרישטין אונ׳ צו אים זאגן קערט אייך
נישט דראן דען זיין סדר איז אזו ער האט אנדרי עסקים אים קאפ אונ׳ מיט דעם
מיינט דער פסוק (תורת חסד על לשונה[45]) דאז איז דיא מידה פון

5   אברהם אבינו ע״ה דער דא האט גומל חסד מיט אורחים גווען דרום אויך ווער זיך
מחזיק איז אין דער מידה טובה פון הכנסת אורחים דער ווייזט דז ער מזרע אברהם
אבינו איז וויא אויך איך איז גשריבן האב (כי גבר עלינו חסדו[46]) איז
ראשי תיבות (גומלי חסדים ביישנים רחמנים) אונ׳ אויף דיא עניינים
פון דען עניים האט דיא היילגי תורה אן גשריבן (פתוח תפתח[47]) דאז איז

10   טייטש עפֿנין דו זאלשט עפֿנין דיין הנט צו דיין ארמן אונ׳ בדערפֿטיגן ער רעט
דרום כפֿל לשון וואו חסרון כיס איז דיא תורה מין מזהיר דרויף אויף גיט דער
פסוק וייטר (נתון תתן[48] הענק תענק[49]) דאז איז טייטש געבן דו זאלשט
געבן אפֿילו מאה פעמים אויף לאדין דו זאלשט אויף לאדין אפֿילו מאה פעמים פון
דיינם גוט דו מיר ארץ ישראל האבן גיהט זיין מיר שולדיג גיווען פון דר תבואה

15   אין דער שייאר אבר איצונדר זיין מיר מחויב צו געבן פון שלשים וואו אונש גו*ט ית״ש
בשערט אז דיא גמרא[50] דרשת דען פסוק (כבד את ה׳ מהוניך[51]) דאז איז טייטש
איר גו*ט פֿון דיין [גוט] אונ׳ פֿון אלים וואו דיך גו*ט ית״ש האט גלייט זעלויגט אז מן
אויך פֿיל פֿרומי זעליגי וויבער גפינט דיא דא גוורניט זיין וען זיא איין קעש אויף
שניידן אדור איין טאפ שמלץ אן הויבן אדור וואו עז איז דא געבן זיא צום אירשטן

20   דען עניים דר טייל אויף דאז האט שלמה המלך ע״ה גזאגט (מרוה גם הוא יורא[52])
דאז איז טייטש דער אנדרי זעט ער ווערט אויך גזעט פון הקב״ה אויך גיט דר
פסוק (יש מפֿזר ונוסף עוד[53]) דר נאך זאגט ער (וחשך מיושר אך למחסור[54])
איז טייטש עש איז אופֿט איינר דר פֿיל איין וועק גיבט אז צדקה דא איז האט ער
זונשטר מער אבור איינר דער דא פֿר מיט זיך פֿון רעכטן וועג פֿערטיגין אונ׳ טוט

25   וידור גו*ט ית״ש נאך דיא וועלט קיין גוטש דער ווערט צו ברענגש דאז מדרש[55] גיט
איין מעשה פון איין פֿרומי אשה אונ׳ איר מאן איז איין גרושיר חסיד גווען דר
האט גרושן דוחק גליטין דא האט אים הקב״ה איין מלאך גשיקט אונ׳ האט אין לאזן
/פֿרעגין

[45]Prov. 31:26.   [46]Ps. 117:2.   [47]Deut. 15:8, 11.   [48]Deut. 15:10.   [49]See Deut. 15:14.   [50]Y. Peah 1 (15b).   [51]Prov. 3:9.
[52]Prov. 11:25.   [53]Prov. 11:24.   [54]Prov. 11:24.   [55]Ruth Zuta 4, 11.

גו*ט 17 P 1609 K 1618

[35a] ורעגן עז זיי דיר זיבן גוטר יאר בשערט ווילשטו זי איצונדר האבן אדור פֿר דיין ענד
דער חסיד האט אים גיענטווערט איך וויל מיין וייב עצה פֿרעגן אזו איז ער גנגין
צו זיין וייב אונ׳ האט איר די זך גזאגט דא האט זי גענטווערט איך וויל זי איצונדר
האבן אזו איז ער אויף דאז פֿעלד גגנגן אונ׳ האט ליים איין גטראגן אום דאש גועלט
5 דען לייטין אזו איין גרושר עני איז ער גוועזין אונ׳ דר נאך איז ער ווידור גגנגן אונ׳
האט איין חפֿורה גפֿונדין מיט גאלד אונ׳ האט מיט וייב אונ׳ קינדר איין גטראגין
איין גרושין סך דר דר נאך איז זיא אין גגין אונ׳ האטש גצילט אונ׳ האט דאז מעשר דר פֿון
אפֿ גליגט דר נאך האט זיא דאש דריט טייל לומדי תורה געבן אונ׳ עניים גשפֿייזט
מיט דען אנדרן דו נוא די זיבן יאר זיין אויש גוועזן דא איז דר מלאך ווידור צו אים
10 קומן אונ׳ גזאגט גיב מיר דען פֿקדון ווידור דו האט אים דר חסיד גענטוור אז איך עז
ניט האב גיטאן אן מיין וייב אזו וויל איך עש ניט געבן אן איר ווישין
אזו איז ער צו זיין וייב גגן אונ׳ האט אירש גזאגט דז דער וויל זיין פֿקדון ווידור
האבן דא האט זיא גזאגט גיא צו אים אונ׳ זאג אים דז ער מיר דריי טאג צייט גיבט
דא די דרייא טאג זיין גיוועזן איז ער ווידור קומן גיב מיר מיין פֿקדון ווידור דא
15 האט זיא אן גהובין קום איך וויל דיר וויל חשבון אזו אונ׳ אזו פֿיל האב איך מקבל גוועשט
אונ׳ דאז האב איך מעשר געבן אונ׳ אזו פֿיל האב איך אלי וואוך אין דר הספֿקה
געבן אונ׳ אזו | פֿיל האב איך ארמי מיידן אויש געבן אונ׳ אזו פֿיל האב איך עניים
לאשין קליידן דאז זאג דיינם הערן דעם דער פֿקדון איז דער דיך גשיקט האט
ווערט ער איין גפֿינדן דער זיין פֿקדון בעשיר פֿר וועזין דא לאש אים
20 דען פֿקדון ווידור נעמן אזו אויא איז דער מלאך צו דער הקדוש ברוך הוא גגין דא האט
הקב״ה גזאגט דיא רעט רעבֿלט לאש איר דען פֿקדון לענגר אזו האט דיא צדקות דען
עושר לענגר ביהלטין מיט איר צדקות נוא קענן מיר פֿר שטין דז הקדוש ברוך
הוא האט דען דרום מזל אונ׳ ברכֿה געבן פֿון וועגן דער גרושי צדקה דיא זיא גטאן
האבן אויף דרשת דיא גמרא[56] אויף דען פסוק (ועניים מרודים תבֿיא בֿית[57])
25 איין איטליבֿר דער זיך אויף אין עני מרחם איז ווערט ער גבֿעגשט מיט כֿ״ד ברכֿות
אז דר ילקוט[58] ברענגט דאז מדרש ר׳ יהודא בר סימן פֿון ר׳ יהושיע בן לוי וועגין דר
האט גזאגט לעולם לא תהא מצות עני קלה בֿעניך) דאז איז טייטש לאז דיר דיא
מצוה/

[56]See B. Bava Batra 9b.   [57]Isa. 58:7.   [58]Yalkut, § 665.

17 K1618; אונ׳ P1609

מצוה פון איין עני ניט גרינג זיין איין דיין אויגין דען ער לערנטש אויז דיא פסוקים [35b]
אז דר פסוק גיט אין ישעיה עש איז דיא הפטורה פון יום כיפור (הלא] פרוש
לרעב לחמיך59) איז טייטש ווער שטו דען הונגרין פון דיינם ברוט זעטין דיא פיר
אונ' [צוווציגן] ברכות דיא דא שטין ווערין דיך אלי אן גין וכן לו להיפך ח'ו פיר אונ'
5 צוווציג קללות די דרשת ער אויף דען דען מזמור ק"ט אויז דען פסוקים (הפקד עליו רשע60
וגו') דר איין עני ניט פר לאזט61 אז דיא גמרא62 דרשת דען פסוק (מסיר אזנו מזעקת
דל הוא יקרא ולא יענה63) דאז איז טייטש דער זיין אורין פר העלט פון איין
ארמן ווען ער צו אים קומט אונ' שרייעט אין זיין ניטן דו ווערט אים הקב"ה אויך ניט
ענטפערין אויך דרשת דאז מדרש דען דען פסוק (כי יעמוד לימין אביון להושיע
10 משופטי נפשו64) דאז איז טייטש וון איין עני זיין פר שעמט אונ' קומט
צו דיר אונ' בעט דא קומן צוווייא מלאכים מיט אים צו גין איינר אויף דער רעלטי הנט
אונ' איינר אויף דער לינקי הנט ווען ער אים פנים יפות אונ' פריינטליד מיט
אים רעט אונ' טוט אים זיין רצון איז דער גוטי מלאך דא אונ' שרייבט אויף אים די ויר
אונ' צוווציג ברכות וואו ער אין אבר ח'ו מבייש איז דא קומט דר ביזי
15 מלאך אונ' שרייבט אויף אים השם ישמרינו די פיר אונ' צוווציג קללות אז דר פסוק גיט
(כי יעמוד לימן אביון להושיע משופטי נפשו65) דאז איז טייטש דר שטן שטיט
בייא אים אונ' מלט דז ער קיין מצוה זאל טון דר ווארטין דז ער זיין משפט זאל ליידן
אויף דאז מאג אויך איוב גמיינט האבן דען דען פסוק (להניח
ברכה בביתך66) וידעת כי שלום אוהליך ופקדת נוך ולא תחטא67) דיא גמרא68 דרשת
20 דען פסוק [צווישן] מאן אונ' וייב אבור איך מאג דען פסוק אויך אזו אויז ליגן אז ער
שפריכט להניח ברכה בביתך69) דאז ווערט רידן אויף איין זקינה דיא דא אים הויז איז אז
דיא גמרא70 גיט (סבתה בבית ברכה בית) עז איז טייטש איין אלט וייב אין
הויז איז איין ברכה דיא קאן מלין מיט איר מעשים טובים אונ' יראת שמים אונ' אירי
תפילה תשובה צדקה אונ' איר גמילות חסד אונ' מלט שלום אין אירן הויז אונ'
25 שטראפט אירי קינדר אונ' אירי גזינד דז זי זיך ניט דורך צנקין אונ' דז מן קיין
קללה נאך שבועה אויז אירין מיילרין לאשט גין אזו איין אשה חשובה קאן מלין מיט
אירי פרומקייט דז אירי קינדר זכות איר זכות גנישין אונ' ברענגט אין הוז ברכה והצלחה /אונ'

59See Isa. 58:7.   60Ps. 109:6.   61See Ps. 109:16.   62B. Shabbat 55a.   63See Prov. 21:13.   64See Ps. 109:31.   65See Ps. 109:31.   66See Ezek. 44:30.   67Job 5:24.   68B. Yevamot 62b.   69See Ezek. 44:30.   70B. Arakhin 19a.

2 K 1618; דלא P 1609 | 4 צו וונציג P 1609 K 1618 | 20 K 1618; צ ווישן P 1609

[36a] אונ' אורך ימים אונ' בפרט ווען איר געשט עניים אין אירין הויז קומן איז זיא זיך
משמח דז איר הש"י מצות צוא שיקט אונ' איז זיא (מקבל בפנים יפות) אונ' גיבט
אין פריינטליכי ווארט אונ' טרישט זיא נעמט מיט אונש פר גוט דאן ווערט שלמה
המלך ע"ה אין דען פסוק גרעט האבן (מאירת יי' בבית רשע ונוה צדיקים
5   יבורך[71]) דא איז איך טייטש דיא פלוכונג פון [גו*ט] איז אין הויז דאש רשע אונ' דיא
וואנונג פון דען צדיקים איז גבענשט מיט אלין ברכות אויף דאז מיינט איוב (וידעת
כי שלום באוהלך[72]) איין זקנה דיא איין צדקת איז דיא טוט וויא איך גשריבן האב
ווערט שלום אין אירין גצעלט מלין אזו ווערט זיא אויך זולכה דז זי ווערט אויך
שלום אין עולם הבא האבן אז מיר גפינדן אז השם יתברך שמו האט גזאגט צו דען
10   צדיקים (ואתה תבא בשלום אל אבותיך[73]) דאש איז טייטש דוא ווערשט קומן אין
עולם הבא צוא דיין עלטרין מיט שלום אז דיא גמרא[74] גיט ווען איין צדיק שטערברט
דא גיאן אים שליחות מלאכים אן קיגן אונ' אנטפגגין אים אונ' שפרעכין (יבואו
בשלום וינוחו על משכבם[75]) דאז איז טייטש דיא צדיקים זאלין קומן מיט שלום אונ'
זעלין רואן מיט מנוחה אויף אירן גלעגר דאז מיינט דיא דא שלום גמלט האט אויף
15   דר וועלט ווערט אויך צו שלום זיין אויף עולם הבא דרום שפרלט ער יבא
בשלום מיט דר ב' עש מיינט אזו ער נעמט דען שלום מיט זיך פון דער וועלט אויף יעני
וועלט דרום זול איין איטלכה גווערנט דראן זיין אונ' דרום לאזן אל אונזרי תפילו' אויז
מיט שלום בזכות זה ווערן מיר זולכה זיין צו דר גאולה פון [משיח] דר דא וועט שלום
אין גנצן עולם מכן אונ' ווערן זולכה לבניין ב"ה זיין אונ' די שכינה ווערט ווידר רואן
20   אונטר ישראל דער אדון השלום איז ווערט אונש לערנן אונ' מגלה זיין די תורה דיא
אייטל שלום איז אז אז דר פסוק גיט כל דרכיה דרכיה נועם וכל נתיבותה שלום[76] אכי"ר

תם ונשלם היום יום ב' ך ימים בחודש [אלול] שנח לפ"ק
ע"י יוסף שמואל בר מרדכי גראזמרק ז"ל ובביתו

---

[71]Prov. 3:33.   [72]Job 5:24.   [73]See Gen. 15:15.   [74]See B. Berakhot 64a.   [75]See Isa. 57:2.   [76]See Prov. 3:17.

---

5 גאט K1618 | 18 {ח}משK1618 | 22 אלר K1618

APPENDIX II

SIMḤES TOYRE LID:
ORIGINAL YIDDISH TEXT

The tombstone in the Old Jewish Cemetery
marking the grave of Rivkah bat Meir Tiktiner,
who was buried in Prague in 1605.

שמחת תורה ליד¹

הללויה.	אחד אלהינו דוא בישט מיין גאט
הללויה.²	דער מיר מיין זיל און' לייב בישאפין האט
הללויה.	בשאפין האשטו הימל און' ערד
הללויה.	דרום דיין לוב איבג גווערד
הללויה.	גוועזן בישטו און' ווערשט איביג זיין 5
הללויה.³	דוא האשט בישפן אונש אל גימין
הללויה.	דוא האשט אל דינג אין דיינר מכט
הללויה.	דרום לובן מיר דיך טאג און' נכט
הללויה.	העלפן קאנשטו אויז נוט און' פיין
הללויה.	דרום לובן מיר דיך אליין 10
הללויה.	וואר הפטיג און' לויטר זיין דיין גבאט
הללויה.	דרום דאנקן מיר דיר דו⁴ וואדר גאט
הללויה.	זיא איז אונש⁵ אל מאל גשטנדן בייא
הללויה.	פון גיהנם ווערט זיא⁶ אונז מכין פרייא
הללויה.	חי וקים⁷ אונזר טרישטר בישטו 15
הללויה.	וויא דוא אונש האשט גזאגט צו
הללויה.⁹	[טושט]⁸ און' מכשט לעבן וועמן דוא בגערשט
הללויה.	דרום דיין לוב נימר אויף הערט
הללויה.	יאגין טושטו דען פיינט דיין
הללויה.	אין גיהנם מוז ער איביג זיין 20
הללויה.	[כ]יגן¹⁰ דיר קאן נימנט בישטין
הללויה.	אז¹¹ ווא איין ווקש אין¹² פייאר מוז ער צו גין
הללויה.	לעבשט איביג אין דיין הימלשן טרון¹³
הללויה.	דען פרומן בהלשטו אירן לון

---

1. The text is based on the transcription by Kh. Shmeruk, *Sifrut yidish be-polin: Meḥkarim ve-iyyunim historiyim* (Yiddish Literature in Poland: Research and Historical Analysis) (Jerusalem, 1981, pp. 66–69, who used the printing Opp. 8° 650 (called by him Version A) and referred for addenda and emendations to Opp. 8° 460 (called by him Version B). These are held by the Bodleian Library, Oxford; see Y. Vinograd, *Thesaurus of the Hebrew Book: Listing of Books Printed in Hebrew Letters since the Beginning of Hebrew Printing circa 1469 through 1863* (Jerusalem, 1993), II, p. 536, no. 199 (Prague, ca. 1610), and II, p. 564, no. 1581 (Prague, n.d.). Vinograd mentions a third print, see ibid., II, p. 539, no. 349 (Prague, n.d.). *Rafe* bars were not incorporated; missing abbreviation marks after "*un*" were tacitly added. For a translation see D. Kay, *Seyder Tkhines. The Forgotten Book of Common Prayer for Jewish Women* (Philadelphia, 2004), pp. 221–223. On this poem, see also K. Hellerstein, "The Name in the Poem: Yiddish Women Poets," *Shofar* 20, 3 (spring 2002), pp. 32–52.
2. Version B: דער מיין זיל און' לייב בישאפין האט הללויה.
3. Version A: אויך האשטו נאך ניט גליטן פיין.
4. Version B: word missing.
5. Version B: word missing.
6. Version B: only ווערטו.
7. Cf., e.g., B. Rosh ha-Shanah 25a.
8. Shmeruk reads [טיטש]ט; Version A: טטיטש.
9. Version B: טיטשט און' דוא מכשט לעבן הללויה; possible erroneous spelling for טושטו.
10. Versions A and B: קיגן (common spelling).
11. Version B: word missing.
12. Version B: אים.
13. Version A: טארן.

הללויה.	מעכטיג בישטו אונזר גאט אליין
הללויה.[14]	דייני (שונאים) מוזן פר לארן זיין
הללויה.	נעבן דיר איז קיין גאט ניט מין[15]
הללויה.	דרום בלייבט הימל אונ' ערד בשטין
הללויה.	ספיר אונ' אידל גישטיין
הללויה.	דיא הובן קיגן דיין ליכט קיין שיין
הללויה.	ער בהילט דאש ליכט אין איביגלייך
הללויה.	זייני פריינד לייכט ער אין הימל רייך
הללויה.	פירט אונש מיט גנאד[16] אין איביקייט
הללויה.	ורט אונש דר געצין אל אונזר טרויארקייט[17]
הללויה.	צירן ווערט ער אונש מיט זיינר קרון
הללויה.	אל דיא תורה[18] הובן גינומן אן
הללויה.	קומט אונש צו הילף מיט זיין הימלשין שאר
הללויה.	אלש דען ווערט זיין ער[19] אופן וואר
הללויה.	רופן ווערט ער מיט צארין גרים
הללויה.	הימל אונ' ערד ווערט ציטרן פון זיינר שטים
הללויה.	שופר משיח ווערט גהערט מיט איין גרושן של[20]
הללויה.	דיא גרעכטין ווערן[21] אויף וואכין אל
הללויה.	[ת]ריסטן[22] ווערט ער זייני ליבה קנעכט
הללויה.	אל דיא אים האבן גדינט רעכט
הללויה.	ריכטן ווערט ער איין סעודה אן
הללויה.	אל דיא זיין ווילן הובן גיטאן
הללויה.	ברענגט[23] הער פון אל דיא פיר זייט
הללויה.	צו אל דיא אין גלות זיין פר שפרייט
הללויה.	קומן ווערט אונז צו הויז דר ווירט
הללויה.	אונז ברענגן משיח דען ווארן הירט
הללויה.	הער צו ירושלים ווערט ער פר זמלן זייני פר שפרייט שאף
הללויה.	דז דש[24] גלות הובן גליטן מיט מענכי שטראף
הללויה.	דאש ווערט אלש ווערן וואר
הללויה.	אז אונזר נביאים שרייבן קלאר

---

14. .אל דיא דיך ביטן העלפשטו פיין
15. Version B: word missing.
16. Version B: this and previous word missing.
17. Version B: word missing.
18. Version B: תורת משה.
19. Version B: word missing.
20. Version A: שטים.
21. Version A: word missing.
22. Versions A and B: טרישטן (common spelling).
23. Shmeruk: בורענגט.
24. Version B: instead of this and previous word: אל די דז.

55	בשיינפרלך ווערט איר²⁵ זעהן איטלכש²⁶ פרומש קינד	הללויה.
	וויא מן עז אין ישעיה²⁷ גישריבן פינט	הללויה.
	תראגנדיגה²⁸ און׳ קינד²⁹ בעטרינש אל גמיין	הללויה.
	דיא ווערן אין איין חברותה זיין	הללויה.
	מיט אונש ווערט ער טיילן זיין גרושי גינאד	הללויה.
60	דער פילן וויל ער אונש אל אונזרין שאד³⁰	הללויה.
	היילין ווערט ער אונז גאט יתברך שמו גאר און׳ גנץ	הללויה.³¹
	דיא בחורים און׳ בתולות ווערן זיך פרייאן אן איינם טאנץ	הללויה.
	רומין ווערט מן אונז דען רעכטן וועג	הללויה.
	ווען זיא ווערן גנעהנן דיא זעלביגן טעג	הללויה.
65	ריכטן ווערן זיא יונג און׳ אלט	הללויה.
	אייהרן שאדן וועלן מיר בצאלין בלד	הללויה.
	מערן וויל איך אייך אז דיא היילגן שאף	הללויה.
	דש גלות ווערט אונש דונקן אז איין³² טרוים אין³³ שלאף	הללויה.
	אפין ווערליך וויל איך אייך ווייזן וואש איך³⁴ פר מאג	הללויה.
70	צו פרייד און׳ צו וואון וויל איך פר קערן אל אייאר קלאג	הללויה.³⁵
	יודן קינדער לענקט אייך אין דען רכטן וועג	הללויה.
	דער לענגן וויל איך אייך³⁶ אייארי טעג	הללויה.
	[ר]יין³⁷ גאלד וויל איך אייך ברענגן פר מעשן גשיר	הללויה.
	פר אייזן וויל איך אייך ברענגן זילבר דר פיר	הללויה.
75	זמלן וויל איך אייך פון דער זונן איוף ביז אן אונטר גנג	הללויה.³⁸
	איין גוט עשן קאן מן ניט [הרן]³⁹ צו לנג	הללויה.
	ציפל איינש⁴⁰ מענטשן ווערן⁴¹ זיך הלטן אן	הללויה.⁴²
	אין אייערן⁴³ ליכט וועלן מיר גאן	הללויה.
	לובן וועלין מיר דען איינגן גאט	הללויה.
80	דער אונש אלי בישאפן האט	הללויה.

25. Version B: word missing.
26. Version A: איטלכם.
27. Jer. 31:8; cf. Isa. 26:17; 7:14.
28. Version A: תראגדיגה.
29. Version A: קינדר.
30. Version B: טא.
31. Version B: היילן ווערט גאט (יתברך שמו) אונש גאר און׳ גנץ הללויה.
32. Version B: word missing.
33. Version B: word missing.
34. Version B: word missing.
35. Version B: words צו, איך, אל missing.
36. Version A: word missing.
37. Version A: מיין; Version B: ריין.
38. Version B: זמלן וויל איך אייך פון דער זוני איוך אייך אונטר גנג הללויה.
39. Shmeruk emendates הערן (*heren*—to listen), however this word makes no sense; better is *"haren"* (to await).
40. Version A: איינם.
41. Version A: ווערג.
42. Version B: ציפל איינש יודן ווערין זיא זיך הלטין אן הללויה.
43. Possible erroneous spelling for זיין.

BIBLIOGRAPHY

Dictionaries, Lexicons, Encyclopedias

Encyclopaedia Judaica. 16 vols. Jerusalem, 1972.

Even Shoshan. Avraham. *Ha-milon he-ḥadash* (The New Dictionary), 4 vols. Jerusalem, 1988.

Gesenius, Wilhelm. *Hebräisches und Aramäisches Handwörterbuch über das Alte Testament* (Hebrew and Aramaic Dictionary). Berlin, 1996.

Grimm, Jakob, and Wilhelm Grimm. *Deutsches Wörterbuch* (German Dictionary). 2nd ed. Ed. M. Heyne. München, 1984.

Jastrow, Marcus. *A Dictionary of the Targumim, the Talmud Babli and Yerushalmi, and the Midrashic Literature.* 2 vols. Jerusalem, 1987.

Lexer, Matthias. *Mittelhochdeutsches Handwörterbuch* (Dictionary of Middle High German). Stuttgart, 1992.

The Responsa Project. Version 6. Bar Ilan University. Ramat Gan, 1998.

Röhrich, Lutz. *Lexikon der sprichwörtlichen Redensarten* (Lexicon of Proverbial Expressions). Freiburg, 1974.

Steinschneider, Moritz. *Catalogus librorum hebraeorum in bibliotheca Bodleiana, jussu curatorum digessit et notis instruxit.* 2nd ed. Berlin, 1931.

Vinograd, Yeshayahu. *Thesaurus of the Hebrew Book: Listing of Books Printed in Hebrew Letters since the Beginning of Hebrew Printing circa 1469 through 1863.* 2 vols. Jerusalem, 1993.

Wander, Karl F. *Deutsches Sprichwörterlexikon* (Lexicon of German Proverbs). Darmstadt, 1964.

Non-Edited Primary Sources

Bobzin, Hartmut, and Hermann Süß (eds.). *Sammlung Wagenseil. Gesamtedition nach dem Verkaufskatalog von 1708* (Wagenseil Collection. Complete Edition according to the Sales Catalogue from 1708 [Microfilms]). Erlangen, 1996.

Den Muser un' Hanhoge. Anonymous. Krakow, 1538 (Jewish National University Library. Jerusalem [JNUL]).

De Rebecca Polona. Eruditarum in Gente Foeminarum Rariori Exemplo. Johann Konrad, Lufft. Altdorf, 1719.

Eyn shoyn Froyenbuykhleyn—Seder Mizvot ha-Nashim. Benjamin Slonik. Basel. 1602 [JNUL].

Iggeret Derekh ha-Shem. Moses of Trani. Venice, 1553 [JNUL].

Meneket Rivkah. Rivkah bat Meir. Prague, 1609 [Old University Library, Erlangen].

Meshiv Ḥema—Minhagim Eshet Ḥayil. Isaac ben Berl Ẓoref. Frankfurt-am-Main, 1715 [JNUL].

Mishlei Ḥakhamim. Judah bar Israel Regensburg. Prague, ca. 1616 [JNUL].

Seder Nashim—Vayberbukh. Samuel Shmelke ben Ḥayyim. Prague, 1620 [JNUL].

Sefer Hazkarot. Prague [Jewish Museum, Prague, MS 113].

Sefer ha-Gan. Isaac ben Eliezer. Krakow, 1579 [JNUL].

Sefer ha-Yir'ah. Anonymous. Trans. Michael Adam. Freiburg (im Breisgau), 1583 [JNUL].

Sefer Ḥayyei Olam. Anonymous. Sabbioneta, 1552 [JNUL].

Sefer Middot. Anonymous. Isny, 1542 [JNUL].

Sefer Mishlei. Anonymous. Krakow, 1582 [JNUL].

Sefer Oraḥ Ḥayyim. Anonymous. Basel, 1602 [JNUL].

Sefer Orḥot Ẓaddikim. Anonymous. Prague, 1581 [JNUL].

Sefer Ẓe'enah u-Re'enah. Jacob ben Isaac Ashkenazi. Hanau, 1622 [JNUL].

Sota, hoc est, liber Mischnicus de uxore adulterii suspecta, una cum Libri En Iacob excerptis Gemarae, versione latina...Accedunt correctiones Lipmannianae. Johann Christoph, Wagenseil. Altdorf, 1674.

Edited Primary Sources

Aggadat Bereshit. Ed. S. Buber. New York, 1959.

Avot de-Rabbi-Natan. 2nd ed. Ed. S. Schechter and M. Kister. New York, 1997.

Ba-midbar Rabbah. In Midrash Rabbah. Bnei Brak, 1958–63.

Bereshit Rabbah. In Midrash Rabbah. Bnei Brak, 1958–63.

Brantshpigl. Moses Henokhs Altshul. Krakow, 1596. Ed. S. Riedel. Moses Henochs Altschul-Jeruschalmi. "Brantspigel." Frankfurt-am-Main, 1993.

Devarim Rabbah. In Midrash Rabbah. Bnei Brak, 1958–63.

Die Fabeln des Kuhbuches. Moses ben Eliezer Wallich, Aron Freimann (ed.). Berlin, Leipzig, 1926.

Kohelet Rabbah. In Midrash Rabbah. Bnei Brak, 1958–63.

Maḥzor Vitry. Ed. Sh. Hurwitz. Nuremberg, 1923.

Mekhilta de-Rabbi Yishmael. Ed. S. Horovitz and I. A. Rabin. Jerusalem, 1960.

Midrash Mishlei. 2nd ed. Ed. S. Buber. Jerusalem, 1965.

Midrash Tanḥuma. 2nd ed. Ed. S. Buber. Jerusalem, 1964.

Midrash Tannaim. 2nd ed. Ed. D. Hoffmann. Jerusalem, 1968.

Midrash Tehillim. 2nd ed. Ed. S. Buber. Jerusalem, 1966.

Midrash Zuta. 2nd ed. Ed. S. Buber. Tel Aviv, 1964.

Mishnah—Shishah Sidrei Mishnah. Ed. H. Albeck. Jerusalem, 1952–1959.

Mishneh Torah. Moses ben Maimon. Ed. Z. Preisler. Jerusalem, 1985.

Ozar Midrashim. Ed. J. D. Eisenstein. Tel Aviv, 1969.

Perush al ha-Torah. Abraham ibn Ezra. In Mikraot Gedolot. Jerusalem, 1964–67.

Perush al ha-Torah. Solomon ben Isaac (Rashi). In Mikraot Gedolot. Jerusalem, 1964–67.

Perush Rabbenu Yonah Gerondi ʻal Avot. Ed. B. D. Kohen. Mishnah Avot. Jerusalem, 1993.

Pesikta Rabbati. 2nd ed. Ed. M. Friedmann. Tel Aviv, 1963.

Pirkei de-Rabbi Eliezer. 2nd ed. Ed. B. Diskin. Jerusalem, 1970.

Seder Eliyahu Rabbah. Ed. M. Ish Shalom. Jerusalem, 1960.

Sefer Gematriyot le Rav-Yehudah he-Ḥasid. Ed. D. Abrams and I. Ta-Shma. Los Angeles, 1998.

Sefer Ha-Ḥasidim. Al-pi nussaḥ ktav yad asher be-Parma. Ed. Y. Wistinetzki. Jerusalem, 1992.

Sefer Ḥasidim. Yehudah ben Shemuel he-Ḥasid [Bologna 1538]. 2nd ed. Ed. R. Margaliot. Jerusalem, 1992.

Sefer ha-Zohar. Jerusalem, 1960.

Sefer Reshit Ḥokhmah. Eliyahu de Vidas. Venice, 1579. Ed. H. J. Waldman. 3 vols. Jerusalem, 1984.

Shemot Rabbah. In Midrash Rabbah. Bnei Brak, 1958–63.

Shir ha-Shirim Zuta. In Midrash Zuta. Ed. S. Buber. Tel Aviv, 1964.

Shulḥan Arukh, Joseph ben Ephraim Karo. Jerusalem, 1963–66.

Sifrei ʻal Sefer Devarim. 2nd ed. L. Finkelstein. New York, 1969.

Sifrei de-Aggadeta 'al Megillat Esther, Panim Aḥerim. 2nd ed. Ed. S. Buber. Jerusalem, 1663/64.

Sifrut ha-Hekhalot. Synopose zur Hekhalot-Literatur (Synopsis of the Hekhalot Literature). Ed. P. Schäper. Tubingen, 1981.

Talmud Bavli. [Venice, 1520–23]. Jerusalem, 1967–72.

Talmud Yerushalmi. Ed. P. Schäfer and H.-J. Becker. Synopse zum Talmud Yerushalmi. 7 vols. Tübingen, 1991–2001.

Torah, Nevi'im, Kethuvim. A New Translation of the Holy Scriptures according to the Traditional Hebrew Text. Philadelphia, 1985.

Torah, Nevi'im, Ketuvim. Jerusalem: Keter, 1988.

Tosefta. 2nd ed. Ed. M. P. Zuckermandel. Jerusalem, 1975.

Va-yikra Rabbah. In Midrash Rabbah. Bnei Brak, 1958–63.

Yalkut Shim'oni. Moshe ha-Darshan. Ed. Y. Shiloni, A. Hyman, and Y. Lerer. Jerusalem, 1973.

Secondary Literature

Abramsky, Chimen, Mociej Jachimczyk, and Antony Polonsky (eds.). *The Jews of Poland*. Oxford, 1986.

Adelman, Howard. "The Literacy of Women in Early Modern Italy." In Barbara J. Whitehead, *Women's Education in Early Modern Italy*. New York, 1999.

Alexander-Frizer, Tamar. *The Pious Sinner: Ethics and Aesthetics in the Medieval Hasidic Narrative*. Tübingen, 1991.

Ashkenazi, Shelomo. *Ha-Isha be-aspeklariyat ha-yahadut* (The Woman as Reflected in Judaism). 2nd ed. 2 vols. Tel Aviv, 1979.

——. *Meḥaberot piyyutim, teḥinnot u-tefillot* (Female Authors of Piyyutim, Tḥinnes and Prayers). *Maḥanayim* 109 (1967), 75–82.

——. *Nashim lamdaniyot* (Learned Women). Jerusalem, 1942.

Assaf, Simḥa. *Mekorot le-toledot ha-ḥinnukh be-yisra'el* (Sources on the History of Jewish Education). 4 vols. Tel Aviv, 1954.

Baskin, Judith R. (ed.). *Jewish Women in Historical Perspective*. Detroit, 1991.

——. *Midrashic Women: Formations of the Feminine in Rabbinic Literature*. Hanover, N.H., 2002.

——. *Women of the Word: Jewish Women and Jewish Writing*. Detroit, 1994.

Baumgarten, Jean. *Introduction à la littérature yiddish ancienne*. Paris, 1993. *Old Yiddish Literature*. Ed. and trans. Jerold C. Frakes. New York, 2005.

—— (ed.). *Le Commentaire sur la Torah (The Torah Commentary): Tseenah ureenah de Jacob ben Isaac Achkenazi de Janow*. Lagrasse, 1987.

Ben Sasson, Ḥayyim H. *Hagut ve-hanhagah: Hashkafoteihem ha-ḥevratiyot shel yehudei Polin be-shilhei yemei ha-benayim*. Jerusalem, 1959.

Benthien, Claudia. *Haut. Literaturgeschichte, Körperbilder, Grenzdiskurse* (Skin: History of Literature, Body Images, Borderline Discourses). Hamburg, 1999.

Berger, Ruth. *Sexualität, Ehe und Familienleben in der jüdischen Moralliteratur (900–1900)* (Sexuality, Marriage, and Family Life in Jewish Moral Literature, 900–1900). Wiesbaden, 2003.

Bernstein, Ignaz. *Jüdische Sprichwörter und Redensarten* (Jewish Proverbs and Aphorisms). 2nd ed. Wiesbaden, 1988.

Biale, Rachel. *Women and Jewish Law: An Exploration on Women's Issues in Halakhic Sources*. New York, 1984.

Bondy, Gottlieb, and Franz Dvorsky. *Zur Geschichte der Juden in Böhmen, Mähren, Schlesien von (906–1620)* (On the History of the Jews of Bohemia, Moravia, Silesia, 906–1620). Prague, 1906.

Bourdieu, Pierre. *Practical Reason: On the Theory of Action.* Cambridge, 1998.

Boyarin, Daniel. *Carnal Israel: Reading Sex in Talmudic Culture.* Berkeley, 1993.

Brilling, Bernhard. "Die Prager jüdische Gemeinde als Fürsprecherin und Vertreterin des deutschen Judentums im 16. und 17. Jahrhundert" (The Jewish Community of Prague as Advocate and Representative of German Jewry in the Sixteenth and Seventeenth Century). *Theokratia* 3 (1973–75), 185–98. Leiden, 1979.

Bublitz, Hannelore, Andrea D. Bührmann, Christine Hanke, and Andrea Seier (eds.). *Das Wuchern der Diskurse: Perspektiven der Diskursanlayse Foucaults* (The Proliferation of Discourses: Perspectives on Foucault's Discourse Analysis). Frankfurt-am-Main, 1999.

Carmoly, Eliakim. "Gallerie der Rabbiner" (Gallery of Rabbis). *Der Israelit. Ein Central-Organ für das orthodoxe Judenthum* 5 (1867), 81; 10 (1867), 164–65.

Dan, Joseph. *Jewish Mysticism and Jewish Ethics.* Seattle, 1986.

——. *Sifrut ha-derush veha-musar.* Jerusalem, 1975.

Davis, Natalie Z. "Glikl bas Judah Leib: 'Arguing with God.'" In *Women on the Margins: Three Seventeenth-Century Lives*, 5–62. Cambridge, Mass., 1995.

Dinse, Hartmut. *Die Entwicklung des jiddischen Schrifttums im deutschen Sprachgebiet* (The Development of Yiddish Literature in the German Speaking Area). Stuttgart, 1974.

Elbaum, Jacob. "Aspects of Hebrew Ethical Literature in Sixteenth Century Poland." In D. B. Cooperman (ed.), *Jewish Thought in the Sixteenth Century*, 146–66. Cambridge, Mass., 1983.

Elbogen, Ismar. *Der jüdische Gottesdienst in seiner geschichtlichen Entwicklung.* Hildesheim, 1995. *Jewish Liturgy: A Comprehensive History.* Trans. Raymond P. Scheindlin. Philadelphia, 1993.

Erik, Max. "Bletlekh tsu der geshikhte fun der elterer yidisher literatur un kultur" (Papers on the History of the Older Yiddish Literature and Culture). *Journal on Jewish History, Demography and Economy, Literary Research, Language Research, and Ethnography* [Yidd.], 1 (1926), 173–77.

Fishman, Isidor. *The History of Jewish Education in Central Europe: From the End of the Sixteenth to the End of the Eighteenth Century.* London, 1944.

Foucault, Michel. *The Order of Things: An Archaeology of Human Sciences.* New York, 1973.

Fox, Marvin. "The Moral Philosophy of the Maharal." In D. B. Cooperman (ed.), *Jewish Thought in the Sixteenth Century*, 167–85. Cambridge, Mass., 1983.

Frakes, Jerold C. *The Politics of Interpretation: Alterity and Ideology in Old Yiddish Studies.* Albany, N.Y., 1989.

Fram, Edward. *My Dear Daughter: Rabbi Benjamin Slonik and the Education of Jewish Women in Sixteenth-Century Poland.* Cincinnati, 2007.

Frankel, Jonathan (ed.). *Jews and Gender: The Challenge of Hierarchy.* Oxford, 2000.

Fuks-Mansfeld, Renate G. "The Impact of Midrash on the Old Yiddish Literature." In A. Kuyt, E. G. L. Schriver, and N. A. van Uchelen (eds.), *Variety of Forms. Dutch Studies in Midrash.* Amsterdam, 1990.

Funkenstein, Amos. *Perceptions of Jewish History.* Berkeley, 1993.

Gaster, Moses (ed.). *Ma'aseh Book: Book of Jewish Tales and Legends.* 2nd ed. Philadelphia, 1934.

——. "The Maasehbuch and the Brantspiegel." In S. W. Baron and A. Marx (eds.), *Jewish Studies in the Memory of G. A. Kohut*, 270–78. New York, 1935.

Gellis, Ya'akov. *Sefer Tosafot ha-shalem: Ozar perushei ba'alei tosafot.* (The complete Sefer Tosafot. A Treasury of the commentaries of the ba'alei tosafot.) Jerusalem, 1989.

Ginzberg, Louis. *Legends of the Jews.* 2nd ed. 7 vols. Philadelphia, 2003.

Goldberg, Sylvie-Anne. *Crossing the Jabbok: Illness and Death in Ashkenazi Judaism in Sixteenth through Nineteenth Century Prague.* Berkeley, 1996.

——. "Von der (Prager) Judenstadt zum jüdischen Prag" (From the Jewish Quarter in Prague to Jewish Prague). In M. Graetz (ed.), *Schöpferische Momente des Judentums.* Heidelberg, 2000.

Greenblatt, Rachel L. "The Shapes of Memory: Evidence in Stone from the Old Jewish Cemetery in Prague." *Leo Baeck Institute Year Book* 47 (2002), 43–67.

Gries, Ze'ev. *Conduct Literature. Its History and Place in the Life of Beshtian Hasidism* [Heb.]. Jerusalem, 1989.

Grossman, Avraham. *Pious and Rebellious: Jewish Women in Medieval Europe.* Waltham, Mass., 2004.

Grünbaum, Max. *Jüdischdeutsche Chrestomathie. Zugleich ein Beitrag zur Kunde der hebräischen Literatur* (Jewish-German Anthology and Contribution to the Lore of Hebrew Literature). Leipzig 1882, reprint, Hildesheim, 1969.

Güdemann, Moritz. *Quellenschriften zur Geschichte des Unterrichts und der Erziehung bei den deutschen Juden* (Sources on the History of Teaching among the German Jews). Berlin 1891, reprint. Amsterdam, 1968.

Halpern, Micah D., and Hanah Safrai (eds.). *Jewish Legal Writings by Women.* Jerusalem, 1998.

Hasan-Rokem, Galit, Tamar S. Hess, and Shirley Kaufman. *The Defiant Muse: Hebrew Feminist Poems from Antiquity to the Present. A Bilingual Anthology.* New York, 1999.

Heilperin, Me'ir. *Ha-Notarikon, ha-simanim veha-kinnuyim.* (The Notarikon, the Characters, and the Epithets.) 2nd ed. Jerusalem, 1930.

Hellerstein, Kathryn. "The Name in the Poem: Yiddish Women Poets." *Shofar* 20, 3 (Spring 2002), 32–52.

Henry, Sondra, and Emily Taitz. *Written Out of History. Our Jewish Foremothers.* New York, 1978, 1988.

Henry, Sondra, Emily Taitz, and Cheryl Tallan (eds.) *The JPS Guide to Jewish Women, 600 B.C.E–1900 C.E.* Philadelphia, 2003.

Herman, Jan. "Die wirtschaftliche Betätigung und Berufe der Prager Juden vor ihrer Ausweisung im Jahre 1541" (Economic Activity and Professions of the Jews of Prague prior to Their Expulsion). *Judaica Bohemiae* 4, 1 (1968), 20–63.

——. "The Conflict between Jewish and Non-Jewish Population in Bohemia before the 1541 Banishment." *Judaica Bohemiae* 6, 1 (1970), 39–53.

Hock, Simon, and David Kaufmann. *Die Familien Prags* (The Families of Prague). Pressburg, 1892.

Horowitz, Eliott. "Jüdische Jugend in Europa: 1300–1800" (Jewish Youth in Europe, 1300–1800). In G. Levi and J.-C. Schmitt (Hg.), *Geschichte der Jugend*, vol. 1, 113–65. Frankfurt-am-Main, 1996.

Hundert, Gershon D. *The Jews in Poland and Russia. Bibliographical Essays.* Bloomington, Ind., 1984.

——. "Jewish Children and Childhood in Early Modern East Central Europe." In D. Kraemer (ed.), *The Jewish Family.* New York, 1989.

Idel, Moshe. *Golem: Jewish Magical and Mystical Traditions on the Artificial Anthropoid.* Albany, N.Y., 1990.

Israel, Jonathan I. *European Jewry in the Age of Mercantilism, 1550–1750.* Oxford, 1985.

Jakobovits, Tobias. "Die jüdischen Zünfte in Prag" (The Jewish Guilds in Prague). *Jahrbuch der Gesellschaft für Geschichte der Juden in der czechoslovakischen Republik* 8 (1936), 57–68.

Kaplan, Lawrence. "R. Mordekhai Jaffe and the Evolution of Jewish Culture." In D. B. Cooperman (ed.), *Jewish Thought in the Sixteenth Century.* Cambridge, Mass., 1983, 266–82.

Karpeles, Gustav. *Geschichte der jüdischen Literatur* (History of Jewish Literature). 2 vols. Berlin, 1909.

Katz, Jacob. *Tradition and Crisis: Jewish Society at the End of the Middle Ages.* 2nd ed. New York, 1993.

Kay, Devra. *Seyder Tkhines: The Forgotten Book of Common Prayer for Jewish Women.* Philadelphia, 2004.

Kayserling, Meyer. *Die jüdischen Frauen in der Geschichte, Literatur und Kunst* (Jewish Women in History, Literature, and Arts). Leipzig, 1879; reprint, Hildesheim, 1991.

Kirshenblatt-Gimblett, Barbara. "Toward a Theory of Proverb Meaning." *Proverbium* 22 (1973), 821–26.

Kisch, Alexander. "Das Testament des Mardochai Meysels" (The Testament of Mordecai Meisel). *Monatsschrift für Geschichte und Wissenschaft des Judenthums* 37 (1892), 25–40, 82–91, 131–46.

——. "Megillat purei ha-kela'im. The Chronicle of Henokh Altshul" [Heb.]. In *Jubelschrift zum Siebzigsten Geburtstage des Professors Dr. Heinrich Graetz*. Breslau 1887, 48–52.

Kisch, Bruno. "Jewish Pharmacists and Doctors in Prague." *Historica Judaica* 8 (1946), 149–80.

Kleinberger, Aharon F. "The Didactics of Rabbi Loew of Prague." *Scripta Hierosolymitana* 13 (1963), 32–55.

Koch, Margarete. *Der Schlegel. Zur Novelle von Rüdiger von Hünchoven: Kritische Ausgabe, Untersuchungen und Übersetzung* (The Club. On the Novella by Rüdiger von Hünchoven: Critical Edition, Studies and Translation). Münster/Hamburg, 1993.

Korman, Ezra. *Yidishe Dikhterins* (Jewish Women Poets). Chicago, 1928.

Lamdan, Ruth. *A Separate People: Jewish Women in Palestine, Syria and Egypt in the Sixteenth Century*. Leiden, 2000.

Lenhard, Doris. *Die rabbinische Homilie: Ein formanalytischer Index* (The Rabbinic Homily: A Form Analytic Index). Frankfurt-am-Main, 1998.

Levine Katz, Yael. *Midreshei Eshet Hayil* (The Midrashim of the Woman of Valor). Ph.D. diss., Bar-Ilan University, 1992.

——. "Nashim lamdaniyot birushalayim" (Learned Women in Jerusalem). *Mabua* 26 (1994), 98–125.

Lieben, Salomon H. "Der hebräische Buchdruck in Prag im 16. Jahrhundert" (Hebrew Book Printing in Sixteenth Century Prague). In S. Steinhertz, *Die Juden in Prag*. Prague, 1927.

——. "Frumet Meisel, ebenbürtige Gattin ihres Mannes Mordechai Meisel" (Frumet Meisel, a Wife Equal to Her Husband Mordecai Meisel). In *Monatsschrift für Geschichte und Wissenschaft des Judentums* 75 (1931), 374–77.

Marcus, Ivan, G. *Rituals of Childhood: Jewish Acculturation in Medieval Europe*. New Haven, 1996.

Margaliot, Re'uven (ed.). *Yehudah ben Shemu'el he-Ḥasid: Sefer Ḥasidim*. 2nd ed. Jerusalem, 1998.

Markus, Jacob Rader. "Etishe Vantshpiglen." *Yivo Bleter* 21 (1943), 201–14.

Muneles, Otto. "Die Rabbiner der Altneuschul" (The Rabbis of the Altneushul). *Judaica Bohemiae* 5, 2 (1969), 92–107.

——. *Epitaphs from the Ancient Jewish Cemetery of Prague* [Heb.]. Jerusalem, 1988.

——. *Prague Ghetto in the Renaissance Period*. Prague, 1965.

——. "Zur Prosopographie der Prager Juden im 15. und 16. Jahrhundert" (On the Prosopography of Fifteenth and Sixteenth Century Jews of Prague). *Judaica Bohemiae* 2, 1 (1966), 3–13.

Neuberg, Simon. *Aspekte der jiddischen Sprachgeschichte am Beispiel der "Zenerene"* (Aspects of the History of the Yiddish Language using the Example of Ze'enah u-Re'enah). Hamburg, 1999.

Niger, Shmuel. "Di yidishe literatur un di lezerin" (Yiddish Literature and the Female Reader). *Der Pinkes* 1 (1913), 85–138.

Niger, Shmuel, and Sheva Zucker. "Yiddish Literature and the Female Reader." In J. Baskin, *Women of the Word: Jewish Women and Jewish Writing*. Detroit, 1994.

Nosek, Bedrich. "Katalog mit einer Auswahl hebräischer Drucke Prager Provenienz" (Catalogue with a Selection of Hebrew Prints of Prague Provenance). *Judaica Bohemiae* 10, 1 (1977), 13–41.

Nulman, Macy. *The Encyclopedia of Jewish Prayer*. Northvale, N.J., 1993.

Rohden, Frauke von. "'Für Frauen und Männer, die wie Frauen sind.' Weibliche und männliche Verhaltensideale im Brantshpigl des Moses Henochs Altschul" ('For Women and Men Who Are Like Women.' Female and Male Ideals of Conduct in Brantshpigl by Moses Henokhs Altshul). In M. Brocke, A. Pomerance and A. Schatz (eds.). *Neuer Anbruch*. *Minima Judaica* 1 (2001), 175–90.

——. "Jüdische Ehe zwischen religiöser Norm und Alltagswahrnehmung im 16. Jahrhundert" (Jewish Marriage between Religious Norms and Daily Live Perceptions in the Sixteenth Century). In A. Holzem and I. Weber (eds.), *Ehe, Familie, Verwandtschaft*. Münster, 2008.

——. *Zur Jiddischen Mussar-Literatur im 16. Jahrhundert: Die Konstruktion von Weiblichkeit und Männlichkeit im Brantshpigl von Moshe Henochs Altschul* (On Sixteenth-Century Yiddish Moral Literature: The Construction of Female and Male in the *Brantshpigl* by Moses Henokhs Altshul). Master's thesis, Free University of Berlin, 1997.

Röll, Walter. "Zum 'Sefer ha-Gan' Jizhaks ben Elieser" (On *Sefer ha-Gan* by Isaac ben Eliezer).

Romer Segal, Agnes. "Yiddish Literature and Its Readers in the Sixteenth Century. Books in the Censors Lists, Mantua 1595" [Heb.]. *Kiryat Sefer* 53 (1978), 779–90.

——. "Yiddish Works on Women's Commandments in the Sixteenth Century." *Studies in Yiddish Literature and Folklore. Monograph Series* 7 (1986), 37–59.

Rosenfeld, Moshe N. "'Der Brandshpigl': An Unknown Edition, and the Identification of Its Author" [Heb.]. *Kiryat Sefer* 55 (1980), 617–21.

Saperstein, Marc. *Jewish Preaching 1200–1800. An Anthology*. New Haven, 1989.

Schnell, Rüdiger. *Frauendiskurs, Männerdiskurs, Ehediskurs: Textsorten und Geschlechterkonzepte in Mittelalter und Früher Neuzeit* (Female Discourse, Male Discourse, Marriage Discourse: Literary Genres and Gender Concepts in the Middle Ages and in the Early Modern Age). Frankfurt-am-Main/New York, 1998.

—— (ed.). *Text und Geschlecht. Mann und Frau in Eheschriften der frühen Neuzeit* (Text and Gender. Man and Woman in Marriage Literature of the Early Modern Age). Frankfurt-am-Main, 1997.

Scholem, Gershom. *Die jüdische Mystik in ihren Hauptströmungen*. Frankfurt-am-Main, 1980. Major Trends in Jewish Mysticism. New York, 1995.

——. *Zur Kabbala und ihrer Symbolik*. Frankfurt-am-Main, 1973. (On the Kabbalah and Its Symbolism. New York, 1965.)

Schudt, Johann Jacob. *Jüdische Merkwürdigkeiten*. Frankfurt-am-Main, 1714–18.

Shepherd, Naomi. *A Price below Rubies. Jewish Women as Rebels and Radicals*. Cambridge, Mass., 1993.

Shmeruk, Khone. *Sifrut yidish be-polin: Mehkarim ve-iyyunim historiyim* (Yiddish Literature in Poland: Research and Historical Analysis). Jerusalem, 1981.

——. "The First Jewish Authoress in Poland: Rivkah Tiktiner and Her Works" [Heb.]. *Gal-Ed* 27–28 (1978), 13–23.

Sixtova, Olga. "Findings from Genizot in Bohemia and Moravia." *Judaica Bohemiae* 33 (1997), 126–34.

Stein, August. *Die Geschichte der Juden in Böhmen und Mähren* (The History of the Jews of Bohemia and Moravia). Brünn, 1904.

Stern, David. *Parables in Midrash. Narrative and Exegesis in Rabbinic Literature*. 2nd ed. Cambridge, Mass., 1994.

Stone, Daniel. *The Polish-Lithuanian State, 1386–1795*. Seattle, 2001.

Süß, Herrmann. *Raritäten der jiddischen Literatur des sechzehnten und siebzehnten Jahrhunderts in der Universitätsbibiliothek; Ausstellungsbegleittext* (Rarities in Sixteenth and Seventeenth Century Yiddish Literature in the University Library; Accompanying Text for the Exhibition). Erlangen, 1980.

Taitz, Emily. "Women's Voices, Women's Prayers: The European Synagogue of the Middle Ages." In S. Grossman and R. Haut (eds.), *Daughters of the King. Women and the Synagogue: A Survey of History, Halakhah, and Contemporary Realities*. Philadelphia, 1992.

Ta-Shma, Israel. "Ḥidat sefer 'Menorat ha-Ma'or' u-fitronah" (The Riddle of the 'Menorat ha-Ma'or' and Its Solution). *Tarbiz* 64 (1995), 395–400.

Timm, Erika. "Das jiddischsprachige literarische Erbe der Italo-Aschkenasen" (The Yiddish Literary Heritage of Italian Ashkenazim). In M. Graetz (ed.), *Schöpferische Momente des europäischen Judentums*. Heidelberg, 2000.

——. "Verwandtschaftsbezeichnungen im Jiddischen, kontrastiv zum Deutschen betrachtet" (Examination of Kinship Terms in Yiddish as Opposed to German). In J. Jährling, U. Mewes, and E. Timm (eds.), *Röllwagenbüchlein. Festschrift für Walter Röll zum 65. Geburtstag*, 443–64. Tübingen, 2002.

Toch, Michael. "Die jüdische Frau im Erwerbsleben des Spätmittelalters" (The Jewish Woman in the Economic Life of the Late Middle Ages). In J. Carlebach (ed.), *Zur Geschichte der jüdischen Frau in Deutschland*, 37–48. Berlin, 1993.

Trachtenberg, Joshua. *Jewish Magic and Superstition: A Study in Folk Religion*. 2nd ed. New York, 1979.

Turniansky, Chava. *Glikl. Zikhronot 1691–1719*. Jerusalem, 2006.

——. "Ha-derashah veha-derashah bikhtav ke-metavkhot beyn ha-tarbut ha-kanonit le-veyn ha-kahal ha-raḥav" (Sermons and Written Sermons as Mediators between the Canonical Culture and the Broad Public). In B. Z. Kedar (ed.), *Ha-tarbut ha-amamit. Koveẓ meḥkarim*, 183–95. Jerusalem, 1996.

——. "Ha-yeẓirah hadu-leshonit be-Ashkenaz: Kiyyum ve-ofiyah" (The Bilingual Literature in Ashkenaz: Its Existence and Character). *Proceedings of the Sixth World Congress of Jewish Studies*, 85–99. Jerusalem, 1980.

——. "Maydlekh in der altyidisher literatur" (Girls in Old Yiddish Literature). In W. Röll and S. Neuberg (eds.), *Jiddische Philologie. Festschrift für Erika Timm*, 7–20. Tübingen, 1999.

——. *Sefer massah u-merivah shel Aleksander ben Yizḥak Pfafenhofen*. Jerusalem, 1985.

Veltri, Giuseppe. *Magie und Halakha: Ansätze zu einem empirischen Wissenschaftsbegriff im spätantiken und frühmittelalterlichen Judentum* (Magic and Halakhah: Approaches toward an Empirical Notion of Science in Late Antique and Early Medieval Judaism). Tübingen, 1997.

——. "'Ohne Recht und Gerechtigkeit': Rudolf II. und sein Bankier Markus Meyzl" (Without Law and Justice: Rudolf II and His Financier, Markus Meisel). In G. Veltri and A. Winkelmann (eds.), *An der Schwelle zur Moderne. Juden in der Renaissance*, 233–55. Leiden, 2003.

Vilimkova, Milada. *Die Prager Judenstadt* (The Jewish Quarter of Prague). Hanau, 1981.

——. "Seven Hundred Years of the Old-New-Synagogue." *Judaica Bohemiae* 5, 2 (1969), 72–83.

Warnock, Robert G. "Proverbs and Sayings in Early Yiddish Literature." In W. Röll and S. Neuberg (eds.), *Jiddische Philologie. Festschrift für Erika Timm*, 175–96. Tübingen, 1999.

Weigel, Sigrid. *Die Stimme der Medusa. Schreibweisen in der Gegenwartsliteratur von Frauen* (The Voice of the Medusa: Writing Styles in Contemporary Literature by Women). Reinbek, 1983.

Weinreich, Max. *Geschichte der jiddischen Sprachforschung* (History of the Research on Yiddish Language). Ed. J. C. Frakes. Atlanta, 1993.

——. *History of the Yiddish Language*. 2nd ed. Chicago/London, 1980.

Weinryb, Bernard. "Historisches und Kulturhistorisches aus Wagenseils hebräischem Briefwechsel" (Historical and Culture-Historical Material from Wagenseil's Hebrew Correspondence). *Monatsschrift für Geschichte und Wissenschaft des Judentums* 83 (1939), 325–41.

Weissler, Chava. "The Religion of Traditional Ashkenazic Women. Some Methodological Issues." *Association for Judaic Studies Review* 12 (1987), 73–94.

——. "The Traditional Piety of Ashkenazic Women." In A. Green (ed.), *Jewish Spirituality from the Sixteenth Century Revival to the Present*. New York, 1987.

——. *Voices of the Matriarchs: Listening to Prayers of Early Modern Jewish Women*. Boston, 1998.

Whitehead, Barbara. *Women's Education in Early Modern Europe: A History, 1500–1800*. New York, 1999.

Wolf, Gerson. "Zur Geschichte der Juden in Österreich. Gemeindestreitigkeiten in Prag von 1567–1678" (On the History of Jews in Austria: Community Conflicts in Prague, 1567–1678). In *Zeitschrift für die Geschichte der Juden in Deutschland* 1 (1887), 309–320.

——. "Zur Geschichte der Juden in Österreich. Verzeichnis der Prager Juden, ihrer Frauen, Kinder und Dienstboten im Jahre 1546" (On the History of Jews in Austria. Register of the Jews in Prague, Their Wives, Children, and Servants, in the Year 1546). In *Zeitschrift für die Geschichte der Juden in Deutschland* 1 (1887), 177–190.

Wolff, Johann Christoph. *Bibliotheca Hebraea*, 4 vols. Hamburg, 1715–33.

Wolfthal, Diane. *Picturing Yiddish: Gender, Identity, and Memory in the Illustrated Yiddish Books of Renaissance Italy*. Leiden, 2004.

Wunder, Meir. *Ateret Rivkah. Arba'ah thinnot nashim 'im tirgum li-leshon ha-kodesh ve-sefer ha-musar Meneket Rivkah* (Rebekah's Crown: Four Yiddish Women's Prayers with a Translation into Hebrew and the Morality Book, Meneket Rivkah). Jerusalem, 1992.

Wyczanski, Andrzej. *Polen als Adelsrepublik*. Osnabrück, 2001.

Ya'ari, Avraham. *Toldot hag simhat torah* (History of the Feast Simhat Torah). Jerusalem, 1989.

Yerushalmi, Yosef Hayim. *Zakhor. Jewish History and Jewish Memory*. Seattle, 1982.

Yudlov, Yizhak. "'Sheyne Thinne' ve-'Orah Hayyim': shnei sifrei yidish bilti yedu'im" ('Sheyne Thinne' and 'Orah Hayyim': Two Unknown Yiddish Books). *Kiryat Sefer* 62 (1989), 457–58.

Zinberg, Israel. *A History of Jewish Literature*. Vol. 7: Old Yiddish Literature from Its Origins to the Haskalah Period. New York, 1975.

Zolty, Shoshana P. *And All Your Children Shall be Learned: Women and the Study of Torah in Jewish Law and History*. Northvale, N.J., 1993.

SCRIPTURAL INDEX

1. Bible

Gen.

1:27	9a
2:7	5a
2:18	9a 12b
2:22	5a
2:23	9a
3:16	14a 21b 22a
12:5	26a
12:16	14a
15:15	36a
16:2	5a
21:12	14a
22:17	28b
24:14	29a
24:20	29a
25:22	4b
26:4	28b
26:19	2a
27:29	2a
28:12	11b 32a
29:2	2a
29:27	9a
29:30	9a
30:3	5a
35:8	2a
39:15	2a
49:28	9b

Exod.

1:21	4a
3:7	2a
15:2	6a
19:3	29a
20:5	12b
20:11	15a
20:12	15a
21:17	14b 25a
23:13	23a
25:33	5b 6b
25:37	5b
29:29	29b
29:42	33b
32:3	14a
32:4	14a
32:8	14a
34:7	12b
35:25	33b
35:31	4a
37:19	5b 6b

Lev.

16:3	10a
16:6	9a
16:11	9a
16:17	9a
19:3	14b
19:17	30b
19:18	32a
19:23–24	27b
20:26	20b
24:16	14b
25:36	34a
26:4	22a
26:6	22a

Num.

14:18	12b
22:6	2a
22:38	2a
23:9	20a
23:21	20a
24:6	20b
24:9	2a
28:6	33b

2. Rabbinic Literature

Talmud Yerushalmi

Talmud Bavli

YIDDISH SUBJECT INDEX

SUBJECT INDEX

lack of historiographical research on, 50,
    54–55
likened to Torah, 85, 102
literature for, 2
needs of, 89
occupations of, 1–2, 3
old, as blessing, 201–202
prudent, 144
reacting to men's behavior, 129–130
religious functions of, 2
reputation of, 40–41
respecting parents, 142–143
responsibility of, 106
rewards for, 33, 37
role of, 32–34, 127, 161
studying Torah, 179
thoughts of, 92, 102
unable to decide *halakhah,* 88
verifying source of men's wealth, 129
wicked, 125–126
working in the home, 40, 194
working out of the home, 39–40
work
    as curse, 152–153
    merits of, 179–181, 194
world, this *(olam ha-zeh),* 116
world to come *(olam ha-ba),* 116, 122–123

Y

Yalkut Shimoni, 22–23
Yiddish moral literature
    and world to come, 116
    as genre, 11–12
    development of, 29–31
    diversity of, 56
    for women, 2, 54–55, 79, 101
    influence of, 28
    nature of, 48–50
    practical use of, 49
    rabbinic opposition to, 24–25, 65–66
    research status of, 55–59
    sources for, 27
    value of, 24–25
Yiddish proverbs, in *Meneket Rivkah,* 21
Yiddish subject index, 303–307
Yishmael, Rabbi, 138

Z

Zarephath, woman from, 192
Ze'enah u-Re'enah, 33, 35, 47, 59, 161, 171,
    177, 179, 184, 201
Zinberg, Israel, 52, 56
Ziphites, 185
Zohar, 26